26TH ANNUAL EDITION
1989 - 2014

Calorie, Fat, Carbohydrate Counter

Alcoholic Drinks (w. Alcohol Cou...	134
Baking Ingredients	135
Bars (Breakfast, Granola, Nutrit...	136
Beverages: Cocoa, Hot Chocolate	35
Coffee & Coffee Drinks	35
Energy, Protein, Diet Shakes	38
Fruit & Vegetable Juices	41
Milk (Plain, Flavored, Mixes)	47
Non-Dairy (Soy, Rice/Cereal/Nut)	49
Soda/Soft Drinks	51
Tea & Iced Tea Drinks	53
Bread & Bread Products, Bagels	54
Breakfast Cereals (Hot & Cold)	57
Cakes, Donuts, Muffins, Pastries	62
Candy, Chocolate, Gum	68
Cheese & Cheese Products/Dips	76
Chicken ~ See Poultry	
Condiments, Salsa, Pickles	80
Cookies, Crackers	81
Crispbreads, Matzo	88
Cream & Creamers	89
Desserts (Puddings, Gelatin Desserts)	90
Eggs, Egg Substitutes, Egg Dishes	91
Fats, Butter, Spreads, Oils, Mayonnaise	93
Fish, Shellfish	95
Flour, Grains	98
Fruit (Fresh/Packaged/Dried/Snacks)	99
Ice Cream & Frozen Yogurt/Novelties	103
Meals, Entrees, Sides:	
Cans/Packaged/Frozen	111
Meats: Beef, Lamb, Pork, Game	123
Sausages/Franks/Hot Dogs	127
Lunch/Deli Meats & Sausages	128
Milk ~ See Beverages	
Nuts, Seeds, Peanut Butter	130
Pancakes & Waffles	132
Pasta & Noodles, Macaroni	133

Rice & Rice Dishes	140
Salads	141
Salad Dressings	142
Sauces & Gravy	144
Seasonings, Flavorings, Spices	147
Snacks (Popcorn, Chips, Pretzels)	148
Soups	152
Soy, Tofu, Supplements/Cough Syrup	156
Sugar, Sweeteners, Honey, Jam	157
Syrups, Dessert Toppings	157
Vegetables (Fresh, Frozen, Canned)	158
Yogurt, Yogurt Drinks & Probiotics	162

Eating Out:
Cafeteria, Sandwiches	165
Fair/Carnival/Stadium Foods	166
Restaurant & International Foods	168

Fast-Food Chains & Restaurants	175-258

A-Z Food Index	282-287

EXTRA DIET GUIDES & COUNTERS

Diabetes Guide	16-21
Alcohol Guide & Counter	23-29
Caffeine Guide & Counter	37
Fats & Cholesterol Guide	259-263
Fiber Guide & Counter	264-269
Protein Guide & Counter	270-274
Salt/Sodium Counter with High Blood Pressure Guide	275-281
Weight Control Guide	2-15

✅ Eat & Drink Sensibly

- Avoid fad diets. Eat 3 sensible portion-controlled meals daily.
- Limit fats, high-fat foods/snacks and sugar. Eat adequate fresh fruit & vegetables.
- Limit soft drinks, energy drinks, fruit juice and alcohol. Quench your thirst on water. (See Sample Meal Plan ~ Page 11)

✅ Exercise Daily

- Aim for at least 30 minutes daily – even in 5-10 minute lots. For motivation, find an exercise buddy, personal trainer or join a gym. *(Extra Notes ~ Page 12)*

✅ Reshape Eating Behaviors

- Be aware of eating and shopping behaviors that lead to overeating.
- Also focus on social and emotional situations that may trigger compulsive eating. *(Extra Notes ~ Page 14)*

✅ Keep a Food & Exercise Journal

- A journal helps you see exactly what you eat and drink, and how much you exercise. *(Extra Notes ~ Page 15)*
- An excellent motivator and proven weight loss aid. Keeps you honest!

✅ Arrange Moral Support

- Gain the support of family and friends.
- Get extra professional help if required, from your doctor, dietitian, psychologist, exercise trainer, or slimming group.
- Beware of family saboteurs who discourage you from adopting a healthier lifestyle!

DOCTOR CHECK-UP

Ask your doctor to check your blood pressure, blood sugar and blood cholesterol levels.

HEALTHY WEIGHTS
~ MEN & WOMEN ~
(Over 18 Years)

Based on weights with least risk of disease or death from heart disease, diabetes, stroke and cancer.

Based on Body Mass Index of 20-25

BMI calculated as: $\dfrac{\text{Weight (kg)}}{\text{Height (m)}^2}$

Height (No Shoes) Ft Ins	Healthy Weight Range (Pounds)
4'7" ~	86-108
4'8" ~	88-110
4'9" ~	92-114
4'10" ~	97-121
4'11" ~	99-123
5'0" ~	101-127
5'1" ~	105-132
5'2" ~	110-136
5'3" ~	112-140
5'4" ~	114-145
5'5" ~	119-149
5'6" ~	123-156
5'7" ~	127-158
5'8" ~	129-162
5'9" ~	134-167
5'10" ~	138-173
5'11" ~	143-178
6'0" ~	145-182
6'1" ~	149-187
6'2" ~	156-193
6'3" ~	158-198
6'4" ~	162-202
6'5" ~	170-211
6'6" ~	172-215
6'7" ~	175-220

Body Fat Distribution & Health

Moderate amounts of body fat do not compromise health. However, excess fat above the hips carries a far greater health risk than fat on or below the hips - better to be a 'pear-shape' than an 'apple-shape'.

Abdominal obesity greatly increases the risk of developing diabetes, heart disease, high blood fats, hypertension, stroke, sleep apnea, arthritis and some cancers. So-called 'cellulite' carries no extra health risk.

Waist Circumference directly reflects the increased health risk of abdominal obesity. Waist size associated with a high health risk:

Men ~ Over 40 inches   **Women** ~ Over 35 inches

Body Mass Index (BMI)

BMI is a general (but not specific) indicator of body fatness. Although BMI alone is not diagnostic, the higher the BMI, the greater the health risk of developing diabetes, high blood pressure and heart disease. BMI does not apply to heavily muscled persons. BMI is used in a different way for children.

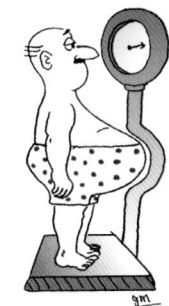

Abdominal obesity greatly increases the risk of ill-health and earlier death.

Check Your BMI: Find your height (no shoes) - look across the row to the weight nearest your own. Then track down to BMI.

Ht	WEIGHT (LBS) ~ ADULTS													
5'1"	100	106	111	116	122	127	132	137	143	148	153	158	185	211
5'2"	104	109	115	120	126	131	136	142	147	153	158	164	191	218
5'3"	107	113	118	124	130	135	141	146	152	158	163	169	197	225
5'4"	110	116	122	128	134	140	145	151	157	163	169	174	204	232
5'5"	114	120	126	132	138	144	150	156	162	168	174	180	210	240
5'6"	118	124	130	136	142	148	155	161	167	173	179	186	216	247
5'7"	121	127	134	140	146	153	159	166	172	178	185	191	223	255
5'8"	125	131	138	144	151	158	164	171	177	184	190	197	230	262
5'9"	128	135	142	149	155	162	169	176	182	189	196	206	236	270
5'10"	132	139	146	153	160	167	174	181	188	195	202	207	243	278
5'11"	136	143	150	157	165	172	179	186	193	200	208	215	250	286
6'0"	140	147	154	162	169	177	184	191	199	206	213	221	258	294
6'1"	144	151	159	166	174	182	189	197	204	212	219	227	265	302
6'2"	148	155	163	171	179	186	194	202	210	218	225	233	272	311
6'3"	152	160	168	176	184	192	200	208	216	224	232	240	279	319
6'4"	156	164	172	180	189	197	205	213	221	230	238	246	287	328
BMI	19	20	21	22	23	24	25	26	27	28	29	30	35	40

BMI Classification:

BMI Below 19
Underweight

BMI 19-24.9
Healthy Weight
(Low Health Risk)

BMI 25-29.9
Overweight
(Moderate Health Risk)

BMI 30-40
Obese (High Health Risk)

BMI Over 40
Morbid Obesity
(Very High Risk)

Interactive BMI Calculator
www.calorieking.com

Calories & Weight Loss

Calories in Food
Calories in food are derived from protein, fat and carbohydrate. Alcohol also provides calories. Vitamins, minerals and water provide no calories.

Calorie Values Per Gram

Fat/Oil	~ 9 Calories
Carbohydrate	~ 4 Calories
Protein	~ 4 Calories
Alcohol	~ 7 Calories

Note that fats have over double the calories of protein and carbohydrate. The higher the fat content of food, the higher the calories.

Sample Calculation

QUARTER POUNDER®
WITH CHEESE
has 510 calories
derived from:

26g Fat (x 9 cals/gram)	= 234
40g Carbohyd.(x 4 cals/gram)	= 160
29g Protein (x 4 cals/gram)	= 116
Total Calories	= 510

Calorie Levels for Weight Loss
Start with a calorie-controlled diet that allows a moderate weight loss of ½ - 1 pound per week. Weight loss is usually much greater in the first few weeks due to extra fluid losses.

Note: It is better to increase exercise rather than lessen food calories too drastically.

Suggested Calories for Weight Loss

Women:	Non-active	1000 - 1200
	Active	1200 - 1500
Men:	Non-active	1200 - 1500
	Active	1500 - 1800
Teenagers:		1200 - 1800

ChooseMyPlate.gov

The MyPlate symbol represents the recommended proportion of foods from each food group. It focuses on the importance of making smart food choices in every food group, every day. Daily physical activity is also important. *(More info: www.ChooseMyPlate.gov)*

Examples of Single Serving Sizes

Grains (Eat 6 servings per day):
- 1 slice wholegrain bread (1 oz)
- ½ bun, small bagel or English muffin
- 4 small crackers or 1 tortilla
- 1 oz ready-to-eat wholegrain cereal
- ½ cup cooked cereal, rice or pasta

Vegetables (Eat 3-5 servings per day):
- 1 cup raw leafy vegetables
- 1½ cups raw chopped vegetables
- ½ cup cooked vegetables
- ½ - ¾ cup vegetable juice

Fruit (Eat 3-5 servings per day):
- 1 medium apple, orange, banana
- ½ cup canned fruit (in own juice)
- ¼ cup dried fruit
- ½ cup fruit juice (unsweetened)
- ¼ medium avocado

Protein (2-3 servings per day):
- 2-3 oz (cooked) lean meat/poultry/fish
- 2 eggs or 6 oz tofu or ¼ cup nuts
- 1 cup (cooked) dried beans or chickpeas

Dairy (2-3 servings per day):
- 1 cup (8 fl.oz) milk/soy (enriched)/yogurt
- 1½ oz cheese or ½ cup cottage cheese

Portion Size Counts!

Food portion size is critical to controlling calorie intake for weight control.

Super-sized food servings have become more common when eating out and in the home. This can mean a day's worth of calories being consumed in one meal; or a snack being equivalent to a full meal.

It is easy to underestimate portion size of foods and drinks, and unwittingly consume excess calories – even if the fat content is low or even zero!

To more accurately estimate portion size of different foods, weigh and measure your food with food scales, measuring spoons and cups. Better control of calories will result.

For a visual idea of portion sizes, visit www.CalorieKing.com See examples (fries and cola) on this page.

Allow for Extra Calories in Packaged Food

The actual weight of packaged foods is usually 5-10% more than the label net weight (the minimum legal weight) – and in some cases up to 50% more. However, manufacturers calculate the calories based on the net weight. For actual calories, weigh the product and calculate the extra calories.

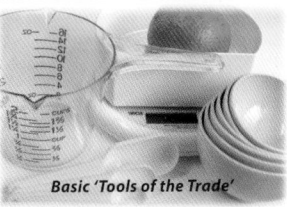

Basic 'Tools of the Trade'

CALORIEKING PORTION WATCH

Fries | Cal | Fat | Carb |

	Cal	Fat	Carb
Small	230	11	29
Medium	380	19	48
Large	500	25	63

CALORIEKING PORTION WATCH

Cola | Cal | Fat | Carb |

	Cal	Fat	Carb
8 fl.oz Cup	100	0	25
12 fl.oz Can	150	0	37
20 fl.oz Bottle	250	0	63
1 Liter Bottle	400	0	100
2 Liter Bottle	800	0	200

3.75 oz

4.65 oz

Actual weight of this bun is 24% more than the stated net weight.

Recommended Fat Intake

► Fat in the Diet

Fats in the diet are essential for good health. However, too much fat can contribute to obesity and a higher risk of heart disease, high blood pressure, diabetes, gallstone and certain cancers.

Dietary fat and oils have over double the calories of carbohydrates and protein. (Example: Changing from whole-milk to non-fat milk halves the calories.)

MAXIMUM DESIRABLE FAT INTAKE (DAILY)	
Calories	**Fat**
1200 cals	30g fat
1500 cals	40g fat
1800 cals	50g fat
2000 cals	60g fat
2200 cals	70g fat
2500 cals	80g fat
3000 cals	110g fat

ZERO GRAMS TRANS FAT

Don't be fooled by **Zero Grams Trans Fat** boldly displayed on some high-fat snacks. They are still high in fat and calories.

Examples: Cheetos 99c pkg ~ 24g fat, 380 cals
Lay's Chips (2¾ oz pkg) ~ 27g fat, 430 calories

0 grams Trans Fat

► Beware low-fat foods

It is a mistake to think that eating low-fat or fat-free foods allows you to eat double the quantity. You can end up with even more calories than eating smaller amounts of regular-fat products.

Food products which are fat-free but high in calories include soda drinks, fruit juices, beer, alcoholic spirits, sugar and candy. Bread, rice and pasta also have negligible fat but need to be eaten in controlled amounts.

Ultimately, **it is food portion size as well as total calories that count** whether from fat, carbohydrate or protein. Remember, cows get fat on grass!

Reduced fat and fat-free foods are not necessarily low calorie. Portion size is still important.

Reduced Fat

3 Cookies
140 Calories

6 oz Fat-Free Muffin:
450 calories

FOOD LABEL MEANINGS

FDA Nutrition Claim Definitions
(All are on a Per Serving Basis)
Low Calorie: 40 Calories or less
Light or Lite: One third fewer calories or, 50% or less fat than regular product
Fat-Free: Less than half a gram of fat
Low-Fat: 3 grams or less of fat
Reduced Fat: 25% less fat than regular product
Fewer or Less Calories: At least 25% fewer calories than regular product

▶ **Meats, Poultry, Fish**

• **Choose lean cuts** of meat with little marbling. **Trim all visible fat** from meat and remove the skin from poultry. Removal of fat after cooking, is okay (to prevent dryness). Choose 'extra lean' ground beef.

• **Avoid high-fat meat products** such as salami, bacon, sausage and franks.

• **Broil or bake. Avoid frying in oil.** Allow casseroles to cool and skim off surface fat.

• **Avoid fried fish,** frozen fish in batter and canned fish in oil.

▶ **Fats & Oils**

• **Use minimal amounts** of all types of fat and oil. All are high in calories.

• **Choose** 'light' and 'reduced fat' spreads but still use sparingly.

• Use minimal amounts of oil when stir-frying. Use no-stick sprays like Pam.

▶ **Salad Dressings & Sauces**

• **Avoid regular mayonnaise and oil dressings.** Choose 'light', 'reduced fat' or 'fat-free' brands.

• **Choose low-fat or fat-free sauces** (mainly tomato-based). Avoid 'pesto', 'alfredo', 'cheese' and 'creamy' sauces.

▶ **Milk, Cheese**

• **Choose low-fat or nonfat milks and yogurts.** Avoid full-cream milk, cream, Half & Half.

• **Cheese:** Choose fat-free, and low-fat cheese. Part-skim ricotta is still high in fat. Low-fat cottage cheese is a good choice. Cheese substitutes can still be high in fat.

▶ **Snacks, Cookies, Candy**

• **Avoid** high-fat snacks such as potato chips, corn/tortilla chips, cheese puffs, buttered popcorn, chocolate and carob bars.

▶ **Desserts/Sweets**

• **Avoid high-fat desserts,** such as cake, pie, pastries, cheesecake, full-fat puddings.

• **Choose** fresh fruits, fresh fruit salad, canned fruit in water pack, low-fat ice cream. Use low-fat yogurt in place of cream.

▶ **Fast-Foods & Take-Out**

Check the Fast-Foods Section of this book for actual fat and calorie counts.

• **Avoid deep-fried foods such as** chicken, french fries and onion rings.

• **Pizzas:** Avoid sausage/pepperoni. Choose vegetarian topping and modest quantity of cheese. Eat a moderate serving. Eat extra salad and fresh fruit.

• **Hamburgers:** Choose medium size, lower fat burgers. Avoid bacon. Have a side salad (with fat-free dressing).

• **Delis:** Choose sandwiches/bread rolls, pitas with low-fat fillings and plain salad. Limit meat/cheese to small portions.

• **Coffees:** Avoid large sizes of latte and frappuccino. Request nonfat milk and no whipped cream. Avoid cookies and pastries.

Extra Information: www.CalorieKing.com

FRYING ADDS FAT!

The greater the surface area of potato exposed to fat or oil, the higher the fat content and calories.

Whole Potato (3 oz)
0g Fat **65 Cals**

Roasted Potato (3 oz)
5g Fat **155 Cals**

Fries (Large cut, 3 oz)
12g Fat **220 Cals**

Fries (Small, 3 oz)
15g Fat **265 Cals**

Potato Chips (3 oz)
30g Fat **450 Cals**

Naturally-Friendly Carbs

- **Carbohydrate foods in their more natural forms** (not overly processed) are essential to good health. They are the main source of fuel for the body, and also provide important vitamins, minerals, antioxidants and fiber – all of which help protect against heart disease, diabetes, hypertension, constipation-related ailments and many other diseases.

Carbohydrate foods (minimally processed) are essential to good health.

Be sure to eat adequate fruit and vegetables (5 - 7 servings) every day.

- Carbohydrates even help the body produce serotonin, the 'feel good' brain chemical that helps control appetite and overeating. Too little serotonin can lead to mood swings and depression.

Carbohydrates are found in different forms in food as:

- Sugars in fruit, sugar cane, milk
- Starches in whole grains, legumes, nuts, seeds and vegetables
- Dietary fiber (See Fiber Guide ~ Page 264)

Glycemic Index & Diabetes ~ Page 21

RECOMMENDED CARBOHYDRATE INTAKE		
Calories (Daily)	Carbohydrate (Grams)	Percent Carbohydrate Calories
1200 cals	100-120g	35-40%
1500 cals	140-170g	40-45%
1800 cals	180-200g	40-45%
2000 cals	200-250g	40-50%
2500 cals	310-350g	50-55%
3000 cals	410-450g	55-65%

How Much Do We Need?

- As shown in the chart, well-balanced diets above 2000 calories contain 50-60% of total calories from carbohydrates.
- At lower calorie levels used for weight control (1200-1500 calories), carbohydrates account for as little as 40% of total calories. This is because protein calories have nutritional priority.
- Carbohydrates & Diabetes ~ *See Page 21*

Low-Carbohydrate Diets

- Popular low-carbohydrate diets are extreme in their recommendations to initially cut carb intake to as little as 20 grams per day – the amount in 1 thick slice of bread, or 1 medium apple, or 1 small potato.

  This greatly increases the risk of nutritional deficiencies and compromises health, particularly if fat intake is excessive through fatty meats, high-fat dairy products, and fried foods.

- While overweight Americans do need to reduce carbohydrate intake, it should be done **sensibly as part of reducing portion size and total calories.**

- Simply eating 'low-carb' food products without regard to portion size, calories or fats, will do little to promote weight loss or good health.

- **Low-carb diets (and indeed any diet) only work if total calories are reduced.**

- Refined sugars should be one of the first targets in reducing carb intake.

FAT MATTERS
CARBS COUNT BUT
CALORIES ARE KING!

Extra Info ~ www.CalorieKing.com

Sugar-free & lower carb products may still be high in calories and fat.

- Many overweight, inactive people consume over 500 calories of refined sugars per day, either self-added or as part of food products. This is equivalent to over 30 level teaspoons – a significant amount in weight control terms. Halving this amount would be reasonable and worthwhile.

  Note: Naturally occurring sugars in fruits, vegetables and milk are fine when consumed in normal recommended amounts. These foods are also rich in other nutrients.

  Refined sugar is referred to as having 'empty calories' because it supplies calories but negligible nutrients and no fiber.

- Most sugar in our diet is 'hidden' in processed foods such as soft drinks, fruit drinks, candy, cookies, cake, jam, sauces, ice cream, desserts, canned foods, and breakfast cereals.

  Certainly enjoy moderate quantities of these foods, but for serious weight control, look for 'low calorie', 'diet' or 'sugar-free'.

  However, be careful not to substitute sugar-rich foods with high-fat foods which might boost calories even more!

- Be aware that sugar comes in different forms such as sucrose, glucose, fructose, malt, high-fructose corn syrup, molasses, honey and maple syrup. Check the label.

- **Sugar alcohols such as sorbitol,** mannitol and maltitol are carb-based and have ½ - ¾ the calories of regular sugar. While not counted as sugar on food labels, they do add to the carb count. Excess amounts can cause bloating, gas and diarrhea.

- **Sugar-free sweeteners** such as *Equal, DiabetiSweet, NutraSweet, Splenda, Sweet'n Low* and *Stevia* make it easy to reduce sugar in drinks and recipes. Use only in moderation. Note: Most recipes can be adapted to contain less sugar with little effect on taste or quality.

Extra Info ~ www.CalorieKing.com

Sugar-free snacks and foods may be higher in fat and calories than the regular product.

Example	~ Creme Wafers (3):
Regular	~ 115 cals, 6g fat
Sugar-Free	~ 160 cals, 10g fat

SUGAR CONTENT OF SOME COMMON FOODS

Teaspoons of Sugar

Coca Cola or *Pepsi*, 12 fl.oz	10
20 fl.oz size	17
Iced Tea, sweetened, 12 fl.oz	8
Chocolate Milk, 12 fl.oz	6
Honey Smacks Cereal, ¾ cup, 1 oz	4
Popcorn, caramel, 1 cup	3.5
Chocolate Bar, 1.5 oz	6
M&M's 1.7 oz pkg	7
Muffin, large, 4 oz	6
Choc Chip Cookie, 1 oz	2
Donut, iced	6
Apple Pie, 1 piece	7
Jell-O, ½ cup	4.5
Jam, 1 Tbsp, ¾ oz	2.5
Syrup, maple, 1 Tbsp	3

Reach for fresh fruit when you want to snack instead of candy or snack products rich in sugar and fat.

The XL Generation

Some 15% of American kids and adolescents are overweight; and childhood obesity has doubled over the last 20 years. Diabetes, high blood pressure and high cholesterol are major problem areas for overweight children and adolescents, as are depression, low self-esteem, sleep apnea and bone joint problems.

To address this problem, cooperation is required between kids, parents, schools and government. Weight control is a family and community affair.

Five Simple Tips To Get Started:

❶ Watch Soda Intake

Limit soda and sugary drinks to one serving on the weekends. Soda should not be an everyday beverage – water should be. When at restaurants or using a soda fountain, choose small servings with ice or choose diet soda instead. Schools should provide water and restrict access to soda as should parents when eating out or in the home!

❷ Cut back on Fast-Foods and Eating Out

Many more calories are consumed when you eat out. Healthy meals prepared at home are best for the whole family.

❸ Say "No" to Super-Sizing

When meals are upsized, loads more calories are consumed. Choose sensible portion sizes when eating out and at home. Use smaller plates and choose smaller packages.

❹ Limit Between-Meal Snacking

Watch out for high-fat and high-calorie snacks – they can have more calories than a meal! Keep your eye on portion sizes and limit salty snack foods and candy to parties and special occasions. Choose fresh fruit, vegetables, nuts and low-fat milk instead.

❺ Get Moving ~ Watch Less TV

Kids need at least 60 minutes of physical activity every day. It's critical for their fitness, and greatly lessens the risk of obesity.

Encourage kids to be active out of school hours. Wearing a pedometer can be highly motivational for kids to move more – as can playing dance video games such as *Dance Dance Revolution*. *Dance Central* (XBox360) and *Wii Fit* (Nintendo) are also excellent fitness motivators.

Limit TV and non-active computer games to just one hour per day. Also limit the accompanying snacks! Include exercise in family activities.

Extra information and tips ~ www.CalorieKing.com

For Healthy, Overweight Persons ~ Not for Persons With Any Medical Condition
~ Please Check With Your Doctor & Dietitian ~

 ## Breakfast (approx. 300 cal)

	1 Small Fruit or ½ oz Dried Fruit
Plus	Cereal: 1½ oz Dry (high fiber)
	or 1 cup cooked Oatmeal
Plus	½ oz Almonds/Seeds
Plus	Milk (from daily allowance) or Yogurt (low-fat)

Daily Milk Allowance (approx.160 calories)
2 cups Non-Fat Milk or 1½ cups Low-fat (1%) Milk
or equivalent Soy Drink, Yogurt, Cheese, Tofu

Fat Allowance (140 calories; 15g Fat)
4 tsp Fat or 6-8 tsp Diet Margarine or 3 tsp Oil
or 1½ Tbsp Mayonnaise or ½ medium Avocado
or 1½ Tbsp Peanut Butter or 30g Nuts/Seeds

 ## Breakfast ~ Choice 2

	1 Small Fruit
Plus	2 Eggs (no added fat)
	or 2 oz Cheese (low-fat)
	or 4 oz Cottage Cheese (low-fat)
	or 2 oz Lean/Canadian Bacon
Plus	1 Tomato
Plus	1 Slice Wholegrain Toast

 ## Between Meals

Water, Coffee, Tea, Diet drinks,
Fruit from main meals; Raw vegetable
pieces, Milk from Daily Allowance

 ## Lunch (approx. 440 calories)

	2 slices Wholegrain Bread (2 oz)
	or 4 Crispbreads/Crackers or 6" Pita
Plus	2 oz lean Meat, Chicken or Turkey
	or 3½oz Tuna (in water) or 2½ oz Salmon
	or 1 oz Cheese or ½ cup (4 oz) Cottage Cheese
	or ½ cup (4 oz) Ricotta Cheese (low-fat)
	or ½ cup (4 oz) Fruit Yogurt (low-fat)
	or ½ cup (4 oz) Bean Salad
Plus	Large Salad (Oil-free dressing)
Plus	1 small Fruit or ½ oz Dried Fruit

Dinner (approx. 360 calories)

	Soup (fat-free)
Plus	3 oz lean Meat (cooked weight)
	or 4 oz Chicken Breast (no skin)
	or 3 oz Chicken Thigh/Leg (no skin)
	or 5 oz Fish (grilled, no fat)
	or ¾ cup (6 oz) Beans (Soy, Kidney, Pinto etc)/Lentils
	or Low-fat Entree (e.g. Lean Cuisine)
Plus	1 small Potato
	or ½ cup Rice/Pasta/Sweet Corn
	or 1 slice Wholegrain Bread
Plus	2-3 servings Vegetables/Salad
Plus	1 small Fruit + Diet Gelatin Dessert

- **Persons who exercise regularly lose more weight** and keep it off longer than non-exercisers.
- **Exercise also improves general health and well-being.** Mood, confidence and self-esteem are enhanced by a sense of control and accomplishment.
- **Exercise is a good way to 'wake up' a sluggish metabolism** and burn extra fat tissue.
- **Aerobic (huff and puff) exercise most days** is great for burning calories and for cardiovascular fitness. But, it is strength training that mainly builds the muscles that burn calories even while we sleep.
- **Strength training is the key to retaining or rebuilding muscles.** As we age, we lose some 6 pounds of muscle per decade. This results in a lower metabolism and fewer calories being burnt.

  Muscles are the furnaces that burn calories. The more muscle you have, the more calories you will burn.

Brisk walking each day is a safe and effective way to burn calories and keep fit.
Try it – you'll like it!

- **Regular strength training (2-3 times weekly)** can increase our metabolic rate for several days following exercise – and an extra 100 calories per day being burnt. While 2-3 pounds of muscle may be gained in the first 8-10 weeks, weight from exercised muscles is okay. It is excess fat (particularly abdominal fat) that is a potential health hazard. Gaining muscle and losing fat also helps body reshaping – even if the scales don't show it.
- **Avoid injury** by beginning with walking, low impact aerobics, or weight-supported exercise (e.g. swimming, cycling). Avoid competitive sports. Allow 2-3 days of recovery between strength training sessions. Get professional advice ~ particularly if you have a medical condition.
- **How Much?** Start with 10-20 minutes per day and progress to 30-60 minutes per day.

  Also walk up stairs instead of using elevators. Take a brisk walk at lunch. Use an exercise bike, treadmill or stair machine while watching TV. Walk the dog.
- **How Often?** While aerobic fitness requires only 3-4 sessions weekly, **weight control is a daily event which requires daily exercise to burn calories.** Add in strength training 2-3 times weekly.
- **For motivation,** find an exercise buddy, personal trainer or join a gym.

Strength training is the key to retain or rebuild muscles.
Muscles burn extra calories even while you sleep.
For extra guidance, seek a qualified trainer or join a gym.

Calories Used in Exercise

LIGHT	MODERATE	HEAVY
130 lbs ~ 3 Cals/Min	130 lbs ~ 5 Cals/Min	130 lbs ~ 8 Cals/Min
170 lbs ~ 4 Cals/Min	170 lbs ~ 6 Cals/Min	220 lbs ~ 12 Cals/Min
220 lbs ~ 5 Cals/Min	220 lbs ~ 7 Cals/Min	170 lbs ~ 10 Cals/Min

LIGHT	MODERATE	HEAVY
Walking, slow	Walking, brisk	Walking (power), Jogging
Cycling, light	Cycling, moderate	Cycling (vigorous), Spinning
Frisbee playing	Swimming, crawl	Swimming, strenuous
Gardening, light	Weight-training, light	Weight-training, heavy
Golf, social	Tennis, moderate	Wrestling/Judo, advanced
Tennis, doubles	Racquetball, beginners	Racquetball, advanced
Housework, cleaning	Aerobics, light	Tae Bo, Kick Boxing
Calisthenics, light	Football, touch	Football, training
Bowling	Basketball, Baseball	Basketball (Pro)
Ping-pong, social	Walking Downstairs	Climbing Stairs
Ice Skating, light	Snow Skiing (downhill)	Skipping Rope
Aquarobics, light	Shovelling snow	Skiing (cross country)
Skate Boarding	Dancing (ballroom)	Aquarobics, advanced
Line/Square Dancing	Rowing, moderate	Dancing (strenuous), Zumba
Tai Chi, Yoga	Volleyball, competitive	Rowing, vigorous
Volleyball		Martial Arts

Note: Only those sports or activities that are sustained over a period of time (e.g running) qualify for heavy exercise. Stop-start sports such as tennis are considered 'moderate'.

Interactive Calculations ~ www.CalorieKing.com/tools

WALKING PROGRAM

		USE DISTANCE, STEPS OR TIME	
Weeks	Distance	Steps Pedometer	Time
1-2	1 mile	2000	20 mins
3-5	1.5 miles	3000	28 mins
6-8	2 miles	3500	35 mins
9-10	2.5 miles	4500	45 mins
11+	3.5 miles	6000	60 mins

10,000 STEPS PER DAY

A pedometer can motivate you to be more active. It clips to your belt or waist band and registers each step.

Aim for 8,000 - 10,000 steps per day, instead of an average of only 3,000 - 4,000 steps.

For Extra Information:
www.CalorieKing.com

Reshaping Eating Behaviors

- Eating is a behavior that is largely controlled by people with whom we live or socialize, places in which we carry out our lives, and our emotions. Become aware of those situations that commonly lead to extra food being eaten.

- We may also be unaware of 'bad' eating habits that can lead to excess calorie intake; e.g. eating quickly, large mouthfuls, eating when tense or bored, finishing a large serving of food when not hungry.

Tips to help uncover and correct those 'bad' or problem eating habits:

- **Don't eat while engaged in other activities;** for example, watching TV, reading. Eat only at the table, not at the fridge or while standing.

- **Don't eat quickly.** Chewing slowly allows time to register a feeling of fullness. Don't use fingers, only utensils. Cut food into smaller pieces. Don't load your fork until the previous mouthful is finished.

Practice saying 'NO' politely but assertively.

- **Don't purchase problem high calorie foods.** Shop from a set list to prevent impulse buying. Avoid shopping with children.

- **Buy snack foods** in the smallest package. The larger the serving size or package, the more you are likely to eat or drink.

- **Plan meals in advance. Stick to a set menu.**

- **Plan a strategy to avoid uncontrolled eating** and drinking at social events, or when your emotions urge you to binge.

  Rehearse repeatedly in your mind exactly what you will do in such situations. Remind yourself several times each day that you are in charge of your actions and that you can be strong-willed. Seek counseling or coaching on various strategies.

- **Distract yourself** when you feel the urge to snack impulsively. Engage in some activity that will distract you from thinking about food. Examples: go for a walk, brush your teeth, phone a friend.

  If you eat out of boredom, find some new hobby or interest that gets you out of the house. Even enrol in an adult education class.

Do you use food as an emotional crutch? If so, professional counseling may be helpful.

The food journal is the most powerful proven aid for dieters. Persons who keep a food and exercise journal not only lose more weight, they also keep it off. Here are some of the reasons:

- **Recording your eating and exercise habits** jolts you into realizing just what you do eat and drink each day; and also whether you exercise sufficiently.

- **Helps you identify problem foods** and drinks with excessive calories and fat.

- **Helps identify moods,** situations and events that lead to excessive eating of unwanted calories. You can then plan to overcome or avoid them.

- **Prevents 'calorie amnesia',** the forgetfulness that leads to rebound weight gain after successful weight loss. Recording puts you back on the right track.

- **Helps you develop greater self-discipline.** You will think twice about overindulging if you have to record it - especially if someone checks your journal regularly. It certainly keeps you honest!

- **Motivates you** to carefully plan your meals and to exercise each day.

- **Serves as a check system** for your doctor, dietitian or counselor to assess your progress and make recommendations.

Write It Down!

"Keeping a journal gives me feedback on exactly what I eat and drink each day.

It helps prevent 'calorie amnesia' and reminds me to exercise each day.

It's a 'must' for successful weight control!"

3 Easy Ways to Track Your Food & Exercise Calories!

CalorieKing Online
Part of a comprehensive personalized program that includes tools, reports and a supportive community.

iPhone
Make smart food choices wherever you are! ControlMyWeight is easy to use & always with you.

Book
A 10-week journal that fits in your pocket. Includes Weekly Summary page and Progress Checklist

Extra Information ~ CalorieKing.com

What is Diabetes?
Diabetes occurs when the body has difficulty processing glucose sugar in the blood.

- **After digestion,** sugar and starches are changed into **glucose** – the simplest form of sugar vital for body energy and growth.
- Insulin is the hormone which acts like a key that opens the door to body cells and allows glucose to enter.
- **Without enough insulin,** glucose builds up in the blood and passes into the urine. High blood glucose levels lead to frequent urination, extreme thirst, and tiredness.
- **Untreated diabetes increases the risk of damage to nerves and blood vessels.** This, in turn, increases the risk of heart disease, stroke, blindness, kidney damage, foot ulcers and gangrene (with amputation), impotence and other complications.

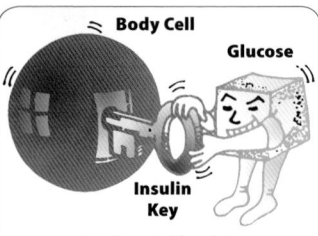

*Insulin acts like a key.
It opens the door to body cells
and allows glucose to enter.*

People with type 1 diabetes and some with type 2 have too few or no keys and require insulin injections.

Others (primarily type 2) make enough insulin but the body doesn't use it as well as it should – particularly if obese and inactive.

SYMPTOMS OF DIABETES
- Frequent urination
- Extreme thirst
- Unusual hunger
- Rapid weight loss
- Extreme fatigue
- Blurred vision
- Skin infections that are slow to heal
- Tingling/numbness in feet

Note: Diabetes can be present even with no symptoms.

DON'T IGNORE DIABETES
IT'S A SERIOUS DISEASE!

TYPE 2 DIABETES
- Occurs in 90% of diabetes cases
- Occurs mainly in adults - particularly in overweight and inactive persons
- Insulin is produced but body cells resist its action and glucose cannot enter cells
- Usually treated with meal planning and physical activity. Sometimes requires medication (pills or insulin)

TYPE 1 DIABETES
- Occurs in 10% of diabetes cases
- Usually in children and young adults
- Pancreas produces little or no insulin. Daily insulin injections (or use of an insulin pump) are necessary, as well as:
  - matching pre-meal insulin to the amount of carbohydrate eaten
  - weight control and regular physical activity

GESTATIONAL DIABETES
- Occurs in some women during pregnancy. It usually disappears after the baby's birth.
- Women who have had gestational diabetes still have a high risk of developing type 2 diabetes within 5 to 10 years.
- Requires weight control, a healthy lifestyle and regular medical checks

Are You At Risk for Diabetes?

Pre-Diabetes ~ An Early Warning!

Pre-diabetes means that your blood glucose levels are higher than normal, but not high enough to be called diabetes.

If you have pre-diabetes, you have a higher risk for getting diabetes later on.

The good news is that you can start taking steps to prevent diabetes by making healthy lifestyle changes – such as losing weight if overweight, and being more physically active.

WHAT'S YOUR RISK?

Find out if you're at risk for diabetes by answering the following questions:

- ☐ I have been told I have pre-diabetes
- ☐ I have a family history of diabetes
- ☐ I am African American, Latino American, Asian American, Native American or a Pacific Islander
- ☐ I have had gestational diabetes (diabetes during pregnancy)
- ☐ I am over age 45
- ☐ I am overweight
- ☐ My waist is larger than: 35 inches (for a woman) or 40 inches (for a man)
- ☐ I get little or no physical activity
- ☐ My blood pressure is higher than 130 over 85
- ☐ My HDL (good cholesterol) is too low
- ☐ My triglycerides (blood fats) are too high

✔ CHECK YOUR RESULT

- If you've put a check mark in two or more of the boxes, you may be more likely to develop type 2 diabetes.

- Talk with your healthcare provider to see if you should have a blood test for diabetes.

BLOOD GLUCOSE CLASSIFICATION OF DIABETES

Normal:	Below 100 mg/dl*
Pre-Diabetes:	100-125 mg/dl*
Diabetes:	Over 125 mg/dl*

(*Fasting Blood Glucose)

KNOW YOUR BGL

(Blood Glucose Level)
Everyone over the age of 45 should have a blood glucose test every three years

Importance of Weight Control

- **Type 2 diabetes** is more common in people who are overweight.

- **Being overweight** means that your insulin doesn't work as well to control blood glucose levels.

- **Losing just 10 to 20 pounds** can help you better manage your diabetes and lower your risk for heart disease.

- **Keys to weight control include:**
- Following a healthy eating plan
- Controlling food portions
- Being physically active most days of the week
- Keeping food records
- Setting realistic goals

- **Work with a registered dietitian** who can help you reach a weight that's ideal for you.

KEEP MOVING!

Every day, do at least 30 minutes of moderate intensity exercise.
(even in 5-minute sets)

It's the key to improving insulin action.
Add muscle strength training 3-4 times a week to double the benefits.

Managing Diabetes

Don't battle diabetes alone. Establish a partnership with your doctor, dietitian, certified diabetes educator, and pharmacist.

Extra Support: • Joslin Diabetes Center
• American Diabetes Association
• American Association of Diabetes Educators
• Juvenile Diabetes Research Foundation
• National Diabetes Education Program

Hints to keep blood glucose within safe limits:

• **Control your food intake.** Know what and when you will eat. Seek referral to a dietitian for expert advice.

• **Exercise regularly.** It assists weight control and can improve sensitivity of body cells to insulin. Plan physical activity into your daily routine.

• **Monitor your blood glucose** at home and work with a blood glucose meter. It will help you become familiar with your blood glucose patterns, and the effects of food, activity and medication.

• **Take insulin or oral medication as prescribed.** If on insulin, know what action to take if hypoglycemia (low blood glucose) occurs. Also educate your family and friends. More Info: www.joslin.org

Be Heart Smart ~ Know Your ABC's

If you have diabetes, you are at a higher risk for heart attack and stroke than someone without diabetes. But you can fight back!

Be smart about your heart!

Take control of the ABC's of diabetes and live a long and healthy life. Talk to your healthcare provider about your ABC targets.

A is for A1C
The A1C (A-one-C) test – short for hemoglobin A1C. It reflects your average blood glucose (sugar) over the last 3 months.
Suggested Target: Below 7%

B is for Blood Pressure
High blood pressure makes your heart work too hard.
Suggested Target: Below 130/80

C is for Cholesterol
Bad cholesterol, or LDL, can build up and clog your arteries. **Suggested Target: Below 100**

Joslin Diabetes Center, an affiliate of Harvard Medical School, is the world's largest diabetes research center, diabetes clinic and provider of diabetes education.

MORE INFORMATION
www.joslin.org or call 800-344-4501

National Diabetes Education Program

Be smart about your heart!

Take control of the ABC's of diabetes and live a long and healthy life.

Talk to your healthcare provider about your ABC targets.

Take action now to lower your risk for heart attack, stroke and other diabetes problems.

* * *

◀ Note: These targets are suggested by the National Institutes for Health and the American Diabetes Association

Guidelines for choosing a healthy diet apply equally to people with or without diabetes. Eating a wide variety of foods that are mainly low in fat, low in refined sugars, and high in fiber, is recommended.

However, actual food quantities, as well as when you eat, will also influence control of blood glucose. Your dietitian will individualize a meal plan to suit your food preferences, lifestyle and medical status.

Eat a well-balanced diet with foods high in fiber and low in saturated fat.

Here are a few tips:

- **Maintain a healthy weight.** If overweight, even a modest weight loss plus daily physical activity can help manage blood glucose in type 2 diabetes.

- **Don't skip meals.** If you take insulin or an oral hypoglycemic agent, regular meals are important.

  If on insulin, eat meals at the same time each day. Eat a similar amount of food at each meal. Eating about the same amount of carbohydrate over the day will make best use of insulin and prevent wide variations in blood glucose levels.

- **Know which foods contain carbohydrate;** and learn how to check the *Nutrition Facts Label* on foods. Check the serving size, total fat and total carbohydrate – not just the sugar content. All carbohydrate breaks down to sugars after digestion.

- **Choose wholegrain breads, cereals and pasta.** Eat fresh fruits, vegetables and legumes. These foods contain more fiber and slow the release of glucose into your blood after a meal.

- **Limit foods high in saturated fat, trans fat and cholesterol.** Enjoy fish, soy foods, and other foods rich in omega-3 fats. *(Extra Notes: Page 259)*

- **Limit sugars and foods high in added sugar** particularly if overweight. Small amounts of sugar as part of a meal may occasionally be okay. Check with your dietitian. *(Extra Notes: Page 9)*

The Plate Method is an easy way to eat healthfully. (See next page)

MAIN MEAL

Vegetables & Salad Greens

Bread · Starch · Grain   Meat · Protein

ALCOHOL TIPS

- **If you drink alcohol, have only moderate amounts:**
  Men ~ 1-2 drinks/day
  Women ~ 1 drink/day
  For some people, safe drinking will mean no alcoholic drinks at all.

  (Also see Alcohol Guide ~ Page 23)

- **Drink along with your food** – especially if you use insulin or diabetes pills.

- **Do not omit any carb food** in exchange for an alcoholic drink. However, non-alcoholic beers (12 fl oz) count as one carb exchange.

- **Alcohol increases the risk of hypoglycemia** (low blood sugar) and drug interactions if you take insulin and certain types of diabetes pills.

- **Check with your doctor and dietitian.**
  Extra Info: www.joslin.org

The Plate Method – An Easy Way to Eat Healthfully

The plate method is a helpful tool to guide your food choices until you see a dietitian for your own meal plan.

For a healthy meal:
- Fill half of your plate with non-starchy vegetables (broccoli, green beans, carrots).
- Fill a quarter of your plate with carbohydrate (wholegrain bread, pasta, potato, brown rice).
- Fill the other quarter of your plate with 3-4 ounces of lean meat, poultry, or fish.
- Use 1-2 teaspoons of tub margarine or a heart-healthy vegetable oil.
- Add a small piece of fruit or 8 ounces of skim/low-fat milk or yogurt.

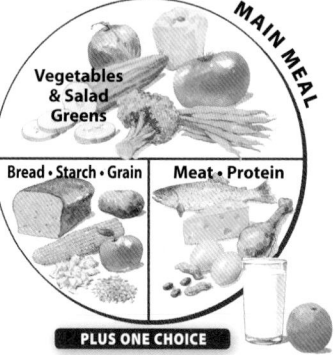

MAIN MEAL

Vegetables & Salad Greens

Bread · Starch · Grain

Meat · Protein

PLUS ONE CHOICE
Milk, Fruit, Dessert or other Carb Food

How Much Carbohydrate Should You Eat?

A dietitian can best determine how much carbohydrate you need at each of your meals, based on your lifestyle, food preferences, and overall diabetes control.

Until you see a dietitian, aim to keep the amount of carbohydrate you eat the same at each of your meals.

CARB CHOICES MEAL PLAN
One Carb Choice = 15 Grams of Carb

 The amount in: 1 slice Bread **or** ¾ cup Cereal (unsweetened) **or** 1 small Potato **or** 1 small Fruit

Breakfast
- Eat 2-3 carb choices (30-45 grams)
- Include a low-fat protein source such as egg whites or skim milk.

Lunch and Dinner
- Eat 3-4 carb choices (45-60 grams carb)
- Include fruit and non-starchy vegetables. Choose small portions of low-fat protein foods.

Snacks: If needed, eat 1-2 carb choices (15-30 grams carb).

Note: Above plan is for adults. Carbohydrate amounts will vary with physical activity level.

Carb Type Affects Blood Glucose

The various forms of carbohydrate affect blood glucose levels in different ways. It is difficult to predict the effect of particular foods, sugars, or meals, simply by their carbohydrate content.

Thus the same amount of carbohydrate from different foods may affect blood sugar levels very differently. Many factors affect the rate of digestion and absorption such as:

- the type of sugar, starch, and fiber
- the degree of processing and cooking (which increases digestion rate)
- the amount of protein and fat (which slow stomach emptying and digestion).

Glycemic Index (GI)

The GI is a method of ranking carbo-hydrate foods on a scale (0-100) according to how they affect blood glucose levels. (See next column.)

The higher the GI value, the greater the food's ability to rapidly raise blood glucose levels, and the more insulin needed by the body (not desirable).

Eating low-GI foods may lead to better control of blood glucose and insulin levels (which in turn lowers the risk of damage to blood vessels and nerves). The slower digestion of low-GI foods may also help to delay hunger pangs and benefit weight control.

Cautionary Notes on GI

Choosing low-GI foods is not a license to eat unlimited amounts. Calorie restriction and portion control for weight control is of prime importance.

Also remember, Low-GI foods are carbo-hydrate foods and must still be counted as part of any dietetic carbohydrate plan.

GI is not meant to be used by itself without regard to portion size, and other dietary recommendations for healthy eating. Foods are not good or bad on the basis of their GI.

While GI may be a helpful tool for some people with diabetes, what is most important is to control the total amount of carbohydrate that you eat.

LOWER-GLYCEMIC FOODS

Slower-Acting Carbohydrates
These foods are more slowly digested and absorbed. They help maintain more even blood glucose levels, as long as excessive amounts are not eaten. Use these foods regularly but still limit portion size for weight control.

Examples:

- Dried beans, peas, lentils
- Nuts and seeds
- Wholegrain breads
- Bran cereals, oats
- Sweet corn, barley, buckwheat
- Wholegrain pasta, basmati rice
- Fresh fruit: apples, avocados, bananas (firm), cherries, grapefruit, grapes, olives, oranges, peaches, pears, plums. Fresh juices.
- Vegetables: broccoli, yam, sweet potatoes, salad greens
- Milk, yogurt, soy drinks
- Dark chocolate
- Sugar alcohols (sorbitol, maltitol)

HIGHER-GLYCEMIC FOODS

Quicker-Acting Carbohydrates
These foods more rapidly raise blood glucose levels. Eat only in moderation.

- White bread, rice cakes, bagels, croissants, doughnuts
- Low-fiber cereals: Cornflakes, *Rice Krispies, Froot Loops*
- White potatoes, white rice
- Watermelon, ripe bananas, cantaloupe, pineapple
- Soda, sugar-sweetened sports and energy drinks
- Sugar, candy, popcorn (plain)
- Ice cream (low-fat), frozen yogurt

High-GI fruits and potatoes are still healthy choices when eaten in moderate amounts.

≫ **Calorie and fat values have been rounded off.** Calories ~ to the nearest 5 or 10 calories. Fat ~ to nearest half gram. **Note:** Trace amounts of fat (less than 0.3 grams) have been treated as zero.

≫ **Carbohydrate figures** in this book are for total carbohydrate, and not **Net Carbs** (which deducts fiber, polydextrose and sugar alcohols from total carbs).

≫ Because manufacturers' figures on labels are rounded off, figures in this book may differ slightly from the label. Serving sizes may also vary.

C ~ Calories
F ~ Fat (grams)
Cb ~ Carbohydrate (grams)

Abbreviations	
tsp	= teaspoon
Tbsp or T	= Tablespoon
oz	= ounce(s)
c	= cup
fl.oz	= fluid ounce(s)
g	= gram(s)
avg	= average
pkg	= package

Volume Measures	
(All measures are level)	
3 tsp	= 1 Tbsp
2 Tbsp	= 1 fl.oz
½ cup	= 4 fl.oz
1 cup	= 8 fl.oz
2 cups	= 1 Pint
2 Pints	= 1 Quart

Note: 8 oz weight is not the same as 8 fl oz volume (space occupied). Dense foods weigh more per set volume. Examples:
1 cup popcorn weighs ½ oz
1 cup milk weighs 8½ oz
1 cup pudding weighs 10 oz

Metric Conversion	
½ oz	= 14 grams
1 oz	= 28.4 grams
2 oz	= 57 grams
3½ oz	= 100 grams
1 fl.oz	= 30 mls
1 cup (8 fl.oz)	= 240 mls
33 fl.oz	= 1 liter (volume)

IMPORTANT DISCLAIMER

* The authors and publishers of this book are not physicians and are not licensed to give medical advice. This book is not a substitute for professional advice. Users should consult their medical professional before making any health, medical or other decisions based on the material contained herein.

* This book is a compilation of original material from other sources intended for educational purposes only. Because food manufacturers constantly change their products, only they are the authoritative source for food's most current nutritional information.

* Persons using the information herein for any medical purposes, such as matching insulin dosage to carbohydrate intake, should not rely solely on the accuracy of figures herein and should independently check food labels or contact the food manufacturer for the latest data.

Canadian Readers:

Please note that figures in this book are based on U.S. food products and restaurants. Equivalent Canadian foods may vary and should be checked independently.

* WARRANTY DISCLAIMER:

THE AUTHOR AND PUBLISHER DISCLAIM ANY LIABILITY ARISING DIRECTLY OR INDIRECTLY FROM THE USE OF THIS BOOK. THE INFORMATION HEREIN IS PROVIDED "AS IS" AND WITHOUT ANY WARRANTY EXPRESSED OR IMPLIED. ALL DIRECT, INDIRECT, SPECIAL, INCIDENTAL, CONSEQUENTIAL OR PUNITIVE DAMAGES ARISING FROM ANY USE OF THIS INFORMATION IS DISCLAIMED AND EXCLUDED.

This information is also provided subject to Family Health Publications' Terms and Conditions found at the website, www.calorieking.com/terms and incorporated herein.

INFORMATION SOURCES
• U.S. Dept. of Agriculture
• U.S. Food Manufacturers
• Food Industry Boards & Councils
• Author extrapolations

FEEDBACK WELCOME!
Please contact the author with your queries and suggestions.
feedback@calorieking.com

- **Health Hazards: Excessive alcohol intake** contributes to obesity, high blood pressure, stroke, heart and liver disease, some cancers, and even impotence. **Concentration and short-term memory** are reduced as well as athletic performance.

  Other alcohol hazards include: Fetal Alcohol Syndrome, stomach upsets, menstrual problems, depression, snoring, sleep problems, work absenteeism, impaired judgement, risky behaviors and social/family problems.

- **Alcohol contributes to obesity** through its high calories and by lessening the body's ability to burn fat. Fat storage is promoted, particularly in the belly – a health danger zone. Alcohol can also stimulate the appetite; and weaken the dieter's resolve!

- **Alcohol is potentially more harmful while dieting:** Blood sugar levels may drop with resultant fatigue and further impairment of concentration, reflexes and driving skills.

Excess alcohol contributes to obesity, high blood pressure and many other health problems

LOWER RISK ALCOHOL LIMITS

WOMEN:
No more than
1 drink per day

MEN:
No more than
2 drinks per day
(Over 65 y.o. ~ 1 drink)

(At least 2 days a week should be alcohol-free)

1 DRINK CONTAINS 14 GRAMS ALCOHOL
→ 12 fl.oz Regular Beer (5% Alc.)
→ OR 14 fl.oz Light Beer (4.2% Alc.)
→ OR 5 fl.oz Wine (12% Alc.)
→ OR 1½ fl.oz Spirits (80 Proof)

Note: You cannot save daily drinks for one occasion.

Binge drinking is particularly harmful:
4 drinks for males or 3 drinks for females (within 2 hours).

For some people, safe drinking means no alcohol at all. Even one drink may impair driving skills, particularly if tired. For women who drink frequently, breast cancer risk is increased by 9% for each drink after the first drink. In men, just 2 drinks a day doubles the risk of cancers of the mouth and throat.

It is advisable not to drink at all if you are:
- pregnant, trying to conceive or breastfeeding
- taking medication or have liver or heart disease (unless approved by your doctor or pharmacist)
- planning to drive, use machinery or play sports
- studying or needing to concentrate
- a child or adolescent

Women and adolescents are more prone to alcohol's ill-effects due to their lower body weight, smaller livers and lesser capacity to metabolize alcohol. As we age, our ability to handle alcohol decreases.

HOW TO CALCULATE ALCOHOL CONTENT

Percent alcohol on label refers to alcohol volume (ml alcohol/100ml).
Note: 100ml = 3½ fl.oz

To convert to grams (weight) of alcohol, multiply the alcohol volume by 0.8 – since 1 ml of alcohol weighs only 0.8 grams.

EXAMPLE:
12 fl.oz Can Beer (5% alcohol)
5% alc. volume
= 5% of 12 fl.oz = 0.6 fl.oz
= 18ml alcohol (Note: 1 fl.oz = 30ml)
Weight (18ml x 0.8) = 14.4g alcohol

GOVERNMENT WARNINGS!

(1) According to the Surgeon General, women should not drink alcoholic beverages during pregnancy because of the risk of birth defects.

(2) Consumption of alcoholic beverages impairs your ability to drive a car or operate machinery, and may cause health problems.

EXTRA INFORMATION

Alcohol & Diabetes ~ See Page 21
Alcohol & The Heart ~ See Page
Tips to Avoid Harmful Drinking ~ Page

Quick Guide

Alc ~ Alcohol (Grams)
Cb ~ Carbohydrate

Beer:
Beer Contains Zero Fat:

	C	**Alc**	**Cb**
Regular Beer (5% Alc. Vol.):			
7 fl.oz Glass	80	8.5	4
12 fl.oz Bottle/Can/Glass	140	14	10
16 fl.oz Bottle/Can	185	19	13
22 fl.oz Bottle	260	26	18
24 fl.oz Can	280	28	14
32 fl.oz Bottle	370	38	28
40 fl.oz Bottle	470	47	35
50 fl.oz Football	590	59	50
Light Beer (4.2% Alc. Vol.):			
7 fl.oz Glass	65	7	4
12 fl.oz Bottle/Can/Glass	110	12	7
16 fl.oz Bottle/Can	145	16	9
22 fl.oz Bottle	200	22	13
24 fl.oz Can	220	24	14
Non-Alcoholic Brews:			
(Less than 0.5% alcohol by volume)			
Average all Brands, 12 fl.oz	70	1	14

Beer ~ Brands

Note: Figures shown are for the United States except for the states of Utah, Colorado, Kansas and Oklahoma who have certain restrictions limiting the alcohol content to not more than 4% by volume (3.2% by weight).

Percentage alcohol listed is by volume - not by weight.
Per 12 fl.oz Serving

	C	**Alc**	**Cb**
Amstel, Light (3.5%)	95	10	5
Anchor: Porter (5.6%)	210	15	23
Steam (4.9%)	165	14	14
Asahi: Kuronama (5.3%)	165	14	14
Select (4.7%)	140	13	11
Super Dry (4.9%)	150	14	11
Bass, Pale Ale (5.1%)	155	14	12
Beck's: Original (5%)	145	14	10
Premier Light (2.3%)	65	7	4
Big Sky: Original IPA (6.2%)	195	18	17
Moose Drool (5.3%)	175	15	16
Scape Goat (4.7%)	155	14	14
Trout Slayer Ale (4.7%)	145	14	12
Blatz: Original (4.6%)	145	13	13
Light (3.9%)	110	11	8
Blue Moon: Belgian (5.4%)	165	15	13
Grand Cru Ale (8.2%)	230	21	19
Harvest Pumpkin Ale (5.8%)	180	17	14
Spring Ale (5.7%)	180	16	15
Summer Ale (5.2%)	150	15	13
Winter Abbey Ale (5.7%)	180	16	14
Bohemia (4.73%)	140	14	12

Brands (Cont)

Alc ~ Alcohol (Grams)

Per 12 fl.oz Serving

	C	**Alc**	**Cb**
Bud Ice, (5.5%)	120	16	4
Bud Light: Regular (4.2%)	110	12	7
& Clamato Chelada (4.2%)	150	12	16
Lime (4.2%)	115	12	8
Lime-A-Rita (8%), 8 oz	220	15	29
Platinum (6%)	140	17	5
Straw-Ber-Rita (8%), 8 oz	200	15	24
Budweiser: Lager (5%)	145	14	11
Black Crown (6%)	165	17	11
Clamato Chelada (5%)	185	14	20
Picante (5%)	200	14	23
Select (4.3%)	100	12	3
Select 55 (2.4%)	55	7	2
Busch: Original (4.3%)	115	12	7
Ice (5.9%)	135	17	4
Light (4.1%)	95	12	3
Carlsberg, Pilsner (5%)	135	14	10
Carta Blanca (4.6%)	145	13	11
Castlemaine XXXX, Bitter (4.6%)	140	14	10
Cerveza, Aguila (4%)	125	11	11
Colt 45, Malt Liquor (5.6%)	155	16	11
Coors: Banquet (5%)	150	14	12
Extra Gold (5%)	150	14	13
Light (4.2%)	100	12	5
Corona: Extra (4.6%)	150	13	14
Light (4.1%)	100	12	5
Dos Equis XX: Amber (4.6%)	145	13	12
Lager (4.6%)	140	13	11
Fosters: Lager (5%)	145	14	11
Premium Ale (5.5%)	145	16	12
Genesee: Lager (4.5%)	150	13	14
Genny Light Lager (3.6%)	95	10	6
George Killian's, Irish Red (5%)	160	14	15
Grolsch: Blonde (2.8%)	120	8	16
Light (3.6%)	95	11	6
Premium (5%)	145	14	10
Guinness: Draught (4%)	125	12	10
Extra Stout (6%)	175	17	14
Hamm's: Original (4.7%)	145	13	12
Special Light (3.9%)	110	12	8
Heineken: Lager (5%)	150	14	12
Special Dark (5%)	165	14	15
Premium Light (3.5%)	100	10	7
Hurricane: Malt Liquor (5.9%)	135	17	4
High Gravity (8.1%)	185	23	14
Icehouse: Original (5.5%)	150	16	10
Light (5%)	125	16	7
Keystone: Ice (5.9%)	140	17	6
Light (4.2%)	105	12	5
Killian's, Irish Red (5%)	165	14	14
King Cobra (6%)	135	17	4

Brands (Cont)

Alc ~ Alcohol (Grams)

Cb ~ Carbohydrate

Per 12 fl.oz Serving

Beer Contains Zero Fat:	C	Alc	Cb
Kirin: Ichiban (5%)	145	14	10
Light (3.2%)	95	9	8
Kokanee Glacier, (5%)	145	14	11
Labatt: Blue (4.7%)	135	14	10
Blue Light (4%)	110	11	8
Landshark, Lager (4.6%)	150	13	13
Leinenkugel's: Original (4.6%)	150	13	14
Summer Shandy (4.2%)	130	12	12
Lone Star: Pale Lager (4.7%)	135	13	12
Light (3.9%)	110	11	9
Lowenbrau, Original (5%)	140	14	12
Magic Hat, #9 (5.1% alc)	155	15	14
Magnum, Malt Liquor (5.6%)	160	16	9
Michelob: Lager (4.8%)	160	14	14
Light (4.1%)	120	12	9
Amber Bock (5.1%)	150	14	12
Golden Draft (4.6%)	120	13	7
Golden Draft Light (4.1%)	110	12	7
Ultra (4.2%)	95	12	2.5
Ultra Amber (3.9%)	90	11	3
Ultra Fruit Flavors (4%)	95	11	5
Mickey's, Malt Liquor (5.6%)	160	16	11
Miller: Chill, 100 Calorie (4.2%)	100	12	4
Genuine Draft /High Life (4.7%)	145	13	13
High Life Light (4.2%)	110	12	7
Lite (4.2%)	95	12	3
MGD 64 (2.8%)	65	8	2.5
Milwaukee's Best:			
Premium (4.3%)	130	12	11
Ice (5.9%)	145	17	7
Light (4.2%)	100	12	4
Minnesota's Best, Original (4.9%)	140	14	10
Modelo, Especial (4.4%)	145	13	13
Molson Canadian: Lager (5%)	135	14	11
'67' Light (3%)	70	9	2
Light (4%)	115	11	10
Moosehead, Lager (5%)	140	14	11
Natural: Ice (5.9%)	130	17	4
Light (4.2%)	95	12	3
Negra Modelo (5.4%)	170	15	15
Newcastle, Brown Ale (4.7%)	140	13	10
Old English "800",			
Malt (5.9%)	160	17	11
Old Milwaukee:			
Lager (4.5%)	150	13	15
Light (4.3%)	125	12	10
Ice (5.5%)	150	16	10
Old Style: Lager (4.7%)	145	13	12
Light (4.2%)	115	12	7
Pabst: Blue Ribbon (4.7%)	145	13	12
Light (3.9%)	110	11	8

Cb ~ Carbohydrate

Per 12 fl.oz Serving Unless Indicated

	C	Alc	Cb
Pacifico, Clara (4.4%)	145	13	13
Piels, Lager (4.3%)	125	12	9
Pilsner Urquell, Lager (4.4%)	155	13	16
Point: Amber Classic (4.7%)	160	14	11
Special Lager (4.6%)	150	13	9
Redbridge, Lager (4.7%)	125	10	12
Red Dog, Lager (5%)	150	14	14
Red Hook: ESB (5.8%)	185	16	16
India Pale Ale (6.5%)	190	13	19
Red Stripe, Jamaican Ale (5%)	155	14	14
Samuel Adams:			
Boston Lager (4.9%)	175	14	19
Sam Adams, Light Lager (4%)	125	13	9
Sapporo, Prem. Lager (4.9%)	140	14	10
Schaefer: Lager (4.6%)	145	13	12
Light (3.9%)	110	11	8
Schell's: Deer (4.8%)	135	14	8
Light (4%)	100	11	7
Schlitz: Pale Lager (4.6%)	145	13	12
Light (3.8%)	110	11	8
Schmidt's: Pale Lager (4.6%)	145	13	13
Light (3.8%)	110	11	8
Sheaf, Stout (5.8%)	190	16	19
Shock Top: Belgian White (5.2%)	165	15	15
Lemon Shandy (4.2%)	130	12	10
Sierra Nevada: Bigfoot (9.6%)	330	28	32
Pale Ale (5.6%)	175	16	14
Glissade Golden Bock (6.4%)	205	18	18
Porter (5.6%)	195	16	18
Sol (4.2%)	130	12	11
Southpaw, Light (5%)	125	14	7
Sparks, Lager (6%)	255	17	35
Steel Reserve:			
High Gravity Malt Liquor (8.1%)	220	23	16
Steel 6 (6%)	160	17	11
Stella Artois: Pale Lager (5.2%)	155	15	12
Cidre (4.5%)	170	13	21
Stroh's: Pale Lager (4.6%)	145	13	12
Light (3.9%)	115	11	7
Tecate: Pale Lager (4.6%)	140	13	12
Light (4%)	110	10	8
Trader Jose:			
Premium Lager (5%), 11.2 fl.oz	145	14	14
Prem. Lager Light (3.8%), 11.2 fl.oz	105	14	8
Weinhard's: Priv. Reserve (4.8%)	150	14	13
Hefeweizen (4.86%)	150	14	13
Widmer, Hefeweizen (4.9%)	165	15	13
ZeigenBock, Amber (4.9%)	145	14	11
Home Brewed Beer:			

Similar to regular beers, according to alcohol content.

Alc ~ Alcohol (Grams) **Cb** ~ Carbohydrate

Non-Alcoholic Brews

Less Than 0.5% Alcohol
Average All Brands:
(Busch NA, Coors NA, Haake Beck, Kaliber, Kingsbury, O'Douls, Old Milwaukee NA, Pabst NA, Stroh's NA, Texas Select):

	C	Alc	Cb
12 fl.oz Can/Bottle	70	1	14
O'Doul's, Amber, 12 fl.oz	90	1	18
Sharp's, 12 fl.oz	60	1	12

Cider ~ Alcoholic

Per 12 fl.oz

	C	Alc	Cb
Ace: Cider (5%), av. all flavors	155	14	12
Joker (6.9%)	135	20	12
Hornsby's: Draft Cider (6%)	170	17	16
Hard Apple Cider (5.5%)	200	15	27
Michelob, Ultra Light Cider (4%)	120	10	10
Woodchuck: Amber (5%)	200	14	21
Dark & Dry (5%)	180	14	16
Granny Smith (5%)	160	14	11
Pear (4%)	150	12	18
Raspberry (4%)	170	12	22
Wyder's: Apple (5%)	150	14	21
Pear (4%)	140	12	22
Raspberry (4%)	120	12	17

Quick Guide

Table Wines:
Average all Varieties (11.5% Alc.)
(Wine Contains Zero Fat)

	C	Alc	Cb
4 fl.oz, 1 small wine glass OR ½ large wine glass	100	12	3
6 fl.oz, (¾ large wine glass)	145	18	5
8 fl.oz, (1 large wine glass)	195	25	7
½ Carafe/Bottle, 12 fl.oz	295	37	10
1 Bottle, 750ml, 25.4 fl.oz	620	78	21

Table Wines

	C	Alc	Cb
Red: Per 4 fl.oz			
Burgundy/Cabernet/Merlot, av.	100	11	4
White: Per 4 fl.oz			
Dry (Chenin; Fume Blanc; Chardonnay)	95	11	4
Sparkling (11%)	95	11	4
Zinfandel Sweet, (Moselle/Sauterne), 4 fl.oz	85	11	2
Skinnygirl ~ See Reduced Alcohol Wine			

Table Wines (Cont)

	C	Alc	Cb
Champagne: Per 4 fl.oz			
Average all types, 1 glass	85	11	2
with Orange Jce (3:1 orange)	75	8	4
with Orange Jce (1:1 orange)	65	5	7
Mulled Wine (Gluhwein), 4 fl.oz	180	14	20
Non-Alcoholic Wine: Less than 0.5% Alcohol			
Ariel: White varieties, average, 4 fl.oz	35	0.5	8
Red varieties, average, 4 fl.oz	25	0.5	5
Reduced Alcohol Wine:			
Average all types, (6%), 4 fl.oz	80	6	10
Skinnygirl, Red/White, (8.5%), 5 fl.oz	100	10	5
Sake (Gekkeikan), (16%), 4 fl.oz	120	15	5
Sangria (Skinnygirl), (4%), 5 fl.oz	130	12	23

Flavored Wines

Average All Brands (6% alcohol)
(Arbor Mist, Wild Vines, Boone's Farm):

	C	Alc	Cb
1 small wine glass, 4 fl.oz	80	6	10
1 large wine glass, 8 fl.oz	160	11	20
1 bottle, 750 ml (25.4 fl.oz)	510	35	64

Dessert Wines

	C	Alc	Cb
Madeira (18%), 2 oz	85	9	5
Marsala (18%), 2 oz	110	9	11
Port, Muscatel (18%), 2 oz	85	9	5
Sherry (15%), 2 oz:			
Dry, 1 Sherry glass	90	7	7
Sweet/Cream, average	90	7	8
Vermouth (Martini & Rossi):			
Extra Dry (18%), 2 oz	65	9	2
Martini Rosso (16%), 2 oz	90	8	8

Cooking Wines

	C	Alc	Cb
Holland House:			
Marsala, (14%), 2 T., 1 fl.oz	45	4	4
Red/White, (10%): 2 T., 1 fl.oz	20	2	1
1 cup, 8 fl.oz	160	24	8
Sherry, (17%), 2 Tbsp, 1 fl.oz	45	5	2

Cooking with Wine:
For alcohol to evaporate, sufficient heat and cooking time (at least 30 minutes) is required.
Red and white table wines would then contain negligible residual calories.
Sweetened wines (marsala/sherry) would contain 10 calories per 1 fl.oz.
Flambé Desserts: Only surface alcohol is burned off, so negligible reduction in alcohol or calories.

Quick Guide — Alc ~ Alcohol (Grams)

Spirits/Liquors:
Includes Bourbon, Brandy, Gin, Rum, Scotch, Tequila, Vodka, Whiskey.
Note: All spirits with same alcohol proof have similar calories and zero fat.

Average All Brands

	C	Alc	Cb
80 Proof (40% Alcohol by Volume):			
1 fl.oz	65	9.5	0
1½ fl.oz (1 shot)	100	14	0
3 fl.oz (Double shot)	195	28	0
½ Bottle, 350 ml (12 fl.oz)	770	113	0
1 Bottle, 700 ml (24 fl.oz)	1540	227	0
86 Proof (43% Alc):			
1 fl.oz	70	10	0
1½ fl.oz (1 shot)	105	15	0
1 Bottle (24 fl.oz)	1670	244	0
100 Proof (50% Alc),			
1½ fl.oz	125	18	0
Shochu (Soju),			
average all types (25% alc), 2 fl.oz	65	12	0

Flavored Spirits

	C	Alc	Cb
Captain Morgan: Per 1½ fl.oz			
Original (35%)	85	12	0.5
Black Label (40%)	100	14	0
Parrot Bay (21%), average	95	7.5	11
Silver Spiced (35%)	95	12	2
Malibu Rum: Per 1½ fl.oz			
Original/Banana (21%)	80	7.5	30
Pineapple (21%)	75	7.5	22
Southern Comfort (35%), 1½ fl.oz	100	12	3

Hard Lemonade & Sodas

	C	Alc	Cb
Margaritaville,			
Spiked Lemonade/Tea (5.5%), 12 fl.oz	225	15	30
Mike's: Per 11.2 fl.oz Unless Indicated			
Lemonade: Hard, Original, (5%), av.	220	14	33
Light (4%)	110	11	14
Harder (8%) average, 16 fl.oz	395	22	22
Margarita (5.5%)	235	14	34
Punch : Hard (5.5%)	230	15	34
Harder (8%): Fruit Punch, 23.5 fl.oz	730	0	96
Mango (8%), 23.5 fl.oz	690	0	87
Sparks: Per 12 fl.oz (Half of 24 oz Can)			
Blackberry; Iced Tea (8%), av.	295	23	34
Lemonade (8%)	275	23	29
Original (6%)	260	17	35
Tilt: Per 16 fl.oz Can			
Blue/Green/Purple (6%),	340	23	45
Pink (6%)	320	23	41
Red/Yellow (6%)	280	23	30
Twisted Tea: Light (4%), 12 fl.oz	115	11	9
Original (5%), average all, 12 fl.oz	210	14	31

Coolers & Premix Cocktails

Ready-To-Drink:
Zero Fat Unless Indicated

	C	Alc	Cb
Bacardi Silver: Per 12 fl.oz			
Lemonade/Sangria (6%), av.	270	17	41
Raz/Strawberry (5%)	240	14	36
Mojito (5%)	240	14	36
Bacardi: Per 4 fl.oz			
Party Drinks (Ready To Pour):			
Bahama Mama; Mai Tai (10%)	130	9	16
Mojito (15%)	160	14	16
Rum Island Ice Tea (12.5%)	150	12	16
Bartles & Jaymes: Per 11.2 fl.oz			
Malt Based Coolers (3.2%):			
Exotic Berry	195	9	31
Margarita	235	9	43
Mojito	245	9	43
Pina Colada	250	9	45
Sangria	230	9	25
Captain Morgan's,			
Parrot Bay (4.1%), all var. av., 11.2 fl.oz	210	10	35
Chi Chi's: Long Is. Iced Tea, 4 fl.oz	145	12	17
Mexican Mudslide, 4 fl.oz (8g fat)	240	1.5	42
Mojito, 4 fl.oz	160	11	21
Pina Colada, 4 fl.oz (6g fat)	240	4	42
White Russian, 4 fl.oz (7g fat)	245	1.5	43
Daily's (6.9%):			
Bag-In-Box Cocktails, 4 fl.oz	110	6	15
Single Serve Bottles, all flav., 8 fl.oz	220	12	30
Jack Daniels, Country Cocktails (5%),			
all varieties, average, 10 fl.oz	245	12	40
Jose Cuervo:			
Margaritas:			
Classic Lime (10%), 6 fl.oz	210	14	29
Golden (12.7%), 4.7 fl.oz	170	14	19
Seagram's:			
Escapes Coolers (3.2%):			
Bahama Mama, 12 fl.oz	150	9	39
Strawberry Daiquiri, 12 fl.oz	170	9	44
Skinnygirl:			
Vodka with flavors (30%), 1½ fl.oz	75	11	0
Cocktails (10%), av., 3 fl.oz	70	8	4
Smirnoff: Per 11.2 fl.oz			
Ice (4.5%):			
Original/Grape, average	205	12	37
Apple/Stawberry Acai, av.	235	12	36
Mango	225	12	33
Pomeg./Raspb./Triple Black	225	12	37
TGI Friday's: Per 6 fl.oz			
On The Rocks:			
Margarita (7.5%)	180	6	28
Long Island Ice Tea (15%)	245	12	27
Mudslide (10%)	355	8	50
Blenders (12.5%), av.	435	10	51

Coolers & Premix Cocktails (Cont)

Ready-To-Drink:

The Club Premix Cocktails: Per 3.4 oz Serving (½ can)	C	Alc	Cb
Censored on Beach; Margarita (7.5%)	105	6	17
Gin/Vodka Martini (21%), average	155	17	0.2
Long Island Ice Tea (15%)	145	12	17
Manhattan (17%)	115	13	5
Mudslide/Pina Colada (10%), average	200	8	16
Screwdriver (7.5%)	95	6	14
Whiskey Sour (10%)	95	8	11

Shooters

Alc ~ Alcohol (Grams)

	C	Alc	Cb
Alabama Slammer	110	14	2
Amaretto Sour	120	6	19
B52	145	14	11
Beam Me Up Scotty	145	13	13
Blue Tequila	160	18	6
Jager Bomb	205	8	30
Jager Bomb, w/ Sugar-Free Red Bull	155	8	18
Jell-O Shot: 3 oz, With 1½ oz Vodka	180	14	19
With Diet Jell-O	110	14	0
Kamikaze	75	8	3
Kool-Aid	160	15	14
Orgasm	100	12	6
Peppermint Patty	195	8	11
Stinger	170	18	12
Surfer on Acid	90	7	11

Cocktail Mixers ~ Non-Alcoholic

Bacardi: Per 8 fl.oz, Prepared from 2 fl.oz Concentrate	C	Alc	Cb
Daiquiris; Rum Runner	120	0	32
Margarita	90	0	25
Mojito	110	0	30
Pina Colada	170	0	36
Baja Bob's: Per 4 fl.oz			
Cranberry Cosmo Martini	10	0	2
Pina Colada	30	0	4
Jose Cuervo,			
Margaritas: Av. all flav., 4 fl.oz	85	0	21
Light (Sugar Free), Lime, 4 fl.oz	5	0	1
Mr & Mrs T:			
Bloody Mary: Original, 5 oz	30	0	7
Bold & Spicy, 4 oz	35	0	7
Mai Tai	130	0	32
Margarita	100	0	26
Pina Colada	170	0	44
Strawberry Daiquiri	180	0	46
TGI Friday's:			
Mudslide, 2.3 fl.oz	110	0	23
Cosmo; Berrytini, 2 fl.oz	80	0	20
Strawb. Daiquiri; Marg., 4 fl.oz	190	0	46

Cocktails

Alc ~ Alcohol (Grams)

Made to Standard Recipes (Standard Size):
(Main Reference: The New American Bartender's Guide)

Zero Fat Unless Indicated	C	Alc	Cb
Adios Mother F.	260	23	23
Bacardi & Coke (with 1½ oz Bacardi)	160	14	17
Bellini, 4.5 fl.oz	95	11	7
Bloody Mary (with 1½ oz Vodka)	125	10	7
Blushin' Russian (20g fat)	405	14	23
Bourbon & Soda (with 2 oz Bourbon)	130	19	0
Brandy Alexander (10g fat)	300	20	15
Chupa Naranjas (with 1½ oz Tequila)	150	16	8
Cosmopolitan	215	24	12
Daiquiri (w/ 2 oz Rum), av. all types	140	19	4
Frozen Daiquiri (with 2 oz Rum):			
Without fruit	155	19	6
With fruit (with 1½ oz Rum)	145	14	11
Grasshopper	260	17	28
Greyhound (with 1½ oz Vodka)	170	14	17
Harvey Wallbanger	200	19	17
Highball (1½ oz Whiskey)	100	14	0
Irish Coffee (10g fat)	205	14	2
Kahlua Mudslide: With milk (3g fat)	145	11	12
With cream (12g fat)	230	11	10
Lemon Drop, 4 fl.oz	130	14	10
Long Island Iced Tea (with 3 oz Cola)	270	19	22
With 3 oz Diet Cola	235	19	22
Mai Tai (with 2 oz Rum)	290	24	33
Manhattan	130	17	5
Margarita	160	18	7
Martini: Dry, with 1.5 oz gin	100	14	0
Sour Apple, w/ 2 oz Vodka/1 oz Schnapps	250	31	10
Mint Julep (with 2½ oz Bourbon)	180	24	4
Mojito (with 2 oz rum)	170	19	9
Moscow Mule	185	14	24
Pina Colada (10g fat), 6 oz	250	15	18
Red Bull & Vodka (with 1½ oz vodka)	210	14	28
With Sugar Free Red Bull	105	14	3
Rum & Coke (with 1½ oz Rum)	160	14	17
Sangria: With 1 oz Fruit Juice, 5 oz	120	12	9
With ½ oz Brandy, 5.5 oz	150	17	9
Screwdriver	160	14	15
Sex On The Beach	235	19	25
Spritzer (with 3 oz Wine)	65	8	2
Tequila Sunrise	200	14	25
Tom Collins (with 2 oz Gin)	210	19	18
Vodka Soda (with 1½ oz Vodka)	100	14	0
Vodka Tonic (with 1½ oz Vodka)	165	14	18
Whiskey Sour (w/ 2 oz Whiskey)	155	19	7
White Russian (10g fat)	240	19	7
Non-Alcoholic:			
Cinderella	45	0	11
Shirley Temple (with 6 oz Ginger Ale)	140	0	34

Liqueurs/Cordials

C **Alc** **Cb**

Per 1 fl.oz

	C	Alc	Cb
Advocaat (36 Proof; 2g fat)	85	4	9
Alizé: Cognac (80 Proof)	70	9	2
Gold/Red Passion (32 Proof)	105	4	11
Amaretto (56 Proof)	100	7	14
Baileys Irish Cream (34 Proof; 5g fat)	95	4	3
Benedictine (80 Proof)	90	9	5
Chambord (33 Proof)	105	4	11
Chartreuse (80 Proof)	100	9	9
Cherry Brandy (48 Proof)	80	6	9
Coffee Liqueur (53 Proof)	115	7	16
Cointreau (80 Proof)	95	9	7
Creme de Cacao (54 Proof)	100	6	15
Creme de Menthe (72 Proof)	125	9	14
Curacao (70 Proof)	95	8	6
Drambuie (80 Proof)	105	9	9
Frangelico (40 Proof)	65	5	12
Galliano (86 Proof)	100	10	8
Grand Marnier (80 Proof)	100	9	7
Kahlua (40 Proof)	85	5	14
Kirsch (68 Proof)	80	8	6
Midori (42 Proof)	80	5	11
Ouzo (80 Proof)	105	9	11
Pernod (80 Proof)	75	9	11
Sambuca (84 Proof)	100	10	11
Schnapps (100 Proof)	115	12	9
Southern Comfort (70 Proof)	65	8	3

Liqueur Coffee & Hot Drinks

Per Standard Drink

Liqueur Coffee, Av. all types	**200**	10	10
Irish, 1½ oz Whiskey & 1 oz whip	205	9	4
Hot Toddy, with 1½ liquor, av. all	**170**	9	19
Mulled Wine (*Glühwein*), 4 fl.oz, av	**195**	14	25

"The doctor told him to cut down to just one glass a day."

TEN TIPS TO AVOID HARMFUL DRINKING

1. **Add up the alcohol** you typically drink each day and on social occasions. How does this compare with 'low risk' amounts? (*See page 23*)

2. **Compare the alcohol content** of different drinks and select the lowest. Request half shots of alcohol in cocktails and mixed drinks. Dilute them and keep topping off with non-alcoholic drinks.

3. **Go easy on 'Light' beers.** At 4% alcohol, on average, they are still high in alcohol compared to regular beer (5% alcohol).

4. **Try low alcohol or non-alcohol** alternatives such as fruit juices and mineral water. Take your own to parties.

5. **Before drinking alcohol,** quench your thirst with water and non-alcohol drinks – particularly after vigorous exercise or sports.

6. **Slow the rate of drinking.** Chugging or drinking fast is the major cause of illness and death from alcohol poisoning.

7. **Avoid drinking in 'rounds'.**

8. **Have a non-alcoholic 'spacer'** between drinks (e.g. mineral water, orange juice).

9. **Don't drink on an empty stomach.** Food slows the rate of alcohol absorption.

10. **Keep track of the number of drinks** and know when to stop. Stick to a set limit.

Note: Alcohol can be very dangerous when taken with prescription or street drugs, or when you are very tired.

Extra Info: www.CalorieKing.com

Cocktail Mixers & Extracts

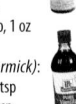

Angostura Bitters, ¼ tsp	2	0	0.5
Grenadine, ½ tsp	6	0	2
Lime/Lemon Juice, 2 Tbsp, 1 oz	10	0	2
Maraschino Cherry, 1 small	8	0	2
Simple Syrup, 1 Tbsp, av.	50	0	14
Sweet & Sour Mix, 2 Tbsp, 1 oz	30	0	7
Tonic Water, 8 fl.oz	80	0	22
Flavor Extracts (*McCormick*):			
Pure Lemon (83%), 1 tsp	0	3.5	0
Pure Vanilla (35%), 1tsp	0	1.5	0

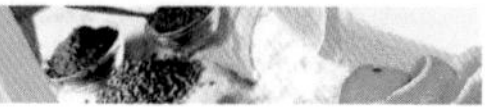

Baking Ingredients	C	F	Cb
Almond Paste, 			
(Marzipan), 2 Tbsp	170	7	24
Apple Pie Filling,			
Sweetened, 9.4 oz	290	0	69
Baking Powder: Regular, 1 tsp	5	0	1
Cream of Tartar, 1 tsp	10	0	2
Baking Mix (*Bisquick*): 			
Original, ⅓ cup, 1½ oz	160	5	26
Heart Smart, 1½ oz	140	2.5	27
Batter Mix (*Golden Dipt*),			
All Purpose, ¼ cup	100	0	20
Blueberries, 1 cup, 5 oz	90	0.5	21
Butter/Margarine, ½ cup, 4 oz	800	88	1
Stick (*Land O' Lakes*), ½ oz	100	11	0
Carob Flour, ½ cup	115	0.5	46
Chocolate Baking Bars: *Average all Brands*			
Sweet (*Baker's*):			
1 oz portion	120	7	16
4 oz bar 	470	28	64
Semi-sweet, 1 oz	140	9	16
Bittersweet, 1 oz	140	12	14
White Baking, 1 oz 	160	9	16
Unsweetened: 1 oz	140	14	8
Grated, 1 cup, 4½ oz	660	69	39
Chocolate Baking Chips: *Average all Brands*			
Milk Choc./Semi Sweet, 1 oz	140	8	18
½ cup, 3 oz	420	24	54
1 cup, 6 oz 	840	48	108
Dark, 1 Tbsp, ½ oz	70	5	3
Mini Kisses (*Hershey*), 1 piece	5	0.5	1
Cocoa Powder:			
Nestle: 1 Tbsp 	15	1	3
⅓ cup, 1 oz	85	5	17
Hershey's: 1 Tbsp	20	0.5	3
⅓ cup, 1 oz	115	3	17
Coconut, Dried:			
Unsweetened, 1 oz	190	18	7
Sweetened/Flaked:1 oz	130	8	15
½ cup, 1.3 oz	195	12	22
Toasted (*Baker's*), 1 oz	170	13	13
Coconut Cream/Milk ~ *See Page 89*			
Coconut Manna (*Nutiva*), 1 Tbsp	100	9	3
Cornstarch, 1 Tbsp	30	0	7
Eggs: Large (1) 	75	5	0
Jumbo (1)	90	6	0.5
Egg White: 1 Egg White	15	0	0
½ cup (4 egg whites), 4 oz	60	0	1
Flour: 			
White: 1 Tbsp, 0.3 oz	25	0	5.5
1 cup, 4.2 oz	400	1	88
Whole Wheat, 1 cup, 4.2 oz	400	2	84

Flavor Extracts: *Av. all Brands*	C	F	Cb
Imitation, 1 tsp 	10	0	2
Pure Extract, 1 tsp	10	0	0.5
Almond; Vanilla, 1 tsp	10	0	0.5
Fruit Pectin: Swtnd, ¼ tsp	5	0	1
Unsweetened, ¼ tsp	0	0	0
Gelatin, dry, unsweetened, 0.25 oz	20	0	0
Glaze (*Duncan Hines*): Choc., 2 T.	150	7	21
Vanilla, 2 Tbsp	140	6	22
Golden Dipt, Batter Mix 			
¼ cup, 1 oz	100	0	23
Honey, ½ cup, 6 oz	515	0	140
Lemon/Orange Peel, ¼ cup	25	0	6
Lighter Bake (*Sunsweet*):			
(Butter & Oil replacement)			
1 Tbsp, ½ oz 	35	0	9
¼ Cup, 2.7 oz	140	0	36
Milk: Whole, 1 cup, 8 fl.oz	150	8	12
2%, 1 cup, 8 fl.oz 	120	5	12
1%, 1 cup, 8 fl.oz	100	2.5	12
Fat-Free, 1 cup, 8 fl.oz	90	0.5	13
Pastry ~ *See Page 134*			
Pie Crusts ~ *See Page 134*			
Pie Fillings, Fruits ~ *See Page 134*			
Lemon Creme, ⅓ cup	130	1.5	28
Mincemeat, 3½ oz 	190	5	45
Pumpkin, 1 cup, 9.3 oz	270	1.5	60
Prune Puree, ¼ cup, 3 oz	220	0	55
Raisins, ½ cup, 2.8 oz	240	0.5	63
Rennin, 0.4 oz pkt	10	0	2
Soy Milk ~ *See Pages 49-50*			
Sprinkles, all types, 1 tsp	20	1	3
Sugar: 1 Tbsp, ½ oz 	55	0	14
1 oz	110	0	28
1 cup, 7 oz	775	0	195
1 lb, 16 oz	1760	0	454
Sweeteners & Sugar Substitutes ~ *See Page 156*			
Vinegar, average all types, 1 oz	5	0	1
Whey, sweet, dry, 1 oz	100	0.5	21
Yeast: Active, dry, ¼ oz pkg	25	0.5	3
Bakers, compressed, 1 oz	30	0.5	5
Fleischmann's, 0.6 oz pkg	0	0	0

For Full Nutritional Data & Product Updates
~ *See Author's Website*
www.CalorieKing.com

Note: Actual weight of bars is usually 5-10% more than label Net Weight. Weigh bar and allow extra calories.

Bars ~ Brands	C	F	Cb

Per Bar

	C	F	Cb
ABB, Steel Bar, av. all var., 2.5 oz	255	5	35
AdvantEdge ~ *See EAS*			
Annie's Homegrown:			
Organic Granola Bars: *Per 1 oz Bar*			
Berry Berry	120	3.5	20
Chocolate Chip	120	4	19
PB & J; Peanut Butter	120	4.5	18
Atkins:			
Advantage Meal: *Per 1.7 oz Bar Unless Indicated*			
Chocolate Chip Cookie Dough, 2 oz	240	11	29
Chocolate Chip Granola	200	9	19
Choc. Peanut Butter, 2 oz	250	14	23
Cookies 'n Crème	180	9	24
Strawberry Almond	200	9	20
(Carbs include 7-15g sugar alcohol)			
Advantage: *Per 1.55 oz Bar*			
Caramel varieties, average	175	10	20
Coconut Almond Delight	200	15	18
Dark Choc. Decadence	150	6	23
(Carbs include 9g sugar alcohol)			
Day Break: *Per 1.25 oz Bar*			
Apple Crisp	150	7	16
Choc. Chip Crisp; Cranb. Alm., av.	145	6	16
Peanut Butter Fudge Crisp	150	7	14
(Carbs include 5-9g sugar alcohol)			
Endulge:			
Caramel Nut Chew, 1.2 oz	130	8	17
Chocolate Caramel Mousse, 1.2 oz	120	4.5	23
Nutty Fudge Brownie, 1.4 oz	170	12	14
Peanut Caramel Cluster, 1.2 oz	140	9	12
(Carbs include 4-12g sugar alcohol)			
Attune Bars:			
Probiotic Bars: *Per 0.7 oz Bar*			
Dark Chocolate	80	6	11
Milk Chocolate Crisp	90	6	12
Mint Chocolate	90	6	12
Balance: *Per 1.76 oz Bars*			
Original varieties; Bare varieties, av.	200	7	21
Dark varieties	180	6	20
Gold varieties, average	200	7	23
Cascadian Farms *(General Mills):*			
Chewy Granola, av. all vars., 1.23 oz bar	135	3	26
Crunchy Granola, all var., 2 bars, 1.4 oz	185	8	27

Per Bar

	C	F	Cb
Clif:			
Original,			
average all varieties., 2.4 oz	240	5	45
Builder's, av. all varieties, 2.4 oz	270	8	30
Kid, ZBar, av. all var., 1.27 oz	125	3.5	23
Max, average all varieties, 3.42 oz	385	13	40
Mojo, average, 1.6 oz	190	11	21
Corazonas:			
Oatmeal Squares: *Per 1.75 oz Bar*			
White Choc. Macadamia	200	8	29
Av. other varieties	185	7	28
Detour:			
Original, Caramel Peanut, 3 oz	350	11	32
Lean Muscle: Av. all var., 1.6 oz	190	7	17
Average all varieties, 3.2 oz	395	15	33
Lower Sugar: Av. all var., 1.4 oz	170	5.5	16
Average all varieties, 2.8 oz	340	11	33
(Carbs include 12-28g sugar alcohol)			
Oatmeal, av. all varieties, 4.25 oz	455	11	61
dotFIT: *Per 2 oz Bar*			
dotBAR: Chocolate Mint	160	5	15
Chocolate Peanut Butter Crunch	190	5	23
Iced Mochaccino	200	5	24
(Carbs include 5.5g sugar alcohol)			
dotSTICK, Iced, average all var.	190	6	26
(Carbs include 8g sugar alcohol)			
EAS:			
AdvantEDGE:			
Carb Control: Crisp Bars, av., 2 oz	240	8	27
Average other varieties, 2 oz	230	8	27
(Carbs include 17-19g sugar alcohol)			
Myoplex 30, average all varieties	350	10	36
Extend Bar: Crunch, av., 1.4 oz	150	2.5	30
Delight, av. all varieties, 1.4 oz	150	3	21
(Carbs include 4-6g sugar alcohol)			
Fiber One: Chewy, av. all, 1 oz	105	3.5	21
90-Calorie Bar, average all, 0.8 oz	90	3	18
FiberPlus *(Kellogg's):*			
Antioxidants: Choc. Chip, 1.25 oz	120	4	26
Nutty Delights, av all var., 1.25 oz	150	8	22
Other varieties, 1.25 oz	130	5	25

Bars ~ Brands (Cont)

	C	F	Cb

Per Bar

Full Bar, Regular, av. all, 1.6 oz — 170, 4, 28
GeniSoy: *Per 1.98 oz Bar*

Protein: Chunky PB Fudge — 220, 6, 30
  Crispy Choc. Mint — 210, 4.5, 33
  Other varieties — 220, 6, 32
General Mills: *Per 1.6 oz Bar*
Milk 'n Cereal Bar,
  Honey Nut Cheerios — 160, 4, 28
Glenny's: *Per 1.1 oz Bar*
Cashew/Cranberry & Almond, av. — 145, 7, 17
Cherry & Almond — 130, 6, 18
Classic Fruit & Nut — 140, 6, 18
Peanuts & Peanut Butter — 170, 13, 10
Glucerna:
Crispy Delights Nutrition Bars,
  Peanut/Choc. Chip, av., 1.4 oz — 145, 5, 20
  (Carbs include 7-8g sugar alcohol)
Mini Snack Bar, average, 0.7 oz — 80, 3, 11
  (Carbs include 2-5 g sugar alcohol)
Gnu Foods: *Per 1.6 oz Bar*
Banana Walnut; Chocolate Brownie — 140, 4, 30
Cinnamon Raisin; Orange Cranberry — 130, 3, 32
Great Value (Walmart):
90 Calories, average all, 0.8 oz — 90, 1.5, 19
Fiber Bar, Oats & Peanut Butter, 1.4 oz — 150, 4.5, 29
Fruit & Grain, low fat,
  average all varieties, 1.3 oz — 135, 2.5, 26
Fruit & Nut, Trail Mix Bar, 1.3 oz — 140, 4, 24
Granola: Choc Chunk, 0.85 oz — 90, 2, 16
  Crunchy Oats & Honey, 1.5 oz — 200, 7, 29
  Sweet & Salty, Almond, 1.25 oz — 160, 8, 20
Health Valley, Cobbler Cereal Bar
Cobbler Cereal Bars, av. 1.25 oz — 130, 2.5, 27
Herbalife,
  Prot. Deluxe!, average, 1.25 oz — 160, 6, 17
HMR, Benefit Bars, av. all, 1.41 oz — 155, 4, 24
Jenny Craig: S'mores, 1.25 oz — 140, 4, 22
  Choc. Caramel P'nut, 1.25 oz — 140, 5, 19
  Choc Chip Snack Bar, 1.2 oz — 140, 3, 23
  Yogurt Dream Bar, 1.2 oz — 130, 4.5, 20
Kashi:
Cereal Bars, av. all var., 1.23 oz — 125, 3, 24
Granola & Seed Bars (2), av., 1.4 oz — 180, 7, 27
Granola Bars:
  Chewy, av. all var., 1.23 oz — 135, 4, 21
  Layered, all varieties, 1.1 oz — 125, 4, 21

Per Bar

	C	F	Cb

Kashi (Cont):
Go Lean:
  Crisp!:
    Chocolate Caramel, 1.58 oz — 150, 3, 28
    Chocolate Peanut, 1.75 oz — 180, 5, 30
    Other varieties, av., 1.58 oz — 165, 4, 27
  Dipped, average all , 1.94 oz — 195, 5, 32
Soft & Chewy, av. all, 1.4 oz — 130, 3, 24
Kellogg's,
  Cinnabon Bar, Original, 1.3 oz — 150, 4.5, 26
Fiber Plus ~ *See page 31*
Nutrigrain ~ *See page 33*
Special K ~ *See page 34*
Kind: *Per 1.4 oz Bar*
Fruit & Nut:
  Almond & Apricot — 180, 10, 23
  Apple Cinnamon & Pecan — 190, 12, 20
  Nut Delight — 210, 16, 14
  Peanut Butter & Strawberry — 190, 11, 19
Nuts & Spices:
  Cashew & Ginger Spices — 200, 14, 16
  Dark Chocolate, all varieties — 200, 13, 16
  Madagascar Vanilla Almond — 210, 16, 14
Plus, average all varieties — 185, 12, 18
Kudos, av. all varieties, 0.85 oz — 100, 3, 17
Labrada:
Protein Bars:
  Lean Body, S'mores Delight, — 360, 14, 33
  Cookie Roll, Chocolate Chip, 2.82 oz — 330, 11, 34
Larabar:
Apple Pie, 1.6 oz — 190, 10, 24
Cherry Pie, 1.7 oz — 200, 8, 30
Chocolate Chip Brownie, 1.6 oz — 200, 9, 31
Peanut Butter & Jelly, 1.7 oz — 210, 10, 27
Lindora, av. all varieties, 1.6 oz — 155, 5, 17
Luna:
Bars For Women,
  average all varieties, 1.7 oz — 180, 4.5, 27
Protein, average all, 1.6 oz — 180, 7, 21
Marathon (Snickers):
Energy: Chewy, av. all var., 2 oz — 210, 8, 26
  Crunchy, Dark Chocolate, — 150, 4.5, 22
Protein, average all, 2.8 oz — 285, 9, 40

Bars ~ Brands (Cont)

Per Bar	C	F	Cb
Market Pantry *(Target):*			
Crunchy Gran., Oat & Honey, 1.5 oz	180	6	28
Cereal Bars: PB Choc Chip, 0.8 oz	100	3	17
Average other varieties	150	5	23
Chewy Bars: Choc Chip, 0.8 oz	100	2.5	18
Choc. Chunk; S'Mores, 0.8 oz	90	1.5	18
Fiber Dark Choc. & Alm., 1.27 oz	140	5	23
Mariani: *Per 1.4 oz Bar*			
Honey Bars: Cranb.; Granola, av.	170	8	23
Sesame	200	14	16
Medifast: Crunch, av., 1.2 oz	110	3	13
(Carbs include 2-3g sugar alcohol)			
Maintenance, C'rmel Nut, 1.5 oz	170	5	22
Met-Rx: *Per 3.5 oz Bar Unless Indicated*			
Big 100, average all varieties	375	6	49
Big 100 Colossal:			
Brownie, Super Choc Fudge	390	12	40
Chocolate Toasted Almond	410	13	46
Crispy Apple Pie	400	10	47
Protein Plus, Mud Pie Fusion, 3 oz	300	9	32
Mojo Bars ~ *See Clif*			
Muscle Milk *(Cytosport): Per 2.6 oz Bar*			
High Protein: Choc. P'nut Caramel	320	11	30
Vanilla Toffee Crunch	310	11	29
Protein Crunch, Choc. PB, 2.9 oz	360	13	30
MuscleTech:			
Nitro-Tech Hardcore, 2.8 oz	310	8	29
Smart Protein:			
Peanut Caramel Crunch, 2.2 oz	290	12	26
Triple Choc., 2.2 oz	270	9	26
Nature's Path:			
Granola Bars:			
5 Bar Box, 1 bar, av., 1.23 oz	145	4	22
10 Bar Box, 2 bars, av. all, 1.4 oz	195	7	28
Nature Valley:			
Crunchy Granola Bars:			
Apple Crisp (2), 1.5 oz	160	6	26
Average other var. (2), 1.5 oz	185	7	28
Chewy, Yogurt coating, av., 1.2 oz	140	3.5	26
Granola Thins, av. all var., 0.6 oz	85	4.5	11
Protein, all varieties, 1.4 oz	190	12	14
Trail Mix, Chewy, av. all, 1.25 oz	135	4	25
Nutri-Grain *(Kellogg's):*			
Cereal Bars: Fruit Flav., av. all, 1.3 oz	120	3	24
Yogurt Bar, Strawberry, 1.3 oz	130	3.5	25
Crunch, (2), all varieties, 1.48 oz	190	7	29

Per Bar	C	F	Cb
Nutrilite *(Amway Global):*			
Meal Bars, all varieties, 1.8 oz	200	7	26
Snack Bar:			
Chocolate Caramel, 0.9 oz	100	3	16
Fudgy Brownie w/ Almds., 0.9 oz	100	3	9
NutriSystem:			
Granola Breakfast Bars:			
Chewy Chocolate Chip	150	2	27
Peanut Butter	160	5	25
Snack Bars: Chewy Peanut	180	9	19
Chocolate Caramel	150	3.5	23
Odwalla:			
Chewy,			
Choc. Alm. Coconut, 1.6 oz	200	8	29
Nourishing: *Per 2 oz Bar*			
Choco-walla	210	5	39
Dark Chocolate Chip Walnut	220	7	36
White Chocolate Macadamia	210	10	27
Protein, Choc. Chip Peanut, 2 oz	230	8	33
Superfood: *Per 2 oz Bar*			
Original	200	3.5	39
Berries GoMega	210	6	36
Blueberry Swirl	200	3	41
Strawberry Pomegranate	200	2	43
Oh Yeah! *(ISS),*			
Orig., Almond Fudge Brownie, 3 oz	350	13	27
Optifast, 800 Bars, av., 1.6 oz	165	4	20
PowerBar:			
Harvest Energy: Fruit & Nut/Nut	210	10	34
Average other varieties	245	5	42
Performance Energy, av. all var.	240	4	45
Protein & Recovery:			
10G Protein, Triple Threat, av. all	230	9	30
20g Protein Plus, av. all varieties	210	5	27
30g Protein Plus, av. all varieties	360	11	34
Power Crunch *(BNRG),*			
Protein Bar, av. all var., 1.4 oz	205	12	10
PR Bar: Double Chocolate, 1.8 oz	200	6	22
Yogurt Berry, 1.8 oz	210	7	22
Granola, Oatmeal Raisin, 1.75 oz	210	7	22
Premier Nutrition:			
Premier Protein:			
Crisp Bars, average all var.,1.8 oz	190	6	26
Protein Bars, av. all var., 2.5 oz	280	7	24
Promax:			
Gluten-Free:			
Chocolate Peanut Crunch, 2.6 oz	300	8	37
Double Fudge Brownie, 2.6 oz	280	7	37
Lower Sugar, av. all var., 2.4 oz	230	7	33
Proti Bars *(Bariatrix),*			
average all varieties, 1.5 oz	160	5.5	16

Note: Actual weight of bars is usually 5-10% more than label Net Weight. Weigh bar and allow extra calories.

Bars ~ Brands (Cont)

Per Bar	C	F	Cb
PureFit, av. all varieties, 2 oz	220	7	25
Pure Protein:			
Baked, all varieties, 1.58 oz	190	8	14
Hi Protein:			
1.75 oz bars, average all varieties	190	5	18
2.75 oz bars, average all varieties	305	10	30
Quaker:			
Chewy Granola Bars:			
25% Less Sugar, Choc. Chip, 0.85 oz	100	3.5	17
90 Calories, av. all varieties, 1 oz	90	2	19
Big, average all varieties, 1.5 oz	170	6	29
Dipps, Caramel Nut	140	6	21
School Days,			
Amazing Apple; Best Berry, 1 oz	100	2	20
Yogurt, all varieties, 1.2 oz	150	4.5	25
Oatmeal To Go:			
Regular, average all varieties, 2.1 oz	220	4	43
High Fiber, Maple Brown Sugar, 2.1 oz	210	4	43
Soft Baked, av. all varieties, 1.48 oz	140	3.5	26
Quest Bar:			
Protein Bar:			
No Sugar Added, av. all flav., 2.12 oz	180	5	23
(carbs include 17-20g fiber/xylitol)			
Revival Soy (Direct):			
Apple Cinnamon	230	3	30
Chocolate Temptation	270	7	32
Peanut Pal	240	6	28
Low Carb, all varieties, average	235	8	31
Slim-Fast:			
Meal Bars:			
Chewy Chocolate Crisp, 1.65 oz	200	6	25
Chocolate P'nut Caramel, 1.58 oz	200	7	21
Sweet & Salty Choc. Almond, 1.58 oz	200	8	21
Snack Bars, av. all flavors	100	3	16
SoyJoy Bars, av. all var., 1 oz	135	6	16
Solo, GI, av. all, 1.75 oz	200	7	26
Special K:			
Cereal Bars, av. all varieties, 0.8 oz	90	1.5	18
Protein Meal, av. all varieties, 1.6 oz	175	5	25
Protein Snack Bars,			
average all varieties, 0.9 oz	110	3	16
Steel Bar (ABB), av. all var., 2.5 oz	250	4	36

Per Bar	C	F	Cb
Supreme Protein:			
High Protein:			
Caramel Nut Chocolate, 3.4 oz	390	15	36
Peanut Butter & Jelly, 3.38 oz	390	15	35
Peanut Butter Crunch, 3 oz	390	18	26
(Carbs include 14-20g Sugar Alcohol)			
thinkThin:			
High Protein:			
Choc. Covered Strawberries, 1.76 oz	200	7	23
2.1 oz Bars, average	235	8	24
(Carbs include 18-22g Sugar Alcohol)			
Bites, av. all var., 0.9 oz	100	4	12
(Carbs include 10g Sugar Alcohol)			
Tiger's Milk:			
Protein Rich, 1.2 oz	140	5	18
Peanut Butter Crunch, 1.2 oz	150	6	18
King Size, av all varieties, 2 oz	225	9	18
Toaster Strudel ~ see page 64			
Trader Joe's:			
Chewy Coated Granola Bars, 6-Packs:			
Chocolate Chip, 1.25 oz	150	4	26
Peanut Butter, 1.25oz	170	8	19
Vanilla Almond, 1.25 oz	150	6	22
Fruit Bars: Fig 1.5 oz	120	2	24
Average other varieties, 1.5 oz	140	2.5	27
Granola Bars, 6-packs:			
Fiberful, 1.25 oz	120	3.5	22
Trail Mix, 1.25 oz	150	5	23
Tri-O-Plex (Chef Jay's):			
High Protein, Ban. Walnut, 4.2 oz	405	14	40
Duo: Caramel Peanut Butter	340	8	45
Bursting Peanut Butter	395	17	35
Usana:			
Choco Chip, 1.4 oz	160	5	17
Go Nuts 'n' Berries, 1.2 oz	150	7	18
Peanutt Bliss, 1.2 oz	160	5	17
Zoe's, Omega-3's, Choc. Delight	190	7	27
Zone Perfect:			
Blueberry Pomegranate, 1.75 oz	210	6	24
Choc, Chip Cookie Dough, 1.5 oz	180	5	24
Dark Chocolate, av. all varieties, 1.5 oz	185	6	22
Fudge Graham, 1.75 oz	210	7	24
Strawberry Yogurt, 1.75 oz	200	6	25
Sweet & Salty, Cashew Pretzel, 1.6 oz	200	7	23

Cocoa & Hot Chocolate **C** **F** **Cb**

Cocoa:

	C	F	Cb
Small (8 fl.oz):			
With Whole Milk	205	8.5	22
With Nonfat Milk	145	1	23
Tall (12 fl.oz): With Whole Milk	280	12	26
With Nonfat Milk	185	1	28
Hot Chocolate:			
Small (8 fl.oz): With Whole Milk	180	7	26
With Nonfat Milk	140	2	27
Tall (12 fl.oz): With Whole Milk	260	10	36
With Nonfat Milk	190	2	37
Cinnabon, Mochalatta Chill, 16 oz	420	17	63
Swiss Miss, Mixes, av., 1 packet	120	2.5	22

Cocoa - Chocolate Mixes

Add extra cals/fat/carbohydrate for milk

Carnation Breakfast Drinks - *See Page 38*

Carnation: *Per 3 Tbsp*

	C	F	Cb
Malted Milk: Original	90	2	15
Chocolate	90	1	18
Ghirardelli:			
Chocolate Mocha, 3 Tbsp, 1.2 oz	120	1.5	29
Double Chocolate, 3 Tbsp, 1.3 oz	120	1.5	30
Hershey's, Cocoa,			
Natural, unsweetened,			
1 Tbsp, 0.2 oz	10	0.5	3
Land O Lakes:			
Arctic White Cocoa, 1.23 oz	160	6	26
Other varieties, 1.23 oz	140	3.5	26
Nestle: *Per Per Single Serve Envelope*			
Chocolate Caramel	100	3	19
Dark Chocolate	100	3	19
Rich Milk Chocolate:			
Regular	80	3	14
Fat Free	25	0	5
No Sugar Added	50	0	9
Nesquik Powder: *Per 2 Tbsp*			
Chocolate; Strawberry	60	0.5	15
Chocolate; Strawb., No Added Sugar	35	1	7
Ovaltine, All Natural Cocoa Mixes,			
average all varieties, 2 Tbsp	40	0	10
Swiss Miss: *Per Single Serve Envelope*			
Breakfast Blends: Great Start	60	1	11
Pick Me Up	110	2	23
Classics:			
Average all flavors	120	2	23
Fat-Free: Original	50	0	10
Marshmallow Lovers	70	0	13

Instant Coffee **C** **F** **Cb**

Powder/Granules: *Regular or Decaffeinated,*

	C	F	Cb
1 level tsp	2	0	0.5
1 rounded tsp	4	0	1
Ground, 3 tsp	7	0	2
Brewed/Percolated, 1 cup, 8 fl.oz	4	0	1
Coffee With Milk/Cream/Creamers: *Per 8 oz Cup*			
Black:	4	0	1
With Whole Milk: Dash, 1 Tbsp	15	0.5	1
2 Tbsp, 1 fl.oz	25	1	2.5
With 2% Milk, 2 Tbsp	20	0.5	2.5
With 1% Milk, 2 Tbsp	20	0.5	2.5
With Fat Free Milk, 2 Tbsp	15	0	2.5
With Soy Milk: 1 Tbsp	10	1	1.5
2 Tbsp, 1 oz	15	0.5	2
With Half & Half: 2 Tbsp	50	3	3
¼ cup, 2 fl.oz	90	6	4
With Cream (light coffee), 2 Tbsp	65	6	2
With Coffee Mate: Liquid, reg., 1 T.	20	1	3
Liquid Fat Free, 1 Tbsp	25	0	2
Powder, 1 heaping tsp	15	1	2
Sugar ~ Add Extra: 1 heaping tsp	25	0	6
Single portion, 1 package	25	0	6
Sweeteners, (Equal/Splenda/Sweet N Low),			
Powder, 1 package	0	0	0

Flavored Coffee Mixes

Chicory:

	C	F	Cb
Instant Coffee, 1 tsp	5	0	1
Coffee Essence, 1 tsp	15	0	4
Caffé D'Vita:			
Mixes, all varieties, average, 3 tsp	60	1.5	11
Sugar Free Mixes, 2 tsp	35	2	3
General Foods International:			
Average all varieties, ½ oz	60	3	10
Sugar-free, av. all varieties, 1 tsp	30	2.5	2
Cappuccino Coolers, all varieties, ½ oz	60	0	15
Hills Bros: *Per 3 Tbsp, 1 oz*			
Cappuccino: French Vanilla	120	4.5	19
Chocolate Hazelnut	110	3.5	19
Classic Cappuccino	120	5	17
Dark Chocolate	110	4	19
Mocha Mint	120	4	20
Nescafe, Memento, 1 stick,			
average all varieties	100	2.5	19
Starbucks, VIA, Iced Coffee,			
all varieties, 1 stick/packet	100	0	24

Coffee Shops/Restaurants

Per 8 fl.oz Cup (Unless Indicated)

	C	F	Cb
Coffee, Regular/Percolated/Filtered	5	0	0
Americano Drip Coffee, 1 cup	7.5	0	1
Cafe Au Lait: 1 cup, 8 fl.oz	60	3.5	5
Nonfat Milk, 1 cup, 8 fl.oz	35	0	5
Caffe Latté:			
8 fl.oz cup: With Whole Milk	110	6	9
With 2% Milk	100	3.5	9
With Nonfat Milk	70	0	10
12 fl.oz: With Whole Milk	180	9	14
With Nonfat Milk	100	0	15
16 fl.oz: With Whole Milk	220	11	18
With Nonfat Milk	130	0	19
Cafe Mocha (Mochaccino): 8 fl.oz	150	6	20
12 fl.oz	230	9	31
16 fl.oz	290	12	41
Cappuccino:			
8 fl.oz cup: With Whole Milk	90	3.5	7
With 2% Milk	80	3	8
With Nonfat Milk	50	0	8
12 fl.oz: With Whole Milk	110	6	9
With 2% Milk	90	3.5	9
With Nonfat Milk	60	0	9
16 fl.oz: With Whole Milk	140	7	11
With 2% Milk	120	3.5	11
With Nonfat Milk	80	0	12
Mocha: *With Cream*			
8 fl.oz: With Whole Milk	200	11	22
With Nonfat Milk	160	6	22
12 fl.oz: Whole Milk	290	15	33
With Nonfat Milk	230	8	34
Iced Mocha: *Without Cream*			
12 fl.oz: With Whole Milk	170	6	26
With Nonfat Milk	130	0	27
Espresso: Single (Solo), 1 fl.oz	5	0	1
Double (Doppio), 2 fl.oz	10	0	2
Espresso con Panna,			
(w/ dollop wh. cream), solo, 1 fl.oz	30	2.5	2
Espresso Macchiato, solo, 1 fl.oz	5	0	1
Frappuccino: Tall, 12 fl.oz	180	2.5	37
Grande, 16 fl.oz	240	3	48
Frappuccino Mocha:			
(With Cream): Tall, 12 fl.oz	280	11	43
Grande, 16 fl.oz	380	15	57
Iced Latte, Similar to Caffe Latte			

McCafe (McDonald's) ~ *See Fast Food, Page 216*
Starbucks ~ *See Fast-Foods Section , Page 243*

Coffee Substitute Mixes

	C	F	Cb
Roasted Cereal Beverages ~ *(No Caffeine)*			
Cafix, Instant Beverage, 1 tsp	5	0	1
Kaffree Roma, Instant Beverage, 1 tsp	10	0	2
Teeccino, Herbal Coffees, 1 tsp	10	0	2

Irish & Liqueur Coffees

	C	F	Cb
Irish Coffee, without sugar	175	10	0
Liqueur Coffee,			
with cream, all varieties, av., 1 fl.oz	100	5	7

Coffee Extras

Chocolate (Cocoa) Topping, ½ tsp	5	0	1
Flavored Syrups: Regular, 2 Tbsp	80	0	20
Sugar-free, 2 Tbsp	0	0	0
Half & Half Cream: 2 Tbsp	40	3.5	1
Single serve pkg, ⅜ fl.oz	15	1.5	0.5
Light whipped cream, 2 Tbsp	15	1.5	1
Marshmallows, miniature (2)	5	0	1
Sugar:			
1 single portion package	20	0	5
1 level tsp	15	0	4
1 heaping tsp	25	0	6
Equal/Splenda/Sweet 'N Low	0	0	0

Coffee Shop ~ Cakes, Cookies

Cookies:	C	F	Cb
Biscotti, 1 oz	140	6.5	18
Chocolate Chip, 3 oz	350	15	54
Oatmeal Raisin, 3 oz	350	12	56
Peanut Butter, 3 oz	410	25	39
White Chocolate Macadamia, 3.33 oz	420	20	55
Cakes/Pastries:			
Almond Croissant, 5 oz	620	35	67
Apple Danish, 5 oz	450	18	67
Banana Walnut, 4.5 oz	410	17	60
Brownie, 3 oz	390	24	42
Bundt, Chocolate, 4 oz	440	21	61
Carrot Cake, 4 oz	400	22	45
Chocolate Cake, 5 oz	530	28	65
Crumble Coffee Cake, 4.5 oz	500	25	65
Cupcake, 3 oz	330	16	43
Pound Cake, av., 3 oz	330	17	40
Cinnamon Roll, 6 oz	500	15	83
Donuts:			
Sugared, 1.75 oz	220	11	27
Glazed, 2 oz	250	12	34
Pretzel, large, 4 oz	290	5	52

Starbucks Bakery Items ~ *See Page 244*

Ready To Drink Coffee C F Cb

Chilled:

Adina: *Per 8 fl.oz Can*			
Double XXpresso	100	2	18
Mayan Mocha	130	2.5	24
Mocha Madness	110	2.5	20
Full Throttle Coffee & Energy ~ *See Page 38*			
International Delight,			
Iced, all varieties, 8 fl.oz	150	2.5	29
Java Monster Energy ~ *See Page 39*			
Kahlua, Cappuccino Shake, 10.5 fl.oz	130	2	24
RealBeanz: *Per 9.5 fl.oz*			
Iced Coffee: All varieties	140	2	27
Diet, Trim & Fit, Cappuccino	60	2	16
Shock Coffee:			
Triple Latte, 8 fl.oz can	150	3.5	27
Triple Mocha, 8 fl.oz can	150	3.5	28
Starbucks: *Per Bottle*			
DoubleShots: *Per 6.f fl.oz*			
Espresso & Cream: Regular	140	6	18
Light	70	4	6
Frappuccino: *Per 9.5 fl.oz Bottle Unless Indicated*			
Caramel/Coffee/Vanilla	200	3	37
Dark Chocolate Mocha, 13.7 fl.oz			
Mocha	180	3	33
Light, Mocha/Vanilla	100	3	12
Iced Coffee, Caramel, 11 fl.oz	110	0.5	21

Starbucks Coffee & Energy ~ *See Page 40*

Caffeine Counter

Moderate caffeine intake is not harmful to healthy adults. However, frequent large amounts (over 350mg/day) may cause dependency ('caffeinism') and adversely affect health. To be safe, limit caffeine to 200mg/day. Avoid if pregnant, breast feeding, a child under 8, have sleep problems, an overactive bladder or heart arrhythmia.

	Caffeine (mg)
Coffee: Instant, weak, 1 level teaspoon	30
Medium, 1 rounded teaspoon	60
Strong, 1 heaping teaspoon	100
Decaffeinated, 1 round teaspoon	2
Bags (Folgers), 1 bag (6-8 fl.oz)	115
Ground, 1 Tbsp, 0.2 oz	60
Bottled (Ready-To-Drink), 9.5 fl.oz	70
Coffee Shop: Brewed, 8 fl.oz	110 -150
Cappuccino: 1 cup, 8 fl.oz	75
Tall, 12 fl.oz	110
Large, 16 fl.oz	150
Decappuccino, decaffeinated	5
Espresso: Regular/Solo	75
Double, (Doppio)	150
Iced Coffee, 12 fl.oz	140
Latte, 1 cup, 8 fl.oz	75
Mocha, 1 cup, 8 fl.oz	90
Hot Chocolate, 8 fl.oz	15
Tea (Black/Green): Weak, 1 cup	20
Medium Strength, 1 cup	40
Strong, 1 cup	70
Decaffeinated Tea, 1 cup	0-5
Herbal Tea, 1 cup	0
Iced Tea, tall glass/can, 12 fl.oz	25-30
Soft Drinks: *Per 12 fl.oz Can*	
Coca-Cola; Pepsi (Regular/Diet)	35
Diet Coke; TAB; RC Cola (Regular)	45
Dr. Pepper; Sunkist Orange	40
Pepsi One; Mountain Dew; Mellow Yellow; Surge	55
Pepsi Max (Regular/Diet) Sun Drop (Reg/Diet)	70
7-Up, Fanta, Sprite, Fresca, Diet Rite Cola	0
Energy Drinks (with added caffeine):	
(AMP, Adrenaline Rush, Full Throttle	
Monster, No Fear, Red Bull, Rockstar)	
Average all brands: 8 fl.oz	80
16 fl.oz	160
NOS Energy, 16 fl.oz	260
Chocolate Bars: Milk Chocolate, 2 oz	20
Dark Chocolate, 2 oz	30
Choc Chip Cookies, 2 medium, 2 oz	6
Chocolate Syrup, 2 Tbsp, 1.4 oz	5
Medicinals: Excedrin, Extra Strength (2)	130
NoDoz Maximum, 1 tablet	200

Energy/Protein Drinks

	C	F	Cb
5-hour Energy, 2 fl.oz	4	0	1
ABB:			
Energy: Speed Shot, 8.5 fl.oz	0	0	0
Ripped Force, 18 fl.oz	90	0	23
Hi-Pro:			
Pure Pro 35 Shake, all flav., 12 fl.oz	160	0.5	5
Pure Pro 50, all flavors, 14.5 fl.oz	240	1.5	7
Recovery,			
Maxx Recovery, all flavors, 18 fl.oz	400	0.5	60
AdvantEDGE *(EAS),*			
Carb Control, av. all flavors, 11 fl.oz	100	2	3
AllSport,			
Body Quencher, all flavors, 20 fl.oz	150	0	40
AMP: *Per 16 fl.oz Can*			
Active: Lemonade	130	0	31
Lemonade, Sugar Free	15	0	0.5
Boost: Original	220	0	58
Original, Sugar Free	10	0	0.5
Cherry; Grape	130	0	31
Focus, Mixed Berry	130	0	31
Arizona,			
Caution Extreme Performance, 11 fl.oz	160	0	40
Atkins, Advantage Shakes, av., 11 oz	155	9	4
Bariatrix, Proti-Max,			
Anytime Shakes, av., 8 fl.oz	100	4	4
Bawls:			
Guarana: Original, 10 fl.oz	120	0	32
Cherry, 10 fl.oz	90	0	32
Blue Sky, Blue Energy, 8.3 fl.oz	120	0	29
Bolthouse: *Per 8 fl.oz*			
Protein Plus:			
Blended Coffee	190	2.5	26
Choc.; Mango; Vanilla, av.	200	2	30
Boost: *Per 8 fl.oz*			
Original, all flavors	240	4	41
Glucose Control, all flavors	190	7	16
High Protein, all flavors	240	6	33
Plus, all flavors	360	14	45
Carnation:			
Breakfast, Essentials Powder:			
All flavors, 1 envelope, 1.3 oz	130	1	27
No Sugar Added, all flav., av., 0.7 oz	60	1	12
Ready To Drink, Rich Milk Choc., 8 fl.oz	240	4	41
Celestial Seasoning, Shots,			
Kombucha, all flavors, 2 oz	30	0	8
CeraSport, EX1 powder, 1 pkt, 8.4 oz	40	0	10
Champion Lyte, Sports Drink	0	0	0

Champion Nutrition:	C	F	Cb
Heavyvwt Gainer 900, av. 4 scps, 5.4 oz	600	7	102
Ultramet, Original, 1 packet, 2.7 oz	280	2	24
Clif Shot,			
Energy Gel, all flavors, 1.2 oz pkt	110	1.5	21
Cocaine, Energy, 8.4 fl.oz can	70	0	18
Curves, Protein Drink:			
Choc.; Vanilla, 2 scps, 1 oz	120	1	12
CytoSport:			
Muscle Milk:			
Powder, all flavors, av., 2 scoops	310	12	18
Ready To Drink: Chocolate, 11 fl.oz	240	11	12
17 fl.oz	320	16	12
Drank, Anti Energy, 16 fl.oz bottle	220	0	54
EAS ~ *See AdvantEdge/Myoplex*			
Ensure: *Per Bottle*			
Clear, 10 fl.oz	180	0	35
High Protein Shake, 14 fl.oz	210	2.5	23
Nutrition Shake, all flavors, 8 fl.oz	250	6	40
Plus, 8 fl.oz bottle	350	11	50
Enterex, Diabetic, all flavors, 8 fl.oz	240	9	27
FRS, Energy, Wild Berry; Cherry Limeade			
average, 12 fl.oz	90	0	22
Fruit₂O *(Veryfine),* 20 fl.oz bottle	0	0	0
Full Throttle: *Per 16 fl.oz*			
Energy: Citrus	220	0	58
Blue Agave; Red Berry	230	0	58
Fuze: *Per 16.9 fl.oz Bottle*			
Blends average, 16.9 fl.oz	185	0.5	43
Juice: Berry Punch, 8 fl.oz	80	0	20
Strawberry Lemonade, 8 fl.oz	100	0	25
Gatorade:			
G Series: *Ready To Drink*			
Endurance, Thirst Quencher: 12 fl oz	80	0	21
32 fl oz bottle	215	0	56
G2 Low Calorie Thirst Quencher:			
12 fl oz	30	0	7
32 fl oz	80	0	19
Prime, Sports Fuel,			
4 fl oz pouch	100	0	25
Recover:			
Post-Game Prot. Drink, 16.9 fl oz	230	0	41
Protein Shake, 330 ml carton	270	1.5	45
Genisoy:			
Protein Powder, Chocolate; Vanilla,			
average, 1.25 oz scoop	125	0	18
Glaceau:			
Smartwater, 8 fl.oz	0	0	0
Vitaminwater, all flav., 20 fl.oz	125	0	33
Glucerna,			
Shakes, all flavors, 8 fl.oz	200	7	27

	C	F	Cb
GNC:			
Lean Shake: Powder, all flav., 2 scoops	200	3	17
Drinks, av. all flavors, 14 fl.oz bottle	170	6	6
Pro Performance:			
100% Whey Protein Powder, Natural Vanilla, 1 scoop, 1 oz	150	2.5	8
Amplified: Mass XXX, Strawberry, 4 level scoops	750	6	124
Wheybolic Extreme 60, all flavors, 3 scoops	280	1	7
Golazo:			
Sports Energy: Av. all flavors, 12 fl.oz	95	0	22
Sugar Free, Mango Lime, 12 fl.oz	10	0	5
Sports Hydration, 20 fl.oz bottle:			
Mandarin; Mango Limon, average	95	0	33
Other flavors	130	0	33
GU, Energy Gel, av. all flavors, 1 packet	100	1	25
Guru, Energy: Regular, 8.3 fl.oz can	100	0	25
Lite,12 oz can	10	0	2
Hammer, Gel, av. all, 1.7 fl.oz, 1.17 oz	90	0	22
Hansen's: Energy Pro, 8 fl.oz	130	0	34
Energy Diet Red, 8 fl.oz	20	0	6
Vidration, all flavors, 8 fl.oz	0	0	0
Herbalife: Nutr. Shake, 1 pkt	90	1	13
With 8 fl.oz non-fat milk	170	1	26
Hollywood Miracle Diet, 4 fl.oz	100	0	25
Hype:			
Energy: Regular/ Organic/MFP, all flavors, 8.4 fl.oz	120	0	28
Enlite, 8.4 fl.oz	25	0	4
Shot, 3.5 fl.oz	45	0	10
Jarrow:			
Whey Protein: Unflavored, 0.8 oz	95	2	2
Chocolate; Vanilla, average, 0.95 oz	105	1	6
Muscle Optimeal, 2 scoops, 1.5 oz	160	1	15
Java Monster: Per 15 fl.oz Can			
Regular, average all flavors	190	3	33
Light, Vanilla	95	3	13
Kellogg's:			
To Go, Breakfast Shakes:			
RTD, all flavors, av., 10 fl.oz bottle	185	5	29
Shake Mix, all flavors, 1 pkt	130	0.5	27
Knudsen: Recharge, av., 8 fl.oz	70	0	23
Simply Nutritious, av. all, 8 fl.oz	120	0	30
Kombucha, Wonder Drink, 8.5 fl.oz	60	0	16
La Brada:			
Powders: Lean Body, 2.8 oz	330	8	24
Lean Body, Mass 60, 6 oz	615	7	76
Carb Watchers, 2.3 oz	250	4.5	12
RTD, Lean Body, 17 fl.oz	260	9	9
Lipovitan, B3, 8.6 fl.oz	130	0	30
Liquid Ice: Regular, 8.3 fl.oz	130	0	32
Sugar Free, 8.3 fl.oz	15	0	0

	C	F	Cb
Liquid Lightning,			
Regular, 8.4 fl.oz	90	0	22
Max Velocity:			
Regular: 8.45 fl.oz can	130	0	33
16 fl.oz can	240	0	62
Sugar Free, 16 fl.oz can	15	0	1
Met-Rx:			
Protein Plus:			
Powder, Choc., 2 scoops	220	1.5	7
Ready To Drink 51, av. all flav.,15 fl.oz	235	2	6
Metabol: Endurance, 2 sc.,1.83 oz	200	5	24
GlyProXTS, 1 scoop, 0.2 oz	20	0	4
Met, 2 scoops, 2.3 oz	260	3	40
Met Max, mix, 2 scoops, 2.2 oz	230	2.5	11
MiO Energy, 1 serving	0	0	0
MLO, Mus-L Blast, Chocolate, 4 scoops	570	3.5	112
Monster, Energy: 16 fl.oz can	200	0	54
Lo-Carb, 16 fl.oz	20	0	6
M-80, 16 fl.oz	180	0	46
Mixxd (with Juice), 16 fl.oz	220	0	54
MRM: All Natural Whey, 1 scoop, 0.9 oz	85	1	1.5
Low Carb Protein, average, 1 scoop	115	2.5	2
Muscle Milk ~ *See Cytosport*			
Muscle Tech: *Dry Powder Only*			
100% Ultra Premium, Mass Gainer, 2 scoops, 11.6 oz	1290	4	261
Mass-Tech Advantage, Milk Chocolate, 5 scoops, 9 oz	1000	9	168
Nitro Tech Lean Muscle, Van., 1.3 oz	140	1.5	1
Myoplex *(EAS):*			
Original Shakes, av. all flavors, 17 fl.oz	300	7	19
Lite, all flavors, 11 fl.oz	170	2	20
Powder: Original Choc. 1 pkt	290	4.5	22
Lite, 1 packet, 1.9 oz	180	2	24
Nature's Best:			
Carbo Power, all flavors, 16 fl.oz	400	0	100
Isopure: Alpine Punch, 20 fl.oz	260	0	25
Mass, all flavors, 20 fl.oz	350	0	53
Zero Carb, all flavors, 20 fl.oz	160	0	0
JavaPro Powders,			
average all flavors, 1.5 scoops, 1 oz	110	1.5	2
No-Fear: Regular, 16 fl.oz	260	0	72
Sugar Free, 16 fl.oz	20	0	2
Noni, Tahitian, 2 Tbsp	15	0	4
NOS:			
Energy: All flavors, 16 fl.oz can	210	0	54
Sugar Free, all flav., 22 fl.oz bottle	20	0	2
Natural Caffeine & Electrolytes, all flavors, 12 fl.oz	10	0	1
Nutrament *(Nestle),* 12 fl.oz	360	10	52
Nutrilite *(Amway):*			
Meal Replacement Shakes, all, 11 fl.oz	140	3	15
Whey Protein Powder, av., all, 1.27 oz	150	1	9

Energy/Protein Drinks (Cont)

	C	F	Cb
Optifast 800 (Nestle):			
High Protein Powder, 1 pkg	200	6	10
Powder 800 Formula, 1 pkg	160	3	20
Ready To Drink Shakes, 8 fl.oz	160	3	20
Optimum Nutrition:			
100%: Whey, 1 oz scoop	120	1	3
Oats & Whey, 1.85 oz scoop	200	1.5	22
Soy Protein, 1.1 oz scoop	120	1.5	1
Optisource (Nestle):			
Very High Protein Drink, 8 fl.oz	200	6	12
Powerade:			
Sports Drink:			
Regular, av. all flav., 12 fl.oz	80	0	22
Zero, 12 fl.oz	0	0	0
PowerBar:			
Performance Energy, 1 pouch	80	0	21
Power Gel, av. all flavors, 1.5 oz pkg	110	0	27
Pro-Cal 100 (R-Kane), all flav., 1 pkt	100	1.5	7
Propel, Workout Water,			
all flavors, 12 fl.oz	0	0	0
Radioactive: Regular, 10.5 oz	150	0	37
16 oz	220	0	56
Sugar Free, all sizes	0	0	0
Red Bull:			
Energy Drink, all flavors:			
8.4 fl.oz	110	0	28
12 fl.oz can	160	0	40
Sugar-Free, 8.4 fl.oz	10	0	3
Resource (Nestle):			
Breeze, 8 fl.oz	250	0	54
Diabetishield, 8 fl.oz	150	0	30
Health Shake: 4 fl.oz	200	4	35
No Added Sugar, 4 fl.oz	200	9	22
Shake Plus, 8 fl.oz	480	16	69
Revenge (Champion Nutrition):			
Sport, Choc.; Vanilla, av., 0.9 oz scoop	125	1.5	6
Strength, Choc.; Vanilla, av., 1.3 oz scp	145	2	8
Revival, Soy Mix, unsweetened:			
Plain, 2 scoops, 0.95 oz	105	1	4
Chocolate Day Dream, 1 package	120	2.5	7
Average other flavors, 1 pkg	115	2	4
Rhino's, Energy Drink, 100ml	50	0	11
Rip It, Energy Fuel, Citrus X, 16 fl.oz	260	0	66
Rockstar: Per 16 fl.oz Can			
Energy Drink: Punched, av.	270	0	62
Sugar Free	20	0	0
Rush: Per 8 fl.oz			
Energy Drink: Regular	140	0	31
Lite	0	0	0
SK Energy, Energy Shot, all flavors, 2 oz	0	0	0

	C	F	Cb
Slim-Fast:			
Protein Meal Shakes: 10 fl.oz			
Ready to Drink,			
Average all flavors	190	6	25
Protein Shake Mixes:			
French Vanilla, 0.9 oz scoop	200	4	30
SoBe: Per 20 fl.oz Can/Bottle			
Energize, Citrus Energy	270	0	67
Lifewater: Average all flavors	100	0	25
O-Cal, average all flavors	0	0	9
(Carbs inlude 7-10g sugar alcohol)			
Vita Boom: Cranberry Grapefruit	250	0	64
Orange-Carrot	220	0	57
Solixir, Energy Drink, av. all, 12 fl.oz	55	0	13
Spiru-Tein: Per 1.2 oz			
Energy Meal:			
Banana; Cappuccino	100	0	10
Black Cherry Chocolate	110	1	13
Starbucks:			
Refreshers, av. all flav., 12 fl.oz	60	0	19
Steaz: Energy, 12 fl.oz	135	0	35
Zero Calorie, Berry, 12 fl.oz	0	0	0
The Sports Club/LA:			
Beachbody Whey Protein Powder,			
Chocolate; Vanilla, 2 scoops, 1.4 oz	130	4	7
Trader Joe's,			
Enhanced Water, 33.8 fl.oz	0	0	0
Twin Lab:			
Endurance Fuel, 1.1 oz scoop	110	0	20
Energy Fuel, 250ml can	0	0	0
Venom: Mojave Rattler, 16 fl.oz	50	0	8
Average other varieties, 16 fl.oz	235	0	57
Verve: Energy, 8.3 fl.oz can	70	0	18
Sugar Free	5	0	1
Weider:			
Creatine ATP, powder, ½ cup, 1.7 oz	210	0	37
Dynamic Weight Gainer, pdr, 4.45 oz	450	2.5	94
Mega Mass 2000, powder, av., 3.5 oz	400	7	62
Training Whey, 1.2 oz scoop	140	1.5	2
Worldwide:			
Carbo Rush, average, 20 fl.oz	270	0	68
Pure Protein Shakes,			
35g Protein, 11 fl.oz	160	1	2
Worx, Energy:			
Original; Extra Strength, 2 fl.oz	0	0	0
XS (Quixtar), Energy Drink, 8.4 oz	10	0	0
Zola, Acai, Original Juice, 12 fl.oz	185	3	39

Quick Guide C F Cb

Orange Juice
Average ~ Fresh

	C	F	Cb
½ Cup, 4 fl.oz	55	0	13
Small Glass, 6 fl.oz	85	0	19
Regular Cup 8 fl.oz	110	0.5	26
Regular Glass, 12 fl.oz	160	0.5	39
10 fl.oz Bottle	140	0.5	32
11.5 fl.oz Can	160	0.5	37
16 fl.oz Bottle	225	1	52
20 fl.oz Bottle	280	1	64

Juices ~ Generic

Average All Brands:

	C	F	Cb
Aloe Vera Juice, unsweetened, 2 oz	10	0	0
Apple Juice: 8 fl.oz	120	0	29
10 fl.oz Bottle	145	0.5	36
16 fl.oz	235	0	58
Carrot Juice: Fresh, 6 fl.oz	35	0	8
Sweetened, 6 fl.oz	75	0	17
Coconut Water, 8 fl.oz	50	0.5	9
Cranberry Juice, Cocktail/Blend	140	0	34
Fruit Blends, av. all, 8 fl.oz	110	0	27
Fruit Nectars, av. all, 8 fl.oz	140	0	36
Grape Juice, 8 fl.oz	155	0	38
Grapefruit Juice, 8 fl.oz	95	0	22
Lemon/Lime Juice: 1 Tbsp	5	0	1
1 cup, 8 fl.oz	50	0.5	16
Concentrate, 1 tsp	0	0	0
Noni Juice:			
Tahitian, 2 Tbsp, 1 fl.oz	15	0	3
Tahiti Traders, 1 fl.oz	20	0	5
Passion Fruit Juice, Fresh:			
Purple, 1 cup, 8 fl.oz	125	0	34
Yellow, 1 cup, 8 fl.oz	80	1.5	14
Papaya/Peach Nectar, av., 8 fl.oz	140	0	36
Pear Nectar, 8 fl.oz	150	0	40
Pineapple Juice, 8 fl.oz	130	0	32
Pomegranate Juice, 8 fl.oz	160	0	40
Prune Juice, 8 fl.oz	180	0	45
Strawb./Raspberry Juice, 8 fl.oz	100	0	23
Tangerine Juice, 8 fl.oz	105	0.5	25
Tomato Juice, 8 fl.oz	40	0	10
Vegetable Juice, 8 fl.oz	45	0	11
Wheat Grass Juice:			
1 fl.oz 'Shot'	10	0	1.5
2 fl.oz 'Shot'	20	0	3

Quick Guide C F Cb

Fruit Smoothies (Jamba Juice; Smoothie King)
Average All Brands

	C	F	Cb
Fruit Only: 8 fl.oz	115	0.5	29
12 fl.oz	175	1	43
16 fl.oz	230	1	58
24 fl.oz	350	1	78
Fruit + Non-Fat Milk/Soy:			
12 fl.oz	135	0	29
16 fl.oz	155	0	37
24 fl.oz	265	1	59
Fruit + Non-Fat Frozen Yogurt/Sherbet:			
12 fl.oz	200	0.5	47
16 fl.oz	265	1	63
24 fl.oz	395	1.5	95

Juice ~ Brands C F Cb

Per 8 fl.oz Unless Indicated

	C	F	Cb
Apple & Eve:			
Cranberry Grape/Pommeg.	140	0	34
Naturally Cranberry	130	0	32
Fruitables, av. all flavors, 6.75 fl.oz	60	0	14
Bolthouse Farms: *Per 8 fl.oz*			
Juice: 100% Carrot	70	0	14
Orange & Carrot	120	0	27
Fruit Smoothies:			
Berry Boost	130	0	30
Blue Goodness	160	0	34
C-Boost	120	0	29
Green Goodness	140	0	33
Strawberry Banana	130	0	32
Bom Dia: *Per 8 fl.oz*			
Acai: Original	110	0	27
+ 10 Superblend	120	0	31
Mango Coconut Splash	60	0	15
Pomegranate	170	0	42
Bright & Early (Minute Maid),			
Orange Juice (Chilled/Frozen)	110	0	30
Campbell's:			
Tomato Juice: 5.5 fl.oz can	30	0	7
8 fl.oz	50	0	10
Cactus Cooler, Orange Pineapple Blast,			
12 fl.oz can	150	0	40

Juice Brands (Cont)

	C	F	Cb

Per 8 fl.oz Unless Indicated

	C	F	Cb
Capri Sun: *Per 6 fl.oz*			
100% Juice: Citrus	100	0	23
Average other flavors	85	0	21
Juice Drinks, (25% Less Sugar),			
average all flavors	60	0	17
Roarin' Waters, all flavors, 6 fl.oz	30	0	8
Clamato:			
Original Tomato Cocktail	60	0	12
Picante	60	0	13
Crystal Geyser:			
Juice Squeeze: *Per 12 fl.oz Bottle*			
Blackberry Pomegranate	170	0	43
Ruby Grapefruit	150	0	36
Average other flavors	135	0	32
Dole: *Per 8 fl.oz*			
Aguas Frescas, average all flavors	110	0	26
Blended Juices:			
Orange Peach Mango	120	0	29
Pina Colada	120	0	29
Pineapple-Orange Banana	120	0	30
Strawberry Kiwi	120	0	31
Fruit Squish'ems, all flavors, 3.2 oz	60	0	14
Florida's Natural: *Per 8 fl.oz*			
Apple Juice	120	0	29
Cranberry Ruby Red	130	0	32
Lemonade, Home Squeezed	110	0	28
Orange: Premium	110	0	26
Mango	110	0	27
Pineapple	130	0	31
Strawberry	110	0	26
Ruby Red Grapefruit, Original	90	0	22
Fuze: *Per 16.9 fl.oz Bottle*			
Banana Colada	180	0.5	43
Other Fruit Flavors	180	0	45
Slenderize, average all flavors	15	0	3
Goya: *Per 12 fl.oz Can*			
Nectar: Guava; Tamarind	240	0	59
Mango	230	0	56
Papaya	220	0	56
Peach	220	0	54
Pear & Passion Fruit	230	0	57
Pineapple & Passion Fruit	220	0	55

Per 8 fl.oz Unless Indicated

	C	F	Cb
Hansen's:			
Juice Box: *Per 6.75 fl.oz Box*			
Awesome Apple; Loud Lemonade, av.	90	0	23
Burstin Berry; Totally Tropical	100	0	24
Strawberry Banana	110	0	27
Other flavors	100	0	24
Junior Juice,			
100% Juice, all flavors, 4.23 oz box	60	0	15
Natural, (64 fl.oz Bottles): *Per 8 fl.oz*			
Apple	120	0	28
Apple Strawberry	110	0	27
Grape	120	0	33
Ruby Red Grapefruit	100	0	25
White Grape	140	0	36
Smoothie Nectar, average, 12 fl.oz	180	0	46
Hawaii's Own, Frozen Concentrate,			
100% Juice, all varieties, av., 8 fl.oz	110	0	28
Hi-C Juice Drinks: *Per 6.75 fl.oz Box*			
Flashin' Fruit Punch	90	0	26
Orange Lavaburst	90	0	26
Poppin' Lemonade	100	0	27
Hood: *Per 8 fl.oz*			
Apple	120	0	31
Fruit Punch; Orange	120	0	30
Lemonade	110	0	28
Jamba Juice ~ *See Fast-Foods Section*			
Juicy Juice *(Nestle):*			
Average all flavors:			
6.75 fl.oz box	100	0	24
4.23 fl.oz box	60	0	15
Kerns:			
Nectars: *Per 11.5 fl.oz Can*			
Guava	210	0	53
Pear; Strawb. Banana, av.	220	0	53
Pineapple Coconut	280	8	53
Strawberry	210	0	52
Kool Aid: *Per 6 fl.oz Containers*			
Jammers: Grape; Cherry	80	0	20
Average other flavors	70	0	19
L & A: *Per 8 fl.oz*			
All Cherry	180	0	45
All Cranberry	60	0	14
Papaya Delight	130	0	32
Pineapple Coconut	140	3	28

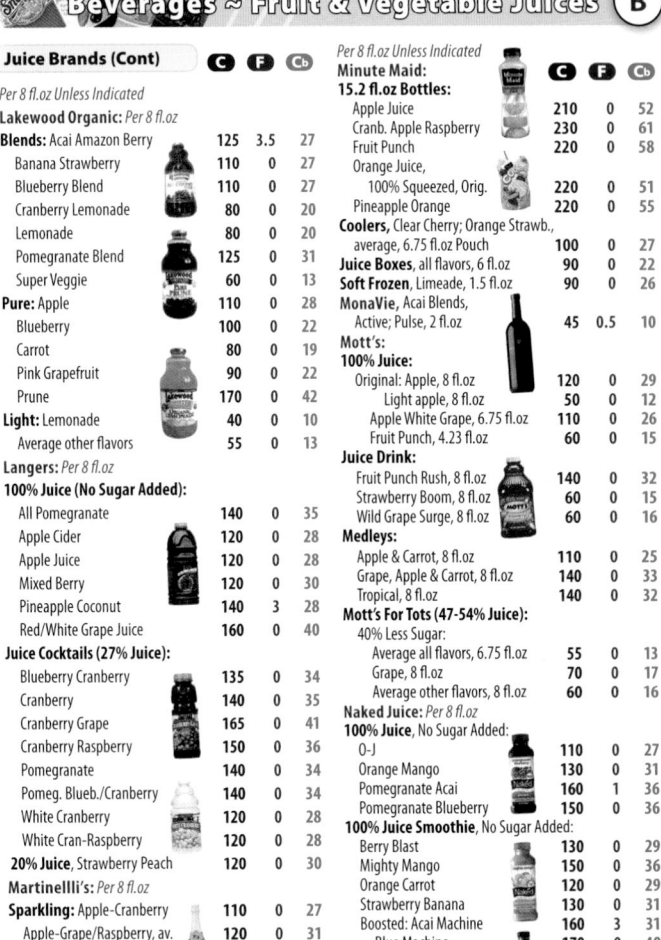

Juice Brands (Cont)

	C	F	Cb

Per 8 fl.oz Unless Indicated

Lakewood Organic: *Per 8 fl.oz*

	C	F	Cb
Blends: Acai Amazon Berry	125	3.5	27
Banana Strawberry	110	0	27
Blueberry Blend	110	0	27
Cranberry Lemonade	80	0	20
Lemonade	80	0	20
Pomegranate Blend	125	0	31
Super Veggie	60	0	13
Pure: Apple	110	0	28
Blueberry	100	0	22
Carrot	80	0	19
Pink Grapefruit	90	0	22
Prune	170	0	42
Light: Lemonade	40	0	10
Average other flavors	55	0	13

Langers: *Per 8 fl.oz*

100% Juice (No Sugar Added):

	C	F	Cb
All Pomegranate	140	0	35
Apple Cider	120	0	28
Apple Juice	120	0	28
Mixed Berry	120	0	30
Pineapple Coconut	140	3	28
Red/White Grape Juice	160	0	40

Juice Cocktails (27% Juice):

	C	F	Cb
Blueberry Cranberry	135	0	34
Cranberry	140	0	35
Cranberry Grape	165	0	41
Cranberry Raspberry	150	0	36
Pomegranate	140	0	34
Pomeg. Blueb./Cranberry	140	0	34
White Cranberry	120	0	28
White Cran-Raspberry	120	0	28
20% Juice, Strawberry Peach	120	0	30

Martinellli's: *Per 8 fl.oz*

	C	F	Cb
Sparkling: Apple-Cranberry	110	0	27
Apple-Grape/Raspberry, av.	120	0	31
Apple-Mango/Pomegranate	150	0	38
Apple-Pear/Marionberry, av.	130	0	32
Apple-Wild Berry	150	0	36

Per 8 fl.oz Unless Indicated

Minute Maid:

	C	F	Cb
15.2 fl.oz Bottles:			
Apple Juice	210	0	52
Cranb. Apple Raspberry	230	0	61
Fruit Punch	220	0	58
Orange Juice,			
100% Squeezed, Orig.	220	0	51
Pineapple Orange	220	0	55
Coolers, Clear Cherry; Orange Strawb.,			
average, 6.75 fl.oz Pouch	100	0	27
Juice Boxes, all flavors, 6 fl.oz	90	0	22
Soft Frozen, Limeade, 1.5 fl.oz	90	0	26

MonaVie, Acai Blends,

	C	F	Cb
Active; Pulse, 2 fl.oz	45	0.5	10

Mott's:

	C	F	Cb
100% Juice:			
Original: Apple, 8 fl.oz	120	0	29
Light apple, 8 fl.oz	50	0	12
Apple White Grape, 6.75 fl.oz	110	0	26
Fruit Punch, 4.23 fl.oz	60	0	15
Juice Drink:			
Fruit Punch Rush, 8 fl.oz	140	0	32
Strawberry Boom, 8 fl.oz	60	0	15
Wild Grape Surge, 8 fl.oz	60	0	16
Medleys:			
Apple & Carrot, 8 fl.oz	110	0	25
Grape, Apple & Carrot, 8 fl.oz	140	0	33
Tropical, 8 fl.oz	140	0	32
Mott's For Tots (47-54% Juice):			
40% Less Sugar:			
Average all flavors, 6.75 fl.oz	55	0	13
Grape, 8 fl.oz	70	0	17
Average other flavors, 8 fl.oz	60	0	16

Naked Juice: *Per 8 fl.oz*

100% Juice, No Sugar Added:

	C	F	Cb
O-J	110	0	27
Orange Mango	130	0	31
Pomegranate Acai	160	1	36
Pomegranate Blueberry	150	0	36

100% Juice Smoothie, No Sugar Added:

	C	F	Cb
Berry Blast	130	0	29
Mighty Mango	150	0	36
Orange Carrot	120	0	29
Strawberry Banana	130	0	31
Boosted: Acai Machine	160	3	31
Blue Machine	170	0	40
Green Machine	140	0	33
Power-C Machine	120	0	29
Red Machine	170	4.5	31

Juice Brands (Cont)

	C	F	Cb

Per 8 fl.oz Unless Indicated

Naked Juice (Cont):

	C	F	Cb
Coconut Water, Pure, 11.2 fl.oz	60	0	14

Nantucket Nectars:

100% Juice: *Per 8 fl.oz*

Peach Orange	130	0	32
Pineapple Orange Banana	140	0	34
Pomegranate Cherry	120	0	29
Premium Orange Juice	110	0	26
Pressed Apple	120	0	30
Juice Cocktail, Cranberry, 8 fl.oz	130	0	33

Juice Drinks: *Per 8 fl.oz*

Orange Mango	120	0	31
Pineapple Orange Guava	120	0	29
Pomegranate Pear	110	0	28
Red Plum Juice	130	0	31
Watermelon Strawberry	110	0	28
Lemonade, Squeezed, 8 fl.oz	110	0	28

Newman's Own: *Per 8 fl.oz*

Lemonade, Regular; Pink	110	0	27
Limeade	140	0	34

Fruit Juice Cocktail:

Gorilla Grape	140	0	34
Orange Mango Tango	130	0	33

Northland:

100% Juice,

Cranb. Blackberry/Raspberry/Grape, average, 8 fl.oz	140	0	36

Ocean Spray: *Per 8 fl.oz*

Juice Cocktails:

Blueberry	110	0	28
Cranberry	120	0	30
With Calcium	130	0	31
Ruby Red Grapefruit	110	0	28
White Cranberry	110	0	27

100% Juice Blends:

Citrus Tangerine Orange	110	0	28
Cranberry Concord Grape	150	0	37
Cranberry Raspberry	140	0	34
White Grapefruit	90	0	21

Juice Drinks:

Cran-Apple	130	0	32
Cran-Grape	120	0	31
CranRaspberry/Strawberry, av.	110	0	28

Per 8 fl.oz Unless Indicated

Ocean Spray (Cont): *Per 8 fl.oz*

	C	F	Cb
Diet Juice Drinks, all flavors	5	0	2
Light Juice Drinks, av. all flavors	50	0	13

Odwalla: *Per 12 fl.oz Bottle*

Blueberry B	210	0	50
Carrot Juice	100	0	22
Chocolate Protein Monster	320	6	40
Mango Tango	220	1	50
Mo'Beta	170	0	40
Orange Honey Passion Wellness	220	0	53
Original Super Food	190	0.5	44
Original Super Protein	290	1	52
Pomegranate Limeade	180	0	44
Strawberry C Monster	240	0	56

Orange Julius

Originals, Orange:

Small, 16 fl.oz	210	0	52
Medium, 17.5 fl.oz	270	0	68
Large, 26 fl.oz	420	0	103

Smoothies ~ See Fast-Foods Section

Orangina, 10 fl.oz bottle	130	0	32

Pom Wonderful: *Per 8 fl.oz*

100% Juice,

Blueberry; Cherry; Pomegranate	150	0	36

Juice Blends: Coconut

	140	0	33
Hula	140	0	35
Mango	140	0	34

R.W. Knudsen: *Per 8 fl.oz*

Organic, 100% Juice: Apple

	120	0	30
Concord Grape	150	0	39
Cranberry Blueberry	120	0	30

Natural, 100% Juice: Mango Peach

	120	0	30
Cranberry Raspberry	130	0	32
Kiwi Strawberry	120	0	30
Razzleberry	120	0	30
Rio Red Grapefruit	140	0	34
85% Juice, Hibiscus Cooler	100	0	25

Just Juice:

Just Black Currant	100	0	15
Just Black Cherry	160	0	37
Just Blueberry	100	0	24
Simply Nutritious: Mega C	140	0	34
Average other flavors	125	0	30

Juice Brands (Cont)

	C	F	Cb

Per 8 fl.oz Unless Indicated
R.W. Knudsen (Cont):
Sparkling Essence:

	C	F	Cb
average all flavors, 10.5 fl.oz	0	0	0
Spritzers: *Per 10.5 fl.oz Cans*			
Black Cherry	120	0	29
Mango Fandango	110	0	28
Red Raspberry	110	0	27
Very Veggie, Original, 8 fl.oz	60	0	12
ReaLemon – ReaLime:			
Lemon/Lime Juice (from concentrate):			
1 teaspoon	0	0	0
2Tbsp, 1 fl.oz	10	0	2.5
Santa Cruz: *Per 8 fl.oz*			
Organic, 100% Juice:			
Apple Juice	120	0	30
Concord Grape; White Grape	160	0	39
Orange Mango	130	0	32
Strawberry Kiwi	120	0	30
25% Juice Drink Boxes:			
Lemon	120	0	29
Grape	100	0	23
Carbonated Beverages: *Per 10.5 fl.oz Can*			
Lemon Lime	130	0	32
Root Beer	130	0	32
Celebratory Style:			
Sparkling Lemonade	110	0	27
Sparkling Limeade	100	0	26
Nectars: Berry	120	0	29
Cranberry	120	0	30
Passionfruit	160	0	38
Seismic *(Amway):*			
Super Juices: *Per 10 fl.oz Bottle*			
Citrus; Berry	180	0	44
Low Sugar Cherry	100	0	26
Simply Orange Juice Company:			
Lemonade; Limeade	120	0	30
Orange Juice,			
with or without pulp	110	0	26
Snap·E· Tom,			
Tomato & Chili Cocktail,			
11.5 fl.oz can	70	0	15
Snapple: *Per 16 fl.oz Bottle*			
Juice Drink Blends:			
Go Bananas; Raspb Peach, average	220	0	55
Grapeade; Lemonade; Orangeade	190	0	46
Fruit Punch	200	0	48
Diet, Cranberry Raspberry	20	0	4

Per 8 fl.oz Unless Indicated

	C	F	Cb
Ssips, Juice Boxes,			
average all flavors, 6 fl.oz box	80	0	21
Stonyfield Farm: *Per 10 fl.oz Bottle*			
Smoothies: Strawberry; Wild Berry	230	3	39
Peach; Strawb. Banana, av.	230	3	41
SunnyD:			
Original: *Per 64 fl.oz Ctn*			
Smooth/Tangy Orange, 8 fl.oz	50	0	14
Blends, 64 fl.oz Containers,			
average all flavors, 8 fl.oz	60	0	15
Baja Juice: *Per 12 fl.oz Bottles*			
Red Punch	170	0	43
Other flavors	190	0	46
Sunsweet: *Per 8 fl.oz*			
Plum Smart: Original	160	0	36
Light	60	0	15
Prune Juice: Original	180	0	42
With Pulp	150	0	44
Light	100	0	26
Trader Joe's:			
All Natural Pasteurized, 32/64 fl.oz Bottle: *Per 8 fl.oz*			
100% Cranberry	70	0	16
Blueberry Pomegranate	140	0	34
Just Blueberry	100	0	24
Just Pomegranate	150	0	37
Mango PassionFruit	130	0	32
Omega Orange Carrot	110	0	26
Organic, 32/64 fl.oz Bottle: *Per 8 fl.oz*			
100% Pomegranate	140	0	35
Apple Juice	120	0	30
Concord Grape Juice	160	0	39
Cranberry	70	0	18
Grapefruit Sunset; Lemonade	120	0	30
Mango Nectar	130	0	32
Pink Lemonade	130	0	32
Strawberry Lemonade	120	0	29
White Grape Juice	160	0	40
Joe's Kids: *Per 6.75 fl.oz Box*			
From Concentrate: Apple	90	0	23
Apple Grape	100	0	24
White Grape	120	0	30
10% Juice, Lemonade	90	0	22
Sparkling Juices, 25.4 fl.oz Botle: *Per 8 fl.oz*			
Blueberry	120	0	30
Cranberry	140	0	35
Pomegranate	130	0	31

Juice Brands (Cont)

	C	F	Cb

Per 8 fl.oz Unless Indicated

Tree Top:
100% Juice Concentrates:

	C	F	Cb
64 fl.oz Bottle: *Per 8 fl.oz*			
Apple Berry/Grape, average	125	0	32
Apple Cranb./Blueberry Pomegr.	120	0	30
11.5 fl.oz Can: *Per Can*			
Apple Berry/Grape, av.	180	0	46
Fruit Punch	170	0	42
6.75 fl.oz Box: *Per Box*			
Apple Pear	100	0	25
Fruit Punch	110	0	26
Grape Juice	110	0	27

Tropicana: *Per 8 fl.oz*

	C	F	Cb
Chilled:			
Orangeade	130	0	33
Punches, average all flavors	125	0	31
Non-Refrigerated:			
100% juice, 10 fl.oz bottoes: Apple	170	0	40
Fruit Medley	170	0	42
20% Juice, 15.2 fl.oz Bottle,			
Cranberry	270	0	67
Farmstand, 46fl.oz bottle,			
average all flavors, 8 fl.oz	120	0	30
Trop50, 50% less sugar, 59 fl.oz bottle,			
average all flavors, 8 fl.oz	50	0	13
Tropics, 59 fl.oz container,			
average all flavors, 8 fl.oz	120	0	30
Twisters, 20 fl.oz bottle,			
average all flavors	300	0	74

V8 Juices & Drinks:

	C	F	Cb
Original/Spicy 100% Vegetable Juice:			
5.5 fl.oz can	35	0	7
8 fl.oz cup	50	0	10
11.5 fl.oz can	70	0	14
12 fl.oz bottle	75	0	15
Splash: Average all flavors, 8 fl.oz	70	0	19
Diet Splash, all flavors, 8 fl.oz	10	0	3
Smoothies: Strawb. Banana, 8 fl.oz	90	0	20
Tropical Colada, 8 fl.oz	100	0	21
V-Fusion: Grape Raspberry, 8 fl.oz	140	0	33
Av. other flavors, 8 fl.oz	110	0	27
Light Varieties, av. 8 fl.oz	50	0	13
Refreshers, av. all, 8 fl.oz	100	0	25
Smoothies, av. all flavors, 8 fl.oz	125	0	31
Sparkling, av. all flavors, 8.4 fl.oz	55	0	13

Per 8 fl.oz Unless Indicated

	C	F	Cb
Veryfine:			
100%: Apple Juice	120	0	29
Orange Juice	120	0	30
Walnut Acres: *Per 8 fl.oz*			
Organic: Apple	110	0	29
Apricot; Raspberry	130	0	32
Cherry	140	0	34
Cranberry	110	0	26
Incredible Vegetable	50	0	12
Mango Nectar	120	0	29
Welch's: *Per 8 fl.oz*			
100% Juice: Grape Juice	140	0	36
Red Grape juice	160	0	41
White Grape	140	0	38
White Grape Cherry/Peach	140	0	34
Cocktails, Refrigerated: *64 fl.oz Ctn:*			
Dragon Fruit Mango	140	0	35
Mango Twist	150	0	38
Strawberry Breeze	130	0	33
Concentrates, 100% Juice,			
Gape;White Grape, 2 fl.oz	140	0	38
Light Juice: *52 fl.oz Bottle*			
Concord/WhiteGrape	45	0	12
Sparkling Juice Cocktail,			
all varieties, average	140	0	34
Zola: *Per 12 fl.oz Bottle*			
Acai: Original	185	3	39
With Blueberry Juice	180	3	38

CALORIEKING PORTION WATCH

ORANGE JUICE	C	Cb
8 fl.oz	110	26
16 fl.oz	220	52
24 fl.oz	330	78
32 fl.oz	440	104

Quick Guide   **C F Cb**

Cow's Milk ~ Average All Brands

Whole (3.25% fat):

	C	F	Cb
2 Tbsp, 1 fl.oz	20	1	1.5
1 Cup, 8 fl.oz	150	8	12
1 Large Glass, 12 fl.oz	220	12	17
1 Pint, 16 fl.oz	295	16	22
1 Quart, 946 ml	590	32	44

Reduced-Fat (2% fat):

	C	F	Cb
2 Tbsp, 1 fl.oz	15	0.5	1.5
1 Cup, 8 fl.oz	120	5	12
1 Large Glass, 12 fl.oz	180	7.5	18
1 Pint, 16 fl.oz	245	10	23
1 Quart, 946 ml	490	20	46

Light/Low-Fat (1% fat):

	C	F	Cb
2 Tbsp, 1 fl.oz	15	0.3	1.5
1 Cup, 8 fl.oz	100	2.5	12
1 Large Glass, 12 fl.oz	150	4	18
1 Pint, 16 fl.oz	205	5	25
1 Quart, 946 ml	410	10	49

Fat Free/Skim:

	C	F	Cb
2 Tbsp, 1 fl.oz	10	0	1.5
1 Cup, 8 fl.oz	90	0.5	13
1 Pint, 16 fl.oz	180	1	26

Protein Fortified,

	C	F	Cb
1 cup	100	0.5	14

Buttermilk: *Average All Brands*

	C	F	Cb
Reduced-Fat (2%), 1 cup, 8 fl.oz	120	5	10
Low-Fat (1%), 1 cup, 8 fl.oz	100	2.5	12

Lactose-Free: *Per 8 fl.oz*

	C	F	Cb
Dairy Ease: Whole	160	9	11
2% Reduced-Fat	130	5	12
Fat-Free	90	0	12
Lactaid 100: Whole	150	8	12
2% Reduced-Fat	130	5	12
1% Low-Fat	110	2.5	13
Fat-Free; Calcium Fort.	80	0	13
Real Goodness, 2% Fat	120	5	7
Smart Balance,			
FF + Omega-3s & Vit. E	110	1	14

Lower Calorie Dairy Drinks: *Per 8 fl.oz Cup*

Calorie Countdown (*Hood*):

	C	F	Cb
2% Reduced-Fat	90	5	3
2% Reduced-Fat, Chocolate	90	5	5
Fat-Free	45	0	3

Goat/Sheep Milk, Kefir   **C F Cb**

Goat's Milk *(Meyenberg):*

	C	F	Cb
Whole, 1 cup, 8 fl.oz	140	7	11
Light/Low-Fat (1%), 8 fl.oz	100	2.5	11
Evaporated, reconst., 8 fl.oz	150	8	11

Kefir: *Per 8 fl.oz*

	C	F	Cb
Lifeway: Original	150	8	12
Greek Style	210	14	12
Green	170	2	25
Lowfat, average all flavors	140	1.5	20
Nancy's: Plain	110	3	14
Fruit flavors, average	180	2.5	34
Trader Joe's: Plain, 1%	110	2.5	8
Strawberry	160	2	21
Sheep's Milk, Whole, 1 cup	265	17	13

Canned & Dried Milk

	C	F	Cb
Condensed: Sweetened, 2 T., 1 fl.oz	130	3	23
Low Fat, 2 Tbsp	120	1.5	23
Fat-Free, 2 Tbsp	110	0	24
Evaporated: Whole, 2 Tbsp	40	3	3
Whole, ½ cup, 4 fl.oz	170	10	13
Carnation: Low Fat, 2 Tbsp, 1 oz	25	0.5	3
½ cup, 4 fl.oz	115	2.5	14
Fat-Free, 2 Tbsp, 1 oz	25	0	4
Dried: Whole, ¾ cup, 1 oz	160	9	12
Skim/Non-Fat, ⅓ cup, 1 oz	80	0	12
Made-up, 1 cup, 8 fl.oz	80	0	12
Buttermilk (sweet cream): 1 oz	110	2	14
Non-Fat, 1 Tbsp	25	0	3
Carnation, Malted, dry, 1 Tbsp	30	0.5	6
Horlick's, Malt Powder, dry, 1 oz	180	4	27

Soy/Non-Dairy Drinks ~ See Page 49

'Whatever happened to sensible portion size?!'

Quick Guide

	C	**F**	**Cb**
Chocolate Milk:			
Average All Brands:			
Whole Milk, (3.3%):			
8 fl.oz cup	250	9	35
1 Pint, 16 fl.oz	415	17	52
Reduced-Fat, (2%):			
8 fl.oz cup	190	5	30
1 Pint, 16 fl.oz	380	10	60
Low-Fat, (1%):			
8 fl.oz cup	160	3	26
1 Pint, 16 fl.oz	315	5	52

Flavored Milk ~ Brands

	C	**F**	**Cb**
Ready-To-Drink: *Per 8 fl.oz Cup Unless Indicated*			
Albertson's, Choc Milk	180	2.5	29
Hood: Chocolate	230	9	31
Low-Fat (1%), Chocolate	170	3	28
Horizon Organic:			
Low-Fat: Chocolate with Omega 3	160	2.5	26
Vanilla with Omega 3	150	2.5	23
Kellogg's:			
To Go, Breakfast Shakes: *Per 10 fl.oz*			
Milk Chocolate	190	5	29
Strawberry; Vanilla	180	5	29
Mixes, average all flavors,			
1 packet	130	0	26
Kroger, Simple Truth,			
Choc Milk, Low-Fat, 1%	150	2.5	22
Land O Lakes:			
Grip 'n Go:			
Swiss Chocolate (2% red-fat), 8 fl.oz	190	5	26
Strawberry (whole milk), 8 fl.oz	190	8	22
Muscle Milk ~ *See Energy Protein Drinks*			
Nesquik:			
Chocolate: Low Fat, 8 fl.oz	150	2.5	25
No Sugar Added, 8 fl.oz	100	2	13
Strawberry, Low Fat, 8 fl.oz	180	2.5	31
Prairie Farms:			
Chocolate, 2% Reduced Fat, 8 fl.oz	180	5	26
Strawberry, 1% Low Fat, 8 fl.oz	160	2.5	28

Flavored Milk (Cont)

	C	**F**	**Cb**
Ready-To-Drink: *Per 8 fl.oz Cup Unless Indicated*			
Ralphs, Chocolate, Low-Fat, 8 fl.oz	210	2.5	36
Skinny Cow, Chocolate, Fat-Free	150	0	26
TruMoo, Choc.; Strawb., av., 8 fl.oz	145	2.5	22
Yoo-Hoo, Chocolate,15.5 fl.oz bottle	230	2	51
Bottled Coffee Drinks ~ *See Page 37*			

Shakes

	C	**F**	**Cb**
Arby's:			
Chocolate; Jamocha, 16 oz	440	12	76
Vanilla, 16 oz	380	12	60
Burger King:			
Chocolate:			
Small, 12 fl.oz	580	17	97
Medium, 16 fl.oz	760	21	131
Large, 20 fl.oz	980	24	174
Other flavors ~ *See Fast Food Section*			
Denny's: *Per 14 oz*			
Chocolate	680	31	90
Strawberry	580	25	78
Vanilla	640	31	80
Hardees, all varieties, av., 16 fl.oz	710	33	86
McDonalds, McCafe Shakes:			
Chocolate & Strawberry:			
12 fl.oz cup	555	16	91
16 fl.oz cup	695	20	114
22 fl.oz cup	850	24	141
Other Restaurants ~ *See Fast-Foods Section*			

Smoothies

	C	**F**	**Cb**
Made Up Ready-To-Drink:			
8 fl. oz Milk/Soy + Fruit: *Per 12 fl.oz*			
Average all flavors:			
With Whole Milk	300	8	50
+ Ice Cream, 1 scoop	400	13	62
With Non-Fat Milk	240	0	50
Kroger/Ralph's Smoothies: *Per 8 fl.oz*			
Mixed Berry	210	2.5	40
Strawberry Banana	200	2.5	37
LALA: *Per 7 fl.oz Bottle*			
Frusion C-Charged Smoothie,			
average all flavors	180	2.5	35
Freshens; Jamba Juice; TCBY ~ *See Fast-Foods*			

Nut, Rice & Cereal Drinks

Per 8 fl.oz Cup

	C	F	Cb
Almond Breeze (Blue Diamond):			
Refrigerated/Shelf Stable, average:			
Original	60	2.5	8
Chocolate	120	3	22
Vanilla	80	2.5	14
Unsweetened, Orig; Vanilla	30	2.5	1
Almond Dream:			
Shelf Stable, Enriched:			
Original	70	3	12
Unsweetened	50	3.5	3
Alpina:			
Oat Based Smoothies: *Per 8.33 oz*			
Original; Cinnamon	180	4	29
Light, Original	110	1.5	19
Amazake, Oh So Simply,			
Rice Shake	150	0	34
Better Than Milk:			
Rice Vegan Powder Mix,			
Original; Vanilla, 2 Tbsp, 0.67 oz	70	0	17
Cacique,			
Horchata Rice Drink	160	3.5	31
Don Jose:			
Cereal Match	100	3	17
Horchata Rice Drink	140	4	25
Pacific:			
Rice Drinks, Plain; Vanilla	130	2	27
Organic Oat, Original/Vanilla, av.	130	2.5	25
Nut Drinks: Hazelnut, Original	110	3.5	19
Chocolate	120	5	19
Organic Almond:			
Original	60	2.5	8
Vanilla	70	2.5	11
Chocolate, single serve container	100	3	19
Rice Dream:			
Refrigerated, Enriched, Original	120	2.5	23
Shelf Stable: Classic Carob	150	2.5	30
Classic/ Enriched Vanilla, av.	130	2.5	27
Horchata	160	2.5	32
Silk:			
True Almond: Original	60	2.5	8
Dark Chocolate	120	3	23
Unsweetened, Orig.; Vanilla	30	2.5	1
Trader Joe's:			
Rice Drinks:			
Unsweetened: Original, Organic	120	2.5	23
Vanilla	130	2.5	26
WestSoy, Rice, Plain; Vanilla	110	2.5	20

Note: Rice/Oat/Nut drinks are very low in protein. Unless enriched with protein (and calcium), they are not suitable for infants as a substitute for milk or calcium-enriched soy drinks.

Soy Milk ~ Ready-To-Drink

Per 8 fl.oz Cup

	C	F	Cb
365 Organic (Whole Foods):			
Original, unsweetened	70	4	4
Chocolate	140	3.5	22
Vanilla	90	3.5	10
Light: Original	70	1.5	9
Vanilla	70	1.5	10
8th Continent:			
Original	80	2.5	7
Complete Vanilla	80	2.5	8
Vanilla	100	2.5	11
Fat-Free: Original	60	0	8
Vanilla	70	0	11
Light: Original	50	2	7
Chocolate	90	1.5	12
Vanilla	60	2	5
Better Than Milk, Original	90	1.5	17
Bolthouse Farms:			
Perfectly Protein Cafe Drinks:			
Green Tea Soy Latte	150	3	25
Vanilla Chai Tea	180	4	27
Edensoy: *Per 32 fl.oz Container*			
Organic: Original	140	5	14
Unsweetened	120	6	5
Carob; Chocolate, av.	175	4	28
Vanilla	160	3	25
Extra: Original	130	4	13
Vanilla	150	3	24
Kidz Dream:			
Smoothies: Berry Blast	100	2	17
Orange Cream	120	2	21
O Organics (Safeway):			
Plain	90	3.5	8
Chocolate	150	4	23
Vanilla	90	3	9
Odwalla: *Per 12 fl.oz Bottle*			
Protein Monster:			
Strawberry	240	5	28
Vanilla	290	5	36
Pacific:			
Super Protein:			
Original	290	1	52
Mango	260	1	42
Pumpkin	240	5	33
Vanilla Al'Mondo	290	8	37
Organic, Original, Unsweetened	90	4.5	4
Select Soy: Original	70	2.5	9
Vanilla	80	2.5	11
Ultra: Original	140	5	12
Vanilla	140	5	14

Soy Milk ~ Ready-To-Drink (Cont)

Per 8 fl.oz Unless Indicated   **C**   **F**   **Cb**

	C	F	Cb
Silk:			
Original	110	4.5	9
Chocolate	120	3	19
Vanilla	100	3.5	10
Very Vanilla	130	3.5	18
Light: Original	60	1.5	5
Chocolate	90	1.5	16
Vanilla	70	1.5	7
Organic: Original	100	4	8
Unsweetened	80	4	4
Slim-Fast ~ See Page 40			
Soy Dream:			
Enriched: Original	100	3.5	9
Vanilla	120	3.5	14
Shelf Stable:			
Classic Vanilla	140	4	18
Enriched: Original	100	4	8
Chocolate	150	4	21
Vanilla	120	4	14
Soy Slender,			
average all varieties	70	3	4
Trader Joe's:			
Soy Milk: Original	110	2	13
Chocolate	130	2.5	23
Vanilla	100	2	16
Organic: Original	130	3	17
Chocolate	120	3	17
Vanilla	130	3	19
WestSoy:			
Organic Plus, (25% Less Sugar):			
Plain	110	4.5	11
Vanilla	110	4.5	11
Low-Fat: Plain	90	2	15
Vanilla	120	2	23
Non-Fat: Plain	70	0	10
Vanilla	80	0	12
Unsweetened: Plain	90	4.5	5
Chocolate; Vanilla, average	100	4.5	6

Soy Powder Mix

   C   **F**   **Cb**

1 oz (¼ cup) mix makes 8 fl.oz Cup

	C	F	Cb
Soy Protein Isolate, dry, 1 oz	95	1	2
Better Than Milk:			
Original, 2 Tbsp	90	1.5	18
Vanilla, 2 Tbsp	90	1.5	18
Genisoy: *Per Scoop*			
Protein Shake Powder:			
Natural, 1 oz	100	0	0
Chocolate, 1.2 oz	120	0	17
Vanilla, 1.2 oz	130	0	18
Now:			
Soy Protein Isolate:			
Plain, ⅓ cup, 0.8 oz	90	0.5	0.5
Natural:			
Chocolate, 1 level scoop, 1.58 oz	160	1.5	9
Vanilla, 1 level scoop, 1.58 oz	180	2.5	13
Revival: *Per Packet*			
Unsweetened Shakes: Plain	105	1	4
Cappuccino; Strawberry Smile	115	2	4
Chocolate	120	2.5	7
Vanilla Pleasure	120	2	6
Average other flavors	115	2	4
Whole Foods:			
Chocolate, with Spirulina, 1 oz	100	1	10
Vanilla, with Spirulina, 1 oz	100	0	11

Coconut Milk Drink

   C   **F**   **Cb**

	C	F	Cb
So Delicious: *Per 8 fl.oz cup*			
Original	70	4.5	8
Vanilla	80	4.5	10
Unsweetened, Original; Vanilla	45	4.5	2
Trader Joes: *Per 8 fl.oz cup*			
Unsweetened	60	5	1
Vanilla	90	5	9
(Enriched with calcium + vitamins D & B12)			

Confucious say:
"Man who eat with one chopstick never have problem with obesity"

50

Quick Guide

Cola Drinks: *Average all Brands*	**C**	**F**	**Cb**
8 fl.oz Cup/Can	100	0	26
12 fl.oz Can	150	0	39
16 fl.oz Bottle	200	0	52
20 fl.oz Bottle	250	0	65
24 fl.oz (Pepsi)	300	0	84
1-Liter Bottle (34 fl.oz)	400	0	100
2-Liter Bottle (68 fl.oz)	800	0	200
Other Soda Drinks: *Per 12 fl.oz, average all brands*			
Club Soda	0	0	0
Cream Soda	190	0	48
Ginger Ale	125	0	31
Lemonade, Regular/Pink	180	0	45
Orange	180	0	45
Root Beer	150	0	39
Tonic Water	125	0	32
Mineral Water: Plain	0	0	0
Sweetened/flavored	150	0	37
With Fruit Juice	120	0	30
Soda Water/Seltzer: Plain/Diet	0	0	0
Sweetened/flavored	155	0	39
With Fruit Juice	160	0	40

Fountain, Movie Theater & Take-Out

Average All Flavors			
Small Cup, 12 fl.oz: No Ice	160	0	40
With ⅓ Ice	120	0	30
Regular, 16 fl.oz: No Ice	215	0	53
With ⅓ Ice	160	0	40
Medium, 22 fl.oz: No Ice	295	0	73
With ⅓ Ice	220	0	55
Large, 32 fl.oz: No Ice	430	0	105
With ⅓ Ice	320	0	80

Note: ⅓ Cup of Ice = ¼ Cup Liquid

Soft Drink ~ Brands

Per 12 fl.oz Unless Indicated			
365 Organic *(Whole Foods)*, Spritzers, all flavors	110	0	28
A&W: Root Beer	175	0	47
Ten	10	0	3
Albertson's:			
Super Chill: Cola	160	0	43
Root Beer	180	0	48
Barq's, Root Beer	160	0	45
Big Red, Soda, 20 fl.oz	250	0	63
Blue Sky, Natural Soda, Cola	160	0	40

Soft Drink Brands (Cont)

Per 12 fl.oz Unless Indicated	**C**	**F**	**Cb**
Bubble Up, Lemon-Lime Soda, 8 fl.oz	110	0	28
Cactus Cooler, 12 fl.oz	150	0	40
Canada Dry: *Per 8 fl.oz*			
Club Soda; Diet Ginger Ale	0	0	0
Ginger Ale; Tonic Water, average	90	0	25
Cheerwine, 12 fl.oz	150	0	42
Coca-Cola:			
Classic; Caffeine Free	140	0	39
Diet Coke, all varieties	0	0	0
Cherry Coke; Vanilla Coke	150	0	42
Country Time *(Dr Pepper/Snapple)*, Lemonade, all varieties, 20 fl.oz	230	0	58
Crush: *Per 20 fl.oz Bottle*			
Grape; Orange	270	0	72
Peach; Pineapple, average	315	0	85
Strawberry	290	0	77
Dad's: Orange Cream Soda	180	0	46
Root Beer	165	0	41
Diet Rite, Pure Zero	0	0	0
Dr Pepper: *Per 12 fl.oz Can*			
Regular	150	0	40
Cherry	160	0	43
Ten	10	0	3
Fanta: Orange	160	0	44
Other flavors	180	0	48
Fresca, all flavors	0	0	0
GuS, average all flavors	95	0	23
Hansen's:			
Natural Cane Sugar:			
Creamy Root Beer	160	0	43
Original Cola	160	0	41
Pomegranate	130	0	35
Hawaiian Punch:			
Aloha Morning, 40% less sugar, all flavors	90	0	20
Maizin Melon Mix; Wild Purple Splash	165	0	44
Average other flavors	100	0	27
Henry Weinhard's: Root Beer	170	0	43
Orange/Vanilla Cream, av.	180	0	44
Hires, Root Beer	170	0	46
IBC: Root Beer	160	0	43
Cream Soda; Black Cherry	180	0	48
Icee: Coca-Cola; Orange Fanta	100	0	27
Lemon Lime Fanta	90	0	24
Minute Maid, Raspb. Lemonade	100	0	27
Jarritos, all flav., 8 fl.oz	110	0	28
Jelly Belly, all flavors	180	0	42
Jolt, Cola, 12 fl.oz	150	0	41

Soft Drink Brands (Cont)

Per 12 fl.oz Unless Indicated

	C	F	Cb
Jones Soda: Cola	170	0	43
Whoopass, 16 oz	200	0	52
Average other flavors	185	0	46
Kool Aid, Bursts, av., 6.75 fl.oz	35	0	9
Mello Yello, Regular	170	0	46
Mountain Dew:			
All flavors	170	0	46
Diet varieties	0	0	0
Mug, Root Beer	160	0	43
Natural Brew:			
Draft Root Beer	170	0	43
Outrageous Ginger Ale	180	0	44
Vanilla Cream Soda	160	0	39
Nehi, Royal Crown Peach	190	0	51
Pepsi:			
Regular; Caffeine Free	150	0	41
Diet Pepsi; Jazz; Pepsi One	0	0	0
Pepsi Next	60	0	16
Perrier, Carbonated Water	0	0	0
Pibb, Xtra	140	0	39
RC Cola: Regular	160	0	43
Ten	10	0	3
Reed's, Ginger Brew,			
all varieties	145	0	38
7·UP: Lemon Lime; Cherry	140	0	39
Diet flavors	0	0	0
Ten, Lemon Lime	10	0	3
Safeway: *Per 8 fl.oz*			
Refreshe: Cola	110	0	29
Grape	140	0	36
Lemon Lime	110	0	27
Mtn Breeze; Strawberry	120	0	30
Santa Cruz: Or. Mango, 10.5 fl.oz	120	0	29
Raspberry Lemonade, 10.5 fl.oz	100	0	26
Average other varieties, 10.5 fl.oz	135	0	33
Schweppes: Ginger Ale	120	0	33
Tonic Water	130	0	33
Shasta: Cream Soda	190	0	47
Cherry Cola	180	0	45
Club Soda: Diet, all flavors	0	0	0
Dr. Shasta	150	0	38
Ginger Ale	130	0	33
Tiki Punch; Pineapple; Or.	200	0	50
Average other flavors	170	0	41
Sierra Mist, Lemon Lime	140	0	37
Slurpee ~ *See Page 236*			
Sprite: Regular, 8 fl.oz	100	0	26
Zero	0	0	0

Per 12 fl.oz Unless Indicated

	C	F	Cb
Squirt, Ruby Red	170	0	45
Stewarts: Root Beer	160	0	41
Grape; Orange 'n Cream	190	0	48
Sun Drop: Citrus Soda, 20 fl.oz	290	0	76
Diet Citrus Soda	10	0	1
Sunkist: Orange	170	0	44
Ten, Orange	10	0	2
TAB	0	0	0
Tampico:			
64 fl.oz Container:			
Blue Raspberry Punch	45	0	21
Pineapple Coconut	105	0	25
Average other flavors	90	0	21
Thomas Kemper:			
Black Cherry	170	0	44
Ginger Ale; Vanilla Cream	150	0	36
Root Beer	160	0	41
Trader Joe's:			
Sparkling:			
French Berry Lemonade:			
1 cup, 8 fl.oz	130	0	31
1 bottle, 33.8 fl.oz	520	0	124
Lime Ade: 1 cup, 8 fl.oz	110	0	28
1 bottle, 33.8 fl.oz	440	0	108
Pink Lemonade: 1 cup, 8 fl.oz	130	0	31
1 Bottle, 33.8 fl.oz	520	0	124
Vernor's, Ginger Soda	140	0	39
Virgil's, Root Beer	160	0	42
Walgreens: *Per 20 fl.oz*			
Orchard Grape Soda	300	0	84
Cola; Zesty Lemon Lime, av.	225	0	65
Root Beer	225	0	75
Zevia, average all flavors	0	0	6
(Contains between 4-7g Erythritol)			

Powdered Soft Drink Mixes

Per 8 fl.oz Prepared, Unless Indicated

	C	F	Cb
Country Time:			
Lemonade; Pink Lemonade	60	0	16
Strawberry Lemonade	80	0	19
Crystal Light: *(Kraft)*			
Fruit Drinks, all flavors, ½ tsp	5	0	0
Pure Fitness, average all flavors, 1 pkt	15	0	4
Flavor Aid, ⅛ package	60	0	16
Kool-Aid, sweetened, 0.6 oz	60	0	16
Tang, Regular, 2 Tbsp, 1 oz	90	0	24

Quick Guide

Teas

	C	F	Cb
Regular: Bag, Loose or Instant			
Brewed, 1 cup, 8 fl.oz	2	0	0.5
(Add extra for sugar/milk)			
Herbal: All flavors, average, 1 cup	2	0	0.5
Bigelow, all flavors	0	0	0
Celestial Seasonings, all flavors	0	0	0
Bubble Milk Tea, w/ Pearls, 8 fl.oz	175	0	41
Chai Tea, 2 Tbsp	120	3.5	21
Starbucks ~ See Fast-Foods Section			

Iced Tea

Average All Brands

	C	F	Cb
Sweetened: 8 fl.oz cup	90	0	22
12 fl.oz glass/can	140	0	35
16 fl.oz bottle	180	0	45
20 fl.oz bottle	225	0	55
Unsweetened, 8 fl.oz	0	0	0

Iced Tea Mixes

Per 8 fl.oz Made-Up

	C	F	Cb
4C Iced Tea:			
Average all flavors, 0.67 oz	70	0	18
Totally Light, all flavors	0	0	0
Crystal Light, sugar free	5	0	0
Lipton:			
Sweetened: Lemon	70	0	18
Mango; Peach	80	0	19
Unsweetened	0	0	0
Diet, all varieties	5	0	1

Bottled & Canned Teas

	C	F	Cb
Arizona: *Per 8 fl.oz*			
Black: Cranberry	80	0	22
Sweet	90	0	23
With Ginseng	60	0	15
Green Tea, average all flavors	70	0	18
Fuze, Iced Lemon	70	0	19
Gold Peak, Lemon, 12 fl.oz	120	0	30
Honest Tea: Black Forrest Berry, 16 fl.oz	60	0	16
Raspberry Fields, 16 fl.oz	70	0	18

Bottled & Canned Teas (Cont)

	C	F	Cb
Lipton:			
Iced Tea: *Per 8 fl.oz*			
Natural: With Lemon	50	0	13
With Pomegranate Blueberry	50	0	13
Natural Green Tea: With Citrus	70	0	19
With Passionfruit Mango	50	0	13
White Tea, with Raspberry	50	0	14
Diet, all flavors	0	0	0
Sparkling,			
Strawberry Kiwi, Diet	0	0	0
Sweet Iced Tea	80	0	23
Minute Maid, Pomeg. Tea, 8 fl.oz	40	0	9
Nestea:			
Iced Tea, with Lemon:			
8 fl.oz	50	0	12
20 fl.oz bottle	125	0	30
Diet, Green/Lemon	0	0	0
POM:			
Antioxidant Super Tea: *Per 16 fl.oz*			
Pomegranate:			
Lychee Green Tea	140	0	36
Peach Passion White Tea	160	0	38
Snapple: *Per 16 fl.oz*			
Green Tea	120	0	31
Diet Green Tea	0	0	0
Lemon/ Raspberry Tea	150	0	37
Diet Lemon/Raspberry Tea	10	0	0
SnapTea: Lemon	120	0	31
Peach Green Tea	160	0	42
Sweet Tea	170	0	46
SoBe, Energize, Green Tea, 20 fl.oz	200	0	52
Ssips, Lemon Iced, 6 fl.oz	70	0	18
Steaz, Green Tea,			
average all flavors, 16 fl.oz	80	0	20
Tazo, Org. Iced Black Tea, 13.8 fl oz	60	0	15
TeaZazz: Original; Peach, 20 fl.oz	50	0	12
Green Tea Lemon, 20 fl.oz	60	0	17
Trader Joe's: *Per 8 fl.oz*			
Organic Tea & Lemonade	100	0	25
Pomegranate Green Tea	60	0	15
Unsweetened *(Kettle/Green)*	0	0	0
Turkey Hill: Iced Tea, 16 fl.oz	180	0	42
Fruit flavors, av., 16 fl.oz	205	0	50
Green Tea, Mango	180	0	42
365 Organic *(Whole Foods):*			
Unsweetened: Black Tea	0	0	0
Green Tea	0	0	0

Note: Most breads have similar calories on a weight basis. However, volume may vary.

For example, 1 oz of bread may equal 1 slice regular bread or 2 slices of a lighter bread. It is best to weigh bread used and calculate using: 1 oz bread = 70 calories, 14g carb.

Quick Guide

Bread	C	F	Cb
White or Wheat: *Average Per Slice*			
Thin or Light, 0.75 oz	50	0.5	9
Sandwich slice, 1 oz	70	1	12
Thick or Large, 1.5 oz	105	1.5	18
Thick, 2 oz	140	2	23
Extra Thick, 3 oz	210	3	35
Whole Loaf: 16 oz	1120	15	185
24 oz Loaf	1680	24	280
Multi Grain/Whole Grain: *Per Slice*			
Sandwich Slice, 1 oz	75	1.5	12
Thick Slice, 2 oz	150	2.5	25
Toast: *Based on same counts as White/Wheat as above*			
1 Slice (1 oz fresh)			
With 1 tsp butter/margarine	105	5	12
With 1 tsp "light" butter/marg.	90	3.5	12
With 2 tsp butter/margarine	140	9	12
With 2 tsp "light" butter/marg.	110	6	12

Breads

Per Slice Unless Indicated	C	F	Cb
12-Grain, 1.5 oz	110	1.5	22
Bran style/Dark, 1 oz	70	1	14
Buttermilk, average, 1.5 oz	110	1	22
Challah, 0.75 oz	85	1.5	17
Chapati, 1 oz	110	3	18
Ciabatta, 2 oz	130	1	26
Cornbread, average, 3 oz	220	6	37
Cracked Wheat Sourdough, 1.5 oz	130	0.5	27
Croissants ~ *See Page 134*			
Crustless Bread, regular, slice, 0.75 oz	40	0.5	8.5
Crusts Only, regular slice, 0.25 oz	30	0	7
English Toasting, 2 oz	140	1.5	27
Flax & Grain, 1.5 oz	120	3	19
Foccacia: Plain, 2 oz serve	150	2.5	28
Cheese & Garlic; Pesto, 2 oz serve	160	6	21
Tomato & Olive, 2 oz serve	150	5	21

Breads (Cont)

Per Slice Unless Indicated	C	F	Cb
French Stick/Baguette, 1 oz	70	1	15
French Toast: Slices, 1.5 oz	140	2	26
Aunt Jemima, Sticks, av., 2 oz	110	2	18
Garlic Bread/Toast:			
Small slice + 1 tsp spread, 0.75 oz	80	5	7
Medium slice + 2 tsp spread, 1.5 oz	160	10	14
Thick slice + 3 tsp spread, 1.8 oz	220	14	20
Pepperidge Farm, 1 slice, 1.4 oz	160	10	15
Hawaiian Sweet Bread, 1.5 oz	110	2	19
Hemp Bread, 1.2 oz	95	2	12
Italian Bread, 2 oz	140	1	28
Lower Carb, (higher protein/fiber), average all brands, 1 oz	60	1.5	9
MultiGrain, 1.5 oz	100	2	21
Naan Flatbread, 2 oz	160	3.5	29
Nut/Health Nut, 1.35 oz	90	1.5	18
Oatmeal/Oatbran Bread, 1.5 oz	90	0.5	18
Pita, average all types:			
Small (4" diam), 1 oz	90	0	18
Large (6½" diam), 2 oz	140	1.5	27
Extra Large (9" diam), 4 oz	300	1.5	60
Popovers, (1), without butter	130	5	18
Pumpernickel:			
Cocktail/Party size	30	0.5	6
Large slice, 1.35 oz	80	0	15
Raisin Bread, 1 oz	80	1	15
Rye: 1 thin slice, av., 1 oz	80	1	14
1 thick slice, 2 oz	150	2	25
Cocktail size, 0.4 oz	25	0.5	4
Sandwich Pockets, 2 oz	140	1.5	27
Sourdough: Regular, 1.5oz	120	1	25
French Style,1 oz	75	0	14
Spelt, 1.6 oz	130	1	24
Sprouted 7-Grain, 1.5 oz	110	0.5	18
Squaw, 1.1 oz	85	0.5	13
Tacos/Tortillas ~ *See Page 172*			
Turkish/Middle Eastern, 1 oz	80	1.5	16
Wheat-Free Breads: Spelt, 1.6 oz	130	1	26
Rice, with Fruit Juice, 1.5 oz	110	2	21
Healthseed Rye, 1.6 oz	90	1	20
Millet, 1.5 oz	100	1	20

Bread ~ Brands

Per Slice Unless Indicated

	C	F	Cb
Ener-G, Gluten-Free Breads:			
Brown Rice Loaf:			
Regular, 1.3 oz	100	3	16
High Fiber Loaf, 1.4oz	90	4.5	16
Tapioca, regular, sliced,1 oz	80	3	11
Ezekiel:			
7 Sprouted Grains, 1.2 oz	80	0.5	15
Sesame, 1.2 oz	80	0.5	14
Whole Grain, 1.35 oz	80	0.5	15
French Meadow: *Per Slice*			
Flax & Sunflower, 1.2 oz	90	1.5	15
Hemp, 1.2 oz	100	2.5	12
Spelt, 1.2 oz	85	0.5	17
Francisco International:			
Extra Sourdough Loaf,			
1 slice, 1.7 oz	130	1	24
French, 2 slices, 1.6 oz	120	1	22
Oroweat:			
3 Seed Oatnut, 1.35 oz	110	2.5	18
100% Whole Wheat, 1.35 oz	90	1	18
Country Buttermilk, 1.35 oz	100	1	19
Honey Wheat Berry, 1.2 oz	80	1	17
Pepperidge Farm: *Per Slice Unless Indicated*			
100% Whole Wheat, Very Thin, 3 slices	110	2	20
15 Grain	100	2	20
Farmhouse, Hearty White	110	1.5	22
Goldfish:			
White/100% Whole Wheat,			
average, 2 slices	100	1.5	23
Italian, with Sesame Seeds	90	1	19
Light Style, average all varieties	130	1	26
Frozen Breads:			
Garlic Bread:			
Five Cheese, 2.25 oz	200	10	20
Parmesan, 2.5"	180	8	21
Premium: Roasted Garlic Toast	150	7	18
Tuscan Inspired Sourdough	170	7	20
Roman Meal: Orig. Multigr., 2 slices	110	1.5	25
Honey Oat Bran, 1.5 oz	110	1.5	20
Sara Lee: Honey Wheat, 1 oz	75	1	14
100% Whole Wheat, 1 oz	70	1	13
45 Cals & Delightful Wheat	45	0.5	9
Schwan's, Frozen:			
Cheese Stuffed Breadsticks, 1.75 oz	130	5	15
French Baguette, ¼ loaf, 1.7 oz	130	0.5	26
Trader Joe's: Gourmet White, 1.5 oz	120	3.5	19
Soft 10 Grain, 1.5 oz	90	1.5	16
Sprouted Rye, 1.2 oz	90	1	15

Biscuits, Bread Rolls & Buns

	C	F	Cb
Biscuits: *Average, 2½" diameter*			
Plain/Butter Milk:			
Prepared from Recipe	210	10	27
Refrig. Dough, Baked	95	4	13
Brown 'n Serve, av., 1 oz	70	1	13
Refrigerated Dough:			
Pillsbury, Buttermilk Biscuit,			
(3), 2.25 oz	150	2	30
Buns:			
Frankfurter/Hot Dog: 1.25 oz	110	1.5	21
1.5 oz size	130	2	25
Hamburger: Regular, 1.5 oz	110	1.5	22
Large, 3 oz	210	3	40
Hoagie/Submarine, Plain, 2.3oz	200	1	38
Rolls:			
Ciabatta Roll, 3.5 oz	230	4	41
Crescent Roll, Original, 1 oz	100	6	11
Dinner:			
1 small, 1 oz	90	1.5	17
1 medium (3" diam),1.5 oz	110	1	23
French: 1 med, 1.3 oz	110	1.5	22
1 large, 3 oz	230	2.5	42
Kaiser:			
Small, 2 oz	200	2.5	35
Large, 3.5 oz	350	4	61
Plain, 6", average all, 2.5 oz	200	1	38
Sourdough, 1.25 oz	110	1	21
Wheat Rolls: Small, 1.2 oz	100	1	17
Medium, 1.75 oz	130	1.5	23
Large, 3.5 oz	260	3	46

Breadsticks, Croutons

	C	F	Cb
Breadsticks:			
Salt Sticks, plain, 1 oz	110	1	20
Fresh baked (1), 2 oz	180	2.5	34
Stella D'oro: Original (1)	45	1	7
Sesame (1)	50	2	7
Croutons: Seasoned, 2 Tbsp, 0.25 oz	35	1.5	4
Pepp. Farm, Zesty Italian, 6 croutons	30	1	5

Bread Products

	C	F	Cb
Bread Crumbs, dry:			
Plain or seasoned: 1 oz	110	1.5	20
1 cup, 3½ oz	385	5	70
Corn Flake Crumbs, 1 oz	120	0	29
Graham Cracker Crumbs *(Keebler),*1 oz	110	2.5	20
Bread Dough, average:			
Frozen, 1 slice, 2 oz	140	2	26
Refrigerated: French, 1" sl.	60	1	13
Wheat; White, 1" slice	80	2	14
Coating Mixes, av., 2 Tbsp., 1 oz	100	0.5	20
Stuffing: Dry mix, average all,1 oz	110	1	10
Prepared, ½ cup, 4 oz	180	9	11

Updated Nutrition Data ~ www.CalorieKing.com
Persons with Diabetes ~ See Disclaimer (Page 22)

B Bread ~ Bagels ◆ Tortillas ◆ Taco Shells

Quick Guide

Bagels
Average All Brands
Plain/Onion:

	C	F	Cb
1 mini/bagelette, 1 oz	65	0.5	13
1 small bagel, 2 oz	145	1	29
1 medium bagel, 3 oz	220	1.5	43
1 large bagel, 4 oz	290	2	57
Bagel Chips, 1 oz	130	4.5	19
Pizza Bagel Bites (Bagel Bites),			
all varieties, av., 4 pieces, 3 oz	190	5.5	27
Bagel Crisps (New York Style),			
all varieties, av., 6 crisps, 1 oz	130	5	17
Bagel Thins (Thomas'), 1, 1.5 oz	110	1	25

Bagel ~ Brands

Per Bagel

	C	F	Cb
Bubba's: Plain; Onion, average	240	2	48
Blueberry	150	0.5	32
Cinnamon Raisin	250	1.5	51
Costco Bakery: Plain	330	1.5	70
Cinnamon Raisin	340	1.5	73
Whole Grain	300	5	56
Lender's, Fresh, NY Style:			
Plain, 3.3 oz	240	2	46
Blueberry, 2 oz	150	0.5	32
Whole Grain, 3.3 oz	250	1.5	48
Whole Wheat, 3.3 oz	210	1.5	41
Panera Bread: Plain	290	1.5	59
Cinnamon & Raisin Swirl, 3.75 oz	320	2	65
Everything, 4 oz	300	2.5	59
Whole Grain, 4.25 oz	340	2.5	67
Sara Lee: Mini, average, 1.3 oz	100	0.5	20
Plain, 3.35 oz	260	1	50
Blueberry, 3.7 oz	280	1	54
Cinnamon Raisin, 3.7 oz	270	1	54
Everything, 3.7 oz	280	3.5	50
Onion, 3 oz	270	1	52
Western, The Alternatives, av., 2 oz	120	0.5	29

Bagel Spreads

Cream Cheese:

	C	F	Cb
Plain: 2 Tbsp, 1 oz	100	9	1
2 oz mini-tub	200	18	2
Reduced Fat: 2 Tbsp, 1 oz	60	5	2
2 oz mini-tub	120	10	4
Flavors: Lox, 1 oz	90	8	2
Honey Nut, 1 oz	80	7	4
Strawberry, 1 oz	90	7	5
Sundried Tomato, 1 oz	80	7	2
Vegetable, 1 oz	90	8	2

English Muffins C F Cb
Average All Brands
Plain/Whole Wheat:

	C	F	Cb
Regular, 2 oz	135	1.5	26
Heavier, 2.5 oz	155	2	31
Super Size, 3.2 oz	190	2	38
Raisin-Cinnamon, 2.2 oz	150	1	30

Note: Actual weight of packaged muffins can be 10-15% heavier than stated net weight.

Rice Cakes

	C	F	Cb
Regular size (1), average, 0.32 oz	35	0.5	7.5
Hain, Mini, Mild Cheddar (10)	70	2.5	11
Lundberg,			
all varieties, 0.65 oz	70	0.5	14
Quaker, Apple Cinn., 0.45 oz	50	0	11

Tortillas & Shells

Tortillas: *Per Tortilla*
Corn Flour:

	C	F	Cb
White/Yellow: 6", 1 oz	55	1	11
7", 1.2 oz	75	1	14
Wheat Flour:			
6", 1.2 oz	100	3	16
8", 1.4 oz	130	4	20
10", 2.3 oz	200	6	31

Shells: *Per Shell, Without Fillings*
Corn Taco Shells:

	C	F	Cb
Mini, 3", 0.2 oz	25	1	3
Medium, 5", 0.5 oz	60	2.5	8
Large, 6½", 0.7 oz	100	4.5	13
Salad Shell, 10"	310	17	34
Tostada Shells, fried:			
White Corn, 5½" diam., 0.4 oz	55	2.5	8
Yellow Corn, 5½" diam., 0.5 oz	80	3.5	11
Sopes, 1 shell, 4" 2 oz	110	1.5	23

La Tortilla Factory: *Per Tortilla*
Corn: Hand Made Style

	C	F	Cb
Regular, 1.4 oz	90	1	14
Grande, 2.5 oz	150	2	25
Wheat/Flour:			
Low Carb:			
Original size, 1.3 oz	50	2	10
Large size, 2.2 oz	80	3	18
100 Calorie, 2 oz	100	1.5	24
Burrito size, 2 oz	170	4.5	24

Mission Foods:
Corn: Yellow/White

	C	F	Cb
Regular size, 0.8 oz	40	0.5	8
Super size, 1 Tortilla, 1.2 oz	70	1	14
Flour: Estilo Casero, 1 Tortilla, 1.8 oz	170	6	24
Homestyle, 1 Tortilla, 2.2 oz	190	4.5	32
Whole Wheat, Soft Taco, 1.6 oz	130	3	22

Quick Guide

Cooked Cereals

	C	F	Cb
Barley, pearled, cooked, 1 cup	195	0.5	44
Buckwheat Groats, roasted:			
Dry, ½ cup, 3 oz	285	2	61
Cooked, 1 cup, 6 oz	155	1	34
Bulgur: Dry, ½ cup, 2.5 oz	240	1	53
Cooked, 1 cup, 6.5 oz	150	1	34
Corn/Hominy Grits:			
Dry: Regular, ¼ cup, 1.4 oz	140	0.5	32
Instant, 0.8 oz packet	75	0	18
W/ Imitation Bacon Bits, 1 oz	100	0.5	20
Cooked, ¾ cup, 6.5 oz	110	0.5	23
Cream of Rice, cooked, ¾ cup, 6.5 oz	95	0	21
Cream of Wheat:			
Cooked: Regular, ¾ cup, 6.5 oz	95	0.5	20
Instant, ¾ cup, 6.5 oz	105	0.5	21
Quick, ¾ cup, 6.5 oz	100	0.5	22
Farina, cooked, ¾ cup, 6 oz	95	0.5	19
Millet, dry, ¼ cup, 1.75 oz	190	2	36
Oat Bran: Raw, ⅓ cup, 1 oz	70	2	19
Cooked, ½ cup, 3.75 oz	45	1	13
Oatmeal:			
Dry: Regular, ⅓ cup, 1 oz	100	1.5	18
Instant: Regular, average, 1 oz	105	1.5	18
Flavored, average, 1.5 oz	165	2	34
Cooked: Regular, ¾ cup, 6 oz	125	2.5	21
1 cup, 8 oz	165	3.5	28
Whole Wheat, cooked, ¾ cup, 6.5 oz	115	0.5	25

Brans, Wheat Germ, Add-Ons

Bee Pollen Granules, 1 Tbsp, 0.28 oz	25	1	2
Bran:			
Oat Bran: Raw, 1 Tbsp, 0.18 oz	20	0.5	3
⅓ cup, 1 oz	100	2	17
Rice Bran: Raw, 1 Tbsp, 0.18 oz	15	1	2.5
¼ cup, 1 oz	95	6	15
Fruit: Dried, average, 1 oz	70	0	18
Banana, ½ medium	55	0	14
Prunes in Syrup (5), 3 oz	90	0	23
Honey, 1 Tbsp, 0.75 oz	65	0	17
Lecithin Granules, 1 Tbsp, 0.35 oz	55	4	0.5
Nuts, Almonds (6), 0.25 oz	40	4	1.5
Psyllium Husks, 1 Tbsp, 0.18 oz	10	0	4
Wheat, unprocessed, 1 Tbsp, 0.10 oz	5	0	2
Wheat Germ: Raw, 1 Tbsp, 0.25 oz	25	0.5	4
¼ cup, 1 oz	105	3	15

Hot/Cooked Cereals ~ Brands

Per Serving, Dry Mix only

	C	F	Cb
Albers,			
Quick Grits, ¼ cup, 1.4 oz	140	0.5	31
B&G:			
Cream of Wheat, Instant: Orig., 1 oz	100	0	20
Maple Brown Sugar, 1.25 oz	130	0	28
Bobs Red Mill,			
10 Grain, ¼ cup, 1.6 oz	140	1	28
Country Choice,			
Quick Oats, ½ cup, 1.5 oz	150	3	27
Dr. McDougall's:			
Big Cup Oatmeal, Organic:			
Apple Flax, 2.25 oz	250	3.5	48
Cranberry Almond & Grains, 3 oz	330	4	64
Hemp Peach, 3 oz	330	5	63
Maple, 2.45 oz	270	3.5	55
Great Value *(Walmart):*			
Instant Oatmeal:			
Maple & Brown Sugar, 1.5 oz	160	2	32
Peaches & Cream, 1.25 oz pkt	130	2.5	22
McCann's:			
Instant Irish Oatmeal:			
Regular, 1 oz package	100	2	19
Apple & Cinn., 1.25 oz	130	1.5	26
Maple & Brown Sugar, 1.5 oz	160	2	32
Malt-O-Meal: Orig., 3Tbsp, 1.2 oz	130	0.5	27
Maple Brown Sugar, ¼ cup	170	0	37
Natures Path:			
Oatmeal:			
Apple Cinnamon, 1.7 oz	210	2.5	40
Hemp Plus, 1 pkt, 1.4 oz	160	2.5	30
Maple Nut, 1.7 oz	210	4	38
NutriSystem:			
Oatmeal, Apple Cinnamon 1 pkt	130	1.5	26
Quaker:			
Grits:			
Instant, all flavors, average, 1 oz	100	0	22
Quick, Original, ¼ cup, 1.3 oz	130	0.5	29
Instant Oatmeal:			
Original, Organic 1 oz	100	2	19
Cinnamon & Spice, 1.5 oz	160	2	32
Maple Brown Sugar, 1.5 oz	160	2	32
Peaches & Cream, 1.25 oz	130	2	27
Old Fash'nd/Quick Oats, ½ c., 1.4 oz	150	3	27
Real Medleys: Blueb. Hazelnut, 2.5 oz	270	7	49
Summer Berry, 2.5 oz	250	3	51
Average other varieties, 2.6 oz	290	8	49
Wegmans:			
Feel Good About Oatmeal:			
Instant, Original, 1oz packet	100	2	19
Maple & Brown Sugar, 1.5 oz pkt	160	2	32

Quick Guide

Cold Cereals
Average All Brands

	C	F	Cb
Bran Flakes, ¾ cup, 1 oz	95	0.5	24
Corn Flakes, 1 cup, 1 oz	100	0	22
Frosted Flakes, ¾ cup, 1 oz	110	0	27
Granola, 100% Nat., ½ cup, 1.7 oz	205	6	35
Oat Bran Cereal, ½ cup, 1.5 oz	145	3	24
Puffed Rice, 1 cup. 0.5 oz	55	0	13
Puffed Wheat, 1 cup, 0.5 oz	45	1	10
Raisin Bran, ½ cup, 1 oz	90	0.5	22
Rice Crisps, 1 cup, 1 oz	105	0.5	24
Shredded Wheat, 1 biscuit, 1 oz	85	0.5	20
Wheat Flakes, ¾ cup, 1 oz	105	1	24

Breakfast/Cereal Bars ~ *See Page 31*

Ready-To-Eat Cereal ~ Brands

Arrowhead Mills: *Per Cup*

	C	F	Cb
Flakes: Amaranth, 1.2 oz	140	2	
Kamut, 1.1 oz	120	1	25
Oat Bran, 1.2 oz	140	2.5	24
Spelt, 1.1 oz	120	1	24
Sprouted Multigrain, 1.3 oz	120	1	26
Breadshop Granola:			
Crunchy Oat Bran, w/ Almds.,1.7 oz	210	8	33
Raspberry 'N Cream, ½ cup, 1.75 oz	220	8	34
Puffed: Corn, 0.5 oz	60	1	12
Kamut, 0.5 oz	50	1	11
Millet, 0.5 oz	60	0.5	11
Rice, 0.5 oz	60	0	14
Wheat, 0.5 oz	60	1	12
Shredded Wheat:			
Bite Size:			
Regular, 1.7 oz	190	1	38
Sweetened, 1.8 oz	200	1	42

Back to Nature: *Per ½ Cup, Unless Indicated*

Granola: Apple Blueberry, 1.75 oz	200	2.5	39
Blueberry Walnut, 1.5 oz	190	6	30
Chocolate Delight, 1.75 oz	220	6	37
Classic, 1.8 oz	200	3	39
Cranberry Pecan, 1.65 oz	180	4.5	36
Honey Almond, 1.48 oz	190	7	29
Organic Cherry Vanilla, 1.75 oz	200	4	38
Sunflower & Pumpkin Seed, 1.75 oz	210	7	30

Barbara's Bakery:

Classics, Organic & Sweetened:

	C	F	Cb
Brown Rice Crisps, 1 oz	120	1	25
Corn Flakes, 1 cup, 1 oz	110	1	25
Honest O's, Original, 1 oz	120	2	22
High Fiber:			
Original, 1.95 oz	180	1.5	42
Cranberry, 2 oz	190	1.5	42
Flax & Granola, 1 cup, 2 oz	200	3	42
Puffins:			
Original, ¾ cup, 0.95 oz	90	1	23
Cinnamon, ⅔ cup, 1 oz	90	1	26
Multigrain, ¾ cup, 1 oz	110	0	25
PB/PB & Choc., av., ¾ cup, 1 oz	110	2	24
Puffs: Crunchy Cocoa, ¾ cup, 1 oz	120	1	24
Fruit Medley, ¾ cup , 1 oz	120	1	26
Morning Oat Crunch:			
Original, 1 cup, 2 oz	210	2	44
Cinnamon Crunch, 1 cup, 2 oz	230	3	43
Vanilla Almond, 1 cup, 2 oz	220	3	42
Shredded Wheat, 2 biscuits, 1.4 oz	140	1	31
Spoonfuls, Multigrain, ¾ cup, 1 oz	120	1.5	24

Cascadian Farm:

Cinnamon Crunch, 1 cup, 1 oz	110	2.5	22
Granola: Ancient Grains, 1c., 2 oz	210	5	38
French Vanilla Almond, ¾ c.,1.75 oz	210	5	38
Oats & Honey, ⅔ cup, 2 oz	230	6	42
Honey Nut O's, 1 cup, 1 oz	110	1	25
Multi Grain Squares,			
1 cup, 1.9 oz	210	1	44
Raisin Bran, 1 cup, 2 oz	180	1	41

EnviroKidz: *Per 1 oz*

Amazon Frosted Flakes, ⅔ cup	120	0	26
Gorilla Munch, ¾ cup	120	1	26
Koala Crisp, ¾ cup	110	1	25
Leapin Lemur, ¾ cup	120	1.5	25
Panda Puffs, ¾ cup	130	3.5	23

Erewhon:

Corn Flakes, 1 cup, 1.2 oz	130	0	30
Crispy Brown Rice: Original, 1 oz	110	0.5	25
W/ Mixed Berries, 1 cup, 1 oz	120	0.5	27
Raisin Bran, 1 cup, 1.8 oz	180	1	40
Rice Twice, ¾ cup, 1 oz	120	0	26
Strawberry Crisps, ¾ cup, 1 oz	120	0.5	28

Ready-To-Eat Cereal (Cont)

	C	F	Cb
Ezekiel 4.9:			
Sprouted Whole Grain Cereals:			
Original, ½ cup, 2 oz	190	1	40
Almond, ½ cup, 2 oz	200	3	38
Cinnamon Raisin, 2 oz	190	1	41
Golden Flax, ½ cup, 2 oz	180	2.5	37
F-Factor, Skinnys 'n Fruit, ½ c., 1.23 oz	70	1	27
General Mills:			
Cheerios: *Per ¾ Cup Unless Indicated*			
Original, 1 cup, 1 oz	100	2	20
Apple Cinn., ¾ cup, 1 oz	120	1.5	24
Banana Nut, ¾ cup, 1 oz	100	1	24
Cinnamon Burst, 1 c., 1.2 oz	120	2	27
Chocolate, ¾ cup, 1 oz	100	1.5	22
Dulce de Leche, ¾ cup, 1 oz	100	1.5	22
Frosted, ¾ cup, 1 oz	100	1	22
Fruity, ¾ cup, 1 oz	100	1.5	23
Honey Nut, ¾ cup, 1 oz	110	1.5	23
Yogurt Burst, Strawberry, ¾ c.,1 oz	120	1.5	24
Multigrain:			
Regular, 1 cup, 1oz	110	1	24
Dark Choc. Crunch, ¾ cup, 1 oz	110	2	23
Peanut Butter, ¾ cup, 1 oz	110	1.5	23
Chex: Corn, 1 cup, 1 oz	120	0.5	26
Apple Cinn; Choc., average, 1 oz	120	2.5	26
Honey Nut, ¾ cup, 1 oz	120	0.5	28
Rice, 1 cup, 1 oz	100	0	23
Vanilla, ¾ cup, 1 oz	120	2	25
Wheat, ¾ cup, 1.65 oz	160	1	39
Cinnamon Toast Crunch, ¾ cup, 1.1 oz	130	3	25
Count Chocula, ¾ cup, 1 oz	100	1.5	23
Fiber One: Original, ½ cup, 1 oz	60	1	25
80 Cal. Honey Squares, ¾ cup, 1 oz	80	1	25
Honey Clusters, 1 cup, 1.8 oz	170	1.5	44
Protein, av. all flavors, 1 cup, 2 oz	220	5	41
Kix: Original, 1¼ cups, 1 oz	110	1	25
Berry Berry; Honey, 1¼ cups, 1.2 oz	120	1.5	28
Lucky Charms, all varieties, average, ¾ cup, 1 oz	110	1.5	23
Total: Original, ¾ cup, 1 oz	100	0.5	22
Raisin Bran, 1 cup, 2.1 oz	160	1	40
Trix, 1 cup, 1 oz	120	1.5	25
Wheaties: Original, ¾ cup, 1 oz	100	0.5	22
Fuel, ¾ cup, 1.95 oz	190	3	46

	C	F	Cb
Great Value *(Walmart):*			
Apple Blasts, 1 cup, 1.2 oz	120	0	29
Crunch Honey Oats, with Almonds, ¾ cup, 1 oz	130	2	26
Frosted Shredded Wheat, 1.85 oz	180	1	42
Fruit Spins, 1 cup, 1 oz	110	1	25
Honey Crunch, ¾ cup, 1 oz	100	0	24
Raisin Bran, 1 cup, 2 oz	210	1	45
Health Valley:			
Crunch-Ems!: Corn, 1 cup, 1 oz	110	0	24
Rice, 1¼ cups, 1 oz	110	0	26
Organic Flakes:			
Amaranth, 1¼ cups, 2 oz	210	2	43
Fiber 7, Multigrain , 1 cup, 1.75 oz	160	1	37
Oat Bran: 1 cup, 1.75 oz	190	1.5	39
With Raisins, 1 cup, 1.9 oz	200	1.5	43
Heartland:			
Granola: Original, ½ cup, 2.25 oz	240	6	40
Harvest Spice, ½ cup, 1.75 oz	210	5	37
Low-Fat Raisin, ½ cup, 2 oz	200	3	40
Hershey's, Cookies 'n' Creme, 1 oz	110	3	21
Kashi:			
7 Whole Grain: Flakes, 1 c., 1.8 oz	170	0.5	41
Honey Puffs, 1 cup, 1 oz	120	1	25
Nuggets, ½ cup, 2 oz	210	1.5	47
Puffs, 1 cup, 0.67 oz	70	0.5	15
GoLEAN: Original, 1 cup, 1.8 oz	160	1	35
Crunch!: Original, 1 cup, 1.9 oz	200	3	38
Honey Almond Flax, ⅔ cup, 1.9 oz	200	5	35
Good Friends, Orig., 1 cup, 1.9 oz	160	1.5	42
Heart to Heart:			
Honey Toasted Oat, ¾ cup, 1.2 oz	120	1.5	26
Oat Flakes & Blueberry Clusters, 1 cup, 1.9 oz	200	2	44
Raisin Vineyard, ¾ cup, 1.8 oz	170	0	40
Whole Wheat Biscuit:			
Av. all varieties, 30 biscuits, 2 oz	180	1	43
Kellogg's:			
All-Bran:			
Original, ½ cup, 1 oz	80	1	23
Bran Buds, ⅓ cup, 1.1 oz	80	1	24
Compl. Wheat Flakes, 1 oz	90	0.5	24
Apple Jacks, 1 cup, 1 oz	110	1	25
Cinnabon, 1 cup, 1.1 oz	120	2	25

continued next page...

Ready-To-Eat Cereal (Cont)

Kellogg's (Cont):	C	F	Cb
Cinnabon, 1 cup, 1.1 oz	120	2	25
Cocoa Crispies, ¾ cup, 1 oz	120	1	27
Corn Flakes, Original, 1 cup, 1 oz	100	0	24
Corn Pops, 1 cup, 1 oz	120	0	27
Cracklin' Oat Bran,			
¾ cup, 1.8 oz	200	7	34
Crispix, Original, 1 cup, 1 oz	110	0	25
Crunchy Nut:			
Golden Honey Nut Flakes,			
¾ cup, 1 oz	120	1	26
Roasted Nut & Honey, ¾ cup, 1 oz	100	1	23
Fiber Plus,			
Cinn. Oat Crunch, ¾ cup, 1 oz	170	1.5	43
Froot Loops: Original, 1 cup, 1 oz	110	1	26
Marshmallow, 1 cup, 1 oz	110	1	26
Frosted Flakes: Orig., ¾ cup, 1 oz	110	0	27
Reduced Sugar with Fiber,			
1 cup, 1 oz	110	0	26
Honey Smacks,			
¾ cup, 1 oz	100	0.5	24
Mini-Wheats, Frosted:			
Big Bites (7), 2 oz	200	1	49
Bite Size, Original (21), 1.9 oz	190	1	46
Little Bites:			
Original, 1 cup, 2 oz	200	1	47
Chocolate, 1 cup, 2 oz	200	2	46
Touch of Fruit In Middle,			
Raspberry (24), 1.95 oz	190	1	45
Mini Wheats, Unfrosted,			
Bite Size (30), 1.95 oz	190	1	45
Mueslix, ⅔ cup, 2 oz	200	3	41
Nutri-Grain Bars ~ *See Page 31*			
Product 19, 1 cup, 1 oz	110	0	25
Raisin Bran: Regular, 1 cup, 2 oz	190	1	46
Crunch, 1 cup, 1.9 oz	190	1	45
Rice Krispies:			
Original, 1¼ cups, 1.15 oz	130	0	29
Frosted, ¾ cup, 1 oz	120	0	27
Treats, ¾ cup, 1 oz	120	1	26

Kellogg's (Cont):	C	F	Cb
Smart Start,			
Antioxidants, 1 cup, 1.8 oz	190	1	44
Special K: Original 1 cup, 1 oz	120	0.5	23
Fruit & Yogurt, ¾ cup, 1 oz	120	1	27
Low Fat Granola, Touch of Honey,			
½ cup, 1.8 oz	190	3	39
Red Berries, 1 cup, 1 oz	110	0	27
Vanilla Almond, ¾ cup	110	1.5	25
Malt-O-Meal:			
Apple Zings, 1 cup, 1.15 oz	130	1	30
Cocoa Dyno-Bites, ¾ cup	120	1	26
Coco Roos, ¾ cup, 1 oz	120	1.5	26
Colossal/Berry Crunch, ¾ cup, 1 oz	120	1.5	26
Frosted Flakes, ¾ cup, 1 oz	120	0	28
Frosted Mini Spooners, 1 cup	190	1	45
Golden Puffs, ¾ cup, 1 oz	100	0	24
Honey Nut Scooters, 1 cup, 1 oz	110	1	24
Raisin Bran, 1 cup, 2 oz	220	1.5	45
Nature's Path:			
Flax Plus:			
Maple Pecan Crunch, ¾ cup	220	7	38
Pumpkin Raisin Crunch, ¾ cup	210	4.5	40
Raisin Bran Flakes, ¾ cup, 2 oz	190	2.5	41
Heritage Flakes, ¾ cup, 1 oz	120	1	23
Honey'd Cornflakes, ¾ cup, 1 oz	120	0	27
Kamut Puffs, 1 cup, 0.5 oz	50	0	11
Multigr. Oatbran Flakes, ¾ cup, 1 oz	110	1	24
Qi'a, all varieties, av., 2Tbsp, 1 oz	135	6.5	14
Optimum Power, Blueb. Cinn. Flax, 2 oz	200	3	38
New England Natural Bakers:			
Granola Pouches:			
All Natural:			
Banana Walnut,			
½ cup, 2 oz	260	12	34
Honey Nut Cinn., ½ cup, 2 oz	270	12	35
Probiotic Raspb., ½ cup, 1.7 oz	200	3	37
Organic:,			
Crispy Fruity Cereal, Gluen Free,			
⅔ cup, 1.9 oz	250	9	39
Muesli, ½ cup, 2 oz	220	5	40
New Morning:			
Fruit-e-O's, Organic, 1 c., 1 oz	120	1.5	25
Oatios, Original, 1 cup, 1 oz	110	2	22

Ready-To-Eat Cereal ~ Brands (Cont)

	C	F	Cb
NutriSystem: *Per Packet*			
Granola, Low-Fat	160	2.5	31
NutriFlakes	110	1	23
Sweetened O's	110	1.5	21
Peace:			
Clusters & Flakes:			
Honey Almond, 2 oz	210	4	40
Average other varieties, 2 oz	235	5	43
Low Fat, Hearty Raisin Bran, 2 oz	190	2	44
Crispy Rice & Flakes,			
Blueberry Pomegranate, 2 oz	240	6	41
Granola, average all varieties, ⅔ cup	240	6	41
Post:			
Alpha Bits, 1 cup, 1 oz	120	1.5	24
Bran Flakes, ¾ cup, 1 oz	100	0.5	24
Good Morenings, average, 1 oz	120	1.5	25
Grape-Nuts: Original, 2 oz	210	1	45
Fit, ⅔ cup, 2 oz	220	3	44
Flakes, ¾ cup, 1 oz	110	1	24
Great Grains:			
Banana Nut Crunch, 1 cup, 2 oz	230	5	42
Cranb. Alm. Crunch, ¾ cup, 1.7 oz	180	3	37
Honey, Oats & Seeds, 1 cup, 2 oz	220	5	37
Protein Blend, av. all varieties, 2oz	230	5	38
Honey Bunches of Oats:			
With Almonds, ¾ cup, 1 oz	130	2.5	26
With Van. Bunches, 2 oz	220	3	46
Honeycomb, 1½ cups, 1 oz	130	1	28
Mini Cinnamon Churros, 1 cup, 1.2 oz	130	3	26
Pebbles, average all varieties, ¾ cup, 1 oz	120	1	24
Raisin Bran, 1 cup, 2 oz	190	1	46
Selects, Blueb. Morning, 1¼ cups, 2 oz	220	3	45
Shredded Wheat, Spoon Size:			
Original, 1.7 oz	170	1	40
Honey Wheat, 2.1 oz	220	2	49
Waffle Crisp, 1 cup, 1 oz	120	2.5	25
Quaker:			
Honey Graham Oh's, 1 oz	110	2	23
King Vitaman, 1½ cups, 1 oz	120	1	26
Life, all types, ¾ cup, 1 oz	120	1.5	25
Natural Granola:			
Apple Cranberry Almond, 1.7 oz	200	6	35
Oats, Honey, & Alm., ½ cup, 1.7 oz	210	5	38
Oatmeal Squares, Honey Nut, 1 cup, 2 oz	210	2.5	44
Whole Hearts, ¾ cup, 1 oz	110	1.5	23

	C	F	Cb
Sweet Home Farm:			
Honey Nut Granola, 1.9 oz	250	10	37
Other varieties, 2 oz	250	8	40
Low-Fat Granola,			
½ cup, 1.9 oz	210	3	44
Stop & Shop:			
Oats & O's, ½ cup, 1.8 oz	110	1.5	22
Raisin Bran, 1 cup, 2 oz	190	1	46
Trader Joe's:			
Clusters: Raisin Bran, 1 cup, 2 oz	190	3	41
Super Nutty Toffee, ¾ cup, 2 oz	250	9	38
Average other varieties,			
⅔ cup, 1.3 oz	145	3.5	26
Corn Flakes, 1 cup, 1 oz	110	0	26
Golden Flax Cereal, 1.7 oz	200	3.5	37
Granola: Mango Passion, 2 oz	240	7	38
Pecan Praline, ½ cup, 1.6 oz	210	7	31
Trek Mix, ⅔ cup, 2 oz	240	8	37
High Fiber, ⅔ cup, 1 oz	80	0.5	23
Honey Nut O's, ¾ cup, 1 oz	120	1.5	24
Joe's O's, 1 cup, 1 oz	110	1.5	22
Shredded Wheats, Bite Size, 1 cup, 1.7 oz	180	1	38
Triple Berry O's, ¾ cup, 1 oz	110	1	25
Toasted Oatmeal Flakes, ¾ cup, 1 oz	110	1	23
Wheats, average all var., 1 cup, 2 oz	200	1	42
Uncle Sam:			
Original, ¾ cup, 1 oz	190	5	38
Raisin Bran, 1 cup, 2 oz	190	1	42
Weetabix,			
2 biscuits, 1.3 oz	130	1	29
Wegmans:			
Blueberry Muffin Squares, ¾ cup, 1 oz	130	3.5	24
Cinnamon Oat Crisps, ¾ cup, 1 oz	120	1	26
Chocolaty Rice Crisps, 1 oz	120	1	26
Corn Flakes, 1 cup, 1 oz	100	0	24
Frosted Flakes, 1 oz	120	0	28
Granola, Vanilla, ⅔ cup	240	6	41
Raisin Bran, 1 cup, 2 oz	190	1	46
Whole Foods (365):			
Corn Flakes, 1 cup, 1 oz	110	0	26
Frosted Flakes, ¾ cup, 1 oz	110	0	27
Hon. Flakes & Oat Clusters,			
¾ cup, 1 oz	120	1	25
Protein & Fiber Crunch, 1 cup, 1.8 oz	190	1	33
Raisin Bran, 1 cup, 2 oz	180	1	44
Wheat Squares:			
Bite Sized, 1.7 oz	180	1	38
Frosted, 1 cup, 1.9 oz	210	1	45

Ready-to-Eat	**C**	**F**	**Cb**

Per Piece/Slice

	C	F	Cb
Angel Food, Plain: Without oil, 2 oz	145	0	33
With oil, 2 oz	145	1	27
With Cream Frosting	255	7	45
Almond Croissant, 5 oz	620	35	67
Apple Danish, 5 oz	450	18	67
Apple Pie ~ *See Pies/Tarts Page 134*			
Baklava, 1½" square, 1.75 oz	200	10	27
Banana Cake, with Butter Cream, 2 oz	230	9	37
Banana Walnut Cake, 3 oz	270	11	40
Bear Claw, 4.5 oz	540	24	71
Black Forest, 3 oz	345	11	59
Brownie: Small, 2" Square, 1 oz	130	8	14
Large, 3 oz	390	24	42
Bundt Cakes, average all types:			
3 oz slice	300	13	42
Mini-Bundt, 5 oz	500	22	70
Cannoli's: Mini, 1 oz	85	3	11
Regular, 2.5 oz	215	8	28
Carrot Cake: Plain, 3 oz	300	16	37
With Cream Cheese Frosting	400	22	48
Cheesecake: Small serving, 3 oz	240	13	26
Large serving, 5 oz	400	21	44
With Low-Fat Cheese/Fruit, 3 oz	170	4	28
Denny's, NY Style, 5oz	510	34	43
Chocolate Cake:			
With Chocolate Frosting, 4 oz	415	18	62
Without Frosting, 1/12 of 9", 3.5 oz	340	14	51
Chocolate Croissant, 4.25 oz	470	26	54
Chocolate Eclair, with custard, 3.5 oz	260	16	24
Chocolate Fudge Cake, 3 oz	270	12	40
Chocolate Meringue, 2.5 oz	320	13	49
Churros, 1 stick, 1.5 oz	165	8	21
Cinnamon Crumb Cake, 2.5 oz	260	9	40
Cinnamon Rolls: Small, 2 oz	220	8	34
Regular, 4 oz	440	16	68
Large, 6 oz	660	24	102
Brands ~ *See Page 67*			
Coffee Cake, 2 oz	180	6	30
Concha: Small, 2 oz	240	9	33
Large (5" diameter), 5.5 oz	615	23	85
Cream Puff, custard filled, 4.6 oz	335	20	30
Cream Horn, 3 oz	210	5	36
Crumble Coffee Cake, 4.5 oz	500	25	65
Danish Pastries:			
Small, 2.5 oz	250	14	25
Large, 5 oz	500	28	50
Donuts ~ *See Page 66*			
Eclair, Chocolate, custard filled, 3.5 oz	260	16	24
Fig Bars, average	160	3	31

Ready-to-Eat (Cont)	**C**	**F**	**Cb**

Per Piece/Slice

	C	F	Cb
Fruit Cake, Dark/Light, 2 oz	185	5	34
Fudge Nut Brownie, 3.5 oz	380	18	54
Gingerbread, from mix, 3" square	210	4	41
Honey Bun, 2.7 oz	310	15	39
Jelly Roll, ½ roll, 1.8 oz	150	2	30
Key Lime Pie, 4.3 oz	400	25	41
Lady Finger, 3 oz	310	4.5	59
Lemon Cake, 4 oz	440	24	49
Lemon Poppy Seed Creme, 1.6 oz	180	9	23
Marble Cake, 4 oz	430	23	50
Mississippi Mud Pie, 4 oz	480	22	67
Mud Cake, 4.5 oz	380	20	44
Muffins ~ *See Page 67*			
Palmier Cookie, large, 4.5 oz	490	25	62
Pineapple Upside Down Cake, 2.5 oz	230	9	36
Peach Melba, 3.5 oz	300	8	52
Pecan Sticky Roll, 6.5 oz	690	22	91
Pecan Twirls, 1.3 oz	170	7	26
Pies & Tarts ~ *See Page 134*			
Pound Cakes: Iced Lemon, 3.5 oz	360	17	50
Marble, 3.75 oz	350	13	53
Raspberry Rugulah, 1.2 oz	110	9	7
Scone, fruit, 2 oz	200	9	30
Sponge Cake: Plain, 2.5 oz	220	10	33
With Chocolate Frosting	290	12	45
With Cream & Strawberry Jam	390	12	69
Starbucks Cakes ~ *Page 244*			
Strawberry Creme Cake, 4.7 oz	400	27	33
Strudel Bites, 0.75 oz	60	2.5	9
Strudel, fruit, av., 4.5 oz	300	17	32
Swiss Rolls, 1 oz	135	6	19
Tiramisu, 4.5 oz	440	22	34
Turnovers, fruit, average, 3 oz	290	15	35

Cupcakes	**C**	**F**	**Cb**

Average all Varieties

	C	F	Cb
Regular:			
Cake only, 1.5 oz	140	5.5	20
Cake + Icing, 2.5 oz	260	13	34
Large, (Muffin Size):			
Cake only, 2.5 oz	235	9	34
Cake + Icing, 5 oz	520	27	67
Mini, (2-Bite):			
Cake only, 0.4 oz	40	1.5	5.5
Cake + Icing, 1 oz	110	5.5	13
Icing Only: Per 1 oz	115	7	13
Thick/Tall amount, 2.5 oz	290	17	32

Cakes ~ Brands	C	F	Cb
Albertson's Bakery:			
Ring Cakes: *Per ⅛ Cake*			
Angel Food, 2 oz	160	0	36
Butter; Chocolate, av., 3 oz	305	15	39
Cake Slices: *Per Slice Unless Indicated*			
Banana Nut Loaf	330	17	39
Butter Creme	110	6	20
Creme Cake (2), 3.2 oz	300	12	43
Cinnamon Streusel (2), 3.2 oz	350	18	43
Bimbo Bakery:			
Concha, Vanilla, 2 oz	260	11	35
Pound Cakes: *Per Slice*			
Panquecitos, 1.75 oz	170	4.5	29
Pecan, 2.25 oz	260	11	36
Raisin, 2.25 oz	240	9	38
Bon Appetit Bakery:			
Banana Bread, 4 oz	440	25	49
Cream Cheese Cake,			
4 oz slice	430	24	49
Danish: Apple (1), 5 oz	210	11	25
Bear Claw (1), 5 oz	240	13	27
Cheese & Berries (1), 5 oz	250	14	26
Vienna Cream (1), 5 oz	240	14	27
Slices: Cheesecake, 4 oz	430	24	49
Lemon Cake, 4 oz	430	24	49
Marble Cake, 4 oz	430	24	54
Walnut Brownie, 3.5 oz	380	18	54
Cheesecake Factory ~ *See Fast-Foods Section*			
Entenmann's: *Per Slice*			
Crumb Cakes: All Butter French, 1.75 oz	210	10	29
Chocolate, 1/8th cake	270	12	39
Danish: Pecan Danish Twist, ⅛ cake	260	16	27
Cheese-Filled Crumb Coffee, 2 oz	200	10	25
Raspberry Danish Twist, 2 oz	220	11	29
Dessert Cakes:			
Banana, 2.25 oz	270	14	36
Carrot, Iced, 2.4 oz	260	12	37
Chocolate Fudge, 2.25 oz	240	10	37
Red Velvet, Iced, ⅛ oz	270	14	36
Loaf Cakes: Chocolate, ⅛ loaf	190	8	29
Cinnamon Crunch, ⅛ loaf	270	14	33
Glenny's:			
100 Calorie:			
Blondie, Choc. Chip, 1.45 oz	100	4	15
Brownies: Chocolate Chip, 1.45 oz	100	4	12
Peanut Butter, 1.45 oz	100	4	15
Muffins/Sweet Rolls ~ *See Page 67*			

Great American Cookies:	C	F	Cb
Cookie Cakes: *Per Slice*			
By the Slice, 4.5 oz	580	27	83
Heart Shaped, 3.5 oz	440	21	64
M&M, 4 oz	500	24	73
Great Value *(Walmart)*:			
Devil's Food Cake (1), 1.4 oz	160	7	23
Swiss Rolls (2), 2.2 oz	250	10	38
Hostess:			
Twinkies, (1)	135	4.5	23
Cup Cakes:			
100 Calorie, Lemon Golden (1)	100	2.5	21
Chocolate, 8-pack, 1 cupcake, 1.5 oz	160	6	26
Ding Dongs, 2.75 oz	350	18	46
Donettes ~ *See Page 66*			
Little Debbie:			
100 Calories: Choc. Cake (1), 1 oz	100	3	17
Yellow Cake with Icing (1), 1 oz	100	3	18
Brownie: Choc Chip (1), 2.2 oz	270	11	41
Fudge (1), 2.2 oz	280	12	40
Chocolate Cup Cake (1)	210	8	33
Cocoa Creme (1), 1.5 oz	170	8	24
Coffee Cake (1)	190	5	35
Devil Creme (1), 1.65 oz	200	9	29
Devil Squares (2), 2.2 oz	260	11	38
Fancy Cake (2)	300	13	44
Frosted Fudge Cake, 1.5 oz	190	9	27
Star Crunch (1)	150	6	22
S'mores (1)	190	7	30
Strawberry Shortcake Roll, 2 oz	240	9	40
Swiss Cake Roll (2), 2.2 oz	270	12	38
Zebra Cake (2), 2.5 oz	320	14	48
Nemo's:			
Brookie (1), 1.5 oz	160	7	26
Cake Squares: Banana, 3 oz	300	12	45
Carrot, 3.6 oz	390	21	47
Chocolate, 3 oz	300	12	47
Crumble Cake: Blueberry (1), 4 oz	390	17	54
Cinnamon Streusel (1), 4 oz	420	18	59
Lemon Rasp. (1), 4 oz	400	19	55
Oreo:			
Brownie,			
Creme Filled, 1.5 oz	190	9	25
Soft Cakesters:			
Chocolate (2), 2 oz	250	12	36
Double Stuf (2), 2.6 oz package	350	18	48
Golden (2), 1.75 oz	220	10	32

Cakes ~ Brands (Cont)

	C	F	Cb
Pepperidge Farm:			
3-Layer Cakes: *Per ⅛ Cake*			
Devil's Food 	220	9	34
Key Lime	230	11	31
Orange Cream	210	9	32
Average other varieties	240	11	33
Cookie Cakes: Choc. Chunk, 1/8 cake	250	12	33
Milano, 1/8 cake	250	15	28
Turnovers (Frozen):			
Apple; Cherry (1) 	260	13	31
Peach; Raspberry (1)	270	13	34
Pop Tarts *(Kellogg's):*			
Fruit/Frosted/Unfrosted, av.	200	5	36
Gone Nutty; Oatmeal Delights,			
average all varieties, 1.76 oz	200	5	35
Mini Crisps, all flavors, 1 pouch, 0.5 oz	60	1.5	11
Safeway Select,			
Molten Chocolate Lava Cake, 4.5 oz	440	26	50
Sara Lee:			
Carrot Cake, ⅙ cake 	340	18	41
Cheesecakes:			
Classic: French, 4.7 oz slice	410	26	38
Strawberry, 4.3 oz slice	320	18	37
New York Style, 5 oz slice	480	29	48
Limited Edition,			
NY Style, Chocolate, 5 oz slice	500	29	55
Original Cream:			
Cherry, 4.75 oz slice 	320	11	50
Classic, 4.25 oz slice	340	18	38
Strawberry, 4.7 oz slice	330	12	51
Coffee Cake, Butter Streusel, ⅙ cake	190	9	24
Pound Cakes:			
All Butter, 1.9 oz slice 	260	9	42
Lemon, 2.7 oz slice	270	9	42
Individual Slices:			
All Butter, 1 oz	100	3	15
Double Choc., 1.8 oz 	180	7	28
Lemon, 1 oz	100	3.5	15
Original, 1.6 oz	160	5	27
Smart Ones *(Weight Watchers):*			
Smart Delights: *4 Pack*			
Brownie à la Mode, 2.2 oz	120	2	36
Chocolate Fudge Brownie, 2 oz	140	3.5	24
Double Fudge Cake, 1.95 oz	140	3	26
Key Lime Pie, 3 oz 	150	3	28
Raspberry Cheesecake	130	3.5	22
Strawberry Shortcake, 2.4 oz	120	4	19
Sundaes, average all varieties	140	3	24
Special K, Pastry Crisps (2),			
all varieties, 1 oz	100	2	20

	C	F	Cb
Tastykake: *Per 3 Cakes*			
Chocolate Creme Cups (2), 1.9 oz	210	8	32
Kandy Kake, Peanut Butter, 1.7 oz	230	12	26
Krimpets, Butterscotch, Iced Van., 2 oz	220	6	39
Toaster Strudel *(Pillsbury):* Per 2 oz			
Boston Cream Pie 	180	7	25
Cream Cheese,			
average all varieties	185	9	24
Fruit flavors, all varieties 	170	7	25
Trader Joe's:			
Bakery Fresh:			
Apricot Almond Tart,			
4 oz slice	450	24	56
Cheesecake Brownie Bites (1)	110	7	9
Chocolate Ganache Cake, 3 oz slice	390	22	44
Flourless Chocolate Cake,			
1 slice, 2 oz	260	17	23
Lemon Cake, 3.25 oz slice	350	19	43
Mini Bundt, Triple Choc., ½ cake	340	21	41
Mini Carrot Cake, 5 oz 	450	19	68
Whoopie Pie (1), 2.5 oz	350	14	54
Bread Cake:			
Banana Bonanza, 2.6 oz slice	250	9	39
Pumpkin Nut, 2.6 oz slice	270	10	43
Walnut Streusel Coffee, 2 oz slice	180	8	25
Zucchini Carrot, 2 oz slice	200	7	32
Loaf Cake:			
Cranberry Pumpkin, 2 oz slice	140	2	30
Pumpkin Nut, 2.6 oz slice	270	10	43
Frozen:			
Apple Raspberry Turnover, 3.2 oz	280	14	34
Chocolate Dilemma Cheesecake:			
Plain, 3.5 oz	320	19	30
Choc. Chip; Triple Choc, av., 3.5 oz	345	20	35
Tuxedo, 3.5 oz	320	17	34
Choc Lava Cake (1), 4 oz	360	23	40
Karat Cake, 3 oz slice	320	19	37
N.Y. Style Cheesecake, 4.5 oz slicce	400	28	32
Tiramisu Torte, 3.2 oz slice	230	12	24
Tarts: 			
Pear, 3.5 oz slice	250	9	39
Raspberry, 5 oz slice	290	10	51
Wild Blueberry, 3.5 oz slice	260	6	52

Cakes ~ Mixes

Prepared as Directed	C	F	Cb
Arrowhead Mills:			
Brownie Mix:			
Regular, 1/20 package, 1 oz	**150**	7	21
Gluten Free, 1/20 package, 1 oz	**160**	8	21
Cake Mix:			
Chocolate, organic, 1/12 pkg., 1.5 oz	**260**	11	39
Vanilla, 1/12 package, 1.75 oz	**260**	10	41
Betty Crocker:			
Bars: Caramelita, 1/16 pkg	**190**	8	28
Reese's, 1/15 package	**180**	13	20
Sunkist Lemon, 1/16 pkg	**140**	4	24
Brownie Mix: *Per 1/20 Package Unless Indicated*			
Dark Chocolate Fudge	**160**	7	24
Fudge	**170**	8	23
Low-Fat Fudge, 1/18 pkg	**140**	3	28
Premium:			
Choc. Chunk, 1/16 pkg	**170**	7	26
Original Supreme, 1/16 package	**190**	8	27
P'nut Butter; Walnut, av., 1/16 pkg	**170**	7	24
Triple Chunk, 1/16 package	**180**	7	28
Ultimate Fudge, 1/16 package	**170**	6.5	26
Cake Mixes: *Per 1/10 Package*			
SuperMoist:			
Butter Recipe Yellow	**240**	9	36
Carrot	**310**	18	35
Cherry Chip	**280**	14	36
Devil's Food	**280**	14	35
French Vanilla	**280**	14	35
Milk Chocolate	**250**	10	35
Average other Chocolate varieties	**280**	14	35

If using No-Cholesterol Recipe, deduct 40 cals and 4g fat.

	C	F	Cb
Cupcakes: *Per 0.8 oz Mix & 0.42 oz Filling*			
FUN da-middles:			
Chocolate Cake, Vanilla Filling	**200**	9	27
Yellow Cake, Chocolate Filling	**190**	9	25
Duncan Hines:			
Brownie Mix: *Per 1/20 Pkg Unless Indicated*			
Decadent, Caramel Turtle, 1/16 pkg	**150**	7	23
Premium: Chewy Fudge	**180**	8	24
Snack Size, 1/12 pkg	**140**	7	20
Milk Chocolate	**160**	8	21
Cake Mix: *Per 1/12 Pkg*			
Classic, Dark Choc. Fudge, 1.4 oz	**220**	11	28

Prepared as Directed	C	F	Cb
Duncan Hines (Cont):			
Decadent: *Per 1/12 Package*			
Apple Caramel	**280**	12	39
Classic Carrot	**265**	11	39
Signature:			
Banana Supreme	**270**	12	36
Coconut Supreme	**250**	11	34
French Vanilla	**270**	12	34
Jell-O:			
No Bake Cheesecake:			
Cherry, 1/9 pkg, 2.4 oz	**290**	11	48
Real Cheesecake, 1/8 pkg, 2.1 oz	**360**	21	42
Krusteaz: Cinnamon Crumb Cake, 2"	**210**	5	39
Lemon; Key Lime Bar, 2½x2" bar	**160**	4.5	29
Pillsbury:			
Brownies, Premium Mix: *Dry Mix Only*			
Caramel Swirl, 1/12 packet, 1.2 oz	**130**	3	26
Cheesecake Swirl, 1/18 pkt, 0.85 oz	**100**	2.5	19
Chocolate Extreme, 1/16 packet, 1 oz	**110**	3	22
Double Chocolate, 1/16 pkg, 1 oz	**110**	2	23
Cakes, Moist Supreme: *Per 1/10 Pkg, Dry Mix Only*			
Classic White/Yellow, 1.5 oz	**160**	4	33
Devils Food, Regular, 1.5 oz	**160**	3	34
Supreme Collection: *Per 1/12 Pkg, Dry Mix Only*			
Apple Spice, 1.8 oz	**160**	3.5	33
Fudge Truffle, 1.8 oz	**200**	4.5	40
Red Velvet, 1.8 oz	**200**	5	41

Cake Frostings

Betty Crocker:	C	F	Cb
Rich & Creamy, av., 2 T., 1.15 oz	**140**	6	23
Whipped, av. all var.,2 T., 0.85 oz	**100**	4.5	15
Cool Whip, all varieties, 0.5 oz	**60**	3.5	8
Duncan Hines:			
Creamy Homestyle, av. all var., 2T.	**140**	6	23
Whipped, av. all varieties, 3 Tbsp	**155**	8	23
Pillsbury: *Per 2 Tbsp*			
Creamy Supreme:			
Choc Fudge; Milk Choc., 1.15 oz	**130**	6	20
Classic White, 1.2 oz	**140**	5	22
Vanilla; Vanilla Funfetti, 1.2 oz	**140**	5	22
Sugar Free, Chocolate Fudge	**100**	6	16
Whipped Supreme, av. all varieties	**100**	5	14

Quick Guide | C | F | Cb

Donuts

Average All Brands

	C	F	Cb
Cake: Plain, 1.75 oz	205	12	23
Chocolate Iced, 2 oz	255	14	29
Sugared, 0.75 oz	205	10	29
Non-Cake, Glazed, 2 oz	225	11	29

Croissant-Donuts

(Includes Cronuts/Frissants)

Average all Brands

	C	F	Cb
Cream-filled, 3.5 oz	430	26	45
Custard-filled, 3.5 oz	360	19	45

Extra Listings ~ *See CalorieKing.com*

(Cronut is a trademark of Dominique Ansel Bakery, New York)

Donuts ~ Brands | C | F | Cb

Albertson's:

Donut Holes:

	C	F	Cb
Glazed Old Fashioned (4)	240	12	31
Powdered Sugar (4)	210	12	24
Gem Donuts: Plain Cake (3)	190	12	20
Cinnamon Sugar (3)	240	15	23
Glazed (1)	140	6	21

Bon Appetit:

Mini Donuts:

	C	F	Cb
Chocolate (4)	270	16	29
Crumb (4)	240	12	32
Powdered (4)	250	12	34

Dunkin' Donuts:

	C	F	Cb
Apple Crumb	490	18	80
Apple N' Spice	270	14	32
Barvarian Kreme	270	15	31
Blueberry Cake	340	17	44
Blueberry Crumb	500	18	84
Boston Kreme	310	16	39
Chocolate Frosted Cake	370	23	45
Chocolate Glazed Cake	370	24	35
Cocoa Boston Kreme	300	16	37
Glazed Cake	360	22	44
Jelly Filled	270	14	32
Powdered Cake	340	22	38
Vanilla Kreme Filled	380	23	42

Extra Listings ~ *See Fast Food Section*

Donuts ~ Brands (Cont) | C | F | Cb

Entenmann's:

8 Pack: *Per Donut*

	C	F	Cb
Chocolate Lovers, 2 oz	300	20	31
Crumb, 2 oz	250	12	36
Frosted Devil's, 2.35 oz	310	18	36
Glazed, 2.25 oz	210	10	32
Rich Frosted, 2 oz	300	20	30

Pop'ems:

	C	F	Cb
Frosted (4), 2 oz	320	23	28
Powdered (4), 2 oz	250	12	32

Great Value (Walmart):

	C	F	Cb
Minis: Chocolate Frosted (4)	280	16	32
Powdered (4)	210	10	30

Hostess:

	C	F	Cb
Mini Donettes: Crumb, 6-pack, 4 oz	430	18	63
Frosted, 6-pack, 3 oz	360	22	38
Powdered, 6-pack, 3 oz	340	17	43

Krispy Kreme:

	C	F	Cb
Apple Fritter, 3 oz	210	14	18
Baseball Donut, 2.4 oz	290	17	33
Chocolate: Iced Cake, 2.5 oz	280	15	34
Iced Custard Filled, 3.15 oz	310	17	36
Iced Glazed Cruller, 2.45 oz	260	12	38
Iced Glazed, 2.25	240	11	33
Iced Kreme Filled, 3.15 oz	360	21	40
Iced Glazed w/ Sprinkles, 2.3 oz	250	12	35
Cinnamon Twist, 2.1 oz	240	15	23
Glazed Cruller, 2 oz	220	12	27

Glazed Doughnut Holes:

	C	F	Cb
Original (4)	200	11	26
Blueberry (4)	190	8	26
Chocolate Cake (4)	190	9	25
Glazed Kreme Filled, 3 oz	340	20	38
Maple Iced Glazed, 2.25 oz	230	11	32
New York Cheesecake, 3.4 oz	350	21	36
Original Glazed, 1.72 oz	190	11	21
Powdered Cake, 1.9 oz	220	11	27
Traditional Cake, 2 oz	190	12	19

Little Debbie,

	C	F	Cb
Donut Sticks (1), 1.65 oz	230	14	25

Tastykake:

	C	F	Cb
Cinnamon, 1.8 oz	210	11	26
Mini: Coated, 3 oz	380	22	42
Powdered Sugar (6), 2.5 oz	280	13	37

Quick Guide

Muffins: Ready-To-Eat

Average All Brands

	C	F	Cb
Small, 1 oz	90	3.5	14
Medium, 2 oz	185	6.5	28
Large, 3 oz	275	10	42
Extra Large, 4 oz	365	13	57
Giant, 6 oz	550	20	84
Super Size, 8 oz	730	27	112

Muffins Ready-To-Eat ~ Brands

	C	F	Cb
Albertsons:			
Minis: Banana Nut (2)	200	12	20
Blueberry (2)	180	10	21
Honey Raisin Bran (2)	170	7	24
Entenmann's: *Per Muffin*			
Single Serve: Powdered Pop'ems (4)	250	12	33
Softee, Frosted Donuts (1)	250	17	24
Great Value (Walmart),			
Double Blueberry (1), 4 oz	430	16	65
Little Debbie: Banana Nut (1), 1.9 oz	210	9	30
Blueberry (1), 1.9 oz	190	8	27
Chocolate Chip (1), 1.9 oz	210	9	28
My Favorite Muffin: *Per 6 oz Muffin*			
Banana Nut	585	33	63
Blueberry	505	24	66
Boston Cream Pie	530	21	78
Chocolate Chip	635	33	81
Lemon Poppyseed	605	30	75
Otis Spunkmeyer:			
Banana Nut, 3.25 oz	360	18	48
Chocolate Chip, 2 oz	230	12	29
Wild Blueberry, 2 oz	200	8	28
Starbucks ~ See Fast-Foods Section			
Trader Joe's: *Per Muffin*			
Apple Cranberry, 4.8 oz	220	5	38
Banana Chocolate Chip, 4 oz	400	18	57
Carrot, 4 oz	320	11	52
Triple Berry, 4 oz	310	11	49
Vitalicious:			
VitaMuffins: All var., av., 2 oz	100	1	24
Large, all varieties, av., 4 oz	200	2	50
Sugar-Free, Banana Nut, 2 oz	90	2.5	21
VitaTops: Average all varieties, 2 oz	100	1.5	25
Sugar free, av. all varieties, 2 oz	90	2.5	22
Weight Watchers,			
Blueb.; Double Choc, av., 2.5 oz	185	2.5	42

Muffin Mixes

Per Muffin, Prepared

	C	F	Cb
Betty Crocker: Banana Nut	170	8	22
Cinnamon Streusel	180	8	26
Wild Blueberry	160	6.5	24
Pouch Mix:			
Banana Nut	120	3	22
Blueberry; Triple Berry	120	2.5	23
Chocolate Chip	130	3.5	22
Fiber One:			
Apple Cinnamon; Blueberry, average	160	6	29
Banana Nut	160	6.5	27
Krusteaz: Banana Nut	250	13	29
Choc Chunk	260	13	33
Lemon Poppyseed	170	4	31
Oat Bran	180	4.5	32
Trader Joe's, Triple Berry	150	2	28

Sweet Rolls & Buns

Note: It is best to weigh for accuracy as actual weight can be 10-50% higher than label weight

Per Sweet Roll or Bun Unless Indicated

	C	F	Cb
Bimbo, Bimbolete, 2.2 oz	250	10	36
Bon Appetit,			
Cinnamon Roll, 2.5 oz	230	8	34
Cinnabon: Classic	880	36	127
Caramel Pecanbon	1080	50	147
Cloverhill Bakery,			
Jumbo Honey Bun, 4.75 oz	600	35	64
Entenmann's:			
Cinnamon Swirl Bun, 3 oz	320	14	44
Little Debbie: Honey Buns, 1.75 oz	230	13	26
Pecan Spinwheels, 1 oz	100	3.5	17
McDonald's:			
Cinnamon Melts, 4 oz	460	19	66
Pillsbury:			
Sweet Rolls, Refrigerated: *Per Roll Unless Indicated*			
Cinnamon, w/ Icing	140	5	23
Reduced Fat	130	3.5	24
Mini-Bites with Icing (3)	160	4.5	26
Orange Flavored, with Icing, 1.7 oz	160	6	26
Twists, Flaky Cinnamon, with Icing	160	7	23
Grands: *Per Roll*			
Cinnabon Cinnamon Roll,			
with Cream Cheese	300	8	54
Caramel Rolls, with Icing, 3.5 oz	310	9	53
Flaky Supreme Cinnabon,			
Cinnamon Roll, with Icing, 3.5 oz	360	17	48
7-Eleven: Iced Honey Bun, 6 oz	820	58	68
Glazed Honey Bun, 5 oz	620	35	70
Sara Lee, Cinnamon Roll, 2.4 oz	260	12	33

Quick Guide

Chocolate	C	F	Cb
Average All Brands			
Milk Chocolate, regular:			
Plain/Nuts/Fruit, average, 1 oz	150	9	17
1.5oz Bar	230	13	25
2 oz Bar	305	17	34
4 oz Block	610	34	68
8 oz Block	1220	68	136
1 Pound, 16 oz	2440	136	272
Dark/White Chocolate: 1 oz	155	9	17
Hershey's, Sugar Free, 5 pieces	110	13	24
Milk Chocolate-Coated:			
Almonds, 5-6, 1 oz	150	10	15
Clusters, Nut, 3 pieces, 1.2 oz	210	14	20
Coffee Beans, 1.4 oz	220	13	22
Cherry Cordial Centers, 2 pcs, 1 oz	145	6	21
Macadamias, 10 pieces, 1.4 oz	220	16	21
Mints, 1 medium, ½ oz	55	1	11
Nougat & Caramel, 1 oz	150	9	15
Peanuts, 12 medium, 1 oz	145	10	14
Raisins, 28 medium, 1 oz	110	4	19
Baking Chocolate:			
Baker's: Bittersweet, 1 oz	140	12	14
Semi-sweet, 1 oz	140	9	16
Nestle, Chips: Dark, 1 Tbsp, ½ oz	70	5	3
Semi-Sweet, 1 Tbsp, ½ oz	70	4	9
Unsweetened, 1 oz	140	14	8
Carob, Plain, 1 oz	155	9	16

Candy ~ Brands & Generic

Per Piece/Serving	C	F	Cb
3 Musketeers: Orig., 1 bar, 2.15 oz	260	8	46
2 To Go, 1.65 oz Bar	200	6	35
Fun Size (3), 1.6 oz	190	6	34
Minis, 7 pieces, 1.4 oz	170	5	32
100 Grand: 1.5 oz bar	190	8	30
Super Size, 2.8 oz	360	14	58
Snack Size (1), ¾ oz	95	4	15
Abba Zabba, 2 oz bar	250	5	48
After Dinner Mints, 1 small	25	1.5	4
After Eight Mint, each	35	1.5	4
Airhead, 1 bar, ½ oz	60	1	14
Almond Joy: 2 bars, 1.6 oz	220	13	26
King Size, 4 bars, 3.25 oz	460	26	54
Snack Size, 0.6 oz bar	80	4.5	10
Pieces (46), 1.4 oz	200	10	27

Per Piece/Serving	C	F	Cb
Almond Roca, 3 pieces, 1.25 oz	200	15	17
Almond: Sugar-coated (15), 1.4 oz	190	7	27
Jordan, 15 pieces, 1.4 oz	180	8	28
Almond Clusters:			
True North, 1 oz	170	12	9
Trader Joe's, 1.2 oz	190	14	13
Altoids, 3 pieces	10	0	2
Andes, Thins (8), av. all var., 1.4 oz	205	13	22
Anthon Berg:			
Creamy Mint (4), 1.4 oz	180	6	31
Marzipan with Plum, in Madeira	120	6	14
Atomic Fireball, 1 piece, 0.3 oz	35	0	9
Baby Ruth: King Size, 3.5 oz bar	500	24	66
2 oz bar	280	14	39
Fun size, 2 bars	170	8	24
Minis, 4 bars	210	11	28
Baci (Perugina),			
1 piece, ½ oz	75	6	7
Baskin-Robbins: Sugar Candy, 3 pcs	60	1	12
Sugar Free, 4 pieces, average, 0.6 oz	40	1	16
(Carbs include 16g sugar alcohol)			
Big Hunk, 2 oz Bar	230	3	47
Bit-O-Honey: 1.7 oz Bar	180	3.5	39
Chews, 6 pieces, 1.4 oz	150	3	32
Bliss (Hershey's):			
Milk/Dark Choc./Caramel, 6 pieces	120	14	25
Meltaway Centers:			
Milk Chocolate, 6 pieces	220	15	24
Raspberry, 6 pieces	220	14	24
Blow Pops, each, 0.6 oz	60	0	14
Bon Bons, 3 pieces	65	0	15
Boston Baked Beans, (11), 0.5 oz	70	2	11
Brach's:			
Almond Supremes (10)	200	14	20
Bridge Mix (15), 1.4 oz	190	10	26
Double Dippers (15), 1.4 oz	210	14	22
Gummi Bears (14), 1.4 oz	130	0	30
Lemon Drops, Sugar Free, 4 pieces	35	0	17
(Carbs include 17g Sugar Alcohol)			
Mandarin/Orange Slices (3), 1.6 oz	150	0	37
Maple Nut Goodies (8), 1.5 oz	190	9	27
Milk Maid Caramels (4), 1.25 oz	150	4	25
Peanut Cluster (3), 1.4 oz	210	15	20
Breath Savers, all varieties, each	5	0	2
Bubble Gum ~ See Page 75			
Bulls Eyes, 3 pieces, 1.2 oz	130	3	23
Buncha Crunch, ⅓ cup, 1.4 oz	180	9	25
Movie Box, 3.2 oz	450	20	65
Burnt Peanuts, (31), 1.4 oz	170	6	29

Candy ~ Brands & Generic (Cont)

Per Piece/Serving	C	F	Cb
Butterfinger: 2 oz bar	270	11	43
King Size (3 bars), 3.5 oz	480	18	75
Fun Size, (1), 0.75	100	4	15
Giant, (Pieces in Chocolate),			
¼ bar, 1 oz	150	8	21
Miniatures:			
1 piece, 0.35 oz	45	2	8
4 pieces, 1.4 oz	180	8	32
Snack Pack, 4 pcs, 1.4 oz	180	7	29
Crisp Bar: Original, 2 oz bar	270	11	43
King Size 3 pieces, 2 oz	310	17	38
Minis, 2 bars, 1.4 oz	210	11	25
Snackerz:			
Single, 1 pouch, 1.25 oz	170	8	23
Fun Size, 2 pcs, 1.2 oz	150	7	21
King Size, 10 pcs, 1.4 oz	190	8	25
Butter Mints, 7 pieces, 0.45 oz	50	0	12
Butterscotch: 3 pieces	60	0	15
Discs (Walgreens), 3 pieces, 0.6 oz	70	0	17
Cadbury: Caramello Bar, 1.6 oz	220	10	29
Caramel Egg, 1.2 oz	170	8	22
Dairy Milk Bar, 7 pieces, 1.4 oz	200	11	23
Mini Eggs (Candy), 12 pcs, 1.4 oz	190	8	28
Candy Apple, medium, 6.5 oz	280	0	71
Candy Cane, medium, 5", 0.5 oz	40	0	14
Candy Corn, 20 pieces, 1.4 oz	150	0	38
Candy Jar Mix (Jewel), 3 pcs, 0.6 oz	60	0	14
Candy Necklace (Smarties), (1), 0.75 oz	90	0.5	20
Caramels: Each, 0.35 oz	40	1	7
Chocolate, each, 0.25 oz	25	0.3	6
Creams (3), 1.25 oz	130	3	23
Caramel Popcorn, ⅔ cup	150	6	23
Cella's,			
Milk Choc. Cherries, 3 pieces, 1.5 oz	160	6	27
Certs, Breath Mints, 1 piece	5	0	2
Charleston Chew:			
Chocolate Bar (1), 1.4 oz	160	4.5	30
Mini Bars, 13 pieces	190	6	34
Charms: Blow Pop	60	0	17
Flat Pop, 0.5 oz	50	0	14
Chew-ets, Peanut Chews,			
Original (4), 1.6 oz	230	12	29
Chewz, 1 roll, 1 oz	120	1	28
Chick O Stick, 2 oz	240	9	42

Per Piece/Serving	C	F	Cb
Chunky Bar (Nestlé),			
King Size, 2.5 oz	340	19	44
Chupa Chups, 1 Pop	50	0	12
Cinn. Buttons (Walgreens), 3 pieces	60	0	16
Cinnamon Disks (Walmart), 3 pieces	70	0	18
Circus Peanuts (Spangler),			
6 pieces, 1.3 oz	165	0	41
CocoaVia, Orig., 0.8 oz	100	6	12
Coconut Stacks, (8)	320	16	46
Coffee Go, Candy, (4)	60	1	12
Conversation Hearts (Necco):			
Small (40), 1.4 oz	160	0	39
1 large	10	0	3
Cookie Dough Bites, 1.4 oz	200	10	27
Cote d'Or: Dark 86% Coca, 4 pcs	270	22	14
Dark, 70%, Orange, 3.5 oz	575	46	34
Dark, Raspberry, 3.5 oz	580	46	34
Milk, Intense, 3.5 oz	575	40	45
Cotton Candy, 1 oz	110	0	28
Cough Drops ~ See Page 75			
Cracker Jack, ½ cup, 1 oz	120	2	23
Creme Savers: 3 pieces, 0.5 oz	60	1	11
Sugar-Free, 3 pieces	30	1	8
Crisped Rice, Choc Chip, 1 bar, 1 oz	115	4	20
Crows, 11 pieces, 1.4 oz	130	0	33
Crunch Bar ~ See Nestle			
Dots, 11 dots, 1.4 oz	130	0	33
Double Dip Stick, 1 stick	15	0.5	4
Dove:			
Milk Choc: Singles Bar, 1.4 oz	220	13	24
Large Tablet Bar, 9 pcs, 1.5 oz	230	13	25
Choc. Covered Almonds, 13 pcs, 1.4 oz	220	15	19
Promises: Milk Choc., 1 pc, 0.3 oz	45	2.5	5
With Caramel, 1 piece, 0.3 oz	40	2	5
With Peanut Butter, 1 pc, 0.3 oz	45	3	4
Swirls, all varieties, 9 pieces 1.5 oz	230	14	25
Dark Choc: Singles Bar, 1.3 oz	220	13	24
Large Tablet Bar, 9 pcs, 1.5 oz	220	14	25
Choc. Covered. Almds, 13 pcs, 1.4 oz	210	15	19
Promises, Almond, 1 piece, 0.3 oz	40	3	4
Swirls, Raspberry, 9 pieces, 1.4 oz	220	14	24
Sugar Free, all varieties, 5 pcs, 1.4 oz	195	15	21
Dum Dum Pops (Spangler), 1 pop	25	0	6
Drops (Hershey's):			
Milk Chocolate, 15 pieces, 1.4 oz	200	12	25
Cookies 'n' Creme, 14 pieces, 1.5 oz	210	11	26

Candy ~ Brands & Generic (Cont)

Per Piece/Serving	C	F	Cb
English Toffee, 1 piece, 0.4 oz	70	4	6
5th Avenue: 2 oz bar	260	12	38
King Size, 3.5 oz	440	20	64
Fannie May:			
Mint Meltaway (1)	230	15	24
Pixie (1), 1.5 oz	210	12	24
Trinidad (1), 1.5 oz	200	12	23
Fast Break (Reese's): 2 oz bar	260	12	35
3.5 oz bar	460	22	62
Ferrero Rocher: 1 piece	75	5	5
3 pieces, 1.3 oz	220	16	16
Rondnoir, 3 pieces, 1 oz	180	13	14
Fifty 50 Snack Bars:			
Milk Chocolate: 5 pieces, 1 oz	135	11	14
Almond, 5 pieces, 1 oz	135	11	13
Crunch Bar, 7 pcs, 1 oz	140	14	16
Dark Chocolate, 5 pieces, 1 oz	120	11	15
(Carbs include 9-12g Sugar Alcohol)			
Fluffy Stuff (Charms),			
Cotton Candy, 1.4 oz	150	0	40
Fondant: Choc-coated, 1.2 oz	125	3	27
Mint, 1 oz	105	0	25
Fran's:			
Gold Bar, Almond (1)	250	14	27
GoldBite, Almond (1)	120	7	13
Fruit Drops, (1), ¼ oz	20	0	4
Fruit Gems (Sunkist), (4), 1.4 oz	130	0	33
Fruit Leathers, average, 0.5 oz	50	0.5	12
Fruit Pastilles (Rowntree), 1 roll	185	0	45
Fruit Roll-Ups (Betty Crocker/Sunkist),			
1 roll, 0.5 oz	50	1	12
Fruit Runts (Walgreens),			
12 pieces	60	0	14
Fruit Flavored Shapes (Betty Crocker),			
all varieties, 0.8 oz	80	0	19
Fudge:			
Chocolate; Mint, 1 oz	130	8	14
Peanut Butter & Chocolate, 1 oz	130	8	13
Brevin's: Cashew, 1 oz	195	9	28
Triple Decker, 1 oz	165	7	25
Ghirardelli:			
3 oz Bars: Dark Chocolate, 4 squares	220	17	23
Filled, Peanut Butter, 4 squares	250	17	22
Intense Dark Bars, Ev'ng Dream, 3 pcs	190	15	20
Squares:			
Dark Chocolate (4), 1.5 oz	210	16	23
Milk & Caramel (3), 1.5 oz	220	12	27
Sea Salt Escape (4), 1.5 oz	210	15	24

Per Piece/Serving	C	F	Cb
Godiva:			
Bars: Milk/Dark, av., 1.5 oz	230	14	26
Extra Dark: 75%, 1.5 oz	230	17	18
85%, 1.4 oz	260	21	14
Chocoiste:			
Dark Chocolate Cherries (12)	190	7	30
Milk Chocolate Cashews (14)	230	15	19
Hearts: Dark Ganache (4)	200	12	23
Milk Praline (4)	220	13	23
Go Lightly:			
Assorted Toffee, 5 pieces, 1 oz	85	2	24
Fruit Chews, 5 pieces, 1 oz	95	2	26
(Carbs include 24-25g sugar alcohol)			
Hard Candy, Assorted (4), 0.5 oz	45	0	15
(Carbs include 15g sugar alcohol)			
Goobers Peanuts, 1 package, 1.4 oz	200	13	21
Good & Plenty (Hershey's), (33), 1.4 oz	140	0	35
GooGoo Clusters, 1 piece, 1.75 oz	240	12	30
Gum ~ See Page 75			
Gum Drops: 1 small, 0.1 oz	15	0	3
5 pieces, 0.5 oz	75	0	15
Gummi (Shur Fine):			
Bears (15), 1.4 oz	130	0	29
Chewy Sweet Tarts (4), 1.5 oz	160	0	36
Worms (9), 1.5 oz	140	0	31
Guylian:			
Bars: Dark Chocolate (3), 1 oz	150	12	11
Milk Choc. with Hazelnuts (3), 1 oz	170	11	15
No Sugar Added Bars:			
Milk Chocolate, 3 squares	150	11	16
54% Cocoa, Dark Choc., 3 squares	140	11	16
Seashells:			
Bar, 1.4 oz	210	13	21
Boxed, Originals (1), 0.35 oz	60	4	6
Truffles (1), 0.5 oz	70	5.5	5
Heath: Original (1), 1.4 oz	210	13	24
King Size, 2.8 oz	410	22	49
Snack Size, 3 pieces, 1.5 oz	230	14	27
Hershey's:			
Cookies 'n' Creme, 1.55 oz Bar	220	12	26
Milk Chocolate:			
Bars: 1.55 oz	210	13	26
With Almonds, 1 bar, 1.4 oz	210	14	21
King Size, 1 Bar, 2.5 oz	370	22	44
Kisses, 9 pieces, av., 1.4 oz	200	13	20
Nuggets: 4 pieces, 1.35 oz	200	13	20
W/ Toffee & Alm., 4 pcs, 1.3 oz	200	13	21
Sugar Free Choc., 5 pieces, 1.4 oz	160	13	24
Extra Dark Choc., 4 pieces, 1.4 oz	180	14	21
Simple Pleasures, 6 pieces, av.	180	8	29
Special Dark Choc., 1.45 oz bar	190	12	25

Candy ~ Brands & Generic (Cont)

Per Piece/Serving	C	F	Cb
Hershey's, (Cont):			
Pot of Gold Chocolate Asstd:			
Carmel, 4 pieces, 1.4 oz	190	10	26
Other varieties, av., 4 pieces, 1.4 oz	210	12	24
Candy-Coated Eggs:			
Milk Chocolate: (8), 1.2 oz	170	8	27
With Almonds (8), 1.2 oz	200	12	18
Honeycomb: Plain, 1 oz	115	0	27
Choc-coated, 2 pieces	180	7	31
Hot Tamales,			
20 pieces, 1.4 oz	150	0	36
Hugs ~ See Kisses			
Jawbreakers (Sathers), (15), 0.6 oz	60	0	16
Jells (Joyva), Raspb., 3 pieces, 1.55 oz	160	0	38
Jelly Beans, average all brands:			
Small Size (Jelly Belly): 1 bean	5	0	1
12 beans, 0.5 oz	50	0	13
Regular Size: 1 bean	10	0	2
10 beans, 1.4 oz	105	0	26
Large Size: 1 bean	15	0	4
10 beans, 1.5 oz	150	0	38
Sugar Free:			
Av. all brands, 25 beans, 1 oz	60	0	26
(Carbs include 26g sugar alcohol)			
Jelly Belly: 25 beans, 1 oz	105	0	26
3.5 oz package	360	0	90
Sugar Free,			
25 beans, 1 oz	60	0	26
(Carbs include sugar alcohol)			
Chocolate Dips:			
All flavors: 1 bean	4	0	1
10 beans	40	1	8
2.8 oz bag	300	8	62
Jelly Rings (Jewel), 5 pieces, 1.4 oz	110	0	26
Jolly Rancher:			
Bites: Soft, 15 pieces	150	1.5	32
Sours, 16 pieces	130	0	34
Crunch 'N Chew, 1.55 oz package	160	0.5	34
Filled Fruity Bites, 22 pieces	140	1	31
Gummies, 9 pieces	120	0	28
Hard Candy, 3 pieces	70	0	17
Jelly Beans/Sours, 1.4 oz	140	0	36
Lollipops (1), 0.55 oz	60	0	15
Jujubes, all varieties (52), 1.4 oz	110	0	28
Juju Bears, 5 pieces	130	0	34
Juju Mix (Sathers), 11 pieces, 1.5 oz	150	0	36
Jujyfruits, 16 pieces, 1.4 oz	120	0	34
Junior Caramels: 13 pieces, 1.5 oz	190	6	33
Mini, 2 boxes, 1.4 oz	140	4	23

Per Piece/Serving	C	F	Cb
Junior Mints: 1.8 oz	220	4	45
16 pieces, 1.4 oz	170	3	35
Justin's, Peanut Butter Cups,			
Milk Choc, 2 cups, 1.4 oz pkg	200	14	18
Kisses (Hershey's):			
Air Delights (11), 1.4 oz	200	12	24
Cookies 'n' Creme (9), 1.5 oz	220	12	26
Hugs (9), 1.4 oz	210	12	24
Milk Chocolate: (1), 0.16 oz	25	1.5	3
(9), 1.4oz	200	12	25
With Almonds (9), 1.4 oz	200	13	22
Caramel Filled (9), 1.5 oz	190	9	27
Special Dark (9), 1.4 oz	180	12	25
Kit Kat (Nestle):			
Milk Chocolate:			
4 piece bar, 1.5 oz	210	11	28
Extra Crispy, 1.6 oz bar	220	12	29
King Size, 8 pieces, 3 oz bar	420	22	56
Minis, 5 pieces	210	11	28
Snack Size, 6 pieces, 1.5 oz	210	11	27
White Chocolate, 4 pieces, 1.5 oz	220	12	26
Peanut Bar (Lance), 2.2 oz package	340	19	29
Lemon Drops: (4), 0.6 oz	60	0	16
Walgreens, Sugar Free (3), 0.6 oz	50	0	17
Lemonhead, (26), 1.4 oz	140	0	36
Licorice:			
All varieties, average, 1oz	100	0	25
Chews (Panda), (1)	10	0	2
Tid Bits (1)	10	0	2
Twists: Black/Red, av., 1 pc	35	0	8
Sugar Free, 1 piece	15	0	2.5
American Licorice Co.:			
Natural Vines: Black (9), 1.4 oz	140	1	33
Strawberry (9), 1.4 oz	150	1	34
Red Vines (4), 1.4 oz	140	0	34
Sip-n-Chew, 1 package 1 oz	100	1	23
Snaps (31), 1.4 oz	140	0.5	33
Sour Punch (6), 1.4 oz	150	0.5	34
Super Ropes (1), 2 oz	200	0	46
Lifesavers: Large size, 1 candy	15	0	3
Regular: All flavors, 1 candy	10	0	3
1 Roll (14 candies), 1.2 oz	140	0	35
Creme Savers 3 pieces, 0.5 oz	60	1	11
Sugar Free (4)	45	1.5	17
Pep-o-mint (3), 0.2 oz	20	0	5
Fruit Splosion (10), 1.4 oz	130	0	31
Sugar-Free Delites,			
Orchard Fruits; Summer Blend (1)	5	0	2
Butter Toffee; European Collection	10	1	3

Candy ~ Brands & Generic (Cont)

Per Piece/Serving

	C	F	Cb
Lik-m-aid (Nestle), Fun Dip, 1 package	50	0	13
Lindt: Lindor Truffles (1), average	75	6	5
Swiss Milk Chocolate Bars:			
70% Cocoa, 4 pieces	220	17	19
Classic, with Hazelnuts, 10 pieces	230	16	20
Raspberry filled, 7 pieces	200	10	25
Dark Choc. Truffles,			
with filling, 7 pieces	240	18	18
Lollipops: Mini, 0.25 oz	25	0	6
Small, 0.5 oz	50	0	12
Medium, 1 oz	100	0	25
Giant (4" diam), 7 oz	790	0	198
M & M's:			
Dark Chocolate: 1.5 oz pkg	210	10	29
Peanuts, 1.5 oz	220	12	25
Milk Chocolate: 28 piece, 1 oz	145	6.5	21
1.5 oz package	210	9	30
1.7 oz package	240	10	34
Almond Choc., 1.5 oz	220	12	25
Minis, 1 tube, 1 oz	150	7	21
Peanut: 28 pieces, 1 oz	155	8	17
1.75 oz pkg	250	13	30
Peanut Butter 1.63 oz package	240	14	26
Premiums: Chocolate Trio, 1.5 oz	230	14	25
Mint Thrills, 1.5 oz	240	14	25
Pretzels, ½ pkg, 1.4 oz	180	6	29
Snack Mix, av. var., ⅓ cup, 1.5 oz	200	9	25
Mamba Sours, Fruit Chews,			
6 pieces, 1 oz	100	1	22
Marshmallow Egg, 1 egg, 1 oz	120	3	22
Mary Jane (Necco), 5 pieces, 1.4 oz	160	3.5	32
Marshmallows: Firm/Soft, 1 oz	90	0	23
Regular size, 4 pieces, 1 oz	100	0	24
Mini-Marshmallow, ⅔ cup, 1 oz	95	0	24
Joyva, Choc-coated Twists, each	95	2	10
Fluff, 2 Tbsp, 0.6 oz	60	0	15
Kraft: Mini, 1 oz	90	0	23
Creme, 0.5 oz	45	0	11
Jet-Puffed, 5 pieces, 1 oz	100	0	24
Funmallows, ⅔ cup, 1 oz	100	0	24
Marzipan, 2 Tbsp, 1.4 oz	160	4	29
Mauna Loa, Mountains, 4 pcs	230	17	21
Mexican Hats, (7), 1.4 oz	120	0	30
Mentos: Regular	10	0	3
Sugar Free	5	0	2
Mike & Ike:			
Original: 2.1 oz package	220	0	55
23 pieces, 1.4 oz	140	0	36
Milk Duds, 1 box, 1.8 oz	230	8	38

Per Piece/Serving

	C	F	Cb
Milky Way (Mars):			
Bars: Single, 2 oz	240	9	37
Fun Size, 2 bars, 1.2 oz	160	6	24
To Go, 1.8 oz	230	9	36
Minis, 5 pieces, 1.5 oz	190	7	30
Midnight Bars: 1.75 oz	230	8	36
Minis, 5 pieces, 1.4 oz	190	7	30
Simply Caramel, 1.9 oz	250	11	37
Mints: Uncoated, 3 pieces	70	0	17
1 mint	7	0	1
1 large mint	15	0	3
Mon Cheri (Ferrero), 4 pieces, 2 oz	260	18	20
Mounds: 1.75 oz bar	230	13	29
King Size, 4 pieces, 3.5 oz	460	26	58
Snack Size, 1 piece, 0.6 oz	80	4.5	10
Mr Goodbar: 1.75 oz bar	250	17	26
King Size, 2.6 oz bar	380	26	38
Munch Bar, 1.4 oz	220	15	18
Necco, Candy Wafers (40), 2 oz	220	0	56
Nestle Crunch: Orig.,1.55 oz bar	220	11	30
Fun Size, 3 bars, 1.4 oz	180	9	26
Miniatures, 4 bars, 1.4 oz	200	10	27
Buncha Crunch, ⅓ cup, 1.2 oz	180	9	25
Crunch Crisp, 1.75 oz	240	13	32
Newman's Own:			
Milk Chocolate: Caramel Cups (3)	160	8	21
Peanut Butter Cups (3)	180	12	17
Dark Chocolate: Caramel Cups (3)	160	9	20
Peanut Butter Cups (3)	180	13	16
Nips, all varieties, 2 pieces, 0.5 oz	60	2	11
Nougat: 3 pieces, 1.5 oz	170	1	39
Chocolate Covered, 2 oz	125	4	22
Nuggets ~ See Hershey's			
Nutrageous Bar (Reese's), 1.8 oz	260	16	28
Oh Henry!: Fun Size, 0.9 oz	120	5	16
1.8 oz bar	230	11	33
Orange Slices:			
Jewel, 3 pieces, 1.5 oz	140	0	35
Walgreens, 4 pieces, 1.6 oz	160	0	39
Pastel Mints (Walgreens), 20 pieces	60	0	14
PayDay Bar: 1.8 oz bar	240	13	27
King Size, 3.5 oz bar	440	24	50
Snack Size, 0.7 oz	90	5	10
Avalanche, 1.8 oz bar	250	13	29
Peanut Bar (Planter's), 1.6 oz	240	14	21
Peanut Butter Cups ~ See Reese's; Newman's Own			
Peanut Brittle: 1 piece, 1.5 oz	190	5	32
Sugar Free (Russell Stover),			
4 pieces, 1.3 oz	140	10	24

Candy ~ Brands & Generic (Cont)

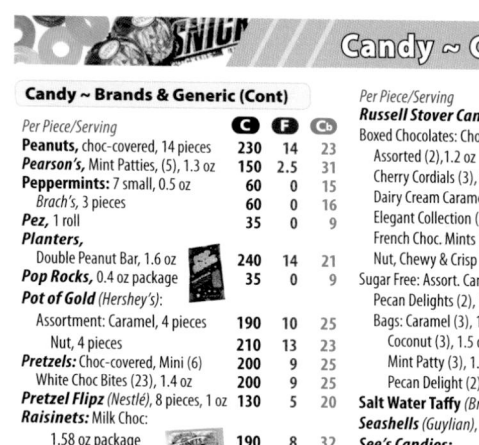

Per Piece/Serving	C	F	Cb
Peanuts, choc-covered, 14 pieces	230	14	23
Pearson's, Mint Patties, (5), 1.3 oz	150	2.5	31
Peppermints: 7 small, 0.5 oz	60	0	15
Brach's, 3 pieces	60	0	16
Pez, 1 roll	35	0	9
Planters,			
Double Peanut Bar, 1.6 oz	240	14	21
Pop Rocks, 0.4 oz package	35	0	9
Pot of Gold (Hershey's):			
Assortment: Caramel, 4 pieces	190	10	25
Nut, 4 pieces	210	13	23
Pretzels: Choc-covered, Mini (6)	200	9	23
White Choc Bites (23), 1.4 oz	200	9	24
Pretzel Flipz (Nestlé), 8 pieces, 1 oz	130	5	20
Raisinets: Milk Choc:			
1.58 oz package	190	8	32
Movie Pack, 3.5 oz	380	16	64
Dark Chocolate, ¼ cup, 1.6 oz	180	8	32
Reese's:			
Clusters, 3 pieces, 1.5 oz	220	12	24
Crispy Crunchy Bar: 1.7 oz	260	18	22
2 pieces, 1.2 oz	170	9	22
King Size, 3 oz	480	32	40
Fast Break, 2 oz bar	260	12	35
Peanut Butter Chips, 1 Tbsp, 0.5 oz	80	4	8
Peanut Butter Cups, Milk Chocolate:			
(2), 1.5 oz	210	13	24
Miniatures (5), 1.5 oz	220	13	26
Minis (11)	200	12	23
Big Cup, 1 cup, 1.4 oz	200	12	23
Sugar Free, Minis (5), 1.4 oz	180	13	27
Dark Chocolate (2), 1.5 oz	210	14	23
Pieces, Peanut Butter (51)	200	9	25
Sticks: 1.5 oz package	220	13	23
King Size, 3 oz package	440	26	46
Snack Size (1), 0.6 oz	90	5	9
Snacksters, 1 package, 0.75 oz	100	4	14
Whipps, 1.5 oz	230	9	37
Rice Krispies Treats (Kellogg's),			
1 bar, average all varieties, 0.8 oz	95	2.5	17
Riesen, Choc. Chew, 4 pieces, 1.25 oz	170	6	28
Rocky Road, Milk/Dark, 1.8 oz bar	240	11	34
Roca Thins, 3 pieces, av. all varieties	210	14	20
Rolo: Regular, all varieties, 1.7 oz roll	220	10	33
Mini Chews, Caramel in milk choc. (11)	190	9	26
Root Beer Barrels, (3), 0.6 oz	60	0	17

Per Piece/Serving	C	F	Cb
Russell Stover Candy:			
Boxed Chocolates: Chocolate Coated			
Assorted (2), 1.2 oz	150	7	22
Cherry Cordials (3), 0.35 oz	150	5	25
Dairy Cream Caramels (2), 1.2 oz	160	7	22
Elegant Collection (3), 1.6 oz	210	10	25
French Choc. Mints (4), 1.4 oz	220	13	22
Nut, Chewy & Crisp Centers (2)	160	8	21
Sugar Free: Assort. Candies (3), 1.6 oz	210	16	24
Pecan Delights (2), 1.2 oz	160	12	19
Bags: Caramel (3), 1.3 oz	180	8	25
Coconut (3), 1.6 oz	160	10	28
Mint Patty (3), 1.5 oz	180	12	24
Pecan Delight (2), 1.2 oz	160	12	19
Salt Water Taffy (Brach's), (5)	170	2.5	36
Seashells (Guylian), 4 shells, 1.6 oz	260	17	24
See's Candies:			
Almond Royal (5), 1.3 oz	190	13	18
Butterscotch Chews (5), 1.5 oz	210	12	27
Krispy's: Caffe Latte (5),1.3 oz	180	8	27
Mint (5), 1.3 oz	170	8	27
Little Pops:			
Butterscotch (4), 0.5 oz	60	2	12
Chocolate (4), 0.5 oz	60	3	10
Vanilla (4), 0.5 oz	50	2	9
Lollypops, average, 0.7 oz	90	3	17
Milk Molasses Chips, 6 pieces, 1.4 oz	180	8	27
Milk Peppermints, 2 pieces, 1.25 oz	150	4	28
Peanut Brittle Bar, 1 oz	150	10	15
Peanut Butter Patties, 2 pieces, 1.2 oz	170	10	16
Peppermint Twists, 0.5 oz	60	0	15
Toffee-ettes, 3 pieces, 1.6 oz	270	21	18
Sugar Free: Dark Bar, 1.5 oz	180	16	24
Dark Walnut Clusters (4), 1.5 oz	230	21	17
Peanut Brittle, 1.5 oz	170	14	17
Skinny Cow:			
Dreamy Clusters, all varieties, 1 pouch	120	6	20
Heavenly Crips, all varieties, 1 bar	110	6	14
Skittles: Original, 2 oz	230	2.5	52
Sour, 1.8 oz	200	2	44
Tropical; Wild Berry, 2.2 oz	250	2.5	56
Fun Size, 1 bag, 0.5 oz	60	1	14
Tear & Share, 4 oz bag	420	4.5	93
Skor, Toffee Bar (1), 1.4 oz	200	12	25
Smarties: Candy Rolls (1), 0.25 oz	25	0	6
Giant, 1 roll, 1 oz	100	0	25

Candy ~ Brands & Generic (Cont)

Per Piece/Serving **C F Cb**

Snickers:
Milk Chocolate:
	C	F	Cb
1.9 oz bar	250	12	33
Fun Size, 2 bars, 1.2 oz	160	8	21
To Go Bar, 1.6 oz	220	10	29
Miniatures: (4)	170	8	22
Sugar Free, 5 pcs	180	13	27
Almond Bar, 1.75 oz	230	11	32
P'nut Butter Squared, 2 bars, 1.8 oz	250	13	30
Dark Chocolate Bar, 1.85 oz	250	12	31
Sno Caps, ¼ cup, 1.4 oz	180	8	30
Soft 'N Chewy, Butter Toffee, 1 piece	30	0.5	5
Sorbee,			
Crystal Light Hard Candy, 4 pieces	25	0	13

(Carbs include Isomalt which has fewer calories than sugar)

	C	F	Cb
Sour Patch: Kids, average, 2 oz	210	0	52
Extreme, 1.8 oz	190	0	47
Spearmint Leaves:			
Jewel, 5 pieces, 1.4 oz	140	0	35
Walgreens, 4 pieces, 1.6 oz	160	0	39
Spree Candies: Original, 15 pieces	50	0	13
Chewy, 8 pieces	60	0	13
Starburst:			
Candy Canes, 0.5 oz	70	0	18
Fruit Chews: Original, 1 piece	20	0.5	4
8 pieces, 1.4 oz	160	3.5	33
Gummibursts, 9 pieces, 1.4 oz	130	0	31
Jellybeans, 1.4 oz	150	0	37
Tropical Fruit, 1.4 oz pack	160	3.5	34
Starlight Mints, 3 pieces, 0.5 oz	60	0	15
Suckers (Walgreens), 1 piece, 0.4 oz	45	0	11
Sugar Babies, Original, 1.4 oz	160	1.5	37
Sugar Coated Peanuts, 1 oz	120	8	10
Sunbursts Sunflowers (Kimmie):			
Choco Rocks Milk, 1.4 oz	210	10	27
Kettle Corn Nuggets, 1.4 oz	200	9	29
Sunburst Milk, 1.4 oz	210	11	23
Swedish Fish, 7 pieces, 1.4 oz	150	0	38
SweeTARTS:			
Orig., 8 pieces, 0.5 oz	50	0	13
Mini Chewy, 23 pieces, 0.5 oz	50	0.5	12
Symphony (Hershey's):			
Milk Choc: 1.5 oz bar	220	14	23
Large Block: 5 pieces, 1.35 oz	200	12	22
W/ Alm. & Toffee, 5 pcs, 1.3 oz	200	13	21

Per Piece/Serving **C F Cb**

	C	F	Cb
Taffy,			
Fruit Chews, 1 piece	20	0.5	4
Take 5 (Hershey's): Orig, 1.5oz	200	11	25
King Size, 2.25 oz	300	16	37
Snack Size, 2 pcs, 1 oz	150	8	19
3 Musketeers: Original, 1.9 oz	240	7	42
2 To Go, 1 bar, 1.6 oz	200	6	35
Fun Size, 3 bars, 1.6 oz	190	6	34
Minis, 7 pieces, 1.4 oz	170	5	32
Tang-a-Roos, 1 roll	25	0	6
Terry's: Chocolate Orange (5), 1.5 oz	230	12	27
Dark Chocolate Orange (5), 1.5 oz	240	13	28
Tic Tac, all varieties, 1 piece	2	0	0
Toblerone: 1.25 oz bar	190	10	22
1.75 oz bar	270	15	31
3.5 oz bar	540	30	63
5.3 oz Package, 5 pieces, 1.55 oz	230	13	27
Toffees, Regular, 1 oz	160	9	18
Tootsie Pops, (1), 0.6 oz	60	0	15
Tootsie Roll: 2.25 oz roll	245	2	55
Midgees, 1.4 oz	140	3	28
Truffles: Reg., 1 piece, 0.4 oz	60	4	6
Large (Godiva), 0.75 oz	110	6.5	12
Extra Large (J.Schmidt), 1.5 oz	220	13	24
Turtles: Original, 1 piece, 0.6 oz	85	5	10
Sugar Free, 1 piece, 0.4 oz	50	3.5	7
Twists: Licorice; Strawb., sugar free,			
7 pieces, 1.4 oz	90	0	25
Twix:			
Caramel: 2 cookies, 1.8 oz	250	12	34
Fun Size, 2 cookies, 1.7 oz	250	14	27
4 To Go, 1 cookie, 0.8 oz	110	5	15
6 To Go, 1 cookie, 0.5 oz	80	4	11
Minis, 3 pieces, 1 oz	150	7	20
Peanut Butter:			
Single, 2 cookies, 1.7 oz	250	14	27
4 to Go, 1 cookie, 0.8 oz	250	12	34
Twizzlers: Cherry Bites (17), 1.4 oz	140	0.5	32
Cherry Nibs, 29 pieces, 1.4 oz	140	1	32
Pull 'n' Peel, Cherry, 1 piece, 1.2 oz	110	0.5	26
Twists Strawb., 1.3 oz	120	0.5	29
U-No Bar, 1.5 oz	250	17	22
Weight Watchers (Whitman's):			
Caramel Medallions (3)	160	9	24
Coconut (3)	150	9	23
English Toffee Squares (3)	150	9	21
Mint Patties (3)	150	9	23
Peanut Butter Cups (4)	180	8	31
Pecan Crowns (3)	160	10	24

Candy ~ Brands & Generic (Cont)

Per Piece/Serving	C	F	Cb
Werther's:			
Caramel Chocolate (6), 1.4 oz	220	13	21
Hard Candy: Original (3), 0.5 oz	70	1.5	14
Sugar-Free Original (5)	40	1.5	14
(Carbs include 14g sugar alcohol)			
Whatchamacallit: 1.5 oz Bar	230	12	28
King Size Bar, 2.5 oz	370	20	45
Whitman's, Boxed Chocolates:			
Sampler (4), 1.6 oz	220	12	27
12 oz Box, 3 pieces, 1.2 oz	170	9	21
Reserve, 7 oz Box, 2 pieces, 1.2 oz	160	9	21
Sugar Free, 10 oz Box, 3 pcs, 1.5 oz	190	13	25
Whoppers, av. all varieties, 18 pcs	190	7	31
Wonka:			
Bar (1), 2.5 oz	360	19	49
Exceptional Bars, 4 pieces, av.	200	13	23
Gobstopper, 9 pieces, 0.5 oz	60	0	14
Laffy Taffy: Ropes, all var., 0.8 oz	80	1.5	18
Stretchy & Tangy, all var., 1.5 oz	150	3.5	29
Nerds, Giant, Chewy, 1.8 oz package	180	0	42
Yogurt Candy,			
Coated Raisins, 27 pieces, 1.4 oz	180	8	28
York: Mints, (3)	10	0	3
Peppermint Pattie, reg, 1.4 oz	140	2.5	31
Pieces (50)	170	8	28
Zagnut, 1.75 oz bar	220	9	35
Zero Bar: 1.8 oz bar	230	14	37
King Size, 3.5 oz	400	14	68

Gum

Per Piece	C	F	Cb
Bazooka	15	0	4
Beechies	6	0	1
Big League Chews	10	0	2
Bubble Yum: Original	25	0	6
Sugarless	10	0	3
Candilicious	30	0	2
Carefree, Sugarless/Regular	5	0	2
Chiclet	5	0	1
Dentyne	5	0	0.5
Double Bubble Ball	20	0	5
Estee, bubble/regular	5	0	2
Extra (Wrigley's), Sugar-Free	5	0	2
Freshen-Up	10	0	3
Hubba Bubba: Regular	25	0	6
Sugar-free, average	14	0	0.5
Ice Breakers	5	0	2
Jolt Gum	5	0	2
Super Bubble	15	0	4
Trident, Orig.; White	5	0	1
Wrigley's, all flavors	10	0	2

Carob Candy

Per Piece/Serving	C	F	Cb
Carob, Plain/Natural, 1 oz	155	9	15
Carob Coated: Raisins, 1 oz	130	8	15
Almonds/Peanuts, 1 oz	150	10	14
Malt Balls, 1 oz	135	8	15
Caramels, 1 oz	110	4	18
Dates, 1 oz	125	5	20
Soybeans	145	9	16
Trail/Party Mix, 1 oz	150	9	15

Cough Drops

Per Drop/Piece	C	F	Cb
Beech Nut, 1 drop	10	0	2
CVS, Honey Lemon Cough Drops	15	0	4
Diabetic Tussin	0	0	0
Halls, Defense Vitamin C: Regular	15	0	4
Sugar Free	5	0	3
Fruit Breezers	15	0	4
Menthol Drops: Regular	15	0	4
Sugar Free	5	0	4
Plus	20	0	5
Listerine (Amer. Chicle), Lozenge	10	0	4
Luden's, Throat Drops: Reg., all var.	10	0	4
Sugar Free	0	0	1
Pine Bros, Cough Drops	10	0	4
Ricola, Cough Drops:			
Natural Herbs	10	0	3
Sugar-Free Lemon Mint	0	0	1
Rolaids, Sodium Free	5	0	1
Sathers, Peppermint Lozenges	15	0	3
Sucrets (Beecham), Lozenges	10	0	2.5
Wintergreen, Lozenges	15	0	3

Eat at least 5 servings of fruit and vegetables every day . . . and Enjoy Better Health!

Quick Guide C F Cb

Firm/Hard Cheeses
American, Cheddar, Jack, Swiss:
Average All Brands
Regular Cheese:

	C	F	Cb
Thin Deli slice, 0.75 oz	80	6	0.5
1 oz slice/piece	110	9	0.5
8 oz package	880	72	3
Cubes: 1" cube, 0.6 oz	70	5.5	0.5
1¼" cube, 1 oz	115	9	0.5
Diced, 1 cup, 4.5 oz	510	41	3
Melted, ¼ cup, 2 oz	245	20	1
Shredded: ¼ cup, 1 oz	110	9	0.5
1 cup, 4 oz	440	36	2

Cheese & Cheese Products

Per 1 oz Unless Indicated C F Cb

	C	F	Cb
Almond (Lisanatti), Chunks, av.	50	1	3
American:			
Regular: 1 slice, 1 oz	105	9	0.5
Kraft, Regular, 0.67 oz slice	60	4.5	1
Land O'Lakes, 1 oz slice	100	9	2
Reduced Fat:			
Alpine Lace, Yellow/White, 0.8 oz	90	6	1
Borden, 1 slice, 0.75 oz	50	3	2
Kraft, 2% Milk, Deli Deluxe, 0.67 oz	60	4	1
Land O Lakes, 2% Milk, 1 oz	90	6	1
Babybel (Laughing Cow), Mini:			
Original (1), 0.75 oz	70	6	0
Light (1), 0.75 oz	50	3	0
Bonbel (1), 0.75 oz	70	6	0
Light Original (1), 0.75 oz	50	3	0
Gouda (1), 0.75 oz	80	6	0
Blue/Bleu: Average all Brands			
Crumbled, ¼ cup, 1 oz	100	8	0
Light, 0.75 oz	35	1.5	2
Brie: Average, 1 oz	95	8	0
Alouette,			
Baby Brie Wedge, 1 oz	110	10	1
Camembert, 1 oz	85	7	0
Caraway, 1 oz	105	8	1
Castello, 1 oz	120	12	0
Cheddar:			
Regular: Medium/Sharp, av., 1 oz	110	9	1
Shredded, ¼ cup, 1 oz	110	9	1
Cracker Barrell: Extra Sharp, 1 oz	120	10	0
Sharp, Shreds, 1 oz	110	9	1

Cheese & Cheese Products (Cont)

Per 1 oz Unless Indicated C F Cb

	C	F	Cb
Cheddar: (Cont):			
Reduced Fat,			
2% Milk, Shredded:			
Borden, ¼ cup, 1 oz	80	6	0
Cracker Barrell, 1 oz	80	6	1
Cheese Curds:			
Fresh: ¼ cup, 1 oz	110	9	0
1 cup, 4 oz	440	36	0
Breaded & Fried:			
A&W, 5 oz	570	40	27
Culver's, Wisconsin, 6.7 oz	670	38	54
Cheese Logs (Kaukauna), average	90	6	4
Cheese Whiz:			
Original, 2 Tbsp, 1 oz	90	7	4
Light, 2 Tbsp, 1 oz	80	3.5	6
Salsa Con Queso,			
2 Tbsp, 1 oz	90	7	4
Cheshire, 1 oz	110	9	1.5
Colby, Regular, 1 oz	110	8	1
Colby-Jack:			
Regular, 1 oz	110	9	1
Kraft, 2% Milk, 1 oz	60	4	0
Cottage Cheese: Average All Brands			
Creamed (4% milk fat):			
2 Tbsp, 1 oz	30	1	1.5
½ cup, 4 oz	110	5	4
With fruit, ½ cup, 4 oz	115	4	5
Reduced-Fat (2%): 2 Tbsp, 1 oz	25	0.5	1
½ cup, 4 oz	100	3	4
Low-Fat (1%): 2 Tbsp, 1 oz	20	0.5	1
½ cup, 4 oz	80	1	3
Fat-Free/Non-Fat: 2 T., 1 oz	20	0	1
½ cup, 4 oz	80	0	5
Cottage Cheese: Brands			
Fiber One, 1% Fat, ½ c., 4 oz	80	2	8
Friendship:			
1% Low-Fat with Pineapple, 4 oz	120	1	16
Nonfat with Pineapple, ½ cup, 4 oz	110	0	17
Pot Style, 2%, ½ cup, 4 oz	90	2.5	3
Hood, with Chive/Onion, 4 oz	90	1	5
Knudsen/Breakstone's:			
Free, Non-Fat, ½ cup, 4 oz	70	0	7
2% Milk Fat, ½ cup, 4 oz	100	2.5	6
On the Go!,			
Low-Fat, 4 oz carton	90	2.5	6
Lactaid, Low-Fat, ½ cup, 4 oz	80	1	7
Light n' Lively:			
Fat-Free, ½ cup, 4.4 oz	80	0	8
Low-Fat, ½ cup, 4.4 oz	80	1.5	6

Cheese & Cheese Products (Cont)

Per 1 oz Unless Indicated	C	F	Cb
Cream Cheese: *Average All Brands*			
Regular/Soft:			
2 Tbsp, 1 oz	95	10	1
3 oz package	290	29	3.5
8 oz package	780	78	9
Light, Plain, 1 oz	60	4.5	2.5
Fat-Free, Plain, 1 oz	30	0	2
Easy Cheese *(Kraft)*,			
American, 2 Tbsp, 1.2 oz	90	6	2
Edam, 1 oz	100	8	0.5
Farmer, Low-Fat, 1 oz	40	2.5	0
Feta: Regular, 1 oz	75	6	1
Crumbled, ½ cup, 2.5 oz	190	15	3
Athenos, Reduced-Fat, 1 oz	60	4	1
Fontina, 2 Tbsp, 1 oz	110	9	0.5
Galaxy, Cheese Substitute:			
Grated Parmesan Flavor, 2 tsp, 0.2 oz	15	0	0
Rice, Mozzarella flavor, 1 sl., 0.6 oz	40	2.5	0.5
Veggy, all varieties, 1 slice, 0.5 oz	40	2.5	0.5
Goat's Milk Cheese:			
Chevre: Original, 2 Tbsp	75	6	0.5
Semi-Soft, 1 oz	100	8.5	1
Hard, 1 oz	130	10	0.5
Chavrie: Regular, 2 Tbsp, 1 oz	50	3.5	1
Caramelized Onion, 2 Tbsp	50	3	4
Logs, average all varieties, 1 oz	80	7	3
Gjetost, fresh, 1 oz	130	8	12
Myzithra, grated, 1 oz	80	4	2
Gorgonzola, 1 oz	100	8	0.5
Galbani, Dolcelatte, 1 oz	95	8	1
Gouda, 1 oz slice	100	8	0.5
Gruyere, 1 oz	115	9	1
Handi-Snacks *(Kraft):*			
Breadsticks 'n Cheez Single, 1 oz	110	4.5	14
Ritz Crackers 'n Cheez Dip, 1 oz	100	6	11
Havarti *(Land O'Lakes)*, 0.75 oz	80	7	0
Italian Pasta Blend *(Sargento)*, 1 oz	90	6	3
Jarlsberg: Average, 1 oz	100	8	0
Reduced Fat, shredded, 1 oz	70	3.5	0
Labneh, (Lebanese Cream Chse), 1.8 oz	70	4	4

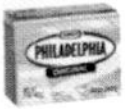
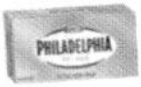
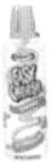
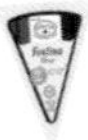
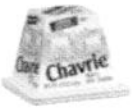
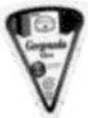
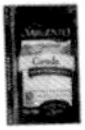

Updated Nutrition Data ~ www.CalorieKing.com
Persons with Diabetes ~ See Disclaimer (Page 22)

Cheese & Cheese Products (Cont)

Per 1 oz Unless Indicated	C	F	Cb
Laughing Cow, Wedges:			
Original Creamy Swiss (1)	50	4	1
Light Varieties, av., (1)	35	2	2
Lifetime, Cholesterol Reducing,			
Low Fat, all varieties, 1 Slice, 1 oz	45	1.5	1
Limburger, 1 oz	95	8	0
Mascarpone, av., 1 oz	125	13	0.5
Mexican:			
Cacique: Asadero, sliced	70	5	1
Cotija	100	8	0
Enchilado; Manchego	90	7	0
Panela	80	6	0
Queso Fresco	80	6	0
Queso Quesadilla	90	7	0
Ranchero	80	6	0
Chi-Chi's, Salsa Con Quéso, Mild	45	3	4
El Mexicano: Asadero, Regular	90	7	0
Cotija, Regular	110	9	0
Kraft, Mexican Four Cheese; Taco, Shredded,	100	8	1
Sargento, 4 Cheese Mexican	110	9	1
Supremo: Quéso Chihuahua, 1 oz	100	8	0
Quéso Oaxaca	80	5	1
Monterey Jack:			
Regular, shredded, 1 oz	100	8	1
Alpine Lace, Co-Jack, 1 oz	70	5	0
Kraft, 1 oz	100	8	1
Mozzarella:			
Regular: Average 1 oz	85	6.5	0.5
Land O'Lakes/Polly-O:			
Slice, average, 1 oz	90	6	1
Shredded, 1 oz	90	6	1
Fat-Free,			
Kraft, Shredded, 1 oz	45	0	2
Light:			
Kraft, 2% Milk Fat, Reduced Fat	70	4	1
Polly-O Lite, Shredded, 1 oz	60	2.5	1
Part Skim:			
Alpine Lace, 25% Reduced Fat	60	4	1
Borden/Kraft, Shredded	80	5	2
Kraft, String	80	6	0
Muenster:			
Regular, 1 oz	105	9	0.5
Low-Fat, 1 oz	85	5	1

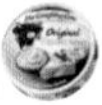
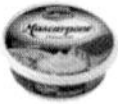
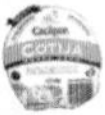
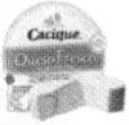
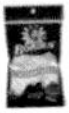
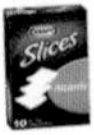
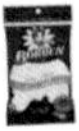
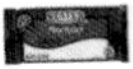

C Cheese

Cheese & Cheese Products (Cont)

Per 1 oz Unless Indicated — **C F Cb**

Item	C	F	Cb
Parmesan:			
Fresh/Block, Dry, 1 oz	110	7.5	1
Grated (Packaged): 1 Tbsp	20	1.5	0
1 oz	120	8	1
½ cup, 1.75 oz	215	14	2
Kraft, Reduced-Fat Topping, 1 Tbsp	20	1	2
Philadelphia:			
Cream Cheese: Original, 2 T. 1 oz	100	9	1
3 oz package	300	27	3
Regular, 1 oz	90	9	2
Creme, Cooking, av. all var., ¼ cup	110	9	4
Flavored:			
Blueberry, 1 oz	80	6	5
Honey Nut; Strawberry, av., 1 oz	80	7	5
Garden Vegetable, 1 oz	80	7	2
Salmon, 1 oz	70	7	1
Light, Plain, 1 oz	70	5	2
⅓ Less Fat: Plain, 2T., 1 oz	70	6	2
Garden Veggie; Chive & On., 1 oz	70	5	2
Neufchatel, 2 T., 1 oz	70	6	1
Fat-Free, Plain, 1 oz	30	0	2
Indulgence:			
Milk/White Chocolate:			
1 Tbsp, 0.6 oz	60	3.5	6
Mini Tub, 1.25 oz	125	7	13
8 oz container	800	47	80
Dark Chocolate, 1 T., 0.6 oz	55	3.5	6
Spread: Regular, 1.1 oz	80	7	2
Flavors, average, 1.2 oz	80	6	5
Whipped:			
Regular, 0.8 oz	60	5	2
Mixed Berry, 0.7 oz	70	5	3
Pizza Four Cheese, shredded, *Kraft/Sargento,* Regular, av., 1 oz	90	7	1
Port de Salut, 1 oz	100	8	0
Port Wine (*Kaukauna/WisPride*):			
8 oz Tub: Average, 1 oz	85	7	3
Lite, 2 Tbsp, average, 1 oz	60	3.5	5
Ball, 1 oz	100	6	4
Log, 1 oz	100	7	4
Provolone: Regular, 1 oz	100	7.5	0.5
Alpine Lace, Reduced-Fat, 0.8 oz	60	4.5	0
Sargento, Deli Style 1 slice, 0.67 oz	50	3	0
Pub (*Rondele*), average all varieties	75	7	1
Quark: 40% fat	45	3	1
20% fat	30	1.5	1
Skim/Non-Fat	20	0	1.5
Queso:			
Anejo/Asadero/Blanco, 1 oz	105	9	1
Chichuahua/De Papa, 1 oz	110	9	2
Rice Cheese Chunks (*Lisanatti*), average, 1 oz	60	3	2
Swiss (*Lifetime*), Fat Free, 1 oz	40	0	1

Cheese & Cheese Products (Cont)

Per 1 oz Unless Indicated — **C F Cb**

Item	C	F	Cb
Ricotta Cheese:			
Whole Milk: 1 oz	50	3.5	1
½ cup, 4.5 oz	215	16	4
Part Skim: 1 oz	40	2	1.5
½ cup, 4.5 oz	170	10	6
Light/Low-Fat: 1 oz	25	1	1.5
½ cup, 4.5 oz	125	5	6
Fat-Free, ½ cup, 4.5 oz	100	0	10
Baked Ricotta, 2 oz	130	9	3
Romano: Block/Loaf	110	8	1
Grated: 1 oz	120	9	1
1 Tbsp, 0.2 oz	20	1.5	0
Roquefort, 1 oz	105	9	0.5
Sheep's Milk, (Manchego), *Trader Joes/Wegman's,* 1 oz	120	10	0
Soy Cheese:			
Trader Joe's, Cheddar flavor, 0.7 oz	45	2	3
Soy Kaas: Cheddar, 1 oz	50	2	8
Monterey Jack, 1 oz	60	4	0
Soy Sation, Chunks, all varieties, 1 oz	60	3	2
Smoked Cheddar, average, 1 oz	110	10	0
Stilton, average, 1 oz	110	10	0
String:			
Regular, average all brands	80	6	0.5
Kraft, Twist-Ums & String-ums, Super Long, 1 stick, 1.1 oz	90	6	1
Light/Lite:			
Frigo, String	60	2.5	0.5
Polly-O, String, 2% Red-Fat, 0.8 oz	60	2.5	1
Sargento: 1 piece, 0.75 oz	50	2.5	1
Part Skim, 0.85 oz	70	4.5	1
Swiss: Regular, 1 oz	110	8	1.5
Alpine Lace, Reduced-Fat, 0.8 oz	70	4.5	1
Kraft Singles, 2% Milk, 0.67 oz	45	2.5	2
Tilsit, 1 oz	100	7.5	0.5
Tybo, 1 oz	100	7	1
Tofutti, Better Than Cream Cheese, all varieties, 1 oz	85	5	9
Velveeta (*Kraft*):			
Original, 1 oz	80	5	3
Reduced Fat, 2% Milk, 1 oz	60	3	4
Extra Thick, 1.2 oz	100	7	3
Mexican: Hot, 1 oz	90	6	3
Mild, 1 oz	80	6	3

Dips/Spreads

Per 2 Tbsp, 1 oz, Unless Indicated

	C	F	Cb
Average All Brands			
Avocado/Guacamole	45	4	2
Baba Ghanoush (Eggplant/Sesame)	70	6	4
Cheese Fondue, ½ cup, 4 oz	260	15	4
French Onion Dip	60	4.5	3
Hummus: 2 Tbsp	50	1	5
½ cup, 4.5 oz	220	4.5	23
Tzatziki (Cucumber/Yogurt)	30	2.5	2
Clearman's, Original Spread	150	16	0
De La Casa, 5 Layer Party Dip	45	2.5	4
Fritos: *Per 2 Tbsp*			
Dips:			
Chili Cheese	45	3	3
Bean; Hot Bean w/ Jalap.	35	1	5
Jalapeno Cheddar Cheese	50	3.5	3
Guiltless Gourmet,			
Black Bean/Spicy Black Bean Dip	40	0	7
Heluva Good Cheese,			
French Onion Dip, 2 Tbsp	50	4.5	2
Hidden Valley,			
For Everything Topping, av.	130	14	3
Kaukauna *(Wisconsin)*:			
Spreadable Cheddar:			
Sharp/Smokey Cheddar	90	7	3
Cheese Balls, all varieties	100	6	4
Cheese Logs, all varieties	100	7	4
Kemps: *Per 2 Tbsp*			
Dips: French Onion	60	5	3
Ranch Style	60	5	2
Top The Tater,			
Taco Fiesta; Veggie Ranch	60	5	2
Kroger, Dips, all varieties	60	5	2
Kraft: *Per 2 Tbsp*			
Dips: Average all varieties	60	5	3
Cheez Whiz: Original	90	7	3
Light	80	3.5	6
Salsa Con Queso	90	7	4
Spreads: Olive & Pimento, 1.2 oz	70	6	3
Old English Sharp; Roka Blue, av	85	8	2
Marzetti: *Per 2 Tbsp*			
Dips: Choc Fruit, 1.4 oz	110	1	25
Caramel Apple, fat free, 1.4 oz	100	0	25
Veggie: Dill, Light, 1 oz	60	5	2
Ranch, Singles, 1.5 oz	180	18	2.5
Ranch, Fat-Free, 1 oz	30	0	6

Dips/Spreads (Cont)

Per 2 Tbsp, 1 oz, Unless Indicated

	C	F	Cb
Marie's:			
Dips: Buttermilk Ranch; Crmy Dill. av.	100	10	2
Guacamole	40	3	3
Nalley's, Ranch Chip Dip	100	10	2
Naturally Fresh: *Per 2 Tbsp*			
Dips: Chocolate	70	0	12
Cream Cheese Strawb.	90	3.5	14
Caramel	100	4	16
Old Dutch:			
Dips: French Onion, 1 oz	50	3	5
Mild Cheddar, 1 oz	40	3	2
Nacho Cheese, 1 oz	35	2.5	2
Old El Paso: *Per 2 Tbsp*			
Dips: Cheese & Red Pepper	35	2	3.5
Thick N' Chunky Salsa	10	0	2.5
Price's: *Per 2 Tbsp*			
Dips: Pimiento Cheese	85	7	3
Light Pimiento	55	3	3
Zesty Jalapeno	75	6	2.5
Stop & Shop: *Per 2 Tbsp*			
Dips: Veggie	100	10	3
Sour Cream French Onion	60	4.5	3
TGI Fridays,			
Spinach, Cheese & Artichoke Dip	30	1.5	2
Toby's, Tofu Pate, 2 Tbsp	80	7	2
Tostitos: *Per 2 Tbsp*			
Dips: Creamy Spinach, 1 oz	50	4	2
Salsa Con Quéso	40	2.5	5
Smooth & Cheesy, 1 oz	50	3.5	4
Wise: *Per 2 Tbsp*			
Dips: French Onion, 1.2 oz	60	5	3
Ranch, 1.2 oz	50	4	3

*New Diet Aid
- The Refrigerator Air Bag!*

POOF!

C Condiments ◆ Salsa

Condiments, Sauces

	C	F	Cb
Average of Brands & Homemade			
Apple Sauce:			
Sweetened, ¼ cup, 2.5 oz	55	0	13
Unsweetened, ¼ cup, 2 oz	25	0	7
Barbecue Sauce:			
Regular: Av. all flavors, 2 Tbsp, 1 oz	40	0	10
Bull's Eye, Original, 1 oz	60	0	14
Bearnaise Sauce, ¼ cup, 2.5 oz	190	19	5
Buffalo Wing Sce: Hon. Mustard, 1 T.	40	3	3
Average other varieties, 1 Tbsp	25	2	2
Cheese, h/made, ¼ cup, 2.5 oz	150	10	12
Chef-Mate, Hot Dog, ¼ cup	70	2.5	9
Chili Sauce *(Heinz)*, 1 Tbsp	20	0	5
Cocktail Sauce: ¼ cup	110	0	15
Walden Farms, Fat-Free, 1 Tbsp	0	0	0
Cranberry Sauce: Av. all varieties, 2 T.	45	0	11
¼ cup, 2.5 oz	110	0	27
Demi Glaze Gold, 2 tsp	30	0.5	3
Honey Mustard *(French's)*, 2 Tbsp	60	0.5	12
Horseradish: 1 tsp	2	0	0
Kraft, 1 tsp	15	1.5	1
Ketchup: Regular, 1 Tbsp	15	0	4
Heinz: Reduced Sugar, 1 Tbsp	5	0	1
Simply Heinz, 1 Tbsp	20	0	5
Mole:			
Dona Maria, av. all varieties., 2 T.	150	10	10
Rogelio Bueno, 2 Tbsp, 1 oz	160	11	12
Mushroom Sce, ½ cup, 2 oz	50	2	5
Mustard, average, 1 tsp	5	0	0.5
Pesto Sauce, ¼ cup, 2 oz	270	28	2
Pizza Sauce, ¼ cup, 2 oz	30	0	6
Seafood Cocktail Sce, ¼ cup	60	0	15
Soy Sauce: Average all, 1 Tbsp	10	0	1
Kikkoman, Lite Soy, 1 Tbsp	10	0	1
Spaghetti Sce, ½ cup, 4.5 oz	135	6	19
Steak Sauce:			
Kraft, A1, 1 Tbsp, 0.5 oz	15	0	3
Lea & Perrins, 1 Tbsp, 0.5 oz	20	0	5
Strawb. Puree Sauce, Unsweet., 2 T.	10	0	2
Sweet & Sour Sauce:			
Contadina, 1.2 oz	40	1	8
Kraft, 1 Tbsp	60	0	13
Tabasco Sauce, 1 tsp	2	0	0
Taco Sauce, average all, 2 Tbsp, 1 oz	10	0	1
Tartar Sauce: *(Heinz)*, 2 Tbsp, 1 oz	120	11	4
Hellmann's, Regular, 2 Tbsp, 1 oz	80	7	4
McCormick, Fat-Free, 2 Tbsp, 1 oz	30	0	7
Teriyaki Sauce *(Kikkoman)*, 1 T., 0.5 oz	15	0	2
Vinegar, White or Wine, 2 T.	4	0	1
White Sauce, ½ cup, 5 oz	130	7	10
Worcestershire Sauce, 1 tsp	5	0	1

Pickles & Relish

	C	F	Cb
Average All Brands			
Bread & Butter Pickles, 4 sl., 1 oz	25	0	6
Chutney, 2 Tbsp, 1.25 oz	50	0.5	11
Dill Pickles:			
Slices, 4 slices, 1 oz	4	0	1
1 large, (3¾"x 1¼" diam.), 2.25 oz	12	0	3
Extra large (4"x 1¾" diam.), 5 oz	30	0	6
Halves: Small, 1 oz	3	0	0.5
Large, 2.5 oz	8	0	2
Gherkins, sweet, 1 medium, 1 oz	30	0	7
Green Chiles, chopped, 2 Tbsp	5	0	1
Horseradish, 1 Tbsp	10	0	2
Jalapenos, pickled (2), 2 oz	10	0.5	2
Jalapeno Relish, 1 Tbsp, 0.5 oz	5	0	1
Mustard, av. all brands, 1 tsp	5	0	0.5
Peppers, Hot/Mild (1), 1.5 oz	20	0	4
Pickled: Beets, ½ cup, 4 oz	75	0	19
Onions, 1 medium, 0.75 oz	10	0	2
Cocktail Onion, 1 onion	2	0	0
Red Cabbage, ½ cup, 3 oz	65	0	15
Pickles: Sweet, 2 Tbsp, 1 oz	35	0	8
Large (3" x ¾ diam.), 1.25 oz	40	0	10
Pickle in a Pouch, 1 large	12	0	3
Relishes:			
Cranberry-Orange, 1 Tbsp	30	0	7
Hot Dog (*Heinzz*), 1 T., 0.5 oz	17	0	3
S'wich Spread, 1 tsp	20	1	5
Sweet Pickle, 1 Tbsp, 0.5 oz	20	0	5
Sweet Cauliflower, 1 oz	35	0	8
Sugar Free Relish, 1 tsp	5	0	1
Sweet Gherkins (2), 1 oz	5	0	1
Sauerkraut,			
Drained, 1 cup, 5 oz	25	0	6

Salsa

	C	F	Cb
Average all Types:			
Regular, w/out oil, 2 T., 1 oz	15	0	3.5
Made with oil, 2 Tbsp, 1 oz	40	3	8
La Victoria, 2 Tbsp, 1 oz	10	0	2
Old El Paso, 1 Tbsp, 1 oz	10	0	3
TGI Friday's, 1.2 oz	15	0	4

Quick Guide   C   F   Cb

Cookies:
Average All Brands: *Per Cookie*

	C	F	Cb
Biscotti: Small, 0.5 oz	70	3	10
Regular, 1 oz	140	6.5	18
Chocolate Chip:			
Small/Thin, 0.5 oz	70	3.5	9
Regular, 1 oz	140	7	18
Large (*Mrs Fields*), 3 oz	350	17	45
Extra Large, 4 oz	555	28	73
Oatmeal/Oatmeal Raisin:			
Small/Thin, 0.5 oz	65	2.5	10
Regular, 1 oz	130	5	20
Large (*Mrs Fields*), 2.5 oz	330	14	44
Extra Large, 4 oz	510	20	78
Peanut Butter:			
Small/Thin, 0.5 oz	70	3.5	9
Regular, 1 oz	135	7	17
Large (*Mrs Fields*), 2.5 oz	330	17	41
Extra Large, 4 oz	540	27	67
Low-Fat Cookies:			
Choc Chip (Low-Fat), (1), 0.5 oz	65	2	10
Oatmeal Raisin (Fat-Free), (1), 1 oz	95	0.5	22
Peanut Butter (Low-Fat), (1), 1 oz	105	5	15

Quick Guide   C   F   Cb

Crackers
Average All Brands: *Per Cracker Unless Indicated*

	C	F	Cb
Cheese Crackers:			
Plain: 1" square	5	0	0.5
Bag, single serving, 1 oz	140	7	16
Cheese/P'nut Butter filled	30	1.5	4
Crispbread, Rye	35	0	8
Grahams, 2½" square	30	0.5	4
Melba Toast, Plain, 1 piece	20	0	4
Matzo, Plain, 1 oz	110	0.5	23
Oyster/Soup, ½ cup	95	2	17
Rice: 1 crackers	70	1.5	11
Oriental Style, 1 oz	130	3.5	23
Saltines, 5 crackers	65	2	11
Snack-type, 1 round cracker	15	1	2
Soda Crackers (*Saltine*), 2	25	1	4.5
Water Cracker (*Carr's*), Original	15	0.5	2.5
Wheat:			
Wheat Thins	10	0.5	1.5
Cheese/P'nut Butter filled	35	2	4

Cookies & Crackers ~ Brands

Per Cookie/Cracker, Unless indicated   C   F   Cb

	C	F	Cb
Albertsons:			
Animal Crackers (6), 1 oz	130	3.5	22
Chocolate Chip:			
Original (3), 1 oz	150	7	20
Chewy (2), 1 oz	130	6	18
Chunky (1), 0.5 oz	80	3.5	10
Chocolate S'wich Cremes: (3) 1 oz	150	6	25
Double Filled (2), 1 oz	140	6	22
Fudge Graham (3), 1 oz	140	7	18
Fudge Wafer (3), 1 oz	140	8	18
Fudge Marshmallow Ring	120	5	19
Pinwheels, Choc. Marshmallow	120	5	20
Vanilla Wafers (9), 1 oz	140	4	25
Graham: Cinnamon (2)	150	3	28
Honey (2), 1 oz	140	2	28
Annie's:			
Bunny Grahams:			
Choc.; Choc Chip, 1 oz	130	4.5	21
Cinnamon, 1 oz	140	4.5	23
Friends, 1 oz	120	4	20
Honey, 1 oz	140	4.5	23
Gluten Free: Cocoa & Vanilla, 1 oz	120	3.5	22
Ginger Snaps; SnickerDoodles, 1 oz	130	4	21
Cheddar Bunnies:			
Regular: 1 oz Snack Pack	140	6	19
7.5 oz Box	1050	45	145
Sour Cream & Onion, 1 oz	150	7	19
White Cheddar, 1 oz	140	6	19
Whole Wheat, 1 oz	140	6	19
Austin:			
Sandwich Crackers: *Per Package*			
Cheese: With Cheddar Cheese	190	10	23
With Peanut Butter	190	10	23
Chocolate Peanut Butter	190	8	26
Toasty, with Peanut Butter	190	9	23
Barbara's Bakery:			
Fig Bars: Raspberry, 1.4 oz	120	0	27
Wheat/Multigrain	110	0.5	26
Snackimals:			
Choc Chip, 1 oz	120	4	19
Double Choc.; P'nut Butter, av., 1 oz	145	6	22
Bear Naked:			
Soft-Baked Granola,			
Double Choc.; Fruit & Nut, av.	130	6	19

Cookies & Crackers ~ Brands (Cont)

Per Cookie/Cracker, Unless Indicated **C** **F** **Cb**

belVita *(Nabisco):*

Breakfast Biscuits:

	C	F	Cb
Crunchy, 1 pack (4 biscuits), average	230	8	36
Soft Baked, 1 biscuit, average	190	7	32

Blue Diamond:

Nut Thins, (17), average all varieties	130	3	23
Artisan Nut Thins , (13), av. all var.	130	3.5	22

Brent & Sam's: *Per 2 Cookies*

Natural: Choc. Chip Pecan	130	7	14
Key Lime White Chocolate	120	6	16
Triple Chocolate Bliss, 1 oz	120	6	16

Carr's: Ginger Lemon Cremes (2)

Ginger Lemon Cremes (2)	140	6	21
Poppy & Sesame Crackers(4)	80	4	10
Rosemary Crackers(4)	70	2.5	11
Whole Wheat Crackers (2)	80	4	10

Cheez•It ~ *See Sunshine, Page 87*

Chips Ahoy! ~ *See Nabisco, Page 85*

Country Choice:

Sandwich Cremes (2), all varieties	130	5	19

Snacking:

Ginger Snaps (5); Vanilla Wafers (7)	140	5	22
Iced Oatmeal (4)	120	4	21

Dr. Kracker:

Crispbread: 100% Whole Wheat (1)

Crispbread: 100% Whole Wheat (1)	80	1	16
Average other varieties (1)	100	4	12
Snackers, average all varieties (8)	125	5	15

Erin Baker's:

Original Breakfast: *Per 3 oz*

Banana Walnut	300	8	53
Peanut Butter	320	11	49

Minis: *Per 1 oz Cookie*

Peanut Butter	110	3.5	16
Dble Chocolate; Oatmeal Raisin, av.	100	2	18

Famous Amos:

Bite Size: Choc. Chip,

4 Cookies, 1 oz	150	7	20
Choc. Chip & Pecans (4)	150	8	18

Sandwich, Creme Filled:

Chocolate (3), 1 oz	160	7	25
Vanilla (3), 1 oz	170	7	25

Per Cookie/Cracker, Unless Indicated **C** **F** **Cb**

Fig Newtons ~ *See Nabisco, Page 85*

Fifty50:

	C	F	Cb
Butter (4)	190	9	24
Average other varieties (4)	165	9	22
Wafers, average all varieties, (6)	165	9	22

Gamesa:

Animalitos, 14 cookies, 1 oz	110	1	25
Arcoiris M/mallow, 2 oz pkg, 6 cookies	220	5	38
Chocolatines M/mallow, 2 cookies, 1 oz	130	5	18
Chokis, Chocolate Chip, 1.4 oz pkg	190	9	27
Emperador: Cream Cookie Sandwich			
Lemon Creme, 1 pkg, 6 cookies	270	8	45
Av. other flavors, 1 pkg, 6 cookies	360	12	57
Fruitbars, average, 1 cookie, 1 oz	110	4.5	18
Giro, 3 cookies, 1 oz	140	6	20
Mamut, Choc Marshmallow,			
1 cookie, 1 oz	130	5	19
Marias, 8 cookies, 1 oz	120	2	24
Sugar Wafers, av., 3 wafers, 1.2 oz	160	7	25

Girl Scouts Cookies:

Caramel DeLites/Samoas (2)	130	6	19
Do-si-dos (3)	160	7	22
Peanut Butter Patties (2)	130	7	15
Savannah Smiles (5)	140	5	23

Goya:

Lady Fingers , 3 cookies	65	0.5	13
Maria, 5 cookies, 1 oz	130	3	19
Wafers, average all flavors,			
4 wafers, 1 oz	150	7	20

Grandma's:

Frosted, average all flavors,

1 cookie	230	9	34

Homestyle: *Per Cookie*

Chocolate Brownie	190	8	21
Chocolate Chip	170	9	22
Oatmeal Raisin	150	6	23
Peanut Butter	170	9	19
Peanut Butter Chocolate Chunks	200	10	22

Sandwich Cremes:

Peanut Butter (5)	200	9	25
Vanilla (5)	190	9	27
Mini's, Vanilla (9)	150	7	22

Cookies & Crackers ~ Brands (Cont)

Per Cookie/Cracker, Unless Indicated **C F Cb**

	C	F	Cb
Great American Cookies:			
Chewy Chocolate Supreme	180	7	27
Chewy Pecan Supreme	230	12	31
Double Fudge with Reese's	230	11	33
Original, w/ Reese's M&M's	240	12	31
Peanut Butter w/ M&M's	250	14	29
White Chunk Macadamia	250	14	30
Double Doozies:			
Original, 5.3 oz	690	34	94
M&M Big Bite, 2.5 oz	340	17	46
Cookie Cakes: 16", 3.5 oz	460	22	67
16" M&M, 4 oz	500	24	73
Heart Shaped, 3.5 oz	440	21	64
Great Value *(Walmart):*			
Chocolate Chip, all varieties (1)	160	7	23
Soft Cookies, Fudge & Cream (1)	150	6	22
Twist & Shout, all varieties (1)	140	6	22
Buttery Rounds, Baked (5)	80	4.5	10
Reduced Fat (5)	70	2	11
Cheese, 1 oz	150	8	18
Joseph's:			
Sugar Free: *Per 4 Cookies*			
Almond; Chocolate Walnut, average	95	3.5	14
Chocolate Chip; Pecan Choc. Chip, av.	95	5	14
Average other varieties	95	4	15
Note: Carb figures include 6 grams Maltitol			
Kashi:			
Chocolate Almond Butter	130	5	19
Happy Trail Mix, Chewy	140	5	21
Oatmeal: Dark Chocolate	130	5	20
Raisin Flax	120	4.5	20
Crackers:			
Country Cheddar (18)	130	4.5	20
Fire Roasted Veggie (15)	120	3.5	19
Honey Sesame (15)	120	3	22
Original 7 Grain (15)	120	3.5	19
Toasted Asiago (15)	130	4.5	21
Heart To Heart Whole Grain, Original; Roasted Garlic (7)	120	3.5	22
Pita Crisps:			
Original 7 Grain with Salt (11)	120	3	22
Zesty Salsa (11)	120	3	23

Per Cookie/Cracker, Unless Indicated **C F Cb**

	C	F	Cb
Keebler:			
Animals: Frosted (8)	160	7	22
Iced (6)	140	4.5	22
Cinnamon Roll (2), all varieties	150	6	23
Chips Deluxe: Original (2)	160	8	19
Soft & Chewy (2)	140	6	21
Chocolate Lovers (2)	170	9	20
Coconut (2)	160	9	18
Peanut Butter Cups (2)	170	9	19
Rainbow: Choc. Chip (2)	160	8	20
Minis, 1.4 oz package	200	10	24
Danish Wedding, (4)	140	7	19
E.L. Fudge: Original (2)	170	7	25
Double Stuffed (2)	180	9	24
Fudge Shoppe:			
Cheesecake Middles, Orig. Grahams (3)	130	7	17
Deluxe Grahams (3)	140	7	18
Fudge Sticks:			
Original (3)	150	8	20
Jumbo (1)	160	8	21
Fudge Stripes: Original (2)	140	6	19
Dark Chocolate (2)	150	7	22
Filled Pretzel Bites, Peanut Butter & Fudge, average, 1 pkg	170	9	21
Grasshopper (4)	140	7	20
Mint Creme Middles, Choc. Graham (3)	130	7	17
Gripz, Chips Deluxe 0.88 oz pouch	120	5	18
Oatmeal, average all varieties	140	6	20
Sandies Cookies:			
Dark Choc. Almond; Pecan Shtbrd, av.	170	10	19
Average other varieites	160	9	19
Vienna Fingers:			
Creme Filled (2)	150	6	23
Reduced Fat (2)	140	4.5	24
Wafers: Vanilla (8)	140	5	22
Mini Vanilla (18)	140	5	22
Crackers:			
Club: Original (4)	70	3	9
Reduced Fat (5)	70	2	12
Grahams: Original (8)	120	3.5	22
Honey (8)	140	4.5	23
Town House: Original (5)	90	5	9
Reduced Fat (6)	60	1.5	12

Cookies & Crackers ~ Brands (Cont)

Per Cookie/Cracker, Unless Indicated

	C	F	Cb
Kraft, Macaroni & Cheese Crackers,			
av. all varieties, 1. oz	150	7	18
Kroger:			
Chip Mates: Orig.(3), 1.5 oz	150	7	22
Chunky (2), 1 oz	120	6	17
Peanut Butter (2), 1 oz	120	7	15
White Chip (2), 1 oz	120	6	16
Chocolate Sandwich:			
Original (3), 1.2 oz	150	6	24
Chocolate Sandwich (2), 1 oz	150	6	23
Double Filled (2), 1 oz	140	6	22
Olde Southern Pecan Shortbread (2)	150	9	16
Vanilla Wafers (7)	130	3.5	23
Crackers:			
Grahams, Original; Honey, (4)	120	3	20
Saltines, Orig., (5), 0.5oz	60	1.5	10
Lance:			
Cookies:			
6 Pack: Nekot, Peanut Butter	240	11	32
Choc-O-Lunch, Vanilla Cream	220	8	34
Van-O-Lunch, Vanilla Cream	230	9	34
Crackers:			
Cracker Creations: *Per 2 Crackers*			
Granola: Choc. Filling, 1.3 oz	190	9	24
Peanut Butter Filling, 1.3 oz	190	9	23
Five Grain,			
Peanut Butter Filling	140	7	16
Sandwich Crackers: *Per 6 Crackers*			
Malt, with Peanut Butter Filling	180	8	20
Nip Chee, Cheddar Cheese	190	9	24
Toastchee:			
Peanut Butter	210	10	25
Toasty, Peanut Butter	180	8	21
Wholegrain, Cheddar Cheese	200	9	26
Little Debbie:			
Apple Oatmeal Pies (1)	140	4.5	24
Chocolate Chip Cream Pie (1)	150	6	23
Cookie Wreaths (1)	100	5	12
Marshmallow Puffs	150	5	25
Oatmeal Creme Pie (1)	170	7	26
Star Crunch(1)	150	6	22
Lu:			
Petit Beurre (4)	140	4	24
Petit Ecolier, all varieties (2)	130	6	17
Pim's, Orange, 1 oz	100	3	17
Manischewitz:			
Crackers:			
Tam Tams: Original (10)	110	4	16
Everything; Garlic (1), av.	140	5	20

Mary's Gone Crackers:

	C	F	Cb
Cookies:			
Chocolate Chip; Double Choc (2)	130	6	19
Ginger Snaps (3)	140	5	23
"N'Oatmeal" Raisin w/out Oats (2)	120	4	20
Crackers,			
all varieties (13)	140	5	21
Miss Meringue:			
Cookies:			
Madeleines:			
Traditional (2), 1.2 oz	160	9	19
Traditional & Dipped (2), 1.2 oz	160	9	18
Meringue Classiques:			
Cappuccino (4), 1 oz	110	0	26
Mint Choc. Chip (4), 1 oz	120	1.5	25
Triple Chocolate (4), 1 oz	120	1.5	25
Vanilla Rainbow/Van. (4), 1 oz	110	0	27
Meringue Minis:			
Chocolate (13), 1 oz	110	0	26
Choc. Chip (12), 1 oz	130	1.5	25
Mint Chocolate Chip (12), 1 oz	120	1.5	26
Vanilla; Rainbow Van. (26), 1 oz	110	0	27
Sugar-Free, Chocolate (30), 0.5 oz	40	0	8
Mother's:			
Chocolate Chip (4), 1 oz	150	7	20
Circus Animal (6), 1 oz	150	7	21
Coconut Cocadas (5), 1.2 oz	160	8	21
Double Fudge (2), 1.3 oz	170	7	27
Iced: Lemonade (4), 1 oz	150	7	19
Oatmeal (4), 1.2 oz	150	6	23
Macaroons (2), 1 oz	170	11	19
Oatmeal (2), 1 oz	130	5	19
Taffy; Van. Cream (2), av., 1.3 oz	185	8	27
Mrs Fields Cookies ~ *See Page 219*			
Murray:			
Cookies, Sugar Free:			
Fudge-Dipped:			
Grahams (4)	140	8	19
Mint Cookies (4)	130	7	17
Vanilla Wafers (4)	150	10	19
Oatmeal (3)	140	7	21
Peanut Butter (3)	150	9	16
Sandwiches, Lemon Creme (3)	130	7	20
Shortbread (8)	130	5	21
Shortbread Pecan (3)	160	11	18
Vanilla Creme Wafers (4)	130	8	19

Note: Carb figures include 4-9g sugar alcohol

Cookies & Crackers ~ Brands (Cont)

Per Cookie/Cracker, Unless Indicated **C** **F** **Cb**

Nabisco:

Cookies:

100 Calorie Packs:

	C	F	Cb
Cookie Crisps, Lorna Doone, Shortbread, 0.7 oz	100	3	16
Thin Crisps, Chips A'hoy, Baked, 0.75 oz	100	3	18

Chips Ahoy!, Chocolate Chip:

Original, 1.1 oz	160	8	22
1.4 oz	190	9	27
Mini Choc. Chips: Go-Pak (14)	150	7	21
Snak Saks (5)	150	7	21
Chewy, 1.1 oz	140	6	21
Chewy Gooey Caramel, (2), 1 oz	140	5	21
Chunky, Choc. Chunk (1), 0.5 oz	80	4	10
Ginger Snaps, (4)	120	2.5	23

Honey Maid:

Grahamfuls, av. all varieties, 1 oz	115	5	17
Grahams: Original (8)	130	3.5	24
Low-Fat (8), av., 1.25 oz	140	2	28
Chocolate, 1.25 oz	140	3.5	27
Honey (8), 1. oz	130	3	24
Mini S'Mores, 1 oz	140	6	21
Mallomars, 1 oz	120	5	18

Newtons: Original Fig (2), 1 oz | 110 | 2 | 22 |
(4), 2.2 oz	220	4	44
Fat-Free (2), 1 oz	90	0	22
100% Whole Grain (2), 1 oz	110	2	22
Strawberry, (2), 1 oz	100	1.5	21
Fruit Thins, (3), av. all var., 1 oz	140	5	21

Nilla Wafers: (8), 1 oz | 140 | 6 | 21 |
| Reduced-Fat (8), 1 oz | 120 | 2 | 24 |

Nutter Butter:

P'nut Butter Sandwich:
16 oz package, (2), 1 oz	130	5	20
1.9 oz package	250	10	37
Bites			
Big Bag, 3 oz pkg	420	18	63
Go-Paks!, 1 oz	140	6	21

Per Cookie/Cracker, Unless Indicated **C** **F** **Cb**

Nabisco (Cont):

Oreo Chocolate Sandwich Cookies:

Chocolate Creme Filling (2)	150	7	21
Cool Mint Filling (1), 1 z	140	7	20
White Cream Filling:			
3 cookies, 1.2 oz	160	7	25
6 cookies, 2 oz	270	11	41
Choc. White Fudge Covered, 3 cookies, 0.7 oz	100	5	13
Double Stuf (2), 1 oz	140	7	21
Mini Bite, Single Serve, 1.25 oz	170	7	25

Oreo Fudge Cremes: Choc., 1.25 oz | 170 | 9 | 24 |
| Golden, 1.25 oz | 180 | 9 | 25 |
| Peanut Butter, 1.25 oz | 170 | 9 | 23 |

Oreo Golden Sandwich Cookies:
Chocolate Creme Filling, 1.2 oz	170	7	24
White Creme filling: (3), 1.2 oz	170	7	25
1.8 oz Cookie	250	10	37
Double Stuf (2), 1 oz	150	7	21

Snackwell's:
Creme Sandwich (2) 1 oz	110	3	20
Devil's Food Cake, Fat-Free, 0.5 oz	50	0	12
100 Cal. Packs, av. all var., 0.75 oz	100	4.5	17

Teddy Grahams: Choc.; Cinn., 0.8 oz | 90 | 3 | 15 |
| Average other varieties, 1 oz | 130 | 4 | 23 |
| Multipack, Choc/Honey/Cinn., 1 oz | 120 | 4 | 21 |

Crackers:

Barnum's Animals: (8), 1 oz | 120 | 3.5 | 24 |
| Snack Saks (17), 1 oz | 140 | 4 | 24 |

Premium:
Original (5), ½ oz	70	1.5	12
Minis, ½ oz	70	2	11
Saltine: Original (5), 0.5 oz	70	1.5	12
Unsalted Tops (5), 0.5 oz	70	1.5	13

Triscuit:
Original (15), 1 oz	120	4	20
Reduced Fat, 1 oz	120	2.5	23
Brown Rice, av. all var	130	4.5	21
Thin Crisps, all varieties, 1 oz	140	5	22

Wheat Thins:
Original (16), 1 oz	140	5	22
Multigrain (15)	140	4.5	22
Av. other var., (16), 1 oz	140	5	22
Flatbread, av. all varieties, (2), 0.5 oz	60	1.5	12

Wheatsworth,
| Stone Ground Wheat (5) | 80 | 3.5 | 10 |

Per Cookie/Cracker, Unless Indicated	C	F	Cb
Newman's Own Organics:			
Alphabet, average all, (10)	120	3	21
Chocolate Cups:			
Milk/Dark: Caramel, average, (3)	160	9	21
Peanut Butter, average, (3)	180	13	17
Dark Chocolate Peppermint (3)	190	11	18
Fig Newman's: Fat-Free, 2 bars	100	0	24
Low-Fat, 2 bars	110	1.5	23
Wheat/Dairy-Free, 2 bars	120	1.5	26
Newman-O's: Original (2)	130	5	19
Chocolate Creme; Mint Creme (2)	120	5	19
Ginger-O's (2)	130	4.5	20
Nonni's:			
Biscotti:			
Original; Decadence (1), av.	95	4	15
Average other varieties (1), 0.8 oz	110	4	17
Bites: Classic Almond (4)	130	6	17
Almond Dark Chocolate (3)	120	6	16
Caramel Milk Chocolate (3)	110	4	18
Oreo Cookies ~ See Nabisco, Page 85			
Payaso:			
Animalitos, ¼ cup, 1 oz	110	2.5	19
Duplex Cremes , (3), 1.1 oz	140	6	21
Marias, (8), 1 oz	120	2.5	22
Esponijitas, Mallows (3), 1 oz	130	2	24
Pepperidge Farm:			
Cookies:			
American Collection: *Per Cookie Unless Indicated*			
Chesapeake, Dark Chocolate Pecan	130	6	17
Lexington, Milk Chocolate, Toffee Almond	130	7	17
Nantucket: Dark Chocolate Double	130	6	18
Sausalito, Milk Chocolate	140	7	17
Tahoe, White Choc. Macadamia	130	6	17
Brussels, (3)	150	7	20
Favorites, Chocolate (2)	130	5	16
Geneva, (3)	160	9	19
Milano: Original; Milk Choc, av., (3)	175	10	21
Double Chocolate (2)	140	8	17
Orange; Raspb. (2), av.	135	8	16
Melts (2), all varieties	140	7	18
Slices (3), av. all varieties	150	8	18
Pirouettes, (2), av. all var.	120	5	19
Tahiti, Coconut (3)	170	10	19
100 Calorie Pouches, average all varieties, 1 pouch	100	4.5	12

Per Cookie/Cracker, Unless Indicated	C	F	Cb
Pepperidge Farm (Cont):			
Crackers:			
Baked Naturals:			
Four Cheese Crisps (20)	140	6	19
Cracker Chips (27), all varieties	135	4.5	23
Pretzel Thins (1)	110	0	24
Golden Butter (4)	70	2	10
Goldfish: Crackers (55), 1 oz	140	5	20
Grahams (35)	140	5	22
Puffs (41)	140	6	20
Harvest Wheat (4)	100	4	14
Jingos! (23), average all varieties	135	4	22
Toasted Wheat Crisps (17)	140	5	21
Ritz:			
Crackers:			
Cheddar; Sour Cream & Onion, 1 oz	140	6	19
Average other varieties, 1 oz	80	4	10
Single Serve:			
With Peanut Butter, 1.3 oz pkg	200	11	21
With Real Cheese, 1.3 oz pkg	200	12	21
Crackerfuls: Regular varieties, 1 oz	135	7	17
Big Stuf Extreme, Peanut Butter, 1.3 oz	180	9	20
Ritz Bits, Cracker Sandwiches:			
Cheese: Single Serve, 1.5 oz	220	1	25
Go-Pak (13), 1 oz	160	9	18
Kickin' Cheddar (1), 1 oz	150	8	17
P'nut Butter: 1 oz	160	8	17
Single Serve, 1.5 oz	200	11	21
Big Bag (12), 1 oz	140	8	16
Toasted Chips, Wstn Ridge Peppercorn Ranch, 1 oz	130	5	19
Safeway Select:			
Cookies:			
Homestyle, Oatmeal Raisin, 1 oz	130	6	18
Indulgent: Double Choc Chunk, 1 oz	130	7	18
Milk Chocolate Macadamia Nut, 1 oz	140	8	17
Gourmet Sandwich Cremes:			
Maple Creme (2), 1 oz	170	7	25
Raspberry Swirl (2), 1 oz	130	5	20
Strawberry Swirl (2), 1 oz	130	6	19
Sedano's:			
Cinnamon, 5 cookies	160	6	24
Marias, 5 cookies, 1 oz	120	3	22
Shar Gluten Free ~ See CalorieKing.com			

Cookies & Crackers ~ Brands (Cont)

Per Cookie/Cracker, Unless Indicated **C** **F** **Cb**

Special K: *Per 1 oz Serving*

	C	F	Cb
Crackers, Multigrain (24), 1 oz	120	3	23
Cracker Chips, av. all varieties	110	2.5	22
Popcorn Chips, av. all varieties	120	2.5	23

Stella D'Oro:
Cookies:

	C	F	Cb
Biscotti, av. all varieties, 0.75 oz	100	4.5	13
Breakfast Treats, average all	90	3	15
Margherite: Chocolate (2)	130	6	19
Vanilla (2)	120	4	20
Roman Egg Biscuits, 1 oz	130	4.5	19
Swiss Fudge (3)	180	9	22

Toast & Sponge:

	C	F	Cb
Almond Toast (2)	100	2	20
Anisette Sponge (3)	90	1	18
Anisette Toast (3), 1 oz	130	1	27

Streit's:
Cookies:
Flavored Wafers:

	C	F	Cb
Chocolate (3)	160	9	19
Lemon (3)	170	10	19
Rolls, Chocolate Cream filled (3)	105	6	12

Sunshine:
Crackers:
Cheez-It Snack: Original: (27), 1 oz

	C	F	Cb
Cheez-It Snack: Original: (27), 1 oz	150	8	17
1.25 oz bag	180	9	20
Colby, 0.75 pouch	110	6	12
Average other varieties (25), 1 oz	145	8	18
Big: Original, 1.25 oz package	180	9	20
Monterey Jack (14), 1 oz	150	8	17
Reduced Fat: Original (29), 1 oz	130	4.5	18
White Cheddar (25), 1 oz	130	4	22

Trader Joe's:
Cookies:

	C	F	Cb
100 Calorie Packs, average	100	2.5	18
Almond Windmill (2), 1 oz	140	6	18
Charmingly Chewy Choc Chip (2), 1 oz	130	5	20
Cherry Granola (2), 1 oz	110	4	18
Chocolate Chip: Small (4), 1 oz	140	7	18
Large, singles, 1.7 oz	280	14	35
Vegan (1), 1 oz	130	6	18
Caramel Cashew (3), 1 oz	140	7	16
Crispy Crunchy Choc Chip (12)	150	9	19
Crispy Oatmeal Choc Chip (12)	150	7	19
Dark Choc Chunks with almonds (3)	140	7	17
Dunkers: Choc. Chip (2), 1.2 oz	160	7	17
Choc. Coated Choc. Chip (2), 1.3 oz	190	9	25

Per Cookie/Cracker, Unless Indicated **C** **F** **Cb**

Trader Joe's (Cont):
Cookies:

	C	F	Cb
Ginger Snaps, Gluten Free, (5), 1 oz	140	6	21
Highbrow Chocolate (2)	140	7	17
Joe Joe's S'wich Cremes, Chocolate/ Vanilla (2), 1 oz	130	6	19
Macarons A La Parisienne (2)	90	3	10
Meringues, Vanilla (4)	110	0	27
Oatmeal Raisin, 1.8 oz	270	12	35
Pecan Southern Style (4), 1 oz	150	9	15
Thins: Meyer Lemon (9), 1 oz	130	4.5	22
Toasted Coconut (8)	130	4.5	22
Triple Ginger (9), 1 oz	130	4	23
Triple Choc Chunk, 1 oz	140	7	20
Ultimate Vanilla Wafers (5), 1 oz	120	6	15
Way More Chocolate Chip (3)	160	11	14
Crackers, Water (4)	60	1	12

Triscuits ~ *See Page 85*

Voortman:
Cookies:

	C	F	Cb
Classics: Almond Krunch (2), 1 oz	140	6	20
Chunky Chip (1), 0.75 oz	100	4.5	14
Wafers, all varieties (3), 1 oz	140	6	20
Sugar Free: Chocolate Chip (1), 0.7 oz	80	5	13
Peanut Butter Wafer (4), 1 oz	150	7	17
Contains 6g of Sugar Alcohols			

Whole Foods (365 Organic):
Cookies:

	C	F	Cb
Choc Chip (2), 1 oz	150	7	21
Classic Fig Bars (2), 1.3 oz	140	2.5	27
Lemon Wafers (7), 1 oz	110	3	19
Oatmeal (2), 1 oz	130	4.5	20
S'wich Cremes; Sugar (2), average	130	5	20

WhoNu?:
Cookies:

	C	F	Cb
Choc. S'wich; Crsply Choc. Chip (3)	155	7	23
Crispy, Chocolate Chip (3)	160	7	22
Vanilla Wafers (8), 1 oz	130	5	20

Cookie ~ Mixes

Prepared as Directed **C** **F** **Cb**

Betty Crocker:
Pouch Mix: *Per 2 Cookies*

	C	F	Cb
Double Choc. Chunk; P'nut Butter, av.	140	6	21
Walnut Chocolate Chip	170	9	20
Average other varieties	145	6	22
Duncan Hines, Chocolate Chip, 2 cookies, 1 oz	180	9	23
Pillsbury, (2) average all varieties	110	2	23

Thaw, Bake & Serve | C | F | Cb

Per Cookie/Cracker Unless Indicated

Pillsbury Cookies:

Refrigerated Cookie Dough: *Per Cookie*

	C	F	Cb
Chocolate Chip Cookie	130	6	18
Peanut Butter	120	5	17
Sugar: Regular	120	5	18
Peppermint, 0.77 oz	100	4.5	14

Ready To Bake:

	C	F	Cb
Chocolate Chip (2)	170	8	23
Chocolate Chunk & Chip (2)	170	8	23
Holiday Cookies, Sugar, av. all varieties, (2)	120	6	15
Sugar Cookie (2)	170	8	22

Big Deluxe Classics: *Per Cookie*

	C	F	Cb
Chocolate Chip	170	8	23
Oatmeal Raisin	150	6	24
Peanut Butter Cup	160	7	22
White Chunk Macadamia Nut	170	9	22
Simply Cookies: Chocolate Chip	150	7	20
Peanut Butter	140	6	19

Refrigerated Sweet Buns/Rolls~ *See Page 67*

Toll House (Nestle): *Per Cookie Unless Indicated*

Refrigerated Dough Bars:

	C	F	Cb
Chocolate Chip	90	4	11
Mini Choc. Chip (3)	160	8	20
Oatmeal Raisin (2)	160	6	24
P'B Chocolate Chip	80	4.5	10
Sugar Cookie	160	7	23

Ultimates Refrigerated Dough: *Per Cookie*

	C	F	Cb
Chocolate Chip Lovers	180	9	23
Chocolate Pecan Deluxe	190	10	22
Choc. P'nut Butter Deluxe	180	9	23
Dark Chocolate Delight	160	8	21
Pecan Turtle Delight	160	7	23

Crispbreads | C | F | Cb

Per Crispbread Unless Indicated

Finn Crisp:

	C	F	Cb
Classic: Traditional Rye	40	0.5	7
Hi-Fibre	40	0.5	6.5
Round: Original	45	0.5	7.5
Sesame	50	1	8
Thin Crisps, Original	20	0	4

Kavli Norwegian:

	C	F	Cb
Crispy Thin (3)	60	0	13
Golden Rye (2)	60	0.5	12
Hearty Thick (2)	60	0	12
Malsovit, Meal Wafers	75	4	7

New York Flatbread Crisps,

	C	F	Cb
Everything, 0.4 oz	50	1.5	7
Ry-Krisp: Natural (2)	50	0	11
Seasoned (2)	60	1	11
Sesame (2)	60	1.5	10

Ryvita:

	C	F	Cb
Crackerbreads, Original; Wholegrain	20	0	4
Crispbreads, Original; Dark	35	0	6.5

WASA:

	C	F	Cb
Crisp'n Light 7 Grain (3)	60	0	13
Fiber, 0.35 oz	35	0.5	8
Hearty; Multi Grain, 0.5 oz	45	0	11
Light Rye (2), 0.5 oz	60	0	14
Whole Wheat, 0.5 oz	50	1	10

Matzos

Manischewitz:

	C	F	Cb
Matzos: Egg 'n Onion, 1 oz	80	0.5	17
Thin Salted/Tea,av., 0.9 oz	95	0	20
Whole Wheat, 1 oz	110	1	21
Yolk Free, 1.2 oz	100	0	20

Crackers:

	C	F	Cb
Tam Tam: Original (10), 1 oz	110	4	16
Everything; Onion (10), 1 oz	140	5	19
Sesame (10), 1 oz	140	6	19

Streit's:

	C	F	Cb
Mediterranean Matzos, 1 Matzo, 1 oz	90	0.5	18
Unsalted Matzos, 1 Matzo, 1 oz	100	0	23

Quick Guide   C F Cb

Cream
Average All Brands

Half & Half Cream:

	C	F	Cb
1 Tbsp, ½ oz	20	1.5	0.5
2 Tbsp, 1 oz	40	3	1
¼ cup, 2 oz	80	6	2

Light: Coffee/table (20% fat): 1 Tbsp 30 | 3 | 0.5

	C	F	Cb
Light: Coffee/table (20% fat): 1 Tbsp	30	3	0.5
2 Tbsp, 1 oz	60	6	0.5

Sour Cream:

	C	F	Cb
Regular: 1 Tbsp, ½ oz	25	2.5	1
1 cup, 8 oz	445	45	7
Low-Fat/Light: 1 Tbsp, ½ oz	20	1.5	1
2 Tbsp, 1 oz	40	3	2
Fat-Free: Av., 2 Tbsp, 1 oz	20	0	4.5
Hood, 2 Tbsp, 1 oz	25	0	4
Knudsen, 2 Tbsp, 1 oz	30	0	5
Kroger, 2 Tbsp, 1 oz	20	0	3
Naturally Yours; Oak Farm, 2 Tbsp	20	0	3

Sour Cream Substitute:

	C	F	Cb
Albertson's, 2 Tbsp, 1 oz	60	5	4
Tofutti, Sour Supreme, 2 Tbsp, 1 oz	85	5	4

Whipping Cream:

	C	F	Cb
Heavy, (37% fat):			
1 Tbsp fluid/2 Tbsp whipped	50	5.5	0.5
¼ cup whipped	105	11	1
½ cup fluid/1 cup whipped	410	44	3.5
Light, (30% fat):			
1 Tbsp fluid/2 Tbsp whipped	45	4.5	0.5
½ cup fluid/1 cup whipped	350	37	3.5

Coconut Cream/Milk

Coconut Cream, (Canned):

	C	F	Cb
Plain/unsweetened: 2 Tbsp, 1 oz	75	6.5	3
½ cup, 4 oz	285	26	12
Sweetened:			
Coco Lopez: 1 oz	130	5	21
½ cup, 4 oz	520	20	84
Coconut Milk: (Canned):			
Thai Kitchen: Lite, ⅓ cup, 2 fl.oz	50	4.5	1
Premium/Organic, 2 fl.oz	115	10	4
Unsweetened, ⅓ cup	140	14	3
Coconut Water, (Center), 1 cup	45	0.5	9

Whipped Toppings   C F Cb
Average All Brands

	C	F	Cb
Cream (Pressurized): 2 Tbsp	20	1.5	1
¼ cup	40	3.5	2
Cream Topping, Lite, 2 Tbsp	20	1	3
Kraft:			
Cool Whip: Regular, Original, ⅓ oz	25	1.5	2
Extra Creamy, 2 Tbsp	25	2	2
Lite, 2 Tbsp, ¼ oz	20	1	3
Free, 2 Tbsp, 0.32 oz	15	0	3
Chocolate; Vanilla, 0.65 oz	60	3.5	8
Dream Whip, 2 Tbsp	10	0	2
Reddi wip:			
Original, 2 Tbsp, 0.28 oz	15	1	1
Extra Creamy, 2 Tbsp, 0.28 oz	15	1	1
Fat-Free, 2 Tbsp, 0.28 oz	5	0	1
Chocolate, 2 Tbsp, 0.28 oz	15	1	1

Creamers (Non-Dairy)

Powder:
Coffee-Mate/Cremora/N-Rich:

	C	F	Cb
Original: Unsweetened, 1 tsp	10	0.5	1
1 heaping tsp	25	2	2
Lite, 1 tsp	10	0	2
Sweetened, 4 tsp	60	2.5	9
Flavors: Av., 4 tsp	60	3	9
Fat-Free, average, 4 tsp	50	0	11

Liquid/Refrigerated:
Per Tablespoon

	C	F	Cb
Bailey's: All flavors, average	35	1.5	5
Fat Free, all flavors	25	0	5
Coffee-Mate: *Per Tablespoon*			
Flavors: Average all	35	1.5	5
Fat-free, all flavors	25	0	5
Sugar free, all flavors	15	1	2
Unflavored: Original	20	1	2
Fat-Free	10	0	1
Low-Fat	10	0.5	1
Natural Bliss: All flavors	35	1.5	5
Vanilla, Low-fat	20	1	3
Hood, Country Creamer, 1 Tbsp	20	1.5	2
International Delight: *Per Tbsp*			
American/Classic/Coffee House:			
Regular, all flavors	35	1.5	6
Fat-free, all flavors	30	0	7
Kroger: *Per Tbsp*			
Coffee Creamers: Original	20	1	3
Caramel Vanilla; Hazelnut	35	1.5	6
Fat-free, Hazelnut	30	0	6
Silk: Original	15	1	1
French Van.; Hazelnut	20	1	3

Ready-To-Serve

	C	F	Cb
Hunt's:			
Snack Pack Puddings: *Per 3.25oz Cup*			
Regular: Chocolate; Butterscotch, av.	115	3	21
Chocolate Fudge	120	3	21
Tapioca	110	2.5	20
Vanilla	100	2.5	20
Fat Free: Chocolate	90	0	20
Tapioca	80	0	19
Sugar Free: Chocolate	70	3	14
Caramel; Vanilla	60	3	10
Fruit Blasts: Lemon Pudding	120	2.5	24
Juicy Gels: Regular, all flavors	100	0	24
Sugar Free, Cherry	10	0	2
Jell-O *(Kraft):*			
Ready To Eat Puddings:			
Banana Split, 3.9 oz	110	2	21
Butterscotch, 3.9 oz	110	1.5	23
Cinnamon Rice, 3.65 oz	110	3	21
Vanilla Rice, 3.65 oz	110	3	20
Kozy Shack:			
Puddings:			
Bread, av. all flavors, 3.5 oz	145	2.5	26
Butterscotch, 4 oz	120	2	23
Chocolate, ½ cup, 4.6 oz	140	2.5	27
Rice:			
Original, ½ cup	130	2.5	24
Cinnamon Raisin, ½ c.	150	2.5	28
European Style, ½ cup	140	2.5	24
No Sugar Added:			
Chocolate, 4 oz	70	1	13
Rice; Tapioca, 4 oz	70	1	14
Flan, Creme Caramel, 1 cup, 4 oz	140	3	27
Lactose Free: *Per 4 oz Cup*			
Chocolate	130	3.5	22
Rice; Tapioca	120	3	20
Kroger: *Per Container*			
Puddings: Butterscotch,	110	2	22
Chocolate, 3.5 oz	110	2.5	21
Swiss Miss:			
Puddings: *Per 4 oz Cup*			
Classic Butterscotch	130	3.5	22
Creamy : Milk Chocolate	150	3.5	27
Vanilla	140	3.5	24
Old Fashioned Tapioca	140	3.5	24
Sugar Free: Chocolate	70	3.5	15
Vanilla	60	3	11

Homemade Puddings

	C	F	Cb
Apple Tapioca, ½ cup	150	0	32
Bread Pudding, ½ cup	250	8	40
Blancmange, ½ cup	140	5	19
Chocolate, ½ cup	190	6	30
Crème Brûlée, ½ cup	400	35	16
Plum Pudding, 2 oz	170	3	32
Rice w/ Raisins, ½ cup	200	4	38
Sponge Pudding, 3.5 oz	340	16	45
Tapioca Cream, ½ cup	110	4	15
Trifle, ½ cup	180	7	26

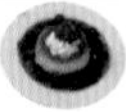

Custards

	C	F	Cb
Custard Mix *(Jello/Royal Flan),* average:			
Dry, ¼ of 2.9 oz package, 0.73 oz	80	0	19
Prepared: Whole milk, ½ cup	155	4	25
2% milk, ½ cup	140	2.5	25
Non-Fat milk, ½ cup	125	0	25
Home Made Egg Custard:			
With Whole Milk, ½ cup	170	8	18
With 2% Milk, ½ cup	155	6.5	18

Gelatin • Parfait • Jell-O

	C	F	Cb
Prepared As Directed			
Jell-O:			
No Bake: Oreo, ⅑ package	370	17	51
Peanut Butter Cup, ⅛ package	360	21	42
Cheesecake: Real, ⅛ package	360	21	42
Strawberry, ⅑ package	290	10	48
Flan, Spanish Style Custard			
with Caramel Sauce, ¼ package	140	3.5	27
Gelatin Dessert Mix: All flav., ¼ pkg	80	0	19
Sugar free, all flavors, ⅛ package	10	0	2
Pudding & Pie Filling: *Prepared As Directed*			
Cook & Serve: Choc. Fudge, ⅙ pkg	150	2.5	27
Banana Crm/Vanilla, ⅙ pkg	140	2.5	27
Sugar & Fat-Free, all flav., ⅙ pkg	70	0	12
Instant Mix:			
Banana Cream, ¼ pkg	150	2.5	30
Butterstotch, ¼ pkg	160	2.5	30
Oreo, ¼ package	180	3.5	33
White Chocolate, ¼ pkg	150	2.5	30
Sugar free, all flavors, ¼ pkg	70	0	12
Ida Mae, Strawberry Parfait	90	2	18
Reser's, Parfaits, av. all flav. 3.88 oz	100	2	19

Meringues

	C	F	Cb
Meringue Swirl, ½ oz	50	0	8
Meringue Shell, 1 oz shell	100	0	16

Chicken Eggs

	C	**F**	**Cb**
Fresh Eggs:			
Raw:			
Small	55	4	0
Medium	65	4	0
Large	70	5	0
Extra Large	80	5.5	0
Jumbo	90	6	0
Egg Yolk, 1 extra large	55	4.5	0
Egg White, 1 extra large	17	0	0
Dried Egg Powder:			
Whole Egg: ¼ cup, 1 oz	170	12	0
1 Tbsp	30	2	0
Egg White, ¼ cup, 1 oz	105	0	0
Egg Yolk, ¼ cup, 1 oz	195	18	0

Egg Substitutes

¼ Cup (Equivalent to 1 Egg) ~ Zero Cholesterol

	C	**F**	**Cb**
All Whites (Crystal Farms), 1.6 oz	25	0	0
Better 'n Eggs (Crystal Farms):			
Regular, ¼ cup, 2 oz	30	0	1
Plus, ¼ cup, 2 oz	35	0	1
Egg Beaters (ConAgra):			
Original, 3 Tbsp, 1.6 oz	25	0	1
Southwestern Style, 3 Tbsp, 1.6 oz	20	0	1
Egg Replacer (Ener-g), 1.5 tsp,	15	0	4
Eggs (Second Nature),			
Egg Whites, Fat-Free,			
¼ cup, 2 fl.oz	35	0	0.5
Egg Substitute (Albertson's), ¼ cup	30	0	1
Naturegg (Burnbrae Farms),			
Simply Egg White, ¼ cup, 2 oz	30	0	1

Other Eggs

	C	**F**	**Cb**
Duck, 1 large, 2.5 oz	130	9.5	0
Goose, 1 large, 5 oz	280	19	0
Quail, 3 eggs, 1 oz	42	3	0
Turkey, 1 large, 3 oz	135	9.5	0
Turtle, 1 egg, 1.75 oz	75	5	0

Omega-3 Fat Enriched

	C	**F**	**Cb**
Eggland's Best, 1 large	70	4	0
Horizon Organic, 1 large	70	4.5	0

Note: Cholesterol content same as regular eggs, but Omega-3 fats inhibit blood cholesterol increase.

Updated Nutrition Data ~ www.CalorieKing.com
Persons with Diabetes ~ See Disclaimer (Page 22)

Cooked Eggs

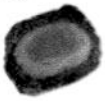

	C	**F**	**Cb**
Boiled Egg: *Same as Raw Egg*			
Hard-Cooked, Small, Peeled	65	4	0
Fried Egg:			
With fat: 1 large egg	105	9	0.5
2 small eggs	175	13	1
No fat/nonstick pan, 1 large	75	5	0.5
Deviled Egg, 2 halves	145	13	0.5
Eggs Benedict, (2),			
on Toast or English Muffin	860	56	25
Eggs Florentine, (2),			
on Toast or English Muffin	890	59	25
Pickled Egg, 1 large	80	5.5	0
Poached Egg, 1 large	65	4	0
Quiche (Homemade):			
Egg & Bacon, 1 slice, 5.3 oz	580	43	27
Ham & Cheese, 1 slice, 5.3 oz	475	33	29
Scotch Egg, 1 egg	300	21	16
Scrambled Eggs:			
1 large egg:			
With 1 Tbsp milk + 1 tsp fat	120	9	1
With 1 Tbsp skim milk/no fat	85	5.5	1
2 large eggs:			
With 2 Tbsp milk + 2 tsp fat	260	20	2
With 2 Tbsp skim milk, w/o fat	180	11	2

Omelets

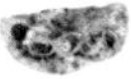

	C	**F**	**Cb**
1 Egg:			
Plain (with 1 tsp fat)	125	10	0.5
With: ½ oz cheese	175	15	0.5
½ oz cheese + ½ oz ham	200	16	0.5
2 Eggs:			
Plain (with 2 tsp fat)	250	20	1
With: 1 oz cheese	360	29	2
1 oz cheese + 1 oz ham	410	32	2
3 Eggs:			
Plain (with 1 Tbsp fat)	360	29	1.5
With: 2 oz cheese	580	47	2.5
2 oz cheese + 2 oz ham	680	53	2.5
Extras, Tomato/Onion/Veggies, 2 oz	20	0	4.5
Egg Substitute (EggBeaters):			
2 eggs (½ cup) + 1 tsp fat	100	4	2
3 eggs (¾ cup) + 2 tsp fat	160	8	3
Extras: 1 oz Cheese	110	9	1
1 oz Ham	50	3	1

Egg Nog

	C	**F**	**Cb**
Average all Brands,			
½ cup, 4 oz	170	9.5	17
Borden, Regular, 4 fl.oz	160	8	18
Hood, Golden, ½ cup, 4 fl.oz	180	9	22
Horizon/Hood, Light/Low-Fat,	140	4	22

Breakfast Sides

	C	F	Cb
Toast:			
Plain, 1 thick slice	85	1	13
With: 2 tsp butter/marg.	155	9	13
3 tsp/1 Tbsp fat	190	13	13
English Muffin:			
Plain, 2 oz	130	1	26
With 3 tsp fat	230	12	26
Bacon, 2 strips	70	5	0
Ham, lean, 2 oz	100	3	0
Hash Browns:			
½ cup, 3 oz	125	6.5	14
1 cup serving, 6 oz	250	13	28
Sausages, 2 oz link	180	16	1.5

Frozen Egg Breakfasts

	C	F	Cb
Aunt Jemima:			
Breakfast Sandwiches: *Per Sandwich*			
Croissant, Sausage, Egg & Cheese	350	23	23
Griddlecake, Ham, Egg & Cheese	240	8	33
Jimmy Dean:			
Breakfast Sandwiches: *Per Sandwich*			
Biscuit, Bacon, Egg & Cheese	310	19	26
Croissant, Sausage, Egg & Cheese	410	28	27
Muffin, Sausage, Egg & Cheese	350	21	26
Omelets: *Per Omelet*			
Three Cheese	290	23	4
Ham & Cheese	250	19	4
Pillsbury,			
Egg Scrambles, Bacon & Veggies	290	15	22
Red Baron:			
Scrambles: *Each*			
Bacon, 5 oz	390	19	38
Sausage; Western, 5 oz	360	17	38
Frozen Pancake/Waffles ~ *See Page 132*			
Toaster Pastries ~ *See Page 64*			

Frozen Egg Rolls

	C	F	Cb
Kahiki: *Each, Without Sauce*			
Chicken, 3.25 oz	140	2.5	24
Pork, 3.25 oz	160	4.5	24
Vegetable, 3.25 oz	130	2	24
Lotus: Chicken; Pork (1)	160	7	25
Vegetarian (1), 3 oz	120	4.5	21
Pagoda Express: *Without Sauce*			
Chicken (1)	140	4.5	20
Pork (1)	180	9	19
Pork & shrimp (1)	170	7	19
Vegetable (1)	130	4.5	20
Trader Joes,			
Vegetable (1), 3 oz	110	4	16

Fast-Foods/Restaurants

	C	F	Cb
Arby's,			
Bacon, Egg & Cheese Croissant	400	26	25
Au Bon Pain, Egg on a Bagel	430	12	58
Bob Evans:			
Omelets: Border Scramble	630	45	15
Ham & Cheddar	485	35	4
Western	495	35	7
Bojangles: Egg & Cheese Biscuit	515	34	35
Bacon, Egg & Cheese Biscuit	550	37	35
Bruegger's:			
Bagels: With Egg & Cheese, 6.8 oz	430	18	63
With Egg, Chse & Sausage, 8.8 oz	500	24	64
Burger King:			
Breakfast Burritos: Sausage	290	17	21
Southwestern	580	35	42
Croissan'wich's:			
Bacon, Egg & Cheese	320	18	25
Ham, Egg & Cheese	310	15	26
Double, Sausage, Egg & Dble Chse	660	48	27
Carl's Jr:			
Burritos: Bacon & Egg	570	34	38
Big Country	710	43	55
Loaded Breakfast	770	48	53
Steak & Egg	640	36	43
Chick-fil-A, Chicken, Egg & Cheese,			
on Sunflower Multigrain Bagel	480	20	48
Del Taco, Egg & Cheese Burrito	400	17	38
Denny's: *With Hashbrowns, Without Bread*			
Omelette:			
Ultimate	870	63	37
Veggie-Cheese	650	44	37
Dunkin Donuts:			
Bacon, Egg & Cheese Croissant	480	27	40
Ham, Egg & Cheese Bagel	440	8	67
Eat 'N Park:			
Omelettes:			
Ham & Cheese	535	35	5
Meat Lovers	725	55	4
Hardee's:			
Loaded Omelet Biscuit	490	28	40
Sausage & Egg Biscuit	560	37	39
IHOP: T-Bone Steak & Eggs, 12 oz	1300	73	73
Omelette, Spinach & Mushroom	1000	82	22
Jack in the Box:			
Biscuits: Bacon, Egg & Cheese	430	25	35
Sausage, Egg & Cheese	560	38	36
McDonald's:			
Biscuit, Bacon, Egg & Cheese, regular	460	26	38
Egg McMuffin	290	12	31
Whataburger, Breakfast Platter,			
with Bacon	640	41	34

Fats ◇ Spreads & Oils (F)

Quick Guide C F Cb

Butter

Average All Brands
Regular: 1 tsp, 0.18 oz — 35, 4, 0
1 Pat/Single Portion, 0.18 oz — 35, 4, 0
1 Tbsp, 0.5 oz — 100, 11, 0
2 Tbsp, 1 oz — 205, 23, 0
1 Stick, ½ cup, 4 oz — 810, 92, 0
1 Pound, 2 cups, 16 oz — 3255, 368, 0
Light: Regular, 40% Fat
1 tsp, 0.18 oz — 25, 3, 0
1 Tbsp,½ oz — 75, 8.5, 0
2 Tbsp, 1 oz — 145, 16, 0
Whipped Butter: Regular
1 tsp, 0.14 oz — 30, 3, 0
1 Tbsp, 0.35 oz — 65, 7.5, 0
1 Stick, ½ cup, 2.66 oz — 545, 62, 0
Whipped Light Butter (Land O Lakes):
1 tsp, 0.15 oz — 15, 1.5, 0
1 Tbsp, 0.4 oz — 45, 5, 0
2 Tbsp, 0.8 oz — 90, 10, 0
Unsalted ~ *Same as Salted*

Flavored Butter/Spreads

Average All Brands
Honey Butter, (60% Fat):
1 Tbsp, 0.5 oz — 90, 8, 4
Downey's, 2% Fat,
1 Tbsp, 0.5 oz — 60, 1, 11
Garlic Butter, (80% Fat):
1 Tbsp, 0.5 oz — 100, 11, 0
Sweet Cream Butter:
Land O Lakes: Reguar, 1 Tbsp — 100, 11, 0
Honey Butter Spread, 1 Tbsp — 70, 6, 4

Butter & Butter Blends

Per 1 Tablespoon
Challenge: Stick, 0.5 oz — 100, 11, 0
Tub, Whipped, 0.3 oz — 70, 7, 0
Brummel & Brown,
Butter Blended with Yogurt, ½ oz — 45, 5, 0
Land O'Lakes:
Sticks: Original, ½ oz — 100, 11, 0
Light, ½ oz — 50, 6, 0
Tubs: Butter With Olive Oil, ½ oz — 90, 10, 0
Light, Whipped, 0.4 oz — 45, 5, 0
Smart Balance:
Butter & Canola, 1 Tbsp — 100, 11, 0
Light Butter & Canola Oil — 50, 5, 0

Ghee (Clarified Butter) C F Cb

(Example: Purity Farms)
Note: Ghee is 100% fat compared to regular butter (80% fat + 20% water)
1 tsp, 0.18 oz — 45, 5, 0
1 Tbsp, ½oz — 120, 14, 0

Light & Reduced Fat Spreads

Per Tablespoon
bestlife, Buttery, 0.45 oz — 60, 6, 0
Benecol: Regular, 0.5 oz — 70, 8, 0
Light, ½ oz — 50, 5, 0
Blue Bonnet:
Stick, Light Spread, 0.5 oz — 50, 5, 1
Tub, Original Soft Spread, 0.5 oz — 60, 6, 0
Country Crock (Shedd's):
Tubs: Regular Spread, 0.5 oz — 70, 7, 0
Light Spread, 0.5 oz — 50, 5, 0
Churn Style, 0.5 oz — 60, 7, 0
Fleischmann's:
Original: Soft Spread, 0.4 oz — 60, 7, 0
Spread, 0.5 oz — 80, 9, 0
Light Spread, 0.5 oz — 40, 4.5, 0
I Can't Believe It's Not Butter!:
Tubs: Original Spread, 0.5 oz — 70, 8, 0
Light, 0.5 oz — 45, 5, 0
Olive Oil Spread, 1 Tbsp — 70, 8, 0
Parkay:
Original Spread, 0.4 oz — 70, 7, 0
Spray, 5 sprays — 0, 0, 0
Squeeze Bottle, 0.5 oz — 70, 8, 0
Promise:
Activ, Light Spread, 0.5 oz — 45, 5, 0
Buttery Spread, 0.5 oz — 80, 8, 0
Light Spread, 0.5 oz — 45, 5, 0
Smart Balance:
Tubs, Buttery Spread:
Original, 0.5 oz — 80, 9, 0
Light Original, 0.5 oz — 50, 5, 0
HeartRight, Light, 0.5 oz — 50, 5, 0
Omega 3: Reg., 0.45 oz — 80, 8, 0
Light, 0.5 oz — 50, 5, 0

Butter Substitutes

Butter Buds:
Butter Flavored Mix, 1 tsp — 5, 0, 2
Butter Flavored Sprinkles, 1 tsp — 5, 0, 2
Earth Balance,
Original, 1 Tbsp — 100, 11, 0
Molly McButter, 1 tsp — 5, 0, 0
Sunsweet, (Butter/Oil Replacement),
Lighter Bake, 1 Tbsp, 0.67 oz — 35, 0, 9

Animal Fats/Lards C F Cb

Average All Types
**Beef Tallow/Drippings, Lard (Pork),
Chicken, Duck, Goose, Turkey:**

1 Tbsp, 0.45 oz	115	13	0
2.25 Tbsp, 1 oz	255	28	0
1 cup, 7.25 oz	1850	205	0
½ pound, 8 oz	2040	227	0

Ghee/Butter/ Oil ~ *See Page 93*

Vegetable Shortening

Average All Types

1 Tbsp, 0.45 oz	115	13	0
2.25 Tbsp, 1 oz	250	28	0
1 cup, 7.25 oz	1810	205	0

Vegetable Oils

Includes almond, avocado, canola, corn, coconut, flaxseed, grapeseed, linseed, mustard, olive, palm, peanut, rice bran, safflower, sesame, sunflower, soybean, wheat germ. Note: Oil is 100% fat.

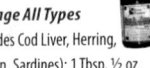

1 tsp, 0.17 oz	45	5	0
1 Tbsp, 0.5 oz	120	14	0
2 Tbsp, 1 oz	240	28	0
1 cup, 7.25 oz	1930	205	0

Fish Oils

Average All Types
(Includes Cod Liver, Herring, Salmon, Sardines): 1 Tbsp, ½ oz   125   14   0

Cooking Sprays/Squeezes

Cooking Sprays: (PAM, Mazola, I Can't Believe It's Not Butter, Weight Watchers, Wesson):
Pam: ¼ second spray   2   0   0
  1-3 second spray   6   1   0
I Can't Believe It's Not Butter,
  Original Spray   0   0   0
Parkay, Buttery Spray   0   0   0

Olestra (Olean) C F Cb

Olestra *(Olean)*   0   0   0
Note: Olean is Proctor & Gamble's brand name for Olestra – a no-calorie cooking oil that gives snacks (like potato chips, tortilla chips and crackers) taste and texture without adding fat or calories.

Examples:
• **Frito-Lay,** Light Products
  (Lays, Ruffles, Tostitos, Doritos)
• **Pringles,** Fat-Free Potato Crisps

Quick Guide

Mayonnaise:
Regular: *Per 1 Tbsp, 0.5 oz Unless Indicated*
Average All Brands   90   10   0
Best Foods; Hellman's; Kraft:
  Original/Real   90   10   0
  ½ cup, 4 oz   720   80   0
Hain, Safflower Mayonnaise   100   11   0
Spectrum, Canola Mayo   100   11   0
Light/Reduced Fat: *Per 1 Tbsp, 0.5 oz*
Best Foods/Hellman's   35   3.5   1
Kraft, Light//Olive Oil   35   3   2
Smart Balance, Omega   50   5   1
Spectrum, Light Canola Mayo,
  Eggless   35   3.5   1
Fat Free:
Kraft: Original, 1 Tbsp   10   0   2
  ½ cup, 4 oz   80   0   16
Sugar Free:
Dukes Mayo, 1 Tbsp   100   12   0
Mayonnaise Style Dressing:
Per 1 Tbsp, 0.5 oz
Best Foods, Sandwich Spread   60   5   2
Kraft:
  Miracle Whip Dressing:
    Original   40   3.5   2
    Light   20   1.5   2
    Fat Free   15   0   3
  Sandwich Shop Mayo:
    Chipotle   40   4   2
    Horseradish-Dijon   40   3.5   2
    Hot & Spicy   100   11   0
Nasoya, Egg & Dairy Free:
  Nayonaise: Regular/Whipped   40   3.5   1
    Light   20   1.5   1

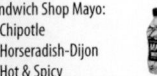

Quick Guide

Fresh Fish **C** **F** **Cb**

Low Oil: *Less than 2.5% fat*

White/Lightly-colored flesh. Examples:
Cod, Flounder, Haddock, Halibut, Mahi Mahi, Perch, Pike,
Pollock, Snapper, Sole, Whiting.

	C	F	Cb
Raw, without bones, 4 oz	100	1	0
Steamed, Broiled, Baked, 4 oz	140	1.5	0
Fried: Lightly Floured, 4 oz	210	8	3.5
Breaded, 4 oz	260	12	8
In Batter, 4 oz	320	16	27

Medium Oil: *2.5-5% fat*

Lightly-colored flesh. Examples: **C** **F** **Cb**
Bluefin Tuna, Catfish, Kingfish, Orange Roughy, Salmon
(Pink), Swordfish, Rainbow Trout, Yellowtail.

	C	F	Cb
Raw, without bones, 4 oz	145	7	0
Baked/Broiled, 4 oz	195	8	0
Fried, 4 oz	230	11	8

High Oil: *Over 5% fat* **C** **F** **Cb**

Darker-colored flesh. Examples:
Albacore Tuna, Mackerel,
Salmon (Atlantic/Chinook/Sockeye), Sardines, Trout.

	C	F	Cb
Raw, without bones, 4 oz	220	14	0
Baked, Broiled, 4 oz	275	17	0
Fried, 4 oz	340	23	12

Cooking Yields (Fin Fish):

4 oz Raw wt. = 3.5 oz Cooked weight
4 oz Cooked wt. = 5 oz Raw weight

Calorie & Fat Variations:

The amount of fat/oil in fish varies with the species, season
and locality. Within the same fish, fat/oil content is generally
higher towards the head.

Fish & Shellfish **C** **F** **Cb**

Edible Weights: (no bones/shell)

	C	F	Cb
Abalone: Raw, 3 oz	90	0.5	5
Fried, 3 oz	160	6	9.5
Ahi Tuna, grilled, 6 oz fillet (w/o fat)	235	2	0
Anchovy: Paste, 1 Tbsp, 0.5 oz	45	2	0
Canned in oil, drained, (5), 0.7 oz	40	2	0
Barracuda (Pacific), raw, 4 oz	130	3	0
Basa/Swai, raw, 4 oz fillet	70	2	0
Bass:			
Sea: Raw, 4.6 oz fillet	125	2.5	0
Baked, 3 oz	105	2	0
Striped: Raw, 1 fillet, 5.5 oz	150	3.5	0
Baked, 3 oz	105	3	0
Freshwater: Raw, 3 oz	95	3	0
Baked, 3 oz	125	4	0

Fish & Shellfish (Cont) **C** **F** **Cb**

Edible Weights: (no bones/shell)

	C	F	Cb
Calamari/Squid:			
Raw, 4 oz	100	1.5	3.5
Baked, 1 cup	190	6.5	5.5
Fried, 3 oz	150	6	7
Catfish:			
Farmed: Raw, 1 fillet 5.6 oz	190	9.5	0
Baked, 1 fillet 5 oz	205	10	0
Wild: Raw, 1 fillet, 5.6 oz	150	4.5	0
Baked, 1 fillet, 5 oz	150	4	0
Breaded, fried, 1 fillet, 3 oz	200	12	0
Caviar, black/red, 1 Tbsp, 16g	40	3	0.5
Clams: Raw (4 large/9 small), 3 oz	70	1	3
Breaded, Fried (20 small), 6.6 oz	380	21	20
Canned, drained, ½ cup, 2.8 oz	115	1	0
Steamed (10 small), 3.3 oz	140	2	5
Clam Juice *(Snow's)*, 1 Tbsp	0	0	0
Cod:			
Atlantic: Raw, 4 oz	95	1	0
Baked, 3 oz	90	1	0
Canned, solids & liquid	90	0.5	0
Pacific: Raw, 4 oz	80	0.5	0
Baked, 3 oz	70	0.5	0
Crab:			
Alaska King, 1 leg, cooked, 4.7 oz	130	2	0
Blue: Raw, 1 crab, 6 oz	150	1	0
Steamed, 3 oz	70	0.5	0
Canned, drained, 6.5 oz can	105	0.5	0
Dungeness: Raw, 1 crab, 5.75 oz	140	1.5	0
Steamed, 4.45 oz	140	1.5	0
Crab Cakes *(Capt. D's)*, (1), 2.8 oz	250	16	16
Crayfish:			
Farmed: Raw, 3 oz	60	1	0
Steamed, 3 oz	75	1	0
Wild: Raw 3 oz	65	1	0
Steamed, 3 oz	70	1	0
Cuttlefish, raw, 3 oz	70	1	1
Dolphinfish ~ *See Mahi-Mahi*			
Eel: Raw, 3 oz	155	10	0
Baked, 3 oz	200	13	0
Fish & Chips *(Red Lobster)*, battered, without condiments	630	26	54
Fish Sandwich *(Burger King)*, without Tartar Sauce	410	12	53
Fish Oil, 1 Tbsp, 0.5 oz	125	14	0
Flounder/Sole:			
Raw, 4 oz	80	2	0
Baked, 3 oz	75	2	0
Frozen Fish ~ *See Pages 114-122*			

Fish & Shellfish (Cont)	C	F	Cb
Edible Weights: Without Bones or Shell			
Haddock: Raw, 4 oz	85	0.5	0
Baked, 3 oz	75	0.5	0
Smoked, 3 oz	100	1	0
Halibut:			
Atlantic: Raw, 4 oz	105	1.5	0
Baked, ½ fillet, 5.6 oz	175	2.5	0
Herring:			
Atlantic, raw, 4 oz	180	10	0
Canned: Plain, drained, 3 oz	130	8	0
In Tomato Sauce, 3.5 oz	140	8	2
Pickled, 2 pieces, 1 oz	75	5	3
Smoked, kippered, 4 oz	245	14	0
Jellyfish: Raw, 4 oz	30	0	0
Dried, Salted, 1 cup, 2 oz	20	1	0
Ling, raw, 4 oz	100	0.5	0
Lobster, Northern:			
1.5 lb Whole Lobster, edible portion:			
Raw, 6.25 oz	140	1.5	0
Boiled, 5 oz	140	1	0
Lobster Salads, average, ½ cup	220	13	5
Lobster Newberg, average, ¾ cup	360	20	9
Lobster Thermidor, av., 1 serving	370	22	15
Lobster Tail,			
Red Lobster, grilled/roasted	170	1	1
Lox, Regular/Nova, 2 oz	65	2.5	0
Mackerel, Atlantic: Raw, 4 oz	230	16	0
Baked, 3 oz fillet	225	15	0
Pacific/Jack: Raw, 4 oz	180	9	0
Baked, 3 oz	170	9	0
Spanish: Raw, 4 oz	160	7	0
Baked, 3 oz	135	5.5	0
Mahi-Mahi/Dolphinfish:			
Raw, 4 oz	95	1	0
Baked, 4 oz	125	1	0
Monkfish: Raw, 4 oz	85	1.5	0
Baked, 3 oz	80	2	0
Mullet, Striped: Raw, 4 oz	135	4.5	0
Baked, 3 oz	130	4	0
Mussels:			
Raw: 4 oz (edible wt)	100	2.5	4
1 cup, 5.25 oz (edible weight)	130	3.5	5
Cooked, moist heat, 3 oz	150	4	6
Ocean Perch:			
Atlantic: Raw, 4 oz	90	2	0
Baked, 3 oz	80	1.5	0
Octopus:			
Common: Raw, 4 oz	95	1	2.5
Boiled, 3 oz	140	2	4
Orange Roughy:			
Raw, 4 oz	85	1	0
Baked, 3 oz	90	1	0

Fish & Shellfish (Cont)	C	F	Cb
Edible Weights: Without Bones or Shell			
Oysters, Common, Raw, 3 oz	70	2	4
Eastern:			
Farmed: Raw, 6 medium, 3 oz	50	1.5	4.5
Cooked, dry heat, 6 med., 2 oz	45	1.5	4.5
Wild: Raw, 6 medium, 3 oz	45	1.5	2.5
Cooked, dry heat, 6 med., 2 oz	45	1.5	2.5
Breaded & Fried, 6 med., 3 oz	175	11	10
Pacific: Raw, 1 medium, 1.75 oz	40	1	2.5
Steamed, 1 medium, 0.9 oz	40	1	2.5
Perch ~ *See Ocean Perch*			
Pike: Northern: Raw, 4 oz	100	1	0
Baked, 3 oz	95	1	0
Walleye: Raw, 4 oz	105	1.5	0
Baked, 3 oz	100	1.5	0
Pollock, Atlantic: Raw, 4 oz	105	1	0
Baked, 3 oz	100	1	0
Pompano, Florida, raw, 4 oz	185	11	0
Red Snapper ~ *See Snapper*			
Roe, raw, 2 Tbsp, 1 oz	40	2	0.5
Sablefish: Raw, 4 oz	220	17	0
Smoked, 3 oz	220	17	0
Salmon:			
Atlantic, Farmed: Raw, 4 oz	235	15	0
Baked, 3 oz	175	10	0
Steaks: Raw, 7 oz	410	27	0
Baked, 6 oz	365	22	0
Atlantic, Wild: Raw, 4 oz	160	7	0
Baked, 3 oz	155	7	0
Steaks: Raw, 7 oz	280	13	0
Baked, 6 oz	310	14	0
Chinook: Raw, 4 oz	205	12	0
Baked, 3 oz	195	11	0
Smoked, 3 oz,	100	3.5	0
King: Raw, 3.5 oz	185	12	0
Kippered, 3.5 oz piece	265	16	0
Smoked & canned, 3.5 oz	150	6	0
Coho:			
Farmed: Raw, 4 oz	180	8.5	0
Baked, 3 oz	150	7	0
Wild: Raw, 4 oz	165	6.5	0
Steamed, 3 oz	155	6.5	0
Pink/Chum: Raw, 4 oz	145	5	0
Baked, 3.5 oz	155	5.5	0
Canned: Drained solids, 11.1 oz	435	16	0
W/o skin & bones, 8.54 oz	330	10	0
Sockeye: Raw, 4 oz	160	6.5	0
Baked, 3 oz	145	5.5	0
Canned, Drained solids, 3 oz	140	6.5	0
Smoked, 3.5 oz	205	7.5	0
Salmon Cake (1), 3 oz	240	15	6

Fish & Shellfish (Cont)   C   F   Cb

	C	F	Cb
Sardines: *Canned, Average all Brands*			
Drained of Oil:			
¼ cup drained, 2.15 oz	130	9	0
3.75 oz can, drained, 3.25 oz	190	11	0
1 large/2 medium, ⅗", 0.8 oz	50	3	0
In Tomato Sauce, 3.75 oz	150	8	3
Sashimi ~ *See Japanese Foods, Page 171*			
Scallops: Raw, 6 lge/15 small, 3 oz	65	0.5	3
Breaded, Fried, 6 pieces, 5 oz	385	20	39
Steamed, 3 oz	95	0.5	0
Sea Bass ~ *See Bass*			
Seafood Salad, Deli Style,			
½ cup, 3.5 oz	250	21	11
Shark: Raw, 4 oz	145	5	0
Baked, 4 oz	185	7	0
Batter-dipped, fried, 4 oz	260	16	7
Shrimp:			
Raw: Small/Medium (4), 0.75 oz	15	0	0
Large (4), 1 oz	20	0	0
Breaded & Fried, 4.75 oz	395	24	27
Steamed, in shell, 3 oz	100	1.5	0
Canned, 1 can, 4.5 oz	130	2	0
Snapper: Raw, 4 oz	115	1.5	0
Baked: 3 oz	110	1.5	0
6 oz fillet	220	3	0
Sole: Raw, 4 oz	80	2	0
Baked, 3 oz	75	2	0
Squid ~ *see Calamari*			
Surimi, (Imitation Crab), 4 oz	110	0.5	17
Swai/Basa, raw, 4 oz	70	2	0
Swordfish: Raw, 4 oz	165	7.5	0
Medium Steak, 6 oz	250	11	0
Baked: Small Steak, 4 oz	205	7	0
Medium Steak, 6 oz	290	13	0
Tilapia, Raw, 4 oz	110	2	0
Baked: 3 oz	110	2.5	0
Trout, Rainbow:			
Farmed: Raw, 4 oz	160	7	0
Baked, 3 oz	145	6.5	0
Wild: Raw, 4 oz	135	4	0
Baked, 3 oz	130	5	0
Tuna:			
Raw: Bluefin, 4 oz	165	5.5	0
Skipjack, Yellowfin, av., 4 oz	120	1	0
Baked: Bluefin, 3 oz	155	5.5	0
Skipjack, Yellowfin, av., 3 oz	110	1	0
Canned: In Water, drained			
Chunk Light, 2 oz	50	1	0
3 oz can	75	1.5	1
5 oz can	125	2.5	1.5

Tuna (Cont):   C   F   Cb

	C	F	Cb
In Water, drained (Cont):			
Solid White: 2 oz	60	0.5	0
5 oz can	150	1.5	0
7 oz can	210	2	0
In Oil, drained:			
Chunk Light: 2 oz	80	4	0
5 oz can	200	10	0
Solid White: 2 oz can	90	4	0
5 oz can	270	12	0
Tuna Salad, Deli Style, ½ cup, 4oz	280	20	8
Whitefish: Raw, 4 oz	150	6.5	0
Baked, 3 oz	145	6.5	1
Smoked, 3 oz	90	1	0
Whiting: Raw, 4 oz	100	1.5	0
Baked, 3 oz	100	1.5	0
Yellowtail: Raw, 4 oz	165	6	0
Grilled, 3 oz	160	6	0

Other Canned/Packaged Fish

	C	F	Cb
Bumble Bee:			
Tuna Salad Kits: *With Crackers*			
Original: 3.5 oz package	300	22	18
With Mayonnaise, 4.9 oz	560	39	30
Fat-Free, 3.5 oz	150	2	24
Lunch on the Run Kit, 8.2 oz	500	26	52
Seafood Salad,			
with Crackers, 3.3 oz pkg	150	5	24
Sensations Bowls:			
Lemon & Pepper Tuna Medley, 4 oz	160	6	2
Spicy Thai Chili Tuna Medley, 4 oz	180	6	11
Chicken of the Sea:			
Albacore White Tuna in Water,			
2.5 oz pouch	80	1.5	0
Pink Salmon, skinless/boneless,			
2.5 oz pouch	90	3	0
Shrimp, medium, 4 oz can	90	1	2
Gorton's ~ *Page 114*			
Kroger ~ *Page 116*			
Starkist:			
Autentico, average all, 2 oz drained	85	5	3.5
Pouch: *Per 2.6 oz Pouch*			
Albacore White Tuna in water	80	1.5	0
Chunk, Light, Tuna in water	70	0.5	0
Lunch-To-Go Kit: Chunk Light Tuna			
With Mayonnaise & Crackers, 4 oz	230	9	20
Tuna Creations: *Per 2.6 oz*			
Herb & Garlic	110	4	2
Lemon Pepper	80	0.5	0
Van De Kamp's *(Frozen)* ~ *Page 122*			

Restaurant Chains

Captain D's Seafood ~ *Page 187*
Long John Silver's ~ *Page 213*
Southern Tsunami ~ *Page 242*

Flours & Grains	C	F	Cb
Amaranth Flour, ½ cup, 3.5 oz	365	6.5	65
Arrowroot Flour, ½ cup, 2.25 oz	230	0	56
Barley: Grain, regular, ½ cup, 2.6 oz	255	1	55
Pearled, raw, 3½ oz	350	1	78
Buckwheat: Grain, ½ cup, 3 oz	290	3	61
Flour, whole-groat, ½ cup, 2 oz	200	2	42
Groats: Roasted, dry, ½ cup, 2.9 oz	285	2	67
Roasted, cooked, 3.5 oz	80	0.5	17
Bulgur: Dry, ½ cup, 2.5 oz	240	1	53
Cooked, ½ cup, 3.2 oz	75	0.5	17
Carob Flour, ½ cup, 1.8 oz	115	0.5	46
Corn Kernels, cooked, av., ½ cup	80	0.5	18
Corn Bran, ½ cup, 1.3 oz	85	0.5	33
Corn Flour/Masa, ½ cup, 2 oz	215	2.5	43
Corn Grits:			
Dry, ½ cup, 2.75 oz	290	1	62
Cooked, ½ cup, 4.25 oz	70	0.5	15
Corn Germ, toasted, ½ cup, 4 oz	100	1.5	22
Cornmeal, all varieties, average:			
3 Tbsp, 1 oz	105	0.5	22
½ cup, 2.5 oz	255	1	54
Mixes, same as above	230	1	48
Cornstarch: 1 Tbsp, 0.3 oz	30	0	8
½ cup, 2.25 oz	245	0	58
Couscous: Dry, 1 oz	110	0	22
1 cup cooked, 5.5 oz	175	0.5	37
Farina: Dry, ½ cup, 3.1 oz	325	0.5	69
Cooked, ½ cup, 4.1 oz	55	0	12
Flaxseed: Whole, 1 T., 0.3 oz	45	3.5	2
Ground, 2 Tbsp, 0.3 oz	60	4.5	4
Garbanzo, (Chick Pea), ½ cup, 1.6 oz	180	3	27
Gluten Free Flour, 3 Tbsp	100	0	24
Matzo Meal, ½ cup, 2.2 oz	230	0.5	48
Millet: Raw, ½ cup, 3.5 oz	380	4	73
Cooked, ½ cup, 3 oz	105	1	21
Oat Bran: Raw, ⅓ cup, 1.1 oz	75	2	21
Cooked, ½ cup, 3.75 oz	45	1	13
Oats, rolled/oatmeal:			
Dry/Groats, ½ cup, 1.5 oz	160	3	28
Cooked, ½ cup, 4.2 oz	75	1	13
Polenta ~ See Cornmeal			
Potato Flour, ½ cup, 2.8 oz	285	0.5	66
Psyllium Husks, 1 Tbsp, 0.15 oz	10	0	4
Quinoa: Dry ½ cup, 3 oz	320	5	59
Cooked, ½ cup, 3.75 oz	130	2	24
Rice Bran, ½ cup, 2 oz	180	12	28
Rice Flour, ½ cup, 2.75 oz	290	1	63

Flours & Grains (Cont)	C	F	Cb
Rice Polish, ½ cup, 3.5 oz	360	0.5	80
Rye Flour:			
Dark, ½ cup, 2.3 oz	210	2	44
Light, ½ cup, 1.8 oz	190	1	41
Medium, ½ cup, 1.8 oz	180	1	40
Rye Grain: ½ cup, 3 oz	280	2	59
Flakes, ¼ cup, 1 oz	100	0.5	21
Semolina Flour, ½ cup, 3 oz	300	1	61
Sorghum, ½ cup, 3.4 oz	325	3	72
Soy Flour:			
Defatted, ½ cup, 3.5 oz	330	1	38
Low-Fat, 1 cup, 3 oz	325	6	33
Full-Fat, 1 cup, 3 oz	365	17	29
Soy Meal, defatted, 1 cup, 4.3 oz	415	3	49
Spelt Flour, ½ cup, 2 oz	190	1	41
Tapioca Pearl:			
Dry, ½ cup, 2.7 oz	270	0	67
3 Tbsp, 1 oz	100	0	25
Teff Seed Flour, 2 oz	215	2	42
Tortilla Flour Mix,			
½ cup, 2 oz	220	6	37
Triticale:			
Grain, 3.4 oz	325	2	70
Flour, wholegrain, ½ cup, 2.3 oz	220	1	48
Wheat Bran, unprocessed, ½ cup, 1 oz	65	1	19
Wheat Flakes, ½ cup, 1.5 oz	160	1	35
Wheat Germ:			
Raw, ¼ cup, 1 oz	105	3	15
Toasted, ¼ cup, 1 oz	110	3	14
Wheat Flour:			
White, All Purpose/Self-Rising:			
1 level Tbsp, 0.28 oz	30	0	6
½ cup, 2.2 oz	230	0.5	48
1 cup, 4.4 oz	455	1.5	95
Whole Wheat, 1 cup, 4.2 oz	405	2	87

FRUIT TIME

Fruit ~ Fresh

Weights As Purchased

	C	F	Cb
Apples, all varieties, average:			
Whole, with skin:			
1 small, 4 oz	55	0	14
1 medium, 5.5 oz	75	0	19
1 large, 8 oz	110	0	28
1 extra large, 11 oz	145	0	36
Flesh only, no skin or core: 1 oz	15	0	3.5
Slices, 1 cup, 4 oz	55	0	14
Candy/Caramel Apple, 1 med., 6.5 oz	245	4	54
Chiquita, Apple Bites, 14 slices, 5 oz	80	0	20
Apricots: 1 small, 1.5 oz	20	0	4
1 medium, 2 oz	25	0	6
1 large, 3 oz	40	0	10
1 extra large, 4 oz	50	0	12
Asian Pear, (Nashi Fruit), 1 medium, 7 oz	85	0	21
Avocado			
Fuerte (Florida) variety:			
¼ medium, 2.7 oz pulp	90	7.5	6
½ medium, 5.4 oz pulp	180	15	12
Mashed, 2 Tbsp, 1 oz	35	3	2
Hass variety (Californian/Mexican):			
Cubes, ½ cup, 2.5 oz	120	11	6
Mashed, 2 Tbsp, 1 oz	50	4	2
¼ cup, 2 oz	95	8	5
Pulp: ¼ medium, 1.5 oz	70	6.5	3
½ medium, 3 oz	140	13	7
1 medium (8.5 oz whole), 6 oz	280	26	14
Salad slices (3), 1 oz	50	4	2

Note: The fat of avocados is heart-healthy. Avocados are very low in sugars; and most of the carbohydrate is fiber. This benefits blood sugar and cholesterol levels. Use in place of butter and other high-fat spreads.

	C	F	Cb
Banana:			
Weight with skin:			
1 baby, 3 oz	50	0	12
1 small (5"), 4 oz	65	0	16
1 medium (7"), 5 oz	80	0	20
1 large (8"), 8 oz	120	0	30
1 extra large (9"), 9 oz	135	0	34
Flesh only, weight without skin:			
Mashed, ½ cup, 4 oz	100	0	25
Slices, ½ cup, 2.5 oz	65	0	16
Green Bananas, weight with skin:			
1 medium (7"), 5 oz	75	0	18
1 large (8"), 7 oz	110	0	27
Blackberries, 1 cup, 5 oz	60	0.5	14
Blueberries, ¼ cup, 1 oz	15	0	4
1 cup or ½ pint container, 5 oz	80	0	20
1 pint container, 10 oz	160	0	40

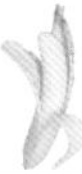

	C	F	Cb
Boysenberries, 1 cup, 4.5 oz	60	4.5	14
Breadfruit, ½ cup, 4 oz	115	0	30
Cactus Fruit:			
1 small, 2 oz	15	0	4
1 medium, 5 oz	40	0	9
1 large, 7 oz	55	0	13
Pulp, no skin, 1 cup, 5.3 oz	60	0	14
Cantaloupe: Flesh, without skin, 1 oz	10	0	2
Pieces/Balls, 1 cup, 5.5 oz	50	0	13
Slices, ½ Circle, without rind:			
1 thin (buffet), (⅛"), 0.5 oz	5	0	1
1 medium (¼"), 1 oz	10	0	2
1 thick (½"), 2 oz	20	0	5
Wedges, length cut, without skin:			
1 thin, 1/16 medium, 2 oz	20	0	5
1 thick, ⅛ medium, 4 oz	40	0	9
Whole, weight with seeds and skin:			
½ small, 20 oz	195	1	46
½ medium, 28 oz	270	1.5	65
½ large, 2.5 lb	370	2	90
Cape Gooseberries, 1 cup, 5 oz	70	1	15
Cherimoya: Pulp, ½ cup, 3 oz	60	0	14
1 Fruit (11 oz), 8 oz edible	170	1	40
Cherries, (Red/White), sweet, raw:			
6 medium or 4 large, 2 oz	30	0	7
1 cup, 4.5 oz	75	0	18
1 cup / ½ lb quantity	130	0	32
Sour, red, raw, 1 cup, 4 oz	50	0	12
Clementine, 1 medium, 2.6 oz	35	0	9
Coconut: raw:			
Young, sweet,			
Pieces: 1 piece (2" x 2"), 1.5 oz	35	2	4
½ cup, 3.5 oz	80	5	9
Mature, hard, 1 piece (2"x 2"), 1.5 oz	160	15	6
Crabapples, slices, ½ cup, 2 oz	40	0	11
Cranberries, fresh, ¼ cup, 1 oz	25	0	6.5
Custard Apple ~ See Cherimoya			
Dates: Medium (1), 0.3 oz	20	0	5
Large Medjool (1), 0.5 oz	40	0	10
Extra Large Medjool (1), 0.9 oz	65	0	16
Chopped, ½ cup, 3 oz	240	0	58
Dragon Fruit, (Pitahaya):			
1 medium, 4" long, 12 oz	60	0	13
1 large, 5" long, 16 oz	80	0	18
Durian, pulp, 4 oz	165	6	31
Elderberries, ½ cup, 2.5 oz	55	0.5	13

Weights As Purchased	C	F	Cb
Feijoa, (Pineapple Guava),			
1 medium, 2 oz	30	0.5	5.5
Figs, green/black:			
1 medium, 2 oz	40	0	10
1 large, 3 oz	60	0	15
Gooseberries, raw, 1 cup, 5 oz	65	1	15
Grapefruit, all varieties, average:			
½ fruit, 10 oz (6 oz flesh)	55	0	13
1 cup sections w/ juice, 8 oz	75	0	18
Grapes: Average, 1 cup, 5.5 oz	105	0	28
1 small bunch, 4 oz	80	0	20
1 medium bunch, 7 oz	140	0	36
1 large bunch, 16 oz	315	0	82
Granadilla, pulp, ½ cup, 4 oz	110	0	27
Guanabana, pulp, ½ cup, 4 oz	75	0	19
Guava, 1 medium, 4 oz	80	1	16
Honeydew:			
1 slice, ¾" thick, 3 oz	30	0	7
1 wedge, (⅛ of 7" diameter),			
12 oz (with rind)	80	0	20
Cubes/Balls, 1 cup, 6 oz	60	0	14
½ small (4½ lb whole)	180	0.5	42
½ medium (6lb whole)	230	1	56
Honey Murcots, 1 only, 5 oz	45	0	11
Jaboticaba, 1 cup, 5.5 oz	55	0	14
Jackfruit, flesh, ⅛ av., 4 oz	105	0	27
Kiwano, ½ medium, 5 oz	35	0	8
Kiwifruit:			
1 Medium, 2.7 oz	45	0	11
1 Large, 3.2 oz	55	0	13
Langsat, Duku 1 medium, 2 oz	25	0	7
Lemons: 1 medium, 5oz	20	0	4
1 wedge, 1 oz	5	0	1
Limes, 1 medium, 2.4 oz	20	0	7
Loganberries, frozen, ½ cup, 2.5 oz	40	0	9
Longans, 5 fruit, 0.5oz	10	0	2.5
Loquats, 4 fruit, 2.25 oz	30	0	8
Lychees, 4 fruit, 2.25oz	30	0	7
Mamey Apple, Cubes, 1 cup, 6 oz	85	1	20
Mandarin Orange:			
1 small, 3 oz	35	0	9
1 medium, 4 oz	45	0	11
1 large, 6 oz	50	0	13
Mango:			
Slices, ½ cup, 3 oz	55	0	14
1 small mango, 7 oz	90	0.5	24
1 medium: 10 oz	130	0.5	34
Side cheek, 4 oz	60	0	14
1 large, 17 oz	220	1	58
1 extra large, 24 oz	310	1.5	82
Marionberries, 1 cup, 5 oz	75	1	15

Weights As Purchased	C	F	Cb
Melons, all varieties, average,			
cubes/balls, 1 cup, 6 oz	60	0	14
Mulberries, 20 fruit, 1 oz	15	0	3
Nashi Fruit/Asian Pear, 1 med. 7 oz	85	0	21
Nectarines: 1 medium, 5oz	60	0	14
1 large, 7 oz	80	0	18
Oheloberries, ½ cup, 2.5 oz	20	0	5
Olives, Pickled: Green, 10 lge, 1.5 oz	60	6.5	1.5
Ripe, Greek Style, 10 medium, 1 oz	70	6	4
Ripe (Black) Californian:			
1 small/medium	5	0	0.2
1 large/extra large	6	0.5	0.5
1 jumbo	7	0.5	0.5
1 colossal	11	1	0.5
Oranges, all varieties, average, weights with skin:			
1 small, (2.5" diam.), 5 oz	45	0	11
1 medium (3") 7 oz	75	0	18
1 large, (3.5") 10 oz	105	0	25
1 extra large, (4"), 14 oz	130	0	30
Flesh/Pulp only, 1 cup, 6 oz	85	0	21
Peel, 1 Tbsp	0	0	0
California Navel (3"), 7 oz	70	0	17
Californian Valencia,			
1 medium (2¾" diam.) 6 oz	60	0	14
Florida Orange, 1 med., 7 oz	70	0	17
Sunkist Navel, large, 14 oz	130	0	30
Papaya:			
1" pieces, 1 cup, 5 oz	60	0	15
1 medium, 16 oz	120	0	30
Green (unripe), ½ cup, 3.5 oz	20	0	5
Passionfruit:			
1 small, 1.5 oz	15	0	3
1 large, 2.7 oz	30	0	6
Pulp, ½ cup, 4 oz	110	0	27
Peaches: 1 baby/donut, 3 oz	30	0	7
1 small, 5 oz	50	0	12
1 medium, 6 oz	60	0	14
1 large, 7 oz	70	0	16
1 extra large, 9 oz	90	0	21
Pears, all varieties, average:			
1 mini, 2.5oz	35	0	8
1 small, 5 oz	75	0	18
1 medium, 7 oz	100	0	25
1 large, 9 oz	130	0	33
1 extra large, 12 oz	170	0	42
Pepino, ½ medium, 4 oz	20	0	4
Persimmons: Native, 1 oz	35	0	9
Japanese (2½"d. x 2½"h), 7 oz	120	0	30
Seedless (Maui), 1 medium, 5 oz	100	0	25

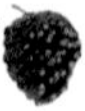

Weights As Purchased	C	F	Cb
Pineapple, average all varieties:			
Weights without skin:			
1 thin slice (1/2"), 2 oz 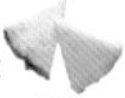	30	0	7
1 thick slice (3/4"), 3 oz	40	0	10
1 cup, chunks, 6 oz	80	0	20
Whole fruit, wt with skin: 			
Baby/Mini, 16 oz	150	0	39
Medium size, 3 lbs	450	1	118
Canned ~ See Page 102			
Pitanga, (Surinam-Cherry) (5), 1.2 oz	10	0	2
Plaintains:			
Fresh/Raw, weight with skin:			
1 medium, 10 oz 	220	0	55
Slices, 1 cup, 5 oz	180	0	44
Cooked:			
Mashed, ½ cup, 3.5 oz	115	0	30
Slices, 1 cup, 5.5 oz	180	0	47
Fried in oil: 10 slices (¼"), 2 oz	160	6	26
1 cup, 4.2 oz	360	14	58
Plums, all varieties, average:			
1 mini/Damson, (1" diam), 0.5 oz	10	0	1.5
1 small (2"), 2.25oz	30	0	7
1 medium (2½"), 3.5 oz	45	0	10
1 large (3"), 5 oz	60	0	14
Plumcot, 1 medium, 6 oz	75	0	18
Pomegranates:			
1 small (3"), 5.5 oz 	70	1	15
1 medium (3.5"), 10 oz	125	2	27
1 large (4"), 16 oz	230	3	50
Seeds/Arils, ¼ cup, 2 oz	40	1	10
Pomelo, flesh, ½ cup, 3.5 oz	35	0	9
Prickly Pear ~ See Cactus Fruit			
Quince, 1 medium, 3.5 oz	55	0	14
Rambuta/Rambotang, 			
Red/Yellow, 1 medium, 2 oz	15	0	4
Raspberries: ½ cup, 2 oz	30	0	7
10 Raspberries, 0.75 oz 	10	0	2
1 Cup, 4.25 oz	65	1	15
1 Pint, 11 oz	160	2	37
Sapodilla: 1 medium, 78oz	140	2	34
Pulp, 1 cup, 8 oz	200	2.5	48
Sapote:			
Black: 1 medium, 4.5 oz 	60	0	14
Pulp only, ½ cup, 4 oz	100	1	22
Mamey, piece, 1 cup, 6 oz	220	1	50
Satsuma Tangerine, 1 medium, 3 oz	45	0	11
Soursop, pulp, 1 cup, 8 oz	150	0.5	38
Starfruit, (Carambola):			
1 medium, (3.5" long), 3 oz 	30	0	6
1 large (4.5"), 4.5 oz	40	0	8
Strawberries: 1 cup, 5.5 oz	50	0.5	12
6 medium/3 large, 2 oz	20	0	4
1 pint container, heaping, 16 oz	130	0	32
Chocolate Dipped, 1 large	45	2.5	6

Weights As Purchased	C	F	Cb
Sugar-Apple (Sweetsop), 			
pulp, ½ cup, 4 oz	120	0	28
Sugar Cane:			
Unpeeled, 1 baton (7" long), 4 oz	30	0	7
Peeled, 1 small stick (3"), 2 oz	35	0	8
Tamarillo, 1 medium, 4 oz 	20	0	3
Tamarind: 1 fruit (3"x1")	5	0	1.5
Pulp, ½ cup, 2 oz	140	0.5	37
Tangelo: 1 small, 4 oz	55	0	13
1 medium, 5 oz 	70	0	17
1 large, 7 oz	95	0	23
Tangerine, 1 med., (2½" diam.), 4 oz	50	0	13
Tangor, 1 medium, 4 oz	35	0	7
Tomatillos:			
3 medium, 3.5 oz 	35	0.5	6
1lb (16 oz) quantity	160	2	27
Tomatoes:			
1 small (2¼" diameter), 3 oz 	15	0	3
1 medium (2¾"), 5 oz	25	0	5
Sliced: 2 thin slices, 1 oz	5	0	1
2 thick (⅜"), 2 oz 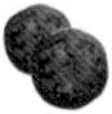	10	0	2
Wedge, 1/4, 1.25 oz	6	0	1
1 large (3½"), 8 oz	40	0.5	9
1 extra large (4"), 12 oz	60	0.5	14
Cherry: 4 medium, 2 oz	10	0	2
1 cup, 5 oz 	25	0	6
Grape, 5 medium, 2 oz	10	0	2
Yellow Tear Drop, 3 medium, 1 oz	5	0	2
Canned Tomatoes/Products ~ See Page 144			
Tree Tomato/Tamarillo, 3 oz	20	0	5
Ugli Fruit, Tangelo type, 5 oz	40	0	8
Watermelon:			
Flesh only, weights without skin:			
1 thin slice (1/2"), ¼ circle, 3 oz	25	0	6
1 thick slice (1"): ¼ circle, 6 oz	50	0	12
½ circle, 12 oz 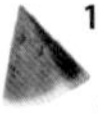	100	1	24
Buffet Slice, small, thin, 1 oz	8	0	2
Cubes or Balls, 1 cup, 5.5 oz	45	0	11
Round Seedless Melon, weight with skin:			
Medium size, 13 lb, (8" diam.):			
Whole melon, 13 lb	1160	5	280
Wedge, ⅛ whole, 26 oz	145	1	35
Mini size, 6 lb, (6.5" diam.): 			
Whole melon, 6 lb	480	2.5	110
Wedge, ⅛ whole, 12 oz	60	0	14

Dried Fruit

	C	F	Cb
Apples, 5 rings, 1 oz	80	0	19
Apricots, 8 halves, 1 oz	65	0	16
Banana Chips, ⅓ cup, 1 oz	180	9	16
Banana Flakes, 4 Tbsp, 1 oz	80	0	20
Cranberries *(Craisins):*			
Original, ¼ cup	130	0	33
Reduced Sugar, ¼ cup	100	0	31
Chocolate Covered, ¼ cup, 2 oz	180	8	28
Dates ~ *See Dates in Fresh Fruit*			
Figs, 3 medium figs, 1 oz	90	0	23
Goji Berries, 3 Tbsp, 1 oz	100	1	20
Mango Slices, 5 pieces, 1.4 oz	25	0	6
Papaya Spears, 2 pieces, 1.4 oz	120	0	30
Peaches, 2 halves, 1 oz	60	0	15
Pears, 3 halves, 2 oz	140	0.5	34
Plums *(Sunsweet)*, (5), 1.4 oz	100	0	24
Prunes/Dried Plums:			
With pits, 3 medium, 1 oz	70	0	17
Without pits, 4 medium, 1 oz	70	0	17
Cooked: With sugar, ½ cup, 5 oz	155	0	38
Without sugar, ½ cup, 4.5 oz	135	0	34
Raisins: 2 Tbsp, 1 oz pack	85	0	20
½ cup, 2.8 oz	220	0.5	56

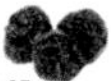

Candied/Glazed Fruit

	C	F	Cb
Apricot, 1 medium, 1 oz	70	0	17
Cherry, Maraschino (1)	8	0	2
Citron/Fruit Peel, 1 oz	85	0	20
Ginger, 1 oz	90	0	21
Pineapple, 1 slice, 1.25 oz	120	0	29
Tamarind, dried, sweetened, 1 oz	70	0	17

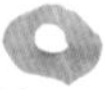

Fruit Leather Rolls

	C	F	Cb
Betty Crocker: Fruit By The Foot,			
1 roll, 0.75 oz	80	0	17
Fruit Gushers, 1 oz	90	1	20
Fruit Roll-Ups, 1 roll	50	1	12
Stretch Island, Leathers, 1 pouch, 0.5 oz	45	0	12

Canned/Bottled Fruit

	C	F	Cb
Solids & Liquids:			
Per ½ Cup, 4½ oz Unless indicated			
Apricots/Peaches/Pears:			
In juice, light	60	0	15
In heavy syrup	105	0	28
In water/diet	35	0	8
Black/Blueberries:			
In heavy syrup	120	0	30
In light syrup	110	0	26

Canned/Bottled Fruit (Cont)

	C	F	Cb
Cherries, pitted:			
In heavy syrup	105	0	27
In light syrup	85	0	22
In water	55	0	15
Maraschino, 1 oz	50	0	12
Fruit Cocktail/Salad:			
In heavy syrup	95	0	25
In juice, light	60	0	16
In water/diet	35	0	10
Gooseberries, light syrup	90	0	24
Grapefruit, in light syrup	75	0	20
Lychees, ½ cup, 4.5 oz	105	0	26
Mixed Fruit: In fruit juices/light syrup	70	0	18
In heavy syrup	90	0	24
In water/diet	40	0	10
Pineapple, all varieties:			
In heavy syrup, 4.3 oz	110	0	26
In own juice, 4 oz	60	0	15
Prunes: With syrup, 3 oz	90	0	23
Stewed in water, ½ cup	135	0	35

Fruit Snack Cups

	C	F	Cb
Deli/Take-Out: Small, 6 oz	70	0	16
Large, 12 oz	140	0	32
Yogurt and Fruit Cup, 15 oz	380	4.5	75
Del Monte:			
Fruit Natural: All varieties, av., 7 oz	100	0	24
No Sugar Added, all varieties, 6.5 oz	55	0	12
Snack Cups: In light Syrup, av., 4 oz	70	0	18
No Added Sugar, Peaches, 4 oz	25	0	11
Dole:			
Fruit Bowls: *Per 4 oz Container*			
Pineapple; Tropical Fruit, average	60	0	15
Average other varieties	75	0	18
Fruit in Gel: *Per 4.3 oz Container*			
Mixed Fruit, in Cherry Gel	60	0	14
Average other fruits, in various Gels	90	0	23

Apple & Fruit Sauces

	C	F	Cb
Apple Sauce:			
Regular/sweetened, 2 Tbsp, 1 oz	20	0	6
4 oz package	90	0	22
Cranberry, Jellied, ¼ cup	110	0	25
Fruit Sauces & Purees:			
All fruit types, average: 2 Tbsp, 1 oz	25	0	6
½ cup, 4 oz	100	0	24
Mott's:			
Apple Sauce: Original, 4 oz	90	0	24
Fruit Flavored, average, 4 oz	90	0	23
Healthy Harvest, all flavors, 3.92 oz	50	0	13
Ocean Spray,			
Cranberry varieties, ¼ cup	110	0	25

Quick Guide

Ice Cream　　C　F　Cb

Average all Flavors:

Regular (10% fat):
Examples: Dreyer's Grand, Hood, Friendly's

	C	F	Cb
½ cup, 4 fl.oz	140	7	16
1 cup, 8 fl.oz	280	14	32
1 pint, 16 fl.oz	560	28	64

Rich/Premium (16-17% fat):
Examples: Baskin Robbins, Ben & Jerry's, Haagen-Dazs

	C	F	Cb
½ cup, 4 fl.oz	250	16	24
1 cup, 8 fl.oz	500	32	48
1 pint, 16 fl.oz	1000	64	96

Reduced-Fat/Light (5% fat):
Examples: Breyers ½ The Fat, Friendly's Light, Hood Light

	C	F	Cb
½ cup, 4 fl.oz	140	5	21
1 cup, 8 fl.oz	280	10	42
1 pint, 16 fl.oz	560	20	84

Fat-Free:
Example: Breyers Fat-Free

	C	F	Cb
½ cup, 4 fl.oz	90	0	21
1 cup, 8 fl.oz	180	0	42
1 pint, 16 fl.oz	360	0	84

Scoop Shops:
Average all Brands
Add extra for cone (see next column)

	C	F	Cb
Kids, 3 fl.oz	125	8	12
Regular, 6 fl.oz	250	16	24
Large, 9 fl.oz	375	24	36

Soft Serve:
Average all Brands

	C	F	Cb
Regular: ½ cup, 4 fl.oz	255	15	25
1 cup, 8 fl.oz	510	30	50
Light: ½ cup, 4 fl.oz	145	3	25
1 cup, 8 fl.oz	290	6	50

Quick Guide

Frozen Yogurt　　C　F　Cb
Average all Brands

	C	F	Cb
Hard: Low-Fat, ½ cup	110	3	19
Non-Fat, ½ cup	110	0	24
Soft: Low-Fat, ½ cup	120	4	17
Non-Fat, ½ cup	100	0	30

Brands ~ *See Ice Cream & Novelties Section*

Quick Guide　　C　F　Cb

Gelato/Ices/Frozen Custard

Gelato: *Per ½ Cup*

	C	F	Cb
Milk base: Vanilla	160	6	25
Chocolate Hazelnut	230	15	21
Water base, ½ cup	100	0	26

Frozen Custard, Choc./Vanilla, av :

	C	F	Cb
½ cup	210	11	23
Single Scoop, 5 oz wt	300	15	38
Double Scoop, 10 oz wt	600	30	76

Ice (Milk base): *Average all flavors*

	C	F	Cb
Hard (4% fat), ½ cup	100	3	15
Soft Serve (3% fat), ½ cup	110	2	19
Shaved Ice, average, 12 fl.oz	160	0	40
Sherbet, average, ½ cup	110	1.5	23
Sorbet, Fruit, fat free, ½ cup	70	0	19
Fruit Ice Pops	80	0	20

Sundaes　　C　F　Cb

Baskin Robbins:

	C	F	Cb
Classic: Banana Royale	620	28	87
Banana Split	1010	34	173
Brownie	920	47	119

Denny's,

	C	F	Cb
Banana Split, 15 oz	810	31	125

Toppings ~ *See Page 195*

McDonald's:

	C	F	Cb
Sundaes: Hot Caramel, 6.4 oz	340	8	60
Hot Fudge, 6.3 oz	330	9	53
Strawberry, 6.4 oz	280	6	49
Toppings, Peanuts, 0.25 oz	40	3.5	1

Ice Cream Cones & Cups　　C　F　Cb

Average all Brands

	C	F	Cb
Wafer Cone/Cup, average	20	0	4
Sugar Cone, average	50	0	14

Waffle Cone:

	C	F	Cb
Small	50	1	10
Large	90	0.5	19

Brands:

	C	F	Cb
Comet, Sugar Cone	50	0	11
Keebler, Sugar Cone	50	0	10
Oreo, Chocolate Cone	50	1	10

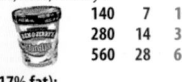

Ice Cream ~ Brands

C F Cb

Baskin-Robbins ~ *See Fast-Foods Section*

Ben & Jerry's:

Scoop Shop Ice Cream: *Hand Scooped, Per ½ Cup*

	C	F	Cb
Americone Dream	250	13	29
Bonnaroo Buzz	250	14	27
Butter Pecan	270	19	19
Choc. Chip Cookie Dough	250	13	28
Chocolate Fudge Brownie	220	12	28
Chocolate Nougat Crunch	250	13	28
Chocolate Therapy	240	13	26
Chunky Monkey	260	16	26
Coconut Seven Layer Bar	270	17	27
Late Night Snack	250	15	27
Mint Chocolate Chunk	240	15	24
NY Super Fudge Chunk	270	18	25
Strawberry Cheesecake	220	13	24
Sweet Cream & Cookies	240	13	26
Vanilla Heath Bar Crunch	270	17	26

Ice Cream, 1 Pint Tubs: *Per ½ Cup*

	C	F	Cb
Banana Split, 3.8 oz	260	14	28
Boston Cream Pie, 3.7 oz	250	13	29
Cake Batter, 3.7 oz	260	16	27
Cherry Garcia, 3.7 oz	240	13	28
Choc. Chip Cookie Dough, 3.7 oz	270	14	33
Chubby Hubby, 3.9 oz	340	21	32
Everything But The..., 3.8 oz	290	17	31
Imagine Whirled Peace	270	16	27
Karamel Sutra, 3.7 oz	260	14	31
Milk & Cookies, 3.5 oz	270	15	30
Peanut Brittle, 3.6 oz	260	15	29
Peanut Butter Cup, 4 oz	360	26	27
Phish Food, 3.7 oz	280	13	39
Red Velvet Cake, 3.6 oz	250	13	30
S'mores, 3.7 oz	280	16	35
Triple Caramel Chunk, 3.7 oz	280	16	32
What a Cluster, 3.7 oz	320	19	31

Frozen Yogurt: *Per ½ Cup*

	C	F	Cb
Fro Yo: Cherry Garcia, 3.8 oz	200	3	37
Choc. Fudge Brownie, 3.7 oz	180	2.5	35
Pfish Food, 3.6 oz	240	6	41
Greek: Rasp. Fudge Chunk, 3.5 oz	200	7	29
Strawberry Shortcake, 3.5 oz	180	5	28
Vanilla with Honey Caramel, 3.5 oz	190	5	30
Sorbet, average all flavors, 3.3 oz	95	0	23

Blue Bunny

C F Cb

Premium Ice Cream: *Per ½ Cup of Pint Container*

	C	F	Cb
Banana Split, 2.6 oz	160	7	21
Bunny Tracks, 2.6 oz	190	11	21
Chocolate Champion, 2.3 oz	130	6	17
Cookies 'n Cream, 2.3 oz	150	7	20

Fat Free, No Sugar Added: *Per ½ Cup, 2.5 oz*

	C	F	Cb
Brownie Sundae	80	0	23
Caramel Toffee Crunch	90	0	23
Vanilla	80	0	20
(Carbs include 5-8 g sugar alcohols)			

Hi Lite: *Per ½ Cup*

	C	F	Cb
Fudge Nut Sundae, 2.3 oz	120	4	19
Homemade Vanilla, 2.3 oz	110	3.5	18
Mint Chip, 2.3 oz	110	3.5	18

Frozen Yogurt, Personals: *Per Container*

	C	F	Cb
All Nat: White Choc., Rasp., 3.6 oz	170	4.5	32
Bordeaux Cherry Choc., 3.6 oz	170	4	31

Bars/Pops ~ *See Page 108*

Breyers:

Original Ice Cream: *Per ½ Cup*

	C	F	Cb
Butter Pecan, 2.23oz	140	6	18
Cherry Vanilla, 2.3 oz	120	3	21
Cookies & Cream, 2.3 oz	140	4.5	21
Mint Chocolate Chip, 2.3 oz	150	8	17
Natural Strawberry, 2.3 oz	140	5	21
Vanilla, Chocolate, 2.3 oz	130	7	16
Fat Free, av. all flavors, 2.3 oz	90	0	21

Half The Fat Ice Cream: *Per ½ Cup*

	C	F	Cb
Cookies & Cream, 2.3 oz	120	4	20
Crmy, Choc. or Vanilla, av., 2.2 oz	105	3	18

No Added Sugar:

	C	F	Cb
Butter Pecan, 2.2 oz	100	6	13
Vanilla, Chocolate, Strawb., 2 oz	80	4	13
(Carbs include 5g sugar alcohol and 4g fiber)			

Blasts!: *Per ½ Cup*

	C	F	Cb
Chips Ahoy, 2.2 oz	140	5	22
Mrs Field's Choc Fudge Brownie, 2.3 oz	140	4	25
Oreo Cookies and Cream Mint, 2 oz	120	4	20
Snickers, 2.4 oz	150	5	19
Strawberry Waffle Cone, 2 oz	130	4	22
CarbSmart, av. all flav, ½ cup, 2.4 oz	115	6	14
(Carbs include 5g sugar alcohol and 4g fiber)			

Ice Cream ~ Brands (Cont)

Bruster's:	C	F	Cb
Ice Cream, Chocolate/Van., av., 3.5 oz	210	12	24
Fat Free, No Added Sugar: *Per ½ Cup*			
Chocolate, 3.2 oz	100	0	26
Choc. Caramel Swirl, 3.3 oz	120	0	31
Cinnamon; Coffee; Vanilla, av. 3.2 oz	100	0	23
Fudge Ripple, 3.2 oz	110	0	30
Frozen Yogurt,			
Chocolate; Vanilla, average, 3.5 oz	150	4.5	24
Carvel Ice Cream ~ *See Fast-Foods Section*			
Clemmy's: *Per ½ Cup*			
Butter Pecan, 2.7 oz	200	15	20
Chocolate; Chocolate Chip, av., 2.7 oz	175	13	22
Coffee; Van. Bean, av., 2.7 oz	160	11	22
Orange Cream, 2.8 oz	120	6	23
P'B Chocolate Chip, 2.8 oz	220	16	22
Toasted Almond, 2.7 oz	170	11	26
(Carbs include 13-15g sugar alcohol)			
Coldstone Creamery ~ *See Fast-Foods Section*			
Dairy Queen/Brazier ~ *See Fast-Foods Section*			
Dippin' Dots:			
Original Dots: *Per ½ Cup, 3 oz*			
Banana Split	160	8	20
Caramel Brownie Sundae	190	9	23
Cookies 'n Cream	180	9	23
Mint Chocolate	170	8	21
Rocky Road	200	10	22
Strawberry	160	8	18
Vanilla	160	8	18
Dove:			
Ice Cream: *Per ½ Cup*			
Mint Choc. Chunk, 2.4 oz	180	11	17
Unconditional Choc., 2.5 oz	200	12	23
Vanilla Choc. Chunk, 2.3 oz	180	11	17
Dreyer's/Edy's:			
Ice Cream: *Per ½ Cup*			
Grand: Chocolate	140	8	17
Mint Chocolate Chip	150	8	18
Neapolitan	130	6	16
Real Strawberry	120	5	16
Vanilla	140	7	16
Slow Churned, ½ The Fat: *Per ½ Cup*			
Chocolate	100	3.5	15
Double Fudge Brownie	120	3	19
Fudge Tracks	120	3.5	19
Mint Chocolate Chip	120	4.5	18
Peanut Butter Cup	130	5	18

Friendly's:	C	F	Cb
Rich & Creamy Ice Cream: *Per ½ Cup*			
Butter Crunch, 2.4 oz	150	7	19
Chocolate Almond Chip	160	9	17
Classic Chocolate, 2.4 oz	150	8	16
Coffee, 2.4 oz	130	7	15
Strawberry, 2.4 oz	140	6	18
Vanilla, 2.4 oz	140	8	15
Vienna Mocha Chunk, 2.4 oz	170	9	19
Smooth Churned Ice Cream: *Per ½ Cup*			
Light: Black Raspberry, 2.2 oz	110	3	18
Choc. Chip Cookie Dough, 2.2 oz	140	5	21
Fudge Swirl, 2.4 oz	130	4	21
Mint Chocolate Chip, 2.2 oz	120	4.5	19
Purely Pistachio, 2.2 oz	130	5	18
Vanilla, 2.2 oz	110	3.5	21
Sundae Cup: *Per Container*			
Original Fudge	300	14	39
Choc. Chip Cookie Dough	330	15	46
Reese's P'nut Butter Cup	430	25	42
Sherbet, all flavors, ½ cup, 3.3 oz	130	1.5	28
Yogurt Frozen,			
average all flavors, ½ cup, 2.6 oz	145	5	24
Gelati-da:			
Gelato: *Per ½ Cup, 4 oz*			
Amaretto Chocolate	150	4.5	23
Choc Mint Milano	120	2.5	22
Coffee Fudge Latte	130	2	22
Limoncello; Vanilla Marsala, average	120	3	21
Red Raspberry	130	1.5	25
Great Value *(Walmart):*			
Ice Cream: *Per ½ cup*			
Chocolate Chip Cookie Dough, 2.32 oz	150	8	19
Peanut Butter Lovers, 2.8 oz	300	16	34
Sherbet, all flavors, 3 oz	110	0	26
Haagen-Dazs:			
Regular: *Tubs, Per ½ Cup*			
Bananas Foster	240	13	27
Butter Pecan	300	22	20
Chocolate Peanut Butter	340	23	26
Cookies & Cream	250	16	22
White Chocolate Raspb. Truffle	280	16	31
Gelato: *Per ½ Cup*			
Black Cherry Amaretto	240	9	35
Sea Salt Caramel	270	11	38
Healthy Choice:			
Greek Frozen Yogurt: *Per 4 fl.oz Ctn*			
Blueberry, 2.5 oz	100	2	19
Dark Fudge Swirl	100	2	17
Vanilla Bean	100	2	17
Average other flavors	100	2	18
Bars ~ *See Page 109*			

Ice Cream ~ Brands (Cont)

Hood:

Ice Cream: *Per ½ Cup, 2.3 oz*

	C	F	Cb
Cookies 'N Cream	150	8	19
Chocolate	140	6	18
Classic Trio	140	7	17
Cookie Dough	160	8	19
Creamy Coffee	140	7	16
Fudge Twister	140	6	20
Golden/Natural Vanilla; Patchwork	140	7	17
Maple Walnut	150	9	17

Light: *Per ½ Cup, 2.2 oz*

Butter Pecan	130	7	16
Chocolate Chip	120	4.5	18
Coffee; Vanilla, average	105	3	16
Maine Blueberry & Sweet Cream	110	2.5	18
Martha's Vineyard Black Raspberry	110	2.5	19
Moosehead Lake Fudge	160	7	21
Under The Stars	160	8	18

Frozen Fat-Free Yogurt: *Per ½ Cup, 2.3 oz*

Maine Blueberry & Sweet Cream	90	0	19
Mocha Fudge	100	0	22
Strawberry	80	0	18
Strawberry Banana	90	0	20

New England Creamery ~ www.CalorieKing.com
Jerseymaid *(Vons): Per ½ Cup*

Ice Cream:

Cookies & Cream	160	8	18
Choc Chip; Mint Choc Chip	150	9	16
Heavenly Hash	165	9	19
Mocha Almond Fudge; Chocolate	150	9	16
Neapolitan; Real Vanilla	140	8	15
Strawberry	130	6	17

Oberweis:
Super Premium Ice Cream: *Per 6 oz Scoop*

Chocolate	480	31	43
Chocolate Peanut Butter	550	39	42
Cookie Dough	500	28	56
Vanilla	460	31	40

Pinkberry:
Frozen Yogurt: *Without Toppings*

Original: Mini, 3.2 oz	90	0	19
Small, 5 oz	140	0	29
Medium, 8 oz	230	0	48
Large, 13 oz	370	0	78
Chocolate Hazelnut	370	0	60
Cookies & Cream	320	4.5	60
Mango; Passionfruit, av.	255	0	53

Purely Decadent:
Soy Based: *1 Pint Carton, Per ½ Cup*

	C	F	Cb
Chocolate Obsession, 3 oz	210	7	27
Peanut Butter Zig Zag	230	12	24

Gluten Free, Cookie Dough, 3.5 oz | 230 | 8 | 36 |

Red Mango:
Frozen Yogurt: *No Toppings Included*

Original: 3.3 oz

Original: 3.3 oz	80	0	19
Small, 4.7 oz	120	0	27
Regular, 7.5 oz	190	0	43
Large, 11.4 oz	290	0	65

Pomegranate: 3.3 oz

Pomegranate: 3.3 oz	90	0	21
Small, 4.6 oz	130	0	30
Regular, 7.5 oz	210	0	48
Large, 11.4 oz	320	0	73

Rice Dream:
Frozen Dessert: *Per ½ Cup, 2.8 oz*

Carob Chip	180	7	28
Cocoa Marble Fudge	170	6	31
Cookies n' Dream	180	7	28
Neapolitan	160	6	26
Strawberry	170	6	30
Vanilla	160	6	26

Bars ~ *See Page 110*

Skinny Cow: *Per Single Serve Cup*

Caramel Cone	160	2.5	33
Chocolate Fudge Brownie	150	2	29

Bars/Sandwiches/Cones ~ *See Page 110*

So Delicious:
Coconut Based: *Per ½ Cup, 3 oz*

Cherry Amaretto	130	6	22
Chocolate	150	9	20
Coconut Almond Chip	180	12	20
Turtle Trails	160	8	26

Soy Based: *Per ½ Cup, 3 oz*

Chocolate Peanut Butter	140	4.5	23
Chocolate Velvet	130	3.5	23
Creamy Vanilla	130	3	24
Mint Marble Fudge	140	3	27
Mocha Fudge	130	3	26
Neapolitan	120	3.5	23

Ice Cream ~ Brands (Cont)

	C	F	Cb
Soy Dream:			
Frozen Dessert: *Per ½ Cup, 2.5 oz*			
Butter Pecan	190	11	23
Choc. Fudge Brownie	170	9	21
French Vanilla; Vanilla	170	9	21
Vanilla Fudge	170	9	23
Stonyfield Farm:			
Frozen Yogurt: *Per ½ Cup, 3 oz*			
After Dark Chocolate	100	0	21
Creme Caramel	130	1.5	26
Gotta Have Vanilla	100	0	20
Stop & Shop:			
Ice Cream: *Per ½ Cup*			
Chocolate	150	8	18
Neapolitan; Vanilla, average	140	7.5	17
Vanilla Fudge Swirl	140	7	18
Light: Moose Tracks	130	5	18
Vanilla	100	3	17
Premium:			
Cookies & Cream	170	9	21
Mint Chocolate Chip	160	9	18
Simply Enjoy:			
Chocolate	210	12	22
Strawberry; Vanilla, average	225	13	25
Tasti D-Lite:			
Soft Serve: *Per 4 fl.oz*			

Calories will vary with density (air in product) and serving size.
Best to weigh product and calculate on 25 cals per 1 oz weight.

	C	F	Cb
Banana	70	1	13
Blueberry Cheesecake	80	1.5	15
Brownie Batter	70	1.5	13
Buttercrunch Mania	90	3.5	13
Chocolate Cookie Dough	80	1.5	14
Marshmallow	80	1	14
Tofutti:			
Premium Pints: *Per ½ Cup*			
Better Pecan	250	15	27
Chocolate	210	13	20
Vanilla	210	13	21
Vanilla Almond Bark	240	15	24
Wild Berry Supreme	190	9	24

TCBY ~ See Page 250

	C	F	Cb
Turkey Hill:			
Premium Ice Cream:			
Black Cherry	130	6	18
Butter Pecan; Choco Mint Chip, av.	160	10	16
Chocolate Peanut Butter Cup	180	11	18
Cookies 'n Cream; Tin Roof Sundae	150	8	19
Rocky Road	170	8	23
Vanilla Bean	140	7	16
Light: Moose Tracks	140	6	20
Vanilla Bean	100	2	17
Average other flavors	130	4	19
All Natural, average all flavors	160	9	17
No Sugar Added:			
Cherry Fudge Ripple	80	0	22
Dutch Chocolate; Vanilla Bean, av.	70	0	20
Moose Tracks	120	5	22
Frozen Yogurt:			
Choc. Chip Cookie Dough	120	2.5	22
Fat-Free: Chocolate Marshmallow	110	0	24
Average other flavors	100	0	19
Sherbet, av. all flavors	120	1	27
Wawa:			
Premium Ice Cream: *1 Pint Container, Per ½ cup*			
Butter Pecan; Mint Choc Chip, av.	180	10	20
Chocolate; Vanilla Bean, average	160	8	20
Cookies & Cream	180	9	21
Strawberry Shortcake	160	7	22
Wegmans: *Per ½ Cup, 2.3 oz*			
Chocolate	130	7	15
Cookies & Cream	160	8	21
French Vanilla; Vanilla, av.	145	7	19
Neapolitan	130	7	17
Peanut Butter Sundae	220	14	20
Premium, Vanilla, ½ Cup, 3.7 oz	270	18	22
Yoplait:			
Go-Gurt!, Frozen Yogurt, 2.3 oz tube	70	0.5	13
Frozen Yogurt:			
Original Fruit flavors, ½ cup, 3.2 oz	115	2	21
Vanilla, ½ cup, 3.2 oz	110	2.5	19
Greek:			
Fruit Flavors, av., 3 oz	130	2	21
Honey Caramel, 3 oz	140	2.5	22
Vanilla, 2.8 oz	120	2.5	17

Ice Cream Bars & Pops ~ Brands

Per Bar/Serving Unless Indicated

	C	F	Cb
Ben & Jerry's:			
Bars: Cherry Garcia	250	14	23
Fudgy Brownies	320	19	23
Half Baked	330	20	35
Big Bear ~ *See Klondike*			
Blue Bunny:			
Bars: Big Fudge, 2.35 oz	90	1	18
Big Star, 1.4 oz	110	7	12
Caramel Ice Cream Crunch, 1.6 oz	120	8	13
Choc. Ice Crm Sundae Crunch, 2.2 oz	170	9	24
Cookies & Cream, 3 oz	250	10	36
English Toffee, 1.6 oz	160	9	19
Orange Dream, 1.9 oz	70	1	15
Root Beer Float, 1.9 oz	60	1	12
King Size: Chocolate Eclair, 2.8 oz	220	12	27
Crunch with Candy Center, 3 oz	340	28	24
Strawberry Shortcake, 2.8 oz	210	11	26
Bomb Pops, Banana Fudge, 4 oz	160	2	31
Champ Cones:			
6 Pack: Caramel Lovers, 3.4 oz	310	16	37
Chocolate Lovers, 3.2 oz	270	13	35
Cookies 'n Cream, 3.2 oz	270	13	37
Vanilla, 3.2 oz	290	16	33
Singles: Caramel Lovers, 3.8 oz	350	19	40
Vanilla, 3.5 oz	330	19	35
King Size:			
Bunny Tracks, 5.9 oz	490	27	57
Strawberry Shortcake, 5.7 oz	400	18	54
FrozFruit:			
Banana & Cream	160	6	27
Chunky Strawberry	130	0	33
Creamy Pina Colada, 4.3 oz	190	3.5	37
Creamy Coconut	210	5	39
Jolly Rancher: Cool Tubes, 3 oz	110	1	23
Ice Pop, 3.9 oz	120	0	24
Ice Cream Sandwiches:			
Birthday Party, 2.5 oz	170	5	29
Mississippi Mud, 4 oz	280	9	46
Simply Vanilla, 2.5 oz	160	5	27
Big: Bopper, 5 oz	490	24	63
Double Strawberry, 4 oz	250	7	42
Mississippi Mud, 4 oz	280	9	46
Neapolitan, 3.8 oz	240	7	40

Per Bar/Serving Unless Indicated

	C	F	Cb
Breyers:			
Carb Smart:			
Fudge Bar	100	7	9
(Carbs include 5g sugar alcohol)			
Vanilla Ice Cream Bar	170	15	9
Vanilla Almond Ice Cream Bar	190	15	11
(Carbs include 2 sugar alcohol)			
Butterfinger *(Nestle):*			
Ice Cream Bar:			
King Size	280	18	27
Loaded	270	17	28
Clemmy's,			
Bars, average all flavors, 2 oz	70	3	16
Cool Classics:			
Arctic Blasters:			
Crispy Bar	160	11	15
Fudge Bar	100	1	21
Ice Cream Bar	150	10	13
Orange Cream	100	2.5	18
Strawberry Shortcake	150	8	20
Toffee Bar	160	11	14
Icepix: Grape; Cherry; Orange	35	0	8
Honeydew; Watermelon; Cantelope	35	0	9
Swirl Pops, Mango-Cherry	80	0	20
Creamsicles: 100 Calorie Bar	100	2	20
Sugar-Free, all flavors	40	0.5	12
(Carbs include 5g sugar alcohol)			
Diana's Bananas:			
Banana Babies:			
Milk/Dark Choc., (1)	130	6	18
Milk Chocolate & Peanuts (1)	215	13	21
Banana Bites,			
1/5 carton, 2 oz	130	8	16
Dove:			
Bars: *Per 2.6 oz Bar*			
Vanilla: With Milk Chocolate	250	16	24
And Almonds	250	17	21
Caramel Swirl & Cashews	250	16	23
Vanilla, with Dark Choc.	250	17	24
Miniatures, Variety Pack, with Milk Chocolate, 5 pcs, 3.2 oz	340	22	32
Dreyer's/Edy's:			
Outshine Fruit Bars:			
Coconut Waters, average all flavors	60	0	15
Creamy Coconut	120	3	20
Grape	60	0	16
Mango; Pineapple	80	0	20
Other varieties, average	70	0	20

Ice Cream Bars/Pops ~ Brands (Cont)

Per Bar/Serving	C	F	Cb
Drumstick (Nestlé): Classic Vanilla	290	16	33
Vanilla Caramel	310	16	38
Simply Dipped: Mint	270	13	37
Vanilla	270	13	37
Lil' Drums, av. all flavors	120	6	16
Super Nugget	310	18	34
Edy's ~ See Dreyer's			
Eskimo Pie (Nestle):			
With Sundae Center	150	9	16
No Sugar Added	150	10	13
Fat Boy:			
Sundae On A Stick:			
Nut Sundae	270	20	23
Toffee Crunch	280	20	26
Vanilla Dipped	260	19	22
Sandwiches: Chocolate, 3 oz	210	9	31
Cookies n' Cream 3 oz	220	8	34
Mint Chocolate Chip, 3 oz	220	9	33
Premium Vanilla, 3 oz	210	8	31
Rasp. Cheesecake, 3 oz	210	7	35
Strawberry, 3 oz	210	7	35
Fresh & Easy, Vanilla Sundae Cone	260	15	29
Fudge Bar (Nestle),			
Regular, 2.8 oz	110	2	21
Fudgesicle, Fudge Bar	100	2	17
Good Humor:			
Bars:			
Orig. Vanilla, 285 oz	250	15	27
Oreo Bar, 2.75 oz	240	13	31
Candy Center Crunch	300	21	27
Chocolate Eclair	210	9	30
Toasted Almond, 2.7 oz	210	10	27
King Cones:			
Vanilla, 2.96 oz	240	12	32
Giant:			
Triple Choc. Brownie, 5.5 oz	380	14	57
Vanilla Chocolate, 5.5 oz	360	17	48
Sandwiches: Choc. Chip Cookie	270	10	44
Giant Neapolitan, 3.35 oz	220	5	40
Giant Vanilla, 3.35 oz	220	5	40
Great Value (Walmart):			
Chocolate Fudge Sticks (2), 3.45 oz	130	1.5	28
Ice Cream Cone, Van., Choc Dipped	270	14	34
Sandwiches: Vanilla, 2.1 oz	160	5	25
Minis, Vanilla, 1.4 oz	100	3.5	16
Pops, Assorted Ice, 1.85 oz	45	0	11

Per Bar/Serving	C	F	Cb
Haagen-Dazs:			
Dark Chocolate Bar, Chocolate	280	20	22
Milk Chocolate Bars:			
Peanut Butter	310	23	21
Raspberry & Vanilla	270	18	24
Salted Caramel	290	19	27
Vanilla & Almonds	300	22	21
Vanilla	280	20	21
Snack Size:			
Coffee & Almond Crunch	190	14	15
Vanilla & Almonds	195	15	13
Healthy Choice: Fudge Bar	80	1.5	13
Mocha Swirl	90	1	17
Frozen Yogurt Bars, av.	85	1	16
Hershey's:			
Cones: Candy Bar Overload	320	12	48
Cookies & Cream; Crazy, av.	120	2	25
Incredible	250	13	28
P-Nutty	210	13	20
Pops, all flavors	35	0	10
Sandwiches:			
99 Cent Vanilla Ice Cream	210	9	30
Giant: Andes Mint	350	16	48
Neopolitan	320	14	43
Vanilla, 6 oz	300	12	43
Signature Bars: Chocolate Eclair	230	10	30
Cookies & Cream	290	15	33
Cotton Candy	280	15	33
Strawb. Shortcake	230	9	34
Hood:			
Bars: Ice Cream Bar	150	11	14
Fudge Stix	70	0	14
Harvey: Cookies 'n Cream	240	14	28
Toffee Crunch	240	14	25
Vanilla	220	13	25
Orange Cream	90	1.5	19
Hoodsie:			
Cups, Chocolate; Vanilla, 3 oz	100	5	12
Sundae Cups, 3 oz	120	5	19
Sandwich, Vanilla	170	6	28
Klondike:			
Bars: Multipacks, Per Bar			
Original Vanilla, 3 fl.oz	250	14	29
Dark Chocolate	240	14	29
Double Chocolate	250	14	29
Heath, English Toffee	230	13	27
Krunch	250	14	29
Neapolitan	240	14	29
Oreo Cookies & Cream	250	15	29
Reese's	260	16	29
Slim-A-Bear	170	9	21
Sandwiches: Each			
Chocolate; Classic Vanilla	180	4.5	31
Oreo	200	7	34

Ice Cream Bars/Pops ~ Brands (Cont)

Per Bar/Serving	C	F	Cb
Luigi's:			
Real Italian Ice: Cherry			
Lemon; Mango	100	0	26
Blue Raspberry; Watermelon	160	0	39
Swirls, av. all flavors	150	0	38
M&M's:			
Cone, Single, 2.6 oz	240	11	32
Cookie Ice Cream Sandwich, 2.8 oz	250	12	33
Magnum: Almond, 2.8 oz	270	18	24
Classic, 2.7 oz	240	16	22
Dark, 2.7 oz	240	17	20
Mint; Mochaccino, 2.7 oz	250	16	24
White, 2.7 oz	250	16	23
Minis: Double Caramel	190	11	19
Gold	170	12	15
Av. other varieties	155	11	14
Minute Maid:			
Juice Bars, all flavors	60	0	15
Soft Frozen Lemonade, all flavors	70	0	19
Nestlé:			
Bars: Crunch	180	12	18
With Sundae Center	170	10	18
Parlour, 2 oz	120	8	11
Strawberry Shortcake	210	10	31
Dibs: Crunch, 26 pieces, 3.4 oz	340	24	30
Chocolate, 3.5 oz	360	25	30
Drumsticks ~ See Page 109			
Ice Pop, Wildberry & Zesty Lemon	90	0	22
Push Up Pops, average	70	1	16
Sandwiches:			
Neapolitan	240	7	40
Vanilla	160	4	29
Toll House, Choc. Chip Cookie S'wich	380	16	54
Popsicle:			
Firecracker, all flavors (1)	35	0	9
Hello Kitty (2)	60	0	14
Marvel Heroes (1)	45	0	11
Scribblers (2)	60	0	16
SpongeBob Pop-Ups (1)	80	1	11
Slow Melts, Mighty Minis, 5 pieces	70	0	16
Reese's, P'nut Butter Ice Cream Cup, 2.45 oz	280	19	22
Skinny Cow:			
Bars: Fudge Bars	110	1	22
Minis Fudge Pops (2)	100	2	19
Truffle Bars, all flavors	100	2.5	19
Cup, Choc. Fudge Brownie, 1 ctn.	145	2	22
Snickers:			
Bars: Regular, 1.75 oz	180	11	18
Mini Bar, 4 pieces	370	22	37
Cone, 2.85 oz	250	13	29
Ice Cream Brownie, 3.3 oz	300	13	41

Per Bar/Serving	C	F	Cb
Snow Cone (Wonder), av. all, 7 fl.oz	60	0	15
So Delicious (Turtle Mountain):			
Coconut Based:			
Mini Bars, Almond	170	10	15
Soy Based:			
Fudge Bar, 2.18 oz	90	2	18
Neapolitan Mini Sandwich, 1.4oz	90	2	18
Soy Dream,			
Lil' Dreamers, Vanilla	100	4	15
Tampico, Freezer Pops, all var., 1.35 oz	30	0	7
Tofutti:			
Cuties: Chocolate	130	6	16
Cookies 'N Cream; Key Lime	130	6	17
Mint Chocolate Chip; Vanilla, av.	130	6	18
Sticks:			
Chocolate Covered Flowers Bar	180	8	23
Chocolate Fudge Treats	30	0	6
Marry Me Bar	170	8	22
Totally Fudge Pops	95	1.5	21
Trader Joe's:			
Fruit Floes: Caribbean	80	0	21
Lime	60	0	16
Strawberry	100	0	24
Bars:			
Coffee Latte & Cream, 1.4 oz	90	6	9
Mango & Cream, 1.4 oz	60	2	10
Mini Mint Sandwich, 1.4 oz	120	6	18
Turkey Hill:			
Sandwiches: Double Decker, 2.47 oz	190	7	30
Vanilla Bean, 2.47 oz	190	7	29
Sundae Cone, Van. Fudge	320	18	33
Twix Bar, 2.43 oz	250	14	28
Wegmans:			
Bars: Fudge, low fat	100	1.5	19
Vanilla, Choc Coated, 1.9 oz	160	11	14
Cones: Nutty Sundae, 2.47 oz	210	11	25
Sundae Nut, 3 oz	260	15	29
Weight Watchers:			
Bars: Choc. Dipped Strawberry	100	4	18
Dark Chocolate:			
Dulce de leche	120	4.5	19
Raspberry Cheesecake	110	4	18
Giant: Chocolate/Cookies & Cream	140	4.5	26
Fudge/Latte Bar, average	100	1	23
Cones, Choc./Dble Caramel, Snack Size	90	2	17
Cups: Chocolate Chip Cookie Dough	150	1.5	32
Mint Chocolate Chip	140	2.5	19
Sandwiches: Vanilla, Snack Size	80	1	18
Round, Vanilla	140	1.5	31
Yoplait ~ See Frozen Yogurt			
Yosicle: Duos! (2), av. all flavors	110	1.5	22
Torpedoes! (2), 2 oz	90	2	16

Canned & Packaged Meals ~ Brands

	C	F	Cb
Amy's: *Per Serve*			
Frozen:			
Asian Meals:			
Stir-Fry: Asian Noodle, 10 oz	300	7	50
Thai, 9.5 oz	310	11	45
Bowls: Baked Ziti, 9.5 oz	390	12	62
Broccoli & Cheddar Bake, 9.5 oz	430	20	44
Pesto Tortellini, 9.5 oz	440	20	40
Burritos: Bean & Cheese, 6 oz	310	9	46
Bean & Rice, 6 oz	320	8	52
Breakfast Burrito, 6 oz	270	8	38
Entrees: Cheese Enchilada, 4.5 oz	240	14	18
Cheese Lasagna, 10.3 oz	380	14	44
Macaroni & Cheese, 9 oz	400	16	47
Roasted Vegetable Lasagna, 9.8 oz	350	11	47
Light & Lean: *Per 8 oz Serve*			
Black Bean & Cheese Enchilada	240	5	44
Pasta & Veggies	210	5	33
Soft Taco Fiesta	220	4.5	40
Pot Pies:			
Broccoli, 7.5 oz	460	24	50
Mex. Tamale; Shepherd's Pie, av., 8 oz	155	3.5	27
Vegetable, 7.5 oz	430	20	54
Snacks: Nacho, Cheese & Bean, 5-6 pcs	220	8	25
Cheese Pizza, 5-6 pieces	210	7	25
Whole Meals:			
Black Bean Enchilada, 10 oz	330	8	53
Black Bean Tamale Verde, 10.5 oz	330	10	55
Southern Dinner, 9 oz	310	7	51
Veggie, Steak & Gravy, 11 oz	380	16	50
Wraps:			
Indian Samosa, 5 oz	250	9	35
Indian Spinach Tofu, 5.5 oz	270	13	28
Teriyaki, 5.5 oz	310	7	51
Atkins: *Per 9 oz Tray/Bowl*			
Frozen:			
Beef Merlot	310	21	9
Chicken & Broccoli Alfredo	330	20	9
Chili Con Carne	320	21	8
Crustless Chicken Pot Pie	330	22	8
Italian Sausage Primavera	330	25	10
Meatloaf w/ Portob. Mshrm Gravy	340	23	11
Bagel Bites:			
Frozen:			
Cheese, Ssge & Pepperoni, 4 pcs	200	6	28
Supreme; Three Cheese, av., 4 pcs, 3 oz	190	4.5	31

	C	F	Cb
B & M:			
Baked Beans: *Per 16 oz Can, ½ cup, 4.6 oz*			
Original; Vegetarian, av.	160	1	31
Barbeque	190	0.5	39
Raisin Brown Bread,			
½" slice, 2 oz	130	0.5	29
Banquet:			
Homestyle Bakes: *Includes Topping*			
Asian Style Fried Rice,			
½ filling & ¼ cup rice	240	1.5	47
Cheesy Chicken Alfredo,			
¾ cup filling & ½ cup pasta	410	21	40
Cheesy Ham & Hashbrowns,			
½ cup filling & ⅓ cup potato	290	15	30
Frozen:			
Dinners: Boneless Pork Rib, 10 oz	320	11	42
Cheesy Smothered Meat Patty, 7 oz	280	16	21
Chicken Fingers, 7 oz	480	21	56
Chicken Pasta Marinara, 6.5 oz	290	14	29
Fettuccine Alfredo, 8 oz	280	11	35
Fish Sticks, 7.5 oz	310	10	44
Fried Beef Steak, 10 oz	390	18	43
Lasagna, with Meat Sauce, 8 oz	250	7	34
Meatloaf, 9.5 oz	280	13	28
Orig. Fried Chicken, 1 pce, 4.25 oz	330	21	12
Pepperoni Pizza, 5.75	340	12	47
Salisbury Steak, 9.5 oz	250	12	24
Spaghetti & Meatballs, 9 oz	330	14	35
Spag. with Popcorn Chicken, 7 oz	270	8	37
Turkey, 9.25 oz	250	7	32
Family: Chicken Alfredo, 8 oz	210	6	29
Country Fried Chkn, 1 pce, 4.25 oz	350	24	11
Fried Chicken,			
Hot & Spicy, 1 pce, 4.25 oz	340	22	12
Lasagna, 8 oz	220	8	27
Pot Pies:			
Chicken; Turkey, av., 7 oz	375	21	35
Chicken with Broccoli, 7 oz	360	20	34
Select Recipe Dinners:			
Chicken Parmigian, 10 oz	350	15	37
Corn Dog Meal, 7.5 oz	460	16	68
Barilla:			
Microwaveables: *Per 9 oz Container*			
Mezze Penne varieties, av., 9 oz	315	4.5	59
Whole Grain varieties, av., 9 oz	315	6	59

Betty Crocker:

	C	F	Cb
Bowl Appetit:			
Cheddar Broccoli Rice	290	6	52
Homestyle Chicken Flavored Pasta	250	5	44
Pasta Alfredo	350	9	55
Teriyaki Rice	250	1	57
Three-Cheese Rotini	340	7	59
Hamburger Helper: *Per 1 Cup, Prepared*			
Beef Pasta	280	12	24
Cheeseburger Macaroni	320	13	30
Cheesy Baked Potatoes	310	12	30
Cheesy Chicken Enchiladas	350	7	42
Cheesy Italian Shells	310	12	27
Crunchy Taco	330	14	33
Salisbury	280	11	27
Helper Complete Meals: *Per 1 Cup, Prepared*			
Cheesy Beef Taco	220	5	35
Chicken & Buttermilk Biscuits	260	9	39
Chicken with Cheesy Rice & Broccoli	230	6	36
Stroganoff	230	8	33
Potatoes: *Per Serving, Prepared*			
Casserole: Au Gratin, ½ cup	150	5	24
Cheddar & Bacon, ½ c.	150	5	24
Roasted Garlic, ½ cup	140	7	17
Scalloped, ⅔ cup	130	3	23
Sour Cream and Chives, ⅔ cup	140	7	17
Flavored Potatoes, prepared, average all varieties, ⅔ cup	145	6	18
Seasoned Skillet:			
Hash Brown, ½ cup	120	4	18
Rstd Garlic & Herb Potatoes, ⅔ c.	170	9	21
Trad'nl Recipe Potatoes, ½ cup	180	9	22
Tuna Helper: *Per 1 Cup, Prepared*			
Creamy Parmesan	270	10	30
Average other varieties	260	10	30
Biggest Loser:			
Refrigerated:			
Simply Sensible: *Per ½ Package*			
Beef Pot Roast & Gravy	220	5	16
Beef Tips & Gravy	200	3.5	21
Lasagna	200	5	28
Medit.-Style Chicken	250	6	36
Zing Chicken	230	1.5	38

Birds Eye:

	C	F	Cb
Frozen:			
Voila!: *Per 1 Cup Prepared Unless Indicated*			
Alfredo Chicken, 1½ cups	280	12	37
Beef & Broccoli Stir Fry	160	6	13
Chicken Florentine	230	6	27
Chicken Parmesan	360	11	50
Garlic Shrimp	230	9	30
Shrimp Scampi	190	2.5	31
Sweet & Sour Chicken	200	1	38
Three Cheese Chicken	210	8	21
Boca:			
Frozen:			
Burger:			
All American Classic, 2.5 oz	90	2	6
Cheeseburger, 2.5 oz	100	4.5	6
Grilled Vegetables, 2.5 oz	80	1	7
Original Vegan, 2.5 oz	100	1	8
Chik'n: Orig. Nuggets, 3 oz	180	7	17
Patties (1), 2.5 oz	160	6	15
Veggie Patties, Bruschetta	90	1.5	9
Boston Market:			
Frozen:			
Dinners: Beef Steak & Noodles, 14 oz	460	14	51
Chicken Parmesan, 14.5oz	550	21	64
Oven Roasted Chicken, 16 oz	320	10	36
Salisbury Steak, 16 oz	630	35	50
Swedish M'balls, 14.5 oz	620	23	69
Buitoni: *Per ½ Package Unless Indicated*			
Refrigerated:			
Ravioli: Chicken Marsala, 1 c., 3.9 oz	280	8	36
Crab, 1 cup, 3.8 oz	300	11	36
Four Cheese, 1¼ cups, 3.7 oz	340	12	42
Tortellini: Herb Chicken, 1 c., 3.8 oz	330	8	52
Spinach Cheese, 1 cup, 3.7 oz	320	7	49
Other Varieties ~ See Page 133			
Bush's Best: *Per ½ Cup, 4.6 oz*			
Baked Beans: Original	140	1	29
Vegetarian	130	0	29
Average other varieties	150	1	32
Black Beans	105	0.5	23
Chili Beans, Pinto w/ sauce	110	1	20
Dark Red Kidney Beans	100	0	22
Garbanzo Beans	105	2	20
Grillin' Beans:			
Black Bean Fiesta	110	1	21
Sweet Mesquite	160	1	32
Texas Ranchero	120	2	20
Average other varieties	165	0.5	35
Refried Beans: Traditional	150	3	24
Fat Free	130	0	24

Campbell's:	C	F	Cb
Beans,			
Pork & Beans, ½ cup	140	1.5	25
Chunky Microwavable Bowls: *Per Cup*			
Firehouse; Roadhouse; Beef & Beans Chili	240	8	26
Spaghetti O's: *Per Cup*			
Original	170	1	35
With Meatballs	240	7	32
With Sliced Franks	220	6	32

Chef Boyardee:	C	F	Cb
Canned: *Per Cup*			
Beefaroni, 8.8 oz	250	9	34
Lasagna,			
w/ Tomato & Meat Sce, 8.8 oz	250	9	32
Ravioli,			
Beef, in Tomato & Meat Sauce:			
Original, 1 cup, 9 oz	230	7	34
99% Fat Free, 1 cup, 8.6 oz	180	2	33
Overstuffed, 9.2 oz	250	6	38
Cheese Ravioli,			
in Tomato Sauce, 8.7 oz	230	6	34
Pepperoni Pizza Ravioli,			
in Zesty Sauce, 9 oz	250	7	38
Spaghetti & Meatballs,			
in Tomato Sauce, 9 oz	260	12	28
Microwaveable: *Per 14.25 oz Bowls*			
Beef Ravioli, in Tom. & Meat Sauce, 8.7 oz	230	7	34
Mini Beef Ravioli,			
in Tomato & Meat Sauce, 8.9 oz	240	7	35
Boxed Pizza Maker Kits:			
Cheese, ⅛ package, 4 oz	260	4	47
Pepperoni, ⅛ pkg, 4 oz	280	7	45
Pizza Sauce, ¼ cup, 2 oz	35	1.5	4

Contessa:	C	F	Cb
Frozen			
World Cuisine: *Per Serving with Sauce, Prepared*			
Beef Mongolian, 12 oz	550	20	75
Chicken Alfredo, 12 oz	520	27	47
Chicken Fried Rice, 12 oz	400	6	62
Jambalaya, 12 oz	360	11	44
Paella, 11 oz	330	4.5	43
Shrimp Stir-Fry, 12 oz	220	1	36

Country Crock *(Hormel)*:	C	F	Cb
Side Dishes:			
Cheddar Broccoli Rice, 7 oz	260	11	32
Elbow Mac. & Cheese, 8 oz	330	14	38
Garlic Mashed Potato, 7 oz	140	7	18
Loaded Mashed Potatoes, 5 oz	190	11	18

Dennison's Chili: *Per Cup*	C	F	Cb
Chili Con Carne:			
Original: With Beans, 9 oz	350	15	31
Without Beans, 8.75 oz	310	16	20
Chili: Orig., with Beans, 9 oz	360	14	38
Chunky, with Beans, 8.8 oz	300	10	32
Hot, with Beans, 9 oz	350	14	36
Vegetarian, 99% fat free, 9 oz	190	1.5	34

Dinty Moore:	C	F	Cb
Big Bowl, 15 oz:			
Beef Stew, 8.32 oz	200	12	13
Chicken & Dumplings, 8.5 oz	220	7	29
Scalloped Potatoes & Ham, 8.5 oz	280	16	23
Hearty Meals, 20 oz Cans:			
Beef Stew, 8.32 oz	200	10	17
Chicken & Dumplings, 8.5 oz	230	8	28
Noodles Chicken, 8.32 oz	170	6	22
Microwave Ready:			
Beef Stew, 7.5 oz	150	6	15
Noodles Chicken, 7.5 oz	190	9	20
Scalloped Pot. & Ham, 7.5 oz cup	240	13	20

Dr. McDougall's: *Per 2 oz Package*	C	F	Cb
Asian Noodle Entree Cups: *Per Cup*			
Pad Thai, 2 oz	200	1.5	42
Spicy Szechuan, 2 oz	200	1	42
Teriyaki, 1.9 oz	200	0.5	42

Eden Organics: *Per ½ Cup (4.6 oz)*	C	F	Cb
Baked Navy Beans w/ Sorghum, Mstrd	150	0	27
Black Eyed Peas	90	1	16
Black Soy Beans	120	6	8
Refried: Black Beans	110	1.5	18
Pinto; Kidney Beans, average	85	1	17

Farmhouse:	C	F	Cb
Rice: *Per 1 Cup, Prepared*			
Chicken Flavor, 6 oz	230	5	43
Long Grain & Wild Herb & Butter	250	7	43
Mexican, 6 oz	230	5	42

French's:	C	F	Cb
French Fried Onions:			
Original; Cheddar:			
2 Tbsp, 0.25 oz	45	3.5	3
¼ cup, 0.5 oz	90	7	6
1 cup, 2 oz	360	28	24
GardenBurger:			
Frozen:			
Veggie Burger: Original, 3 oz	110	3	16
Black Bean Chipotle, 2.5 oz	90	3	16
garden lites: *Per 7 oz Serving*			
Frozen:			
Butternut Squash Souffle	180	2	35
Zucchini Marinara/Portabella	110	4	19
Gorton's:			
Frozen:			
Battered Pollock Fillets:			
Beer Battered (2), 3.6 oz	230	14	20
Crispy Battered (2), 3.8 oz	240	14	20
Lemon Pepper Battered (2), 2.7 oz	270	18	20
Breaded Pollock Fillets:			
Crunchy (2), 3.8 oz	250	13	23
Garlic & Herb (2), 3.5 oz	260	15	21
Grilled Fillets:			
Garlic Butter Pollock (1), 3.5 oz	80	3	0
Lemon Butter Salmon (1), 3.2 oz	100	3	1
Signature Tilapia (1), 3.2 oz	80	2	2
Shrimp:			
Crispy Beer Battered (9), 3.5 oz	240	12	25
Popcoron (22), 3.5 oz	260	13	26
Skillet Crisp (8), 3.35 oz	180	8	18
Great Value *(Walmart):*			
Frozen:			
Breakfast Bowls: *Per 8 oz*			
Sausage & Gravy	380	23	23
Sausage	480	33	20
Complete Skillet Meals: *Per ½ Package*			
Chicken Florentine & Farfalle	575	32	40
Shrimp Scampi & Linguini, 12 oz	550	23	58
Meals: Cheese Manicotti, 7.9 oz	320	16	24
Lasagna, 7.58 oz	280	9	36
Southwest Style Chicken & Pasta, 7.97 oz	410	22	26
Party Size:			
Mexican Style Lasagna, 7.97 oz	380	17	38
Three Cheese Ziti, 7.47 oz	280	9	35

Health Valley:	C	E	CP
Vegetarian Chili: *Per 8.65 oz Cup*			
3 Bean Chipotle	200	3	37
Black Bean Mango	210	3	41
Average other varieties	200	3	37
Heinz, Vegetarian Beans,			
½ cup, 4 oz	140	0.5	27
Healthy Choice:			
Frozen:			
100% Natural Cafe Steamers:			
Asian Potstickers, 10 oz	360	5	69
Portabella Spinach Parmesan, 9.4 oz	270	7	39
Pumpkin Squash Ravioli, 9.2 oz	310	6	52
Tortellini Primavera Parm., 9 oz	230	5	37
Asian/Mediterranean Cafe Steamers:			
Balsamic Garlic Chicken, 10 oz	250	3.5	36
Beef Teriyaki, 10 oz	300	6	44
Grilled Basil chicken, 10.6 oz	270	6	35
Baked: 4 Cheese Ziti Marin., 9.2 oz	310	5	46
Italian Sausage Pasta, 8.5 oz	270	6	40
Roasted Chicken & Potatoes, 9.7 oz	180	3.5	21
Complete Meals:			
Beef Pot Roast, 11 oz	250	6	32
Chkn Parmigiana, 11.5 oz	340	9	49
H'mestyle Salisbury Steak, 12.5 oz	320	7	45
Extra Product Listings ~ *www.CalorieKing.com*			
Hormel:			
Compleats: *Per Meal*			
Modern Classics:			
Beef & Broccoli	280	6	37
Herb Crusted Fish	270	5	40
Traditional Classics:			
Beef Pot Roast	250	6	32
Beef Strips Portabella	280	7	35
Chicken Parmigiana	340	9	49
Classic Meatloaf	330	7	51
Country Herb Chicken	250	5	34
Golden Roasted Turkey Breast	270	4	38
Honey Roasted Chicken	250	4	36
Lemon Pepper Fish	330	4	58
Oven Roasted Turkey Breast	270	4	38

continued next page...

Hormel (Cont):	C	F	Cb
Chili with Beans: *Per 8.7 oz Serving*			
Regular; Hot; Chunky	260	7	33
Turkey	210	3	28
Vegetarian	190	1	35
Chili without Beans: *Per 8.3 oz*			
Chunky/Hot Chili	215	9	19
Turkey	190	3	16
Kid's Kitchen: *Per 7 oz Microwave Cup*			
Beans & Franks	220	1	43
Beef Ravioli	230	4	38
Macaroni & Beef	230	4	35
Pasta & Chicken	170	3	27
Stars & Franks	160	1	30
Hot Pockets:			
Frozen			
Sandwiches: *Per Sandwich*			
Crispy Buttery Crust: BBQ Rcpe Beef	330	13	44
Cheeseburger	310	12	39
Ham & Cheese	300	12	37
Crispy Crust: Five Cheese Pizza	350	17	37
Pepperoni Pizza	350	19	33
Croissant Crust:			
Chicken, Broccoli & Cheddar	300	14	35
Ham & Cheese	320	16	35
Garlic Buttery Crust: Four Chse Pizza	320	13	39
Meatballs & Mozzarella	330	15	38
Pepperoni Pizza	320	15	34
Pretzel Bread,			
Bacon Chedd Chse Melt	320	14	36
Seasoned Crust: Bacon, Egg & Chse	340	15	37
Philly Steak & Cheese	310	12	38
Snackers:			
Baked Mac & Cheese Bites, 3.3 oz	220	8	28
BBQ Recipe Honey Chicken, 3.3 oz	200	5	31
Fiesta Nacho Bites, 3.3 oz	210	8	29
Hungry Jack,			
Easy Mash'd Cheesy, Homestyle,			
⅔ cup, prepared	80	0	19
Hungry Man:			
Frozen:			
Dinners: Boneless Fried Chicken	800	38	85
Boneless Pork Ribs	810	36	98
Classic Fried Chicken	1030	62	63
Country Fried Chicken	560	26	53
Home-Style Meatloaf	660	35	61

Hungry Man (Cont):	C	F	Cb
Frozen (Cont):			
Pub Favorites:			
Beer Battered Chicken	760	34	74
Grilled Beef Patty	530	32	36
Grilled Bourbon Steak Strips	480	11	71
Honey Bourbon Chicken Strips	620	24	69
XXL Sandwiches: *Per Box*			
Angus Beef Charbroil	740	47	52
BBQ Pork Ribs	690	39	62
Buffalo Fried Chicken	650	27	73
Chicken Parmesan	610	29	63
Crispy Fried Chicken	670	32	64
Hunt's, Manwich Sloppy Joe,			
Original, ¼ cup, 2.25 oz	40	0	9
José Olé:			
Frozen:			
Breakfast Burritos:			
Egg & Bacon, 4 oz	260	9	33
Egg & Sausage, 4 oz	270	10	34
Premium Burritos:			
Chicken Monterey (1)	270	6	41
Steak & Cheese (1)	300	10	40
Premium Chimichangas:			
Chicken & Cheese (1), 5 oz	330	11	45
Steak & Cheese (1), 5 oz	350	14	41
Snacks:			
Mini Chimichangas,			
Steak & Cheddar (3)	370	20	37
Mini Quesadillas,			
Grilled Chicken & 3 Cheese (4)	210	8	25
Mini Tacos, Beef & Cheese (4)	230	12	23
Taquitos: Chicken, Corn Tortillas, (3)	200	8	26
Steak & Cheese, Flour Tortillas, (2)	250	12	26
Kashi:			
Frozen:			
Steam Meals: *Per Package Unless Indicated*			
Chicken & Chipole BBQ, ½ pkg, 10 oz	310	6	50
Chicken Fettuccini, 9.5 oz	270	7	38
Roasted Garlic Chicken Farfalle, 9.5 oz	280	9	39
Sesame Chicken, 9.5 oz	300	9	42
Spinach & Artichoke Pasta, 9.5 oz	280	9	41
Kid Cuisine: *Per Meal*			
Frozen:			
Cheese Stuffed Crust Pizza	330	7	54
Chicken Breast Nuggets, 8 oz	430	18	54
Fish Stix, 7.58 oz	320	11	45
Fried Chicken, 10 oz	530	22	53
Hot Dog, 7.2 oz	320	5	55
Mac & Cheese, 10.6 oz	420	11	69
Pancakes, 7.23 oz	400	15	59
Popcorn Chicken, 8.64 oz	370	12	53
Spaghetti & Mini Meatballs, 10.2 oz	290	6	45

Knorr: Sides, Prepared as Directed	C	F	Cb
Asian: Chicken Fried Rice	290	7	48
Teriyaki Noodles	280	9	45
Teriyaki Rice	280	7	48
Cajun, Garlic Butter Rice	260	4	48
Fiesta: Mexican Rice	280	6	48
Spanish Rice	280	6	49
Taco Rice	270	6	46
Pasta: Alfredo	290	10	39
Alfredo Broccoli	300	10	39
Butter	260	6	39
Butter & Herb	260	7	39
Cheesy Cheddar	270	7	39
Parmesan	290	10	39
Stroganoff	260	7	39
Rice: Cheddar Broccoli	280	6	48
Chicken Flavor Broccoli	270	5	48
Chicken Flavor	280	6	48

Kraft:	C	F	Cb
Macaroni & Cheese Dinner: Per Cup, Prepared			
Original flavor, 2.5 oz	400	19	47
Alfredo, 2.5 oz	400	17	51
Premium White Cheddar, 2.5 oz	400	18	51
Thick 'N Creamy, 2.5 oz	410	17	50
Deluxe: Four Cheese, 3.5 oz	320	10	46
Sharp Cheddar, 3.5 oz	320	9	46
Velveeta Potatoes: Per ½ Cup, Prepared			
Cheesy: Au Gratin	190	7	24
Bacon Scalloped	200	7	27
Cheesy Mashed, Twin Pack	180	9	21
Shells & Cheese, Original, 4 oz	360	12	49

Kroger:	C	F	Cb
Kitchen Creation Skillet Dinners: Per Cup, Prepared			
Creamy Broccoli	300	12	33
Creamy Pasta	300	13	33
Double Cheeseburger	320	13	30
Lasagna	280	12	26
Stroganoff	320	14	27
Frozen:			
Healthy Meals Made Simple: Refrigerated, Per Cup			
Braised Beef Pot Roast & Gravy	220	5	15
Lean Beef Tips & Gravy	210	4	20
Lem. Herb Chkn w/ Rice	170	1.5	23
Sweet & Spicy Chicken	270	1.5	48

Kroger (Cont):	C	F	Cb
Frozen (Cont):			
Meals Made Simple:			
Beef Stir Fry, 1¾ cups	180	4	26
Chicken Florentine, 2¼ cups, 6.9 oz	320	18	22
Chicken Stir Fry, 1½ cups	180	2	25
Shrimp Fried Rice, 1¼ cups, 8 oz	240	0	44
Oven Ready:			
Breaded Calamari Rings (10), 3 oz	200	10	21
Coconut Shrimp (5), with 1 oz sweet chili sauce	350	20	34
La Choy:			
Beef Pepper Oriental, 1 cup	80	1	11
Beef Chow Mein, 1 cup	80	1	11
Chicken Chow Mein, 1 cup	100	4	11
Chow Mein Noodles, ½ cup	130	5	19
Creations: Per Cup, Prepared			
Sweet & Sour Chicken	320	4.5	46
Sweet Sesame Chicken	340	9	38
Teriyaki Chicken	310	6	40

Lean Cuisine:	C	F	Cb
Frozen:			
Culinary Collection: Per Complete Meal			
Baked Chicken	240	7	30
Beef & Broccoli	270	5	43
Beef Chow Fun	320	5	54
Beef Portabello	200	6	24
Beef Pot Roast	190	4	25
Chicken with Almonds	270	4	44
Chicken Parmesan	310	9	39
Flatbread Melts:			
Chicken Ranch Club	370	9	52
Sun-Dried Tom. Basil Chicken	360	8	52
Lemon Pepper Fish	300	8	40
Paninis: Chicken Club Panini	360	9	45
Chicken, Spinach & Mushroom	300	7	40
Philly-Style Steak & Cheese	330	9	42
Roasted Turkey & Veggies	200	7	18
Salisbury Steak	260	8	23
Shrimp Alfredo	200	4	29
Spring Rolls:			
Fajita Style Chicken (2)	200	7	20
Garlic/Thai Chicken (2), average	200	8	24
Thai Style Chicken	280	6	37

Meals ◆ Entrees ◆ Sides ~ Canned/Packaged Ⓜ

Lean Cuisine (Cont):	C	F	Cb
Frozen (Cont):			
Market Collections:			
Asiago Cheese Tortelloni	280	7	41
Chicken Margherita	310	7	40
Shanghai Style Shrimp	250	3	41
Sweet & Spicy Ginger Chicken	290	2	45
Simple Favorites:			
Asian Style Pot Stickers	260	4	49
Cheese Ravioli	230	5	34
Macaroni and Cheese	250	4	40
Spa Collection:			
Butternut Squash Ravioli	260	7	40
Lemongrass Chicken	240	4	38
Salmon with Basil	250	2	38
Pizzas ~ See Page 136			

Extra Product Listings ~ www.CalorieKing.com

Lean Pockets:			
Frozen:			
Sandwiches: Per Single Pocket			
Garlic Buttery Crust, Pepp. Pizza	290	7	42
Pretzel Bread: BBQ Recipe Chicken	260	4	42
Chicken Japaleno Cheddar	270	8	35
Three Cheese & Spinach	250	7	36
Seasoned Crust:			
Bacon, Egg & Cheese	260	9	37
Four Cheese Pizza	270	6	40
Sausage, Egg & Cheese	270	9	39
Whole Grain Crust:			
Garlic Chicken White Pizza	260	7	40
Ham & Cheese	270	8	40
Supreme Pizza	220	7	33
Three Cheese Broccoli	250	6	40

Lightlife:			
Smart Cutlets:			
Original (1), 3 oz	110	1	7
Classic Marinara, 5 oz	150	1.5	13
Spicy Sweet & Sour (1), 5 oz	210	1.5	29
Smart Wings: Buffalo (4), 3 oz	100	2.5	6
Honey BBQ (4), 3 oz	110	0	15
Smart Tenders:			
Lemon Pepper (3), 3 oz	100	0	7
Savory Chick'n (3), 3 oz	100	0	7

Lunchables:	C	F	Cb
Per Package without Drink			
Crackers Stackers:			
Bologna & American Cheese	320	17	32
Turkey & American Cheese	330	16	37
Extra Cheesy Pizza	270	9	30
Ham & Cheddar, with Crackers	260	13	22
Nachos, Cheese Dip & Salsa	380	21	40
Pizza, with Pepperoni	300	13	32
Turkey & Cheddar, with Crackers	260	13	22
Lunchmakers (Armour): Per Package			
Cheese Pizza	360	9	53
Nachos	480	17	77

Marie Callender's:			
Frozen:			
Bakes: Per Cup			
Bacon & Cheddar	360	21	30
Chicken & Rice	300	14	27
Chicken & Spinach Lasagna	320	14	33
Grilled Chicken Alfredo	270	10	30
Sundried Tomato Alfredo Pasta	280	12	24
Vermont White Cheddar Mac n Chse	350	20	31
Comfort Bakes: Per Meal			
Braised Beef Pot Roast, 11 oz	210	4	28
Chicken & Broccoli Alfredo, 10 oz	350	11	34
Three Meat & Four Cheese Lasagna 10.5 oz	370	12	42
Dinners: Per Meal			
Beef & Broccoli, 13 oz	370	9	50
Cheesy Chicken & Rice, 13 oz	380	12	45
Chicken Parmigiana, 13 oz	530	27	47
Country Fried Chicken, 16 oz	560	27	61
Golden Battered Fish Filet, 12 oz	410	11	58
Meatloaf, with Gravy, 14 oz	450	17	43
Salisbury Steak, 14 oz	420	19	39
Pasta Al Dente:			
Penne Chicken Modesto, 10 oz	410	17	43
Tortellii Romano, 10 oz	420	13	58

	C	F	Cb
Maruchan:			
Bowls, all varieties, 3.3 oz bowl	380	16	50
Ramen, Noodle Soup, 3 oz block/package, av.	380	16	52
Instant Lunch Noodles, average, 1 package	290	11	39
Yakisoba: *Per 4 oz Package*			
Chicken/Teriyaki Beef Flavor, av.	520	21	72
Sweet & Sour Flavor	560	22	78
Michael Angelo's: *Per Cup, Prepared*			
Frozen:			
Natural: Chicken Parmesan, 10 oz	390	8	51
Four Cheese Lasagna, 10 oz	410	13	47
Meat Lasagna, 10 oz	400	11	45
Stuffed Manicotti, with Sauce, 10 oz	380	15	36
Signature: Chicken Alfredo, 11 oz	410	23	47
Herb Roasted Chicken, 5.4 oz	110	3.5	6
Shrimp Scampi, 10 oz	540	28	46
Minute Rice:			
Ready To Serve: *Per 4.4 oz Container, Prepared*			
Brown/Chicken Rice Mix, average	230	5	42
White/Yellow Rice	195	4	38
Steamers: *Per 1 Cup, 6.5 oz*			
Broccoli & Cheese Rice	200	3.5	37
Spanish Rice	280	6	51
Morningstar Farms:			
Frozen:			
Burgers: *Per Patty*			
Grillers Original (1)	130	6	5
Mushroom Lovers (1)	110	5	6
Spicy Black Bean (1)	110	4	13
Entrees: *Per Entree*			
Lasagna, with Sausage-Style Crumbles 10 oz	270	6	14
Three-Bean Chili, w/ Griller's Crumbles,1 cup, 9 oz	170	2.5	32
Chik'n: Buffalo Wings (5)	200	9	19
Chik'n Nuggets (4)	190	9	19
Patties: Chik, Original (1)	140	5	16
Grillers Chik'n Veggie (1)	80	3	7
Newman's Own:			
Frozen:			
Skillets: *Per ½ Package, 12 oz*			
Chicken: Fettuccine Alfredo	410	12	49
Florentine & Farfalle	370	10	42
Parmigiana & Penne	490	25	47
Italian Sausage & Rigatoni	510	28	48

	C	F	Cb
Nissin:			
Chow Mein: *Per 4 oz Package*			
Chicken Flavor	480	18	70
Spicy Chicken Flavor	560	30	64
Teriyaki Beef	520	20	68
With Shrimp	540	24	68
Cup Noodles:			
Beef/Chicken/Shrimp, 1 cup	300	13	38
Top Ramen, average, 3 oz pkg	380	14	52
Old El Paso:			
Dinner Kits: *Per Serving, Prepared with Chicken*			
Chicken Soft Taco	300	10	30
Enchilada	390	16	27
Mexian Style Rolls:			
Cheese Quesadillas (6), 3 oz	210	9	26
Cheesy Taco Flavor (6), 3 oz	210	8	26
Tortilla Stuffer, Garlic Chili Chicken, with meat, ⅓ cup, 1.75 oz	80	2	11
Pasta Roni: *Per Cup, Prepared*			
Angel Hair Pasta varieties, average	310	14	40
Butter & Herb Italiano	300	11	41
Chicken & Broccoli	360	15	49
Chicken Flavor	300	12	40
Fettuccine Alfredo	450	24	44
Four Cheese Corkscrew	370	15	49
Stroganoff	350	13	48
Tomato Parmesan	270	9	40
White Cheddar & Broccoli	300	13	39
P.F. Chang's: *Per ½ Package, 11 oz*			
Frozen:			
Beef with Broccoli	390	20	30
General Chang's Chicken	390	13	51
Mongolian Style Chicken	350	9	43
Orange Chicken	450	16	58
Sweet & Sour Chicken	370	10	58
Szehuan Style Shrimp	280	8	39

Most packaged noodle soups are high in calories and fat.

Their promotion of '0 Grams Trans Fat' does not make them heart-healthy.

They are still high in saturated fat as well as salt/sodium.

Rice-A-Roni:	C	F	Cb
Classic Favorites: *Per Cup, Prepared*			
Beef; Herb & Butter; Rice Pilaf, av.	310	9	52
Broccoli Au Gratin	350	16	46
Chicken Flavor	300	9	50
Chicken & Broccoli	220	5	40
Spanish Rice	260	8	44
Nature's Way: Ital. Cheese & Herb	340	12	52
Long Grain & Wild Rice	250	7	43
Parmesan & Romano Cheese	280	9	42
Whole Grain Blends:			
Chicken & Herb Classico	260	8	41
Roasted Garlic Italiano	270	9	41
Spanish	250	8	42

Rosarita:	C	F	Cb
Kidney Beans, ½ cup, 4.5 oz	110	0	20
Chili Beans, ½ cup, 4.6 oz	130	0.5	24
Refried Beans: *Per ½ Cup*			
Traditional	120	2	18
Non-Fat, Refried Beans	100	0	18

Safeway Select:	C	F	Cb
Frozen:			
Beef Salisbury Steak, 9.35 oz	410	28	23
Chicken Cacciatore, 8.75 oz	290	10	34
Fettucini Alfredo, 11.5 oz	380	12	55
Five Vegetable Lasagna, 10.6 oz	330	8	48
Homestyle Baked Chicken, 9 oz	260	11	31
Orange Chicken, 9 oz	360	7	61
Penne Pasta, 8 oz	300	11	42
Pot Roast, 9 oz	270	11	23
Spaghetti with Meat Sauce, 12 oz	450	16	61
Swedish Meat Balls, 11.5 oz	470	24	48
Three Cheese Tortellini, 7.5 oz	350	16	38

S & W: *Per ½ Cup*	C	F	Cb
Black Beans, 4.5 oz	110	0.5	22
Chili Beans,			
in Zesty Tomato Sauce, 4.55 oz	130	1.5	23
Kidney Beans, 4.65 oz	110	0	22
White Beans, 4.5 oz	110	0.5	21

Seapak ~ *See www.calorieking.com*

Simply Asia:	C	F	Cb
Noodle Bowls: *Per 8.5oz Bowl*			
Roasted Peanut	460	12	75
Sesame Teriyaki	390	13	82
Soy Ginger	420	6	84
Spicy Mongolian	430	6	86

Simply Asia (Cont):	C	F	Cb
Noodles & Sauce: *Per ⅓ package*			
Sesame Teriyaki	300	3	60
Soy Ginger	320	4.5	60
Spicy Kung Pao	350	7	63
Quick Noodles: *Per 8.8 oz Tray*			
Honey Teriyaki	430	3.5	85
Pad Thai	460	3	93
Szechwan Garl. Chow Mein	460	7	83

Smart Ones *(Weight Watchers):*	C	F	Cb
Frozen:			
Classic Favorites: *Per Meal*			
Angel Hair Marinara	200	4	34
Chicken Enchiladas Suiza	290	5	49
Lasagna with Meat Sauce	250	5	39
Lasagna Florentine	320	10	44
Lemon Herb Chicken Piccata	250	2	45
Macaroni & Cheese	260	2	50
Pasta Primavera	250	4	41
Pasta with Ricotta & Spinach	290	6	44
Ravioli Florentine	270	5	43
Salisbury Steak	230	8	21
Spaghetti with Meat Sauce	250	5	39
Swedish Meatballs	270	6	35
Three Cheese Macaroni	300	6	48
Traditional Lasagna w/ Meat Sauce	290	6	44
Tuna Noodle Gratin	220	3.5	38
Smart Beginnings: *Per Meal*			
Breakfast Quesadilla	230	7	29
Canad. Bacon English Muffin	210	6	27
English Muffin S'wich	210	5	28
Three Cheese Omelet	210	8	18
Smart Creations: *Per Meal*			
Chicken Fettucini	290	6	40
Chicken Parmesan	290	6	35
Homestyle Turkey Breast,			
with Stuffing	260	5	39
Meatloaf	230	6	23
Teriyaki Chicken & Vegetables	250	3	43

So Yah!:	C	F	Cb
Tofu Shirataki Fettuccine:			
Creamy Coconut Curry	190	10	21
Sesame Ginger Sauce	170	8	19

Stagg Chili:

	C	F	Cb
Chili with Beans: *14.3 oz Can, 1 cup*			
Classic	330	17	27
Chunkero	320	16	28
Dynamite Hot	340	17	30
Fiesta Grille	280	13	25
Ranch House Chicken	240	8	26
White Chicken Chili	260	12	20
Low-Fat: Turkey Ranchero, 1 cup	250	5	32
Vege Garden Four-Bean, 1 cup	200	1	37
No Beans, Steakhouse, 1 cup	320	22	14

Stouffer's:
Frozen:
Satisfying Servings For One: *Per Package*

	C	F	Cb
Baked Ziti	520	18	68
Bourbon Steak Tips	490	17	61
Chicken Fettuccini Alfredo	840	38	94
Five Cheese Lasagna	330	14	33
Lasagna Italiano	290	12	30
Lasagna with Meat & Sauce	260	9	28
Macaroni & Cheese	340	16	36
Meatloaf	530	26	40
Monterey Chicken	530	21	54
Salisbury Steak	630	34	41
Savory Beef & Vegetables	360	16	34
White Meat Chicken Pot Pie	590	34	54

Signature Classics For One: *Per Package*

	C	F	Cb
Baked Chicken Breast	240	8	17
Beef Pot Roast	320	8	41
Beef Stroganoff	380	17	34
Cheesy Spaghetti Bake	460	24	39
Creamed Chipped Beef	140	7	11
Fettuccini Alfredo	630	35	63
Green Pepper Steak	240	4	34
Meatloaf	320	16	23
Salisbury Steak	360	19	22
Spaghetti with Meatballs	360	12	45
White Meat Chicken Pot Pie	670	38	64

Simple Dishes For One:

	C	F	Cb
Cheddar Potato Bake, ½ pkg	270	17	21
Creamed Spinach, ½ pkg	200	16	8
Macaroni & Cheese, ½ pkg	340	16	33
Spinach Souffle, ⅓ pkg	150	10	9

Stouffer's (Cont):
Frozen:
Skillets For Family: *Per ½ Package*

	C	F	Cb
Broccoli & Beef	350	6	57
Cheesy Meatball Rigatoni	470	21	48
Chicken Alfredo	410	10	48
Chicken & Dumplings	370	13	40
Garlic Chicken	330	6	45
Garlic Shrimp	310	10	40
Grilled Chicken & Vegetables	360	9	43
Homestyle Beef	340	12	37
Savory Chicken & Rice	330	6	50
Teriyaki Chicken	270	4	41
Yankee Pot Roast	300	8	38

Swanson:
Frozen:
Dinners: *Per Package*

	C	F	Cb
Chicken Nuggets	590	25	71
Rib Style Boneless Pork	540	23	71
Salisbury Steak	450	22	44

Skillets: Alfredo Chicken

	C	F	Cb
Alfredo Chicken	370	12	42
Beef Lo Mein	360	6	55
Chicken Parmesan	430	14	60
Garlic Chicken	420	15	51
Teriyaki Chicken	290	2.5	51

Tasty Bite:
Vegetarian Entrees: *Per ½ Package, 5 oz*

	C	F	Cb
Bengal Lentils	160	6	20
Bombay Potatoes	130	4	19
Jaipur Vegetables	180	11	12
Jodhpur Lentils	110	2.5	16
Madras Lentils	150	6	18
Punjab Eggplant	150	9	13

TGI Friday's:
Frozen:

	C	F	Cb
Beer Battered Onion Rings, 3 rings	180	8	26
Boneless Chicken Bites, with Buffalo Sauce, 6 pieces	150	3.5	16
Cheese & Bacon Loaded Fries, 3 oz	210	11	20
Chicken Parmesan Sliders, 3.1 oz	260	13	27
Cream Cheese Stuffed Jalap., 2.7 oz	230	12	19
Dill Pickle Chips, w/ Horseradish Sce	200	11	22
Mozzarella Sticks, with Marinara Sauce, 1 stick	100	5	10
Potato Skins, Cheddar & Bacon (3)	200	10	21

Thai Kitchen:

	C	F	Cb
Take-Out Meals: *Per ½ Package*			
Original Pad Thai	250	2	54
Thai Basil & Chili	250	3	50
Thai Peanut	270	5	51
Noodle Carts: *Per 9 oz Tray*			
Pad Thai	460	2	104
Thai Peanut	510	9	96
Rice Noodle Soup Bowls,			
all varieties, average, 2.5 oz	240	2	50
Stir-Fry Rice Noodles: *Per ½ Package*			
Original Pad Thai	390	3.5	84
Thai Peanut	390	2	87

Tofurky:

	C	F	Cb
Deli Slices: Pepperoni, 8 slices, 1 oz	60	0.5	6
Roast Beef; Bologna, 3 slices, 1.8 oz	100	3	5
Holidays: Tofky Roast & Gravy, ⅕ pkt	590	11	46
Tofurky Feast, ⅙ package, 5.2 oz	300	7	16
Sausages: Beer Brats (1), 3.5 oz	260	13	8
Italian Sausage (1), 3.5 oz	270	13	12
Kielbasa (1), 3.5 oz	240	12	12

Trader Joe's:

	C	F	Cb
Baked Beans, Organic,			
all varieties, average, ½ cup	140	0	29
Black Beans:			
Regular, ½ cup	110	0	19
Cuban Style, ½ cup	100	0.5	19
Chicken Chili with Beans, 1 cup	290	9	32
Pasta, Shells & White Cheddar, 1 cup	280	6	47
Potatoes: Garlic Mashed, ½ cup	150	7	19
Cheddar Cheese Au Gratin, ½ cup	140	5	21
Turkey Chili w/ Beans, 1 cup	240	4.5	30
Frozen:			
Butter Chicken w/ Basmati Rice, 1 cup	270	8	33
Chicken Chow Mein, ⅓ package, 6.7 oz	210	2	35
Chicken Quesadilla (1), 6 oz	320	16	26
Citrus Glazed Chicken with Rice, 8 oz	270	5	40
Mac & Cheese: Regular, 1 cup, 7 oz	360	15	42
Reduced Guilt, 7 oz	270	6	40
Shrimp Stir Fry, 6.4 oz	70	0.5	6
Spaghetti & Beef Meatballs,			
1 cup, 9 oz	380	14	48
Spicy Beef & Broccoli,			
1.75 cups	430	13	64
Thai Vegetable Kao Soi, 12.6 oz	430	20	55
Vegetable Pad Thai, 10.5 oz tray	520	21	74
Pies: Chicken Pot Pie, ½ pie, 8 oz	360	22	28
Shepherd's Pie, 1 cup, 8 oz	170	3	21

Tyson:

Frozen:

	C	F	Cb
Any'tizers Snacks:			
H'style Chicken Fries (7), 3.2 oz	230	13	14
Stuffed Chicken Cordon Bleu,			
Minis, 3 pieces, 3 oz	200	12	11
Wings: Buffalo Style Hot Wings			
bone-in, 3 oz	190	13	3
Honey BBQ, 3 oz	190	12	8
Hot & Spicy, 3 oz	190	13	1
Wyngz, Boneless: Buffalo Style, 3 pcs	150	7	8
Honey BBQ, 3 oz	200	8	20
Mango Habanero Flavored, 3 oz	140	6	11
Better For You: *Per 3 oz Serving*			
Grilled & Ready Chicken Breast Strips:			
Regular	100	2.5	1
Fajita	110	4	1
Honey BBQ Seasoned			
Southwestern	100	2.5	2
Grilled & Ready,			
Seasoned Steak Strips	140	6	1
Heat & Eat:			
Beef: Pot Roast in Gravy	180	8	4
Seasoned Meatloaf	320	23	16
Steak Tips: In Bourbon Sauce	190	5	17
In Burgundy Sauce	170	9	7
Ham, Maple & Brown Sugar Glazed,			
5 oz	180	3.5	18
Pork: Roast, in gravy, 5 oz	190	10	5
Loin in Sweet Tangy BBQ Sce, 5 oz	190	7	15
To Go Products:			
Mini Chicken Sandwich:			
Original, breaded	390	16	46
With Cheese	440	20	47
BBQ, pulled	310	8	40
Buffalo style, grilled	300	8	37

Uncle Ben's:

	C	F	Cb
Country Inn: *Per Cup, Prepared with Water Only*			
Broccoli Rice Au Gratin	200	2.5	41
Chicken & Vegetable Rice	200	1.5	44
Chicken Flavored Rice	200	1	41
Oriental Style Rice	200	1	43
Long Grain & Wild Rice: *Per Cup, Prep'd w/ Water Only*			
Original	190	0.5	42
Herb Roasted Chicken	200	1.5	41
Roasted Garlic & Olive Oil	210	1	43
Ready Rice: *Per Package, Heat & Serve*			
Butter & Garlic Flavored	220	4	41
Garden Vegetable	200	2.5	41
Roasted Chicken Flavored	210	3	42
Teriyaki Style	220	3	42

continued next page...

Uncle Ben's (Cont):	**C**	**F**	**Cb**
Ready Whole Grain Medley,		
average all varieties, 1 pkt	210	3	41
Van Camp's:		
Baked Beans,		
Original, ½ cup, 4.75 oz	160	1	30
Beanee Weenees, Smkd Hickory, 7.75 oz	320	9	45
Pork & Beans, 28 oz can, ½ cup, 4.6 oz	110	1	23
Van De Kamp's:		
Frozen:		
Battered Crispy Pollock Fillets, 3.9 oz	210	3.5	21
Beer Battered Fillets, 3.8 oz	210	10	21
Breaded: Butterfly Shrimp, 4 oz	330	16	31
Crunch Popcorn Fish, 4.12 oz	270	13	25
Crunchy Fish Fillets, 1.75 oz	90	4	13
Crunchy Fish Sticks, 3.35 oz	230	10	22
Whole Foods (365):		
Chickenless Nuggets,		
breaded (4), 2.8 oz	180	7	16
Meatless Meatballs, 2 oz	110	4	9
Meatless Burgers (1), 2.5 oz	120	4.5	7
Pasta Rings in Tomato Sauce, 1 cup	150	1	31
Vegetarian Chili, 1 cup	130	2	25
Worthington/Loma Linda:		
Big Franks: 1 link, 1.8 oz	110	6	3
Low-fat, 1 link, 1.8 oz	80	2.5	3
Chili, 1 cup, 8.10 oz	280	10	25
Choplets, 2 slices, 3.2 oz	90	1	4
Diced Chik, 2 oz	50	0	2
FriChik, Original, low fat, 2 pieces, 3 oz	80	2.5	4
Linketts (1), 1.25 oz	70	4	1
Little Links (2), 1.6 oz	90	5	3
Redi-Burger, ⅝" slice, 3 oz	120	2.5	7
Super Links (1), 1.5 oz	110	8	2
Tender Rounds (6), 2.8 oz	120	4.5	6
Vegetable Skallops, ½ cup, 3 oz	90	1	4
Vegetarian Burger, ¼ cup, 1.9 oz	70	1.5	4
Veja-Links (1), 1 oz	50	3	1
Frozen:		
Chic-ketts, 2 slices	110	5	3
Dinner Roast, ¾" slice	180	11	6
FriPats, 1 pattie, 2.25 oz	130	6	5
Leanies, 1 link, 1.4 oz	100	7	2
Meatless:		
Chicken Style Roll, ⅜" slice	90	4.5	2
Smoked Turkey Roll, ⅜" slice	130	8	4
Prosage Links (2), 1.6 oz	80	3	3
Stakelets, 2.5 oz piece	150	7	7
Stripples, 2 strips, 0.56 oz	60	4.5	2

Yves Veggie Cuisine:	**C**	**F**	**Cb**
Refrigerated/Frozen:		
Brats:		
Veggie Classic (1), 3.5 oz	160	5	9
Zesty Italian (1), 3.5 oz	150	5	9
Breakfast:		
Patties (2), 1.8 oz	80	2	4
Canadian Bacon, 3 slices	80	0.5	2
Burgers: Meatless Beef Burger (1)	110	4	8
Meatless Chicken (1)	100	3	5
Deli Slices:		
Meatless: Bologna, 4 slices	80	2.5	2
Ham, 4 slices	100	2	5
Pepperoni, 6 slices	80	1	4
Roast without the Beef, 4 slices	110	2.5	4
Salami, 4 slices	80	0	4
Smoked Chicken, 4 slices	100	1.5	5
Turkey, 4 slices	100	1.5	5
Ground Rounds:		
Meatless: Turkey, ⅓ cup, 1.95 oz	60	1	4
Taco Stuffers, ⅓ cup, 1.95 oz	90	2.5	5
Hot Dog:		
Good Dog (1), 2 oz	70	3.5	1
Hot Dog (1), 1.5 oz	50	0.5	2
Jumbo Hot Dog (1), 2.75 oz	110	3	5
Tofu Dog (1), 1.5 oz	45	1	2
Skewers & Strips:		
Chicken Skewers (1)	100	1	7
Meatless Beef/Chicken Strips,		
average, 2.8 oz	115	1	4
Veggie:		
Shrimp, 3 oz	50	1.5	8
Shrimp Scampi, 3.5 oz	100	7	8
Tuna, Sesame Ginger, 3.5 oz	250	20	8
Zatarain's:		
New Orleans Style: *Per Dry Mix Only*		
Black Beans & Rice, Original, 2.3 oz	220	0.5	47
Caribbean Rice Mix, 3 Tbsp	160	1	34
Chicken Creole Rice Mix, 1.34 oz	140	1	29
Chicken Flavor Rice, 2 oz	210	0.5	44
Garlic & Herb & Rice Mix, 1.34 oz	130	0.5	29
Rice Pilaf, 2.5 oz	250	1	54
Smothered Chicken Rice Mix, 1.6 oz	160	0.5	34
Yellow Rice, 2 oz	200	0.5	44
Frozen:		
Meals: *Per 10.5 oz Serve Unless Indicated*		
Blackened Chicken Alfredo	500	21	56
Jambalaya Flavored w/ Ssge, 12 oz	490	10	86
Red Beans & Rice w/ Sausage, 12 oz	540	17	79

Note: Cooking reduces weight of meat by 20-45% due to water and fat losses. Average weight loss is 30%. Actual loss depends on cooking method and cooking time.

Examples:

4 oz raw weight = approx. 3 oz cooked weight

4 oz cooked weight = approx. 5½ oz raw weight

What 3 oz Cooked Meat Looks Like:

• Rectangular piece (4" x 2½" x ½" thick)

• Deck of cards (3½" x 2½" x ⅝" thick)

Quick Guide

Sirloin (Choice Grade):
External fat trimmed to ⅛"
Broiled, Edible Portion (no bone)

C   F   Cb

Small/Regular Serving, 3 oz, cooked weight:
(from 4-4½ oz raw)

	C	F	Cb
Lean + external fat (⅛"), 3 oz	220	13	0
Lean + marbling, 3 oz	185	9	0
Lean only, 3 oz	160	6	0

(No external fat or marbling)

Medium Serving, 5 oz, cooked weight:
(from approximately 7 oz raw)

Lean + external fat (⅛"), 5 oz	365	22	0
Lean + marbling, 5 oz	310	15	0
Lean only, 5 oz	265	10	0

Large Serving, 8 oz, cooked weight:
(from approximately 11-12 oz raw)

Lean + external fat (⅛"), 8 oz	585	36	0
Lean + marbling, 8 oz	500	24	0
Lean only, 8 oz	425	15	0

Extra Large Serving, 12 oz, cooked weight:
(from approximately 16-17 oz raw)

Lean + external fat (⅛"), 12 oz	875	54	0
Lean + marbling, 12 oz	745	36	0
Lean only, 12 oz	640	22	0

Pan Fried:
Sirloin (Choice), medium serving,

Lean + external fat (⅛"), 5 oz	445	30	0

Other Steaks

C   F   Cb

Filet Mignon (Tenderloin):
1 Medium steak, 6 oz raw weight:
Broiled, with ¼" fat trim:

Lean + fat (¼"), 4 oz	360	27	0
Lean only, 3.5 oz	230	12	0

New York/Club Steak:
Top Loin/Short Loin:
1 steak, regular (9.25 oz raw, ¼" fat):

Broiled: Lean + fat (¼"), 6.25 oz	580	43	0
Lean + marbling, 5.5 oz	400	25	0
Lean only, 5.25 oz	360	20	0

Porterhouse Steak:
1 Medium, 6 oz raw weight, without bone, broiled:

Lean + fat (¼"), 4.25 oz	410	33	0
Lean only, 3.5 oz	210	11	0

1 Large, 12 oz raw weight, without bone, broiled:

Lean + fat (¼") 8.5 oz cooked	820	66	0
Lean only, 7 oz cooked	420	22	0

T-Bone Steak: *Broiled or Grilled*
Medium Size: *8 oz raw weight, without bone*
Approximately 6 oz cooked:

Lean + fat (¼"), 5 oz	400	28	0
Lean only, 4 oz	265	12	0

Large Size: *12 oz raw weight*
Approximately 9 oz cooked:

Lean + fat (¼"), 7 oz, without bone	560	39	0
Lean only, 6 oz, without bone	400	18	0

Extra Large Size: *20 oz raw weight*
Approximately 16 oz cooked:

Lean + Fat (¼"), 12 oz, without bone	960	66	0
Lean Only, 10 oz, without bone	660	30	0

Also See Fast-Foods & Restaurants Section ~
Lone Star Steakhouse; Outback Steakhouse

Beef – Individual Cuts

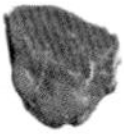

Average All Grades
Edible Weight, Without Bone

		C	F	Cb
Brisket, whole, braised:				
Lean + fat (¼" trim), 3 oz		330	27	0
Lean + marbling, 3 oz		250	17	0
Lean only, 3 oz		185	9	0
Chuck blade, braised:				
Lean + fat (¼"), 3 oz		310	24	0
Lean + marbling, 3 oz		295	22	0
Lean only, 3 oz		245	13	0
Flank: Raw, 4 oz		175	8	0
Braised, 3 oz		225	14	0
Broiled, 3 oz		155	6	0
Round, bottom, braised:				
Lean + marbling, 3 oz		190	7.5	0
Lean only, 3 oz		185	6.5	0
Round, eye/tip, rstd:				
Lean + fat (¼"), 3 oz		205	11	0
Lean, w/ marbling, 3 oz		150	5	0
Round, top: *Per 3 oz, Cooked Weight*				
Braised, Lean + fat		210	10	0
Lean only		170	4	0
Broiled, Lean + fat		180	8	0
Lean only		160	5	0
Pan-fried, Lean + fat		235	13	0
Lean only		195	7	0

Beef Ribs

	C	F	Cb
Back Ribs: *7" long, visible fat trimmed to ¼"*			
10.3 oz raw w/ bone or 3.5 oz cooked, braised, w/o bone			
1 average rib	410	34	0
3 ribs	1230	102	0
Short Ribs: *2½" long, visible fat trimmed to ¼"*			
6 oz raw with bone or 2.52 oz cooked, braised, w/o bone			
1 average rib	320	28	0
3 ribs	960	85	0

Ground Beef

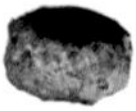

	C	F	Cb
Ground Beef, Raw: *Per 4 oz*			
70% lean (30% fat)	380	34	0
75% lean (25% fat)	335	29	0
80% lean (20% fat)	290	23	0
85% lean (15% fat)	245	17	0
90% lean (10% fat)	200	12	0
95% lean (5% fat)	155	6	0
Baked/Broiled: Regular (70%), 3 oz	230	16	0
Lean (80%), 3 oz	215	14	0
Extra lean (90%), 3 oz	185	10	0
Pan-Broiled:			
Regular (70%), 3 oz	230	15	0
Lean (80%), 3 oz	210	14	0
Extra lean (90%), 3 oz	195	10	0
Ground Beef Patties: *Average, 23% Fat*			
Raw, 4 oz	330	25	0
Broiled, 3 oz (from 4 oz raw)	250	19	0

Quick Guide

Roast Beef	C	F	Cb
Round (Eye/Tip, average): *Average All Cuts*			
Small/Regular Serving: *3 oz*			
(2 thin slices/1 thick slice)			
Lean + fat (⅛" fat trim)	180	9	0
Lean only	145	4	0
Medium Serving: *5 oz*			
(3-4 thin slices)			
Lean + fat (⅛" fat trim)	300	15	0
Lean only	245	6.5	0
Large Serving, 8 oz: *3 thick slices*			
Lean + fat (⅛" fat trim)	480	24	0
Lean only	385	11	0

Roast Dinner Extras

	C	F	Cb
Gravy: Thin, 2 Tbsp	20	0.5	3.5
Thick, 2 Tbsp	50	2	0.5
1 Ladle/4 Tbsp	100	4	1
Veggies: Beans, green, ½ cup	20	0	5
Cauliflower with cheese sauce, 4 oz	135	9	15
Corn, kernels, ¼ cup	35	0	9
Carrots, ¼ cup	20	0	3
Peas, ¼ cup	35	0	6
Potato:			
Baked in jacket: Plain, 1 large	280	0	63
With sour cream, 2 Tbsp	270	5	64
With whipped butter, 1 Tbsp	350	8	63
Roasted with fat, 1 small	155	8	30
Sweet Potato/Yam, 1 medium	105	1	24
Yorkshire Pudding, 1 oz	90	3.5	11
Beef Kebab: *Cooked*			
Beef & Veggies, 2 oz	160	10	4
If very lean meat	100	4	4

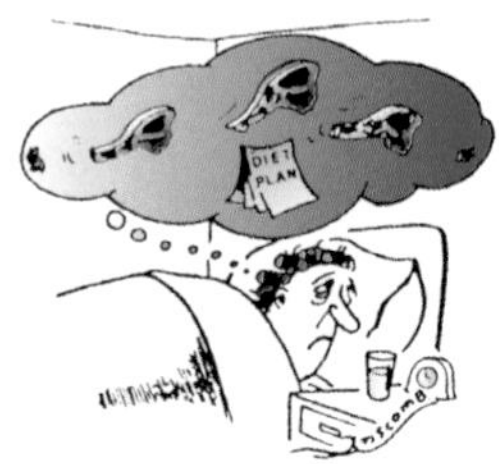

"347 ~ 348 ~ 349..."

Lamb

	C	F	Cb
Choice Grade:			
Leg (Whole), roasted:			
Lean + fat, 3 oz	220	14	0
Lean only, 3 oz	160	7	0
Leg (Sirloin Half), roasted:			
Lean + fat, 3 oz	250	18	0
Lean only, 3 oz	175	8	0
Leg (Shank Half), roasted:			
Lean + fat, 3 oz	190	11	0
Lean only, 3 oz	155	6	0
Loin Chop, broiled:			
1 chop (raw weight, 4.25 oz):			
Lean + fat (2.25 oz edible)	180	12	0
Lean only (1.6 oz edible)	85	3.5	0
Rib Chop, broiled:			
1 chop (raw wt., 3.5 oz):			
Lean + fat (2.5 oz edible)	255	21	0
Lean only (1.75 oz edible)	105	6	0
Shoulder (Arm/Blade):			
Braised: Lean + fat, 3 oz	295	21	0
Lean only, 3 oz	240	12	0
Broiled: Lean + fat, 3 oz	240	17	0
Lean only, 3 oz	170	8	0
Roasted: Similar to Broiled			
Cubed Lamb (Leg/Shoulder):			
For stew or kebab:			
Braised, lean only, 3 oz	190	8	0
Broiled, lean only, 3 oz	160	6	0

Veal

	C	F	Cb
Edible Weights:			
Leg (Top Round):			
Braised: Lean + fat, 3 oz	180	6	0
Lean only, 3 oz	175	5	0
Pan-fried, breaded:			
Lean + fat, 3 oz	195	8	9
Lean only, 3 oz	185	6	9
Pan-fried, not breaded:			
Lean + fat, 3 oz	180	7	0
Lean only, 3 oz	155	4	0
Roasted: Lean + fat, 3 oz	135	4	0
Lean only, 3 oz	130	3	0

Veal (Cont)

	C	F	Cb
Loin Chop: *1 chop, 7 oz raw weight*			
Braised: Lean + fat, 3 oz	240	15	0
Lean only, 3 oz	190	8	0
Roasted: Lean + fat, 3 oz	185	11	0
Lean only, 3 oz	150	6	0
Rib, roasted: *Lean + fat, 3 oz*	195	12	0
Lean only, 3 oz	150	7	0
Shoulder, Arm/Blade, roasted:			
Lean + fat, 3 oz	155	7	0
Lean only, 3 oz	140	5	0
Sirloin, roasted:			
Lean + fat, 3 oz	170	9	0
Lean only, 3 oz	145	6	0
Cubed for Stew, braised:			
Leg/Shoulder, lean only, 3 oz	160	4	0
(1 lb raw yields approximately 9.25 oz cooked)			

Pork

	C	F	Cb
Fresh Pork: *Cooked Weight, without bone):*			
4 oz raw weight = approx. 3 oz cooked weight			
Blade Steak, broiled:			
Lean + fat, 3 oz	220	15	0
Lean only, 3 oz	190	11	0
Country Style Ribs, broiled/roasted:			
Lean + fat, 3 oz	280	22	0
Lean only, 3 oz	210	13	0
Spareribs, braised: *Lean & fat, 6 oz*			
(from 1 lb raw weight)	675	52	0
Leg (Ham), whole, roasted:			
Lean + fat, 3 oz	230	15	0
Lean only, 3 oz	180	8	0
Loin Chops, broiled: *Average*			
(From 1 chop: 5 oz raw weight with bone			
or 4 oz raw weight, without bone)			
Lean + fat, 3 oz	200	11	0
Lean only, 3 oz	165	7	0
Loin Roast, roasted:			
Lean + fat, 3 oz	210	13	0
Lean only, 3 oz	180	8	0
Rib Chops, (Boneless), broiled:			
Lean + fat, 3 oz	220	14	0
Lean only, 3 oz	185	9	0
Rib Roast:			
Lean + fat, 3 oz	215	13	0
Lean only, 3 oz	180	9	0

Pork (Cont) | C | F | Cb

Sirloin Chop, broiled:

	C	F	Cb
Lean + fat, 3 oz	180	8	0
Lean only, 3 oz	165	6	0

Sirloin Roast, roasted:

Lean + fat, 3 oz	175	8	0
Lean only, 3 oz	170	7	0

Tenderloin (Boneless), roasted:

Lean + fat, 3 oz	125	4	0
Lean only, 3 oz	120	3	0

Ground Pork:

Raw, average, ¼ lb, 4 oz	300	24	0
Broiled, 3 oz	250	18	0
Pan-fried, drained, 3 oz	260	19	0

Bacon

Raw: 1 med. slice, 0.75 oz	95	9	0
1 thick slice, 1⅓ oz	175	17	0
(1 lb raw yields approximately 5 oz cooked)			

Broiled/Pan-Fried:

1 medium slice, 0.3 oz	40	3	0
3 medium slices, 0.8	125	10	0
2 thin slices, 0.5 oz	75	6	0
1 thick slice, 0.85 oz	65	5	0

Canadian Bacon:

Cooked: 1 slice, 1 oz	45	2	0.5
2 slices, 2 oz	90	4	1
Bacon Bits, 1 Tbsp, 0.25 oz	35	2	0
Breakfast Strips, Broiled, 1 sl., 0.42 oz	50	4	0

Ham | C | F | Cb

Boneless Ham, cooked:

Regular, (approximately 13% fat):

Roasted, 3 oz	150	8	0
Extra Lean (5% fat), Roasted, 3 oz	125	5	0

Whole Ham, cooked:

Lean + fat (as purchased) Roasted, 3 oz	210	15	0
Lean only, Roasted, 3 oz	135	5	0

Canned Ham: Similar to boneless ham

Chopped, canned, 3 oz	200	16	0
Ham Patties, cooked, (1), 2.25 oz	220	20	1
Ham Steak, extra lean, 2 oz	70	2.5	0

Lunch Slices ~ See Deli Meats, Page 128

Game & Other Meats | C | F | Cb

Bison Steak,

lean, 6 oz (raw)	205	4	0
Boar (wild), roasted, 3 oz	140	4	0

Buffalo Steak,

New West Foods, 4 oz	70	3	0
Caribou, roasted, 3 oz	140	4	0
Deer/Venison, roasted 3 oz	135	3	0

Goat (Capretto):

Raw, 3 oz	95	2	0
Roasted, 3 oz	120	2.5	0

Ostrich:

Blackwing Ostrich Meats:

Sport Jerky, 0.5 oz piece	25	0	0
Sausage Patties (2) 2 oz	60	0.5	0

New West Foods:

Ground Ostrich, 4 oz	165	7	0
Ostrich Steak, 4 oz steak	130	2.5	0
Rabbit: Roasted, 3 oz	165	7	0
Stewed, 1 cup, diced, 5 oz	290	12	0

Variety & Organ Meats

Brain (Lamb): Braised, 3 oz	125	9	0
Pan-fried, 3 oz	230	19	0
Chitterlings, pork, simmered, 3 oz	260	25	0
Ears, pork, simmered, 1 ear, 4 oz	185	12	0
Feet, pork: Simmered, 3 oz	200	14	0
Cured, pickled, 3 oz	170	14	0
Hormel, 2 oz	80	6	0

Head Cheese (Pork Snouts/Ears/Vinegar/Spices),

1 oz slice	50	4	0
Heart, Beef, braised, 3 oz	140	4	0
Jowl, pork, raw, 4 oz	750	80	0
Kidneys, braised, 3 oz	140	5	0
Liver (beef): Raw, 4 oz	150	4	4
Braised, 3 oz	140	4	3
Pan-fried, 3 oz	185	7	7
Pancreas, pork, braised, 3 oz	185	8	0
Pork Cracklins, 0.5 oz	80	6	0
Pork Hocks, 1 piece, 6 oz	340	23	0
Scrapple, pork, 2 oz	120	8	8
Spleen, pork, braised, 3 oz	130	3	0
Stomach, pork, raw, 4 oz	185	12	0

Sweetbreads:

Beef./Lamb, cooked, 3 oz	125	4	0
Tail, pork, simmered, 3 oz	340	31	0
Tongue: Raised Veal, 3 oz	170	9	0
Beef/Lamb/Pork, av., 3 oz	235	17	0
Tripe, beef, raw, 3 oz	85	3.5	0

Quick Guide

Franks & Weiners
Average All Brands

	C	F	Cb
Regular (Pork Mix): *Per Frank*			
Regular (10/16 oz package), 1.5 oz	140	13	1
Bun Length/Jumbo, 2 oz	185	17	2
Extra Long, 2.75 oz	255	24	2
Small/Cocktail, each	30	3	0.5
Beef Franks: *Per Frank*			
Regular (10/16 oz package), 1.5 oz	140	13	2
Bun Length/Jumbo, 2 oz	175	17	2.5
¼ lb Dog, 4 oz	375	35	5

Franks & Weiners

	C	F	Cb
Ball Park: *Per 2 oz Frank Unless Indicated*			
Angus Beef:			
Original; Bun Size, 2 oz	170	15	3
Lower Fat, 1.87 oz	130	10	2
Beef: Original, Bun Size, 2 oz	190	16	4
Fat Free, 1.75 oz	50	0	7
Lite, 1.75 oz	110	7	5
Deli Style, 1.75 oz	150	12	2
GrillMaster,			
Hearty Beef, 2.9 oz	250	21	2
Jumbo, 2.5 oz	240	20	5
Singles, 1.6 oz	150	13	3
Cheese, with Turkey, Beef & Pork	190	16	5
Meat: Original; Bun Size	180	15	5
Lite, 1.75 oz	100	7	4
Singles, 1.6 oz	140	12	3
Turkey, Original	110	7	6
Foster Farms, Chicken; Turkey, 2 oz	140	12	1
Hebrew National: *Per Frank*			
Beef: Regular, 1.72 oz	150	14	1
¼ Pounder, 4 oz	360	33	3
Jumbo, 3 oz	270	25	2
97% Fat-Free, 1.6 oz	40	1	3
Beef Frank in a Blanket, 5 pcs, 3 oz	300	24	12
Jennie-O: *Per Frank*			
Turkey Franks: 1.2 oz	70	6	1
Jumbo, 2 oz	120	10	2
Oscar Mayer: *Per Frank*			
Beef: Classic, 1.59 oz	130	12	1
Light Beef, 1.59 oz	90	7	2
Cheese Dogs, 1.6 oz	140	13	1
Turkey: Classic, 1.6 oz	100	8	2
Classic Bun Length, 2 oz	120	10	3
Shelton's: *Per Frank*			
Uncured: Chicken, 1.2 oz	70	6	0
Smoked Chicken, 3 oz	245	20	0
Turkey, 1.2 oz	60	4.5	1
Zacky Farms, Chkn; Turkey, av, 2 oz	115	10	4

Quick Guide

Fresh Sausages

	C	F	Cb
Pork/Beef: *Average All Types*			
Small: Raw, 4" link, 1 oz	85	7.5	0
Broiled/Pan-fried	80	7	0
Medium: Raw, 1.5 oz	170	15	0
Broiled/Pan-fried	165	14	0
Large: Raw, 3 oz	255	22	0
Broiled/Pan-fried	245	21	0
Italian: Raw, 3.2 oz	315	28	1
Cooked, 2.4 oz	230	18	3
Chorizo: Beef Chorizo, 2.5 oz piece	250	23	5
Pork Chorizo, 2 oz piece	250	23	5

Note: Fat is lost in broiling/pan frying.
Cooked weight = approx. 60-70% raw weight

Smoked Sausages

	C	F	Cb
Per Link:			
Butterball,			
Turkey, 2 oz	100	6	2
Eckrich, Grillers, all varieties, av, 2 oz	185	16	2
Hillshire Farm:			
Angus Beef, 2 oz	170	15	3
Cheddar Wurst, 2 oz	180	16	2
Chicken Hardwood, 2 oz	100	7	3
Johnsonville ~ See CalorieKing.Com			

Breakfast Sausages/Patties

	C	F	Cb
Butterball: *Fully Cooked*			
Turkey: B'fast Sausage Links (3), 2.5 oz	110	6	2
Sausage Patties (2), 2.5 oz	110	6	2
Jennie-O, Turkey Breakfast Sausage,			
Lean, 2 oz	90	5	0
Jimmy Dean: *Fully Cooked*			
Heat 'N Serve:			
Sausage Links:			
Pork: Regular (3), 1.9 oz	210	19	2
Maple (3), 2.4 oz	260	26	5
Turkey (3), 2.4 oz	100	7	1
Sausage Patties:			
Pork: Original (2), 1.8 oz	200	17	2
Maple (2), 2.4 oz	260	22	3
Turkey (2), 2.4 oz	100	7	1
Breakfast Sandwiches ~ See Page 92			
Jones Dairy Farm:			
All Natural Golden Brown Sausages: *Fully Cooked*			
Maple Pork (3), 2.1 oz	240	22	2
Mild Pork (3), 2.1 oz	250	24	1

Vegetarian Patties:
Boca ~ See Page 117
Garden Burger ~ See Page 118

Bagel, Corn & Hot Dogs

Hot Dogs, Ready-To-Go:
Includes Ketchup/Relish; w/o Mayo

	C	F	Cb
Regular, 1.5 oz frank, 1.5 oz bun	260	15	22
Bun Length, 2 oz frank, 1.5 oz bun	290	18	21
Jumbo Dog, 2 oz frank, 2 oz bun	360	20	36
¼ lb Beef Dog, 2 oz bun	480	15	36
Mile Long Dog, 2.6 oz dog, 1.5 oz bun	360	24	23

Corn Dogs:
Beef/Pork Frank, average, 2.6 oz	170	10	16

Foster Farms:
Corn Dogs:
Chili Cheese: (1), 2.7 oz	190	9	21
Honey Crunchy:			
Regular (1), 2.7 oz	190	8	23
Jumbo (1), 3.95 oz	280	15	26
Mini (4), 2.7 oz	210	12	18

State Fair:
Beef Corn Dog (1), 2.7 oz	230	11	26
Classic Corn Dog (1), 2.7 oz	190	8	23
Fiesta (1), 2.7 oz	180	9	19

Bagel Dogs:
Einstein Bros/Noah's N.Y. Bagels,
Asiago/Original with Cheddar, av.	545	28	56
Vienna Beef: Bageldog (1), 6.5 oz	470	18	56
Mini (1), 3 oz	220	13	16

Hot Dog Toppings/Extras:
American Cheese, 1 slice, 1 oz	110	9	1
Chili Con Carne, ¼ cup	50	2	5.5
Ketchup, 1 Tbsp	15	0	4
Mustard, 1 Tbsp	20	0	1
Onions, chopped, 1 Tbsp	5	0	1
Pickle Relish, 1 Tbsp	20	0	5
Sauerkraut, ½ cup	20	0	5

Deli/Lunch Meats & Sausage

	C	F	Cb
Beef Jerky/Meat Snacks,			
Berliner (pork/beef), 1 oz	65	5	1
Beerwurst (Beef):			
Small (2¾"diam), 1/16" sl.	20	2	0
Large (4" diam), 1/8" slice	75	7	0.5
Beerwurst (Pork):			
Small (2.75"diameter), 1/16" slice	15	1	0
Large (4"diameter), 1/8" Slice	55	4	0.5
Blood Sausage, 1 oz	100	9	0.5

Deli/Lunch Meats & Sausages (Cont)

	C	F	Cb
Bologna:			
Beef Bologna: 1 slice, 1 oz	90	8	1
Light, 1 slice, 1 oz	60	4	2
Oscar Mayer: Light, 1 slice, 1 oz	60	4	2
98% Fat Free, 1 oz	25	0.5	3
Boar's Head, Ring, 2 oz	150	13	1
Pork: 1 Slice, 1 oz	65	6	1
Fat-Free, 1 slice, 1 oz	20	0	2
Turkey Bologna, average, 1 oz	60	5	0.5
Bratwurst: Average, 1 oz	80	7	1
Bob Evan's, Beer, 2.2 oz link	170	14	0
Braunschweiger, (Pork/Liver/Sausage),			
Oscar Mayer, 2 oz slice	190	17	1
Chicken, average:			
1 thick or 2 thin slices, 1 oz	30	1	1
2 oz slice	60	2	2
Hillshire Farm,			
Rotiss. Seas'nd Chicken Breast, 2 oz	50	0.5	2
Corned Beef, average, full fat, 1 oz	60	5	0.5
Ham, Sliced:			
Baked/Broiled, 1 oz slice	35	1	1
Oscar Mayer, Baked, 1 slice	60	2	0
Honey/Brown Sugar, av., 1 oz	35	1	1
Prosciutto, average, 1 oz	70	5	0
Ham & Cheese Loaf, average, 1 oz	70	5	1
Italian Sausage, 2.6 oz	250	20	3
Kielbasa: Polish Sausage, 2 oz	65	5	1
Beef, 2 oz link	190	17	1
Hillshire Farm,			
Polska, 2 oz	180	16	3
Knockwurst, av., 1 oz	90	8	0.5
Linguica *(Gaspar's),* 2 oz	130	9	1
Liverwurst, 1 oz	65	5	2
Liver Pate, fresh, average, 1 oz	90	8	1
Mortadella, 1 oz	105	9	0
Olive Loaf: Average, 1 oz	70	5	2
Oscar Mayer, 1 oz	80	6	3
Pancetta ,			
Boars Head, 1 slice	50	4.5	0

Deli/Lunch Meats & Sausages (Cont)

	C	F	Cb
Pastrami (Beef):			
Boar's Head:			
1st cut Brisket, 2 oz	90	4	2
Cap-off Top Round, 2 oz	70	2.5	1
Hillshire, Deli Select, 7 slices, 2 oz	60	1	1
Peppered Beef, 1 oz slice	40	2	1
Pepperoni, 5 slices, 1 oz	140	13	0
Pickle Loaf, av., 1 oz	70	5	5
Pickle & Pepper Loaf,			
Boars Head, 2 oz	150	13	2
Proscuitto/Proscuitti, av., 1 oz	70	5	1
Roast Beef, Lean, 1 oz	40	2	0
Salami: Beef, av., 1 oz	80	7	1
Oscar Mayer, Hard, 1 slice, 1.76 oz	100	8	1
Beer Salami, average, 1 oz	50	4	0.5
Oscar Mayer, Cotto, 1 slice, 1 oz	70	6	1
Dry, Hard, av., 4 slices, 1 oz	100	8	1
Genoa: Average, 1 oz	100	8	1
Stick, 1.75 oz	175	14	2
Bridgford, Italian, 1 oz	120	11	0
SPAM (Hormel): *Per 2 oz Serving*			
Classic: 2 oz serving	180	16	1
7 oz can	630	56	3.5
12 oz can	1080	96	6
Spam Lite: 2 oz	110	8	1
12 oz can	660	48	6
Other Spam Products:			
Hickory Smoked, 2 oz	170	16	2
Hot & Spicy, 2 oz	180	16	2
Oven Roasted Turkey, 2 oz	80	4	2
Spam with Bacon, 2 oz	180	16	1
Spam with Cheese, 2 oz	170	15	2
Spam Spread, 2 oz	140	12	0
25% Less Sodium	180	16	1
Spam Singles:			
Classic, 3 oz package	210	16	0
Lite, 3 oz package	160	11	2

Deli/Lunch Meats & Sausages (Cont)

	C	F	Cb
Summer Sausage:			
Armour, 2 oz	190	17	2
Hillshire Farm, 2 oz	190	16	1
Treet *(Armour),* Luncheon Loaf, Original, 2 oz	140	11	4
Turkey, average: 1 oz slice	30	1	0.5
¾ oz slice	22	0.5	0.5
Turkey Breast:			
Butterball, Oven Roasted:			
Thick Slice, 1 slice 1 oz	30	0.5	2
Thin Slices, 4 slices, 1.9 oz	60	1.5	3
Hillshire, Deli Select,			
Oven Roasted, 6 slices, 2 oz	50	0.5	2
Turkey Ham, 1 slice, 1 oz	35	1.5	0.5
Turkey Pastrami, 1 oz	35	1.5	1
Turkey Roll, 1 oz	40	2	0.5
Turkey Loaf, 1 oz	30	1	0.5
Vegetarian Deli ~ *See Page 118*			

Meat Spreads

	C	F	Cb
Average All Brands: *Per ¼ Cup, 2 oz*			
Chicken, white meat	130	10	2
Ham, Deviled	140	11	0
Liverwurst	190	16	2
Roast Beef	130	10	2
Sandwich Spread	140	10	9
Turkey	110	7	2
Underwood: *Per 2 oz*			
Chicken, White Meat	140	11	2
Deviled Ham	180	15	1
Liverwurst	160	13	4
Roast Beef	130	10	2

Paté

	C	F	Cb
Les Trois Petit Cochons: *Per 2 oz*			
Black Peppercorn	200	19	2
Chicken & Pork Livers with Truffle	140	11	2
Country Pate	200	22	1
Smoked Salmon	110	9	2
Old Wisconsin Pate,			
Braunschweiger, 2 oz	210	18	3

Nuts

Per 1 oz Unless Indicated	C	F	Cb
Acorns, raw 1 oz	110	7	12
Almonds: Dried/Dry Roasted:			
Whole: 12 medium size, ½ oz	85	7.5	3
23-25 medium size, 1 oz	170	15	6
½ cup, 2½ oz	420	37	13
Ground, 1 cup, 3.4 oz	545	47	20
Sliced, ½ cup, 1.6 oz	260	22	10
Slivered, ½ cup, 2 oz	310	27	12
Chocolate Coated (5-6), 1 oz	150	10	15
Honey Roasted, 1 oz	170	14	8
Oil Roasted (*Blue Diamond*), 1 oz	170	16	5
Brazil Nuts, 8 medium, 1 oz	185	19	3.5
Cashews, dry or oil roasted:			
14 large/18 med./26 small: 1 oz	165	14	9
½ cup, 2.4 oz	375	31	20
Honey Roasted, 1 oz	165	13	10
Chestnuts:			
Average, dried, 1 oz	105	1	22
Raw/Fresh, 5-6 nuts, 1 oz	60	0	13
Canned, water chestnuts, sliced/whole/drained, 1 oz	30	0	7
Coconut, Fresh:			
1 piece, 2"x2"x ½", 1 oz	185	18	7
Shredded, fresh, ½ cup, 1.4 oz	140	13	6
Dried (Desiccated):			
Sweetened: Shredded, 1 oz	145	10	14
Grated, ½ cup, 1.3 oz	185	13	18
Unsweetened, 1 oz	185	18	7
Cream (canned), ½ cup, 5.2 oz	285	26	12
Milk (canned), unsweetened, ¼ cup, 2 fl.oz	100	10	3
Water (center liquid), ½ cup,4.25 oz	25	0	4.5
Filberts or Hazelnuts:			
Shelled, 18-20 nuts	180	17	4.5
Chopped, ¼ cup, 1 oz	180	18	5
Ground, ¼ cup, 0.6 oz	120	12	3
Ginkgo Nuts, canned, 14 med., 1 oz	32	0.5	6.5
Hickory, 30 small nuts, 1 oz	200	18	5
Macadamia Nuts, Shelled:			
Raw, 7 medium/14 small, 1 oz	200	21	4
½ cup, 2.3 oz	480	51	10
Dry Roasted, 1 oz	205	22	4
½ cup, 2.4 oz	480	51	9
Choc. coated, 2-3 pieces, 1 oz	170	12	14
Mixed Nuts: Raw, 18-22 nuts, 1 oz	170	15	7
Oil Roasted, all types	170	16	6
Sweet Roasts, 26 pieces, 1 oz	160	12	10
Planters, Dry Roasted/Honey	160	12	9
Nut Toppings, chopped, 1 Tbsp, 0.25 oz	40	4	1.5

Per 1 oz Unless Indicated	C	F	Cb
Peanuts, dry or oil roasted, average:			
Small handful, ½ oz	85	7	3
⅕ cup, 1 oz	165	14	6
½ cup, 2.5 oz	415	35	15
3 oz bag	500	42	18
7 oz bag	1160	98	42
Planters:			
Cocktail, all varieties	170	14	5
Honey Roasted, 1 oz	160	13	7
Spanish Redskins, 1 oz	170	15	4
Sweet N' Crunchy, 1 oz	140	8	15
Japanese Style Peanuts, Coated in Crunchy Shell, ¼ cup, 1 oz	150	8	13
Raw: Shelled, 1 oz	160	14	4.5
In shell, 1 oz	115	110	3
Pecans, roasted:			
10 halves, 0.5 oz	95	10	2
20 Halves, 1 oz	195	20	4
1 cup, halves, 3.5 oz	680	71	14
Pilinuts, dried, ¼ cup, 1 oz	215	24	1
Pine Nuts, dried, 1 Tbsp, 0.3 oz	70	7	1.5
Pistachios, raw:			
Shelled, 45 nuts, ½ cup, 1 oz	160	13	8
Unshelled, ½ cup, 2 oz	165	14	7
Lance, Roasted, 1.5 oz	120	9	6
Sesame Nut Mix, 1 oz	160	13	9
Soy Nuts: Dry Roasted	130	6	9
½ cup, 3 oz	390	18	28
Dr Soy, Chocolate coated, 1 oz pkg	140	7	13
Trail Mix *(Planters):*			
Daybreak, Berry Almond, 1.5 oz	180	7	27
Energy Mix, 1.5 oz	250	20	14
Fruit & Nut	140	9	14
Nut & Chocolate, 1.25 oz	150	9	14
Nuts, Seeds & Raisins, 1.1 oz	160	11	11
Spicy Nuts & Cajun Sticks	150	11	10
Sweet & Nutty, 1.1 oz	150	9	13
Walnuts, average all types:			
7-10 halves, 1/2 oz	90	9	2
15-20 halves, 1 oz	175	17	3
Chopped, 1/2 cup, 2.2 oz	380	36	6
Ground, ¼ cup, 0.7 oz	130	13	3

Quick Guide

	C	F	Cb
Peanut Butter: *Average All Brands*			
1 level tsp, 0.2 oz	35	3	1
1 level Tbsp, 0.6 oz	100	8.5	3.5
1 oz Quantity	165	14	6
½ cup, 5 oz	835	72	29

Peanut Butter ~ Brands

	C	F	Cb
Jif: Regular, all varieties, 2 Tbsp	190	16	8
Reduced Fat, all var., 2 Tbsp	190	12	15
Natural, all varieties, 2 Tbsp	190	16	8
To Go: Crmy/Crunch, 1.5 oz cup	250	22	11
Reduced Fat, 1.7 oz cup	250	16	20
Whipped: Creamy, 2 Tbsp	140	12	6
Chocolate flavored, 2 Tbsp	150	11	11
Laura Scudder's, Natural,			
Smooth; Nutty, 2 Tbsp	210	16	6
Peanut Wonder, Original, 2 Tbsp	100	2	13
Peter Pan:			
Natural, Creamy/Crunchy, 2 Tbsp	210	17	6
Creamy/Crunchy, Red.-Fat, 2 Tbsp	200	13	14
Creamy, Whipped, 2 Tbsp	150	12	5
Planters, Creamy/Crunchy, 2 Tbsp	180	15	8
Smucker's, Goober,			
Grape/Strawberry, 3 Tbsp	235	12	25
Skippy: Natural, Creamy/Chunky, 2 T.	190	16	6
Reduced Fat, all var., 2 Tbsp	180	12	15
Dark Chocolate Spread, 2 Tbsp	200	14	12

Peanut Butter & Jelly Sandwich

	C	F	Cb
1 sandwich: *With 2 oz Bread*			
Thin Spread, 1 Tbsp Peanut Butter			
+ 1 Tbsp Jelly	310	10	48
Thick Spread, 2 Tbsp Peanut Butter			
+ 2 Tbsp Jelly	480	19	67

Nut & Chocolate Spread

	C	F	Cb
Nutella:			
1 Tbsp, 0.7 oz	100	6	11
2 Tbsp, 1.3 oz	200	12	21
Note: Nutella contains approx. 50% sugar & 13% hazelnuts			

Other Nut & Seed Butters

Per 1 Tbsp, 0.5 oz

	C	F	Cb
Almond Butter	100	10	3.5
Cashew Butter	95	8	4.5
Hazelnut Butter; Pecan Butter	110	10	2
Pistachio Butter	90	6.5	4.5
Sesame Butter (Tahini)	90	8	3
Soy Nut Butter	75	5	4

Seeds

	C	F	Cb
Alfalfa Seeds,			
sprouted, ½ cup, 0.5 oz	5	0	1
Caraway/Fennel, 1 tsp	7	0.5	1
Chia Seeds: 1 Tbsp, 0.35 oz	45	3	4
3 Tbsp, 1 oz	140	8.5	12
Cottonseed Kernels,			
roasted, 1 Tbsp	50	3.5	2
Flax Seeds,			
3 Tbsp, 1 oz	140	9	9
Lotus Seeds,			
dried, ½ cup, 0.5 oz	55	0.5	10
Poppy Seeds, 1 tsp	15	1	1
Pumpkin/Pepita Seeds, whole:			
Roasted/Tamari, 1 oz	150	12	4
½ cup, 4 oz	590	48	15
Dried (hulled), ¼ cup, 1 oz	155	13	5
Safflower Kernels, dried, 1 oz	150	11	10
Sesame Seeds:			
Dried, 1 Tbsp, 0.3 oz	50	4.5	2
Roasted/Toasted, 1 oz	160	14	7.5
Sunflower Kernels/Seeds:			
Dried, ¼ cup w/out hulls, 0.25 oz	200	18	7
Dry Roasted: 1 Tbsp, 0.3 oz	45	4	2
¼ cup, 1 oz	165	14	7
Oil Roasted, ⅓ cup, 1 oz	170	14	6.5
Watermelon Seeds,			
dried, ¼ cup, 1 oz	150	13	4

𝒩ut eaters are healthier and live longer, say scientists.

Nuts are a nutritious source of protein, vitamins, minerals, fiber, healthy fats, and antioxidants.

The fat and fiber of nuts can help reduce blood cholesterol. Their protein and fiber also promotes meal satiety (fullness) and reduces hunger levels – of benefit in weight control.

Eat nuts instead of high-sugar snacks, candy and soft drinks. Add chopped nuts to breakfast cereals.

Updated Nutrition Data ~ www.CalorieKing.com
Persons with Diabetes ~ See Disclaimer (Page 22)

Quick Guide   C   F   Cb

Pancakes:

Plain: *Average All Types*

	C	F	Cb
Small (3" diameter), 0.75 oz	50	2	6
Medium (4" diameter), 1.25 oz	85	3.5	11
Large (6" diameter), 2.5 oz	175	7.5	22

Add Extra for Syrups/Butter

	C	F	Cb
Pancake Syrup: Regular, 1 Tbsp	50	0	12
¼ cup, 4 Tbsp	185	0	49
Lite, 1 Tbsp	25	0	6.5
¼ cup, 4 Tbsp	100	0	27

Butter/Margarine:

	C	F	Cb
Regular, 1 Tbsp	100	11	0
Whipped, 1 Tbsp	65	7.5	0

Waffles:

	C	F	Cb
Homemade, 7" waffle, 2.5 oz	220	11	25
Frozen + Toasted, (4" diam.), 1 oz	105	3	16

Pancake Brands   C   F   Cb

Prepared As Directed

Aunt Jemima: *Prepared*

Mixes:

	C	F	Cb
Original, 4 - 4"	250	8	36
Original Complete, 2 - 4"	160	1.5	32
Buttermilk, 4 - 4"	180	6.5	23
Whole Wheat Blend, 3 - 4"	200	6.5	30

Bisquick: *Prepared*

Complete Pancake/Waffle Mix:

	C	F	Cb
Shake 'n Pour, Buttermilk (3)	220	3	43
Simply Buttermilk (3)	210	4	39

Hungry Jack: *Prepared*

Mixes:

	C	F	Cb
Complete, Buttermilk, 3 - 4"	150	1.5	32
Traditional, Original:			
With 2% Milk, Oil, Egg, 3 - 4"	250	8	37
W/ Skim Milk, Oil, Egg Wh., 3 - 4"	180	1	37
Extra Light & Fluffy, 3 - 4"	150	2	37

Easy Packs:

	C	F	Cb
Blueberry Wheat	160	2.5	32
Buttermilk	150	1.5	31

Northern Pines,

	C	F	Cb
3-4", 3.5 oz, prepared	200	3.5	38

Frozen Breakfasts   C   F   Cb

Aunt Jemima:

	C	F	Cb
French Toast: Cinnamon, 2 slices	210	4	35
Homestyle, 2 slices	210	4	34
Sticks, Cinnamon (4)	260	2.5	39
Pancakes: Blueberry (3)	260	6	45
Buttermilk (3)	250	6	41
Low-Fat (3)	210	2	42
Homestyle (3)	250	6	42
Mini Pancakes (10)	280	8	45

Eggo *(Kellogg's):*

	C	F	Cb
French Toaster Sticks, (2), average	225	6	37
Pancakes: Blueberry (3)	260	8	42
Buttermilk Minis (11)	280	9	44
Waffles: Homestyle (2)	190	7	27
Strawberry (2)	190	6	29

Krusteaz:

	C	F	Cb
French Toast, Cinnamon Swirl	230	5	36
Pancakes:			
Blueberry (3)	270	3	51
Buttermilk, 4.5", (3)	210	3	39

Pillsbury:

Pancakes:

	C	F	Cb
Buttermilk (3)	230	4	45
Mini Buttermilk (11)	240	4	45

Frozen Waffles   C   F   Cb

	C	F	Cb
Aunt Jemima: Buttermilk (2)	190	5	29
Homestyle; Blueberry, (2), average	170	5	28

Eggo *(Kellogg's):*

	C	F	Cb
Blueberry (2)	190	6	29
Chocolate Chip (2)	200	7	31
Homestyle (2)	190	7	27
Nutri-Grain:			
Blueberry (2)	180	5	31
Whole Wheat (2)	170	6	26

Kashi:

	C	F	Cb
7 Grains & Sesame (2)	150	5	25
Blueberry (2)	150	5	25
Nature's Path: Fig & Flax (2)	200	9	27
Homestyle (2)	210	7	34
Red Berry (2)	190	9	27
Van's: 8 Whole Grains, Berry (2)	170	5	28
Belgian, Homestyle (2)	190	5	32
Wheat Gluten Free,			
Apple Cinnamon (2)	230	7	39
Mini, Chocolate Chip (8)	160	4	28

Spaghetti/Pasta

- Pasta includes all shapes and sizes; (e.g. spaghetti, fettuccini, elbows, shells, twists, sheets, cannelloni, linguini, tubes, ziti).
- All regular pasta products have the same cals/fat/carbs on a weight basis.
- 1 oz Dry = approximately 2.5 -3 oz cooked.

Dry Spaghetti/Pasta

	C	F	Cb
1 oz quantity	105	0.5	21
1lb box/pkg, 16 oz	1685	7	339
Elbows, 1 cup, 3.75 oz	380	2	80
Shells, small, 1 cup, 3¼ oz	330	1.5	69
Spirals, 1 cup, 3 oz	305	1.5	64

Cooked Spaghetti/Pasta

Plain, All Types (no added fat):

	C	F	Cb
Firm/Al Dente (8-10 minutes), 1 oz	42	0.5	8.5
Medium (11-13 minutes), 1 oz	37	0.5	7.5
Tender (14-20 minutes), 1 oz	32	0.5	7
Longer cooking increases water absorbed			
Spaghetti: ½ cup, 2.5 oz	90	0.5	18
Medium serving, 1 cup, 5 oz	225	1.5	44
Large serving, 2 cups, 10 oz	450	3	88
Extra large, 3 cups, 15 oz	675	5	132
Elbows/Spirals, 1 cup, 5 oz	220	1.5	43
Small Shells, 1 cup, 4 oz	180	1	36
Protein-fortified: Dry, 1 c., 3.35 oz	350	2	63
Cooked, 1 cup, 5 oz	230	0.5	45
Spinach/Vegetable: Dry, 1 cup, 3 oz	310	1	61
Cooked, 1 cup, 5 oz	180	0.5	38
Whole-wheat: Dry, 1 cup, 3.75 oz	365	1.5	79
Cooked, 1 cup, 5 oz	175	1	37

Fresh Pasta (Refrigerated)

Average All Brands:
Plain/Spinach/Tomato:

	C	F	Cb
As purchased, 4.5 oz	370	3	70
Cooked, 1 cup, 5 oz	185	1.5	35
Home-made, w/o egg, cooked, 1 c. 5 oz	175	1	35
Buitoni:			
Cut Pasta:			
Angel Hair, 3 oz	230	2	43
Fettuccine/Linguine, 3 oz	240	2	45
House Foods:			
Tofu Shirataki Noodles:			
Traditional, 1.6 oz	0	0	1
Angel Hair/Fettuccini, Macaroni/Spaghetti, 4 oz	20	0.5	3
Nasoya, Shirataki Spaghetti, Pasta Zero, ⅔ cup, 4 oz	0	0	4

Buitoni: *Per 1 Cup Unless Indicated*

	C	F	Cb
Agnolotti: Butternut Squash, 3.7 oz	300	12	37
Wild Mushroom, 3.8 oz	280	10	34
Ravioli: Beef & Sausage, 3.8 oz	260	8	33
Chicken Marsala, 3.9 oz	280	8	36
Light 4-Cheese, 1¼ cup, 3.3 oz	260	6	37
Tortellini: Herb Chicken, 3.9 oz	330	8	52
Mixed Cheese, 3.7 oz	320	8	48
Tortelloni: Italian Sausage, 4 oz	350	10	51
Spinach & Ricotta, 3.7 oz	270	7	39
Other Varieties ~ See Page 112			
Pasta Sauces ~ See Page 144			

Macaroni & Cheese

Packaged (Kraft) ~ See Page 116
Restaurant: *Average*

	C	F	Cb
Side Serve, 6 oz	265	13	26
Medium serve, 1 cup, 9 oz	350	17	34
Large serve, 2 cups, 18 oz	700	34	68

Noodles

	C	F	Cb
Plain/Egg: Dry, 1 oz	110	1.5	20
1 cup, 1.35 oz	145	1.5	27
Cooked: 1 oz	40	0.5	7
½ cup, 2.75 oz	110	1.5	20
1 cup, 5.5 oz	220	3.5	40
Stir-Fried: 1 cup, 5.5 oz	270	9	40
2 cup serving, 11 oz	540	18	80
Low Carb Noodles, Quest Pasta, 4 oz	10	0	3
(Carbs from glucomannan fiber)			
Yolk Free (Cooked):			
Manischewitz, Yolk Free, 2 oz	200	1	41
Chinese: Cellophane/Rice, dry, 1 oz	100	0	25
Chow Mein/hard, dry, 1 oz	150	9	16
Japanese: Soba: Dry, 1 oz	95	0.5	21
Cooked, 1 cup, 4 oz	115	0.5	24
Somen: Dry, 1 oz	100	0.5	21
Cooked, 1 cup, 6 oz	230	0.5	49
Japanese Style Pan Fried, Yaki-Soba (Maruchan's), av., 5.6 oz	260	3	50
Ramen Noodles ~ See Page 117			
Rice Noodles: Dry, 3.5 oz	365	0.5	83
Cooked, 1 cup, 6.2 oz	190	0.5	44
Yakisoba, Stir Fry, 3.5 oz	430	6	52
House Foods, Tofu Shirataki, 4 oz	20	0.5	3
Chikara, Udon, average, 7.5 oz pkt	250	1.5	52

Simply Asia/Thai Kitchen ~ See Pages 119 & 121

Egg Roll/Won Ton Wrappers

	C	F	Cb
Egg/Spring Roll (1), 0.8 oz	65	0	15
Won Ton Wrapper (1), 0.25 oz	20	0	4

Quick Guide

	C	F	Cb
Fruit Pies: *Average All Brands, 9"*			
Apple; Blueberry; Cherry:			
Small Serving, ⅛ pie, 4.8 oz	350	16	49
Medium Serving, ⅙ pie, 6.5 oz	465	22	65
Large Serving ¼ pie, 9.5 oz	700	33	98
Whole Pie (9"), 38 oz	2800	131	392
Other Pies: *Per Serving, ⅙ of 8" Pie*			
Chocolate Cream Pie	345	22	38
Custard: Egg	220	12	22
Coconut	330	18	35
Lemon Meringue	305	10	53
Peach	260	12	39
Pecan	440	23	57
Pumpkin Pie	315	14	41

Fruit Pies ~ Brands

	C	F	Cb
Denny's Restaurant,			
Apple Pie, 7 oz	480	22	67
Hostess:			
Cherry Pie, 4.5 oz	480	20	69
Lemon Pie, 4.5 oz	490	22	69
Marie Callender's Restaurant,			
Banana Cream, 8.2 oz slice	570	32	63
Mrs Smith's:			
Classsic Pies: *Per ⅙ Pie, 4.5 oz*			
Apple	320	14	47
Coconut Custard	330	18	35
Cherry	320	14	44
Dutch Apple	340	14	52
Original Flaky Crust: *Per ⅛ Pie, 4.6 oz*			
Cherry	360	18	46
Peach	340	19	41
Sara Lee:			
Creme Pies:			
Chocolate, ⅕ pie, 3.9 oz	450	27	50
Coconut, ⅙ pie, 4.5 oz	370	20	44
Key Lime, ⅕ pie	410	17	60
Lemon Meringue, ⅕ pie, 4.6 oz	390	13	64
Oven Fresh Pies: *Per 9" Pie, 4.6 oz Slice*			
Apple	340	16	43
Cherry	340	17	44
Peach	320	15	42
Seasonal: Pumpkin, 4.6 oz	270	10	41
Sthrn Sweet Potato, 4.6 oz	280	9	46
Tastykake: Apple	270	11	40
Coconut Cream	370	20	42
Lemon	300	14	44

Croissants

	C	F	Cb
Average all Brands			
Plain/Butter/Cheese: Mini, 1 oz	115	6	13
Small, 1.5oz	170	9	19
Medium, 2 oz	230	12	26
Large, 2.5oz	290	15	32
Sweet Croissants:			
Almond Filled, 3 oz	330	18	39
Chocolate Filled, 3 oz	360	19	43
Dunkin' Donuts, Plain Croissant	330	13	37
Sara Lee:			
French Style: Original, 1.75 oz	185	9	21
Mini, 1 oz	230	11	26

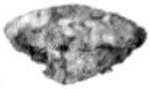

Croissant Sandwiches ~ *See Page 165*

Pastry & Pie Crust

	C	F	Cb
Pie Crust, Baked, 9" diameter shell:			
1 Pie Shell, 6.5 oz	970	64	87
2-crust Pie, 9", 11.25 oz	1660	109	150
Filo Pastry: 4 sheets, 2.5 oz	210	2.5	40
Athens, Filo Dough, 5 sheets, 2 oz	160	1	31
Puff:			
Pepperidge Farm, ½ sheet	480	30	48
Bake & Fill Shell (1)	180	11	18
Arrowhead Mills,			
Graham Cracker Pie Crust, ⅛ of 9"	110	5	14
Keebler:			
Ready Crust: *Per ⅛ of 9" Crust*			
Chocolate	100	4.5	14
Graham: Regular	110	5	14
Reduced Fat	100	3.5	15
Shortbread Crust	110	5	14
Marie Callenders,			
Deep Dish Pie Crust, ⅛ pie, 1 oz	140	10	11
Mrs Smith's,			
Deep Dish, ⅛ pie, 1 oz	130	7	14
Nabisco:			
Honey Maid, Graham, ⅙ of 9", 1 oz	150	8	18
Nilla, Pie Crust, ⅙ of 9", 1 oz	140	8	18
Pillsbury, Rolled, ⅛, 0.9 oz	100	6	12
Trader Joe's, Pie Crust, ⅛ pie, 1.2 oz	190	13	17

Pie Fillings ~ Canned

	C	F	Cb
Apple/Blueb./Cherry/Strawb., average:			
Sweetened: ⅓ cup, 3.2oz	90	0	22
1 cup, 9.5 oz	270	0	66
1 can, 21 oz	600	0	150
Light/Lite, ⅓ cup, 3.2 oz	60	0	15
Unsweetened, ⅓ cup, 3.2 oz	35	0	8
Lemon Cream/Creme, ⅓ cup, 3.2 oz	130	1.5	28

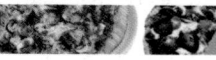

Pizzas ~ Ready To Eat (C) (F) (Cb)

Figures Based On Pizza Hut

Chicken Supreme:
Medium Size (12"):
Hand Tossed/Classic Crust:

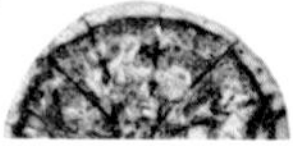

	C	F	Cb
⅛ Pizza (1 slice)	190	6	24
½ Pizza (4 slices)	760	24	96
Whole Pizza (8 slices)	1520	48	192

Pan/Deep Dish:

⅛ Pizza (1 slice)	230	9	27
½ Pizza (4 slices)	920	36	108
Whole Pizza (8 slices)	1840	72	216

Thin Crust:

⅛ Pizza (1 slice)	190	6	23
½ Pizza (4 slices)	760	24	92
Whole Pizza (8 slices)	1520	48	184

Meat Lovers:
Medium Size (12"):
Hand Tossed/Classic:

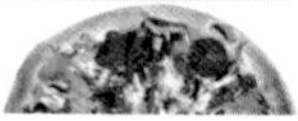

⅛ Pizza (1 slice)	280	15	23
½ Pizza (4 slices)	1120	60	92
Whole Pizza (8 slices)	2240	120	184

Pan/Deep Dish:

⅛ Pizza (1 slice)	320	18	26
½ Pizza (4 slices)	1280	72	104
Whole Pizza (8 slices)	2560	144	208

Thin Crust:

⅛ Pizza (1 slice)	280	16	22
½ Pizza (4 slices)	1120	64	88
Whole Pizza (8 slices)	2240	128	176

Pepperoni:
Medium Size (12"):
Hand Tossed/Classic Crust:

⅛ Pizza (1 slice)	210	10	23
½ Pizza (4 slices)	840	40	92
Whole Pizza (8 slices)	1680	80	184

Pan/Deep Dish:

⅛ Pizza (1 slice)	260	13	26
½ Pizza (4 slices)	1040	52	104
Whole Pizza (8 slices)	2080	104	208

Thin Crust:

⅛ Pizza (1 slice)	210	10	21
½ Pizza (4 slices)	840	40	84
Whole Pizza (8 slices)	1680	80	168

Supreme:
Medium Size (12")
Hand Tossed/Classic Crust:

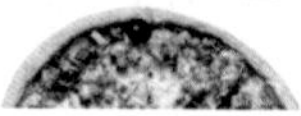

⅛ Pizza (1 slice)	240	11	24
½ Pizza (4 slices)	960	44	96
Whole Pizza (8 slices	1920	88	192

Pan/Deep Dish:

⅛ Pizza (1 slice)	280	14	27
½ Pizza (4 slices)	1120	56	108
Whole Pizza (8 slices)	2240	112	216

Thin Crust:

⅛ Pizza (1 slice)	230	12	23
½ Pizza (4 slices)	920	48	92
Whole Pizza (8 slices)	1840	96	184

Individual Personal Pizzas (6"):
Pan/Deep Dish:

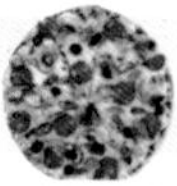

Cheese	590	25	68
Chkn Supreme	590	21	69
Pepperoni	620	28	68
Supreme	730	38	69
Veggie Lovers	540	20	69

Large (14"):
Hand Tossed:

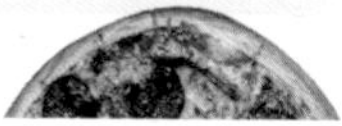

Cheese: ⅛ Pizza	290	11	34
½ Pizza	1160	44	136
Chicken Supreme: ⅛ Pizza	280	9	35
½ Pizza	1120	36	140
Meat Lover's: ⅛ Pizza	400	22	34
½ Pizza	1600	88	136
Pepperoni: ⅛ Pizza	310	13	34
½ Pizza	1240	52	136
Supreme: ⅛ Pizza	340	16	35
½ Pizza	1360	64	140
Veggie Lover's: ⅛ Pizza	260	8	35
½ Pizza	1040	32	140

Extra Large, Single Slices:
(Example: *Sbarro's*)

Cheese	460	13	60
Pepperoni	730	37	61
Sausage	670	31	60
Supreme	630	27	63

P Pizza ~ Frozen

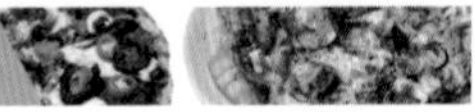

Frozen Pizzas

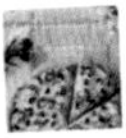

	C	F	Cb
Amy's: *Per ⅓ Pizza*			
Cheese Pizza	290	12	33
Mushroom & Olive	260	10	33
Pesto	310	12	39
Roasted Vegetable	280	9	42
Whole Wheat Crust, Cheese & Pesto	360	18	37

	C	F	Cb
California Pizza Kitchen:			
Crispy Thin Crust: *Per ⅓ Pizza*			
Margherita	320	16	31
Sicilian Recipe	360	18	30
Spinach & Artichoke	350	19	29
White	320	17	30
Small Pizzas: Per Whole Pizza			
BBQ Recipe Chicken; Margh., av	400	15	43
Four Cheese	400	18	40
Hawaiian	350	12	43
Sicilian	430	21	40
Original Restaurant Style Crust:			
BBQ Recipe Chicken, ⅓ Pizza	390	13	46
Hawaiian Recipe, ¼ pizza	290	11	33
Thai Style Chicken, ⅓ pizza	360	13	41

	C	F	Cb
Celeste:			
Pizza For One: Original, 1 pizza	320	14	42
Deluxe; Zesty Four Cheese	335	15	39
Meatball	420	22	40
Pepperoni; Four Cheese	350	16	39
Sausage & Pepperoni	380	19	41

	C	F	Cb
DiGiorno: *Per Slice, Unless Indicated*			
Cheese Stuffed Crust:			
Bacon Cheeseburger, ⅙ pizza, 4.5 oz	310	13	34
Bacon Sausage & Pepperoni, ⅕ pizza, 5 oz	350	17	33
Five Cheese, ⅕ Pizza, 5.3 oz	380	16	40
Pepperoni, ⅕ pizza, 5.3 oz	380	16	40
Three Meat, ⅙ pizza 4.8 oz	340	16	34
Supreme, ⅙ pizza, 5.1 oz	350	16	34
Classic Thin Crust, Supreme, ⅕ pizza, 5 oz	310	14	32
Crispy Flatbread Pizza: *Per ⅓ Pizza*			
Pepperoni & Roasted Peppers, 4.5 oz	340	20	26
Tuscan Style Chicken, 4.6 oz	290	14	25

	C	F	Cb
DiGiorno (Cont):			
Garlic Bread: *Per ⅙ Pizza*			
Four Cheese, 5 oz	350	11	47
Pepperoni, 5 oz	380	17	40
Supreme, 4.25 oz	300	12	36
Small Pizzas, Cheese Stuffed Crust: *Per 1/2 Pizza*			
Four Cheese, 4.2 oz	320	15	34
Pepperoni, 4.2 oz	330	16	34
Three Meat, 4.6 oz	360	18	34
Ultimate Toppings: *Per ⅕ Pizza*			
Four Meat, 5 oz	380	18	35
Pepperoni, 4.9 oz	360	17	34
Supreme, 5.3 oz	360	17	35

	C	F	Cb
Freschetta:			
Brick Oven: *Per ⅕ Pizza Unless Indicated*			
5 Italian Cheese, ¼ Pizza	380	19	40
Chicken Club, ¼ Pizza	360	15	41
Pepperoni & Italian Style Cheese	350	18	33
Rstd Portab. M'shrms & Spinach	270	11	35
Three Meat Medley	350	19	32
Zesty Italian Supreme	330	16	33
Naturally Rising: *Per ⅙ of Large Pizza Unless Indicated*			
4 Cheese Medley, ⅕ Pizza	380	14	46
Canadian Bacon P'apple	280	8	39
Classic Sprme; Meat Medley, av.	345	15	39
Sausage & Pepperoni	370	16	40
Signature Pepperoni	340	14	39

	C	F	Cb
Jeno's: *Per Pizza*			
Crispy 'N Tasty: Cheese, 6.85 oz	460	22	50
Pepperoni, 6.8 oz	490	26	48

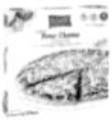

	C	F	Cb
Kashi:			
Thin Crust: *Per ⅓ Pizza*			
Four Cheese	260	8	36
Mediterranean	290	9	37
Mushroom Trio & Spin.	250	9	28

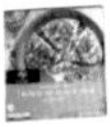

	C	F	Cb
Kroger:			
3 Minute Microwave: *Per 8 oz Pizza*			
3-Meat	500	17	64
Cheese	490	16	66
Combination	520	20	64
Pepperoni	530	20	65
Supreme	490	18	63
French Bread, Pepperoni, 5 oz	380	17	42

	C	F	Cb
Lean Cuisine:			
Culinary Collection: *Per 6 oz Pizza*			
Deep Dish:			
Spinach & Mushroom	340	7	52
Three Meat	380	9	55

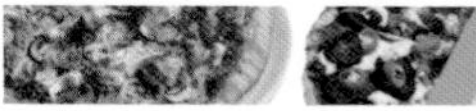

Frozen Pizzas (Cont) C F Cb

		C	F	Cb
Lean Cuisine (Cont):				
Culinary Collection (Cont): *Per 6 oz Pizza*				
Traditional:				
Four Cheese		350	6	57
Mushroom		300	5	50
Pepperoni		380	9	56
Simple Favorites: *Per Pizza*				
French Bread Pizzas:				
Cheese; Deluxe, av.		340	7	53
Pepperoni		310	8	48
Red Baron:				
Classic Crust: *Per ¼ Pizza*				
4 Cheese, 5.15 oz		380	16	40
Pepperoni, 5 oz		370	16	40
Sausage & Pepp.,5.3 oz		400	19	41
Fire Baked: *Per ¼ Pizza*				
4 Cheese, 4.9 oz		360	15	40
Pepperoni, 5.25 oz		370	17	40
Spicy Pepperoni, 4.9 oz		350	16	39
Thin & Crispy Crust: *Per ⅓ Pizza*				
5 Cheese, 5 oz		360	16	40
Pepperoni, 5.25 oz		400	19	40
Pizza For One, Deep Dish: *Per Pizza*				
Hawaiian, 5.3 oz		350	13	47
Meat-Trio, 5.6 oz		400	18	46
Sausage, 5.8 oz		430	20	46
Singles:				
French Bread:				
5 Cheese & Garlic, 1 pizza		430	23	41
Pepperoni, 1 pizza		380	15	43
Original Crust:				
4-Cheese; Supreme, av., ½ pizza		400	14	54
Pepperoni, ½ pizza		410	14	55
Personal Pan: Meat-Trio,½ pizza		370	17	42
Pepperoni, ½ pizza		340	14	41
Safeway Select:				
Pizzeria Crust:				
Cheese Trio, ¼ pizza		340	15	34
Fajita Chicken Ole, ⅕ pizza		250	10	29
Pepperoni & Sausage, ⅕ pizza		320	17	30
Self Rising: *Per ⅙ Pizza*				
Four Cheese		300	9	41
Pepperoni		350	14	41
Sausage & Pepperoni		340	13	41
Ultra Thin Crust: *Per ⅓ Pizza*				
Garlic Chicken		320	12	31
Margherita		330	17	28
Primo Italiano Meat		330	16	27

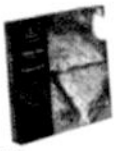

		C	F	Cb
Smart Ones *(Weight Watchers): Per Pizza*				
Stone-Fired: Four Cheese		380	7	64
Pepperoni		410	9	63
Stouffer's: *Each*				
French Bread Pizzas: *Per Pizza*				
Two Per Box: Deluxe, 6 .19 oz		430	21	44
Sausage & Pepperoni, 6.25 oz		460	24	43
Nine Per Box: Cheese, 5.88 oz		380	16	43
Pepperoni, 5.68 oz		430	21	44
Tombstone:				
Original: *Per ¼ Pizza*				
Canadian Style Bacon		320	12	37
Extra Cheese		350	15	36
Pepperoni		390	20	36
Pepperoni & Sausage		360	17	37
Thin Crust: *Per ¼ Pizza*				
Three Cheese		310	15	28
Pepperoni; Sausage, average		315	16	28
Brick Oven Style: Cheese, ⅓ pizza		350	15	37
Pepperoni; Supreme, av., ¼ pizza		315	16	29
Tony's:				
Original Crust: *Per ⅓ Pizza*				
Hamburger, 5.1 oz		350	13	45
Pepperoni, 4.8 oz		350	14	45
Supreme, 5.5 oz		380	16	46
Singles: *Per Pizza*				
French Bread: Pepperoni, 5 oz		380	17	42
Supreme, 5.3 oz		370	16	42
Totino's:				
Crisp Crust Party Pizza: *Per ½ Pizza*				
Cheese		320	15	35
Classic Pepperoni		360	19	35
Combination		360	19	36
Hamburger		350	18	36
Pizza Rolls:				
Cheese (6), 3 oz		210	8	28
Pepperoni (6), 3 oz		220	9	26
Trader Joe's:				
3 Cheese, ⅓ pizza		310	9	42
Parlanno, ¼ pizza		340	16	34
Pizza 4 Formaggi, ⅓ pizza		310	9	42
Spinach, ⅓ pizza		300	12	38

Quick Guide

Chicken

	C	F	Cb

From 3lb ready-to-cook chicken

Breast/Wing Quarter:

	C	F	Cb
Roasted: With skin	300	15	0
Without skin	185	5	0
Fried, batter dipped	530	30	17

Leg Quarter:
Thigh & Drumstick:

	C	F	Cb
Roasted: With skin	270	16	0
Without skin	185	8	0
Fried, batter dipped	435	25	15

KFC ~ See Fast-Foods Section

Per 4 oz Edible Portion

Average of Light Meat: *Per 4 oz Without Bone*

Roasted: With skin	250	12	0
Without skin	175	4.5	0
Stewed: With skin	230	12	0
Without skin	180	4.5	0
Fried: Batter-dipped, with skin, 4 oz	315	17	11
Flour-coated, with skin, 4 oz	280	14	2

Average of Dark Meat: *Per 4 oz Without Bone*

Roasted: With skin	290	18	0
Without skin	235	11	0
Stewed: With skin	265	17	0
Without skin	220	10	0
Fried: Batter-dipped, with skin, 4 oz	340	21	11
Flour-coated, with skin, 4 oz	325	19	5

Chicken Parts

	C	F	Cb

Broilers or Fryers: *Edible Weights (no bone)*
Breast: *Per ½ Breast*

Raw: With skin, 5 oz	250	14	0
Without skin, 4.25 oz	140	3	0
Roasted: With skin, 3.5 oz	195	8	0
Without skin, 3 oz	140	3	0
Stewed: With skin, 4 oz	200	8	0
Without skin, 3.25 oz	145	3	0
Fried: Batter-dipped, w/ skin, 5 oz	365	19	13
Flour-coated, with skin, 3.5 oz	220	9	2

Drumstick: *Per Drumstick*

Roasted: With skin, 2 oz	115	6	0
Without skin, 1.5 oz	75	2.5	0
Stewed: With skin, 2 oz	115	6	0
Without skin, 1.5 oz	80	3	0
Fried: Batter-dipped, w/ skin, 2.5 oz	195	11	6
Flour-coated, with skin, 1.75 oz	120	7	1

Chicken Parts (Cont)

	C	F	Cb

Broilers or Fryers (Cont): *Edible Weights (no bone)*
Thigh Portion:

Raw: With skin, 3.3 oz (4¼ oz with bone)	200	14	0
Without skin, 2.4 oz	80	3	0
Roasted: With skin, 2.25 oz	155	10	0
Without skin, 2 oz	110	6	0
Stewed: With skin, 2.5 oz	160	10	0
Without skin, 2 oz	105	5	0
Fried: Batter-dipped, with skin 3 oz	240	14	8
Flour-coated, with skin, 2.25 oz	165	9	2

Wing: *Per Wing, Bone In*
Raw Weight, 3.2 oz

Raw: With skin	110	8	0
Without skin	35	1	0
Roasted: With skin	100	7	0
Without skin	45	2	0
Fried: Batter-dipped, with skin	160	11	5
Flour-coated, with skin	105	7	1
Stewed, with skin, 4 oz	100	7	0

Buffalo Wings ~ See Fast-Foods Section

Neck: Simmered, with skin	95	7	0
Without skin	30	1	0

Skin Only: *Skin from ½ Chicken*

Raw skin, 2.75 oz	275	26	0
Roasted skin, 2 oz	255	23	0
Stewed skin, 2.52 oz	260	24	0
Fried, flour-coated, 2 oz	280	24	5
Fried, batter-dipped, 6.75 oz	750	55	44

Roasters: *Average of Light & Dark Meat*

Roasted: With skin, 4 oz	250	15	0
Without skin, 4 oz	190	8	0
Light Meat, without skin, roasted	175	5	0
Dark Meat, without skin, roasted	200	10	0

Stewing Chicken: *Per 4 oz, average of Light & Dark Meat*

Stewed: With skin	325	22	0
Without skin	270	14	0
Light Meat, without skin	240	9	0
Dark Meat, without skin	290	17	0

Capon Chicken:

Roasted: With skin, 4 oz	260	13	0
½ Chicken, with skin, 22.5 oz	1460	74	0

Chicken Offal & Stuffing:

Giblets: Simmered, 1 cup	230	7	0.5
Fried, flour-coated, 1 cup	400	20	6
Gizzard, simmered, 1 cup	210	4	0
Heart, simmered, 1 cup	270	12	0.2
Liver: Raw, 4 oz	130	5.5	0
Simmered, 1 cup	215	8.5	1
Liver Pate, Fresh, 1 Tbsp, 0.5 oz	30	2	1
Stuffing, average, ½ cup	180	9	22

Chicken Products   C F Cb

Bumble Bee:
Chicken In Water: *Per 2 oz Drained*

	C	F	Cb
Premium White	70	3	0
Premium Breast	70	1	0

Foster Farms:

	C	F	Cb
Chicken Breast Strips, grilled, 3 oz	110	2	0
Wings: Chipotle, 3 wings, 3 oz	190	13	4
Honey BBQ Glazed, 3 wings, 3 oz	190	11	7
Hot 'n' Spicy, 3 wings, 3 oz	190	14	1

Tyson:
Anytizers, Frozen:
Wings:

	C	F	Cb
Hot Wings, Buffalo Style (3)	190	13	3
Honey BBQ Seasoned (3)	190	12	8

Wyngz, Boneless:

	C	F	Cb
Buffalo Style, 3 pieces, 3 oz	150	7	8
Sweet Garlic Glazed, 3 pcs, 2.8 oz	130	5	10

Duck, Goose, Quail   C F Cb

	C	F	Cb
Duck: Roasted,			
With skin, 3 oz	290	24	0
Without skin, 3 oz	170	10	0
½ duck, with skin, 13.5 oz	1290	108	0
Goose: Roasted with skin, 3 oz	260	19	0
Without skin, 3 oz	200	11	0
Pheasant, cooked, 3 oz	210	10	0
Quail, cooked, 1 whole, 6 oz	385	24	0

Turkey   C F Cb

Fryer-Roasters: *Per 3 oz Serving*
Roasted:

	C	F	Cb
Light Meat: With skin	140	4	0
Without skin	120	1	0
Dark Meat: With skin	155	6	0
Without skin	140	4	0

½ of Whole Turkey: (Approx. 3.25 lbs raw weight without neck and giblets; 1.8 lbs cooked weight)

	C	F	Cb
Roasted: With skin	1650	74	0
Without skin	1125	31	0

Ground Turkey, raw: (4 oz raw wt. = 3 oz ckd wt.)

	C	F	Cb
85% lean, regular, 4 oz	170	10	0
93% lean: Average, 4 oz	160	8	0
Jennie-O, 4 oz	170	8	0
Trader Joe's, 4 oz	150	8	0
94% lean,			
Foster Farms, 4 oz	150	7	0
Breast, no skin, 4 oz	115	1	0
Patties: Small, 3 oz	130	7	0
Medium, 4 oz	170	10	0

Turkey Parts   C F Cb

Roasted, Edible Weights, without bone:
Breast, (½), (from 17.25 oz raw weight with bone):

	C	F	Cb
With skin, 12 oz (no bone)	525	11	0
Without skin, 10.75 oz	415	2	0
Back (½): With skin, 4.5 oz	265	13	0
Without skin, 3.5 oz	165	6	0

Leg (Thigh & Drumstick):
(from 1 lb raw weight with bone)

	C	F	Cb
With skin, 8.5 oz (without bone)	410	13	0
Without skin, 7.75 oz	355	8.5	0

Wing: (From 7.25 oz raw weight)

	C	F	Cb
With skin, 3 oz (without bone)	185	9	0
Without skin, 2 oz (with bone)	100	2	0
Neck: Simmered, 1 neck,			
9 oz (with bone)	275	11	0
Giblets, simmered, 1 cup, 5 oz	240	7	3

Young Hens (Roasted)   C F Cb

Light Meat:

	C	F	Cb
With skin, 3 oz	175	8	0
Without skin, 3 oz	135	3	0
Dark Meat: With skin, 3 oz	200	11	0
Without skin, 3 oz	165	7	0

Young Toms ~ *Similar to Young Hens*

Turkey Products   C F Cb

Foster Farms: *Cooked & Frozen*
Meatballs, cooked:

	C	F	Cb
Homestyle (3)	160	9	3
Italian Style (3)	160	8	5
Hormel, Turkey Breast,			
in water, 5 oz can, 2 oz	50	1	0

Jennie-O:

	C	F	Cb
Bacon, cured, 1 sl., 0.5 oz	30	2.5	1
Bratwurst, lean,			
1 link, 3.85 oz	170	10	2
Burgers, uncooked,			
All Natural, White Meat, 5.25 oz	200	15	0
Meatballs, Fully Cooked: Italian, 3 oz	180	13	2
Home Style, 3 oz	180	13	3
Spam, Oven Roasted Turkey, 2 oz	80	4	0
Trader Joe's,			
Italian Turkey Meatloaf, 3 oz	140	8	5
Valley Fresh, Premium White,			
in water, 97% fat free, 2 oz	80	1.5	0

White Rice | C | F | Cb

Raw:

	C	F	Cb
Glutinous, 1 cup, 6.5 oz	685	1	151
Long Grain, 1 cup, 6.5 oz	675	1	148
Short Grain, 1 cup, 7 oz	715	1	158
Wild Rice, 1 cup, 5.5 oz	570	2	120

Cooked Rice: *Boiled/Steamed*

Short/Medium Grain:

	C	F	Cb
½ cup, 3.25 oz	140	0	30
1 cup (½ Pint), 7.2 oz	265	0.5	59
2 cups (1 Pint), 13 oz	480	1	106

Long Grain:

	C	F	Cb
½ cup, 2.75 oz	100	0	22
1 cup, 5.5 oz	205	0.5	44
Glutinous/Sticky, 1 cup, 6 oz	170	0.5	37
Parboiled, ½ cup, 3 oz	105	0.5	22

Precooked/Instant:

	C	F	Cb
Dry, ½ cup, 3.5 oz	380	1	82
Cooked, ½ cup, 3 oz	95	0.5	21

Wild Rice,

	C	F	Cb
Cooked, 1 cup, 5.75 oz	165	0.5	35

Brown Rice | C | F | Cb

Average of Short or Long Grain

Raw/Dry:

	C	F	Cb
½ cup, 3.25 oz	340	2.5	71
1 cup, 6.5 oz	685	5.5	143
Cooked: ½ cup, 3.5 oz	110	1	22
1 cup, 7 oz	220	2	46

Rice Dishes | C | F | Cb

Chinese Fried Rice:

	C	F	Cb
½ cup, 2.5 oz	140	4.5	21
1 cup, (½ Pint), 5 oz	280	9	42
2 cups, (1 Pint), 10 oz	565	18	84

Mexican Style Rice:

	C	F	Cb
Taco John's, Cilantro Lime, 6 oz	190	3.5	34
Taco Time, Mexi, 3.5 oz	80	0.5	17

Rice-A-Roni ~ *See Page 119*

	C	F	Cb
Rice with Raisins/Pinenuts, 1 cup	400	11	60
Rice Pilaf: Restaurant, 1 cup	275	7.5	46
O'Charley's, A La Carte, 1 order	190	5	30

Rice Pudding,

	C	F	Cb
Kozy Shack, Original, 1 pudding cup	130	3	22
Risotto, 1 cup	420	12	70
Saffron Rice, 4 oz	175	7	25
Spanish Rice: 1 cup, 5 oz	390	9	72
El Pollo Loco, Small, 4.5 oz	170	2.5	32
Taco Cabaña, Small	120	0.5	25
Sticky Rice, 1 cup, 5 oz	155	0.5	34
Sushi Rice: 1 Tbsp	25	0	5
1 cup, 5.2 oz	390	0	77

Other Packaged Rice Products:

Uncle Ben's / Zatarain's ~ *See Page 121*

CalorieKing.com Recipes

See the CalorieKing website for a salubrious selection of healthy recipes – all analyzed for calories, fat, protein, carbohydrate, fiber and sodium.

Choose from:
- **Starters/Appetizers**
- **Salads**
- **Entrees: Meat, Fish and Chicken**
- **Vegetarian**
- **Desserts**
- **Cakes, Cookies**
- **Drinks**

www.CalorieKing.com/recipes

HEALTHY RECIPE TIPS

- **Use non-fat milk** in place of whole or 2% milk
- **Use low-fat yogurt** in place of sour cream
- **Skim fat** from surface of soups and casseroles after cooling
- **Add extra vegetables** to soups and hot entrées
- **Cakes/cookies/muffins:** Replace most or all the fat/oil with applesauce and/or prune puree (Example, *Sunsweet Lighter Bake*)
- **Drinks:** Replace sugar with no-calorie sweeteners such as *Equal, Stevia, Splenda* and *Sweet 'N Low*

Deli Salads

	C	F	Cb
Average All Outlets			
Antipasto Salad, ½ cup	135	8	13
3-Bean Salad, ½ cup	90	4.5	12
Bulgur Salad, ½ cup	70	2	12
Caesar Salad, Classic, 1 cup	200	14	15
Side Salad, without Dressing	25	0	6
Carrot Raisin: With Dressing, ½ cup	135	12	6
Without Dressing, ½ cup	20	0	5
Chef's Salad: Regular, w/o Dressing	620	37	8
With 2 oz Thousand Island Drssng	860	61	8
Chicken Salad, ½ cup/scoop, 4 oz	280	21	2
Coleslaw: Traditional, ½ cup	150	8	18
W/ Low Cal Dressing, ½ c.	50	2	8
Corn, Mexican, ½ cup	240	12	33
Cucumber: Non-Oil Dressing, ½ cup	60	0	14
With Oil Dressing, ½ cup	140	12	8
Eggplant Salad, ½ cup	75	5	7
Fettucini, with veges, ½ cup	135	6	16
Garden Salad, without Dressing, 1 cup	10	0	2
Greek Salad, 1 cup	105	8	7
Greek Vegetables, 1 cup	110	8	6
Lobster Salad, ½ cup, 4 oz	250	21	11
Macaroni Salad, ½ cup, 5 oz	360	26	26
Nicoise, 1 cup	450	32	18
Pasta Salad, ½ cup	200	11	17
Potato Salad: Dijon, 3 oz	120	7	13
With Mayonnaise, ½ cup, 4 oz	215	15	17
Lowfat, ½ cup	110	1.5	21
Rice Salad, ½ cup	150	10	13
Saffron Rice, 4 oz	175	7	25
Spinach Salad, 1 cup	180	13	13
Tabouli, ½ cup	125	7	13
Three Bean Salad, ½ cup	90	4.5	12
Tomato & Mozzarella, ½ cup	180	14	10
Tortellini, with Basil Pesto, ½ cup	150	9	15
Waldorf, with Mayo, ½ cup	110	7	12
Signature Salads: *Per 6 oz Serving*			
(Supplied to Deli's and Institutions)			
Antipasto Salad	510	50	4
Artichoke Salad, marinated	400	41	8
California Medley	120	7	15
Cheese Agnolotti	250	8	23
Chicken Salad	420	33	11
Crabmeat Flavored	450	38	20
Egg Salad	300	23	14
Fresh Button Mushroom	190	16	6

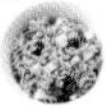

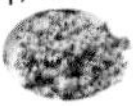

Signature Salads (Cont): *Per 6 oz*	C	F	Cb
Fresh Button Mushroom	190	16	6
Ham Salad	400	32	14
Prima Pasta Salad	360	30	18
Seafood Pasta Del Mar	170	10	21
Seafood, Crab & Shrimp	420	34	20
Shrimp Salad	360	32	8
Tuna Salad	450	36	14
~ Also See Fast-Foods & Restaurants Section			

Fresh Salad Packs

	C	F	Cb
Pre-Packaged (Supermarkets):			
Dole:			
Kits: *Per 3.5 oz, Includes Dressing*			
Asian Island Crunch	130	7	15
Caesar	150	12	8
Perfect Harvest	160	12	11
Southwest	140	10	10
Salad Blends: *Without Dressing*			
American; Mediterranean, 3 oz	15	0	3
Arugula; Baby Spinach, 3 oz	20	0.5	3
Fresh Express:			
Complete Salad Kits: *Per 3½ oz, Prepared*			
Asian	120	5	17
Caesar: Regular	150	12	7
Lite	90	6	7
Supreme	160	14	6
Pear Gorganzola	130	6	17
Gourmet Cafe: Tuscan Pesto Chkn	140	9	8
Waldorf Chicken	170	9	19
Ready Pac:			
Complete Salad Kits: *Per 3.5 oz*			
Baby Spinach, 2 cups	140	3	24
Caesar Lite, 2 cups	110	6	9
Classic Caesar, 2 cups	170	13	10
Santa Fe Caesar, 1¾ cups	150	12	7

Salad Toppings

	C	F	Cb
Bac'n Pieces,			
McCormick, 1Tbsp, 0.25 oz	30	1	2
Bacon Bits,			
Hormel, 1Tbsp	25	1.5	0
Bac-os,			
Betty Crocker, 1 Tbsp	30	1.5	2
Chow Mein Noodles,			
dry, ½ cup	120	7	13
Croutons, 2 Tbsp, 0.3 oz	40	1	7
Olives, 5 medium	25	2	0
Salad Toppins,			
McCormick, 4 tsp	35	1.5	3
Sunflower Seeds, 1 Tbsp, 0.3 oz	45	4	1.5
Toasted Sliced Almonds, 2 T., 0.5 oz	85	7	3
Tortilla Chips, 12 chips, 1 oz	140	7	19

Brands ~ Salad Dressings   **C F Cb**

Salad Dressings
Average All Brands: Per 2 Tbsp, Approx 1 fl.oz

Balsamic Vinaigrette:

	C	F	Cb
Regular	90	9	3
Light, 2 Tbsp	45	4	2
Fat Free, 2 Tbsp	25	0	6
Blue Cheese: Regular, 2 Tbsp	145	15	1.5
Regular, ¼ cup, 2 oz	280	30	3
Light, 2 Tbsp	30	1	4
Caesar: Regular, 2 Tbsp	165	17	1
Regular, ¼ cup, 2 oz	310	34	2
Light, 2 Tbsp	35	1.5	5.5
Coleslaw: Regular, 2 Tbsp	125	11	8
Regular, ¼ cup, 2 oz	245	21	15
Light, 2 Tbsp	110	7	14
French: Regular	145	14	5
Regular, ¼ cup, 2 oz	260	25	9
Light, 2 Tbsp	65	4	9
Fat/Oil-Free, 2 Tbsp	40	0	10
Italian: Regular, 2 Tbsp	85	8.5	3
Regular, ¼ cup, 2 oz	165	16	6
Light, 2 Tbsp	55	5.5	2
Fat/Oil-Free, 2 Tbas	15	0	2.5
Ranch: Regular, 2 Tbsp	145	16	2
Regular, ¼ cup, 2 oz	290	30	4
Light, 2 Tbsp	60	4	6.5
Fat-Free, 2 Tbsp	35	0.5	8
Thousand Island: Reg., 2 T.	115	11	4.5
Regular, ¼ cup, 2 oz	210	20	9
Light, 2 Tbsp	60	3.5	7
Fat-Free, 2 Tbsp	40	0.5	10

Enjoy a healthy salad but don't drown it in high-fat salad dressings.

Use 'light' dressings to halve the fat and calories.

Annie's Naturals: Per 2 Tbsp

	C	F	Cb
Organic: Buttermilk	70	6	1
French	110	11	3
Papaya Poppy Seed	90	8	5
Thousand Island	90	8	5
Vinaigrettes: Pomegranate	70	7	2
Red Wine & Olive Oil	140	15	0
Sesame Ginger	90	8	4
Shitake & Sesame	120	13	1

Bernstein's: Per 2 Tbsp

	C	F	Cb
Creamy Caesar	120	13	1
Herb Garden French	130	12	6
Italian	110	12	1
Restaurant Recipe Italian	120	12	1
Sweet Herb Italian	130	11	8
Fat-Free, Cheese & Garlic Italian	10	0	2
Light Fantastic: Cheese Fantastico	25	1.5	3
Roasted Garlic Balsamic	45	3.5	3

Best Foods: Per 1 Tbsp Unless Indicated

	C	F	Cb
Dijonnaise, 1 tsp	5	0	1
Mayonnaise: Canola	40	4	1
Light	35	3.5	1
Low-Fat	15	1	2
Mayonesa, Lemom-Lime	90	10	0
Olive Oil, 2 Tbsp	60	6	1
Real Mayonnaise	90	10	0
Tartar Sauce, 2Tbsp	80	7	4

Cardini's: Per 2 Tbsp

	C	F	Cb
Aged Parmesan Ranch	150	16	1
Caesar: Original	160	17	1
Fat-Free Caesar	40	0	9
Light Caesar	80	7	5
Honey Mustard	120	11	6
Roasted Asian Sesame	120	10	7
Vinaigrette, Balsamic:			
Regular	100	8	5
Lite	50	3	5

Great Value (Walmart): Per 2 Tbsp

	C	F	Cb
Caesar	120	12	2
Ranch: Bacon	140	14	1
Buttermilk	110	11	2
Chipotle	120	13	2
Classic	130	14	1
Zesty Italian	70	6	3

Hidden Valley: Per 2 Tbsp

	C	F	Cb
Cole Slaw	150	15	5
Ranch Originals: Regular	140	14	2
Light Original	80	7	3
Old-Fashioned Buttermilk	130	14	2

Salad Dressings S

Brands ~ Salad Dressings (Cont)

Hidden Valley (Cont):	C	F	Cb
Ranch, average other varieties	135	14	2
Farmhouse Originals:			
Dijon Mustard Vinaigrette	100	9	4
Homestyle Italian	100	10	3
Southwest Chipotle	100	10	2
Kraft: *Per 2 Tbsp*			
Regular Dressings:			
Caesar Vinaigrette, with Parmesan	70	6	3
Catalina	90	6	9
Classic Caesar	120	12	2
Creamy Italian	100	11	2
Greek Vinaigrette	110	11	2
Honey Dijon Vinaigrette	90	7	6
Parmesan Romano	140	14	2
Ranch	110	11	2
Roka Blue Cheese	120	13	1
Sweet Honey Catalina	100	8	8
Thousand Island	130	12	4
Tuscan House, Italian	130	13	3
Free: Caesar	50	0	11
Honey Dijon	50	0	12
Italian	15	0	3
Peppercorn Ranch	50	0	11
Light: Asian Toasted Sesame	50	2.5	7
Balsamic Vinaigrette	25	1	3
Creamy Caesar	35	2	4
Zesty Italian	25	1.5	2
Seven Seas:			
Green Goddess	130	13	2
Viva Robust Italian	90	9	2
Reduced Fat: Viva Italian	45	4	2
Red Wine Vinaigrette	45	4	3
Marie's: *Per 2 Tbsp*			
Blue Cheese, Premium Super	160	17	1
Caesar	170	19	1
Ranch, all varieties	170	19	1
Classics:			
Chunky Blue Cheese	160	17	0
Coleslaw	140	13	7
Creamy Italian Garlic	170	19	1
Creamy Ranch	170	19	1
Thousand Island	150	15	4
Specialty: Honey Dijon	130	12	5
Jalapeno Ranch	160	17	1

Marzetti's:	C	F	Cb
Organic: Caesar	150	16	1
Blue Cheese	130	14	1
Parmesan Ranch	140	14	2
Chunky Blue Cheese	150	15	0
Classic Ranch	160	17	1
Thousand Island	150	15	5
Newman's Own: *Per 2 Tbsp*			
Regular: Balsamic Vinaigrette	90	9	3
Creamy Caesar	170	18	1
Family Recipe Italian	130	13	1
Olive Oil & Vinegar	150	16	1
Parmesan & Rstd Garlic	110	11	2
Ranch	150	16	2
Light: Italian	60	6	1
Raspberry & Walnut	70	5	7
Organic:			
Light Balsamic Vinaigrette	45	4	3
Tuscan Italian	100	11	2
Wish-Bone: *Per 2 Tbsp*			
Creamy: Chunky Blue Cheese	150	14	1
Creamy Caesar	180	18	1
Creamy Italian	110	10	4
Deluxe French	120	11	5
Ranch	130	13	2
Russian	110	6	14
Sweet 'n Spicy	140	12	7
Thousand Island	130	12	5
Light: Blue Cheese	70	6	2
Creamy Caesar	70	6	2
Honey Dijon	70	5	6
Italian	35	2.5	3
Parmesan Peppercorn Ranch	60	5	2
Ranch	70	5	2
Thousand Island	60	5	4
Vinaigrette: Balsamic & Basil	50	4	3
Asian with Sesame & Ginger	70	5	5
Raspberry Walnut	70	4	7
Fat-Free:			
Chunky Blue Cheese	30	0	7
Ranch	30	0	6
Oil & Vinegar:			
Balsamic Vinaigrette	60	5	3
House Italian	110	10	3
Red Wine Vinaigrette	70	5	6
Robusto Italian	80	7	4

Updated Nutrition Data ~ www.CalorieKing.com
Persons with Diabetes ~ See Disclaimer (Page 22)

Gravy

	C	F	Cb
Homemade Gravy, average:			
Thin, little fat, 2 Tbsp, 1 oz	20	1	3
Thick: 2 Tbsp, 1.25 oz	50	2	9
¼ cup, 2.5 oz	100	4	18
McCormick:			
Brown, 1 Tbsp	25	0.5	3
Turkey, 1 Tbsp	20	0.5	4

Gravy-In-Jars

	C	F	Cb
Boston Market,			
Classic Beef, ¼ cup, 2 oz	30	1	4
Campbell's, Slow Roast,			
Beef/Chicken/Turkey, ¼ cup, 2 oz	25	1	3
Heinz: Per ¼ Cup, 2 oz			
Homestyle: Classic Chicken	30	2	3
Savory Beef	30	1	4
Sausage	45	1.5	4
Other varieties, average	20	0.5	3
Fat-Free, all varieties	20	0	4
Safeway, all varieties, ¼ cup, 2 oz	20	0.5	4

Tomato Products

	C	F	Cb
Whole/Chopped/Crushed/Diced:			
Regular: 1 cup, 8.5 oz	50	0	10
In Aspic, ½ cup	50	0	12
With Green Chili, 1 c., 8.5 oz	60	0	16
Stewed, ½ cup, 1.7 oz	40	1.5	4
Wedges in Tomato Juice, 1 cup	70	0.5	18
Salsa, average, 2 Tbsp, 1 oz	25	0	6
Tomato Ketchup:			
Regular: 1 Tbsp, 0.5 oz	15	0	4
Single Serve, 1 packet	10	0	3
Heinz, One-Carb,			
1 Tbsp, 0.5 oz	5	0	1
Tomato Paste:			
Regular: 2 Tbsp, 1 oz	25	0	6
¾ cup, 6 oz	140	1	32
Tomato Puree, ½ cup, 4.5 oz	50	0	10
Tomato Sauce:			
Regular, ½ cup, 4.4 oz	50	0	11
Spanish Style, ½ cup, 4.3 oz	40	0	9
With Mushr., ½ cup, 4.3 oz	45	0	10
With Onions, ½ cup, 4.3 oz	50	0	12
Tomato Seasoning, 3 tsp	20	0	4
Sundried Tomatoes:			
Natural, 5-6 pieces, 0.4 oz	20	0	5
In Oil, drained, 6 pieces, 0.5 oz	40	2.5	4

Sauces ~ Brands

	C	F	Cb
A-1:			
Marinades: *Per Tablespoon, ½ oz*			
Chicago Steakhouse	20	1	3
Ginger Teriyaki	25	0	5
New York Steakhouse	20	0	4
Steak Sauce: Bold & Spicy	20	0	5
Cracked Peppercorn	15	0	4
Kobe Sesame Teriyaki	25	0	4
Smoky Mesquite	30	0	8
Steak Sauce	15	0	3
Supreme Garlic	25	0	5
Thick & Hearty	25	0	6
Barilla:			
Pasta Sauces: *Per ½ Cup*			
Marinara; Tom. & Basil, av.	70	1	15
Mushroom	80	2.5	12
Rstd Garlic; Traditional, av.	70	1	14
Spicy Marinara	60	1.5	13
Sweet Peppers; Three Cheese, av.	70	1	13
Tuscan Herb	70	0.5	14
Bertolli:			
Alfredo Sauces: *Per ¼ Cup*			
Four Cheese Rosa; Regular, average	110	10	3
Garlic	100	10	2
Mushroom	80	7	2
Traditional: *Per ½ Cup*			
Italian Sausage	90	3	14
Olive Oil & Garlic	80	3	14
Tomato & Basil	70	2	13
Best Foods/Hellmann's,			
Tartar Sauce, 2 Tbsp	80	7	4
Buitoni:			
Pasta Sauces:			
Alfredo: Regular, ¼ cup	140	12	4
Light, ¼ cup	90	6	4
Marinara: Regular ½ cup	70	3	10
With Roasted Garlic, ½ cup	60	1	10
Pesto: With Basil, ¼ cup	270	26	4
Reduced Fat, ¼ cup	230	17	8
Bull's Eye: *Per 2 Tbsp*			
Original BBQ Sauce	60	0	14
Regional: Carolina/Memphis/Kansas	50	0	11
Texas Style	45	0	10
Catelli: *Per ½ Cup*			
Pasta, Garden Select Six Vegetable:			
Country Mushroom	70	1.5	11
Diced Tomato & Basil	70	1	12
Meat Sauce	80	2.5	11
Pizza Sauce, Tomato & Basil	60	1.5	11

Brands (Cont)

	C	F	Cb
Cento: *Per ½ Cup*			
Clam, Red	60	2	6
San Marzano Pasta:			
Arrabbiata	70	3.5	6.5
Marinara	100	9	6
Passata, crushed or pureed	25	0	8
Classico:			
Alfredo: *Per ¼ Cup*			
Creamy	80	7	3
Roasted Red Pepper	60	4	4
Pesto: *Per ¼ Cup*			
Basil Pesto	240	23	5
Sun-Dried Tomato Pesto	100	6	9
Red Sauces: *Per ½ Cup*			
Signature Recipes Sauce:			
Caramelized Onion & Rstd Garlic	70	1.5	12
Fire Roasted Tomato & Garlic	60	1.5	10
Florentine Spinach & Cheese	60	3	7
Mushrooms & Ripe Olives	60	1	10
Spicy Red Pepper	50	1.5	8
Sun-Dried Tomato	80	4	9
Traditional Favorites: Four Cheese	60	1.5	10
Italian Sausage,			
w/ Peppers & Onions	70	2.5	10
Roasted Garlic	50	1	8
Tomato & Basil	45	0.5	8
Colgin, Liquid Smoke, 1 tsp	0	0	0
Contadina:			
Pizza Sauce: *Per 2.2 oz*			
Flavored with Pepperoni	35	1	5
Original; Four Cheese	30	0.5	6
Tomato Sauce, average	20	0.5	4
Crosse & Blackwell:			
Meat: Ham Glaze, 1 Tbsp	25	0	7
Mint Meat Sauce, 1 tsp	5	0	1
Seafood:			
Cocktail, ¼ cup, 2.5 oz	80	0	20
Shrimp, ¼ cup, 2.5 oz	80	0	21
Dave's Gourmet: *Per ½ Cup*			
Pasta Sauces:			
Butternut Squash	100	4	17
Organic: Red Heirloom	45	1.5	7
Rstd Garlic & Sweet Basil	45	1.5	7
Del Monte:			
Spaghetti Sauces: *Per ½ Cup*			
With Four Cheeses	80	1	14
Mushrooms; Traditional	70	1	14
Average other varieties	75	1	16
Sloppy Joe Sauce, Orig., ¼ cup	50	0	11

	C	F	Cb
Emeril's:			
Pasta Sauces: *Per ½ Cup*			
Homestyle Marinara	90	3	14
Kicked Up Tomato	80	3.5	11
Roasted Gaaahlic	80	3.5	12
Roasted Red Pepper	70	3.5	9
Vodka Sauce	110	7	12
Francesco Rinaldi: *Per ½ Cup*			
Hearty: Super Mushroom	110	4.5	17
Three Cheese	90	2	16
Traditional: Original	80	3	14
Meat Flavored	90	3.5	14
Mushroom	80	3	13
French's,			
Worcestershire Sce, 1 Tbsp	5	0	1
Heinz: *Per 1 Tbsp*			
57	20	0	5
Barbecue Sauces, all flavors	35	0	9
Chili Sauce	20	0	5
Cocktail Sauce, Original,			
¼ cup, 2.2 oz	60	0	15
Horseradish Sauce	75	6	3
Tomato Ketchup: Regular	20	0	5
Reduced Sugar	5	0	1
Worcestershire Sauce, 1 Tbsp	5	0	1
House of Tsang: *Per 1 Tbsp*			
Bangkok Peanut Sauce	45	2.5	4
Ginger Flavored Soy	20	0	4
General Tsao	45	0.5	10
Hibachi Grill: Kobe Steak	50	4	3
Sweet Ginger Sesame	40	1	8
Tokyo Teriyaki	40	0	10
Hoisin, 1 tsp	15	0	4
Oyster Flavored	30	0	7
Saigon Sizzle	45	2	7
Sweet & Sour Stir-Fry	35	0	9
Hunt's:			
BBQ Sauce, Original, 2 Tbsp	60	0	15
Hickory & Brown Sugar BBQ Sce, 2 Tbsp	70	0	18
Manwich, Sloppy Joe Sauce,			
Original, ¼ cup, 2.25 oz	35	0	7
Pasta Sauce: *Per ½ Cup*			
Four Cheese	60	1	10
Garlic & Herb	40	1	8
Meat Flavor	60	1	10
Mushroom	50	0.5	10
Traditional	60	1	11

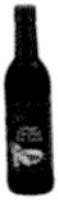

Brands (Cont) | **C** | **F** | **Cb**

Kikkoman:
Asian Authentic:

	C	F	Cb
Black Bean Sauce, with Garlic, 2 Tbsp	50	1	6
Hoisin Sauce, 2 Tbsp	80	0	19

Marinades: *Honey Mustard, 1 Tbsp* | 30 | 0 | 6

	C	F	Cb
Roasted Garlic	25	0	4
Soy Sauce	10	0	0
Teriyaki	15	0	2
Sweet'n Sour, 2 Tbsp	60	0	13

Knorr:
Classic Sauce: *Per Whole Package*

	C	F	Cb
Bernaise, dry mix only	100	0	20
Hollandaise, dry mix only	100	0	20

Kraft:

	C	F	Cb
Barbecue Sauces, average, 2 Tbsp	65	0	15

Specialty Sauce: *Cocktail, 2 Tbsp* | 60 | 0.5 | 11

	C	F	Cb
Coleslaw Dressing, 1.15 oz	110	8	9
Horseradish, 1 oz	100	9	4
Sandwich Spread, 1 Tbsp	35	2.5	3
Sweet'n Sour, 2 Tbsp	60	0	13
Tartar, Original, 1 Tbsp	60	4.5	4

Las Palmas:

	C	F	Cb
Green Enchilada Sauce, 2 oz	25	1.5	3
Red Chili Sauce, 2 oz	15	0.5	2

La Victoria,

	C	F	Cb
Red/Green Enchilada Sauce, av., 2 oz	25	1	3.5

Lawry's:
30 Minute Marinade: *Per Tbsp*

	C	F	Cb
Caribbean Jerk	30	0	7
Herb & Garlic; Lemon Pepper	10	0	2
Mesquite, w/ Lime Juice	10	0	2
Steak & Chop, w/ Garl. Pepp.	5	0	1
Sesame Ginger, w/ Mandarin	30	0	7

Packet Seasonings: *Dry*

	C	F	Cb
Fajitas; Taco, average, 2 tsp	15	0	3
Other varieties, average, 2 tsp	20	0	4

Lea & Perrins:

	C	F	Cb
Marinade In-A-Bag, all varieties, 0.5 oz	15	0	4
Marinade for Chicken, 1 Tbsp., 0.5 oz	10	0	3
Steak Sauce, Bold, 1 Tbsp, 0.6 oz	20	0	5
Worcestershire Sauce, Original, 1 tsp, 5 ml	5	0	1

McCormicks:
Seafood Sauces:

	C	F	Cb
Cajun Style, 2 T., 1.1 oz	15	0	3
Cocktail, Original/Extra Hot, ¼ cup	90	0.5	19
Scampi, 2 T., 1 oz	160	17	2
Tartar: Original, 2 Tbsp	140	14	3
Fat Free, 2 Tbsp, 1 oz	30	0	7

Mrs. Dash:
Marinades: *Per 1 Tbsp*

	C	F	Cb
Garlic Herb	15	0	3
Lime Garlic	15	0	3
Steakhouse	15	0	3
Sweet Teriyaki	35	0	9

Newman's Own: *Per ½ Cup*

	C	F	Cb
Five Cheese	80	3	10
Fra Diavolo	70	3	10
Marinara; Sockarooni	70	2	12
Roasted Garlic & Peppers	70	2.5	11
Tomato & Basil Bombolina	90	4.5	13
Vodka	110	5	11

O Organics *(Von's): Per ½ Cup*

	C	F	Cb
Marinara; Roasted Garlic, av.	60	1.5	9
Mushroom; Tomato Basil	50	1.5	8

Old El Paso:
Enchilada Sauce:

	C	F	Cb
Green Chile, ¼ cup	25	1.5	4
Other varieties, ¼ cup	20	0	4
Salsa, Thick & Chunky, all var., 2 Tbsp	10	0	2
Taco Sauce, all varieties, 1 Tbsp	5	0	1

Pace: *Per 2 Tbsp*

	C	F	Cb
Chunky Salsa	10	0	3
Picante Sauce	10	0	3
Salsa Con Queso	45	3	3

Prego: *Per ½ Cup*

	C	F	Cb
100% Natural: Marinara	80	3	10
Flavored with Meat	80	2.5	13
Fresh Mushroom; Traditional	70	1.5	13
Italian Sausage & Garlic	90	3	13
Mini Meatball	100	3	13
Pizza Sauce, Pizzeria Style	80	3	10
Roasted Garlic & Herb	80	3	13
Three Cheese; Tom. Basil & Garlic, av.	80	2	13

Chunky Garden:

	C	F	Cb
Combo	70	1.5	13
Mushroom Supreme, with Baby Portobellos	90	3	13

Heart Smart: *Trad.; Mushroom* | 70 | 1.5 | 13

	C	F	Cb
Ricotta Parmesan	90	2.5	13
Pizza Sauce, Pizzeria Style	70	2	12

Premier Japan,

	C	F	Cb
Hoisin; Teriyaki, 1 Tbsp	15	0	3

Progresso: *Per ½ Cup*
Recipe Starters:

	C	F	Cb
Creamy Roasted Garlic	70	5	5
Fire Roasted Tomato	60	1.5	10
Average other varieties	90	7	5

Brands (Cont)

Ragu:

	C	F	Cb
Chunky: *Per ½ Cup*			
Mushroom & Green Pepper	80	2	13
Average other varieties	90	2.5	14
Light varieties, average	60	1	12
Old World Style: *Per ½ Cup*			
Flavored with Meat	70	2.5	10
Marinara	80	2.5	11
Mushroom	70	2	11
Traditional	80	2	11
Pizza: Homemade Style, ¼ cup	30	1	5
Quick Sauce, Traditional, ¼ cup	45	1.5	6
Robusto!: *Per ½ Cup*			
7-Herb Tomato	90	3	13
Chopped Tomato, Olive Oil & Garlic	100	4	13
Roasted Garlic	80	2.5	14
Sauteed Onion & Garlic	90	3.5	13
Six Cheese	90	3	13
White: *Per ¼ Cup*			
Classic Alfredo	90	8	2
Light Parmesan Alfredo	60	4	2
Roasted Garlic Parmesan	100	9	3
Safeway Select:			
Salsa, all varieties, average, 2 Tbsp	15	0	3
Select Sauces: *Per ½ Cup*			
Arrabbiata	110	8	10
Artichoke Pesto	60	2	9
Four Cheese	80	3.5	11
Marinara	60	2	10
Spicy Red Bell Pepper	50	1	9
Sundried Tomato & Olive	60	1.5	11
Tomato Alfredo; Vodka	130	10	9
Steel's, Spiced Cranberry Sauce,			
no sugar added, 2 Tbsp	30	0	8
Taco Bell, Jalapeno Sauce, 2 T., 1 oz	110	11	3
Tony Roma's:			
Bold & Spicy BBQ Sauce, 2 Tbsp	50	0	12
Carolina Honeys BBQ Sauce, 1.2 oz	70	0	18
Trader Joe's:			
BBQ Sauce,			
Kansas City Style, 2 Tbsp	60	0	14
Tomato Basil Marinara, ½ cup	80	4.5	10
Walnut Acres,			
Organic Pasta Sauces,			
all varieties, average, ½ cup, 4.5 oz	50	1	9

Seasonings & Flavorings

	C	F	Cb
Auromatic Bitters (Angostua), 1 tsp	15	0	4
Bacon Bits, average, 1 Tbsp	35	2	2
Bacon Chips (Durkee), 1 Tbsp	30	1	2
Bac-Os (Betty Crocker), 1Tbsp	30	1.5	2
Blends (Mrs Dash), 1 tsp	0	0	0
Butter Buds, 1 tsp	5	0	2
Flavor Enhancer (Accent), 1 tsp	0	0	0
Flavor Sprinkles (Molly McButter), Natural/Cheese, 1 tsp	5	0	1
Garlic Bread Sprinkle, 1 tsp	8	0.5	1
Garlic Salt, 1 tsp	2	0	0
Italian Seasoning, 1 tsp	4	0	1
Lemon Pepper Seasoning, 1 tsp	7	0	1
Meat Tenderizer, av., 1 tsp	7	0	1
Salad Crunchies (McCormick), 1 tsp	10	0.5	2
Salt, Reg., Sea Salt, Lite Salt	0	0	0
Seasoning (Old Bay), ¼ tsp	0	0	0
Seasoning Mix (Vegit), ¼ tsp	0	0	0
Seasoning Mixes, av., ¼ pkg	70	1	9
Taco Seasoning, av., ¼ pkg	30	0.5	4
Bragg's, Liquid Aminos			
Old El Paso: Chili Season. Mix, 1 Tbsp	8	0.5	1.5
Cheesy Taco Seasoning Mix, 1 Tbsp	10	0.5	1
Taco/Burrito Seasoning Mix, 2 tsp	15	0	4
Fajita Seasoning Mix, 1 tsp	5	0	1.5

Spices & Herbs

	C	F	Cb
Average all types, 1 tsp	5	0	1
All Purpose, 1 tsp	0	0	1
Allspice, ground	5	0	1
Chili Powder	8	0	1
Cinnamon, ground	6	0	2
Curry Powder	6	0	1
Garlic Powder	9	0	2
Nutmeg, ground	12	0	1
Onion Powder	7	0	2
Parsley, dried	4	0	1
Pepper, average	6	0	1
Saffron	2	0	0
Salt-Free Blends, 1 tsp	0	0	0
Tumeric, ground	8	0	1
Seeds: Fenugreek	12	1	2
Mustard, Poppyseed	15	1	1
Other varieties, average	7	0	1

Home-Popped Popcorn

	C	F	Cb
Popping Corn Kernels, 2 Tbsp, 1 oz	110	1	26
(makes approximately 5 cups)			
Air-popped, without oil: Plain, 1 oz	110	1	22
1 cup, 0.2 oz	20	0	5
Oil-popped, Plain, 1 oz	145	8	16
1 cup, 0.4 oz	55	3	6
Popcorn Oil, 1 Tbsp	120	14	0

Microwave Popcorn

Average all Brands: *Per 1 Cup Popped, Unless Indicated*

	C	F	Cb
Butter: Regular, 1 cup	35	2	4
Light, 1 cup	25	1	4
Act II Popcorn:			
Butter: 1 cup	25	1	4
4½ cups, 1 oz	120	5	19
94% Fat-Free Butter: 1 cup	20	0.5	4
6½ cups, 1 oz	130	2.5	28
Butter Lovers: 1 cup	40	2	4
4½ cups, 1 oz	120	4	19
Xreme Butter: 1 cup	25	1	4
4½ cups	120	4	19
Jolly Time:			
Blast O Butter:			
Regular, 1 cup	40	2	4
Light, 1 cup	30	1.5	4
Extra Butter: 1 Cup	40	2.5	4
4 cups	160	11	16
Newman's Own:			
Butter Flavor, Microwave:			
Regular, 3½ cups	130	5	18
Light, 3½ cups	120	4	19
94% Fat Free, 3½ cups	110	1.5	20
Orville Redenbacher's:			
Family Favorites:			
Butter: 4 cups	170	12	17
Light, 5½ cups	120	5	19
Movie Theater Butter, 4 cups	170	12	16
Ultimate Butter, 5 cups	170	12	16
Sweet & Savory:			
Cheddar Cheese, 4½ cups	180	14	15
Sea Salt & Vinegar, 5 cups	150	7	21
Pop Secret: *Per Cup*			
94% Fat-Free, Butter	15	0	3
Butter; Extra Butter, average	30	2	3
Homestyle; Movie Theater Butter, av.	30	2	3

Bagged Popcorn

	C	F	Cb
Average All Brands (Ready-to-Eat)			
Regular/Plain: ½ oz package	80	5	8
1 oz package	160	10	16
4 oz package	640	40	64
2 oz Box (store/airport)	320	16	32
3 oz Bag (9" high x 5" wide)	480	24	48
Caramel Popcorn, with nuts, 1 cup, 1.5 oz	230	12	39

Bagged Popcorn ~ Brands

	C	F	Cb
Boston's, Lite, 3½ cups, 1 oz	140	4.5	20
Cracker Jack: Original, 1 cup, 2 oz	240	4	46
Butter Toffee Flavored, 1 cup, 2 oz	220	2	50
Crunch 'N Munch:			
Buttery Toffee: ⅔ cup, 1.1 oz	150	6	22
1 cup, 1.6 oz	220	9	32
Caramel: ⅔ cup, 1.1 oz	160	8	20
1 cup, 1.6 oz	230	12	29
12 oz box	1745	87	218
Fiddle Faddle:			
Average all varieties: 1 oz	120	2	24
1 cup, 2 oz	240	4	48
6 oz box	720	12	144
PopCorners, Butter/Kettle, 1 oz	120	3.5	21
Popcorn Indiana:			
Kettlecorn:			
Original, 2 cups, 1 oz	130	5	21
Cinn. Sugar, 2½ cups, 1 oz	130	4.5	21
Popcorn: Aged White Cheddar	150	9	14
Bacon Ranch, 2½ cups, 1 oz	150	10	13
Movie Theater, 2 cups, 1 oz	160	12	13
Seasalt, 3 cups, 1 oz	130	6	18
Poppycock:			
Original/Pecan Delight, av:			
½ cup, 1 oz	155	8	20
1 cup, 2 oz	310	16	40
Cashew Lovers, ½ cup, 1 oz	150	6	20
Chocolate Lovers, ½ cup, 1.15 oz	160	7	22

Movie Theater Popcorn

	C	F	Cb
Small, (7 cups): Plain	385	21	44
With Butter (3 pumps, 0.75 oz)	570	42	44
Medium, (15 cups): Plain	825	45	94
With Butter (4 pumps, 1 oz)	1075	73	94
Large, (20 cups): Plain	1100	60	124
With Butter (6 pumps, 1.5 oz)	1485	102	124
Butter: 1 Pump, 0.25 oz	65	7	0
4 Pumps (2 Tbsp), 1 oz	250	28	0

Corn & Tortilla Chips

	C	F	Cb
Average All Brands			
Corn Chips:			
Average all types: 1 oz	150	8	18
8 oz bag	1200	64	144
Fritos, Original, 32 chips, 1 oz	160	10	15
Tortilla Chips: Average, 1 oz	140	7	18
(1 oz = approx. 12 chips or 13 strips)			
Doritos: Original, 1 oz	140	7	18
Salsa Verde, 1 oz	140	7	19
Baked! Nacho Cheese, 1 oz	120	3.5	21
Kettle, Tias, av. all flavors, 1oz	145	8	17
Popchips: Original, 1 oz	120	4	18
3 oz Bag	360	12	54
Snyder's: White/Yellow Corn	140	4.5	23
Restaurant Style, 1 oz	130	5	20
Tostitos:			
Average all flavors, 1 oz	145	7	19
Baked! Scoops, 1 oz	120	3	22
Utz: White/Yellow Corn	140	7	18
Restaurant Style	130	6	18

Potato Chips/Crisps

	C	F	Cb
Average All Brands			
Regular:			
Plain or flavored, (4 chips)	30	2	3
1 oz package (20 chips)	150	10	15
4 oz quantity	600	40	60
14 oz package	2100	140	210

Chips/Crisps ~ Brands

	C	F	Cb
Lay's *(Fritolay):*			
Regular, average all flavors, 1 oz	160	10	15
Reduced Fat, Kettle, 1 oz	140	6	19
Fat Free, Light Original, 1 oz	75	0	17
Baked, Original, 1 oz	120	4	18
Popchips, av. all flavors, 1 oz	120	4	18
Pringles:			
Original, 1 oz	150	9	15
Large can, 6 oz	900	54	90
Snack Stacks: Original, 1 tub	100	6	10
Other flavors, 1 tub	110	7	11
Reduced Fat, all flavors, 1 oz	140	7	15
Fat Free, all flavors, 15 crisps, 1 oz	70	0	15
Multi Grain, all flavors, 1 oz	140	7	17
Cheez Ummms, all flavors, 1 oz	150	9	15
Ruffles: Regular, av. all flavors, 1 oz	160	11	15
Baked!, average all flavors, 1 oz	120	3.5	22
Sun Chips, Original, 16 crisps, 1 oz	140	6	18

Pretzels

	C	F	Cb
Average All Brands			
Hard-Baked Pretzels: *Each*			
1 oz quantity	110	1	23
Sticks, thin, 2¼" (9/oz)	12	0	3
Twists, thin, ¼" thick, (5/oz)	25	0	5
Dutch (2¾"x 2⅝"), 0.5 oz	55	1	11
Snyders, Sourdough, 0.75 oz	100	0	22
Soft Pretzel Twists, average: *Each*			
Plain: Small, 2 oz	210	2	43
Medium, 4 oz	390	3.5	80
Large, 5 oz	485	4.5	100
Big Cheese, 1.76 oz	130	3	22
New York Street Vendors, 7 oz	660	6	135
Trader Joe's, Peanut Butter filled, 1.1 oz	140	8	14
Snyder's: Milk Chocolate Dips, 1 oz	140	6	19
White Creme Dips, 1 oz	130	6	19

Pretzels ~ Brands

	C	F	Cb
Flipz: Milk Choc, 8 pieces, 1 oz	130	5	20
White Fudge, 7 pcs, 1 oz	130	5	20
Rold Gold *(Frito-Lay):*			
Braided Twists,			
Honey Wheat (8), 1 oz	110	1	24
Pretzel Sticks, 1 oz	110	0	23
Rods/Tiny Twists, av., 1 oz	110	1	23
Sourdough, 1 pretzel	90	1	19
Tiny Twists, Fat-Free, 1 oz	110	0	23
Snyder's of Hanover:			
Gluten Free Pretzel Sticks (30)	110	1.5	25
Homestyle (15), 1 oz	120	1	25
Pieces, Bacon Cheddar , 1 oz	140	7	17
Rods (3), 1 oz	120	1	24
Sticks (28), 1 oz	110	1	23
Thins (11), 1 oz	110	0	23
SuperPretzel:			
Soft: Original (1), 2.25 oz	160	1	34
Sweet Cinnamon (1),			
with topping, 2.5 oz	200	2	42
Bites (5), 1.87 oz	140	0.5	32
Softstix (2), 1.75 oz	130	3	22
Pretzelfils: Pizza (2), 1.85 oz	120	2	20
Pepperjack; Mozzarella, (2), average	130	4.5	19
Utz: Hard (1)	90	0	18
Cinnamon, 1 oz	120	1.5	24

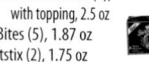

Snacks   C   F   Cb

Note: Actual weight of packaged snacks is usually 5-10% more than label Net Wt. For accuracy, weigh snack and allow extra calories, fat and carbs for any extra weight.

	C	F	Cb
Apple Chips *(Seneca)*, av., 1 oz	140	7	20
Bagel Crisps *(N.Y. Style)*, 6 crisps, 1 oz	130	6	17
Baguette Chips *(Pillsbury)*, 21 chips	130	5	20
Banana Chips *(T.Joe's)*, 13 chips, 1 oz	160	11	13
Beef Jerky *(Jack Link's)*, av., 1 oz	85	1	5
Beef Sticks *(Slim Jim)*, Orig., 2 oz	150	3	10
Jack Links, Original, 1.5 oz	160	13	2
Bugles, Original; Nacho Cheese, 1 oz	160	9	18
Cheese Balls *(Utz)*, 1 oz serving	150	9	16
Cheese Nips, 1.25 oz package	170	7	22
Cheese Puffs, average, 1 oz	160	10	15
Cheese Twists, 1 oz	140	8	15
Cheerios, Snack Mix, average, ⅔ cup, 1.1 oz	120	3	21
Cheetos:			
Crunchy: Av all flavors, 1 oz	155	11	13
4 oz package	640	40	60
Baked!; Fantastix, all varieties, av., 1 oz	130	5	19
Simply Natural, White Cheddar Puffs, 1 oz	150	9	16
Cheez-It Crackers *(Sunshine)*:			
Original, 1.25 oz package	180	9	20
Original Big (13), 1 oz	150	8	17
Colby, 0.8 oz pouch	110	6	12
Mozzarella (25), 1 oz	150	7	19
Reduced Fat: Original, 1 oz	130	4.5	20
White Cheddar, 1 oz	130	4	22
Chester's: Fries, Flamin' Hot, 1 pkg	140	8	16
Puffcorn, Cheese, 1 oz	160	11	14
Chex Mix, *(General Mills)*, Traditional, 1 oz	120	3.5	21
Chips Ahoy!, Choc Chip Cookies:			
1.4 oz Single Serve Pack	190	9	27
Minis: Go-Pak!, 1 pkg, 3.5 oz	525	25	70
Snak Saks, 1 oz	150	7	21
Chicharrones ~ See Pork Skins			
Churros *(Rubio's)*, 9", 1.6 oz	170	8	22
Combos:			
Crackers, av. all flavors· ⅓ cup, 1 oz	140	6	18
Pretzels, average all flavors, 1 oz	135	5	19
Cool Cuts, Carrot & Ranch, 2.3 oz	70	5	5
Corn Chips ~ See Page 149			
Corn Nuts: Av all flav., 1 oz	130	4.5	20
1.7 oz bag	210	8	34
Corn Puffs/Twists, (32 approx), 1 oz	160	11	15
Dunkin Stix *(Dolly Madison)*, (3)	490	25	63

Snacks (Cont)   C   F   Cb

	C	F	Cb
Edamame, Seapointe, Dry Roasted, 1 oz	130	4	10
Fig Newtons:			
Original, 1.1 oz	110	2	22
Fat-Free, 1 oz	90	0	22
Fritos: Corn Chips, all varieties, av., 1 oz	150	10	15
Flavor Twists, Honey BBQ, 1 oz	150	9	16
Funyuns, Onion Flavored, 1 oz	140	7	18
Goldfish, av. all flavors 1 oz	140	5	20
Gold-n-Chees *(Lance)*:			
Snack Mix, 1 oz	150	10	17
Tube, 1 oz	150	8	18
Gripz, *(Sunshine)*, Mighty Tiny, 0.9 oz	120	6	17
Hot Peanuts *(Munchies)*, 1.65 oz	310	25	10
Munchies Snack Mix *(Frito-Lay)*:			
Cheese Fix, ¾ cup	140	7	18
Flaming; Totally Ranch, ¾ c.	140	6	19
Munchos, 16 pieces, 1 oz	160	10	16
Nabisco:			
Toasted Chips: Ritz, av. all flav., 1 oz	130	5.5	20
Wheat Thins, 1 oz	130	5	19
Nutter Butter, Sandwich Cookies:			
Singles, 1.9 oz pkg	250	10	37
Bites: 1.25 oz pkg	170	7	24
Milk Choc-Covered, 2.54 oz pkg	350	17	48
Onion Rings *(T.G.I. Friday)*, 1 oz	130	6	19
Oreo Cookies:			
Double Stuf, 1.5 oz pkg	210	10	30
Mini Bite Size: (9 cookies), 1.25 oz	170	7	25
3 oz Bag	400	17	60
Snak-Saks, 8 oz package	1120	48	168
Oreo Cakesters, soft, 2 oz	250	12	36
Oriental Mix Rice Snacks, 1 oz	125	3.5	21
Peanut Butter Nuggets, (10), 1 oz	140	6	15
Pepitas, dried or roasted, ¼ cup, 1 oz	155	14	3
Pirate's Booty:			
Aged White Cheddar, 4 oz bag	520	20	76
Chocolate, 4 oz bag	560	32	68
Pita Chips, (9), average, 1 oz	130	4	18
Plaintain Chips:			
Goya, 34 chips, 1 oz	150	8	20
PopCorners, Butter/Kettle, 1 oz	120	3.5	21
Popcorn ~ See Page 148			
Pork Cracklins, 1 oz	160	12	0
Pork Skins/Rinds: 1 oz	160	10	0
Baken-ets, 1.25 oz	200	13	0
Mission, Chiccarones, 3 oz package	480	27	0
Potato Chips ~ See Page 149			
Potato Skins *(TGI Friday)*, Cheddar & Bacon, 2.85 oz	150	8	19

Snacks (Cont)

	C	F	Cb
Puffed Wheat,			
Sabritones, Chili & Lime, 1 oz	150	10	13
Pretzels ~ See Page 149			
Rice Cakes:			
Lundberg, (1), average, 0.7 oz	75	0.5	16
Quaker: Plain, lightly salted, 0.3 oz	35	0	7
Chocolate (1), 0,5 oz	60	1	12
Rice Chips:			
Lundberg, average, 1 oz	140	7	18
Quaker, Popped White Cheddar & Herb, 16 chips, 1 oz	130	5	19
Sandwich Crackers:			
Austin, Cheese Crackers:			
With Cheddar, 1.38 oz	190	10	23
With Peanut Butter, 1.3 oz	190	10	23
PB & J Flavored, 1.38 oz	190	8	26
Lance:			
Nip Chee, 6 pieces	190	9	24
Toasty, 6 pieces	180	8	24
Toast Chee, 6 pieces	210	10	25
Ritz Bits:			
Cheese: 1.5 oz package	220	13	24
Go-Pak: 13 crackers, 1 oz	150	9	17
3.5 oz Pak	520	29	58
P'nut Butter: 1.25 oz pkg	170	10	20
Big Bag, 3 oz	450	25	50
Sesame Sticks,			
SunRidge Farm, 1.1 oz	170	11	14
Smart Puffs,			
Pirates Booty, 1 oz	140	7	16
Snack Mix,			
Quaker, Baked Cheddar, 1 package	230	8	34
Soy Crisps, average, 1 oz	120	3	17
Soy Nuts: Dry Roasted, ¼ cup, 1 oz	130	6	9
Choc-coated, 1 oz	140	7	13
Sun Chips,			
Fritolay, average, 1 oz	140	6	19
Takis: Fajitas, 1 oz	140	7	17
4 oz package	560	28	68
Tings,			
Robert's, 2 oz bag	300	16	36
Tortilla Chips/Tostitos ~ Page 149			
Trail Mix (Nuts/Seeds/Dried Fruit):			
Regular, 3 Tbsp, 1 oz	140	9	13
Tropical, 3 Tbsp, 1 oz	130	7	16
Turkey Jerky: Teriyaki, 1 oz	80	1	8
Trader Joe's, Original, 1 oz	60	0.5	6
Veggie Crisps,			
Snyder's, 1 oz	140	7	18
Wasabi Peas, ¼ cup, 1 oz	120	3	19
Yogurt Pretzels, 1.5 oz	190	8	28
Yogurt Raisins,			
Sun-Maid, 1 oz	120	4.5	18

Fruit Snacks

	C	F	Cb
Betty Crocker: Fruit Gushers, 0.9 oz	90	1	20
Fruit by the Foot, 1 roll, 0.75 oz	80	1	17
Fruit Roll Ups, 1 roll, 0.5 oz	50	1	12
Fruit Flavored Shapes, all varieties, 0.9 oz	80	0	19
Sunkist: Fruit Snacks, 1 pouch	80	0	19
Fruit Smoothie Blitz, 1.3 oz	140	1	32

Vending Machines

	C	F	Cb
Bugles, Nacho Cheese, 1.5 oz	220	12	25
Cheese Balls (Utz), 1 oz	150	9	16
Cheetos, Crunchy, 2 oz	320	21	26
Cheeze-It, Snack Mix, 1.5 oz	195	6.5	30
Chex Mix, average, 1.75 oz	220	5	42
Chester's Fries, 1 oz	140	8	16
Choc Chip Cookies:			
Chips Ahoy, 1.4 oz	190	9	27
Famous Amos, 2 oz	280	13	38
Grandma's, (2), 2.8 oz	350	14	53
Chocolate Bars:			
Hershey's, Milk Choc., 1.55 oz	210	13	26
Kit Kat, 1.5 oz	210	11	26
Snickers, 2.07 oz bar	280	14	35
Donut, plain cake, 1.4 oz	160	9	18
Doritos, 1.75 oz	245	12	32
Fritos, Corn Chips, Orig., 1.75 oz	280	17	26
Fruit Pie,			
Hostess, 4.5 oz	480	20	68
Granola/Cereal Bars, av., 1 oz	140	3	26
M & M's:			
Milk Chocolate, 1.7 oz	240	10	34
Peanuts, 1.75 oz	250	13	30
Oreo Cookies, 2 oz	270	11	41
Peanut Butter Cups,			
Reese's, 1.5 oz	210	13	26
Popcorn, plain, 1 oz	160	10	16
Pop Chips, 0.8 oz	100	3	16
Pork Skins, 1.5 oz	240	15	0
Potato Chips: 1 oz	150	10	15
Baked! (Ruffles), 1.1 oz	140	4	24
Potato Skins (TGI Friday's),			
Cheddar Bacon, 1.75 oz	150	8	19
Pretzels,			
Snyder's, Old Time, 1 oz	120	1	24
Raisins, ½ oz package	45	0	11
Rice Krispies Treat	90	2	17
Skittles, 2 oz	220	2.5	50
Starburst, Fruit Chews, Orig., 2. oz	240	4.5	48
Tortilla Chips, 1 oz	140	7	18

S · Soups

Homemade & Restaurant

Restaurant & Take-Out:
Average All Preparations, Per 8 fl.oz

	C	F	Cb
Bean Medley	200	3	34
Beef Consomme	30	0	2
Borscht, with Sour Cream	130	8	14
Bouillabaisse	400	15	10
Chicken & Corn	290	14	20
Chicken & Wild Rice	80	4	9
Chicken Consomme	50	0	2
Chicken Curry	180	8	18
Chicken Jambalaya	160	7	8
Chicken Noodle	80	2	12
with Chicken	160	4	12
Chicken Soup	80	2	6
Chili with Beans	250	12	25
Clam Chowder	240	15	17
Corn & Crab	120	3	18
Corn Chowder	150	8	16
Cream of Broccoli	200	12	20
Cream of Potato	150	6.5	17
Cream of Mushroom	200	13	15
Fish Chowder	220	15	6
French Onion	420	15	25
Gazpacho	50	0	5
Lentil Soup	250	9	28
Lobster Bisque	320	15	10
Matzo Ball, with 1 large ball	180	7	24
Minestrone	125	2.5	18
Mulligatawny	300	15	8
Pea & Ham	240	10	25
Potato & Bacon	170	7	19
Pumpkin, Creamy	210	10	26
Shark Fin Soup	100	4	8
Spicy Shrimp Soup, 1 bowl	160	7	10
Split Pea Soup	180	2.5	30
Vegetable (Fat Free)	75	0	18
Vegetable Beef	80	2	10
Vichyssoise	200	9	15
Watercress	90	4	13

Other Soups ~ *See International & Fast-Foods Sections (Arby's, Au Bon Pain, Boston Market, Dunkin' Donuts, Denny's, Schlotzsky's, Sizzler, Souplantation, Sweet Tomatoes, Zoup!)*

Homemade Soups: *Calculate calories, fat and carbohydrates from recipe ingredients.*

Bouillon Cubes & Powders

Bouillon Cubes: *Average all types*	C	F	Cb
Regular, 1 cube	5	0	1
Extra Large, 1 cube	20	1	1
Powders, average, 1 tsp	10	0	1

Herb-Ox:
Instant Broth & Seasoning,

	C	F	Cb
Beef, 1 envelope, 0.14 oz	5	0	1
Chicken, 1 envelope, 0.14 oz	5	0	1

Soup ~ Brands

	C	F	Cb

Amy's:
Heat & Serve (Organic): *Per 1 Cup, Unless Indicated*

	C	F	Cb
Alphabet	80	0	16
Chunky Vegetable	60	0	13
Cream of M'shrm, ¾ cup	150	9	13
Curried Lentil	230	8	30
Fire Roasted Southwestern Veggie	140	4	21
Lentil	180	5	25
Lentil Vegetable	160	4	24
Rustic Italian Vegetable	140	6	18
Split Pea	100	0	19
Thai Coconut	140	10	13
Tuscan Bean & Rice	160	4.5	25

Andersen's: *Per 1 Cup*

	C	F	Cb
Split Pea	130	1	24
Split Pea with Real Ham	140	1	23
Tomato	130	3.5	22

Bertoli: *Per ½ package, 12 oz*
Meal Soups: Chicken Minestrone

	C	F	Cb
Chicken Minestrone	370	18	32
Roasted Chicken & Rotini Pasta	290	12	28
Ricotta & Lobster Ravioli, in Seafood Bisque	380	16	41
Tomato Florentine & Tortellini w/ Chicken	410	19	36

Campbell's:
Chunky: *Per 8 fl.oz Cup*

	C	F	Cb
Baked Potato w/ Ched. & Bacon Bits	190	9	23
Chicken Corn Chowder	190	10	20
Classic Chicken Noodle	120	3	15
Hearty: Beef Noodle	120	2	17
Italian Style Wedding, with Meatballs & Spinach	120	3	15
Tomato with Pasta	150	1	30

Campbell's (Cont):	C	F	Cb
Classic Condensed Soup: *Per ½ Cup 4 fl.oz*			
Bean with Bacon	160	3	25
Beef with Veggies & Barley	80	1	15
Chicken Noodle	60	2	8
Cream of Broccoli	90	5	9
Cream of Celery/Mushroom	100	7	9
Cream of Potato	90	2	16
Homestyle Chicken Noodle	70	2	10
Old Fashioned Tomato Rice	110	1.5	23
Split Pea with Ham & Bacon	180	2	29
Tomato	90	0	20
Gourmet Bisques: *Per 8 fl.oz Cup*			
Golden Butternut Squash	110	2	21
Sweet Potato Tomatillo	160	8	19
Thai Tomato Coconut	170	5	27
Tomato Roasted Garlic Bacon	210	8	31
Homestyle: *Per 8 fl.oz Cup*			
Butternut Squash Bisque	110	3	19
Creamy Chicken & Herb Dumplings	160	8	16
Creamy Gouda Bisque with Chicken	140	6	15
Chicken Noodle	90	2.5	10
Harvest Tomato with Basil	110	1	23
Italian-Style Wedding	120	3.5	15
Maryland-Style Crab Soup	80	0.5	14
Mexican-Style Chicken Tortilla	130	2	20
Minestrone	100	1	18
New England Clam Chowder	170	10	15
Potato Broccoli	160	9	17
Southwest-Style Chicken Chili	130	2.5	20
Vegetable	90	0.5	18
Zesty Tomato Bisque	110	2	19
Light: Chicken Noodle	70	1	9
New England Clam Chowder	120	4	15
Italian-Style Wedding	80	2	11
Southwestern-Style Vegetable	60	0	12
Healthy Request, Chunky: *Per 8 fl.oz Cup*			
Beef with Country Vegetables	100	1	16
Chicken Corn Chowder	140	3	22
Chicken Noodle	110	2.5	14
New Eng. Clam Chowder	130	3	20
Split Pea & Ham	160	2.5	22
Microwaveable Soup On The Go: *Per 10.75 oz*			
Chicken & Stars	70	1.5	10
Chicken w/ Mini Noodles	70	2	11
Creamy Chicken	130	9	10
Creamy Broccoli	160	11	13
Creamy Tomato Parmesan Soup	220	7	35
New England Clam Chowder	160	11	13
Vegetable Beef	70	1	11

Campbell's (Cont):	C	F	Cb
Slow Kettle Style: *Per 8 fl.oz*			
Braised Beef Stew, with Vegetables & Wine	150	3	19
Portobello Mushroom & Madeira Bisque	250	18	16
Sthwest Style Chkn Chili	190	2	28
Tomato & Sweet Basil Bisque	260	14	30
Tuscan Style Chicken	140	2.5	17
Health Valley:			
Fat Free, 40% Less Sodium: *Per 8 fl.oz Cup*			
Organic: Black Bean Vegetable	110	0	25
Corn & Vegetable	100	0	22
Lentil & Carrot	110	0	24
Split Pea & Carrots	120	0	26
Tomato Vegetable	70	0	17
Specialty: *Per 8 fl.oz Cup*			
Organic: Cream of Chicken	110	6	11
Cream of Celery	90	5	11
Healthy Choice:			
Canned: *Per 8 fl.oz Cup*			
Bean & Ham	180	2.5	28
Chicken & Dumplings	150	3	22
Chicken with Rice	110	2	17
Chicken Tortilla	140	1.5	23
Country Vegetable	100	0	19
New England Clam Chowder	110	1.5	20
Split Pea & Ham	160	2.5	27
Tomato Basil	100	0	22
Microwaveable Bowls: *Per 8 fl.oz Cup*			
Beef Pot Roast	110	1.5	17
Chicken Tortilla	140	1.5	23
Chicken with Rice	90	2	13
Country Vegetable	100	0	20
Hearty Vegetable Barley, 8.8 oz	140	1	30
Imagine:			
Broths:			
Organic: Beef	20	1	1
Free Range Chicken	10	0	1
Vegetable Broth	20	0	2
Chunky Style:			
Chicken & Dumplings	130	4.5	18
Cream of Mushroom	100	3.5	15
Italian Vegetables & Beans	120	1.5	24

S Soups

	C	F	Cb
Imagine (Cont):			
Creamy: *Per 8 fl.oz Cup*			
Creamy: Acorn Squash & Mango	70	1.5	14
Portobello Mushroom	80	3	10
Potato Leek	70	1.5	12
Sweet Pea	80	1.5	14
Tomato Basil	90	1.5	17
Kettle Cuisine: *Per 10 oz*			
Aztec Chili with Beans	190	4	32
Caribbean Jerk Chicken	220	6	31
Carrot Ginger	110	4	18
Cream of Crab	330	26	15
Manhattan Clam Chowder	130	3	17
North Atlantic Haddock Chowder	290	19	14
Gluten Free:			
Beef, Barley & Vegetable	110	3	13
Chicken Noodle	100	2	10
Cream of Broccoli			
with Monterey Jack	260	20	14
Minestrone	140	3	22
Tomato Basil	100	4	14
Knorr:			
Cubes: *Per ½ Cube, 1 Cup, Prepared*			
Beef; Chicken, average	15	1.5	1
Vegetable	20	1	1
Homestyle Stock: *Per 1 Tsp*			
Beef	10	1	0
Chicken	10	2	0
Lipton:			
Cup-a-Soup: *Per Envelope*			
Chicken Noodle, Original	50	1	8
Cream of Chicken	60	1.5	12
Hearty Chicken Noodle	60	0	10
Recipe Secrets: *Per 1 Tbsp Dry Mix*			
Onion	20	0	4
Onion Mushroom	25	0	7
Savory Herb with Garlic	25	0	6
Manischewitz:			
Cans: *Per ½ Cup Soup*			
Chicken Consomme, Clear	15	0	2
Chicken Kreplach	40	1	6
Chicken Noodle	60	1.5	7
Quart Jars: *Per 6 fl.oz*			
Borscht with Beets	50	0	13
Borscht, Low Calorie	15	0	4
Ready To Serve,			
Matzo Ball Chicken, 1 cup, 8 fl.oz	120	4.5	12
Maruchan:			
Instant Lunch,			
av. all flavors., 1 pkg	290	12	38
Ramen, all flavors, 1 pkg, 3 oz	380	14	52

	C	F	Cb
Nissin:			
Souper Meal: *Per ½ of 4.3 oz Ctn*			
Chicken Flavor, w. Vege Medley	290	13	38
Picante Shrimp Flavor, Hot & Spicy	270	11	36
Top Ramen, all flavors, 3 oz	380	14	53
Pacific Foods:			
Condensed: Cream of Chicken, ½ cup	90	3.5	10
Cream of Mushroom, ½ cup	100	2.5	18
Creamy Organic: *Per ¼ of 32 fl.oz Container*			
French Onion	30	1	5
Cashew Carrot Ginger Bisque	120	5	19
Curried Red Lentil	140	5	20
Rst Pepper & Tomato	110	2	16
Progresso:			
Broths: Beef, 1 cup	20	0	3
Chicken, 1 cup	20	0	1
Chili: Pork/Beef w. Beans, 1 cup	320	20	24
White Chicken w. Beans, 1 cup	210	6	24
Heart Healthy: *Per Cup*			
Creamy Tomato w. Basil	120	3	22
Creole Style Chkn Gumbo	110	2	18
Homestyle Vegetable Beef	120	2	19
Italian Wedding w. Meatballs	80	3	11
Savory Garden Vegetable	90	0	21
S'West Black Bean & Vegetable	110	2	22
Reduced Sodium: *Per 1 Cup*			
Beef & Vegetable	130	1	23
Chicken Noodle	90	2	13
Minestrone	120	2	22
Rich & Hearty: *Per 1 Cup*			
Chkn & Homestyle Noodles	110	3	14
Chicken Corn Chowder	200	9	23
New Engl. Clam Chowder	180	8	22
Savory Beef Barley Vegetables	110	1.5	17
Traditional: *Per ½ Can, 1 Cup*			
Chicken Noodle	100	2.5	12
Chicken & Sausage Gumbo	130	4	18
Italian-Style Wedding	120	4	15
Split Pea with Ham	140	1	24
Vegetable Classic: *Per ½ Can, 1 Cup*			
French Onion	50	1	9
Green Split Pea with Bacon	160	2.5	29
Garden Vegetable	90	0	20
Minestrone	100	2	20
Tomato Rotini	130	0.5	28
Light: *Per ½ Can, 1 cup*			
Beef Pot Roast	80	2	10
Chicken Pot Pie Syle	100	3	16
Italian Style Vegetable	70	0	16
Vegetable & Noodle	60	0.5	13

Safeway (Vons):	**C**	**F**	**Cb**
Signature Soups: Per Cup			
Broccoli & Cheesy Cheddar	250	18	12
Chunky Chicken Noodle	160	5	14
Fiesta Chicken Tortilla	110	2	15
Italian-Style Wedding	120	4	14
Pacific Coast Clam Chowder	320	20	27
Tuscan Tomato & Basil Bisque	290	22	20
Swanson:			
Broth: Per 8 fl.oz Cup			
Beef	15	0	1
Chicken	10	0.5	1
Organic Chicken	15	0.5	1
Vegetable	15	0	3
Flavor Boost: Per Pouch			
Beef	10	0	2
Chicken	35	2	3
Vegetable	20	0	4
Tabatchnick:			
Frozen:			
Dairy: Per 7.5 oz Pouch			
Corn Chowder	130	4.5	21
New England Potato	130	4.5	20
Gluten Free: Per 7.5 oz Pouch			
Southwest Bean	220	5	36
Split Pea	140	0	34
Vegetarian Chili	200	3.5	32
Low Sodium: Per 7 .5oz Pouch			
Barley Mushroom	80	1	17
Split Pea	140	0	34
Vegetable	90	1.5	17
Meat: Per 7.5 oz Pouch			
Frenchman's Onion	60	1.5	11
Wilderness Wild Rice	90	0.5	19
Parve: Per 7.5 oz Pouch			
Barley Mushroom	80	1	17
Black Bean	220	2.5	39
Minestrone	110	1.5	20
Shelf Stable: Per ⅔ Cup, 5.3 fl.oz			
Broth: Classic Chicken	5	0	0
Kosher Chicken	10	0	1
Soup: Creamy Tomato	70	2	14
Rstd Red Pepper & Tomato	70	2.5	13
Wisconsin Cheddar Cheese	150	11	10
Thai Kitchen:			
Rice Noodle Soup Bowls: Per Bowl			
Hot & Sour	250	4	51
Lemongrass & Chili	250	3.5	52
Spring Onion	260	4.5	50
Roasted Garlic	250	3	52
Thai Ginger	260	3	52

Trader Joe's:	**C**	**F**	**Cb**
28 fl.oz Cans: Per Cup			
Chunky, Low Fat:			
Lentil with Vegetables	140	3	21
Minestrone	110	2.5	19
14.5 oz Cans: Per Cup			
Organic: Black Bean	140	1.5	26
Lentil Vegetable, ½ can	160	4	24
Split Pea	100	0	19
10.75 oz Can,			
Low Sodium, Minestrone	200	4	37
15 oz Can,			
Low Fat, Chicken Noodle, 1 cup	90	1	14
32 fl.oz. Cartons: Per Cup			
Butternut Squash	90	2	16
Carrot & Ginger	80	1	17
Creamy Corn & Rstd Pepper	110	2	23
Latin Style Black Bean	70	1	12
Sweet Potato Bisque	130	1	28
Organic: Butternut Squash	70	0	17
Tom. & Rstd Red Pepper	100	3.5	15
Low Sodium, Crmy Tomato	90	3.5	15
17.6 fl.oz Cartons: Per Cup			
Beef, Barley with Veggies	100	0.5	16
Chicken Noodle with Veggies	100	1	16
Whole Foods: Per Cup			
365 Organic:			
Chicken Noodle	100	1.5	12
Lentil	70	0	15
Minestrone	140	1.5	23
Southwestern Black Bean	120	1	23
Tomato Basil	90	2	16
Wolfgang Puck: Per Cup			
Organic:			
Butternut Squash	200	11	22
Chicken & Dumplings	140	7	14
Classic Minestrone	120	2.5	20
Corn Chowder	210	13	20
Free Range Chicken Noodle	90	3	11
Hearty Garden Vegetable	130	4	22
Hearty Lentil & Vegetable	150	1	28
New Engl. Clam Chowder	150	7	18
Signature Tortilla	140	3.5	21
Tomato Basil Bisque	150	6	21

Soybean Products | C | F | Cb

Cheeses (Soy) ~ *See Page 78*
Miso Soy Bean Paste:

	C	F	Cb
Cold Mountain: Light Yellow, 1 tsp	10	0	1
Mellow Red, 1 tsp	15	0	3
Red, 1 tsp	10	0	1

Miso Soup (dry mix):

	C	F	Cb
1 Tbsp., dry mix	35	1	5
1 cup, prepared	35	1	5
Natto, ½ cup, 3 oz	160	7	14
Okara (Tofu fiber residue), ½ c., 2 oz	47	1	8
Tempeh: 1 piece, 3 oz	180	8	12
Fried, 3 oz	250	14	14
Seitan *(Westsoy)*, Strips, 3 oz	120	2	4
Soybean Protein *(TVP)*, 1 oz	95	0	8
Soy Bean Paste, 1 tsp	10	0	0

Soy Beans ~ *See Page 160*
Soy Drinks ~ *See Page 49*

Tofu ~ Brands | C | F | Cb

Azumaya Tofu:

	C	F	Cb
Extra Firm; Firm, av., 3 oz	70	4	2
Soft (Silken), 3.2 oz	45	2	1

House Foods: *Per 3 oz*
Premium Tofu: Extra Firm

	C	F	Cb
Extra Firm	80	4.5	2
Firm	70	4	2
Medium Firm (Regular)	60	3.5	2
Soft (Silken)	60	3	2
Organic Tofu: Firm	70	4	2
Extra Firm	70	3.5	2
Ethnic: Tokusen Kinugoshi, Extra Soft	80	4	3
Sukui; Soon (Extra Soft)	45	2	2
Yaki Tofu (Broiled)	90	5	2

Mori-Nu Tofu:
Morinaga Silken:

	C	F	Cb
Soft, 3 oz, 1" slice	45	2.5	2
Firm, 3 oz, 1" slice	50	2.5	2
Extra Firm, 3 oz, 1" slice	45	1.5	2
Organic, Silken 3 oz, 1" slice	50	2.5	2
Lite, Firm, 3 oz, 1" slice	30	1	1
Nasoya: Extra Firm, 3 oz	80	4	3
Firm, 3 oz	70	3.5	2
Silken, 3.2 oz	45	2	1
Soft, 2.8 oz	60	3	1

Tofuplus:

	C	F	Cb
Extra Firm, 3 oz	80	4	2
Firm, 3 oz	70	3	2
Sprouted, Super Firm, 3 oz	100	5	3

Supplements | C | F | Cb

	C	F	Cb
Aloe Vera Juice, undiluted, 2 fl.oz	5	0	1
Brewer's Yeast: Tablets, 2 tabs	4	0	0.5
Flakes, 1 heaping Tbsp, 0.3 oz	30	0.5	4
Powder, 1 heaping Tbsp, 0.5 oz	50	0.5	6
Calcium Chews: *CVS*, 1 chew	20	0	3
Trader Joe's, Chocolate,1 chew	20	1	3
Cod Liver Oil, 1 Tbsp	125	13	0
Fiber Choice, 2 tabs	15	0	4
Fiber,			
Fibersure, 1 heaping tsp	25	0	6
Fish Oil Capsules, (1), av.	10	1	0
Flax Oil:			
Capsules (2)	10	1	0
Barlean's, softgels (3)	110	11	0
Garlic Tablets/Capsules, each	3	0	0
Glowelle:			
Beauty Drink, 8 fl.oz	100	0	24
Powder Stick (1)	50	0	12
Lecithin Granules, 1 Tbsp	55	4	0.5
Metamucil, Powder:			
Orange (Smooth Texture),			
1 rounded Tbsp	45	0	12
Sugar-Free, 1 rounded tsp	20	0	5
Pink Lemonade, Sugar-Free,			
1 rounded tsp	20	0	5
Fiber Wafers, (2)	120	5	17
Capsules:			
Heart & Digestive (6)	10	0	3
Strong Bones (5)	10	0	3
Protein, Powders, av., 1 oz	100	0.5	0
Seaweed: Dried, 1 oz	85	0.5	22
Soaked, drained, 1 oz	15	0.5	3
Spirulina, 1 tablet	2	0	0.5
Vitamins/Minerals: Tabs/Caps (1)	2	0	0
Vitamin E Capsules, each	5	0.5	0
Viactiv Chews, Choc. (1)	20	0.5	4

Cough & Pharmaceutical

	C	F	Cb
Antacids: Av., 1 tablet	4	0	1
Liquid, 1 Tbsp	6	0	1
Antacid Sodium Counts ~ *See Page 280*			
Cough/Cold Syrups:			
Regular: With sugar, 1 Tbsp	35	0	9
With alcohol, 1 Tbsp	46	0	9
Diabetic Tussin, Sugar Free, 1 T.	0	0	0
Cough Drops/Lozenges ~ *See Page 75*			
Sudafed, Syrup 1 tsp	14	0	3
Tylenol, Liquid: Child, 1 tsp	17	0	4
Extra Strength, 1 tsp	11	0	3

Sugar

	C	F	Cb
White Sugar, granulated:			
1 level teaspoon, 4g	15	0	4
1 heaping teaspoon, 6g	25	0	6
1 Tablespoon, 12g	50	0	12
1 ounce, 1 oz	110	0	28
1 cup, 7 oz	775	0	200
1 lb (16 oz)	1760	0	454
Single Portion Packages:			
1 stick	15	0	4
1 packet	15	0	4
1 cube	10	0	2.5
Brown Sugar: 1 Tbsp	50	0	13
1 ounce, 1 oz	110	0	28
1 cup, not packed, 5 oz	550	0	140
1 cup, packed, 7.75 oz	835	0	216
Powdered/Confectioners:			
Sifted, 1 cup, 3.5 oz	390	0	100
Unsifted, 1 cup, 4.25 oz	465	0	120
Cinnamon Sugar, 1 tsp	15	0	4
Dextrose, 1¼ tsp	15	0	4
Fructose, powder, 1 tsp	15	0	4
Glucose, 1 oz	110	0	27
Glucose Tablets, (1)	20	0	5
Palm Sugar, 3 Tbsp	45	0	11
Piloncillo, (Brown Sugar), 3oz	325	0	81
Turbinado Sugar, 2 Tbsp, 1 oz	110	0	27

Sugar Substitutes

	C	F	Cb
Agave, 1 Tbsp, 0.7 oz	60	0	16
DiabetiSweet, 1 teaspoon	9	0	4.5
(Carbohydrate as Sugar Alcohol)			
Domino, Light, ½ tsp	5	0	2
Equal: Tablet (2)	0	0	0
Granular, 1 tsp	0	0	0
Packet (1)	0	0	0
Nectresse, 1 packet	0	0	0
NutraSweet, 1 tsp	0	0	0
Splenda, Granulated No Calorie Sweetener:			
1 tsp	0	0	0
1 cup	95	0	24
Packets, all flavors	0	0	0
Sugar Blend,Orig/Brown, ½ cup	385	0	96
Stevia, single serving	0	0	0
Sugar Twin, 1 packet	0	0	0
Sweet 'N Low, 1 packet	0	0	0
Truvia, 1 packet	0	0	0
Walgreens, Wal-Sweet, 1 packet	0	0	0
Whey Low, 1 tsp	0	0	1

Syrups, Molasses, Agave

Syrups, Plain: *Average All Brands*
(Corn/Rice/Maple/Pancake/Sundae/Waffle)
Includes Aunt Jemima, Cary's, Karo, Hershey's,
Hungry Jack, IHOP, Log Cabin, Mrs Butterworth's

	C	F	Cb
Regular/Dark/Light Color:			
1 Tbsp, ½ fl.oz	55	0	14
¼ cup (4 Tbsp)	220	0	55
Single Portion, 1.5 oz pkg	170	0	42
Lite, 1Tbsp, 1 oz	25	0	6
Sugar-Free: 2 Tbsp, 1 oz	18	0	5
Maple Grove, Cozy Cottage, 2 Tbsp	10	0	3
IHOP, 4 Tbsp, 2 oz	20	0	7
Fruit Syrups, (IHOP), ¼ cup, 2 oz	200	0	52
Honey Cream Syrup, ¼ cup, 2 oz	220	0	55
Molasses: Dark/Light: 1 T, 0.7 oz	60	0	15
1 cup, 11.88 oz	975	0.5	252
Blackstrap, 1 Tbsp, 0.75 oz	47	0	13
Agave Nectar, av. all flavors,			
1 Tablespoon, 0.75 oz	60	0	15

Flavored Syrups/Ice Cream Toppings

	C	F	Cb
Hershey's: *Per 2 Tbsp*			
Average all flavors	105	0	26
Lite	45	0	12
Smuckers: *Per 2 Tbsp*			
Magic Shell, average all flavors	220	17	16
Spoonables: Average all flavors	115	1	28
Sugar Free: Caramel; Chocolate	90	0	24
Strawberry	25	0	9
(Carbohydrate figures includes 9g-17g Sugar Alcohol)			
Sundae Syrups: Regular, av. all flavors	105	0	25
Sugar Free, average all flavors	90	0	24
(Carbohydrate figures includes 15g Sugar Alcohol)			

Honey, Jam, Preserves

Average All Brands	C	F	Cb
Honey: 1 tsp, 0.25 oz	22	0	5.5
1 Tbsp, 0.75 oz	65	0	17
1 ounce, 1 oz	85	0	23
1 cup, 12 oz	1030	0	269
Single Portion, 0.5 oz package	45	0	11
Jams/Jellies/Marmalade/Preserves:			
Regular: 1 tsp, 0.25 oz	20	0	5
1 Tbsp, 0.75 oz	55	0	14
1 ounce, 1 oz	80	0	20
Single Portion, 0.5 oz pkg	40	0	11
Apple/Fruit Butters, 1 T., 0.6 oz	20	0	4
Fruit Spreads: Regular, 1 tsp	15	0	4
Low Sugar, 1 tsp	8	0	2
Jelly: Regular, average, 1 tsp	18	0	4.5
Imitation, Low Calorie, 1 tsp	4	0	1

V Vegetables & Legumes ~ Fresh

Vegetables

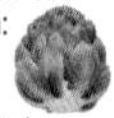

Vegetables	C	F	Cb
Alfalfa Sprouts, ½ cup, 0.5 oz	5	0	0.5
Artichokes, Globe/French:			
1 medium, 4.5 oz	60	0	13
1 large, 5.7 oz	75	0	17
Artichoke Heart, plain, 2 pieces	15	0	3
Asparagus, raw/frozen:			
Cuts & Tips, ½ cup, 4.3 oz	20	0	3
Spears, 3 medium	10	0	2
Bamboo Shoots, cooked, ½ cup, 2 oz	7	0	1
Beans, Green/Snap/String:			
10 beans (4" long), 2 oz	20	0	4
Pieces, ½ cup, 3 oz	30	0	7
Dried Beans (Kidney, Brown, Lima, Navy, Pinto, White):			
Raw: 2 Tbsp, 1 oz	95	0.5	18
1 cup, 7 oz	665	3	126
Cooked: 1 oz	35	0	7
½ cup, 3 oz	105	0	21
Bean Sprouts, average, ½ cup, 2 oz	15	0	3.5
Beets (Beetroot):			
Raw, 1 beet (2" diam.), 4 oz	35	0	8
Cooked, 1 cup, slices, 3 oz	35	0	8
Canned ~ *See Page 161*			
Beet Greens, cooked, ½ cup, 2.5 oz	20	0	4
Bell Pepper ~ *See Peppers*			
Bitter Melon/Gourd, 1 cup, 1.5 oz	15	0	1.5
Blackeye Peas, cooked, ½ cup, 3 oz	100	0.5	18
Bok Choy (Chinese Chard), cooked, 3 oz	10	0	1.5
Breadfruit, ¼ small fruit, 3 oz	100	0	26
Broadbeans (Fava Beans):			
Green, raw, (in pod): 4 pods (3½ oz with shells, 1.2 oz beans)	30	0	6
1 cup beans, without shell, 4.5 oz	110	1	22
Mature Seeds: Raw, 1 cup, 5.3 oz	510	2.5	87
Cooked, ½ cup, 3 oz	95	0	17
Broccoflower, ⅕ head, 3.5 oz	35	0	7
Broccoli: Raw, chopped, 1 cup, 3 oz	30	0	6
3 Florets, 2.5 oz	25	0	5
1 Spear (5" long), 1.1 oz	10	0	2
1 Whole: Medium, 14 oz	135	1.5	26
Large, 21 oz	205	2	40
1 Head (no stalk), 11 oz	105	1	21
1 Stalk, small (5" long), 5.3 oz	50	0.5	10
Brocco Sprouts, ½ cup, 1 oz	15	0	2
Brussels Sprouts: Cooked, ½ cup, 2.8 oz	30	0.5	6
2 Sprouts, 1.5 oz	15	0	3
Butterbeans, cooked, ½ cup, 3 oz	90	0	16
Cabbage, average other flavors:			
Raw: 1 leaf, large, 1 oz	5	0	2
Shredded, 1 cup, 2.5 oz	15	0	4
½ large head (7" diam), 22 oz	150	1	35
Cooked, shredded, ½ cup, 2.5 oz	15	0.5	3.5

Vegetables (Cont)

Vegetables (Cont)	C	F	Cb
Cactus Leaf (Nopales):			
1 leaf, 4.5 oz	20	0	4
1 cup (slices), 3 oz	15	0	3
Carrots, regular thick variety:			
1 small, 4 oz	45	0	11
1 medium, 6 oz	70	0	16
1 large, 8 oz	95	0	22
Chopped, 1 cup, 4.5 oz	50	0	12
Grated, 1 cup, 4 oz	45	0	11
Slices, 1 cup, 4.5 oz	50	0	12
Sticks (4"), 4-5, 1.5 oz	20	0	4
Long thin variety, 1 medium, 2.2 oz	25	0	6
Baby: Snack size, 3 medium, 1 oz	10	0	2.5
Snack Pack, 3 oz	30	0	7
Cassava, raw, 1 cup, 2.5 oz	330	0.5	78
Cauliflower, raw: Pieces, 1 cup, 3.5 oz	25	0	5
½ medium head, 10 oz	70	0	15
Cooked, 3 florets, 2 oz	10	0	2
Celeriac, ½ cup, raw, 2.75 oz	35	0	7
Celery: 1 large stalk, 11", 2.2 oz	10	0	2
4 Strips, thin sticks, 0.5 oz	5	0	1
Chopped, 1 cup, 3.5 oz	15	0	3
Chard (Swiss), ½ cup, cooked, 3 oz	20	0	3.5
Chayote Squash: 1 medium, 7 oz	40	0	9
Pieces, 1 cup, 4.5 oz	25	0	6
Chickpeas, (Garbanzo Beans):			
Dry, 1 cup, 7 oz	730	12	121
Cooked, 1 cup, 5.75 oz	270	4	45
Chicory Greens, 1 cup, 1 oz	7	0	1.5
Chili Peppers ~ *See Peppers*			
Chinese Long Bean, slices, 1 cup, 3.2 oz	45	0	8
Chives, chopped, 1 Tbsp	1	0	0
Choy Sum, 3 oz	15	0	3
Cilantro, (Coriander), 1 cup	5	0	0.5
Collards, cooked, ½ cup, 3 oz	25	0	5
Corn, Yellow/White:			
Raw: Kernels, ½ cup, 3 oz	80	0.5	19
Ear (5"x 1¾"), 5.5 oz	155	1	37
Cooked: Kernels, ½ cup, 3 oz	77	0.5	18
Cob, small, 2.25 oz	60	0.5	14
Ear, large, 5.5 oz	120	1	28
Courgette ~ *See Zucchini*			
Cowpeas ~ *See Blackeye Peas*			
Cress, garden, raw, 1 cup, 1.75 oz	15	0	3
Cucumber, average other flavors:			
Slices, ½ cup, 2 oz	10	0	2
Green, 1 medium (9"), 11 oz	45	0	11
Persian, 1 medium (8"), 6 oz	25	0	5
Daikon Radish, ½ cup, slices, 2 oz	9	0	2
Dandelion Greens, raw, ½ cup, 1 oz	10	0	2.5
Edamame, (Immature green soybeans):			
Shelled, ½ cup, 2.6 oz	110	5	8
With shells, 10 pods, 1.25 oz	30	1	3

Vegetables (Cont)	C	F	Cb
Eggplant, raw: 4 oz	30	0	7
½ cup, 1" pieces, 1.5 oz	10	0	2
1 slice, fried, 1 oz	75	4	10
Endive, Belgian/French: Raw,			
1 medium head (6"), 2.5 oz	12	0	3
Fennel, 1 cup, sliced, 3 oz	25	0	7
Gai Choy Cabbage, cooked, 1 cup, 6 oz	20	0	3
Gai Lan, (Chinese Kale), cooked, 1 cup	35	0.5	7
Garbanzo Beans ~ *See Chick Peas*			
Garlic, 1 clove	4	0	1
Ginger: ¼ cup slices, 1 oz	20	0	5
Crystallized (sugared), 7 pieces, 1.5 oz	130	0	35
Horseradish, raw, 1 pod, 0.5 oz	5	0	1
Jerusalem Artichoke, raw, ½ cup	55	0	13
Jicama, raw, sliced, ½ cup, 2.25 oz	25	0	6
Kale, 1 cup, chopped, 2.5 oz	35	0.5	7
Kohlrabi, cooked, ½ cup, 1.75 oz	17	0	5
Leek, cooked, 1 whole, 4.5 oz	40	0	9
Lentils, green/brown: Dry, 1 oz	100	0.5	17
1 cup, 6.75 oz	675	3	115
Cooked, ½ cup, 3.5 oz	115	0.5	20
Lettuce: 1 cup, chopped/shredded, 2 oz	7	0	1
Butterhead, 2 leaves, 0.5 oz	2	0	0.5
Cos/Romaine, shredded, 1 cup	10	0	2
Iceberg: 1 outer leaf, 0.5 oz	2	0	0.5
1 medium head, 16 oz	75	1	16
Lima Beans, baby, cooked, ½ cup, 3 oz	105	0	20
Lotus Root, cooked, 10 slices, 3 oz	60	0	14
Mung Bean Sprouts, ½ cup, 2 oz	15	0	3
Mushrooms, average all varieties:			
Raw, diced/siced, 1 cup, 3 oz	20	0	3
Pieces, 1 cup, 1.25 oz	8	0	1
Fried/Sauteed, 6 oz	220	16	10
Grilled, pieces, ½ cup, 2.5 oz	20	0.5	4
Shitake, dried, 1 oz package	90	0	22
Mustard Greens, raw, ½ cup, 1 oz	7	0	2
Okra: Raw, 8 pods, 4 oz	30	0	7
Cooked, ½ cup, 2.75 oz	20	0	4
Onions, Raw: 1 small, 2.5 oz	30	0	7
1 medium, 4 oz	50	0	11
1 large, 5.5 oz	65	0	15
1 jumbo, 16 oz	190	0.5	46
Chopped: ½ cup, 3 oz	35	0	8
1 Tbsp, 0.4 oz	5	0	1
Slices: 1 cup, 4 oz	50	0	12
1 medium slice (⅛"), 0.5 oz	5	0	1
1 large slice (¼"), 1.3 oz	15	0	4
Flakes, dried·/4 cup, 0.5 oz	50	0	12
Rings, breaded & fried, 2 rings	80	5	9
Scallions, ½ cup, 2 oz	15	0	3
Spring, chopped, ½ cup, 2 oz	15	0	3

Vegetables (Cont)	C	F	Cb
Parsley, chopped, ½ cup, 1 oz	10	0	2
Parsnip: 1 medium, 4 oz	85	0	20
Cooked, slices, ½ cup, 2.75 oz	55	0	13
Peas: Green, raw, ¼ cup, 1.5oz	30	0	5
With pods, 0.5 lb	70	0	13
Snow Peas, 10 pods, 1.2 oz	15	0	3
Split: Dry, hulled, 1 oz	100	0.5	17
Cooked, 1 cup, 7 oz	230	1	42
Peppers:			
Sweet, 1 medium, 4.2 oz	30	0	7
Bell: 1 medium, 4.2 oz	30	0	7
raw, chopped, ½ cup, 2.5 oz	20	0	5
2 rings (5" diam. x ¼" thick)	3	0	1
Chili: Green/Red, 1.5 oz	20	0	5
Habanero, 1 only, 0.3 oz	10	0	2
Pigeon Peas, cooked, ½ cup, 3 oz	95	1	17
Pimientos, 3 medium, 3.5 oz	25	0	5
Poi, ½ cup, 4.2 oz	135	0	33
Potatoes:			
Raw (with skin):			
1 baby, 2 oz	45	0	10
1 small, 6 oz	135	0	30
1 medium, 8 oz	180	0	40
1 large, 12 oz	270	0	60
1 extra large, 16 oz	360	0	80
Baked, (no added fat), large, 10 oz (raw wt):			
Plain: With skin, 7 oz (cooked wt)	185	0	42
W/o skin, 5.5 oz (cooked wt)	145	0	34
With Skin/Toppings:			
With 2 tsp fat	270	8	58
With Grated Cheese, 1 oz	370	9	58
With Plain Yogurt, 2 Tbsp	260	1	60
With Sour Crm & Chives, 2 Tbsp	320	6	60
Mashed:			
With milk plus fat, ½ cup, 4 oz	120	4.5	18
KFC Style without gravy, 4 oz	90	3	15
Loaded (fat/cream/cheese/bacon):			
Side serving, 6 oz	180	9	22
Large serving, 12 oz	360	18	44
Potato Skins, baked w/ cheese topping,			
½ whole, 4 oz	240	13	22
French Fries: Small serving, 2.6 oz	250	13	30
Medium serving, 4 oz	380	20	47
Frozen, uncooked, 18 fries, 4 oz	165	5.5	28
Oven-heated, 18 fries, 4 oz	165	5.5	28
Take-Out, 1 cup, 5 oz	440	25	60
Au Gratin, ½ cup, 4.3 oz	160	9	14
Pancakes, 2 small, 2 oz	120	6.5	12
Puffs, fried, 4 puffs, 1 oz	55	2.5	8
Scalloped, 8.5 oz	220	9	26

Updated Nutrition Data ~ www.CalorieKing.com
Persons with Diabetes ~ See Disclaimer (Page 22)

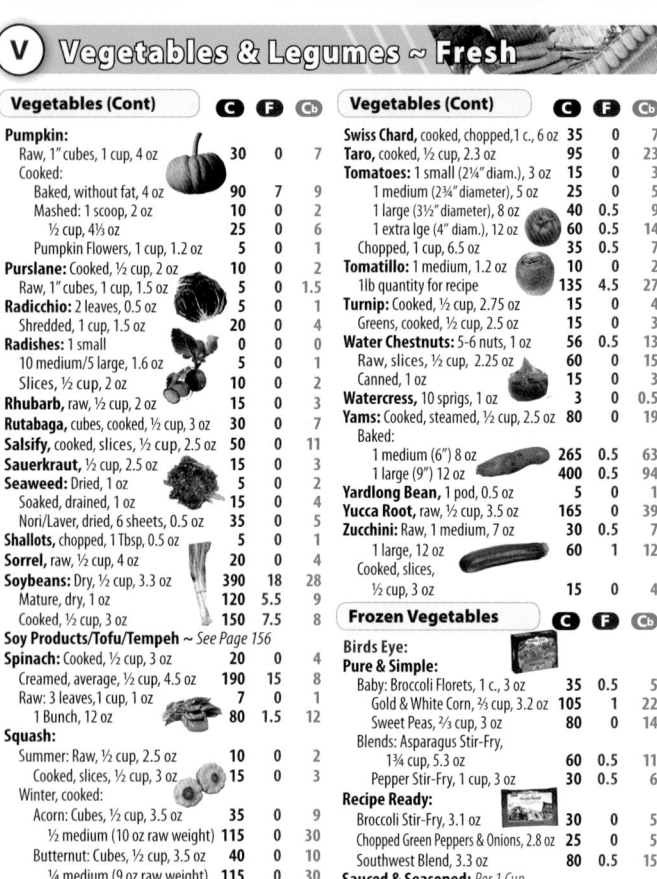

Vegetables (Cont) | C | F | Cb

Pumpkin:
Raw, 1" cubes, 1 cup, 4 oz	30	0	7
Cooked:			
Baked, without fat, 4 oz	90	7	9
Mashed: 1 scoop, 2 oz	10	0	2
½ cup, 4⅓ oz	25	0	6
Pumpkin Flowers, 1 cup, 1.2 oz	5	0	1

Purslane: Cooked, ½ cup, 2 oz | 10 | 0 | 2
| Raw, 1 cup, 1.5 oz | 5 | 0 | 1.5 |

Radicchio: 2 leaves, 0.5 oz | 5 | 0 | 1
| Shredded, 1 cup, 1.5 oz | 20 | 0 | 4 |

Radishes: 1 small | 0 | 0 | 0
| 10 medium/5 large, 1.6 oz | 5 | 0 | 1 |
| Slices, ½ cup, 2 oz | 10 | 0 | 2 |

Rhubarb, raw, ½ cup, 2 oz | 15 | 0 | 3
Rutabaga, cubes, cooked, ½ cup, 3 oz | 30 | 0 | 7
Salsify, cooked, slices, ½ cup, 2.5 oz | 50 | 0 | 11
Sauerkraut, ½ cup, 2.5 oz | 15 | 0 | 3

Seaweed: Dried, 1 oz | 5 | 0 | 2
| Soaked, drained, 1 oz | 15 | 0 | 4 |
| Nori/Laver, dried, 6 sheets, 0.5 oz | 35 | 0 | 5 |

Shallots, chopped, 1 Tbsp, 0.5 oz | 5 | 0 | 1
Sorrel, raw, ½ cup, 4 oz | 20 | 0 | 4

Soybeans: Dry, ½ cup, 3.3 oz | 390 | 18 | 28
| Mature, dry, 1 oz | 120 | 5.5 | 9 |
| Cooked, ½ cup, 3 oz | 150 | 7.5 | 8 |

Soy Products/Tofu/Tempeh ~ See Page 156

Spinach: Cooked, ½ cup, 3 oz | 20 | 0 | 4
Creamed, cooked, ½ cup, 4.5 oz	190	15	8
Raw: 3 leaves, 1 cup, 1 oz	7	0	1
1 Bunch, 12 oz	80	1.5	12

Squash:
Summer: Raw, ½ cup, 2.5 oz	10	0	2
Cooked, slices, ½ cup, 3 oz	15	0	3
Winter, cooked:			
Acorn: Cubes, ½ cup, 3.5 oz	35	0	9
½ medium (10 oz raw weight)	115	0	30
Butternut: Cubes, ½ cup, 3.5 oz	40	0	10
¼ medium (9 oz raw weight)	115	0	30
Spaghetti, ½ cup, 1.75 oz	15	0	3

Succotash, cooked, ½ cup, 3.3 oz | 110 | 1 | 23
Sweetcorn ~ See Corn

Sweet Potatoes:
Cooked with skin (w/o fat),			
1 medium, 4 oz	105	0	24
Without skin, mashed, ½ cup, 5.5 oz	125	0	29
Fries (Alexia, Julienne syle),			
approximately 12 pieces, 3 oz	140	5	24

Vegetables (Cont) | C | F | Cb

Swiss Chard, cooked, chopped, 1 c., 6 oz | 35 | 0 | 7
Taro, cooked, ½ cup, 2.3 oz | 95 | 0 | 23

Tomatoes: 1 small (2¼" diam.), 3 oz | 15 | 0 | 3
1 medium (2¾" diameter), 5 oz	25	0	5
1 large (3½" diameter), 8 oz	40	0.5	9
1 extra lge (4" diam.), 12 oz	60	0.5	14
Chopped, 1 cup, 6.5 oz	35	0.5	8

Tomatillo: 1 medium, 1.2 oz | 10 | 0 | 2
| 1lb quantity for recipe | 135 | 4.5 | 27 |

Turnip: Cooked, ½ cup, 2.75 oz | 15 | 0 | 4
| Greens, cooked, ½ cup, 2.5 oz | 15 | 0 | 3 |

Water Chestnuts: 5-6 nuts, 1 oz | 56 | 0.5 | 13
| Raw, slices, ½ cup, 2.25 oz | 60 | 0 | 15 |
| Canned, 1 oz | 15 | 0 | 3 |

Watercress, 10 sprigs, 1 oz | 3 | 0 | 0
Yams: Cooked, steamed, ½ cup, 2.5 oz | 80 | 0 | 19
Baked:			
1 medium (6") 8 oz	265	0.5	63
1 large (9") 12 oz	400	0.5	94

Yardlong Bean, 1 pod, 0.5 oz | 5 | 0 | 1
Yucca Root, raw, ½ cup, 3.5 oz | 165 | 0 | 39

Zucchini: Raw, 1 medium, 7 oz | 30 | 0.5 | 7
1 large, 12 oz	60	1	12
Cooked, slices,			
½ cup, 3 oz	15	0	4

Frozen Vegetables | C | F | Cb

Birds Eye:
Pure & Simple:
Baby: Broccoli Florets, 1 c., 3 oz	35	0.5	5
Gold & White Corn, ⅔ cup, 3.2 oz	105	1	22
Sweet Peas, ⅔ cup, 3 oz	80	0	14
Blends: Asparagus Stir-Fry,			
1¾ cup, 5.3 oz	60	0.5	11
Pepper Stir-Fry, 1 cup, 3 oz	30	0.5	6

Recipe Ready:
Broccoli Stir-Fry, 3.1 oz	30	0	5
Chopped Green Peppers & Onions, 2.8 oz	25	0	5
Southwest Blend, 3.3 oz	80	0.5	15

Sauced & Seasoned: Per 1 Cup
Green Beans & Spaetzle,			
in Bavarian Sauce	95	4.5	10
Pasta & Veggies in Creamy Cheese Sauce	125	3	21

Steamfresh:
Pure & Simple Blends:
Baby Broccoli Blend, 1 cup	65	1.5	8
Baby Potato Blend, ¾ cup	50	0.5	10
Brocc. & Cauliflower, 1 cup, 3.35 oz	30	0.5	4.5
With Carrots, ¾ cup, 3 oz	35	0.5	5.5

Frozen Vegetables (Cont)	C	F	Cb

Green Giant:

Create A Meal Stir Fry: *Unprepared*

	C	F	Cb
Lo Mein, 1.6 cups	130	1	27
Sweet & Sour, 1.25 cups	140	0	34
Szechuan, 1.3 cups	70	1	14
Teriyaki, 1.25 cups	60	0	14
Just for One:			
Broccoli & Cheese Sauce, 4.25 oz	40	1	7
Caulifl. & Cheese Sauce, 4.25 oz	40	1	8
Seasoned Steamers: *Per ¾ Cup, Frozen*			
Honey Dijon Carrots, 3 oz	60	2	10
Mediterranean Blend, 3 oz	80	3	11
Valley Fresh Steamers:			
Prepared, with Cheese Sauce:			
Broccoli, ⅔ cup, 3.88 oz	60	2.5	7
Broccoli, Cauliflower & Carrots, ⅔ cup, 4.23 oz	60	2.5	8
Garden Vegetable Medley, 3.5 oz	60	0.5	12
Prepared, Without Sauce:			
Broccoli Cuts, ½ cup	15	0	3
Mixed Vegetables, ½ cup	50	0	12
Sweet Peas, ½ cup	50	0	12

Ore-Ida: *Per 3 oz Unless Indicated*

Fries:

	C	F	Cb
Classic: Golden Crinkles	120	4.5	19
Golden	130	3.5	21
Steak	110	3	19
Extra Crispy Easy, Golden Crinkles	170	6	25
Extra Crispy: Fast Food Fries	150	6	24
Golden Crinkles	160	7	22
Seasoned Crinkles	150	6	22
Tater Tots	170	9	20
Premium:			
Country Style French	130	4.5	20
Crispers	230	14	23
Golden Twirls	150	6	23
Texas Crispers	150	7	20
Grillers: Golden Thick Cut Potatoes	130	5	19
Seasoned Thick Cut Potatoes	140	5	21
Hash Browns: Golden Patties (1)	140	8	15
Potatoes O'Brien	60	0	13
Shredded Hash Browns Pattie (1)	70	0	16
Onion: Chopped, 2.85 oz	20	0	5
Gourmet Rings, 2.68 oz	185	9	24
Onion Ringers, 2.85 oz	180	10	21
Steam n' Mash, Cut Russet, 3.35 oz	70	0	16
Tater Tots: Regular	160	8	20
Crispy Crowns	170	10	19

Canned/Bottled	C	F	Cb

Solids & Liquid

Artichoke Hearts:

	C	F	Cb
Fancifoods: Plain, 1 oz (1)	8	0	1
Marinated, ¼ bottle, 1 oz	25	1.5	2
Asparagus: Drained, 3 spears	10	0	1.5
Pieces, ½ cup, 4.3 oz	25	0.5	3
Bamboo Shoots, 1 cup, 4.5 oz	25	0	4
Bean Salad, ½ cup, 4.35 oz	90	0	20
Beans: Baked, ½ cup, 4.5 oz	120	0.5	27
Butter, ½ cup, 4.5 oz	90	0	16
Green, ½ cup, 2.5 oz	15	0	3
Italian, ½ cup, 4.5 oz	30	0	6
Kidney, ½ cup 3.5 oz	105	0.5	19
Lima, ½ cup, 4.5 oz	80	0	15
Pinto, ½ cup, 4.5 oz	105	1	18
Beets: Sliced, ½ cup, 3 oz	25	0	6
Crinkle/Pickled, ½ cup	80	0	20
Carrots: Sliced, ½ cup, 2.5 oz	20	0	4
Del Monte, Honey Glazed, ½ cup	75	0	18
Corn: Kernels, ½ cup, 4.5 oz	80	0.5	18
Creamed style, ½ cup, 4.5 oz	90	0.5	23
Garbanzo/Chick Peas, ½ c, 4.2 oz	145	1.5	27
Hearts of Palm, (1), 1.2 oz	7	0	1
Mushrooms: ½ cup, 2.5 oz	20	0	4
In Butter Sauce, 2 oz	20	1	2
Onions: Cocktail (1)	0	0	0
Pickled, 1 medium, 0.5 oz	10	0	2
Peas, ½ cup, 3 oz	60	0.5	10
Peppers: Hot Chili, Jalapeno, (1), 1 oz	5	0	1
Red/Green, 1 oz	5	0	1
Sweet, undrained, 2.5 oz	13	0	3
Jalapeno, with liquid, ½ cup chopped	20	0.5	3
Fried, drained, 2 Tbsp, 1 oz	60	5	3
Salsa, average all varieties, 2 Tbsp	10	0	2
Sauerkraut, drained, 1 cup, 5 oz	25	0	6
Spinach, ½ cup, 3.5 oz	25	0.5	3.5
Succotash: Cream Style, ½ cup	100	0.5	23
W/ whole kernels, undrained, ½ cup	80	0.5	18
Sweetcorn ~ *See Corn*			
Sweet Potato, ½ cup, 3.5 oz	90	0	24
Tomatoes, Sundried: Nat., 5-6 pieces	20	0	5
In Oil, drained, 6 pieces, 0.5 oz	40	2.5	4
Tomato Products ~ *See Page 144*			
Vegetables, mixed, ½ cup, 4 oz	45	0	8
Yams: In Light Syrup, ½ cup, 4 oz	105	0	25
Candied, ½ cup, 5 oz	170	0	46
Zucchini, in Tomato Sauce, ½ cup, 4 oz	30	0	8

Quick Guide

	C	F	Cb
Yogurt: *Average All Brands: Per 8 oz Container*			
Plain Yogurt: Whole	140	8	10
Low-Fat	145	3.5	16
Fat-Free	125	0.5	17
Fruit Flavored: Whole	225	8	32
Low-Fat	230	3	43
Fat-Free, regular	215	0.5	43
Fat-Free, no sugar added	80	0	15
Yogurt Parfait/Deli Cups:			
With Fruit Pieces: (⅔ Yogurt + ⅓ Fruit)			
Small, 8 oz cup	140	3	20
Large, 12 oz cup	210	4.5	30
With Fruit + Granola:			
Small, 8 oz cup (+ 0.75 oz Granola)	235	7	30
Large, 12 oz cup (+ 1.25 oz Granola)	400	13	58

Yogurt ~ Brands

	C	F	Cb
Activia: *Per 4 oz Container Unless Indicated*			
Fiber/Fruit flavors, average	115	2	21
Greek, fat free, av., 5.3 oz	130	0	19
Light flavors, fat free, all flav.	60	0	10
Alpina, Greek:			
Authentically Strained: *Per 5.3 oz*			
Fruit Flavors, average	120	0	19
Vanilla Bean	120	0	18
Artisan Granolas: *Per 6 oz*			
Plain	170	2.5	22
Fruit Flavors, average	210	4.5	29
Bon Yurt: *Per 5.3 oz Container*			
Cookies & Cream	180	3.5	33
Average other flavors	150	1.5	28
Amande:			
Almond Milk Yogurt: Plain, 8 oz	170	9	19
Fruit Flavors, 6 oz	150	6	23
Vanilla, 8 oz	220	8	26
Axelrod:			
32 oz Containers:			
Fat Free, Plain, 8 oz	130	0	19
Low Fat, Plain, 8 oz	140	2.5	18
6 oz Containers:			
Fat Free, Fruit flavors, av.	90	0	17
Low Fat, Fruit flavors, av.	180	1.5	36
Brown Cow: *Per 6 oz Container*			
Cream Top:			
Fruit On The Bottom:			
Apricot Mango	170	6	23
Cherry-Vanilla	180	6	28
Strawberry; Vanilla Bean	240	4	34

	C	F	Cb
Brown Cow (Cont):			
Cream Top:			
Smooth & Creamy: Plain	130	7	9
Coffee; Vanilla	160	7	19
Low Fat, Peach	150	2	26
Greek: Blueberry; Vanilla, av.	200	11	20
Maple	210	10	23
Cabot: *Per 8 oz Serving*			
32 oz Containers, Greek Style:			
Plain	310	22	12
Lowfat (2%): Plain	180	5	12
Strawberry; Vanilla Bean	240	4	34
Chobani:			
Champions: *Per 3.5 oz Container*			
Vanilla Choc. Chunk	120	3	14
Av. other flavors	100	1.5	13
Flip: *Per 5.3 oz Container*			
Almond Coco Loco	230	10	25
Honey Bee Nana	130	2.5	18
Key Lime Crumble	180	5	24
Strawberry Sunrise	160	2.5	25
Greek, Low Fat: *Per 5.3 oz Container*			
Coconut Blend	170	4.5	19
Key Lime	160	3	21
Strawberry Banana	150	3	17
Greek, Non-Fat: *Per 6 oz Container*			
Black Cherry	140	0	22
Blueberry & Strawberry	70	0	14
Vanilla	130	0	18
Dannon:			
Activia ~ See Activia			
All Natural: *Per 6 oz Container Unless Indicated*			
Low Fat, Coffee/Lemon/Van.	160	2.5	26
Non-Fat, Plain	80	0	12
Plain, 8 oz	160	8	12
Danimals,			
Crunchers, all flav., 3.5 oz	100	1.5	18
Fruit On The Bottom: *Per 6 oz Containers*			
Blueberry; Cherry	140	1.5	26
Average other flavors	150	1.5	27
Light & Fit: Av. all flavors, 6 oz	80	0	16
Quarts, av. all flav., 8 oz	110	0	21
Carb & Sugar Control,			
all flavors, 4 oz cup	45	1.5	3
Oikos: *Per Single, 5.3 oz Container, Unless Indicated*			
Traditional, Fruit flavors	160	4.5	14
Fat-Free: Plain	80	0	6
Fruit On Bottom, av.	125	0	20
Quarts, Vanilla, 8 oz	190	0	29
Emmi: *Per 6 oz Container*			
Swiss: Plain, lowfat	110	2.5	10
Average other flavors	110	3	28

Brands (Cont)	C	F	Cb
Fage: *Per 5.3 oz Container Unless Indicated*			
Total Classic: Plain, Single Serve, 7 oz	190	10	8
Fruit Flavors, average	170	6	17
Total 2%:			
Plain, Single Serve, 7 oz	150	4	8
Fruit Flavors, average	140	2.5	17
Total 0%,			
Strawberry, Single Serve, 5.3 oz	120	0	17
Horizon Organic: *Per 8 oz Cup*			
Fat-Free: Plain	80	0	12
Vanilla	170	0	33
Whole Milk: Plain	160	7	14
Vanilla	220	6	32
Tuberz, 1 tube	60	0.5	11
Kemps:			
Greek, Fat Free,			
average all varieties, 5.3 oz	155	0	26
'Light' 80 Cals, av., 6 oz	80	0	16
La Yogurt: *Per 6 oz Container*			
Low Fat: Original, average all flavors	150	1.5	29
Rich & Creamy, av. all flavors	180	1.5	35
Sabor Latino,			
Low Fat, av. all flavors	185	1.5	37
LALA: Plain, 8 oz	130	2.5	17
Fruit Flavors, av., 6 oz	150	1.5	30
Pina Colada, 6 oz	160	2	30
Liberte:			
Greek: Plain, 5.3 oz	90	0	7
Flavors, average, 5.3 oz	135	0	21
Lucerne: *Per 6 oz Container*			
Low-Fat, av. all flavors.	170	2	32
Fat-Free: Plain	80	0	13
Light Fat-Free, fruit, 6 oz	90	0	17
Mountain High: *Per 8 oz*			
32 oz Containers:			
Original Style: Plain	170	6	19
Strawberry; Vanilla	210	6	30
Low-Fat: Plain	140	2.5	18
Strawberry; Vanilla	180	2.5	29
Fat-Free: Plain	120	0	18
Vanilla	160	0	30
Nancy's: *Per 8 oz Container*			
Natural:			
Whole Milk: Honey Yogurt, Plain	180	8	17
With Fruit on Top, av.	230	5	41
Lowfat: Lemon	150	3	16
Vanilla	140	3	15
Average other flavors	175	2.5	28
Organic:			
Low Fat, Plain; Lemon	140	3	16
Nonfat, Plain, 6 oz	90	0	13

	C	F	Cb
Oikos ~ *see Dannon & Stonyfield*			
O Organics, Blended Low-Fat,			
average all flavors, 6 oz	160	2.5	26
Publix:			
Fat-Free, Plain, 8 oz	140	0	23
Swiss Style, Low-Fat, 8 oz	240	2.5	41
Roberts: *Per 6 oz Ctn*			
Low-Fat, average all flavors	165	1.5	32
Fat-Free, all flavors	90	0	15
Silk: *Per 6 oz Container*			
Fruity & Creamy:			
Blueberry	140	3.5	22
Peach Mango; Strawb.	150	3.5	25
So Delicious:			
Cultured Coconut Milk: Plain, 4 oz	80	4.5	12
Chocolate, 6 oz	170	7	27
Pina Colada; Raspb. av., 6 oz	140	6	22
Greek: Plain, 6 oz	130	5	22
Blueberry, 6 oz	130	4.5	25
Stater Bros: *Per 6 oz Container Unless Indicated*			
Plain	105	1.5	14
Fruit on the Bottom, av. all flavors	170	1.5	34
Blended Low-Fat, av. all flavors	155	1.5	29
32 oz Tubs: Non-Fat, Plain, 8 oz	120	0	18
Low Fat, 8 oz	140	2	19
Stonyfield Organic:			
Fruit On Bottom: *Per 6 oz Container*			
Fat Free: Chocolate Underground	170	0	36
Average other flavors	115	0	22
Low Fat, Fruit Varieties	120	1.5	21
Greek: *Per 5.3 oz Containers*			
Plain	80	0	6
Chocolate	140	0	23
Honey	120	0	18
Vanilla	110	0	13
Smooth & Creamy (32 oz Ctn): *Per 8 oz Serving*			
Fat Free: Plain	110	0	16
French Vanilla	170	0	33
Low Fat: Plain	120	2	15
French Vanilla	170	2	30
Fruit; Banilla, av.	200	2.5	36
Whole Milk: Plain	160	9	13
French Vanilla	220	8	31
Stop & Shop:			
Blended, Light, Non Fat,			
average all flavors, 6 oz	90	0	16
Fruit On The Bottom,			
Low Fat, average all flavors, 6 oz	170	1.5	31
Trader Joes:			
French Village: *Per 32 oz Containers*			
Non-Fat: Plain, 8 oz	120	0	17
Vanilla, 8 oz	180	0	34
Cream Line, Plain, 8 oz	170	10	12
6 oz Container, av. all flav.	130	0	26

continued next page

Brands (Cont) | C | F | Cb

Trader Joes (Cont):	C	F	Cb
Greek Style: Plain, 8 oz	260	18	14
Apricot Mango; Honey, av., 8 oz	300	15	28
Low-Fat: With Almonds/Granola:			
Pomegranate, 4.6 oz	140	2.5	27
Vanilla, 4.6 oz	160	7	20
Organic Non-Fat:			
Plain, 5.3 oz	90	0	7
Honey; Vanilla, av., 5.3 oz	130	0	20
Squishers, Org., low fat, 1 tube, 2 oz	60	1	10
Voskos, Greek, Non-Fat, av., 8 oz	200	0	30
Wallaby Organic, Blended,			
Low-Fat, av. all flavors, 6 oz	150	2.5	26
Wegmans: *Per 6 oz Container*			
Blended Non Fat, Light: Blueb.	100	0	14
Other Berry varietes	80	0	14
Fruit On The Bottom, Lowfat:			
Strawberry	180	2	35
Other fruit flavors, average	160	2	29
Greek, Non-Fat: Plain	90	0	8
Fruit flavors, average	140	0	20
Vanilla	120	0	15
Whole Foods (365):			
Non-Fat: Plain, 6 oz	90	0	13
Fruit flavors, av., 6 oz	145	0	30
Greek, non-fat, 5.3 oz	150	0	25
Whole Soy: Plain, 6 oz	150	4.5	19
Av. other flavors, 6 oz	170	3.5	33
YoCrunch: *Per 6 oz Container Unless Indicated*			
Cookies & Candy Crunch:			
Strawberry: With Nestle Crunch pieces	190	4	34
With Oreo Cookie pieces	170	2	29
Vanilla, with pieces, av. all flavors	180	4	32
Fruit Parfaits, with Granola, all var.	160	1	31
100 Calorie, av. all flavors., 4 oz	100	1.5	19
Yoplait: *Per 6 oz Container Unless Indicated*			
Original: 99% Fat-Free, all flavors	170	1.5	33
Thick & Creamy, all flavors	180	2.5	31
Light: Fat-Free, Fruit flavors	90	0	16
Thick & Creamy, all flavors	100	0	21
With Granola, all flavors	190	2.5	35
Fruitful, average all flavors	170	5	24
Fruplait, av. all flavors, 4 oz ctn	115	1	22
Greek, 0% Fat:			
100 Calories, Fruit Flavors, 5.3 oz	100	0	14
Blended Fruit Flavors, 5.3oz	140	0	24
Splitz, av. all flavors., 3.25 oz ctn	90	1	17
Trix, Fruit flavors, av., 4 oz cup	100	0.5	20
Lactose Free, all flav., 6 oz	170	1.5	33

Brands (Cont) | C | F | Cb

Yoplait (Cont):	C	F	Cb
Splitz, av. all flavors, 3.25 oz ctn	90	1	17
Trix, Fruit flavors, av., 4 oz cup	100	0.5	20
Whips!: Chocolate flavors,			
4 oz cup	160	4	25
Fruit flavors, 4 oz cup	140	2.5	25
Yoplait Kids, all flavors, 3 oz cup	70	1	13

Yogurt Drinks & Probiotics

	C	F	Cb
Alpina, Yogurt Smoothie,			
average all flavors, 7 oz	120	2	19
BioKult, Cultured,			
all flavors, 2.1 oz bottle	35	0	8
Cacique, Yonique,			
average other flavors, 7 fl.oz	200	1.5	35
Dannon: Activia, all flavors, 7 fl oz	160	3	27
DanActive, av. all flav., 3.1 fl oz	80	1.5	13
Danimals, Smoothies,			
all flavors, 3.1 fl.oz	60	0.5	10
Dan-o-nino, all flav., 3.1 fl.oz	70	0.5	15
Glen Oaks, 32 fl.oz Containers,			
average all flavors, 8 fl.oz	150	2.5	28
Good Belly: *Per 2.7 fl.oz Bottle*			
Probiotics: BigShot, all flavors	60	1	11
Plus, average all flavors	50	0	12
Straightshot, Plain, 2.7 fl oz	30	0	6
Kemps, Yo-J Drink, 16 fl.oz Bottle,			
all flavors, 8 fl. oz	120	0	27
LaLa:			
Lalacult, 5 pack, 1 bottle	35	0	7
Proactive: Prune, 6.3 oz bottle	180	3	36
Average other flavors, 6.3 oz bottle	155	3.5	30
Yogurt Smoothies av. 7 fl.oz	175	4.5	29
Lifeway:			
Kefir Smoothie:			
32 fl. oz Container: Original, 8 fl.oz	150	8	12
Lowfat: Choc. Truffle, 8 fl.oz	160	2	25
Other flavors, 8 fl.oz	140	2	20
Ralphs,			
Smoothies, average, 7 fl.oz	200	2.5	37
Stonyfield Organic:			
Super Smoothies: Av. all flav., 10 oz	230	3	40
4-pack, average other flavors, 6 oz	140	2	22
Yakult, 2.7 fl.oz bottle	50	0	12
Yoplait, Frozen Smoothies,			
½ Pouch (4 fl.oz) prep'd w/ 4 fl.oz skim milk			
Blueberry Pomegranate, 1 cup, 8 fl.oz	120	1.5	21
Chocolate Banana, 1 cup, 8 fl.oz	130	1	24
Strawberry Banana, 1 cup, 8 fl.oz	110	1.5	21
Greek, Mixed Berry, 1 cup, 8 fl.oz	160	2	27

Cafeteria-Style Foods | C | F | Cb

Average All Preparations:

	C	F	Cb
Beef Stroganoff, 5 oz	195	13	7
Beef Stroganoff, with 4 oz noodles	350	14	36
Chicken Lasagna, 1 piece	300	11	32
Chicken Chop Suey, with 4 oz rice	245	4	37
Deep Dish Burrito, 7 oz	265	13	20
Ground Beef Casserole, 2 scps, 6 oz	245	13	17
Italian Meat Sce, for Spaghetti, 5 oz	150	9	9
with 5 oz Spaghetti	350	10	49
Lasagna, 1 piece	275	11	25
Meatloaf, 3 oz	205	13	4
Ranch Beans, 2 scoops, 6 oz	350	11	45
Red Beans & Rice, 7 oz	280	9	37
Scalloped Potato/Ham, 2 scoops, 6 oz	160	6	20
Stuffed Shells in Sauce, (1)	105	3	17
Swedish Meatballs, (3)	205	12	9
Sweet & Sour Pork/Rice, 9 oz	240	3	40
Swiss Steak, w/ Mushroom Gravy, 6 oz	280	11	4
Tator Tot Casserole, 2 scoops, 6 oz	260	15	20
Tenderloin Tips/Mshrm Gravy: 5 oz	210	13	3
With 5 oz noodles	395	15	38
Tuna Noodle Casserole, 2 scoops, 6 oz	180	6	17
Turkey Tetrazzini, 2 scoops, 6 oz	195	7	17
Vegetable Lasagna, 1 piece	250	13	21

Croissants | C | F | Cb

	C	F	Cb
Unfilled, medium 1.5 oz	180	10	21
Filled: With Ham (2 oz), garnish	280	14	24
With Ham (2 oz), Cheese (2 oz)	470	30	20
With Chick (2 oz) Cheese (2 oz)	470	30	20
With Turkey/Ham/Cheese (2 oz ea.)	580	36	20
Au Bon Pain: Ham & Cheese	390	21	35
Spinach & Cheese	290	17	28

7-Eleven ~ See Page 236

Bagels | C | F | Cb

	C	F	Cb
Plain: Large, 4 oz (without filling)	320	2	65
With 2 oz Cream Cheese	500	27	54
With 2 oz Lox (Smoked Salmon)	400	4	65

Also see Bagels Section ~ Page 54
Fast-Foods Restaurants ~ Page 175
Au Bon Pain ~ Page 179
Bruegger's ~ Page 185
Einstein Bros Bagels ~ Page 199

Sandwiches | C | F | Cb

No Spreads Unless Indicated:
Includes 2 Slices Bread ~ 3 oz

	C	F	Cb
BLT, (5 strips Bacon, 2 Tbsp Mayo)	600	40	46
Breaded Chicken & Garnish	540	28	46
Chicken Salad with Mayo., 5 oz	580	30	49
Chopped Liver Egg Mayonnaise	630	25	44
Corned Beef with Mustard, 5 oz	560	28	44
Egg Salad, with Mayonnaise	570	29	49
Egg Salad Club, with Bacon & Mayo	780	53	49
Grilled Cheese, (3 oz)	540	30	44
Ham, (4 oz), Cheese (4 oz), & Mayo	910	56	44
Lobster Salad, (4 oz), w/ Mayo.	530	25	45
Overstuffed Tuna Salad, (7 oz)	870	39	75
Philly Cheese Steak Sandwich	550	23	42
Reuben, (6 oz Beef/Pastrami, 2 oz Cheese, 2 Tbsp Dressing)	920	60	28
Roast Beef, (4 oz), with Mustard	460	12	45
Roast Pork, (4 oz), with Apple Sauce	500	16	55
Shrimp Salad Club, w/ Bacon & Mayo	800	57	48
Sloppy Joe with Sauce, (7 oz)	600	30	45
Steak Sandwich, (5 oz cooked)	680	32	41
Triple Cheese Melt, (4 oz)	720	45	46
Tuna Salad, (5 oz), with Mayonnaise	610	30	49
Turkey Breast, (5 oz), w/ Mayo.	460	18	44
Turkey Breast, (5 oz,) with Mustard	360	7	44
Turkey Club, with Bacon & Mayo.	830	38	31
Vegetarian, with Avocado & Cheese	820	49	72

7-Eleven ~ Page 236
Schlotzsky's ~ Page 237
Subway ~ Page 245

Wraps & Roll-Ups | C | F | Cb

Average All Types
Meat/Chicken/Fish/Veggie:

	C	F	Cb
Small, approximately 9 oz	500	25	48
Regular, approximately 15 oz	830	40	80
Large, approximately 22 oz	1400	70	134

Fast-Foods Restaurants ~ Page 175
Au Bon Pain ~ Page 179
Sonic Drive-In ~ Page 241
Subway ~ Page 245
WAWA ~ Page 254

Updated Nutrition Data ~ www.CalorieKing.com
Persons with Diabetes ~ See Disclaimer (Page 22)

Fair & Carnival Foods

	C	F	Cb
Barbeque Chicken/Meats:			
Chicken, ½ chicken, 15 oz	740	24	34
Grilled Chicken Pita, with dressing	680	19	82
Teriyaki Chicken, on stick, w/ dress.	250	6	4
Pork Ribs, 18 oz	1360	68	21
Turkey Leg: Regular, 19 oz	1135	54	0
Caveman (2lb Turkey Leg, with 1lb Bacon)	2360	177	3
Bacon: Fried, on-a-stick, with syrup	230	16	5
Choc-covered Bacon, 4.5 oz dish	640	43	30
Beef Stew over Rice, 2 cups	440	14	61
Butter Balls, deep fried, 4 Balls	460	38	24
Cheese Curds, Breaded & fried, Culver's, 6.7 oz	670	38	54
Corn Dogs: Regular, 4 oz	250	14	23
Jumbo, 6 oz	375	21	36
Pretzel-Wrapped Dog	300	16	30
Papa Pup, on-a-stick	400	24	32
Pronto Pup, on-a-stick	170	9	16
Corn On The Cob, 8"(1), 16 oz	200	1	42
Finger Foods:			
Artichoke, fried, 9 pieces	250	14	24
Chicken Nuggets, (6)	340	17	26
Chicken Strips, (4), 4.5 oz	445	21	33
Onion Rings, 3 rings	310	13	40
Onion Flower	1320	72	140
Shrimp, Fried, 10-12 pieces, 5 oz	555	30	36
Spam, deep-fried in batter, 2 pieces	330	24	18
Gator:			
Big Gator, Nuggets/Hushpuppies	550	31	54
Stick Gator, 1 sausage	250	20	4
Greek:			
Baklava, 2" square	245	13	32
Falafel, 11.6 oz	660	27	85
Greek Salad, 14 oz	520	48	17
Gyro, 7.5", 12 oz	680	40	55
Spanakopita, 8 oz	200	7.5	1
Hamburgers:			
⅓ **Pound Burger**, 7.5 oz	670	41	26
Cheeseburger, 6 oz	550	36	25
Hot Dogs: With Bun			
Regular: No extras	215	14	28
With Chili, 6 oz	450	32	32
With Chili & Cheese, 7.3 oz	500	36	31
⅓ **Pound Hot Dog**	550	41	32
Foot Long Hot Dog	470	26	41
Jumbo, Bratwurst/Kielbasa, average	800	60	28

Fair & Carnival Foods (Cont)

	C	F	Cb
Mexican:			
Burrito, with Bean/Beef, 17 oz	1100	41	104
Carne Asada, 14.5 oz	820	44	58
Cheese Quesadilla, 1.75 oz	480	27	40
Chicken Taco, 3.3 oz	210	12	15
Fish Taco, 5 oz	270	13	31
Jalapeno Pepper, choc-covered (3)	270	15	31
Nachos with Cheese, 9" plate	860	59	70
Tamale, 3.5 oz	180	8	21
Taquito, 5 oz	370	17	43
Pizza:			
Pizza Bread, Pepperoni, ½ loaf, 12 oz	1115	32	151
Pizza on-a-stick, 1 piece	535	28	55
Personal Pizza: Per 7"			
Cheese	670	24	80
Pepperoni	795	35	80
Ham & Pineapple	800	31	87
Potatoes & Fries:			
Australian Battered Potatoes	1290	66	155
Baked Potato, 14 oz	435	0.5	100
Fries: French, 7 oz	560	24	79
Cheese Fries, 10 oz	645	38	62
Chili Fries, 10 oz	700	36	83
Curly Fries, 7 oz	620	30	78
Jamaican Jerk Fries, 7 oz	640	34	77
Sweet Potato, baked, 14 oz	405	0.5	97
Tornado, on-a-stick	210	15	18
Salads/Sides:			
Chili, 1 cup	280	11	24
Cole Slaw, 5 oz	350	21	37
Pickle, whole (6")	30	0	8
Potato Salad, 5 oz	290	15	35
Sandwiches: 7½" Roll			
Ham, 11 oz	645	39	47
Hot Pastrami, 9 oz	760	17	62
Roast Beef, 11 oz	620	36	46
Philadelphia Cheese Steak, 13 oz	680	36	49
Turkey, 11 oz	665	24	65
Drinks:			
Icee, 16 fl.oz	235	0	59
Shakes, average, 16 fl.oz	690	33	85
Slushies: Horchata, 16 fl.oz	280	8	50
Lemonade, 18 fl.oz	210	0	52
Orange Julius, 20 fl.oz	490	10	96
Strawberry Julius, 20 fl.oz	430	0	98
Soft Frozen Lemonade, 12 fl.oz	300	0	78
Smoothies, Berry Flavors, 16 fl.oz	350	1	80

Fair & Carnival Foods (Cont)

	C	F	Cb
Cakes, Pastries:			
Funnel Cake, Plain (1)	760	44	80
Toppings:			
Apple Cinnamon, 2 oz	85	3	16
Cinnamon & Sugar, 2 tsp	40	0	10
Strawberry & Cream, 2 oz	70	0	16
Cheesecake on-a-stick, 6 oz	655	47	56
Churro, (1), 9", 1.6 oz	170	8	22
Cream Puff, (1)	500	43	22
Fried Twinkie, (1)	420	34	45
Puff-on-a-Stick, (4), 8.6 oz	995	86	44
Strawberry Crepe, 4.3 oz	280	14	36
Twinkie Dog, (Sundae)	500	14	89
Candied Apple, 7 oz	330	0	80
Cookies:			
Sweet Martha, (1), ¾ oz	90	4	14
Deep Fried: Oreos, tray (5)	890	48	108
Cookie Dough on stick, 3 pieces	670	32	89
Cotton Candy:			
Small, 1 oz	110	0	27
Large, 2.25 oz	250	0	62
Family Size, 5.5 oz	610	0	151
Dirt Dessert, 1 cup, 9.3 oz	405	12	69
Donuts, Jumbo Twist, (1), 7.5 oz	905	49	109
Fried Dough/FryBread:			
Plain: 7", 3.7 oz	390	19	47
9", 4¾ oz	510	25	61
Toppings: Cinnamon Sugar, 2 tsp	40	0	10
Butterscotch; Caramel, 2 Tbsp	115	0	29
Hot Fudge, average, 2 Tbsp	110	4	22
Cheese Powder, 2 tsp	70	3	2
Honey, 1 Tbsp, ¾ oz	65	0	17
Fudge, 1.5 oz	200	11	25
Ice Cream & Frozen Treats:			
Deep-fried Klondike Bar ,w/ syrup	430	16	18
Dippin' Dots Ice Cream, 6 oz cup	380	20	46
Frozen Banana, choc. coated, 5 oz	240	4	53
Frozen Yogurt, in sugar cone, 14 oz	475	2	94
Ice Cream: Small, sugar cone, 10 oz	775	42	83
Large, sugar cone, 14 oz	935	54	96
Sherbet, 8 oz	270	4	59
Snow Cone, with 3 oz syrup	270	0	68
Strawberry, Choc. Dipped, 1 piece	125	7	15
Popcorn:			
Plain: Small, 3 oz	450	24	48
Large, 6 oz	900	48	96
Kettle Corn: Small, 5 oz	600	15	110
Large, 10 oz	1200	30	220
Pretzels, Soft, 4.5 oz	340	2	70
S'more, on stick	270	16	27

Stadium Foods

	C	F	Cb
Burgers:			
Bacon Burger, 8.3 oz	470	25	34
Cheeseburger, 8.3 oz	450	23	33
Hamburger, 7.8 oz	400	19	33
French Fries, 6.4 oz	470	34	39
Fruit Cup, 6 oz	80	0	20
Hot Dogs:			
Chili Dog, 7.7 oz	520	29	45
Hot Dog, 6.4 oz	465	21	50
Jumbo Dog, 6 oz	440	25	38
Kraut Dog with Sauerkraut, 7.8 oz	490	27	41
Individual Pan Pizza (6"): *Per Pizza*			
BBQ Chicken	630	24	71
Cheese	630	27	71
Pepperoni	660	30	71
Nachos, 40 chips, with 4 oz cheese	1100	59	132
Sandwiches:			
Chicken: With Bacon, 8.3 oz	530	31	41
With Cheese, 8.3 oz	510	29	40
Without Cheese, 7.7 oz	460	25	40
Polish Sausage Sandwich, 7 oz	565	33	46
Snacks:			
Brownie, 2.5" x 4.5"	360	18	44
Cheese Sauce, 1.25 oz	100	8	4
Cheetos, 2.75 oz package	440	28	42
Chocolate Chip Cookie, 2.3 oz	280	12	40
Churro, (1), 10", 2.1 oz	210	10	26
Doritos, Nacho, 2.75 oz package	390	20	45
King Size Candy:			
Butterfinger, 3.75 oz	480	18	75
Nestle Crunch, 2.75 oz	390	21	85
Lay's, Chips, 2.75 oz package	440	28	42
Peanuts, in shell, 8 oz	930	80	24
Popcorn: Small (9 cup size)	575	35	56
Large (15 cup size)	950	58	93
Pretzel, Soft, Reg., 5.5 oz	490	3.5	101
Red Vines, 5 oz box	500	0	117
Snow Cone: With 3 oz syrup	270	0	68
With 6 oz syrup	540	0	136
Beverages:			
Orange Juice, 12 fl.oz	180	0	2
Beer:			
Heineken, 16 fl.oz	200	0	16
Miller: Draft, 16 fl.oz	195	0	17
Lite, 16 fl.oz	125	0	4
Jack Daniels, Punch, 12 fl.oz	235	0	34
Wine, White, 9 fl.oz	190	0	6
Soda, (with ½ ice), average:			
20 fl.oz	160	0	40
32 fl.oz	260	0	65
Starbuck's, Coffee, Frappuccino, 9.5 fl.oz	200	3	37

Asian & Chinese Dishes

	C	F	Cb
Appetizers:			
Crab Cake, 2¼ oz	125	10	1
Dumplings: *Per Dumpling*			
Pork: Steamed	80	4.5	5
Fried	90	6	5
Vegetable, steamed	35	1	5
Egg Rolls, Mini, 3 rolls	100	3	11
Spring Roll:			
Small, 1.5 oz	85	4	9
Medium, 3 oz	170	8	17
Large, 5 oz	290	15	29
Wonton, 1 only	75	4	5
Soup: Egg Flower, bowl 12 oz	90	2	16
Hot & Sour Soup, bowl 12 oz	110	3.5	14
Rice: Plain, 1 cup, 6.5 oz	320	2	66
2 Cups, 13 oz	640	4	132
Fried: 1 cup, 5 oz	365	11	55
Large dish, 16 oz	950	28	67
Noodles, Chinese Egg, cooked, 1 cup	200	4	37
Entrees & Mains: *Per Serving*			
Almond Chicken, 6 oz	270	10	21
BBQ Pork, 5.5 oz	440	23	15
Beef in Black Bean Sauce, 8.5 oz	390	17	17
Broccoli Beef, 6 oz	370	21	13
Chicken & Broccoli, 5.5 oz	160	8	10
Chicken Skewers, 3 oz	210	9	18
Chop Suey:			
Chicken, 5 oz	140	9	2
Pork, 5 oz	170	12	3
Chow Mein, Beef/Chicken, 8 oz	390	12	59
Crab Puff/Rangoon, 1 dumpling	190	11	13
Crispy Fried Chicken, 8 oz	485	33	12
Egg Drop Soup: With Noodles, 1 cup	110	3	16
Without Noodles, 1 cup	60	3	4
Egg Foo Yung with Sauce, 1 cup	270	15	16
Kung Pao Chicken, 5.5 oz	240	15	12
Lemon Chicken, 5 oz	525	21	57
Lo Mein, stir-fried, 8 oz	705	42	49
Omelet, Chicken/Shrimp, 16 oz	990	82	10
Orange Chicken, 5.5 oz	500	27	42
Steamed Whole Fish,			
½ Sockeye Salmon	646	36	23
Sweet & Sour:			
Fish, 20 oz	1160	58	106
Pork, 5.5 oz	400	23	35
Vegetable Combo, with oil, 6 oz	367	5	66
Vegetables, Steamed, without oil, 6 oz	135	1	29
Sauces: Mandarin Sauce 1.5 oz	70	0	17
Potsticker Sauce, 1.5 oz	35	0	8
Bubble Tea, average, 12 fl oz	280	0.5	68
Fortune Cookie, each	32	0.5	7

Cajun & Creole

	C	F	Cb
Alligator, cooked, 4 oz	160	2	0
Baked Herb Chicken, 1 serving	850	53	2
Bouillabaisse	400	15	10
Cajun Fried Turkey, 1 serving	630	25	0
Cocktail Sauce, 2 Tbsp	30	0	6
Couche-Couche, ½ cup	80	0	17
Crawfish Bisque, 1 serving	500	10	10
Crawfish, cooked, 2 oz	45	0.5	0
Creole Jambalaya,			
1 serving	550	30	15
Frog Legs, steamed (2)	45	0	0
Guinea Fowl, flesh, 4 oz, cooked	160	4	0
Hogshead Cheese, ¼ cup	80	5.5	0
Jambalaya, Shrimp & Crabmeat	520	14	12
Red Beans & Rice, 1 serving	400	17	52
Roasted Quail, with Bacon, on Toast	550	25	15
Remoulade Sauce, 2 Tbsp, 1 oz	110	11	2
Shrimp Creole, 1 serving	450	20	10
Stuffed Smothered Steak,			
with 1 cup Rice	890	50	50
Turtle, cooked, 3 oz	120	3	0

Canadian

	C	F	Cb
Bagels, Montreal-Style:			
Plain, 100g/3.5 oz	300	2	60
Poppyseed, 100g/3.5 oz	310	4	58
Sesame, 100g/3.5 oz	320	6	56
Bannock: Plain 33g/1.2 oz	120	3	20
With currants/raisins, 85g/3 oz	215	9	32
Meals:			
Baked Beans in Maple Syrup,			
1 cup, 250g/8.8 oz	320	1	62
Donnairs (*Pizza Delight*):			
Famous, regular, 250g/8.8 oz	510	21	60
Super, regular, 310g/11 oz	685	34	62
Poutine:			
A&W, 330g/12 oz	610	33	58
Boston Pizza, regular, 400g	610	30	67
Burger King, Classic, 330g	680	36	72
Harvey's, 240g/8.5 oz	730	41	63
McDonald's, 1 serving	510	29	44
Swiss Chalet,			
Chalet -Style, 340g/12 oz	150	12	195
Shish Taouk:			
Chicken: 1 skewer, 200g/7 oz	270	25	9
Wrap, 455g/16 oz	1150	12	195
Tassot:			
Beef, 283g/10 oz	430	28	12
Goat, 100g/3.5 oz	360	36	9
Toutiere, 170g/46oz	600	42	35

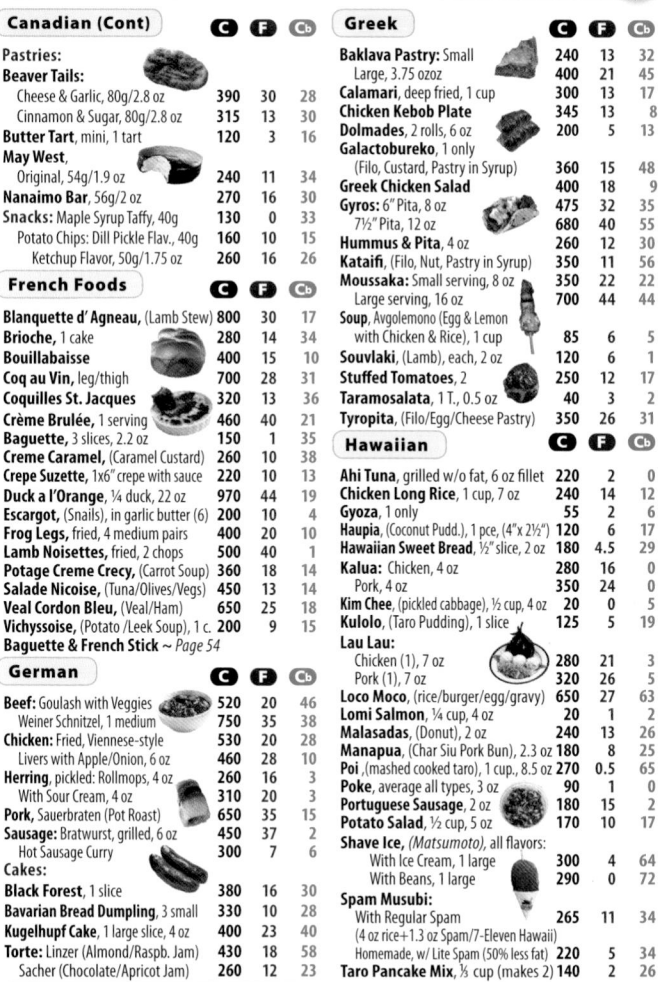

Canadian (Cont) | C | F | Cb

Pastries:
Beaver Tails:
Cheese & Garlic, 80g/2.8 oz	390	30	28
Cinnamon & Sugar, 80g/2.8 oz	315	13	30
Butter Tart, mini, 1 tart	120	3	16
May West			
Original, 54g/1.9 oz	240	11	34
Nanaimo Bar, 56g/2 oz	270	16	30
Snacks: Maple Syrup Taffy, 40g	130	0	33
Potato Chips: Dill Pickle Flav., 40g	160	10	15
Ketchup Flavor, 50g/1.75 oz	260	16	26

French Foods | C | F | Cb

Blanquette d' Agneau, (Lamb Stew)	800	30	17
Brioche, 1 cake	280	14	34
Bouillabaisse	400	15	10
Coq au Vin, leg/thigh	700	28	31
Coquilles St. Jacques	320	13	36
Crème Brulée, 1 serving	460	40	21
Baguette, 3 slices, 2.2 oz	150	1	35
Creme Caramel, (Caramel Custard)	260	10	38
Crepe Suzette, 1x6" crepe with sauce	220	10	13
Duck a l'Orange, ¼ duck, 22 oz	970	44	19
Escargot, (Snails), in garlic butter (6)	200	10	4
Frog Legs, fried, 4 medium pairs	400	20	10
Lamb Noisettes, fried, 2 chops	500	40	1
Potage Creme Crecy, (Carrot Soup)	360	18	14
Salade Nicoise, (Tuna/Olives/Vegs)	450	13	14
Veal Cordon Bleu, (Veal/Ham)	650	25	18
Vichyssoise, (Potato /Leek Soup), 1 c.	200	9	15
Baguette & French Stick ~ Page 54			

German | C | F | Cb

Beef: Goulash with Veggies	520	20	46
Weiner Schnitzel, 1 medium	750	35	38
Chicken: Fried, Viennese-style	530	20	28
Livers with Apple/Onion, 6 oz	460	28	10
Herring, pickled: Rollmops, 4 oz	260	16	3
With Sour Cream, 4 oz	310	20	3
Pork, Sauerbraten (Pot Roast)	650	35	15
Sausage: Bratwurst, grilled, 6 oz	450	37	2
Hot Sausage Curry	300	7	6
Cakes:			
Black Forest, 1 slice	380	16	30
Bavarian Bread Dumpling, 3 small	330	10	28
Kugelhupf Cake, 1 large slice, 4 oz	400	23	40
Torte: Linzer (Almond/Raspb. Jam)	430	18	58
Sacher (Chocolate/Apricot Jam)	260	12	23

Greek | C | F | Cb

Baklava Pastry: Small	240	13	32
Large, 3.75 oz oz	400	21	45
Calamari, deep fried, 1 cup	300	13	17
Chicken Kebob Plate	345	13	8
Dolmades, 2 rolls, 6 oz	200	5	13
Galactobureko, 1 only			
(Filo, Custard, Pastry in Syrup)	360	15	48
Greek Chicken Salad	400	18	9
Gyros: 6" Pita, 8 oz	475	32	35
7½" Pita, 12 oz	680	40	55
Hummus & Pita, 4 oz	260	12	30
Kataifi, (Filo, Nut, Pastry in Syrup)	350	11	56
Moussaka: Small serving, 8 oz	350	22	22
Large serving, 16 oz	700	44	44
Soup, Avgolemono (Egg & Lemon			
with Chicken & Rice), 1 cup	85	6	5
Souvlaki, (Lamb), each, 2 oz	120	6	1
Stuffed Tomatoes, 2	250	12	17
Taramosalata, 1 T., 0.5 oz	40	3	2
Tyropita, (Filo/Egg/Cheese Pastry)	350	26	31

Hawaiian | C | F | Cb

Ahi Tuna, grilled w/o fat, 6 oz fillet	220	2	0
Chicken Long Rice, 1 cup, 7 oz	240	14	12
Gyoza, 1 only	55	2	6
Haupia, (Coconut Pudd.), 1 pce (4"x 2½")	120	6	17
Hawaiian Sweet Bread, ½" slice, 2 oz	180	4.5	29
Kalua: Chicken, 4 oz	280	16	0
Pork, 4 oz	350	24	0
Kim Chee, (pickled cabbage), ½ cup, 4 oz	20	0	5
Kulolo, (Taro Pudding), 1 slice	125	5	19
Lau Lau:			
Chicken (1), 7 oz	280	21	3
Pork (1), 7 oz	320	26	5
Loco Moco, (rice/burger/egg/gravy)	650	27	63
Lomi Salmon, ¼ cup, 4 oz	20	1	2
Malasadas, (Donut), 2 oz	240	13	26
Manapua, (Char Siu Pork Bun), 2.3 oz	180	8	25
Poi, (mashed cooked taro), 1 cup, 8.5 oz	270	0.5	65
Poke, average all types, 3 oz	90	1	0
Portuguese Sausage, 2 oz	180	15	2
Potato Salad, ½ cup, 5 oz	170	10	17
Shave Ice, (Matsumoto), all flavors:			
With Ice Cream, 1 large	300	4	64
With Beans, 1 large	290	0	72
Spam Musubi:			
With Regular Spam	265	11	34
(4 oz rice + 1.3 oz Spam/7-Eleven Hawaii)			
Homemade, w/ Lite Spam (50% less fat)	220	5	34
Taro Pancake Mix, ⅓ cup (makes 2)	140	2	26

Hawaiian (Cont)

C F Cb

Plate Lunches:

	C	F	Cb
Chicken Katsu, (9 oz:) With Rice	1110	48	108
+ Macaroni Salad, ¾ cup	1360	68	123
or Tossed Salad + 2Tbsp Fr. Dress.	1240	61	111
Hamburger, (5 oz): With Rice	710	24	81
Gravy + Macaroni Salad	1135	49	112
Mahi Mahi, (7 oz): With Rice	650	12	90
+ Macaroni Salad + Tartar Sce	1150	58	109
or Macaroni Salad, w/o Tartar ce	935	34	108
or Tossed Salad + 3 Tbsp Fr. Dress.	815	27	96
or Tossed Salad, without dressing	670	12	93
Teri Beef, (5 oz): With 2 scoops Rice	790	23	94
+ Macaroni Salad, ¾ cup	1095	47	113
or Tossed Salad, without dressing	800	23	95

Indian & Pakistani

C F Cb

Per Serving, Meat dishes allow 4 oz meat/serving

	C	F	Cb
Aloo Samosa, each	155	12	12
Alu Gosht Kari, (Meat/Potato Curry)	600	40	23
Chicken Korma	500	35	6
Chicken Pilaf	700	53	50
Chicken Tikka	260	16	2
Chicken Vindaloo	400	20	8
Chapati/Roti, 7" diameter, 1 piece	60	0.5	11
Dahl, (Lentil Puree):			
1 cup, without oil	230	1	37
1 Tbsp Tadka (oil topping)	120	13	0
Dhakla, (Lentil Dish), 1" square, 1 oz	105	5	13
Dhansak, ½ cup	105	3.5	11
Gosht Kari	460	25	17
Lamb Pilaf	520	35	40
Lassi, (Sweet or Mango), 1 cup, 8 oz	160	4	24
Masala Gosht, (Beef/Tomato/Gravy)	400	25	18
Mulligatawney Soup	300	15	8
Murgh Tikka, 1 cup	300	4	7
Naan Flatbread, 2 oz	160	3.5	29
Pappadum, 1 large/2 small	50	3	5
Pesrattu, (Lentil Crepe), 9", 2.6 oz	130	5	15
Pork Vindaloo Curry, without Rice	620	47	3
Rajmah, 1 cup	225	5	35
Rogan Josh,			
without Rice/Potatoes	500	30	3
Shahi Korma, (Braised Lamb)	430	28	3
Tandoori Chicken:			
Breast	260	13	5
Leg/Thigh portion	300	17	6

Italian Dishes

C F Cb

Entrees:

	C	F	Cb
Baked Ziti: Small	370	27	32
Regular	575	42	49
Breadstick, 2 oz piece	120	2.5	25
Broccoli Fettucine Alfredo, regular	815	23	125
Bruschetta, 2 slices	380	17	53
Calzones, av. all varieties	840	34	101
Cannelloni, 1 tube, 6 oz	280	15	18
Cheese Breadstick, 2.4 oz piece	180	8	20
Cheese Ravioli, with sauce	495	17	65
Chicken Alfredo	775	29	82
Chicken Parmigiana, 11 oz	520	22	16
Chicken Scallopine, dinner	1110	71	68
Eggplant Parmigiana	900	39	78
Fettucine Alfredo: Lunch, 9 oz	885	65	63
Dinner, 15 oz	1475	108	104
Linquine & Seafood, dinner	1130	71	79
Manicotti Formaggio	800	38	57
Meat Lasagne:			
Small, 10 oz	440	23	39
Large, 16 oz	700	36	60
Meat Ravioli	725	22	102
Minestrone Soup, 1 bowl	110	2	18
Penne Rustica: Lunch	1300	71	76
Dinner	1540	80	101
Ravioli, over-stuffed, average	990	67	57
Panini Sandwich:			
Chicken, 16 oz	900	38	81
Meats, average, 18 oz	940	39	81
Vegetarian, 18 oz	750	31	83
Pizza, Ready-To-Eat ~ *See Page 135*			
Spaghetti & Meatballs:			
With Tomato Sauce: Kids	500	20	58
Medium/Lunch	1080	63	89
Large/Dinner	1430	81	119
With Meat Sauce: Kids	550	25	56
Medium/Lunch	1300	79	84
Large/Dinner	1700	103	110
Veal Marsala, dinner	1320	66	132
Veal Parmigiana, dinner	1270	65	116
Vegetable Primavera	610	8	116
Salad,			
Caprese , 11 oz	445	34	10
Desserts:			
Gelato: Vanilla (Milk Base), ½ cup	200	15	18
Choc. Hazelnut (Milk), ½ cup	370	29	26
Water Base, ½ cu	100	0	25
Lemon Ice,	180	0	45
Tiramisu, 1 piece, 5 oz	400	29	30
Further listings ~ *See Fast-Foods Section*			

Japanese

	C	F	Cb
Sashimi: (Sliced Raw Seafood/Beef)			
Ika (Squid), 4 oz	105	2	0
Hamachi (Yellowtail), 4 oz	165	6	0
Maguro (Yellowfin Tuna), 4 oz	120	1	0
Niku (Beef), 5 oz	200	10	0
Saba (Mackerel), 4 oz	160	7	0
Suzuki (Sea Bass), 4 oz	110	0.5	0
Tako (Octopus), 4 oz	95	1	0
Sushi Rice: Cooked, 1 Tbsp	25	0	5
1 cup, 5.25 oz	380	3	82
Sushi (Maki) Rolls: *Per Piece*			
Average all types (California Roll; Cream Cheese with Crab; Eel; Salmon; Shrimp; Tuna; Yellowtail; Vegetable)			
Small (1.2" diam. x 1.2" high), 0.8 oz	25	0.5	3.5
Medium (1¾" diam. x 1¾" high), 1.6 oz	50	1	7
Large (2" diam. x ⅞" high), 2 oz	60	1.5	9
Sushi Packs: *Per Pack*			
Average all types: 6 large pieces	370	5	55
9 medium pieces	360	6	60
12 small pieces	265	3	45
Futomaki (thick roll), 6 pieces	380	5	72
Hand Roll (Cone), 4 oz	120	2	18
Inari (rice filled soybean pocket), 4 pces	420	9	73
Sushi-Nigiri, (fish on rice), average all varieties, 1 piece	70	0.5	12
Sushi Plate, Assorted: 6 pieces	420	3	36
Combination (Sushi & Sushi Rolls) 2 Sushi + 6 small & 3 medium rolls	400	7	72
Dipping Sauces: Average, 2 Tbsp	30	0	7
Ginger Vinegar Dressing, 2 Tbsp	20	0	5
Edamame, (young green soybeans):			
Boiled beans (no pods), 4 oz	160	7	12
Steamed (in pods), 4 oz	60	3	5
Katsu-don, Pork with Rice	1100	39	141
Miso Soup, with Tofu pieces, 1 cup	85	3	11
Sake Wine, (16% alcohol), 3 fl.oz	115	0	7
Seaweed Salad, 1.5 oz	20	2	0
Sukiyaki, (Beef/Tofu/Veggies), 8 oz	400	24	32
Tempura:			
3 large shrimp & veggies	320	18	25
1 shrimp only	60	4	3
Teppan Yaki, (Steak, Seafood & Veggies), 10 oz serving	470	30	15
Teriyaki: Beef, 4 oz	350	25	4
Chicken, 4 oz	260	9	7
Salmon, medium, 6 oz	270	8	3
Yakatori, 1 skewer, 2.5 oz	140	5	1

Kosher/Deli Foods

	C	F	Cb
Bagel/Bialy, 1 small, 2 oz	160	2	32
Beiglach, (Cheese Knish)	350	17	35
Blintzes: Average, 1 only	120	1	25
With Sour Cream & Preserves	370	10	30
Borscht, (Without Sour Cream): 1 cup	85	3	14
Diet/Reduced Calorie, 1 cup	30	1	7
Cabbage Roll, (meat/rice), 5 oz	170	6	21
Chicken Broth: 1 cup	80	8	0
With vegetables	100	8	5
With noodles	150	9	16
Lowfat, plain, 1 cup	25	1	0
Cholent, 1 medium serving, 1 cup	350	16	48
Chopped Liver: 1 serving, 3 oz	110	6	5
With Egg Salad, ¼ cup	100	7	3
Farfel, dry, ½ cup	90	0.5	21
Gefilte Fish Balls:			
Regular, 2 oz	55	2	4
With Jelled Broth	80	2	6
Cocktail size, 1 oz	30	1	2
Sweet: Medium, 2 oz	65	2	4
With Jelled Broth	95	2	9
Hallah, (Yeast Bread), 1 slice, 1 oz	85	2	14
Herring: Smoked, 2 oz	120	8	0
In Sour Cream, 2 oz	150	10	0
Kasha, cooked, ½ cup	100	0.5	20
Kipfel, (Vanilla/Almdond Cookie), 1 pce	60	2	7
Knaidlach ~ *See Matzo Balls*			
Knish: Kasha/Potato, 1 only	130	4	22
Cheese, 1 only	350	17	35
Kreplach, beef, 1 piece	40	1	6
Kugel, potato/noodle, 1 serving	300	20	25
Latkes, (Potato Pancake): 2 oz	200	11	22
3 Latkes w/ Sour Cran Apple Sauce	750	25	95
Lochshen: Plain, 1 cup	130	2	26
Pudding, 1 cup	380	13	48
Lox, (Smoked Salmon), 2 oz	65	2	0
Mandelbrot, (Almond Bread), 1 slice, ¼" thick	45	2	5
Matzo, 1 oz board	110	0.5	21
Matzo Balls: 2 small, or 1 large, 2"	90	3	12
Extra large ball, 3"	180	6	24
Matzo Ball Soup:			
Cup w/ 2 small or 1 large ball	150	5	27
Bowl w/ Chkn & Noodles	325	13	34
Jerry's Deli, large bowl	560	17	56
NY Cheesecake, 4 oz	350	24	26
Pierogi, potato/cheese, 1 piece	90	4	11
Reuben S'wich, w/ ½ lb Corned Beef	920	60	28
Schmaltz, (Rend'd Chicken Fat), 1 T.	90	10	0

Korean Food
	C	F	Cb
Bibimbab, (Veg. & Beef on Rice), 1 cup	565	15	89
Bulgogi, (Barbeque Beef), 3.5 oz	325	12	15
Galbi (Short Ribs), 16 oz	975	61	16
Gujeolpan, (Pancake with Meat & Vegetables), 1 cup with 1 pancake	340	11	39
Japchae, (Noodle w/ Veggies & Meat), 1¼ cups	365	19	34
Sides:			
Kimchee, (Cabbage Relish), ½ cup	30	0	6
Namool, (Assorted Vegetables), 1 cup	125	6.5	9
Soups: Per Serving			
Muguk, (Radish & Chive Soup), 6 oz	105	7	6
Samgyetang, (Ginseng Chkn Soup):			
Without Chicken Skin, 1 cup	520	11	60
With Chicken Skin, 1 cup	725	35	60
Yuk Gae Jang, (Spicy Beef Soup), 1¼ cups	180	13	5

Lebanese/Middle East
	C	F	Cb
Baba Ghannouj, 2 Tbsp, 1 oz	70	6	2
Baklava, (Pastry, Nuts, Syrup), 1 pastry, 13/4 oz	245	18	18
Cabbage Rolls, (Cabb. Leaf, Meat, Rice), 1 roll, 3 oz	100	3	12
Cous Cous, (Semolina, Milk, Fruit, Nuts), 1 cup	400	21	43
Falafel, (Chick Pea Fritter), Fried, 1 medium, 1 oz	60	4	4
Hummus, ¼ cup, 2.2 oz	105	3	5
Fried Kibbi, (Wheat, Meat Pinenuts), 1 piece, 3 oz	180	8	15
Kafta, (Ground Lamb, Ssge on Skewer), 1 skewer, 1½ oz	85	5	2
Kibbeh Naye, (raw Lamb, Bulgur & Spice) 1 cup, 9 oz	450	18	28
Lebanese Omelet, 1 serving, 4 oz (Egg, Spinach, Pinenuts, Onion)	200	12	13
Pilaf, (Rice, Onion, Raisins, Apr., Spice) 1 cup	400	11	60
Shawourma, (Spit-Roast Beef), 4 oz serving	280	15	2
Shish Kabob, 1 stick, 2.5 oz	130	7	2
Spinach Pie, 1 piece, 3.5 oz	290	21	20
Sweet Almond Sanbusak, (Pastry, Almonds, Spices), 1 piece	200	15	11
Tabouli, 1 serving, 4 oz	125	7	13
Tahini Sauce, average, 1 Tbsp	90	8	2

Mexican
	C	F	Cb
Burritos (Taco Bell): Bean	370	10	56
Supreme Beef	420	16	53
Chili, plain, ¼ cup	90	6	8
Chili con Carne: With Beans, 1 cup	310	17	15
Without Beans, 1 cup	370	28	10
Chimichangas, Beef, 5 oz	400	19	43
Chorizo Sausage, 2 oz	265	23	0
Churro, (1), 1.5 oz	150	8	18
Corn Chips, ½ cup, 1 oz	160	10	17
Enchilada, average	330	10	49
Fajitas, Chicken	200	7	20
Guacamole, average, 2 Tbsp, 1 oz	45	4	2
Horchata: (Don Jose), 1 cup, 8 fl.oz	140	4	25
Cacique, 1 pint bottle, 16 fl.oz	320	7	62
Margarita, with 1.5 oz Tequila	160	0	6
Masa, (Pre-mixed for Tamales), 1 oz	80	5	9
Menudo:			
With Hominy, 1 cup	240	9	19
Without Hominy, 1 cup	170	9	2
Nachos: With cheese, peppers, 1 portion, 6-8 nachos, 7 oz	600	33	60
With cheese, peppers, beef, peppers, 1 portion, 6-8 nachos, 9 oz	570	31	56
Del Taco: Regular, 4 oz	300	19	30
Macho Nachos, 17 oz	1000	56	94
Taco Bell, BellGrande®, 10.75 oz	780	40	84
Nopal Cactus Salad, 1 cup	130	9	11
Papas Fritas, (1), 6 oz	325	18	40
Piloncillo, (Brown Sugar):			
1 Tbsp, 0.5 oz	50	0	13
Cone, small, 3", 3 oz	325	0	81
Quesadilla, Cheese	490	28	39
Queso Fresco, ¼ cup	80	4.5	2
Refried Beans, ¾ cup, 6 oz	160	3	26
Rice Pudding, (Arroz Con Leche), 4 oz	140	3	24
Soup, Black Bean, 1 bowl	200	3	34
Tacos (Taco Bell):			
Crunchy: Regular	170	10	12
Supreme	200	12	15
Soft: Crispy Potato	270	13	31
Grilled Steak	250	14	19
Taco Salad with Salsa	840	52	85
Taco Sauce, average, ¼ cup	15	0	3
Taco Shell, regular	50	2	8
Tamales, Beef/Chicken, av. 4.5 oz	250	11	27
Taquitos, Beef & Cheese, 4.5 oz	330	15	36
Tostada (Taco Bell)	250	10	29
Tortilla, Corn, 6" diameter	70	1	14
Tortilla Chips, 1 oz	150	8	18
Soup, Black Bean, 1 bowl	200	3	34

Extra Food Listings ~ See Fast Food Section
(Examples: Del Taco, Taco Bell, Taco Cabana, Taco Time)

Mexican (Cont)

	C	F	Cb
Breads:			
Bolillos, 1 roll, 3.5 oz	240	4	42
Mexican Cornbread, 4" square	210	11	19
Pan de Leche, 1 roll, 1.3 oz	110	2.5	20
Telera, 2 oz	150	1.5	19
Cakes, Cookies, Pastries Pan Dulce:			
Banderilla, 1 piece	140	10	8
Bigotes, 7"	570	22	44
Capirotada, (Bread Pudding), 10 oz	810	38	107
Cinnamon Cookies, 2	125	8	13
Concha, av. all varieties:			
Small (3" diameter), 2.5 oz	250	8	38
Medium (4" diameter), 3.5 oz	350	11	53
Large (5" diameter), 5.5 oz	550	18	84
Cream Puff, with Custard, 4.25 oz	255	14	25
Cuernos, (Horns), 3 oz	340	17	41
Donut, large, 4", 3.5 oz	440	21	58
Elotes, 3.5 oz	450	24	51
Empanadas, average all varieties:			
Medium, 3 oz	300	14	42
Large, 4 oz	400	19	56
Fiesta Cookie, (1), 2.25 oz	280	8	47
Galletas Mixtas:			
Small, 1 oz	100	2.5	16
Medium, 2 oz	200	5	32
Large, 3 oz	300	7.5	48
Guayaba, 3.25 oz	360	14	53
Jelly Roll, (1), 3.25 oz	240	4	46
Mantecadites, 4.5 oz	670	42	64
Mini Cupcake, (1),1.75 oz	180	8	25
Muffins/Nino Enbuelto, large, 6 oz	465	11	48
Nuez, 3.25 oz	380	17	52
Ojo de Buey, 4 oz	360	15	55
Orejas, 1 medium, 3 oz	310	15	39
Pan Dulce, 1 bun	330	10	45
Panquecitos, 2.5 oz	260	11	36
Piedras, 4 oz	470	15	76
Polvorones: Small, 1.5 oz	180	9	24
1 large, 3 oz	370	18	48
Pound Cakes, mini, 3.5 oz	380	16	52
Puerquitos, 3.5 oz	350	12	55
Rebanadas, 3.5 oz	390	18	51
Roles De Canela, (Cinn. Roll), 4.5 oz	490	15	81
Roscas, 1 piece, 2.75 oz	360	18	44
Semitas, (Bimbo), 1 piece, 2.2 oz	210	6	33
Sopapillas, (flaky pastry puffs): 1 piece	100	7	10
With Honey & Cream	200	14	18
Strawberry Crema Roll, 2.5 oz slice	240	5	45
Extra Food Listings ~ See CalorieKing.com			

Polish

	C	F	Cb
Cabbage Rolls, w/ Sour Cream, 2 small	220	10	30
Chicken Casserole, w/ Mshrms, 1 cup	520	27	5
Kielbasa, (Sausages, Onions, fried), 2 large	350	28	2
Meatballs, in sour cream, 3 x 1½" balls	300	16	11
Pierogi, Fruit/Vegetables, 3" ball	80	2	15
Pork Goulash, (Pork/Vegetable Stew)	550	21	38
Pot Roast, with Vegetables	630	21	28

Soul Foods

	C	F	Cb
Breakfast Sausage, fried, 2 patties	250	17	0
Brunswick Stew, 1 cup, 8.5 oz	320	14	19
Cornbread, homemade, 3 oz	200	7.5	28
Fatback, 0.5 oz	110	11	0
Ham Hock, pickled, 3 oz	200	12	0
Hog Maw, 1 oz	70	4.5	0
Hominy, cooked, ¾ cup	110	0.5	25
Hush Puppies, 5 pieces	260	12	35
Kale, cooked, ½ cup	20	0.5	4
Opossum, roasted, without bone, 3 oz	190	9	0
Oxtail, cooked, without bone, 2 oz	85	4.5	0
Pig's Ear, ¼ ear	50	3	0
Pig's Foot, ½ foot	70	4.5	0
Pig's Tail, ⅓ tail	115	10	0
Poke Salad, cooked, ½ cup	16	0.5	3
Pork Brains, braised, 3 oz	115	8	0
Pork Chitterlings, simmered, 3 oz	260	25	0
Pork Cracklings, 0.5 oz	80	6	0
Pork Neck Bones, cooked, no bone, 2 oz	100	4.5	0
Pork Skin, 1 cup	70	4.5	0
Pork Tongue, ⅓ tongue	75	5.5	0
Sousemeat, 1 oz	60	4.5	0
Succotash, ½ cup	80	1	17
Sweet Potato Pie, ⅛ of 9" pie	250	12	34
Tripe, 2 oz	55	2	0
Vienna Sausage:			
2 small, 1 oz	90	8	1
1 small, 0.5 oz	45	4	0.5

Restaurant & International Foods

Spanish

	C	F	Cb
Arroz Abanda, (Fish with Rice)	340	8	31
Arroz Con Pollo, (Rice/Chkn Salad)	500	23	50
Clams Marinara, 8 clams	330	16	22
Cochifrito, (Lamb with Lemon/Garlic)	650	25	5
Cochinillo Asado, (Rst Suckling Pig), 2 slices	300	15	3
Cocido Madrileno, (Madrid-Style Boiled Dinner)	450	27	18
Flan de Leche, (Caramel Custard)	325	9	52
Fritadera de Ternera, (Sauteed Veal)	450	27	2
Gazpacho, 1 bowl	60	0	15
Mole Poblano, ½ cup	205	14	16
Paella a la Valenciana, (Chicken & Shellfish Rice)	900	42	70
Pollo a la Espanola, (Chicken)	475	30	4
Ternera al Jerez, (Veal with Sherry)	660	29	6
Zarzuela, (Fish & Shellfish Medley)	530	27	40

Thai Foods

	C	F	Cb
Appetizers: Satay Pork, 1 oz	100	4	2
Spring Roll, 1 oz	110	6	13
Soups, Tom Yam (Hot & Sour): Spicy Shrimp/Seafood:			
1 cup	100	4	6
1 bowl	160	7	10
Vegetarian, 1 cup	50	0	11
Curries: Chicken with Ginger, 1 cup	390	34	4
Thick Red Curry with Beef, 1 cup	600	50	7
Thai Chicken Curry, 1 cup	340	23	4
Massaman Curry, 1 cup	680	57	8
Green Curry with Pork, 1 cup	480	44	5
Pad Thai, large serving, 18 oz	990	38	125
Fish: Steamed with Spicy Thai Sce	450	8	46
Crispy Fried, 5 oz	290	15	9
Spicy Chicken, stir-fry	450	22	14
Spicy Garlic Tofu, stir-fry	340	18	18
Sticky Thai Rice: Plain 1 cup, 6 oz	170	0.5	36
With Coconut & Sesame Seeds, 1 cup	880	28	120
Stir-fried Rice Noodles, 1 cup 5.5 oz	270	9	40
Stir-fried Vegetables, 1 cup	100	3	18
Salads: Green Papaya Salad	160	0	40
Spicy Prawn, 9 shrimp	170	3	15
Thai Beef Salad, 1 serving	260	9	15
Thai Chicken, 1 serving	330	9	17
Thai Noodle, 1 serving	410	13	45
Satay Chicken & Peanut Sauce, 1 satay stick	390	24	20
Sauce, Peanut Satay, ½ cup, 4 oz	160	10	13

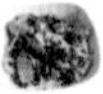

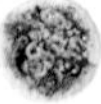

Vietnamese

	C	F	Cb
Banh Cuon, (Steam Rice w/ Pork), 1 roll	105	7	8
Bo Nuong, (Beef Satay), 2 sticks	265	9	4
Bo Xao Dau Phong, (Ginger Beef with Onion, Fish Sce)	750	30	10
Ca Chien Gung, (Whole Snapper/Ginger)	600	16	6
Canh Chay, (Vegetable/Tofu Soup)	80	3	13
Cari Chicken, 1 cup	475	29	16
Cari Chicken, with Rice Noodle, 1 cup curry & 1 cup noodles	660	29	60
Cari Chicken, with Steamed Rice, 1 cup curry & 1 cup rice	650	29	55
Cuu Xao Lan, (Curried Lamb and Veggies in Coconut)	900	40	80
Ga Chien, (Crisp Chick + Plum Sauce)	900	40	105
Ga Nuong, (Chicken Satay + Sauce)	240	10	4
Ga Xao Rau, (Marinated Chicken Braised with Vegetables)	800	26	100
Gio Lua, (Lean Pork Pie), ⅛ of pie	245	12	0
Goi Cuon, (Cold Spring Rolls), 1 roll	60	1	7
Rau Cai Xao Chay, (Stir Fried Veggies)	400	15	65
Thit Bo Vien, (Beef Balls), 6 balls	225	14	2
Thit Heo Goi Baup Cai, (Spicy Cabb. Rolls with Pork), 1 roll	200	7	11
Soup: Per Bowl, ½ Cup			
Bun Bo Hue, (Hot & Spicy Soup): Without Pork Feet	340	9	35
With Pork Feet	830	45	35
Chicken & Rice Noodle Soup	400	3	55
Pho Bo, (Beef Noodle Soup)	410	7	59
Pho Ga, (Chicken Noodle Soup)	460	6	58
Pho Tai, (Rare Beef & Noodle Soup)	440	7	73
Salad, Goi Du Du, (Green Papaya), ½ cup	155	3	29
Sauce, Nuoc Cham (Hot Sauce)	5	0	1

Gourmet & Miscellaneous

	C	F	Cb
Ants Eggs/Larvae, 1 Tbsp	20	0	0
Ants, chocolate coated, 3 Tbsp	140	7	2
Bee Maggots, canned, 3 Tbsp	65	2	0
Caviar, black/red, 1 Tbsp	40	3	0
Caterpillars, canned, 2 oz	60	2	0
Frog Legs, fried, 1 pair (large)	125	7	0
Haggis, boiled, 4 oz	350	24	22
Locusts, roasted, 1 oz	35	1	0
Silkworms, raw, 1 oz	60	2	0
Snails in garlic butter, 6 large	200	10	4
Snake, roasted, 4 oz	160	6	0

Fast - Foods & Restaurants

©2013 Allan Borushek

Nutritional data is based on U.S. outlets

For More Restaurants & Full Nutritional Data ~ See CalorieKing.com

	Page
A&W; Applebee's	**176**
Arby's	177
Atlanta Bread Co.	178
Au Bon Pain	178
Auntie Anne's	179
Back Yard Burgers; Baja Fresh	180
Baskin-Robbins	181
Big Apple Bagels	182
Biggby; Blimpie	182
Bob Evans	183
Bojangles; Boston Market	184
Boston Pizza Canada	184
Braum's; Bruegger's	185
Buca di Beppo	**185**
Burgerville	185
Burger King	186
California Kitchen; Captain D's	187
Caribou Coffee; Carl's Jr	187
Carvel; Cheesecake Factory	188
Charley's Grilled Subs	188
Chevy's Fresh Mex	188
Chick-Fil-A; Chili's	189
Chipotle; Chuck E. Cheese	190
Church's Chkn; Cici's; Cinnabon	190
Claim Jumper	191
Coldstone Creamery	191
Cosi; Costco; Cousins Subs	191
Culver's; D'Angelo's	192
Dairy Queen	193
Daphne's Greek Caffe; Davanni's	193
Del Taco; Denny's	194
Dippin' Dots; Donato's Pizza	195
Domino's Pizza	196
Don Pablos; Dunkin' Donuts	197
Eat 'N Park	198
Edo Japan; Einstein Bros	199
El Pollo Loco; Fatburger	200
Fazoli's	200
Firehouse Subs; Five Guys	201
Flame Broiler; Freshens	201
Godfather's Pizza	202
Gold Star Chili; Golden Corral	202
Great American Bagel Co	203
Green Burrito	203
Great Steak & Potato Co	203
Haagen-Dazs; Hardee's	204
Hissho Sushi	205
Hot Dog On A Stick	205

	Page
Hungry Howie's Pizza	**206**
In-N-Out Burger	206
IHOP	206
Jack in the Box; Jack's	207
Jamba Juice; Jersey Mike's	208
Jimmy John's; Johnny Rockets	209
KFC	210
Krispy Kreme; Krystal	211
La Rosa's Pizzeria; La Salsa	212
Little Caesars; Lone Star	213
Long John Silver's	213
Macaroni Grill	214
Manhattan Bagel	215
Marie Callender's; Max & Erma's	215
McAlister's Deli	216
McDonald's	216
Mimi's Cafe	218
Mr. Goodcents; Mr. Hero	218
Mrs Fields Cookies	219
My Favorite Muffin	219
Nathan's Famous; Ninety Nine	219
Noodles & Co; O'Charley's	220
Nothing But Noodles	220
Olive Garden	221
Old Spaghetti Factory	221
On The Border; Orange Julius	221
Outback Steakhouse	222
Panda Express	222
Panera Bread; Papa Gino's	223
Papa John's; Papa Murphy's	224
Pei Wei Asian; Pepe's Mexican	224
Perkins	225
Peter Piper Pizza; P.F. Chang's	226
Pita Pit; Pizza Hut	227
Pizza Ranch	228
Popeye's; Port of Subs	228
Pret A Manger	229
Pretzelmaker	229
Qdoba; Quiznos Subs	230
Rally's/Checker; Ranch 1	231
Red Hot & Blue; Red Lobster	231
Red Robin	232
Roly Poly	232

	Page
Round Table Pizza	**233**
Rubio's Fresh Mexican Grill	233
Ruby Tuesday	234
Runza	235
Ryan's Grill; 7-Eleven	236
Salad Works; Sarku Japan	236
Sandella's Flatbread Cafe	236
Schlotzsky's	237
Shakey's; Shari's	238
Sheetz	239
Sizzler; Skyline Chili	240
Smoothie King	241
Snappy Tomato; Sonic Drive-In	241
Souplantation	242
Southern Tsunami	242
Starbucks	243
Steak Escape	244
Steak 'n Shake; Subway	245
Sweet Tomatoes	246
Swiss Chalet	246
Taco Bell	247
Taco Cabana	248
Taco Del Mar	248
Taco John's; Taco Mayo	249
Taco Time	249
Target Food Court; TCBY	250
TGI FRiday's	250
ThunderCloud; Tim Hortons	251
T.J. Cinnamons	252
Togo's Eatery	252
Tropical Smoothie Cafe	253
Tubby's	253
Uno Chicago Grill	253
Villa Fresh Italian; Vocelli Pizza	254
Wahoo's Fish Taco	254
WAWA	254
Wendy's	255
Whataburger; White Castle	256
Wienerschnitzel	257
Winchell's; Wing Street	257
Woody's Bar-B-Q	257
Yoshinoya; Z Pizza	258
Zaxby's	258

A&W® (Feb '14)

	C	F	Cb
Burgers:			
Hamburger	380	19	33
Cheeseburger	420	21	37
Double Cheeseburger	680	38	44
Bacon Cheeseburger	530	30	39
Bacon Dble Cheeseburger	760	45	45
Papa Burger	690	39	44
Papa Single Burger	470	25	38
Sandwiches:			
Crispy Chicken	550	25	52
Grilled Chicken	400	15	31
Chicken Strips, 3 pces	500	29	32
Hot Dogs: Plain	310	19	23
Coney Chili Dog	340	20	26
Coney Chili Cheese Dog	380	23	28
Fries/Sides:			
French Fries: Small/Kids, 2.5 oz	200	8	28
Regular, 4 oz	310	12	45
Large, 5.5 oz	430	17	61
Cheese Fries: 6 oz	390	18	50
Chili Cheese Fries, 7 oz	410	17	52
Cheese Curds, Regular, 5 oz	570	40	27
Corn Dog Nuggets: 5 pieces	180	8	20
8 pieces	280	13	32
Onion Rings: Reg., Breaded, 4 oz	350	16	45
Large, 5.5 oz	480	27	62
Dipping Sauces: BBQ, 1 oz	40	0	10
Honey Mustard, 1 oz	100	6	12
Ranch, 1 oz	160	17	2
Sweets & Treats:			
Polar Swirl: M&M; Oreo, av	700	25	107
Reese's	740	31	97
Sundaes: Chocolate	320	8	53
Caramel; Hot Fudge, av.	345	10	56
Soft Serve Cone, Vanilla, 5.5 oz	260	7	41
Floats:			
A&W Root Beer: Medium, 20 oz	350	5	77
Large, 32 oz	640	10	136
Diet, 20 oz	170	5	30
Freeze, A&W Root Beer, 16 oz	370	8	68
Milkshakes: Strawb., Small, 16 oz	670	29	90
Chocolate; Vanilla, average:			
Small, 16 fl.oz	710	30	100
Medium, 20 oz	890	38	123
Smoothies: Pineapple Banana, 16 oz	400	6	85
Strawberry, 16 oz	360	6	70
Strawberry Banana, 16 oz	390	6	78
Sodas:			
A&W Root Beer: Reg., 20 oz	270	0	72
Diet, 20 oz	0	0	0
Pepsi: Small, 16 oz	200	0	56
Regular, 20 oz	250	0	70

Applebee's® (Feb '14)

	C	F	Cb
Appetizers: As Served			
Boneless Wings: Classic Buffalo	1230	76	66
Honey BBQ	1250	55	116
Hot Buffalo	1240	77	67
Dips: Bleu Cheese	240	26	1
Ranch	200	21	1
Classic Wings: Honey BBQ	880	36	59
Hot Buffalo	870	57	10
Chili Cheese Nachos	1420	87	118
Crunchy Onion Rings	1290	56	181
Mozzarella Sticks (9)	930	48	84
Chicken: Includes Standard Sides			
Chicken Fried Chicken	1150	56	104
Chicken Tenders: Basket	1100	62	98
Platter	1420	80	123
Crispy Orange Chicken	1520	49	208
FreshBurgers: Without Fries			
Bacon Cheddar Cheeseburger	970	63	51
Cheeseburger	940	61	51
Cowboy Burger	1280	74	99
Hamburger	790	48	49
Quesadilla Burger	1400	105	43
Pasta: As Served			
Cajun Shrimp	1010	46	92
Chicken Broccoli Alfredo	980	44	91
Three-Cheese Chicken Penne	1090	47	106
Sandwiches: Without Sides			
Applebee's Reuben	980	54	74
Oriental Chicken Rollup	1180	62	122
Roast Beef, Bacon & Mshrm Melt	860	45	57
Seafood: As Served			
Blackened Tilapia	410	15	36
Double Crunch Shrimp	1320	71	104
Hand-Battered Fish & Chips	1730	128	97
New England Fish & Chips	1690	126	92
Sizzling Entrees: Includes Sides			
Bourbon Street Chicken & Shrimp	610	26	31
Bourbon Street Steak	650	36	33
Skillet Fajitas:			
Chicken	1290	46	144
Shrimp	1270	47	145
Steak	1330	48	146

Continued Next Page...

Updated Nutrition Data ~ www.CalorieKing.com
Persons with Diabetes ~ See Disclaimer (Page 22)

Applebees® cont... (Feb '14)

	C	F	Cb
Steaks & Toppers: *Without Sides*			
House Sirloin, 9 oz	330	17	1
New York Strip, 12 oz	480	24	1
Ribeye, 12 oz	670	47	3
Shrimp 'N Parmesan Sirloin	600	34	5
Steak Combos: With Fried Shrimp	670	36	38
With Grilled Shrimp	560	30	3
With Honey BBQ Chicken	620	18	38
Toppers: Grilled Onions	45	2.5	3
Sauteed Garlic Mushrooms	130	13	3
Shrimp 'N Parmesan	280	18	4
Under 550 Calories: *Includes Sides*			
Creamy Parmesan Chicken	460	13	34
Lemon Parmesan Shrimp	490	14	64
Napa Chicken & Portobellos	450	13	31
Roma Pepper Steak	510	27	26
Signature Sirloin w/ Garlic Shrimp	510	23	31
Salads: *Regular, Without Dressing*			
Fiesta Chicken, Chopped	700	31	67
Fried Chicken	680	41	30
Oriental Grilled Chicken	590	20	53
Pecan Crusted Chicken	890	46	78
Sides: *As Served*			
Caesar Salad, Small, with Dressing	300	26	12
Chili Bowl	400	24	17
Garlic Mashed Potatoes	250	14	29
House Salad, without Dressing	230	15	12
Loaded Baked Potato	400	23	41
Loaded Mashed Potatoes	460	31	31
Soups: *Per Bowl*			
Chicken Noodle	170	4.5	18
Chicken Tortilla	220	9	24
Clam Chowder	380	26	24
French Onion	370	23	25
Tomato Basil	290	17	29
Desserts: *As Served*			
Butter Pecan Blondie	1130	61	133
Shooters: Chocolate Mou.	470	32	44
Hot Fudge Sundae	430	21	54
Strawberry Cheesecake	380	23	38
Triple Choc. Meltdown	960	52	122

Arby's® (Mar '14)

	C	F	Cb
Sandwiches:			
Beef 'n Cheddar: Classic	450	20	45
Mid	560	27	45
Roast Beef: Classic	360	14	35
Mid	460	21	35
Max	560	27	35
Ultimate Angus:			
Philly	590	27	48
Three Cheese & Bacon	630	30	45
Chicken:			
Chicken Bacon & Swiss, Crispy	600	29	49
Crispy Chicken	540	27	48
Market Fresh Sandwiches:			
Roast Turkey & Swiss	700	28	77
Roast Turkey, Ranch & Bacon	800	35	76
Wraps:			
Roast Turkey & Swiss	490	25	38
Roast Turkey, Ranch & Bacon	580	32	38
Chicken:			
Prime Cuts: Chicken Tenders (3)	350	17	25
Chicken Tenders (5)	590	28	42
Optional/Regional Items:			
Chicken Cordon Bleu Sandwich,			
Crispy	620	31	47
Homestyle Fries: Small	360	17	49
Medium	480	22	66
Large	610	28	82
Melts: Arby's	340	13	37
Ham & Swiss	300	9	35
Regular Combos: *Includes Small Curly Fries and Small Pepsi*			
Beef 'n Cheddar, mid	1140	49	141
Chicken, Bacon & Swiss, Crispy	1180	51	145
Reuben Sandwich	1220	52	158
Roast Turkey & Swiss Sandwich	1280	50	173
Fries:			
Curly Fries: Small, 4.5 oz	400	22	47
Medium, 6 oz	540	29	62
Large, 7 oz	630	35	74
Potato Cakes: 3 cakes	340	20	37
4 cakes	460	27	50
Snack 'N Save:			
Jalapeno Bites: 5 bites	280	16	31
8 bites	460	25	49
Mozzarella Sticks: 4 sticks	420	21	35
6 sticks	620	32	52
Steakhouse Onion Rings, 5 rings	410	20	51
Turnovers: Apple with Icing	430	18	64
Cherry Turnover with Icing	390	13	64

Continued Next Page...

Arby's® cont... (Mar '14)

Market Fresh Salads: Without Dressing

	C	F	Cb
Chopped Farmhouse:			
Crispy Chicken	420	23	24
Roast Turkey	230	13	8
Dressings: *Per 1.5 oz packet*			
Balsamic Vinaigrette	130	12	5
Buttermilk Ranch	210	22	2
Dijon Honey Mustard	180	16	8
Kids Meals:			
Curly Fries, 2.75 oz	240	13	28
Jr Roast Beef Sandwich	210	8	22
Jr Turkey & Cheese Sandwich	220	6	23
Prime Cut Chicken Tenders (2), 3 oz	230	11	17
Sliced Apples, 2.2 oz	35	0	9
Breakfast: *Per Serving*			
Biscuits: Bacon, Egg & Cheese	470	27	35
Ham, Egg & Cheese	420	21	34
Sausage, Egg & Cheese	620	43	36
Croissants: Bacon, Egg & Cheese	400	26	25
Ham, Egg & Cheese	350	20	24
Sausage, Egg & Cheese	550	42	26
Sourdoughs:			
Bacon, Egg & Cheese	480	22	45
Ham, Egg & Cheese	430	16	44
Sausage, Egg & Cheese	630	38	46
Wraps: Bacon, Egg & Cheese	510	27	43
Ham, Egg & Cheese	420	20	42
Sausage, Egg & Cheese	640	41	44
Sauces: Arby's, ½ oz	15	0	3
Bronco Berry, 1 oz	60	0	15
Cheddar Cheese, 1.5 oz	50	3.5	4
Horsey, 0.5 oz	50	5	3
Marinara, 1 oz	25	0.5	3
Spicy Three Pepper, ½ oz	25	1	3
Tangy BBQ, 1 oz	45	0	11
Dipping Sauces: Buffalo, 1 oz	10	1	1
Honey Mustard, 1 oz	140	13	5
Ranch, 1 oz	100	11	1
Shakes: *Per Regular Size*			
Chocolate, 22 oz	570	15	99
Vanilla, 22 oz	470	15	75
Sodas: *Without Ice*			
Average all flavors:			
Small, 16 fl.oz	200	0	50
Medium, 22 fl.oz	280	0	70
Large, 32 fl.oz	400	0	100
Iced Tea, no added sugar, 18 fl.oz	5	0	1

Atlanta Bread Co® (Feb '14)

Signature Sandwiches:

As Per Menu Board Components

	C	F	Cb
ABC Special on French Baguette	780	37	62
Bella Chicken on Medit. Focaccia	740	38	52
California Avoc. on Onion Focaccia	740	60	41
Salmon Banh-Mi on Ciabatta	560	12	77
Turkey Bacon Avoc. on Nine Grain	740	36	70
Paninis: Chicken Pesto	780	36	79
Chicken Cordon Bleu	670	19	80
Cuban	740	31	77
Italian Vegetarian	570	16	84
Steakhouse	800	39	68
Turkey Club	900	41	92
Salads: *Without Dressing or Bread*			
Balsamic Bleu Salad	390	18	52
Chopstix Chicken Salad	360	14	35
Greek Salad	260	18	17
House Salad	200	13	12
Salsa Fresca Salmon Salad	280	11	23
Soups: *Per 10 oz*			
Baked Potato Chowder	230	13	22
Broccoli Cheese	240	16	13
Chicken & Dumpling	260	16	23
Corn Chowder	340	16	45
Minestrone	250	11	27
New England Clam Chowder	230	10	23
Wisconsin Cheese	260	14	22

For Complete Menu & Data ~ see CalorieKing.com

Au Bon Pain® (Feb '14)

	C	F	Cb
Bagels: *Per Bagel*			
Asiago Cheese	370	8	56
Cinnamon Crisp	410	7	77
Everything	300	2	58
Honey 9 Grain	310	2	63
Jalapeno Double Cheddar	320	8	52
Cream Cheese Spreads: *Per 2 oz*			
Honey Pecan, 2 oz	200	16	10
Lite Cream Cheese	120	9	5
Vegetable	170	16	3

Continued Next Page... ...

Au Bon Pain® cont... (Feb '14)

Breakfast Sandwiches: | C | F | Cb

	C	F	Cb
Egg on a Bagel	430	12	58
With Bacon	510	17	58
With Cheese	480	16	58
Sausage, Egg Whites & Cheddar, on Skinny Wheat Bagel	480	32	23
Smoked Salmon & Wasabi on Onion Dill	410	10	62

Cafe Sandwiches: Per Whole Sandwich

	C	F	Cb
Black Angus Roast Beef & Cheddar	510	18	52
Black Forest Ham & Cheddar	640	17	92
Classic Chicken Salad	450	11	60
Grilled Chicken	480	13	55
Tuna Salad	470	14	60
Turkey & Swiss	740	30	79

Signature Sandwiches: Per Whole Sandwich

	C	F	Cb
Black Angus Roast Beef & Herb Cheese	520	14	71
Caprese	550	27	52
Chipotle Turkey & Avocado	670	32	59
The Veggie	640	27	79
Turkey Club	600	24	52

Wraps: Chicken Caesar

	C	F	Cb
Chicken Caesar	610	30	52
Mediterranean	610	31	65
Southwest Tuna	710	40	55
Thai Peanut Chicken	550	16	73

Harvest Rice Bowls:

	C	F	Cb
Roasted: Angus Steak Teriyaki	730	20	107
Mayan Chicken	630	16	92

Soups: Per Medium 12 oz Bowl

	C	F	Cb
Baked Stuffed Potato	380	24	33
Chicken Gumbo	190	9	22
Corn & Green Chili Bisque	270	16	26
Cream of Chicken & Wild Rice	270	15	26
Italian Wedding	180	10	15
Vegetarian Chili	270	2.5	47
Wild Mushroom Bisque	190	9	23

Specialty Soups: Per 12 fl.oz Bowl

	C	F	Cb
Beef & Vegetable Stew	340	19	26
Macaroni & Cheese	530	29	46
Turkey Chili	340	9	44

Au Bon Pain® cont... (Feb '14)

Salads: Without Dressing | C | F | Cb

	C	F	Cb
Chef's, 9 oz	270	12	8
Chicken Caesar Asiago	260	9	20
Chicken Cobb, with Avocado	410	24	15
Southwest Chicken	350	11	42
Thai Peanut Chicken, 10.5 oz	190	4.5	20
Tuna Garden, 12 oz	270	12	20
Turkey, Apple, Brie & Spinach	430	25	30
Dressings: Balsamic Vinaig., 2 oz	110	9	7
Bleu Cheese, 2 oz	310	33	2
Caesar, 2 oz	270	28	4
Sesame Ginger, 2 oz	230	20	12
Thai Peanut, 2 oz	160	8	12

Bakery: Per Item

	C	F	Cb
Brownie, Choc Chip, 4 oz	440	21	62
Cakes: Red Velvet Cupcake, 3.1 oz	400	22	46
Pound Cakes: Iced Lemon, 4.5 oz	470	21	66
Marble, 4 oz	450	24	54
Cookies: English Toffee, 2.3 oz	320	16	42
Shortbread, 2.25 oz	340	20	37
Croissants: Almond, 4.6 oz	500	31	48
Apple & Cinnamon, 3.4 oz	240	8	38
Chocolate, 4 oz	470	25	57
Raspberry Cheese, 4 oz	360	16	48
Sweet Cheese, 3.9 oz	430	23	48
Muffins: Blueberry, 4.7 oz	490	19	73
Berry Yogurt, Low-Fat, 3.9 oz	300	3	62
Carrot Walnut, 4.7 oz	540	25	73
Raisin Bran, 4.7oz	420	11	78
Beverages: Caffe Latte, 16 fl.oz	140	7	12
Caramel Macchiato, 16 fl.oz	210	7	29
Peach Iced Tea, 24 fl.oz	270	0	67
Strawberry Smoothie, 16 fl.oz	310	0.5	66

For Complete Nutritional Data ~ see CalorieKing.com

Auntie Anne's® (Feb '14)

Pretzels: With Butter | C | F | Cb

	C	F	Cb
Cinnamon Sugar	470	12	84
Garlic	350	5	63
Jalapeno	330	5	65
Original	340	5	65
Original Stix, 6 sticks	340	5	65
Sesame	400	10	63
Sour Cream & Onion	360	5	68
Sweet Almond	390	6	74

Continued Next Page ...

Auntie Anne's® cont... (Feb '14)

Dipping Sauces:

	C	F	Cb
Caramel Dip, 1.5 oz	130	3	23
Cheese Dip; Hot Salsa Cheese, av., 1.1 oz	95	8	3
Light Cream Cheese, 1.25 oz	80	6	1
Marinara Sauce, 2 oz	45	1	7
Sweet Dip, 1.4 oz	130	0	32
Sweet Mustard, 1.25 oz	60	2	10

Beverages: Per Serving
Frozen Lemonade Mixer: Per 12 fl.oz

	C	F	Cb
Blue Raspberry; Strawberry	240	0	60

Back Yard Burgers® (Feb '14)

Burgers:

	C	F	Cb
American Cheeseburger, ⅓ lb	780	48	46
Back Yard Classic Burger, ⅓ lb	680	39	46
Bacon Cheddar	870	55	47
Black Jack	890	62	44
Bleu Cheeseburger: ⅓ lb	730	43	46
Double ⅔ lb	1170	77	46
Cheddar Cheeseburger: ⅓ lb	790	48	47
Double ⅔ lb	1295	87	48
Jr Burger	530	27	47
Mushroom Swiss	790	48	45
Pepper Jack, ⅓ lb	770	48	46
Swiss Cheeseburger: ⅓ lb	790	48	46
Double ⅔ lb	1290	87	46

Chicken Sandwiches:

	C	F	Cb
Blackened Chicken	530	23	51
Chicken Club	700	41	48
Crispy Chicken	590	26	65
Chicken Tender	660	33	64
Grilled Chicken	345	4.5	46

Specialities:

	C	F	Cb
Back Yard Dog	320	18	29
Chicken Tender Basket	465	25	33
Chili Cheese Dog	635	45	32
Loaded Smoked Sausage	575	39	30
Original Smoked Sausage	450	28	32
Veggie Burger (just "Veggie")	400	13	67
Turkey Burgers: Classic	595	36	44
Club	750	53	45
Wild Turkey Burger	705	48	45
Wild Turkey Wrap	385	26	23

Fries:

	C	F	Cb
Seasoned: Regular, 6 oz	700	49	64
Large, 9 oz	1050	73	96
Sweet Potato, Regular, 5 oz	555	43	43

Back Yard Burgers® cont... (Feb '14)

Salads:
Without Dressing Unless Indicated

	C	F	Cb
Chicken: Blackened	555	37	17
Grilled	450	26	16
Caesar, Blackened Chkn w/ drsg	770	64	17
Chopped, Blackened Chkn w/ drsg	1010	68	58

Dressings: Per Serving

	C	F	Cb
Bleu Cheese	220	24	1
Gorgonzola Vinaigrette	170	15	6
Honey Mustard	240	23	7
Ranch	150	15	2

Desserts: Per Serving

	C	F	Cb
Cobblers: Apple	360	14	59
Blackberry	285	7.5	51
Cherry	345	12	59
Pecan	740	26	119
Shakes: Per 12 fl.oz			
Chocolate	760	36	100
Strawberry/Vanilla	730	32	100

Baja Fresh® (Feb '14)

	C	F	Cb
Burritos: With Standard Menu Board Components			
Baja: With Carnitas	830	45	67
With Chicken	790	38	65
With Steak	850	46	67
Bean & Cheese: With Carnitas	1010	42	98
With Chicken	970	35	96
With Steak	1030	43	97
Vegetarian, without Meat	840	33	96
Mexicano: With Carnitas	830	20	119
With Chicken	790	13	117
With Steak	860	21	118
Ultimo: With Chicken	880	38	84
With Steak	950	44	85
Vegetarian, Grilled Veggie	800	33	94
Fajitas: As Served, Without Tortilla Chips			
Chicken, with Corn Tortillas	860	24	105
Chicken, with Flour Tortillas	1140	33	147
Nachos: As Served			
Grande: With Cheese	1890	108	163
With Chicken	2020	110	164
With Steak	2120	118	163

Continued Next Page...

Baja Fresh® cont... (Feb '14)

Quesadillas: With Grilled Flour Tortilla and Standard Menu Board Components

	C	F	Cb
With Cheese	1200	78	84
With Chicken	1330	80	84
With Steak	1430	87	84
Vegetarian	1260	78	94

Tacos: With 2 Grilled Corn Tortillas & Standard Menu Board Components

Americano Soft, av. all varieties	240	11	21
Crispy Wahoo	250	13	27
Original Baja, average all varieties	215	6.5	28

Salads: With Standard Menu Board Components Without Dressing

Baja Ensalada:

With Carnitas	370	18	20
With Chicken	310	7	18
With Shrimp	230	6	18
With Steak	450	18	18

Tostada:

With Carnitas	1180	62	100
With Shrimp	1120	55	99
With Steak	1230	63	98

For Complete Nutritional Data ~ see CalorieKing.com

Baskin Robbins® (Mar '14)

Ice Creams: Per 4 oz Scoop

	C	F	Cb
Classic Flavors: Cherries Jubilee	240	12	30
Chocolate	260	14	33
Jamoca Almond Fudge	260	15	29
Mint Chocolate Chip	260	16	28
Nutty Coconut	300	19	28
Old Fashioned Butter Pecan	280	18	25
Oreo Cookies 'n Cream	280	15	32
Peanut Butter 'n Chocolate	320	20	30
Pistachio Almond	280	19	22
Pralines 'n Cream	280	14	35
Rainbow Sherbet	160	2	33
Reese's P'nut Butter Cup	300	17	32
Vanilla	260	16	27
Very Berry Strawberry	220	11	27
World Class Chocolate	280	16	31
Seasonal Flavors: Baseball Nut	270	14	30
Cotton Candy	250	12	31
Easter Egg Hunt	290	16	34
German Chocolate	300	17	34
Rum & Raisin	240	11	30
Strawberry Cheesecake	260	13	31

Baskin Robbins® cont... (Mar '14)

Cones:

	C	F	Cb
Cake	25	0	5
Mixed Berry Waffle	130	3	23
Sugar	45	0.5	9

Desserts:

Brownie a la Mode, 1 slice, 2.77 oz	260	13	36

Soft Serve:

Cups: Vanilla: Kid's, 3 oz	130	4.5	18
Regular, 6 oz	250	9	37
Large, 9 oz	380	14	55

Parfaits: Per Regular 15 oz Size

Oreo	740	27	114
Reese's	990	63	86
Strawberry 'n Almonds	600	27	76

31 Below' Mix-In: Per 16 oz Medium Cup

Butterfinger	840	32	127
Choc. Chip Cookie Dough	860	30	132
Heath	940	43	121
Oreo	750	28	110
Reese's P'nut Butter Cup	830	40	100

Sundaes:

Banana Royale	620	28	87
Big Easy Banana Split	1070	40	169
Brownie	920	47	119
Choc. Chip Cookie Dough	990	43	138
Classic Banana	1010	34	173
Made with Snickers	1000	46	138
Reese's, Peanut Butter Cup	1220	80	109
Two Scoop	530	29	61

Beverages:

Fruit Blast: Per Medium, 24 fl.oz

Mango	500	1.5	123
Strawberry Citrus	350	0	87

Milk Shakes: Per Medium, 24 fl.oz

Choc. with Choc. Ice Cream	930	40	129
Mint Chocolate Chip	890	44	109
Strawb. w/ Strawb. Ice Cream	780	31	109

Smoothie: Per Medium, 24 fl.oz

Mango Banana	630	2	150
Strawberry Banana	520	1	126
Tropical Banana	550	1.5	132

Big Apple Bagels® (Feb '14)

Bagels:

	C	F	Cb
Regular flavors, average all, 5 oz	340	2	70

Choice Bagels: Per Bagel

	C	F	Cb
Blueberry Cobbler	390	8	70
Cheddar Nacho	350	6	60
Cinnamon Bun	400	8	70
Cinnamon Danish	395	8	72
Quiche Lorraine	355	8	54
Strawberry White Chocolate	365	4	72
Swiss Melt	370	8	58
White Chocolate Swirl	395	8	70

Cream Cheese: Per 2 Tbsp, 1 oz

	C	F	Cb
Plain	90	9	2
Plain, Lite	60	4.5	3
Other varieties, average	90	8	2
Whipped: Classic Plain	70	7	1
Brown Sugar Cinnamon	70	5	5
Reduced-Fat Spring Veggie	60	5	2

Overstuffed Sandwich,

	C	F	Cb
Manhattan Club	1120	40	120

Specialty Sandwiches:

	C	F	Cb
All-American Duo	750	28	78
Big Apple Club	795	37	75
Chicken Caesar	610	19	78
Turkey Club	780	34	75

Toasted Sandwiches:

	C	F	Cb
Cafe Chicken Melt	815	32	80
Roast Beef Parmesan Grinder	585	15	76
Tuna Melt	640	23	75

Breakfast,

	C	F	Cb
Morning Classic	485	11	73

For Complete Nutritional Data ~ see CalorieKing.com

Biggby Coffee® (Feb '14)

Hot Drinks:

	C	F	Cb

Per Tall, 16 fl.oz, w/o Whipped Cream & Sugar Unless Indicated

	C	F	Cb
Caffe Latte: With 2% Milk	175	7	16
With Non-Fat Milk	115	0	16
With Soy	160	5	19
Cappuccino: With 2% Milk	105	4.5	10
With Non-Fat Milk	70	0	10
With Soy	95	3	11
Chai Latte: With 2% Milk	315	7.5	51
With Non-Fat Milk	255	0	51
Cocoa Carmella: *With Sugar*			
With 2% Milk	325	9	51
Add Whipped Cream	405	15	55
Mocha Mocha: *With Sugar*			
With 2% Milk	295	7.5	48
Add Whipped Cream	375	14	52

Biggby Coffee® cont... (Feb '14)

Cold Drinks: Per Tall, 16 fl.oz

	C	F	Cb

Frozen Hot Chocolate: With 2% Milk, Sugar & Whipped Cream

	C	F	Cb
Regular	565	18	93
Mint	560	18	93
Raspberry	565	18	94

Freeze Specials,

	C	F	Cb
Almond Blizzard Creme Freeze, with Whipped Cream	570	17	97

For Complete Menu & Data ~ see CalorieKing.com

Blimpie® (Feb '14)

	C	F	Cb

Cold Deli Subs:

Per 6" White Sub, with Standard Menu Board Toppings

	C	F	Cb
Blimpie Best	450	18	47
BLT	430	22	43
Club	410	13	49
Ham & Swiss	410	14	47
Roast Beef & Provolone	430	15	44
Tuna without Cheese	460	21	41
Turkey & Provolone	410	14	47

Wraps: Includes Dressing

	C	F	Cb
Chicken Caesar	590	26	56
Southwestern	490	18	57

Hot Deli Subs: Per 6" White Sub with Standard Menu Board Toppings

	C	F	Cb
Meatball	560	29	47
Pastrami	430	16	42
VegiMax	520	21	55

Salads: Regular, Without Dressing

	C	F	Cb
Buffalo Chicken	200	8	11
Garden	30	0	6
Tuna Salad	270	19	6
Ultimate Club	270	14	11

Dressings & Sauces: Per 1.5oz

	C	F	Cb
Creamy Caesar	210	21	4
Creamy Italian	180	18	4

Soups: Per 8.5 oz Serving

	C	F	Cb
Chicken Noodle	130	4	18
Cream of Broccoli with Cheese	250	19	13
Harvest Vegetable	100	1	19
New England Clam Chowder	170	3	28
Vegetable Beef	80	2	13

Desserts:

	C	F	Cb
Brownie	230	10	28
Cookies: Oatmeal Raisin	160	8	23
Sugar	320	15	42

For Complete Nutritional Data ~ see CalorieKing.com

Bob Evans® (Feb '14)

Starters:	C	F	Cb
Breaded Garlic Mushrooms, 11 oz	460	18	63
Country Fair Cheese Bites	950	66	49
Crispy Panko Breaded Shrimp (5)	345	24	18

Sandwiches & Burgers:

Big Farm Burgers: Regular	725	42	50
Bacon Cheeseburger	900	58	51
Favorite Burger	835	51	48
Smokehouse Burger	1170	78	65

Sandwiches:

Farm Favorites: Chicken, Fried	660	26	61
Chicken, Grilled	520	17	48
Farm-Grill: Chicken Club, Fried	670	27	61
Chicken Club, Grilled	535	18	48
Knife & Fork Turkey	755	39	62
Pot Roast	650	36	49
Turkey Bacon Melt, full size	555	25	48

Dinners: Without Sides Unless Indicated

Beef: Country Fried Steak w/ Gravy	605	41	42
Meatloaf, 1 slice	345	23	15
Spaghetti with Meat Sce, 21.5 oz	785	35	87

Chicken:

Chicken-N-Noodles: Deep-Dish	665	30	72
Slow Roasted, 13.5 oz	225	4	31
Chicken Penne Pasta	870	56	53
Chicken Pot Pie, slow roasted	860	56	63
Garlic Butter Grilled Chkn Breast	160	4	1
Fish: Garlic Butter Salmon, 8 oz	255	9	1
Potato-Crusted Flounder, 5 oz	245	12	13
Wildfire Salmon, 8.5 oz	310	9	15
Turkey: Slow-Roasted, 3 oz	95	3	2
Turkey & Dressing, 15.5 oz	605	27	53
Side Dishes: Coleslaw, 3.5 oz	210	14	19
Baked Potato, Plain, 10 oz	195	0	50
Bread & Celery Dressing, 6 oz	295	16	29
French Fries, 7 oz	495	21	71
Hash Browns, 4.5 oz	315	9	53
Home Fries, 5 oz	180	6	28
Loaded Baked Potato, 12 oz	395	16	53
Loaded Home Fries, 5.1 oz	270	16	22
Macaroni & Cheese, 7 oz	305	15	29
Mashed Potatoes, 5 oz	190	9	24
Gravy: Beef, 2.25 oz	20	1	2
Chicken Roasted, 2 oz	50	4	3
Country, 3 oz	55	2	8

Bob Evans® cont... (Feb '14)

Sauces:	C	F	Cb
Hollandaise, 1 oz	25	1	3
Wildfire BBQ, 1 oz	60	0	15

Soups: Per Bowl

Beef Vegetable	165	3	25
Cheddar Baked Potato	330	19	26
Farm Festival Bean	200	3	28

Salads: Large, Without Dressing

Cobb, 14.5 oz	515	31	10
Cranberry Pecan Chicken, 14 oz	620	36	34
Heritage Chef, 12.5 oz	400	25	11
Wildfire Grilled Chicken, 13.5 oz	390	13	37

Dressings: Per 3 oz

Blue Cheese	410	44	5
Buttermilk Ranch	290	29	3
Sweet Italian	255	23	12

Breakfast:

Biscuit Bowls: Sausage, 19 oz	975	59	76
Spinach, Bacon & Tomato, 18.5 oz	1015	60	79

Hotcakes: *Without Topping*

Buttermilk (1), 3.1 oz	175	4	31
Cranberry Multigrain (1), 4.2 oz	225	2	48
Loaded Hash Browns, 6.5 oz	520	25	57
Omelets: Border Scramble	630	45	15
With Egg Lites	415	23	14
Farmer's Market	535	38	13
Western	495	35	7
Pot Roast Hash, 14.5 oz	760	53	29
Sunshine Skillet, 11.5 oz	435	24	38

Fit From The Farm:

Breakfast:

Be Fit Breakfast	350	3	68
Veggie Omelet w/ Fruit/Toast/Jelly	310	6	43

Salad: Apple Cranberry Spinach,

with Reduced Fat Raspb. Drssng	370	14	48

Kid's Menu: French Fries, 4.5 oz | 320 | 13 | 46 |

Fried Chicken Strips (1), 1.5 oz	135	8	10
Mac & Cheese, 7 oz	300	9	45
Mini Cheeseburger (1)	275	15	21
Plenty-O-Pancakes,			
Plain, w/o Topping, 11.5 oz	710	18	130
Smiley Face Potatoes, 3 oz	270	16	29
Sundae, Fudge Blast, 4 oz	215	9	31
Dessert: Coconut Cream Pie, 7 oz sl.	515	29	59
French Silk Pie, 5.5 oz slice	660	44	60
Peanut Butter Brownie Bites (8)	930	45	22

Fast - Foods & *Restaurants*

Bojangles® (Feb '14)

Sandwiches:

	C	F	Cb
Cajun Filet: Regular	495	27	43
Club	640	39	44
Grilled Chicken: Regular	375	15	33
Club	520	27	34

Biscuit: Plain

	C	F	Cb
Plain	280	14	33
Bacon, Egg & Cheese	550	37	35
Cajun Filet	515	28	45
Country Ham	355	18	33
Egg & Cheese	515	34	35
Gravy Biscuits	390	20	43
Sausage	420	27	33
Steak	555	35	44

Fixins': Per Individual Serve Unless Indicated

	C	F	Cb
Bo-Tato Rounds	230	14	24
Cole Slaw	255	20	18
Dirty Rice	165	6	24
Macaroni & Cheese	240	7	33
Mashed Potatoes 'N Gravy	150	6	21
Seasoned Fries: Individual	215	14	20
Medium size	300	20	27
Picnic size	530	35	49

Salads: Chicken Supreme

	C	F	Cb
Chicken Supreme	460	18	33
Garden	190	9	9
Grilled Chicken	305	11	11

Sweets:

	C	F	Cb
Bo-Berry Biscuit (1)	375	15	55
Cinnamon Twist (1)	270	12	36
Sweet Potato Pie	410	23	48

For Complete Nutritional Data ~ see CalorieKing.com

Boston Market® (Feb '14)

Sandwiches:

Per Whole With Set Menu Board Toppings

	C	F	Cb
All-White Chicken Salad	970	65	63
Roast Beef Brisket Dip Carver	820	44	58
Roasted Turkey Carver	850	46	62
Rotisserie Chicken Carver	750	34	62

Individual Meals: Without Sides

	C	F	Cb
Beef Brisket, regular, 4 oz	230	13	0
Meatloaf, regular, 7.5 oz	480	30	25
Rotisserie Chicken, half, 12 oz	640	33	2

Boston Market® cont... (Feb '14)

Salads:

Per Whole, With Dressing, Without Cornbread

	C	F	Cb
Chicken Caesar, 10.8 oz	440	29	16
Mediterranean, 13.4	550	39	15
Southwest Santa Fe, 13.7 oz	530	30	30

Sides:

	C	F	Cb
Creamed Spinach, 6.3 oz	260	21	11
Fresh Steamed Vegetables, 4.8 oz	80	5	8
Fresh Vegetable Stuffing, 5.5 oz	220	10	28
Garlic Dill New Potatoes, 4.5 oz	100	2	20
Garlicky Lemon Spinach, 6 oz	110	9	7
Gravy, 1 oz	10	0	2
Poultry, 1 oz	10	0	2
Green Beans, 4.25 oz	90	6	9
Macaroni & Chse, 7.4 oz	280	11	33
Mashed Potatoes: Regular, 7.oz	240	10	32
Loaded, 7 oz	310	16	31
Rice Pilaf, 6.6 oz	190	3	37
Sweet Potato Casserole, 7.4 oz	450	13	83

Soups:

	C	F	Cb
Chicken Noodle, 14 oz	230	8	22
Chicken Tortilla	440	24	39

Desserts:

	C	F	Cb
Apple Pie, 5.75 oz slice	430	21	59
Chocolate Brownie (1), 4.7 oz	530	26	74
Chocolate Cake, 1 Slice, 5 oz	580	32	67

For Complete Nutritional Data ~ see CalorieKing.com

Boston Pizza® Canada (Feb '14)

Starters:

	C	F	Cb
Oven Roasted Wings, 8.4 oz	580	37	7
Poutine,14 oz	610	30	67
Southwest Potato Skins, 13.3 oz	620	33	61
Spinach & Artichoke Dip, 13.7 oz	720	42	65

Gourmet Pastas: Full Order, Without Garlic Toast

	C	F	Cb
Boston's Lasagna	760	23	104
Montréal Smoked Meat Pasta	870	16	139
Pesto Chicken Penne	1210	48	136

Gourmet Pizza: Per Individual Pizza

	C	F	Cb
Classics: Bacon Double Chseburger	790	41	64
Deluxe	730	33	65
Hawaiian	660	24	72
Pepperoni	630	30	60

Continued Next Page...

Updated Nutrition Data ~ www.CalorieKing.com
Persons with Diabetes ~ See Disclaimer (Page 22)

Boston Pizza® Canada cont... (Feb '14)

Gourmet Pizza (Cont): Individual

	C	F	Cb
Originals: Boston Royal	710	30	69
Spicy Buffalo Chicken	840	56	59
Sandwiches: Without Sides			
Boston Brute	800	24	108
Montréal Smoked Meat Sandwich	910	59	40
Pepperoni & Bacon Pizzaburger	1040	88	51
Pesto Chicken Burger	540	25	50
Salads: With Dressing			
Chopped Chicken	280	9	17
Crispy Chicken Pecan, 23.25 oz	1150	93	33
Santa Fe, 18.6 oz	710	51	64
Desssert: NY Cheesecake	600	32	76
The Panookie, with ice cream	880	38	133

For Complete Nutritional Data ~ see CalorieKing.com

Braum's® ~ see CalorieKing.com

Bruegger's® (Feb '14)

Bagels:

	C	F	Cb
Chocolate Chip, 4.1 oz	330	3.5	65
Jalapeno Cheddar, 5.5 oz	440	9	75
Plain, 4.1 oz	300	2	60
Sesame; Whole Wheat, av., 4.1 oz	310	3.5	61
Breakfast Bagel S'wiches: Plain Bagel, with			
Standard Toppings			
Smoked Salmon	460	10	66
Spinach & Cheddar Omelet	490	16	63
Western	670	34	67
Deli Sandwiches: With Standard Toppings			
BLT on Hearty White Bread	720	42	62
Chicken Breast on Plain Bagel	550	6	81
Garden Veggie on Plain Bagel	360	2	72
Ham On Honey Wheat Bread	500	13	62
Hot Paninis: On Ciabatta With Standard Toppings			
Four Cheese & Tomato	570	26	59
Harvest Turkey	690	24	84
Primo Pesto Chicken	560	19	58
Roast Beef Cheddar Melt	630	26	72
Turkey, Artichoke, Mozzarella	520	14	61
Signature & Classic Sandwiches: With Standard			
Toppings			
Herby Turkey on Sesame Bagel	570	15	75
Leonardo da Veggie on Plain Softwich	490	14	70
Thai Peanut Chicken on Plain Bagel	580	11	91
Turkey Chipotle Club on Honey Wheat	400	17	36

Bruegger's® cont... (Feb '14)

Cafe Salads: Without Dressing

	C	F	Cb
Blue Apple, 7 oz	300	14	20
Chicken Almond, 11 oz	260	14	8
Chicken Caesar, 6 oz	190	7	11
Dressings: Balsamic Vinaig., 1 oz	60	6	3
Caesar, 1 oz	80	7	0
Ranch	90	10	1
Dessert Bars:			
Chocolate Chunk Brownie, 2.7 oz	340	17	42
Marshmallow Chews, 2.7 oz	290	7	54
Toffee Almond, 2.7 oz	350	17	44

For Complete Menu & Data ~ see CalorieKing.com

Buca di Beppo® (Oct '13)

Antipasti:

	C	F	Cb
Bruschetta, 5.35 oz	230	10	4
Fried Calamari, 5.65 oz	330	21	19
Fried Mozzarella, 14.7 oz	940	42	77
Baked Pasta Specialties: Per Small Size			
Baked Rigatoni, 16.9 oz	830	40	79
Baked Ziti, 11.25 oz	650	25	74
Lasagna, 11.9 oz	480	24	31
Entrees: Per Small Size			
Chicken Glorioso, 11.8 oz	480	22	24
Chicken Limone, 6.4 oz	360	25	2
Chicken Saltimbocca, 8.2 oz	450	32	10
Prosciutto Stuffed Chicken, 11 oz	670	36	33
Veal Parmigiana, 10 oz	400	19	25
Specialty Pasta: Per Small Size			
Chicken & Sausage Ziti, 12.5 oz	800	45	67
Chicken Carbonara, 11.1 oz	860	46	72
Linguine Fruttie Di Mare, 14 oz	550	11	75
Shrimp Florentine, 11 oz	660	29	68

Burgerville® (Feb '14)

Burgers:

	C	F	Cb
Original Hamburger, with Spread	330	17	31
Cheeseburger, with Spread	380	21	31
Dble Beef Chseburger, w/ Spread	480	29	31
Half Pound Colossal Cheeseburger,			
with Spread	740	43	41
Pepper Bacon Chsebgr, w/ Mayo	660	41	38
Tillamook Chseburger, with Mayo	600	35	41
Sandwiches:			
Crispy Chicken, with Spread	560	27	57
Deluxe Crispy Chicken, with Spread	710	39	58
Turkey Club, with Mayo & Cheese	610	38	40
French Fries: Small, 2.75 oz	220	11	28
Regular, 5 oz	400	19	50
Large, 6.5 oz	510	25	65

For Complete Menu & Data ~ see CalorieKing.com

Burger King® (Mar '14)

	C	F	Cb
Fire Grilled Whoppers: Without Cheese, With Mayo			
Whopper	650	37	50
Double Whopper	900	56	50
Triple Whopper	1160	75	50
Whopper JR.	300	16	27
Flame Broiled Burgers: With Standard Toppings			
Bacon Cheeseburger	290	13	27
Cheeseburger	270	12	27
Double Cheeseburger	360	19	27
Hamburger	230	9	26
Chicken & Fish Sandwiches: With Standard Toppings			
Original Chicken, with Mayo	640	36	53
Spicy Crispy Chicken, with Mayo	640	38	57
Chicken Nuggets:			
4 pieces	190	11	13
10 pieces	470	29	34
20 pieces	950	57	67
Big Fish, with Tartar Sce	530	27	54
Chicken Strips:			
Home-style: 3 pieces	340	17	26
5 pieces	570	28	44
Dipping Sauces: Per 1 oz			
BBQ; Sweet & Sour, average	45	0	11
Buffalo	80	8	2
Honey Mustard	90	6	8
Ranch; Zesty Onion Ring, average	145	15	2
Sides:			
French Fries: Salted			
Small, 4.25 oz	340	15	49
Medium, 5.75 oz	410	18	58
Large, 7 oz	500	22	72
Fresh Apple Slices, 2 oz	30	0	7
Onion Rings: Small (15)	320	16	41
Medium (20)	410	21	53
Satisfries, small	270	11	41
Garden Fresh Salads: With Dressing			
Chicken BLT:			
With TenderCrisp Chkn	640	45	30
With TenderGrill Chicken	440	29	11
Chicken Caesar:			
With TenderCrisp Chkn	650	43	39
With TenderGrill Chicken	450	27	20
Dressings: Per 1.75 oz Packet			
Ken's: Apple Cider Vinaigrette	210	18	10
Avocado Ranch	170	17	4
Honey Mustard	220	18	13

Burger King® cont... (Mar '14)

Breakfast:	C	F	Cb
Biscuits: Bacon, Egg & Cheese	450	27	33
Ham, Egg & Cheese	430	23	35
Sausage, Egg & Cheese	550	36	34
Burritos:			
Sausage	310	19	22
Southwestern	600	38	43
Croissan'wich: Bacon Egg & Chse	370	22	31
Egg & Cheese	330	19	31
Ham Egg & Cheese	390	20	33
Double Croissan'wich:			
Bacon, Egg & Cheese	440	27	32
Ham, Bacon, Egg & Cheese	470	27	34
Ham, Egg & Cheese	480	26	36
Ham, Sausage, Egg & Cheese	600	39	35
Sausage, Bacon, Egg & Cheese	580	39	33
Sausage, Egg & Cheese	790	57	35
French Toast Sticks:			
3 pieces	230	11	29
5 pieces	380	18	49
Hash Browns: Small, 2.95 oz	250	16	24
Medium, 5.95 oz	500	33	48
Large, 7.9 oz	670	44	65
Hot Oatmeal: Original	140	3.5	23
Maple & Brown Sugar	270	4	55
Muffin Sandwiches:			
Bacon, Egg & Cheese	300	14	27
Ham, Egg & Cheese	310	13	28
Sausage, Egg & Chse	430	26	28
Platters:			
Pancake, with Sausage & Syrup	660	31	83
Ultimate Breakfast, 18 oz	1420	79	139
Desserts:			
Cookies: Chocolate Chip (2)	330	15	47
Oatmeal Raisin (2)	310	13	46
Pies: Dutch Apple Pie	340	14	51
Hershey's Sundae Pie	310	19	32
Shakes:			
Chocolate: Small, 12 fl.oz	580	17	97
Medium, 16 fl.oz	760	21	131
Large, 20 fl.oz oz	980	24	174
Vanilla: Small, 12 fl.oz	550	16	91
Medium, 16 fl.oz	730	20	124
Large, 20 fl.oz	930	23	163
Beverages:			
Coca Cola Classic: Small, 20 fl.oz	190	0	51
Medium, 30 fl.oz	290	0	77

For Complete Nutritional Data ~ see CalorieKing.com

Updated Nutrition Data ~ www.CalorieKing.com
Persons with Diabetes ~ See Disclaimer (Page 22)

Captain D's Seafood® (Feb '14)

Fish: Without Sides

	C	F	Cb
Breaded Flounder,	235	14	12
Catfish, 1 order, 2.82 oz	250	18	16
Country Style Fish, 1 piece	180	11	19

From The Grill: Without Sides

Grilled Salmon, 1 piece	240	11	1
Seasoned Tilapia, 1 piece	225	9	0.5
Shrimp Scampi, 1 order	655	35	64
Stuffed Flounder, 1 order	260	14	14

Other Favorites:

Cheese Sticks, full order	500	32	34
Jalapeno Poppers, 1 piece	115	7.5	10

Seafood:

Bite-Sized Shrimp	490	27	45
Crab Cake, 1 piece	190	10	10
Stuffed Crab, 1 piece	140	10	10

Side Dishes:

Baked Potato (1)	195	0	45
Cole Slaw, 1 order	180	12	15
French Fries, 1 order	365	26	29
Hushpuppy, (1)	80	4	9
Dessert, Chocolate Cake, 1 order	300	10	48

Caribou Coffee® (Feb '14)

Without Whipped Cream Unless Indicated

Classic Hot Coffees: Per Medium

	C	F	Cb
Coffee Of The Day, with 2% Milk	90	3.5	9
Espresso, 4 oz	0	0	0
Cappuccino, with 2% Milk	70	3	6
Latte, with 2% Milk	200	8	19
Macchiato, with 2% Milk	20	1	1

Hot Chocolate: Per Medium, With Whipped Cream

Milk Chocolate, 2% Milk	550	33	51

Specialty, Mint Condition,

Milk Chocolate, 2% Milk	570	31	67

Cold Beverages: Per Medium

Iced Americano	5	0	0
Iced Latte, with 2% Milk	90	3.5	8
Iced Mocha, Milk Choc., 2% Milk	320	9	47

Coolers: Per Medium, With Whipped Cream

Caramel	500	16	88
Chocolate	620	24	97
Vanilla	480	16	85

Smoothies: Per Medium

Mango Orange Key Lime	450	0	113
Strawberry Banana	380	0	88
White Peach Berry	330	0	80

Snowdrift: Per Medium, With Milk Chocolate

Cookies & Cream, with 2% Milk	610	17	98
Mint, with 2% Milk	480	12	80

Carl's Jr.® (Mar '14)

Charbroiled Burgers:

	C	F	Cb
Big Hamburger	480	18	56
Famous Star with Cheese	670	37	57
Kid's Hamburger	270	10	33
Super Star with Cheese	940	57	59
The Big Carl	930	58	55
The Six Dollar Burger: Original	950	58	62
Guacamole Bacon	1070	69	56
Low-Carb	560	42	9
Western Bacon	990	55	73
Western Bacon Cheeseburger	740	34	74

Chicken Sandwiches:

Charbroiled: BBQ Chicken	390	7	50
Chicken Club	580	27	45
Santa Fe Chicken	560	28	46
Spicy Chicken Sandwich	460	24	47

Chicken Tenders, hand breaded,

5 pieces, without Sauce	440	21	21
Chicken Stars, 6 pieces, w/o Sce	260	16	18

Fish,

Charbroiled Atlantic Cod S'wich	420	15	51

Turkey Burgers: Regular

Regular	490	22	45
Jalapeno	490	22	43
Teriyaki	470	14	55

Breakfast: Bacon & Egg Burrito

Bacon & Egg Burrito	570	34	38
Breakfast Burger	820	43	70
Hash Brown Nuggets:			
Medium, 3.8 oz	350	23	32
Large, 6 oz	560	37	52
Loaded Breakfast Burrito	770	48	53
Sourdough Breakfast Sandwich	470	23	39
Steak & Egg Burrito	640	36	43

Fries: Chili Cheese, 11.2 oz

Chili Cheese, 11.2 oz	810	46	80
CrissCut Fries, 5 oz	450	29	42
Natural Cut: Small, 4.25 oz	300	15	39
Medium, 6 oz	430	21	55
Large, 6.5oz	460	22	59
Onion Rings, 4.5 oz	530	28	61

Salads: Without Dressing or Croutons

Chicken: Crispy	350	16	29
Original Grilled	280	12	26
Garden, Side	110	4.5	14

Dressings: Per 2 oz Package

Blue Cheese	320	34	1
House	220	22	3
Low-Fat Balsamic	35	1.5	5

Malts, with Ice Cream:

Oreo Cookie	780	39	94
Other flavors, average	765	35	99

Shakes, with Ice Cream:

Oreo Cookie	710	38	79
Vanilla; Choc.; Strawb. av.	695	34	85

Carvel® (Feb '14)

Carvelanche: Per Medium, 16 oz

	C	F	Cb
Butterfinger	850	45	104
M&M's; Reese's, average	880	48	99

Classic Sundaes: Per Small, 12 oz

Caramel	700	36	84
Hot Fudge	540	30	60
Strawberry	610	34	67

Sundae Dashers: Per Small, 12 oz

Banana's Foster	660	23	105
Fudge Brownie	850	45	102
Mint Chocolate Chip	770	42	95
Peanut Butter Cup	1060	60	95
Strawberry Shortcake	580	29	74

Take Home Treats: Brown Bonnet | 390 | 23 | 43

Flying Saucers: Chocolate	230	10	33
Deluxe, with Sprinkles	350	16	49

Thick Shakes: Per 16 oz

Chocolate	650	27	93
Strawberry	600	31	70
Vanilla	660	31	86

Thick Shake Floats: Per 16 oz

Chocolate	790	34	109
Strawberry	750	39	85
Vanilla	810	39	102

Checkers®

Same Menu & Data as Rally's ~ See Page 231

Cheesecake Factory® (Feb '14)

10" Cheesecake: Per Slice

	C	F	Cb
Chocolate Raspberry Truffle	1210	n/a	106
Original: W/ Strawberries	940	n/a	71
Low Carb	640	n/a	41
Reese's P.B. Chocolate Cake	1690	n/a	173

Small Plates & Snacks: Per Dish, As Served

Crispy Crab Bites	350	n/a	10
Ssg. & Ricotta Flatbread	440	n/a	34
Vietnamese Tacos	860	n/a	150

Glamburgers & Sandwiches: Without Sides

Chicken Almond Salad	1480	n/a	83
Factory Burger	730	n/a	52
Turkey Burger	1130	n/a	57

Specialties: Per Dish, As Served

Crispy Chicken Costoletta	2540	n/a	103
Famous Factory Meatloaf	1560	n/a	115
White Chicken Chili	580	n/a	41

Salads: As Served, Includes Dressing

Herb-Crusted Salmon	760	n/a	22
Santa Fe Salad	1690	n/a	98
Skinnylicious Spicy Chicken	430	n/a	40

Charley's Grilled Subs® (Feb '14)

Subs: Regular 7½" Includes Standard Toppings, Without Sauce or Dressings Unless Indicated

	C	F	Cb
Bacon 3 Cheese Steak	635	32	55
Buffalo Chicken, with Sauce	525	16	59
Chicken Bacon Club	570	25	54
Chicken Cordon Blue	570	18	55
Chicken Teriyaki, with Sauce	520	16	59
Italian Deli Deluxe	585	28	53
Mushroom Swiss Steak	520	19	57
Philly Cheesesteak	520	19	56
Philly Chicken	515	16	58
Philly Steak Deluxe	525	19	58
Sicilian Steak	640	31	53
Turkey Cheddar Melt	470	12	53
Ultimate Club	560	23	54

Salads: Cheese or Dressings not included

Grilled Chicken, Teriyaki/Buffalo, av.	210	7	13

Fries: Large | 635 | 55 | 51

Cheddar	525	30	55
Cheddar Bacon	555	30	55

Breakfast:

Omelets: Bacon; Ham, average | 410 | 28 | 9

Veggie	355	23	13

Sandwiches:

Bacon/Ham, Egg & Cheese, av.	540	23	55
Sausage, Egg & Cheese	605	29	54
Steak, Egg & Cheese	620	25	55

For Complete Menu & Data ~ see CalorieKing.com

Chevys Fresh Mex® (Feb '14)

Burritos: As Served

	C	F	Cb
Fajita Carnitas	1260	51	144
Fajita Chicken	1240	46	142
Fajita Steak	1300	54	142

Fresh Mex Combos: As Served

Chevys Super Cinco	1920	100	171
Mar Y Tierra Combo	1230	54	108
Taste of Chevys	1480	68	155

Fresh Mex Innovations: As Served

Enchiladas: Chipotle Chicken | 1070 | 65 | 93

Farmers' Market	1130	72	101
Shrimp & Crab	1250	80	94

Tacos: As Served

Mesquite Grilled: Chicken | 980 | 28 | 123

Steak	1050	38	123
Fish	920	27	123

Grande Salads: Without Dressing Unless Indicated

Sizzling Fajita Chicken w/ dressing	1220	90	51
Santa Fe Chopped	660	39	26
Tostada Steak	1560	100	91
Soup, Tortilla, 1 bowl	420	18	38
Tortilla, El Machino (1), 6"	140	4	22
Tortilla Chips	430	20	56

Updated Nutrition Data ~ www.CalorieKing.com
Persons with Diabetes ~ See Disclaimer (Page 22)

Chick-fil-A® (Mar '14)

Chick-fil-A Sandwiches: W/o Sauce | C | F | Cb

	C	F	Cb
Chargrilled Chicken	310	4	46
Chargrilled Chicken Club	430	12	46
Regular Chicken	440	18	41
Cool Wrap, Grilled Chicken, without dressing	330	12	28
Chicken:			
Chick-n-Strips, breaded, 4 count	470	24	21
Nuggets: Breaded, 8 count	270	13	10
12 count	400	19	15
Breakfast:			
Bagel, Chicken, Egg & Cheese	480	20	48
Biscuits: Chicken	440	20	48
Bacon, Egg & Cheese	450	23	44
Sausage, Egg & Cheese	670	45	44
Burritos: Chicken	440	19	43
Sausage	500	28	40
Chick-n-Minis, 1 box, 3 pieces	280	11	30
Cinnamon Cluster	430	17	63
Hash Browns, 2.7 oz	240	15	25
Oatmeal: Multigrain w/ toppings	290	11	50
Without toppings	140	2.5	28
Salads: Without Dressing or Toppings			
Asian	330	13	24
Cobb	430	22	22
Grilled Market	180	4	13
Condiments:			
Charred Tom. Crispy Bell Peppers	80	6	6
Garlic & Butter Croutons, 0.5 oz	70	3	9
Harvest Nut Granola, salad portion	60	3	8
Dressings:			
Buttermilk Ranch, 1.5 oz	280	30	2
Honey Mustard, fat-free	100	0	23
Light Italian, 1.5 oz	25	1.5	3
Sauces: BBQ	45	0	11
Buffalo, 0.75 oz	10	0	1
Buttermilk Ranch, 0.75 oz	110	12	1
Chick-fil-A, 1 oz	140	13	6
Honey Roasted BBQ, 0.5 oz	60	5	2
Sides:			
Chicken Salad Cup, 6 oz	360	24	7
Cole Slaw, medium	360	31	19
Waffle Potato Fries: Small	310	16	37
Medium	400	21	48
Large	520	27	63
Dessert, Chocolate Chunk Cookie	330	14	35
Milkshakes: Chocolate, large	730	27	110
Vanilla, large	650	27	89
Sundaes: Cookie	400	13	66
Mini Sundae	170	3.5	33

Chili's® (Feb '14)

Appetizers: As Served | C | F | Cb

	C	F	Cb
Bottomless Tostada Chips w/ Salsa	910	45	112
Crispy Onion & Jalapeno Stack	1060	84	67
Classic Nachos: Chicken, regular	980	63	40
Fajita Beef, regular	1090	73	39
Sthwestern Eggrolls w/ Avoc. Ranch	770	40	81
Triple Dipper:			
Big Mouth Bites w/ Ranch	790	53	44
Original Chicken Crispers	630	42	30
Hot Spin. & Artichoke Dip w/ Chips	600	40	48
Burgers: As Served, with Fries			
Classic Bacon	1340	78	104
Oldtimer, with Cheddar Cheese	1160	59	104
Southern Smokehouse Bacon	1610	96	121
Chicken: As Served, with Set Sides			
Chicken Crispers	1550	82	141
Monterey Chicken	890	45	57
Ribs: Full Rack, As Served			
Original	1630	85	132
Memphis Dry Rub	1670	87	135
Southwest Favorites: As Served			
Fajitas: Without Tortillas & Condiments			
Chicken	390	13	24
Steak	570	36	23
Trio	650	34	30
Condiments only (1)	170	15	7
Flour Tortillas only (3)	250	7	41
Quesadillas: As Served			
Bacon Ranch Chicken	1740	132	70
Bacon Ranch Steak	1850	142	69
Steaks: As Served, with set sides			
Classic Ribeye	1260	77	59
Classic Sirloin, 6 oz	860	48	59
Country-Fried Steak	1250	62	122
Sides: Homestyle Fries	410	17	60
Loaded Mashed Potatoes	350	19	33
Mashed Pot. w/ Black Pepper Gravy	280	13	36
Southwest Mac 'n' Cheese	490	30	38
Sweet Potato Fries	420	21	53
Salads: Includes Dressing			
Boneless Buffalo Chicken	1030	67	59
Caribbean with Grilled Shrimp	660	32	79
Quesadilla Explosion	1430	96	88
Stupendously Sweet Endings: Per Slice			
Brownie Sundae	1090	40	171
Cheesecake	750	47	69
Molten Chocolate Cake	1160	63	145

For Complete Menu & Data ~ see CalorieKing.com

Fast - Foods & Restaurants

Chipotle® (Feb '14)

Tortillas:

	C	F	Cb
Crispy: Corn Tortilla (Taco), (3)	180	6	27
Taco Shells (3)	180	6	27
Flour Tortillas (Burrito), (1)	290	9	44
Soft Corn Tortillas (Taco), (3)	210	3	42
Soft Flour Tortillas (Taco), (3)	270	7.5	39

Meal Components:

Barbacoa, 4 oz	170	7	2
Black/Pinto Beans, average, 4 oz	120	1	23
Brown Rice, 4 oz	160	4	31
Carnitas, 4 oz	190	8	1
Cheese, 1 oz	100	9	0
Chicken, 4 oz	190	6.5	1
Fajita Vegetables, 2.5 oz	20	0.5	4
Guacamole, 3.5 oz	150	13	8
Lettuce, 1 oz	5	0	1
Steak, 4 oz	190	6.5	2

Condiments:

Salsa: Chili Corn, 3.5 oz	80	1.5	15
Green Tomatillo, 2 oz	15	0	3
Red Tomatillo, 2 oz	40	1	8
Tomato, 3.5 oz	20	0	4
Sour Cream, 2 oz	120	10	2
Extras, Chips, serving, 4 oz	570	27	73

Chuck E. Cheese® (Feb '14)

Appetizers:

	C	F	Cb
Buffalo Wings, Traditional (1)	80	5	0
Cheesy Breadstick, with Marinara, and Light Ranch Dressing	110	6	9

Oven Baked Sandwiches:

Ham & Cheese	620	24	70
Italian Sub	730	36	70

Pizzas: Per Medium Slice

BBQ Chicken	145	4	21
Canadian Bacon & Pineapple	160	4	22
Cheese	150	4	21
Pepperoni	180	7	21
Super Combo	180	7	22
Veggie Combo	160	5	22

Platters: Sandwich, 1/12 Platter | 185 | 8 | 20 |
| Veggie, 1/8 Platter | 130 | 11 | 7 |

French Fries,

W/ Ketchup & Light Ranch, 8 oz	645	33	83

Desserts: Apple Dessert Pizza, 1 sl. | 105 | 1 | 21 |
| Chocolate Cake (8"), 1 slice | 290 | 13 | 41 |
| Cinnamon Stick, w/ Toppings (1) | 70 | 2 | 11 |

Church's Chicken® (Feb '14)

Chicken: Per Serving

	C	F	Cb
Original: Breast, 1 piece	200	11	3
Leg, 1 piece	110	6	3
Thigh, 1 piece	330	23	8
Wing, 1 piece	300	18	7
Spicy: Breast, 1 piece	320	20	12
Leg, 1 piece	180	11	8
Thigh, 1 piece	480	35	20
Wing, 1 piece	430	27	17
Tender Strips, average, 1 piece	120	6	6

Sides: Per Small Serving

Baked Macaroni & Cheese, 6.3 oz	260	8	24
Cajun Rice, 6 oz	290	17	27
Cole Slaw, 4.15 oz	150	10	15
French Fries, 1.6 oz	140	6	19
Honey Butter Biscuits (1), 2 oz	240	12	28
Mashed Potatoes & Gravy, 6 oz	110	2	21
Okra, 1.95 oz	170	11	17
Sweet Corn Nuggets (6), 3.5 oz	240	7	40

Sauces: Per Packet

BBQ; Sweet & Sour, av.	40	0	10
Creamy Jalapeno	125	13	2
Honey Mustard	140	13	4
Ranch	140	15	2

Cici's Pizza® (Feb '14)

Buffet: Per 1/10 of 12" Pizza

	C	F	Cb
Alfredo	125	2.5	19
BBQ	155	3	25
Beef	165	4	21
Cheese; Ham & Pineapple, av.	150	4	21
Pepperoni & Jalapeno	155	4.5	20
Sausage	150	3.5	20
Spin. Alfredo; Zesty Ham & Chedd.	130	3.5	19

To-Go: Per 1/10 of 15" Pizza

Alfredo	170	4	23
BBQ	250	6.5	36
Beef	210	6.5	25
Sausage	235	10	25
Spinach Alfredo	165	5.5	23
Zesty Pepperoni	190	8	23

Cinnabon® (Feb '14)

	C	F	Cb
Baked Goods: Cinnabon Bites (6)	620	24	88
Cinnabon Stix (5)	390	21	46
Caramel Pecanbon (1)	1080	50	147
Bites (6)	800	39	100
Classic Cinnabon (1)	880	36	127
Sweet Roll Icing, Frosting Cup, 1.4 oz	180	11	20

Claim Jumper® (Feb '14)

Appetizers: As Served

	C	F	Cb
Southwest Eggrolls	1190	53	114
Three Cheese Potatocakes (3)	1075	71	80

Burgers & Sandwiches: Without Sides

	C	F	Cb
Grilled Cobb Sandwich	1210	78	78
Widow Maker Burger	1370	87	84

Meals:

Favorites: With Menu Set Sides & Toppings

	C	F	Cb
Country Fried Steak	2030	107	189
Giant Stuffed Chicken Baker	990	34	118
Meatloaf & Mashed Potatoes	1300	75	117

Pizza & Pasta:

	C	F	Cb
California Works, Classic Crust	1295	64	127
Parmesan Crusted Pasta	975	47	83

Specialties: With Roasted Vegetables

	C	F	Cb
BBQ Baby Back Pork Ribs, Full Rack	1745	111	111
Roasted Tri-Tip	800	47	19

Seafood: With Menu Set Sides & Sauces

	C	F	Cb
Fish & Chips	1195	74	82
Lobster Tail Dinner	715	46	42

Entree Salads: Without Dressing Or Bread

	C	F	Cb
Californian Citrus Chkn, Charbroiled	865	53	58
Seared Ahi Spinach	515	24	31

Soups: Per Bowl

	C	F	Cb
New England Clam Chowder	525	45	23
Potato Cheddar	710	61	31

Sweets: Choc. Motherlode Cake | 2770 | 144 | 340 |
| Italian Lemon Cake | 1240 | 62 | 158 |

Coldstone Creamery® (Feb '14)

Ice Creams:

	C	F	Cb
Amaretto: Like it	330	20	33
Love it	530	31	53
Gotta have it	790	47	80

Sorbet:

	C	F	Cb
Strawberry Mango: Like it	220	0	55
Love it	350	0	87
Gotta have it	520	0.5	131

For Complete Nutritional Data ~ See CalorieKing.com

Cosi® (Feb '14)

Flatbread Pizza: Individual

	C	F	Cb
Original Crust: Margherita	805	30	94
Original Crust: Margherita	805	30	94
Pepperoni	855	33	92
Traditional Cheese	715	21	92

Melts: With Original Flatbread

	C	F	Cb
Chicken TBM	790	35	54
Pesto Chicken	635	24	51
Steakhouse Gorgonzola	780	44	65

Cosi® cont... (Feb '14)

Sandwiches: W/- Orig. Flatbread

	C	F	Cb
Buffalo Bleu	565	25	47
Hearth Roasted Veggie	375	10	57
Italiano	810	47	49
TBM	`695	43	50

Soup: Per 5 oz Bowl, Without Flatbread

	C	F	Cb
Chicken Queso Tortilla	95	4	10
Tomato Basil	215	20	9

Salads: Includes Dressing

	C	F	Cb
Cosi Cobb, 14 oz	710	54	19
Greek, 14 oz	515	47	19
Signature, 14 oz	645	45	51
Steakhouse, 14 oz	650	53	14

Costco Food Court® (Oct '13)

Pizza: Per Slice

	C	F	Cb
Combo, 11 oz	680	29	72
Cheese, 10 oz	700	28	70
Pepperoni , 9 oz	620	24	68

Dogs, Hot Dog, Polish Ssg., 7 oz | 550 | 33 | 39 |

Salads:

	C	F	Cb
Chicken Caesar, w/ dress., 20.5 oz	670	40	35
Quinoa, ½ cup	110	6	12

Meals: Cheese Burger Fry Combo | 860 | 45 | 72 |
Chicken Bake 12.75 oz	770	25	78
Ital. Sausage Sandwich, 12.5 oz	700	42	46
Turkey Wrap, 14.5 oz	810	38	65

Beverages: Hot Latte, 9.5 fl oz | 190 | 5 | 24 |
Hot Mocha, 11.25 fl oz	310	9	45
Latte Freeze, 15.5 fl.oz	240	7	32
Mocha Freeze, 16.25 fl .oz	320	7	49

Desserts: Ice cream Bar, 8 oz | 870 | 65 | 60 |
Berry Sundae, 12.25 oz	410	0	87
Chocolate Gelato, 8.5 oz	410	9	82
Pistachio Gelato, 7.75 oz	480	13	82
Yogurt, 12 oz	390	0	82

Cousins Subs® (Feb '14)

Subs: Per 7½" Italian Bread

	C	F	Cb
BLT, with Mayo	600	36	49
Cheese Steak	680	32	50
Chicken Cheddar Deluxe, w/ Mayo	680	37	53
Club, with Mayo	720	39	55
Double Cheese Steak	1090	63	50
Garden Provolone	880	54	65
Italian Special, w/ Dressing	980	65	52
Philly Cheese Steak	710	37	52

Continued Next Page...

Cousins Subs® cont... (Feb '14)

7½" Subs (cont): With 7½" Italian Bread

	C	F	Cb
Roast Beef & Cheddar, with Mayo	710	35	52
Tuna with Mayo Blend	720	42	52
Turkey Breast w/ Mayo	530	25	53
French Fries: Small, 2.75 oz	250	13	30
Medium, 4 oz	365	19	43
Large, 5.25 oz	485	25	57
Salads: With Dressing			
Almond Berry Chicken	480	20	46
Gourmet Garden with Chicken	500	31	24
Turkey Bacon Delight	500	32	25
Soups: Cheddar Cauliflower, reg.	115	5	13
Chicken & Dumplings, reg.	150	4	17
Chili, regular	220	8	26
Cream of Brocc., w/ Cheese, reg.	170	7	13
Vegetable Beef, regular	70	2	11

For Complete Nutritional Data ~ see CalorieKing.com

Culver's® (Feb '14)

ButterBurgers:	C	F	Cb
Original: Single; Kids	330	15	31
Double	460	23	31
Triple	590	31	32
Cheddar with Bacon, Single	540	33	31
Cheese: Single	400	21	32
Double	600	35	33
Culver's Bacon Deluxe: Single	595	39	35
Double	790	53	35
Culver's Deluxe: Single	515	32	35
Double	710	46	35
Mushroom & Swiss, Single	430	23	33
Sourdough Melt, Single	435	21	35
Corn Dog, Kids	210	13	17
Chicken Tenders, Breaded, 4 pcs	560	28	40
Sandwiches: Beef Pot Roast	365	16	33
Crispy Chicken	450	19	51
Grilled Reuben Melt	610	31	43
North Atlantic Cod Filet	815	48	57
Pork Tenderloin	600	29	63
Shaved Prime Rib	575	29	44
Sides:			
Chili Cheddar Fries	610	36	54
Mashed Potatoes, w/ Gravy, reg.	140	2	26
Wisconsin Cheese Curds, 6.5 oz	610	37	46
Dinners: As Served			
Butterfly Jumbo Shrimp, 6 pieces	1095	60	113
Fried Chicken, 2 pieces	1565	92	102
North Atlantic Cod, Fried, 2 pieces	1640	114	97

Culver's® cont... (Feb '14)

Soups:	C	F	Cb
Broccoli Cheese, 10.5 oz	240	14	16
Chicken Noodle, 10.5 oz	110	2	14
Potato with Bacon, 10.5 oz	225	9	28
Salads: Without Dressing			
Chicken Cashew w/ Grilled Chkn	450	24	16
Cranberry Bacon Bleu, with Grilled Chicken	350	12	18
Garden Fresco w/ Gr. Chicken	320	12	15
Side Salad	55	3	6
Dressings:			
Chunky Bleu Cheese, 1.75 oz	310	33	2
French Dressing, 1.75 oz	190	13	19
Ranch, 1.75 oz	230	24	3
Thousand Island, 2 oz	220	18	14
Concrete Mixers: Per Medium			
Chocolate	1010	50	127
Cookie Dough	1010	56	110
Sundaes: Per 2 Scoops With Whipped Topping			
Banana Split	1090	63	115
Caramel Cashew	965	52	104
Fudge Pecan	985	62	96
Beverages: Choc. Malt, med.	1010	45	135
Chocolate Shake, medium	925	44	120

D'Angelo's® (Feb '14)

	C	F	Cb
Traditional Sandwiches: Per Medium Size, Menu Board Toppings Only, without Bread			
Angus Cheeseburger	520	36	2
Baked Stuffed	510	37	11
Italian Toasted	840	69	14
Meatball & Cheese	770	59	25
Pastami & Swiss	500	37	2
Add Sandwich Bread: Per Medium Size			
Classic Italian Sub	310	3.5	58
Pokket	160	0	34
Wraps: Menu Board Toppings, Without Wraps			
Buffalo Chicken, Whole	520	36	17
Chicken Caesar, Whole	620	42	25
Add Wraps: Honey Wheat, 4 oz	310	8	55
Flour Tortilla Wrap, 4 oz	310	9	49
Dressings: Caesar, 1.5 oz	200	21	3
Greek, 1.5 oz	210	24	1
Ranch, 1.5 oz	150	15	2
Salads: Entree Size, without Bread			
Caesar, with Dressing	630	53	28
Chicken Caesar, with Dressing	770	55	30
Chicken Cobb, without Dressing	310	17	11
Greek, without Dressing	240	13	17
Soup: Per Bowl			
Extreme Broccoli & Cheddar	370	28	18
Hearty Beef Stew	330	12	34
Main Lobster Bisque	540	43	24
New England Clam Chowder	480	27	46

For Complete Menu & Data ~ see CalorieKing.com

Dairy Queen® (Mar '14)

Burgers & Sandwiches:

	C	F	Cb
Burgers:			
Cheeseburger: Original	380	19	34
Double	580	34	35
GrillBurgers:			
¼ lb Bacon Cheese	620	36	41
½ lb Burger, with Cheese	770	46	43
½ lb Flame Thrower	1010	71	39
¼ lb Mushroom Swiss	560	33	39
Sandwiches: Crispy Chicken	610	30	50
Grilled Chicken	360	16	32
Baskets:			
Chicken Quesadilla	1050	53	102
Chicken Strips: 4 pce w/ Country Gravy	1110	54	116
6 piece, with Country Gravy	1250	65	115
Hot Dogs: Regular	300	18	23
Chili Cheese	390	25	25
Salads: *Without Dressing*			
Crispy Chicken	470	26	29
Grilled Chicken	330	15	13
Sides:			
DQ French Fries, regular, 5 oz	380	17	54
DQ Onion Rings, 4 oz	360	16	48
Desserts: *Per Medium*			
Blizzard Treats: Banana Cream Pie	690	25	103
Butterfinger	720	26	111
Cookie Dough	1030	41	151
Heath	860	38	119
Oreo Cookies	790	30	117
Reese's Peanut Butter Cups	760	32	103
Strawberry CheeseQuake	690	25	100
DQ Blizzard Cakes (10"):			
Oreo, ⅒ cake	540	23	76
Reese's P'nut Butter Cup, ½₂ cake	580	27	77
DQ Dipped Cone, Chocolate, med.	470	22	61
DQ Sundaes: *Per Medium, 8.25 oz*			
Caramel	430	11	75
Hot Fudge	440	15	67
Strawberry	360	10	61
Malts: *Per Medium*			
Caramel	830	24	136
Chocolate	790	23	130
Strawberry	710	22	112
Moo Latte: *Per Medium, With Whipped Topping*			
Cappuccino	570	19	90
French Vanilla	630	19	106
Mocha	690	27	104

For Complete Nutritional Data ~ see CalorieKing.com

Daphne's Greek Cafe® (Feb '14)

Starters:

	C	F	Cb
Original Hummus & Pita	300	15	37
Fire Feta & Original Pita	310	17	31
Pita Sandwiches: *Without Fries, Rice or Salad*			
Crispy Shrimp	390	19	40
Fire Roasted Vegetables	350	18	39
Fresh Carved Gyros	660	47	40
Grilled Chicken	370	15	33
Plates: *Without Sides, Pita Bread or Tzatziki*			
Mix & Match:			
Crispy Shrimp	120	6	7
Falafel	180	11	16
Fresh-Carved Gyros	320	27	7
Grilled Chicken Kabob	150	4	4
Grilled Steak Kabob	170	9	4
Grilled Salmon	330	22	0
Classic Greek Salads: *Without Dressing*			
Crispy Shrimp	350	19	28
Falafel	540	31	49
Grilled Chicken	330	15	21
Dressings: Classic Greek	110	12	2
Lite Greek	60	6	2
Sides: Fire Roasted Vegetables	50	3	5
Fries	310	16	39
Multigrain Pita Chips	170	5	27
Original Pita Bread	180	6	28
Seasoned Rice Pilaf	250	6	47
Tabouli Salad	80	1	17

Davanni's® (Feb '14)

Half Hoagies: *Includes 6" White Bun and Standard Toppings*

	C	F	Cb
Assorted	490	30	39
BLT	645	44	40
Chicken & Bacon w/ Honey Mstrd	505	22	46
Chicken Parmigiana	445	16	40
Club	495	27	40
Italian Sausage	620	38	46
Southwestern Chicken	535	26	43
Three Cheese	525	33	39
Tuna Melt	645	44	42
Turkey	455	24	39
Turkey Bacon Chipotle	565	33	39
Veggie	445	24	43
Calzones: Sausage, Peppers & On.	925	50	83
Pepperoni & Sausage	960	56	80
Pizzas: *Per Slice*			
Five Meat: Thin Crust	255	13	19
Traditional Crust	305	13	30
Solo, Thin Crust	655	3	44
Veggie: Thin Crust	220	10	19
Traditional Crust	275	10	30
Works: Thin Crust	265	14	19
Traditional Crust	315	15	30

Fast - Foods & *Restaurants*

Del Taco® (Feb '14)

Breakfast:	C	F	Cb
Burritos: Breakfast	290	13	28
½ lb Sausage & Egg	500	26	38
½ lb Steak & Egg	460	20	40
Egg & Cheese	400	17	38
Hash Brown Sticks: 5 pieces	230	17	18
8 pieces	360	27	28
Quesadilla, Bacon & Egg	410	22	32
American Grill:			
Burgers: Cheeseburger	430	22	40
Double Del Cheeseburger	720	48	40
Crinkle Cut Fries: Kids, 3 oz	160	10	17
Regular, 4 oz	210	13	22
Medium, 6 oz	320	19	34
Macho, 8.75 oz	470	28	49
Chili Cheddar Fries, 10.5 oz	570	34	41
Burritos:			
Classic Grilled Chicken	530	33	40
Macho Beef	960	43	71
Macho Chicken	870	30	100
Macho Combo	940	34	100
Nachos: 4 oz	300	19	30
Macho, Steak or Chicken, 19 oz	1040	53	101
Quesadillas:			
Cheddar; Spicy Jack, average	460	27	32
Chicken Cheddar/Spicy Jack, av	550	31	35
Tacos:			
Al Carbon, Chicken or Steak, av.	150	4.5	19
Bacon Ranch Grilled Chicken, 4 oz	240	13	17
Beer Battered Fish	280	17	27
Macho	300	17	16
Regular	130	7	9
Salads: Deluxe Beef Taco	820	47	66
Deluxe Chicken	770	43	64
Desserts: Cinnamon Churro, 1.8 oz	220	15	23
Caramel Cheesecake Bites, 2 Bites, 4.3 oz	460	28	43
Premium Shakes: Per 16 oz			
Chocolate	560	11	105
Strawberry; Vanilla, av.	520	11	95

Denny's® (Mar '14)

Breakfast:	C	F	Cb
Favorites:			
Banana Pecan Pancake, 17 oz	750	15	131
Blueberry Pancake, with Scrambled Eggs	590	18	85
Country Fried Steak & Eggs, with hashbrowns	690	43	46
Moons Over My Hammy, without Sides	740	46	40
Omelettes: *With Hash Browns, without Bread*			
Meat Lovers	1020	73	37
Ultimate	870	63	37
Veggie-Cheese	650	44	37
Skillets: *As Served*			
Hearty Breakfast	990	46	36
Santa Fe, 14 oz	710	52	30
Ultimate, 15 oz	740	56	34
Slams:			
All American, w/o side choices	770	65	5
French Toast, 15 oz	780	45	66
Lumberjack, w/o side choices, 15 oz	1000	60	73
The Grand Slamwich, with Hash Browns, 21 oz	1530	102	97
Sides: Buttermilk Biscuit (1)	190	9	24
English Muffin, w/o Margarine (1)	130	1	25
Hash Browns, 5 oz	210	12	26
Pancakes: *Without Margarine, Syrup or Toppings*			
Buttermilk, 2 cakes	340	4	67
Hearty Wheat, 2 cakes	310	1.5	64
Lunch:			
Burgers: *Without Sides, Unless Indicated*			
Bacon, Avocado Cheeseburger	970	64	50
Bacon Slamburger, 15 oz	880	49	55
Double Cheeseburger	1120	67	49
Mushroom Swiss, 18 oz	720	38	51
Sandwiches: *Without Sides*			
Bacon Lovers BLT, 10 oz	680	46	40
Club, 11 oz	630	33	51
Hickory Grilled Chicken	900	47	68
The Super Bird, 11 oz	540	27	43

continued Next Page...

Denny's® cont... (Mar '14)

	C	F	Cb
Dinners: W/out Sides Unless Indicated			
Bourbon Chicken Skillet, 22 oz	890	30	78
Brooklyn Spag. & Meatballs, 23 oz	1220	61	108
Chicken Strips, with Bread, 10 oz	760	29	84
Fish & Chips, w/ French Fries, 23 oz	1330	73	132
Slow-Cooked Pot Roast, 16 oz	690	33	91
T-Bone Steak: With Bread			
12 oz	820	35	24
With Breaded Shrimp, 15 oz	1050	59	56
Dinner Sides:			
Broccoli, 3 oz	25	0	4
French Fries, salted, 6 oz	510	28	59
Golden-Fried Shrimp, 6 pieces	190	8	20
Hash Browns, 1 serving	210	12	26
Mac 'n Cheese, 3 oz	140	9	9
Red-Skinned Potatoes, 4 oz	205	9	28
Smoked Chedd. Mashed Pot., 1 sve	130	5	18
Soups: Per Bowl, Without Bread			
Broccoli & Cheddar	370	16	48
Chicken Noodle	140	4	17
Vegetable Beef	170	4	23
Salads: With Dressing, w/out Bread, Unless Indicated			
Caesar, 8 oz	450	29	38
Cranb. Apple Chicken, 14 oz	450	14	46
Fried Chicken Strip Cobb Salad, with Bread, 19 oz	1060	56	91
Dressings: Per 1 oz			
Bleu Cheese	110	11	1
Caesar	100	10	0
French	75	5	8
Honey Mustard	120	10	8
Ranch	120	13	0
Desserts: As Served			
Apple Pie, 7 oz	480	22	67
Banana Split, 15 oz	810	31	125
Caramel Apple Crisp, 13 oz	740	21	134
Hot Fudge Brownie à la Mode, 9 oz	830	37	122
NY Style Cheesecake, 5 oz	510	34	43
Toppings: Caramel, 1.5 oz	190	1	44
Hot Fudge, 1.5 oz	150	6	23
Strawberry, 1.5 oz	60	0	14
Beverages:			
Lemonade Iced Tea, 15 oz	70	0	19
Strawberry Lemonade, 15 oz	200	0	50

For Complete Nutritional Data ~ see CalorieKing.com

Dippin' Dots® (Feb '14)

	C	F	Cb
Flavored Ices: Per ½ Cup, 3 oz			
Sour Blue Razz	60	0	14
Other varieties	100	0	26
Frozen Yogurt,			
Strawberry Cheesecake, ½ cup	100	0	21
Ice Cream: Per ½ Cup			
Banana Split	160	8	20
Choc. Chip Cookie dough	220	10	29
Peanut Butter Chip	170	8	21
Strawberry	160	8	18
Frappes: Per 12 fl.oz			
Caramel	210	9	23
Mocha	220	9	25

Donatos Pizza® (Feb '14)

	C	F	Cb
Pizzas:			
Signature: Thin Crust, ¼ Large Pizza			
Classic Trio	630	32	51
Founder's Favorite	660	34	51
Hawaiian	540	24	52
Signatures: Thicker Crust, ¼ Large Pizza			
Founder's Favorite	730	33	70
Mariachi Beef	600	23	70
Mariachi Chicken	610	21	70
Pepperoni	670	30	69
Serious Cheese	650	23	69
The Works	690	32	70
Vegy	560	21	69
No Dough Signatures: Per Whole Pizza			
Hawaiian	400	25	19
Mariachi Beef	450	27	21
Mariachi Chicken	530	26	23
Pepperoni	480	32	17
Pepperoni Zinger	410	26	18
Serious Cheese	460	31	18
The Works	490	33	18
Oven Baked Subs: Per Whole Sub, White Bread			
Big Don Italian	670	33	63
Meatball	930	52	74
Pepperoni	800	46	62
Steak Hoagie, with Marinara	670	30	65
Stromboli: 3 Meat	660	26	72
Deluxe	790	35	82
Pepperoni	680	29	72
Desserts: Apple Timpano, 1 slice	200	3.5	37
Cinnamon Timpano, 1 slice	260	10	37
Cinnamon Twists (2 sticks)	230	4	45

For Complete Nutritional Data ~ see CalorieKing.com

Domino's® (Mar '14)

12" Hand Tossed:
Per Slice, ⅛ Pizza, Includes Base Sauce and Cheese

	C	F	Cb
Bacon, Beef & Sausage	275	14	27
Beef, Green Pepp., On. & Mshrm	200	8	25
Black Olives, Green Peppers, Onions, Mushrooms, Tomatoes	190	7	25
Ham & Pineapple	200	6.5	26
Pepperoni	215	9	25
Pepperoni & Sausage	240	11	26
Sausage	230	10	26
Sliced Ital. Ssg., Beef & Pepperoni	265	14	26

14" Thin Crust: *Per Slice, ⅛ Pizza, Includes Base Sauce and Cheese*

	C	F	Cb
Bacon, Beef & Sausage	325	19	21
Beef, Green Pepp., On. & Mshrm	220	12	19
Black Olives, Green Peppers, Onions, Mushrooms & Tomatoes	210	11	19
Ham & Pineapple	220	10	21
Pepperoni	240	13	19
Pepperoni & Sausage	275	16	20
Sausage	260	15	21

14" Brooklyn: *Per Slice, ⅙ Pizza, Includes Base Sauce and Cheese*

	C	F	Cb
Beef, Green Pepp., On. & Mushroom	270	13	26
Black Olives, Green Peppers, Onions, Mushrooms, Tomatoes	250	12	26
Ham & Pineapple	265	12	29
Pepperoni	290	15	26
Pepperoni & Sausage	340	19	27
Sausage	320	18	28

12" Feast Hand-Tossed: *Per Slice, ⅛ Pizza*

	C	F	Cb
America's Favorite	250	12	27
Bacon Cheeseburger	270	13	26
Deluxe	230	10	27
ExtravaganZZa	290	14	28
MeatZZa	280	14	27
Ultimate Pepperoni	260	13	25

14" Feast Hand Tossed: *Per Slice, ⅛ Pizza*

	C	F	Cb
America's Favorite	350	17	36
Bacon Cheeseburger	380	19	36
Deluxe	320	14	36
ExtravaganZZa	390	19	37
MeatZZa Feast	380	19	36
Ultimate Pepperoni	360	18	34

12" Legends Thin Crust: *Per ¼ Party Pizza*

	C	F	Cb
Buffalo Chicken	380	22	26
Cali Chicken Bacon Ranch	490	33	28
Fiery Hawaiian	390	22	32
Memphis BBQ Chicken	370	19	33
Philly Cheese Steak	360	21	26

Domino's® cont... (Mar '14)

Chicken Wings: *W/out Dipping Sauce*

	C	F	Cb
Barbeque, 4 wings	250	13	14
Hot, 4 wings	200	13	5

Chicken Dipping Cups: *Per 1.5 oz Container*

	C	F	Cb
Blue Cheese	240	25	2
Kicker Hot	50	4.5	3
Ranch	200	21	2

BreadBowl Pasta: *Per ½ Bowl*

	C	F	Cb
Chicken Alfredo, 10.85 oz	700	26	93
Chicken Carbonara, 11.6 oz	740	28	94
Italian Sausage Marinara, 11.85 oz	730	27	97
Pasta Primavera, 11 oz	670	24	94

Oven Baked Sandwiches: *Per Sandwich*

	C	F	Cb
Buffalo Chicken with Blue Cheese	830	41	74
Chicken Bacon Ranch	870	45	72
Chicken Parmesan	750	30	73
Italian	820	41	70
Italian Ssg. & Peppers	860	45	74
Mediterranean Veggie	680	29	72
Philly Cheese Steak	690	28	70
Sweet & Spicy Chicken Habanero	800	32	83

Salads: *Per Serving Without Dressing*

	C	F	Cb
Garden Fresh	70	3.5	5
Grilled Chicken Caesar	90	3.5	5

Salad Dressings & Condiments: *Per 1.5 oz Package*

	C	F	Cb
Blue Cheese	240	25	2
Buttermilk Ranch	230	24	2
Creamy Caesar	210	21	2
Golden Italian	210	22	2
Light Italian	20	1	3

Bread Side Items:

	C	F	Cb
Breadsticks: 1 stick, without sauce	110	6	11
8 sticks, without sauce	880	48	88

Cheesy Bread:

	C	F	Cb
1 stick, without sauce	120	6	11
8 sticks, without sauce	960	48	88

Bread Dipping Sauces: *Per Container*

	C	F	Cb
Garlic, 1 oz	250	28	0
Marinara, 2 oz	25	0	5

Cinna Stix:

	C	F	Cb
1 stick, without icing	120	6	14
8 sticks, without icing	960	48	112

	C	F	Cb
Sweet Icing, *Dipping Cup*	250	2.5	57
Dessert, *Chocolate Lava Crunch Cake*	350	17	47

Updated Nutrition Data ~ www.CalorieKing.com
Persons with Diabetes ~ See Disclaimer (Page 22)

Don Pablos® (Feb '14)

Start The Fiesta: Per Entire Plate

	C	**F**	**Cb**
Don's Boneless Wings: *Without Bleu Cheese Dressing*			
Buffalo	750	48	49
Chipotle Honey BBQ	1010	59	94
Blue Cheese Dressing	360	38	7
Flautas, without Guacamole	505	29	40
Taquitos, without Guacamole	560	39	28
Optional Guacamole, #30 scoop	70	6	1
Nachos:			
Cantina: With Chicken	1060	46	108
With Beef	1185	55	109
Quesadillas: *Without Guacamole*			
Cheese, small	950	66	50
Mesquite Grilled, Steak, small	860	53	54
Dips: *Per Entire Plate, Without Chips or Tortillas*			
Bowls: Queso Blanco	1080	88	14
Prairie Fire Bean	715	43	53
Entrees: *Per Meal, Without Sides*			
Burritos: Chicken	1025	53	79
Fajita Steak	1025	50	79
Carnitas: Pork	790	31	82
Cold Set, Side	160	11	18
Chimichangas: Chkn, smaller Cheese	785	37	64
Spicy Beef De Oro	1360	79	89
Sizzlin' Fajitas: *With Proteins, Onions & Peppers*			
Combo - Steak & Chicken	580	28	34
Mesquite-Grilled: Chicken	570	27	58
Steak	680	36	36
Fajita Fixin's: 7" Flour Tortilla (3)	375	11	60
Combo Cheese Toppings, 1 oz	110	9	1
Corn Tortillas (4)	60	1	12
Guacamole, #30 scoop	70	6	4
Sour Cream, #30 scoop	80	8	2
Tortilla Chips (13), 1 serving	190	2	39
Enchiladas: Cadillac Chicken	875	43	60
Cadillac Steak	1015	53	65
Don's Combos: *Without Sides*			
Cinco Combo	1175	66	64
El Matador	960	54	59
Mexicano	715	43	31
Numero uno Favorito	870	56	65
Presidente	990	52	70
San Angelo	1025	51	85
Fresh Salads: *Without Dressing*			
Caesar: With Chicken	815	27	96
With Steak	945	38	99
Southwest: *Without Extra Dressing*			
With Buffalo Sauce	950	57	73
With Chipotle-Honey BBQ Sauce	1215	67	118
Sides:			
Mexican Rice, 3 oz	120	2	23
Refritos, 5 oz	215	7	27
Seasoned French Fries, 7 oz	345	16	46
Seasoned Vegetables, 6 oz	110	5	16

Dunkin' Donuts® (Mar '14)

Bagels:	**C**	**F**	**Cb**
Plain; Onion; Wheat, average	310	1	64
Blueberry; Cinnamon Raisin, av.	320	1	67
Everything	340	3	67
Sesame Seed	350	4.5	65
Sour Cream & Onion	330	1.5	66
Danish: Apple Cheese	330	16	41
Cheese	330	17	39
Strawberry Cheese	320	16	40
Donuts: Apple 'n Spice	270	14	32
Bavarian Kreme	270	15	31
Boston Kreme	310	16	39
Bow Tie Donut	310	15	39
Chocolate Frosted Cocoa	270	13	33
Chocolate Kreme Filled	370	21	42
French Cruller	220	15	18
Jelly	270	14	32
Old Fashioned Cake	320	22	33
Powdered Cake	340	22	38
Strawberry Frosted	280	15	32
Sugar Raised	230	14	22
Vanilla Kreme Filled	380	23	42
Muffins:			
Blueberry: Regular	460	15	76
Reduced Fat	410	10	75
Chocolate Chip	550	21	83
Coffee Cake	590	24	86
Corn; Honey Bran Raisin, av.	450	15	73
Munchkins: Jelly Filled (4)	320	16	36
Plain Cake; Cinnamon Cake (4)	240	14	24
Sandwiches: *On French Roll Unless Indicated*			
Bacon Ranch Chicken	660	27	69
BBQ Chicken	590	19	74
Chicken Salad Croissant	580	38	42
Ham & Cheese	440	14	54
Roast Beef	460	16	54
Texas Toasted Grilled Cheese	510	30	41
Tuna Salad: On a Plain Bagel	570	24	69
On English Muffin	400	24	34
Wrap	520	37	25
Turkey Cheddar Bacon	460	14	55

Continued Next Page... ...

Dunkin' Donuts® cont... (Mar '14)

Breakfast:	C	F	Cb
Hash Browns, 9 pieces	200	11	22
Oatmeal:			
Original, w/ Dried Fruit Topping	270	4	54
Brown Sugar Flavored Oatmeal, with Dried Fruit Topping	300	4	61
Bagels:			
Bacon, Egg & Cheese	460	11	67
Egg & Cheese	410	7	67
Ham, Egg & Cheese	440	8	67
Sausage, Egg & Cheese	620	26	67
Big N' Toasted, Regular	530	28	43
Biscuits: Bacon, Egg & Cheese	470	27	38
Chicken	540	28	51
Sausage, Egg & Cheese	630	43	38
Croissants: Bacon, Egg & Cheese	480	27	40
Egg & Cheese	440	24	40
Ham, Egg & Cheese	460	25	40
Sausage, Egg & Cheese	650	43	41
Egg White Flatbreads:			
Turkey Sausage	280	8	32
Veggie	280	10	32
English Muffins:			
Bacon, Egg & Cheese	290	10	34
Ham, Egg & Cheese	280	8	34
Sausage, Egg & Cheese	450	26	32
Wake-Up Wraps:			
Egg & Cheese	150	8	13
Egg White Turkey Sausage	150	6	14
Egg White Veggie	150	7	14
Ham, Egg & Cheese	170	8	14
Sausage, Egg & Cheese	260	17	14
Hot Beverages: Per Medium Size			
Chocolate: Original	320	11	58
Mint	310	10	52
Dunkaccino	350	16	51
Cold Beverages: Per Medium Size			
Coolatta: Orange, 24 fl.oz	310	0	80
Strawberry Fruit, 24 fl.oz	350	0	86
Vanilla Bean, 24 fl.oz	630	9	138
Iced Coffee: Per Medium Size, Without Cream			
Regular, without sugar	15	0	2
Caramel Mocha	180	0	41
Peppermint Mocha	190	0.5	46
Lattes: Per Medium, With Whole Milk			
Caramel Mocha	260	0.5	53
Caramel Swirl	350	9	55

Eat 'N Park® (Feb '14)

Breakfast:	C	F	Cb
Bananas Foster French Toast, 2 slices	495	15	82
Omelettes: Ham & Cheese	535	35	5
Meat Lover's	725	55	3
Pancakes:			
Buttermilk: Plain (1)	75	1	15
Blueberry (1)	85	1	17
Scramblers:			
All-American w/ sausage	705	39	55
Skinny	355	14	32
Waffles: Belgian (1)	280	12	35
Strawberry (1)	375	17	48
Appetizers:			
Fried Cheese Sticks	535	36	26
Fried Ravioli	455	31	30
Grilled Chicken Quesadilla	905	56	52
Onion Rings Basket	365	24	34
Burgers:			
Black Angus: American Grill	615	37	30
Mushroom & Onion	575	31	31
Superburger	1085	73	28
Classic: Black Angus	455	22	28
Black Angus Bacon Cheeseburger	570	31	28
Black Angus Cheeseburger	505	26	28
Garden Burger	290	5	43
Original, Superburger	565	38	27
Sandwiches: With Menu Board Standard Add-Ins			
BLT	490	15	65
Buffalo Chicken Wrap	835	48	61
Chargrilled Chicken	345	7	31
Gourmet Grilled Cheese	795	58	27
Hot Turkey	500	8	71
Santa Fe Turkey	740	50	31
Shredded Pot Roast	530	31	28
Turkey Club	835	49	51
Whale of a Cod Fish	880	42	76
Dinners: Without Sides			
Baked Chicken Parmigiana:			
W/ Marinara Sauce	960	38	99
W/ Meat Sauce	985	41	95
Baked Lemon Sole, 2 fillets	390	19	11
Chicken Fillets, 5 pieces	530	26	28
Cod Floridian, 2 fillets	240	3	8
Mile-High Meatloaf	900	57	19
Smothered Ground Sirloin Steak	445	27	8
Spaghetti Marinara	695	8	129
Spaghetti with Meat Sauce	835	16	146
Whitefish w/ Mac & Cheese 2 fillets	750	34	58

Continued Next Page....

Updated Nutrition Data ~ www.CalorieKing.com
Persons with Diabetes ~ See Disclaimer (Page 22)

Eat 'N Park® cont... (Feb '14)

Salads: Without Dressing	C	F	Cb
Buffalo Chicken Salad	610	33	42
Garden Salad	95	3	16
Grilled Chicken Salad	445	20	30
Steak Salad	740	46	33
Dressings: Per 2 oz			
Bleu Cheese	245	25	3
Citrus Lime Vinaigrette	70	6	13
French, Fat Free	75	0	18
House Ranch	215	21	4
Poppy & Sesame Seed	390	32	26
Desserts:			
Ice Cream, 2 scoops	230	12	27
Pies: Apple Pie, 1 slice	525	27	67
Blackberry Pie, 1 slice	565	28	75
Coconut Cream Pie, 1 slice	490	27	55
Dutch Apple Pie, 1 slice	375	14	61
Sundaes: Caramel Fudge	400	19	56
Oreo	505	21	74

Edo Japan® (Feb '14)

Bento Box: Without Teriyaki Sauce	C	F	Cb
Beef Yakisoba, 20.25 oz	840	29	102
Chicken Yakisoba, 20.5 oz	790	24	102
Sizzling Shrimp, 22 oz	790	15	122
Sukiyaki Beef, 20.25 oz	880	27	120
Teriyaki Dishes: Without Teriyaki Sauce			
Chicken, 15 oz	570	11	80
Chicken & Shrimp	640	14	82
Hawaiian Chicken, 15.5 oz	580	11	85
Sukiyaki Beef, 14.75 oz	580	15	80
Soup: Per 33 oz Bowl			
Beef Udon	750	16	117
Chicken Udon	700	12	117
Maki Sushi: Per 6 Pieces			
California Roll, 7.6 oz	430	17	61
Spicy Tuna Roll, 6.5 oz	300	2.5	54
Nigiri Sushi: Per 1 Piece			
Ebi (Steamed Prawn), 1.65 oz	70	0.5	12
Salmon Sashimi, 0.7 oz	30	1.5	1

Einstein Bros® (Feb '14)

Breakfast:	C	F	Cb
Egg Paninis: Spinach & Bacon	770	38	72
Green Chili & Turkey Sausage	650	22	71
Egg Sandwiches: Ham & Swiss	490	16	59
Turkey Sausage & Cheddar	540	20	59
Egg White Sandwiches:			
Asparagus, Mushroom, Swiss	270	11	30
Southwest Turkey Sausage	350	14	33
Egg Wraps: Santa Fe	660	33	60
Spicy Elmo	630	34	59
Bagels:			
Bagel Thin Singles:			
Everything	160	2	29
Other varieties, average	135	1.5	26
Classics, Plain; Everything, average	265	1.5	56
Gourmet Bagels: Dutch Apple	350	6	69
Green Chile	350	8	58
Power Bagel	290	5	53
Six-Cheese	330	6	59
Spinach Florentine	320	6	56
Pizza Bagels: Cheese	400	11	59
Pepperoni	440	15	59
Signature Bagels: Asiago Cheese	310	5	56
Blueberry	300	1	65
Chocolate Chip	290	2.5	58
Cinnamon Sugar	290	2.5	63
Cranberry; Onion, average	270	1	60
Garlic	270	2.5	56
Poppy Seed; Sesame	280	3	56
Potato	270	4	52
Bagel Dogs: With Cheddar Cheese			
Original	540	27	56
Asiago	550	28	56
Bagel Melts:			
Ham & Swiss	490	15	60
Chicken & Mozzarella	530	15	61
Turkey & Cheddar	490	15	58
Lunch Paninis:			
Italian Chicken	850	37	72
Turkey Club	800	37	74
Wraps:			
Buffalo Chicken	620	31	59
California Chicken	700	35	64
Chipotle Turkey	630	29	69
Cream Cheese: Per 1.25 oz Schmear			
Reduced Fat:			
Garlic Herb/Garden Veggie	110	9	5
Honey Almond; Strawberry, av.	120	9	10
Plain; Sun Dried Tomato & Basil	110	9	4
Onion and Chive	120	11	5

199

El Pollo Loco® (Feb '14)

	C	F	Cb
Chicken Burritos:			
Chicken Avoc., 17.9 oz	950	53	74
El Tradicional, 14.7 oz	780	31	86
Poblano, 18.6 oz	910	39	93
Spicy Chipotle, 17 oz	860	35	86
Chicken Meal: Skinless Breast,			
without Torilla Strips			
or Dressing on Salad	265	8	11
Flame-Grilled Chicken: Skin On			
Breast	220	9	0
Leg	90	4	0
Thigh	220	15	0
Wing	90	5	0
Bowl: Pollo	610	10	87
Ultimate Pollo	960	34	92
Premium Salads: Without Dressing			
Chicken Tostada, with Shell, 17.3 oz	860	42	77
Grilled Chicken,			
without Tortilla Strips, 10.3 oz	170	4	10
Dressings: Per Container			
Creamy Cilantro: 1.3 oz	190	20	1
Light, 1.5 oz	70	5	6
Ranch, 1.5 oz	230	24	2
Soup:			
Chicken Tortilla with Tortilla Strips:			
Small, 10.8 oz	210	9	19
Large, 23.6 oz	450	19	40
Under 500 Calories:			
BRC Burrito	430	12	63
Chicken Tostada Salad, without			
shell or dressing	430	13	43
Fire Grilled Skinless Breast Meal	240	5	12
Grilled Chicken Salad, w/o drssng	240	8	20
Chicken Taco al Carbon	160	6	18
Sides:			
Black Beans, 6 oz	200	0	35
Cole Slaw, 4 oz	130	10	9
Corn Cobbette, 2 pcs, 6.2 oz	160	5	25
French Fries, 3.8 oz	330	17	40
Gravy, 1 oz	10	0	2
Macaroni & Cheese, 5.5 oz	250	15	22
Mashed Potatoes, 5 oz	110	1.5	23
Pinto Beans, 6 oz	200	4	29
Sweet Potato Fries, 3.6 oz	330	20	34
Tortilla Chips & Guacamole, 7.5 oz	740	46	77

El Pollo Loco® cont... (Feb '14)

	C	F	Cb
Condiments:			
Pico de Gallo, 1.5 oz	15	1	2
Salsa: Avocado, 1.5 oz	30	2.5	2
House; Roja, av.,1.5 oz	15	0	3
Sour Cream, 1.3 oz	80	7	1
Dessert, Caramel Flan, 5.1 oz	260	12	34

For Complete Nutritional Data ~ see CalorieKing.com

Fatburger® (Feb '14)

	C	F	Cb
Burgers: Without Extras			
Burgers: Small	400	21	37
Medium	590	31	46
Large	850	41	69
Turkeyburger	480	21	50
Veggieburger	510	20	60
Hot Dogs: Without Extas			
Chili Cheese	480	27	35
Regular Hot Dog	320	15	32
Sandwiches: Without Extras			
Chicken: Crispy	560	27	53
Grilled	430	14	42
Fish	560	31	55
Fries: Fat Fries; Skinny Fries, av.	385	17	53
With Chili, average	485	23	57
With Chili & Cheese, average	595	32	58
Add-Ons: American Cheese, 1 slice	70	5	1
Cheddar Cheese, 1 slice	110	9	1
Mayonnaise, 1 serving	90	10	1
Relish, 1 serving	20	0	5
Sides: Chili Cup	200	11	10
With Cheese & Onions	320	20	12
Onion Rings	540	29	64
Shakes: Chocolate	910	45	115
Cookies & Ice Cream	1180	59	163
Maui Banana	940	44	126
Peanut Butter	950	53	114
Strawberry; Vanilla, average	885	44	112

For Complete Nutritional Data ~ see CalorieKing.com

Fazoli's® (Feb '14)

	C	F	Cb
Oven-Baked Pasta: Per Serving			
Alfredo Bowtie	800	42	68
Baked Ziti	690	30	69
Chicken Broccoli Penne	950	44	74
Chicken Parmigano	930	34	103
Penne Romano	900	46	74
Penne with Creamy Basil Chicken	990	53	70
Spaghetti	660	24	78
Twice-Baked	750	35	68
Italian Melts: Chicken Asiago	670	30	52
Crispy Chicken Parma	830	36	73
Sicilian Sausage	670	32	53

Continued Next Page....

Updated Nutrition Data ~ www.CalorieKing.com
Persons with Diabetes ~ See Disclaimer (Page 22)

Fazoli's® cont... (Feb '14)

Lighter Options Pasta:	C	F	Cb
Baked Chicken Penne & Peppers	350	13	35
Chicken Mushroom Alfredo	390	17	36
Three Cheese Baked Ravioli	330	18	25

Flatbread Pizzas: Per Pizza

Chicken Margherita	500	20	55
Tuscan Chicken	390	11	54

Samplers: Per Serving

Classic Sampler Platter	890	25	122
Spicy Sampler	1020	34	125
Ultimate Sampler Platter	1150	29	166

Submarinos:

Fazoli's Original	830	44	70
Smoked Turkey Basil	760	39	69
Ultimate M'ball Smasher	980	54	75

For Complete Nutritional Data ~ see CalorieKing.com

Firehouse Subs® (Feb '14)

	C	F	Cb
Subs: Per Medium White Sub, With Standard Toppings and Dressings			
Chicken Salad	820	48	60
Engine Company; Engineer, av.	695	36	59
Ham	730	36	70
Hero	770	37	64
Hook & Ladder	700	36	64
Italian	910	57	64
Meatball	820	50	60
Roast Beef	710	36	54
Tuna	1000	68	67
Turkey	670	34	58
Veggie	720	45	60
Chili, Bowl	340	17	25
Salads: Without Dressing			
Chief's Salad: With Chicken	370	18	17
With Chicken Salad	490	29	20
With Ham	410	17	31
With Tuna	670	48	27
With Turkey	350	15	19

Five Guys® (Feb '14)

Burgers:	C	F	Cb
Bacon Burger	780	50	39
Bacon Cheeseburger	920	62	40
Cheeseburger	840	55	40
Hamburger	700	43	39

Five Guys® cont... (Feb '14)

Burgers: (Cont)	C	F	Cb
Little: Bacon Burger	560	33	39
Bacon Cheeseburger	630	39	40
Cheeseburger	550	32	40
Hamburger	480	26	39
Dogs: Bacon Dog; Cheese Dog	620	42	40
Bacon Cheese Dog	695	48	41
Hot Dog	545	35	40
Fries: Little Fry, 8 oz	525	23	72
Regular, 15 oz	955	41	131

Flame Broiler® (Feb '14)

Bowls: Per Bowl	C	F	Cb
Chicken; Beef; Half & Half, average	610	17	69
Beef/Chicken Veggie, average	535	16	53
The Works	630	15	78
Mini Bowls,			
Chicken; Beef; Half & Half, av.	380	7	48
Plates: Per Plate			
Beef; Chicken; Chicken & Beef, av.	855	27	91
Rib	730	23	92
Works	820	24	96

Freshens® (Feb '14)

Smoothies: 100% Juice (20 fl.oz)	C	F	Cb
Blended Fruit Classics:			
Caribbean Craze; Maui Mango	260	0	65
Citrus Mango	390	7	83
Jamaican Jammer	290	0	63
Orange Sunrise	260	3	57
Strawberry Kiwi	290	0	73
Strawberry Squeeze	250	0	54
Tropical Pineapple	380	4	88
High Protein: Peanut Butter	460	12	59
Strawberries 'n Cream	370	1	61
Rainforest Energy:			
Acai; Brazillian, average	285	3	65
Mangosteen	320	0	80
Fro-Yo Blasts: Per 12 fl.oz			
Cookie Dough	490	6	103
Oreo Overload	370	4	78
Indulgent Shakes: Per 16 fl.oz w/o Whipped Cream			
Chocolate	440	2.5	95
Oreo Cream	530	6	110
Strawberry	400	2	87
Breakfast Crepes:			
Denver; Steak & Eggs, av.	470	25	26
Wake Up	420	22	23
Savory Golden Crepes: Fajita Chkn	500	13	58
Fajita Steak	530	19	55
Honey Mustard Chicken	470	14	52
Dessert Crepes:			
Cheesecake Supreme	510	20	69
The Guilty Pleasure	540	13	91

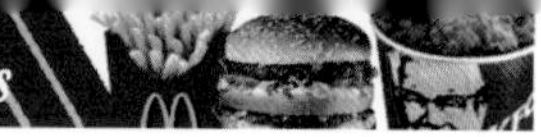

Godfather's Pizza® (Feb '14)

Golden Crust Pizza: Per Slice	C	F	Cb
Cheese: Medium, ⅛ pizza	220	8	25
Large, 1/10 pizza	250	9	28
Combo: Medium, ⅛	290	13	27
Large, 1/10 pizza	330	15	30
Super Combo: Medium, ⅛ pizza	320	15	28
Large, 1/10 pizza	370	18	31
Original Crust Pizza:			
Cheese: Mini, ¼ pizza	150	4	20
Medium, ⅛ pizza	260	7	34
Jumbo, 1/12 pizza	350	10	44
Combo: Mini, ¼ pizza	200	8	21
Medium, ⅛ pizza	350	14	36
Jumbo, 1/12 pizza	480	20	47
Super Combo: Mini, ¼ pizza	220	9	22
Medium, ⅛ pizza	350	14	36
Jumbo, 1/12 pizza	520	23	48
Thin Crust Pizza:			
Cheese: Medium, ⅛ pizza	170	8	15
Large, 1/10 pizza	210	10	17
Combo: Medium, ⅛ pizza	240	13	17
Large, 1/10 pizza	280	16	20
Super Combo: Medium, ⅛ pizza	290	16	19
Large, 1/10 pizza	330	19	20
Calzones: *Per Medium Calzone*			
Cheese	1660	51	200
Combo	1450	40	199
Pepperoni	1410	39	195
Sides:			
Breadstick (1)	110	2	20
Cheesestick, medium, ⅛	200	7	24
Garlic Toast: 1 piece	150	9	15
With Cheese, 1 piece	210	12	16
Hot Chicken Wings (4), breaded	180	12	4
Potato Wedges, 4 oz	175	8	24

Gold Star Chili® (Feb '14)

Meals:	C	F	Cb
Burrito, Gold Star Chili	970	33	126
Burrito Bowl, Grilled Chicken	905	29	111
Chili By The Bowl:			
Gold Star	205	10	10
Low Carb Coney	740	59	9
Tex Mex	225	9	18
Coneys: Regular	225	12	21
Cheese	310	19	21
Ways, Regular:			
2-Way	395	10	54
3-Way	680	34	55
4-Way, Bean	825	34	81
5-Way	895	34	82
Ways, Super, 5-Way	1180	48	122

Gold Star Chili® cont... (Feb '14)

Sandwich,	C	F	Cb
Crispy Chicken	355	20	24
Salads: *Without Dressing*			
Cafe	305	13	34
With Crispy Chicken	495	25	43
With Grilled Chicken	410	16	36
Caesar Salad	190	5	25
With Crispy Chicken	375	16	35
With Grilled Chicken	290	7	27
South of the Border Chili	685	36	62
Fries: Regular	400	16	58
Cheese	575	30	59
Chili Cheese	680	36	63
Firehouse	425	16	64

Golden Corral® (Feb '14)

Breakfast:	C	F	Cb
Bacon & Cheese Quiche, 1 slice	290	21	15
Corned Beef Hash, Grilled, 1 cup	440	28	26
Creamed Chipped Beef, 1 cup	320	18	20
French Toast, Plain, 1 slice	200	6	29
Hash Brown Casserole, 1 cup	260	10	28
Sausage Links (1)	120	11	1
Sausage Patties (1)	100	9	0
Meals: *Without Sides*			
Hot Buffet:			
Awesome Pot Roast, 3 oz	100	4.5	5
Baked Fish w/ Shrimp & Sce, 3 oz	160	10	2
Baked Florentine Fish, 1 piece	180	12	2
BBQ: Chicken Leg Quarter, 1 pce	490	22	21
Pork, 3 oz	170	8	5
Bone-In Catfish, 3 oz	210	14	7
Bourbon Street Chicken, 3 oz	170	9	4
Breaded Bay Scallops (10)	140	6	13
Coconut Shrimp (5)	200	12	16
Crab Cakes (1)	180	15	8
Hickory Bourbon Chkn Tenders (1)	140	2	17
Meatloaf, 1 slice	220	11	11
Sirloin Steak, 4.5 oz	230	9	1
Salad Buffet: *Per ½ Cup Unless Indicated*			
Caesar, without dressing, 1 cup	110	8	8
Cajun Potato	230	17	15
Chicken	240	20	3
Coleslaw	110	9	6
Seafood	140	10	9
Spinach Bacon, 1 cup	120	9	4
Tuna	190	13	5
Dressings: Balsamic Vinaig., 2 T.	20	0	5
Caesar, 2 Tbsp	150	15	2
Ranch, 2 Tbsp	110	12	2

Updated Nutrition Data ~ www.CalorieKing.com
Persons with Diabetes ~ See Disclaimer (Page 22)

(The) Great American Bagel Co® (Feb '14)

	C	F	Cb
Bagels:			
Asiago Cheese	520	16	72
Cheddar Herb	390	8	66
Cinnamon Raisin	380	3.5	76
Jalapeno Cheddar	370	7	63
Plain	360	4	71
Spinach Tomazzo	640	20	86
Tomazzo	520	13	77
Paninis: On Regular Baguette			
Chicken Pesto	770	35	70
Ham & Swiss	600	26	58
Philly Beef	920	40	92
Turkey Club	680	29	67
Sandwiches: Asiago Omelet	720	29	80
Blt	550	17	72
Chicken Parmigiana	740	22	81
Ham	460	9	71
Roast Beef	465	9	71
Turkey	435	5	72
Cream Cheese Filling: Per 1 oz			
Plain	100	10	1
Strawberry; Vegetable, average	90	8	4
Pastries:			
Cookies: Chocolate Chunk, 4 oz	110	3.5	19
Oatmeal Raisin, 4 oz	120	5	18
Muffins: Blueberry, 4.25 oz	430	16	64
Banana Nut, 4.25 oz	430	18	61

Green Burrito® (Feb '14)

	C	F	Cb
Burritos:			
Bean & Cheese	470	19	54
Beef, Bean & Cheese	500	22	51
California: Chicken	470	21	45
Steak	480	21	44
Chicken Especial	580	25	58
Mexicano: Chicken	550	23	56
Steak	560	23	55
Specialties:			
Super Nachos:			
Chicken	950	51	93
Ground Beef	1000	55	93
Taco Salad: Chicken	830	48	68
Ground Beef	880	52	67
Steak	840	47	67
Tacos: Crispy Taco	220	13	20
Ground Beef, hard shell	210	12	15
Southwest Chicken, soft	310	21	19
Street Tacos: Chicken	150	7	15
Steak	160	7	14
Sides: Beans, 6.35 oz	290	13	29
Chips, 2 oz	300	17	35
Guacamole, 1.4 oz	60	5	3

(The) Great Steak & Potato Company® (Feb '14)

	C	F	Cb
Breakfast Sandwiches:			
Bacon, Egg & Cheese, 7.6 oz	600	36	39
Sausage, Egg & Cheese, 9 oz	700	47	39
Steak, Egg & Cheese, 10 oz	600	34	40
Sandwiches: 7"			
Bacon Cheddar Cheesesteak, 12.2 oz	720	32	62
Buffalo Chicken Philly, 13.8 oz	660	24	65
Chicagoland Cheesesteak, 13.3 oz	680	29	63
Chicken Bacon Ranch, 15.2 oz	990	56	66
Chicken Cordon Bleu, 13.4 oz	580	16	78
Great Steak Cheesesteak, 13.6 oz	740	37	62
Gyro, 11.9 oz	580	30	52
Ham Delight/Explosion, av., 14 oz	710	34	71
Orig. Philly Cheesesteak, 11.8 oz	650	26	62
Reuben, 11.9 oz	690	33	61
Super Steak Cheesesteak, 15 oz	750	37	64
Turkey Philly, 13.1 oz	670	30	64
Ultimate Chicken Philly, 14.6 oz	730	33	64
Veggie Delight, 11.7 oz	510	19	64
Wisconsin Inside-Out, 6.2 oz	560	27	57
Baked Potatoes:			
The Great Potato: Chicken, 12.5 oz	500	22	37
Ham, 12.3 oz	420	16	43
Steak, 13 oz	520	26	37
Turkey, 12.3 oz	390	13	39
The King, 8.4 oz	490	29	31
Fries:			
Great Fry: Kids, 6.25 oz	270	13	36
Regular, 10.25 oz	440	20	60
Large, 12.5 oz	540	25	72
Coney Island Fry, Regular, 12.7 oz	570	30	61
King Fry, regular, 11.4 oz	630	39	52
Nacho Fry, regular, 11.8 oz	510	27	53
Salads: Without Dressing			
Chef Salad, 16 oz	260	11	15
Great Salad: Grilled Chicken, 19 oz	380	13	18
Grilled Steak, 19.4 oz	400	23	18
Wedge: Grilled Chicken, 14.8 oz	270	12	11
Grilled Steak, 15.3 oz	290	16	11
Salad Dressings: Ranch, 1 oz	170	18	1
Thousand Island, 1 oz	130	12	4

Haagen-Dazs® (Feb '14)

Classic Flavors: Per ½ Cup	C	F	Cb
Butter Pecan	300	22	20
Caramel Cone	320	20	30
Cherry Vanilla	230	14	22
Chocolate	260	17	22
Chocolate Chip Cookie Dough	300	18	30
Chocolate Peanut Butter	340	23	26
Coffee	250	17	20
Creme Brulee	300	17	32
Dulce de Leche	270	16	27
Green Tea	250	17	20
Midnight Cookies & Cream	290	17	29
Mint Chip	280	18	25
Pineapple Coconut	230	13	25
Pistachio	280	19	22
Pralines & Cream	270	16	28
Rocky Road	290	17	29
Rum Raisin	240	16	21
Vanilla Bean	270	17	24
Frozen Yogurt: Per ½ Cup			
Coffee	180	2.5	31
Vanilla	170	2.5	29
Vanilla Raspberry Swirl	150	1	31
Gelato: Per ½ Cup			
Black Cherry Amaretto; Limoncello	240	9	35
Cappuccino	230	10	32
Sea Salt Caramel	270	11	38
Stracciatella	270	13	34
Sorbet: Per ½ Cup			
Mango	150	0	38
Orchard Peach; Strawberry, av.	130	0	31
Raspberry; Zesty Lemon, av.	115	0	29

Ice Cream Bars/Cones ~ See Page 109

Hardee's® (Mar '14)

Burgers:	C	F	Cb
Big Hot Ham 'N' Cheese	410	18	31
Cheeseburgers: Small	330	15	32
Double, 7 oz	420	22	33
Hamburger, Small	280	12	32
Original Turkey Burger	390	17	31
Thickburgers:			
Original, 1/3 lb	850	54	56
Bacon Cheese, ⅓ lb	890	59	54

Hardee's® cont... (Mar '14)

Burgers (Cont):	C	F	Cb
Thickburgers (Cont):			
Double, ⅔ lb	1200	81	58
Frisco, ⅓ lb	880	59	46
Little Thickburger	580	39	33
Little Thick Cheeseburger, 6 oz	430	23	33
Low-Carb, ⅓ lb	470	36	9
Monster, ⅔ lb	1330	95	51
Mushroom 'N' Swiss, ⅓ lb	710	41	52
Six Dollar	980	66	63
Sandwiches:			
Chicken: Charbroiled BBQ Chicken	330	6	50
Charbroiled Chicken Club	540	31	38
Hand Breaded Chicken Fillet	530	32	38
Fish, Charbroiled Cod	380	18	39
Breaded Chicken Tenders: Without Sauce			
3 pieces, 4.5 oz	260	13	13
5 pieces, 7.5 oz	440	21	21
Sides:			
Beer Battered Onion Rings, 4.5 oz	410	24	45
Natural Cut Fries: Small, 4 oz	360	18	47
Medium, 5.85 oz	490	24	63
Large, 6.8 oz	530	26	69
Kids Meals: Includes Kid's Fries & Small Drink			
Cheeseburger	550	26	61
Chicken Tenders	400	19	37
Hamburger	500	22	61
Breakfast:			
Biscuits: Bacon, Egg & Cheese	460	26	38
Biscuit 'N' Gravy	460	26	49
Chicken Fillet	550	32	47
Cinnamon 'N Raisin	300	15	40
Country Fried Steak	510	31	44
Loaded Omelet	490	28	40
Monster	730	49	40
Sausage and Egg	560	37	39
Big Country Platter, Bacon, without syrup, jam & butter	880	43	93

Continued Next Page...

Hardee's® cont... (Mar '14)

Breakfast (Cont):

	C	F	Cb
Bowl, Low Carb	660	52	10
Burrito, Loaded	580	34	46
Platter, with Bacon	760	45	51
Sandwiches, Frisco	450	19	45

Sunrise Croissants:

With Bacon	440	30	27
With Ham	450	28	30
With Sausage	590	44	28

Breakfast Sides:

Grits	100	3	16
Hash Rounds: Small, 2.92 oz	260	15	23
Medium, 4.23 oz	370	22	38
Large, 5.75 oz	510	30	45

Desserts:

Apple Turnover w/o Cinn. Sugar	270	13	35
Chocolate Chip Cookie: Fresh (1)	290	15	35
Wrapped (2)	240	10	36
Single Scoop Ice Cream:			
Bowl, 4 oz	240	13	27
Cone, 4.4 oz	290	13	37

Drinks:

Hot Chocolate	150	3	18
Ice Cream Malts: Per 14.6 oz Cup			
Chocolate	780	35	99
Strawberry	770	35	97
Vanilla	780	35	98
Ice Cream Shakes: Per 14 oz Cup			
Chocolate; Strawberry, average	705	34	86
Vanilla	700	33	86

For Complete Nutritional Data ~ see CalorieKing.com

Hissho Sushi® (Feb '14)

Starters: Per Serving

	C	F	Cb
Baby Octopus Salad, 3.5 oz	150	2	18
Spring Rolls: Regular (2), 4.9 oz	135	2	18
Garden (2), 4.9 oz	130	3	23
Grilled Chicken (2), 4.9 oz	140	4	19
Ocean Salmon (2), 4.9 oz	150	5	16
Ocean Tuna (2), 4.9 oz	155	4	16

Hissho Sushi® cont... (Feb '14)

Maki Sushi: Per 6 Pieces Unless Indicated

	C	F	Cb
Rolls: Blazing California	265	2	53
Boston	265	2	53
California	275	3	56
Crab Salad	270	3	53
Crunchy	285	3	53
Dynamite: Salmon	295	5	51
Shrimp	285	3	52
Tuna	290	4	49
Yellowtail	295	4	51
Inari	285	4	54
Nippon Favorite: Salmon, 16 pcs	330	2	65
Tuna, 16 pieces	330	2	64
Philadelphia	345	10	56
Snow Crab	280	3	56
Sushicado: Salmon, 12 pieces	510	7	92
Shrimp, 6 pieces	300	3	56

Specialty Items: Per 4 Pieces

Rolls:			
Caterpillar	330	5	60
Grande Finale	280	5	48
Living Color	250	3	43
Mango Tango	250	5	37
Salmon Lover	305	8	42
Sriracha Party	450	8	77
Tempura Shrimp	255	3	52
TNT: Salmon	290	4	52
Shrimp	280	2	52
Tuna	290	3	50
Wasabi Crunch	335	7	53

Hot Dog on a Stick® (Feb '14)

Menu Items:

	C	F	Cb
American Cheese on a Stick	260	16	21
Beef Hot Dog on a Bun	380	20	33
Turkey Hot Dog on a Stick	240	13	23
Veggie Dog on a Stick	220	8	24
Pepperjack Cheese on a Stick	240	14	19
Sides, French Fries, 4.5 oz	400	21	49
Dessert, Funnel Cake Sticks, (10)	210	8	31
Beverages: Per Regular Size, 16 fl.oz			
Lemonade: Original	150	0	38
Sugar Free	15	0	3
Lime	230	0	57

Fast - Foods & *Restaurants*

Hungry Howie's Pizza® (Feb '14)

Counts may vary in Florida.

Pizzas: Per Slice

	C	F	Cb
Cheese: Small, 1/8 pizza	170	4	23
Medium, 1/8 pizza	180	4.5	24
Large, 1/10 pizza	200	5	25
X-Large, 1/12 pizza	240	6	33

Oven Baked Subs: Per 1/2 Sub

Deluxe Italian	505	18	61
Ham & Cheese	475	15	61
Steak & Cheese	490	15	64
Turkey Club	555	15	63
Vegetarian	530	21	64

Sides: Boneless Wings, 3 pieces

Boneless Wings, 3 pieces	145	5	12
Howie Wings, 5 wings	180	13	0

Salads: Serves 2, Small Size, Without Dressing

Antipasto	230	15	6
Chef	230	13	8
Garden	40	0.5	7
Greek	250	15	16

Dressings: Per 1 oz

Creamy Italian	120	12	2
Greek	110	11	2
Ranch	180	19	1
Thousand Island	140	14	4

In-N-Out Burger® (Feb '14)

Burgers:

	C	F	Cb
Hamburger: With Onion	390	19	39
With Mustard/Ketchup, w/o Spread	310	10	41
Protein Style w/ Lettuce Wrap, w/o Bun	240	17	11
Cheeseburger: With Onion	480	27	39
With Mustard/Ketchup, w/o Spread	400	18	41
Protein Style w/ Lettuce Wrap, w/o Bun	330	25	11
Double Double: With Onion	670	41	39
With Mustard/Ketchup, w/o Spread	590	32	41
Protein Style w/ Lettuce Wrap, w/o Bun	520	39	11

French Fries, 4.5 oz

French Fries, 4.5 oz	395	18	54

Drinks: Milk, 10 fl.oz

Milk, 10 fl.oz	180	6	18
Coca-Cola, 16 fl.oz	195	0	54
Dr Pepper; 7-Up, av., 16 fl.oz	200	0	53
Lemonade, 16 fl.oz	180	0	40
Root Beer, 16 fl.oz	220	0	60

Shakes:

Chocolate, 15 fl.oz	590	29	72
Strawberry, 15 fl.oz	590	27	81
Vanilla, 15 fl.oz	580	31	67

IHOP® (Feb '14)

Pancakes:

Buttermilk: *With Menu Toppings*

	C	F	Cb
Full Stack (5)	750	22	115
Short Stack (3)	470	15	69
Chocolate Choc. Chip, Buttermilk Style (4)	710	23	110
Double Blueberry (4)	690	17	118
Strawberry Banana (4)	760	17	137

Condiments:

Syrup: Blueberry; Maple, 1 fl.oz	110	0	26
Boysenberry; Strawberry, 1 fl.oz	100	0	26
Sugar-Free Syrup, 1 fl.oz	15	0	5

French Toast & Waffles: W/ Toppings Unless Indicated

French Toast: Original	720	30	92
Berry Brioche	770	29	114
Strawberry Banana	880	28	138
Waffle, Belgian	400	20	47

Savory Crepes:

Chicken Florentine	1020	64	53
Garden Stuffed	1230	92	56

Sweet Crepes:

Blueberry-Fruit Topped	1180	70	117
Cheese Blintzes	1210	89	71
Danish Fruit	1110	68	111

Hearty Omelettes: Without Pancakes or Sides

Big Steak	1290	92	51
Garden	920	77	14
Hearty Ham & Cheese	950	69	17
Spinach & Mushroom	1000	82	22

Breakfast Combinations: As Served, w/o Syrup

Biscuits & Gravy Combo with Country Gravy	1440	92	112
Breakfast Sampler	1220	76	82
Chicken Fried Chicken & Eggs, with Country Gravy	1270	71	104
Chorizo & Egg	1440	86	110
T-Bone Steak & Eggs, 12 oz	1300	73	73

Sandwiches & Burgers: Without Sides

Bacon Cheddar Chicken Sandwich	950	58	53
Chicken Clubhouse Super Stacker	1000	59	61
Mels: Ham & Egg	1190	74	67
Spinach, Rstd Red Pepp. & Chse	1270	89	69
Turkey & Bacon Club Sandwich	780	42	57

Hearty Dinner Favorites: Without Sides

Chicken Fried Chicken, with Country Gravy	840	41	89
French Onion Pot Roast	940	47	88
Simple & Fit Grilled Glazed Chicken	400	15	30
T-Bone Steak, 12 oz	1020	57	67

Updated Nutrition Data ~ www.CalorieKing.com
Persons with Diabetes ~ See Disclaimer (Page 22)

Jack in the Box® (Mar '14)

Sandwiches & Burgers:

	C	F	Cb
Bacon Ultimate Cheeseburger	905	56	44
Hamburger: Original	280	11	32
With Cheese	320	14	32
Jumbo Jack:			
Original	490	23	44
With Cheese	570	30	45
Junior Bacon Cheeseburger	390	21	32
Sirloin Cheeseburger, with Bacon	1030	71	52
Sourdough Jack	660	41	40
Sourdough Cheesesteak Melt	450	25	40
Ultimate Cheeseburger	820	49	44

Chicken & Fish:

	C	F	Cb
Chicken Sandwich	410	21	42
With Bacon	470	25	42
Chicken Strips: Crispy, 4 pieces	560	24	53
Grilled, 4 pieces	250	7	5
Fish Sandwich	390	15	46
Jack's Spicy Chkn S'wich	530	20	61
With Cheese	600	25	62
Sourdough Gr. Chicken Club	540	26	38

Breakfast:

	C	F	Cb
Biscuit: Bacon, Egg & Cheese	430	25	35
Sausage, Egg & Cheese	560	38	36
Breakfast Jack: Regular	280	11	30
With Bacon	310	14	30
Croissants: Sausage	560	39	32
Supreme	450	27	32
Sandwiches: Extreme Sausage	660	47	32
Sourdough	410	21	35
Ultimate	520	25	42
Hash Brown	190	13	17
Meaty Burrito, with salsa	620	37	40

Snacks & Sides:

	C	F	Cb
Bacon Cheddar Pot. Wedges, 8.8 oz	600	41	58
Chiquita Apple Bites, med.	70	0	17
Egg Rolls (3), w/o sauce	440	22	46
Mozzarella Cheese Sticks:			
3 Pieces	280	16	22
6 Pieces	560	33	43
Stuffed Jalapenos:			
3 Pieces	220	12	21
7 Pieces	510	29	49
Onion Rings (8), 4.25 oz	450	28	45
Seasoned Curly Fries, med., 4.5 oz	430	25	46

Healthy Dining:

	C	F	Cb
Chicken Fajita, without Salsa	320	11	33
Chicken Teriyaki Bowl	690	6	133
Grilled Chicken Strips,			
w/ Teriyaki Dipping Sce	310	8	16

Jack in the Box® cont... (Mar '14)

Salads: No Dressing or Condiments

	C	F	Cb
Chicken Club with Grilled Chicken	360	20	12
Grilled Chicken	250	9	14
Southwest Chicken,			
with Grilled Chicken Strips	350	15	28
Croutons	50	3	10
Dressings: Bacon Ranch	220	23	3
Creamy Southwest	190	19	3
Light Ranch	130	13	2
Low Fat Balsamic Vinaigrette	25	1.5	3

Sauces:

	C	F	Cb
Dipping Sauce: Barbecue, 1 oz	40	0	10
Buttermilk House, 1 oz	130	13	3
Frank's Red Hot Buffalo, 1 oz	10	0	2
Sweet & Sour, 1 oz	45	0	11
Tartar, 0.5 oz	150	16	2
Sandwich Sauce:			
Mayo-Onion, 0.5 oz	90	10	0
Soy,, 0.25 oz	5	0	1
Taco, 0.25 oz	0	0	0

Shakes & Desserts:

	C	F	Cb
Chocolate Overload Cake	300	7	57
Churros, Mini (5)	350	18	42
New York Style Cheesecake	310	17	32
Shakes: 16 oz, with Whipped Topping			
Chocolate	800	38	101
Oreo Cookie	810	43	92
Strawberry	780	38	95
Vanilla	700	38	76

For Complete Nutritional Data ~ see CalorieKing.com

Jack's® (Feb '14)

Sandwiches:

	C	F	Cb
Big Bacon Cheeseburger	610	41	31
Big Jack Burger	530	33	35
Cheeseburger	380	21	31
Chicken Fillet Sandwich	490	24	40
Double Big Jack Cheese Burger	850	59	35
Double Cheeseburger	540	33	31
Grilled Chicken Sandwich	380	16	32
Hamburger	340	18	31
Chicken, Chicken Fingers, 3 pieces	300	14	14
Fries, regular	310	13	42
Breakfast: Egg & Cheese Biscuit	360	21	31
Sausage, Egg & Cheese Biscuit	520	35	32
Steak Biscuit	480	28	43

For Complete Menu & Data ~ see CalorieKing.com

Jamba Juice® (Feb '14)

	C	F	Cb
Smoothies:			
All Fruit: *Original Size, 22 fl.oz*			
Mega Mango	340	0.5	85
Peach Perfection	300	0.5	75
Pomegranate Paradise	340	0.5	85
Classics: *Per 16 fl.oz*			
Banana Berry	290	1	68
Mango-A-Go-Go	290	1	69
Peach Pleasure; Pomeg. Pick-Me-Up	260	1	61
Strawberry Surf Rider	320	1	78
Creamy Treats: *Per 16 fl oz*			
Chocolate Moo'd	430	4	86
Orange Dream Machine	350	1	76
Peanut Butter Moo'd	480	10	83
Fit 'n Fruitful, all var., av., 16 fl.oz	285	4.5	53
Fruit & Veggie: *Per 16 fl.oz*			
Apple & Greens; Berry upBEET, av.	225	1	50
Orange Carrot Karma	180	0.5	43
Tropical Harvest	230	0.5	56
Make It Light, all var., av., 16 fl.oz	180	1	42
Pre Boosted: *Per 16 fl.oz*			
Acai Super-Antioxidant	260	4	54
Orange C-Booster	250	1	59
Protein Berry Workout	290	0	54
Probiotic Fruit & Yogurt Blends,			
average all flavors, 16 fl.oz	240	0	49
Fresh Squeezed Juices: *Per 12 fl.oz*			
Carrot	100	0.5	22
Orange	170	0.5	39
Shots: *Single*			
Wheatgrass Detox, 1 fl oz	5	0	1
Breakfast:			
Steel-Cut Oatmeal: *As Served, with Fruit & Brown*			
Sugar Unless Indicated			
Plain, without fruit	220	3.5	44
Berry Cherry Pecan	340	9	62
Average other Fruit Flavors	285	4	59
California Flat Bread: *Per Flatbread*			
Four Cheesy, 5.75 oz	420	16	46
Smokehouse Chicken, 6 oz	390	10	53
Baked Goods: *Per Item*			
Apple Cinnamon Pretzel, 5 oz	380	4	76
Berry Agave Bar, 3 oz	220	12	26
Cheddar Tomato Twist	240	4.5	41
Cinnamon Swirl	250	11	33
Sourdough Parmesan Pretzel, 5 oz	410	10	67
Fuit & Yogurt Parfaits: *Per 16 oz*			
Berry; Mango Peach Toppers, av	465	9	89
Chunky Strawberry	570	17	93

Jersey Mike's Subs® (Feb '14)

	C	F	Cb
Cold Subs: *Per Regular, on White,*			
without Vinegar, Oil or Mayo Unless Indicated			
#1 BLT	570	23	67
#2 Jersey Shore Favorite	560	15	70
#3 American Classic	560	15	69
#5 Super Sub	580	16	71
#6 Roast Beef & Provolone	720	22	67
#7 Turkey Breast & Provolone	525	12	64
#8 Club Sub with Mayonnaise	890	49	70
#9 Club Supreme w/ Mayonnaise	935	49	69
#10 Albacore Tuna	910	56	70
#13 Original Italian	680	24	72
#14 Veggie	720	30	72
Hot Subs/Cheese Steaks: *Per Regular on White Roll*			
#15 Meatball & Cheese	890	48	75
#17: Chicken Philly	620	22	69
Steak Philly	595	21	65
#43: Chipotle Chicken	920	52	71
Chipotle Steak	875	51	68
#18 Chicken Parmesan	635	19	80
#19 BBQ Beef	700	13	87
#20 Pastrami & Swiss	560	14	64
#56: Big Kahuna Steak	670	25	69
Big Kahuna Chicken	690	29	67
Cold Wraps: *With Flour Tortilla, w/o Vin./Oil or Mayo*			
#1 BLT	590	29	60
#2 Jersey Shore Favorite	580	22	64
#3 American Classic	580	22	63
#5 Super Sub	600	22	65
Salads: *Without Dressing*			
Chef, 16 oz	240	10	12
Grilled Chicken Caesar, 12.5 oz	510	35	11
Tossed, 12 oz	50	0.5	11
Tuna, 18 oz	690	60	15
Dressings: *Per 2 Tbsp, 1 oz*			
Caesar	150	15	2
Chipotle Mayo	180	20	0
Golden Italian	110	11	3
Ranch	120	12	2
Russian	160	16	4
Desserts: Cookie, Choc Chip, 1.5 oz	190	6	22
Chocolate Brownie, 1.5 oz	170	7	23
Drinks: Mountain Dew, 22 oz	310	0	84
Mug Root Beer, 22 oz	290	0	79
Tropicana Twister Orange, 22 oz	360	0	96

Updated Nutrition Data ~ www.CalorieKing.com
Persons with Diabetes ~ See Disclaimer (Page 22)

Jimmy John's® (Feb '14)

Subs: (8")

	C	**F**	**Cb**
Figures Based on French Bread w/ Standard Toppings & Mayo, Unless Indicated			
#1 Pepe	590	30	50
#2 Big John	500	23	47
#3 Totally Tuna without dressing	680	35	53
#4 Turkey Tom	475	20	49
#5 Vito with Italian Vinaigrette	605	31	52
#6 Vegetarian	650	39	52
JJBLT	560	31	52

Giant Club Sandwiches: *Figures Based on French Bread w/ Standard Toppings & Mayo, Unless Indicated*

#7 Gourmet Smoked Ham	760	35	70
#8 Billy Club	790	37	68
#9 Italian Night w/ Mayo & Vinaig.	935	54	72
#10 Hunter's Club	800	38	66
#11 Country Club	750	34	69
#12 Beach Club	810	43	71
#13 Gourmet Veggie Club	970	60	72
#14 Bootlegger	660	27	66
#15 Club Tuna without dressing	1000	56	73
#16 Club Lulu	720	35	71
#17 Ultimate Porker, with 9-grain wheat bread	730	36	72

Plain Slims: *Figures Based on French Bread without Toppings, Dressing or Mayo*

Slim 1 Ham & Cheese	530	13	67
Slim 2 Roast Beef	440	5.5	64
Slim 3 Tuna Salad	775	36	69
Slim 4 Turkey Breast	410	3	65
Slim 5 Salami Capicola & Cheese	615	23	66
Slim 6 Double Provolone	570	21	66

Sides:

Jimmy Chips: BBQ, 1 oz	160	9	17
Jalapeno, 1 oz	150	8	17
Regular, 1 oz	150	9	16
Sea Salt & Vinegar, 1 oz	150	8	17
Thinny, 1 oz	130	5	19
Jumbo Kosher Dill Pickle	20	0	4

Johnny Rockets® (Feb '14)

Original Hamburgers:

	C	**F**	**Cb**
Hamburger #12	970	61	60
Original Burger	870	55	58
Rocket: Single	950	60	56
Double	1420	97	56
Route 66	1000	68	52
Smoke House: Single	1100	66	70
Double	1700	115	70
Streamliner	420	11	59
Chicken Tenders, without Sauce	880	56	42

Hot Dogs: *With Condiments*

Regular	550	24	63
Chili Cheese Dog	770	51	42

Rocket Melts: *Without Sides*

Patty Melt, on Rye Bread	880	54	53
Tuna Melt, on White Bread	810	52	45

Sandwiches:

BLT, on White Bread	480	26	49
Chicken Club, on White Bread	920	36	77
Grilled Chicken, on Hamburger Bun	590	26	52
Philly Cheese Steak, w/ Amer. Cheese, on Hoagie Roll	750	38	55
Tuna Salad, on White Bread	750	48	47

Breakfast: *With Menu Set Components*

Patty n' Eggs:

Beef, with White Toast	1370	89	90
Turkey, with Sourdough Toast	1260	83	88
Boca, with Wheat Toast	1100	61	100
The Works	1000	70	55

Starters:

Chili Bowl, 9 oz	610	48	17
Fries: American Fries, 7 oz	480	19	69
Bacon Cheese Fries, 13 oz	830	44	82
Cheese Fries, 12 oz	740	37	82
Chili Cheese Fries, 14 oz	1000	56	93
½ Rings & ½ American Fries, 8 oz	660	29	79
Onion Rings, 9 oz	880	40	90
Rocket Wings, Traditional, without Dressing, 7 wings	660	49	19

Desserts: Apple Pie a la mode | 840 | 49 | 94 |

Super Sundae w/ Hot Fudge, 11 oz	660	41	65

Beverages:

Coke, 20 oz	240	0	67
Fanta Orange, 20 oz	270	0	74
Minute Made Lemonade, 20 oz	240	0	65

Deluxe Shakes:

Chocolate Vanilla Twist, 12 oz	910	50	102
Oreo Cookies & Cream, 12 oz	1030	61	110
Strawberry Banana, 11.5 oz	900	50	99

KFC® (Mar '14)

Chicken Pieces: Per Piece

	C	F	Cb
Original Recipe:			
Breast, 5.75 oz	320	14	13
Drumstick, 1.75 oz	120	7	3
Thigh, 3.4 oz	290	21	8
Whole Wing, 2 oz	140	8	5
Original Recipe Bites: 6 Bites	200	9	7
10 Bites	330	15	12
Extra Crispy: Breast, 6.4 oz	490	29	20
Drumstick, 2 oz	160	10	5
Thigh, 3.8 oz	370	26	15
Whole Wing, 2 oz	210	15	8
Kentucky Grilled:			
Breast, 4.25 oz	220	7	0
Drumstick, 1.5 oz	90	4	0
Thigh, 2.5 oz	170	10	0
Whole Wing, 1.25 oz	80	4.5	1
Spicy Crispy:			
Breast, 6.17 oz	520	34	23
Drumstick, 2 oz	150	10	5
Thigh, 3.5 oz	350	27	11
Whole Wing, 1.65 oz	160	12	6

Strips & Filet:

	C	F	Cb
Extra Crispy Tenders:			
2 Strips, 4 oz	250	13	11
3 Strips, 6 oz	380	20	17
Original Filet, 3.5 oz	200	9	6

Wings: Without Dipping Sauce

	C	F	Cb
Fiery Buffalo, Hot	70	4	5
Honey BBQ, Hot	80	4	8
Hot	70	4	3

Dipping Sauces: Per 0.9 oz Container

	C	F	Cb
Bacon/Creamy Ranch	140	15	1
Creamy Buffalo	70	7	2
Honey BBQ	40	0	9
Honey Mustard	120	10	6
KFC Signature Sauce	70	5	5
Orange Ginger	50	0	11
Spicy Chipotle	70	3.5	8
Sweet & Sour	45	0	12

KFC Famous Bowls & Pot Pie:

	C	F	Cb
Famous Bowl: Snack Size, 6.5 oz	270	12	28
18.5 oz	690	30	80
Chicken Pot Pie, 14 oz	790	45	66

KFC® cont... (Mar '14)

Sandwiches: With Sauce

	C	F	Cb
Chicken Littles	310	18	23
Colonal's Original	450	20	41
Crispy Twister	610	32	52
Doublicious	530	27	42
Honey BBQ	320	3.5	47

Value Boxes:

	C	F	Cb
Drumsticks: Original	400	22	37
Extra Crispy	450	25	39
Grilled	380	19	34
Popcorn Chicken	700	39	61
Thighs: Original	540	32	42
Extra Crispy	660	41	49
Grilled	460	25	34
Wings: Fiery Buffalo	510	28	50
BBQ	540	28	57
Hot	490	27	45

Salads: Without Dressing or Croutons

	C	F	Cb
Caesar, Side	40	2	2
Crispy Chicken BLT	350	18	18
Crispy Chicken Caesar	330	17	16
House Side Salad	15	0	3

Dressings & Add-Ins:

	C	F	Cb
Creamy Parmesan Caesar, 2 oz	260	26	4
Light Italian, 1 oz	15	0.5	2
Original Ranch Fat Free, 1.5 oz	35	0	8
Croutons, Parm. Garlic, 1 pouch	70	3	8

Sides: Per Single Portion

	C	F	Cb
BBQ Baked Beans, 4.5 oz	210	1.5	41
Biscuit, 2 oz	180	8	23
Cole Slaw, 4.2 oz	170	10	19
Corn on the Cob (3"), 2.5 oz	70	0.5	16
Cornbread Muffin, 2 oz	210	9	28
Macaroni & Cheese, 4.75 oz	170	6	22
Mashed Potatoes, with Gravy, 5 oz	120	4	19
Potato Wedges, 3.8 oz	290	15	35

Desserts:

	C	F	Cb
Apple Turnover, 2.85 oz	230	10	32
Reese's Peanut Butter Pie, 2.6 oz	310	19	31
Sweet Life Sugar Cookie, 1.1 oz	160	7	21

Kilwins® ~ see CalorieKing.com

Kolache® ~ see CalorieKing.com

Krispy Kreme® (Feb '14)

Doughnuts:	C	F	Cb
Apple Fritter	400	20	50
Caramel Kreme Crunch	390	20	50
Chocolate Iced Glazed Cruller	260	12	38
Chocolate Iced Cake	280	15	34
Chocolate Iced Custard Filled	310	17	36
Chocolate Iced Glazed	240	11	33
Chocolate Iced, Kreme Filled	360	21	40
Chocolate Iced Glazed w/ Sprinkles	250	12	35
Cinnamon Apple Filled	290	16	33
Cinnamon Bun	260	16	28
Cinnamon Twist	240	15	23
Dulce de Leche	300	18	31
Glazed: Chocolate Cake	300	15	41
Cinnamon	200	11	25
Cruller	220	12	27
Kreme Filled	340	20	38
Lemon Filled	290	16	35
Maple Iced	230	11	32
Original	190	11	21
Raspberry Filled	290	16	36
Sour Cream	310	14	43
Powdered: Cake	220	11	27
Strawberry Filled	290	16	33
Sugar	190	11	20
Traditional Cake	190	12	19
Doughnut Holes: Orig. Glazed (4)	200	11	26
Glazed Cake, Chocolate (4)	190	9	25

Kool Kreme:

Doughnut Shakes: *Per 12 oz*	C	F	Cb
Original Glazed	600	26	80
Chocolate Cake	650	30	86
Raspberry Filled	630	26	87
Doughnut Sundaes:			
Orig. Glazed	460	17	69
Chocolate Cake	560	21	89
Strawberry Cake	560	20	90

Chiller Beverages: *Without Whipped Cream Topping*
Orange You Glad; Very Berry, average:

	C	F	Cb
12 fl.oz	175	0	43
20 fl.oz	295	0	71

Kremey Chillers: *Includes Whipped Cream Topping*

Berries & Kreme: 12 fl.oz	620	28	92
20 fl.oz	960	40	150
Oranges & Kreme: 12 fl.oz	630	28	92
20 fl.oz	970	40	150

For Complete Menu & Daa ~ See CalorieKing.com

Krystal® (Feb '14)

Burgers:	C	F	Cb
Big Angus: Original	550	35	46
Dble, w/ Bacon & Cheese	850	59	48
Krystal:			
Original	130	6	70
Double	290	13	33
Bacon Cheese	200	11	20
Chik	300	16	27
Double Cheese	350	17	34
Pups: Chili Cheese	230	14	16
Corn	240	14	22
Plain	150	8	15
Fries:			
Chili Cheese, 8.25 oz	570	29	62
French, medium, 4.25 oz	310	13	46
Sides:			
Chik'n Bites, small, 3 oz	200	7	20
Salad, Crispy Chicken, 11 oz	370	21	20
Breakfast Items:			
Biscuits:			
Bacon, Egg & Cheese	440	24	34
Chik	400	18	43
Gravy	350	18	41
Plain	260	13	32
Sausage	420	28	32
Sandwich, Krystal Sunriser	200	11	16
Scramblers:			
Original: With Bacon	330	16	27
With Sausage	420	26	27
4-Carb Scrambler,			
With Sausage	620	52	3
Desserts:			
Apple Turnover, fried	220	8	34
Lemon Icebox Pie	320	9	56
Drinks: *Per 16 fl.oz, with ¼ ice*			
Coca-Cola,			
Classic	120	0	32
Diet Coke	0	0	0

For Complete Menu & Data ~ see CalorieKing.com

For Menu Updates,
Check Author's Website
www.CalorieKing.com

Fast - Foods & *Restaurants*

LaRosa's Pizzeria® (Feb '14)

Pizzas:

	C	F	Cb
Focaccia Style: *Per Slice, ⅒ of Medium Pizza*			
Florentine	240	13	24
Roma	300	18	23
Hand Tossed: *Per Slice, ⅛ of Medium Pizza*			
Cheese	230	8	29
Double Pepperoni	300	14	29
Big 4: Meat	325	15	29
Pick 4	280	11	30
Veggie	240	7	30
Multigrain Wheat: *Per ½₂ of 12" Pizza*			
Pepperoni-Sausage	190	11	14
Average other varieties	125	5	15
Pan Crust: *Per Slice, ⅛ of Medium Pizza*			
Cheese	300	16	30
Double Pepperoni	370	22	30
Big 4: Meat	325	15	29
Pick 4	275	11	30
Veggie	235	7	30
Traditional Crust: *Per Slice, ⅛ of Medium Pizza*			
Cheese	200	10	19
Double Pepperoni	280	16	20
Big 4: Meat	285	16	20
Pick 4	240	12	20
Veggie	200	8	21
Calzones: *Per Calzone, No Dipping Sauce*			
Cheese & Pepperoni	960	45	101
Cheese	840	34	101
Philly Cheesesteak	870	39	90
Sausage Pelucci	1040	52	92
Classic Hoagys: Baked Meatball	700	29	75
Original Steak	740	33	69
Pasta Dinner: *Without Bread, Soup or Salad*			
Cheese Ravioli	660	26	80
Lasagna, with Meat Sauce	735	38	84
Spaghetti: With Alfredo Sauce	975	50	104
With Meatballs	870	28	119
With Meat Sauce	700	18	104
With Traditional Sauce	640	12	113
Ziti Chicken Alfredo	980	42	102
Ziti Sausage Pelucci	765	20	115
Appetizers: Garlic Fries, 11 oz	630	34	74
Four Taste Sampler, 6.63 oz	475	26	48
Fried Cheesesticks, 6.2 oz	450	22	45
Garlic Bread, 2 pcs, 2.6 oz	300	14	38
Kitchen Chips, 10 oz	570	27	71
Onion Twists, 10 oz	910	57	91
Rondo: Pepperoni, 4.6 oz	545	36	35
Spinach/Cheese, av., 4.5 oz	405	22	35

For Complete Nutritional Data ~ see CalorieKing.com

La Salsa Fresh Mexican® (Feb '14)

Appetizers:

	C	F	Cb
Salsa & Chips: Regular, 14.5 oz	700	32	87
With Guacamole, 14.5 oz	970	55	103
Chips (15), 1.4 oz	200	10	25
Nachos:			
Black Beans: With Carnitas	1570	83	141
With Chicken	1600	83	148
With Steak	1580	84	142
Pinto Beans: With Carnitas	1560	83	139
With Chicken	1590	83	146
With Steak	1565	84	139
Burritos: Without Chips			
Black Beans: With Cheese	1100	48	132
With Carnitas	1205	51	132
With Chicken	1240	52	139
With California Steak	815	35	89
Pinto Beans: With Cheese	1070	48	115
With Chicken	1200	52	122
With Steak	1175	54	115
Baja Fish Burrito	875	53	58
Overstuffed Grilled Burrito:			
With Carnitas	1200	59	108
With Chicken	1260	59	110
With Steak	1290	66	109
Grande, Black Beans:			
With Carnitas or Chicken, average	810	34	92
With Steak	820	35	91
Tacos: Without Chips			
Baja Fish	395	22	29
Baja Shrimp	320	19	30
Guadalajara Carnitas	320	15	30
Mexico City, Chicken or Steak, av.	190	4	27
Quesadillas: Without Chips			
Classic: Carnitas	960	58	57
Chicken	955	57	58
Steak	965	59	57
Grande, Pinto Beans, with choice of meat, average	1130	61	90
Grande, Black Beans, with choice of meat, average	1140	61	91
Favorites: Without Chips			
Stuffed Fajita Quesadilla:			
With Carnitas or Chicken, av.	860	51	54
With Shrimp	800	49	54
With Steak	885	55	53
Fire Roasted Bowls:			
Black Beans: W/ Chicken	730	32	74
With Steak	735	34	73
Without Meat	630	29	71
Pinto Beans: W/ Chicken	730	32	73
With Steak	720	34	70
Without Meat	620	29	69

212

Updated Nutrition Data ~ www.CalorieKing.com
Persons with Diabetes ~ See Disclaimer (Page 22)

Little Caesars® (Feb '14)

14" Pizza: Per Slice, 1/8 Pizza	**C**	**F**	**Cb**
Optional: 3 Meat Treat	340	17	32
Hula Hawaiian: W/ Ham	280	9	35
W/ Canadian Bacon	280	9	35
Ultimate Supreme	310	13	33
Veggie	270	10	33
Deep Dish: Just Cheese	340	15	38
Pepperoni	380	18	38
Hot-N-Ready:			
Just Cheese	250	9	32
Pepperoni	280	11	32
Baby Pan! Pan!,			
Cheese & Pepperoni, 1 pan	360	18	33
Caesar Wings: *Per Wing*			
BBQ: Regular	80	5	3
Spicy	70	5	1
Buffalo, Mild or Hot	70	5	1
Garlic Parmesan	90	7	1
Lemon Pepper	90	8	0
Oven Roasted	70	5	0
Caesar Dips: *Per 1 oz Container Unless Indicated*			
BBQ; Buffalo Ranch	160	17	2
Buffalo	100	10	2
Buttery Garlic, 0.5 oz	130	14	0
Cheezy Jalapeno	140	15	2
Ranch	170	18	2
Bread: *Per Piece*			
Crazy Bread, 1 stick	100	3	15
Crazy Sauce, 4 oz	45	0	10
Italian Cheese Bread	130	6	13
Pepperoni Cheese Bread	150	8	13

Lone Star Steakhouse® (Oct '12)

Appetizers: Per Serving	**C**	**F**	**Cb**
Chicken Tenders: Original, 3.5 oz	320	19	27
Buffalo Style, 3.5 oz	300	19	23
Lone Star Wings, mild, 3.5 oz	305	20	5
Spin. & Artichoke Dip, 3.5 oz	160	13	4.5
Texas Rose, 3.5 oz	285	19	25
Meals: *Without Sides, Toppings & Sauce*			
Mesquite Grilled Steaks:			
Chopped Steak, 9.6 oz	710	52	0
Five Star Filet, 6 oz	335	18	2
NY Strip, 9.6 oz	525	28	0
Texas Ribeye, 12.5 oz	710	40	5.5

Lone Star® cont... (Oct '12)

Meals (Cont): Without Sides, Toppings & Sauce | | | |
Ribs Combo:	**C**	**F**	**Cb**
Baby Back Ribs:			
With Chicken, 10.45 oz	740	30	46
With Sirloin, 10.2 oz	655	33	7.5
Grilled Pork Chops: 3.5 oz	190	10	0
5.9 oz	315	16	0
Seafood:			
Fried Shrimp Entree, 11.65 oz	865	40	97
Grilled Shrimp: 3.5 oz	60	2	5.5
11 oz	190	7	17
Lobster Tail, 3.5 oz	150	1	14
Lobster & Lobster, 3.95 oz	165	1	15
Sweet Bourbon Salmon: 6oz	240	11	0
9 oz	360	16	0
Burgers:			
Bubba, 15.65 oz	1085	57	67
Bacon Bleu,13.45 oz	820	37	51
Cheeseburger, 14 oz	895	45	50
Lonestar, 12.15 oz	640	27	48
Swiss & Mushroom, 15.2 oz	845	38	53
Chili, 10 oz bowl	345	18	14
Salads: *Per Serving, Includes Dressing*			
Dinner, Caesar, 6.25 oz	145	11	8
Grilled Chicken Caesar	480	24	19
Lettuce Wedge	395	34	10
Steakhouse	710	53	2
Sides: *Per Serving*			
Garlic Mashed Potatoes, 1/2 cup	130	5	19
Macaroni & Cheese: 3.5 oz	80	4	8
8 oz	185	9	18
Steak Fries, 8 oz	610	26	86
Texas Rice, 8 oz	100	3.5	14

Long John Silver's® (Feb '14)

	C	**F**	**Cb**
Sandwiches & More:			
Chicken Tenders, 1 piece 2.4 oz	190	11	13
Ciabatta Jack: Chicken Sandwich	430	44	57
Fish Sandwich	570	35	45
Tacos: Baja Fish, 1 taco, 7oz	600	40	44
Chicken Strip Taco, 1 taco, 6.2 oz	560	36	44

Continued Next Page....

Long John's® cont... (Feb '14)

Seafood:

	C	F	Cb
Battered: Alaskan Pollock, 1 piece, 3.25 oz	230	15	14
Cod, 1 piece, 3 oz	230	15	10
Shrimp, 3 pieces, 1.5 oz	130	9	5
Breaded Catfish, 1 piece, 4.2 oz	300	17	26
Crab Cake, 1 cake, 2.2 oz	190	10	18
Hold The Batter: Cod, 1 piece 1.7 oz	45	3	0
Shrimp, 3 pieces, 1 oz	25	2	0
Snack Box: Breaded Clam Strips	280	18	20
Popcorn Shrimp, 3 oz	240	12	28

Sauces & Condiments:

Dipping Sauces:

	C	F	Cb
Cocktail, 1 oz	25	0	6
Tartar, 1 oz	100	8	6
Louisiana Hot Sauce, 1 tsp	0	0	0
Ketchup, 1 pouch, 1 oz	30	0	8
Malt Vinegar, 0.5 oz	0	0	0

Sides:

	C	F	Cb
Breaded Mozzarella Sticks (3)	170	10	12
Broccoli Cheese Soup, 1 bowl, 7.5 oz	220	18	8
Clam Chowder, 1 bowl	170	8	19
Cole Slaw, 4 oz	200	15	15
Corn Cobbette w/ Butter Oil, 3.5 oz	150	10	14
Crumblies, 1 oz	180	14	12
Fries, 4 oz	210	10	27
Hushpuppy, 2 pups, 1.5 oz	160	9	18
Jalapeno Cheddar Bites (5), 1 oz	250	16	18
Rice, 5 oz	180	1	37

For Complete Menu & Data ~ see CalorieKing.com

Macaroni Grill® (Feb '14)

	C	F	Cb
Tapas & Antipasti: Per Whole Appetizer as Served			
Calamari Fritti	850	51	58
Goat Cheese Peppadew Peppers	360	18	42
Mac & Chse Bites w/ Dip	990	78	45
Parmesan Fries	790	57	61
Spicy Ricotta Meatballs	370	29	17
Meals: Per Whole Entree, as Served			
Carne: Chianti BBQ Steak	1920	121	81
Pan-Roasted Pork Chop	1370	91	58
Pesce: Grilled King Salmon	1110	68	71
Parmesan-Crusted Sole	1550	104	99
Pasta: Carbonara	1260	68	101
Carmela's Chicken	930	31	111

Macaroni Grill® cont... (Oct '13)

Meals (Cont): Per Whole Entree

	C	F	Cb
Pasta (Cont): Lobster Ravioli	710	41	39
Mama's Trio	1430	99	77
Mushroom Ravioli	900	62	52
Penne Rustica	1160	49	110
Classics: Eggplant Parmesan	950	56	76
Fettuccine Alfredo, Chicken	1470	88	94
Lasagne Bolognese	630	40	27
Mom's: Ricotta Meatballs & Spaghetti Bolognese	1190	70	95
M'balls & Spag. Pomodoro	960	55	91
Chicken: Caprese	560	22	31
Grilled Spiedini	410	11	38
Marsala	810	35	61
Scallopine	1180	81	55
Under a Brick	1440	115	24

Flatbreads: Per Whole Meal, as Served

	C	F	Cb
Mushroom, & Goat Cheese	910	46	83
Roasted Chicken & Arugula	1060	50	83

Pizza: Per Whole Meal, as Served

	C	F	Cb
Italian Sausage	1100	52	100
Margherita	840	31	101
Primo Pepperoni	980	41	97

Salads: Includes Dressing

	C	F	Cb
Bibb & Blue	680	56	23
Market Chop	1010	71	33
Salad Sampler	1030	80	36
Warm Spinach	340	25	17

Soups: Per 8 oz Bowl

	C	F	Cb
Minestrone	310	14	32
Pomodorina	190	12	16

Dessert: Per Serving

	C	F	Cb
Gelato: Dark Chocolate	260	12	36
Double Vanilla	290	12	40
Homemade Chocolate Cake	990	56	114
Lemon Passion	580	33	65
New York Style Cheesecake	760	52	61
Sorbet, Blood Orange	170	0	41
Tiramisu	690	48	54

For Complete Nutritional Data ~ see CalorieKing.com

Manhattan Bagel® (Feb '14)

Bagels: Per Bagel

	C	F	Cb
Blueberry, 3.75 oz	300	1	65
Chocolate Chip, 3.75 oz	290	2.5	58
Cinnamon Raisin, 4 oz	330	1	70
Egg; Jalapeno Cheddar, av., 4 oz	320	2	67
Everything, 4.25 oz	330	2	68
Poppy, 4.25 oz	340	3	68
Pumpernickel, 3.5 oz	240	1.5	53
Salt, 4.25 oz	320	1	68
Sesame Seed, 4.5 oz	360	5	68
Cream Cheese: Plain, 1.25 oz	120	12	2
Plain, Reduced-Fat, 1.25 oz	110	9	4

For Complete Nutritional Data ~ see CalorieKing.com

Marie Callender's® (Feb '14)

Appetizers: Per Serving

	C	F	Cb
Crispy Chicken Tenders, 12.87 oz	870	47	72
Crispy Green Beans, 10.5oz	810	52	75
Mozzarella Sticks, 8.64 oz	690	42	46
Burgers and Sandwiches: With Fries			
Original Burger	1290	87	84
Albacore Tuna Melt	1430	92	99
Grilled Ham Stack	1260	81	96
Roasted Turkey Croissant Club	1450	97	95
Main Meals: Per Complete Meal as Served			
Comfort Classics:			
Artichoke & Mushroom Chicken	1070	74	38
Callender's Fish & Chips	1280	92	85
From The Grill: Gr. Rosemary Chkn	900	49	43
Gr. Atlantic Salmon, Cajun style	630	37	25
St. Louis BBQ Ribs	1090	72	58
Pasta Perfecto: Includes Garlic Bread			
Chicken & Broccoli Fettuccini	1540	87	119
Double Shrimp Pasta	1500	96	97
Pies, Chicken Pot Pie, w/out sides	1140	79	70
Fresh Crisp Salads: Includes Dressing			
Chinese Chicken	910	33	107
Gorgonzola, Pecan & Field Greens	990	53	79
Traditional Caesar, with Chicken	700	43	28
Sides: Cornbread,			
with Honey Butter, 3 oz	340	21	33
French Fries, 4 oz	380	20	45
Loaded Mashed Potatoes, 6.15 oz	340	23	23
Macaroni & Cheese, 6.35 oz	230	9	26
Soups: Per Bowl			
Chicken Noodle	130	0.5	22
Clam Chowder	270	13	22
Hearty Vegetable	90	3	13
Split Pea & Ham	220	13	17

Marie Callender's cont... (Feb '14)

Breakfast: As Served

	C	F	Cb
Griddle Greats:			
Belgian Waffles	600	19	99
Buttermilk Pancake Stack	720	30	99
Old Fashioned French Toast	830	31	123
Hashers: Country	1320	82	90
Tex-Mex	1180	71	99
Homestyle Choices:			
Country Fried Steak & Eggs	1580	70	179
Grilled Ham & Eggs	1170	47	146
Marie's Magnificent Six:			
With Bacon	750	36	80
With Sausage	910	52	81
Omelettes: BTA	1610	84	160
Denver	1380	65	149
Spanish	1550	78	165
Quiche: Bacon, 1 slice	990	79	45
Ham, 1 slice	1030	83	39
Desserts: Per Slice Unless Indicated			
Pies: Apple	630	39	66
Banana Cream, with Meringue	510	24	66
Chocolate Cream, with Meringue	570	26	77
Pumpkin, with Whipped Cream	530	23	70
Razzleberry	650	29	71

For Complete Nutritiona Data ~ see CalorieKing.com

Max & Erma's® (Feb '14)

Appetizers:

	C	F	Cb
Black Bean Roll-Ups w/o dressing	560	13	92
Wings: Buffalo (6)	820	81	5
Sweet Chili (6)	650	32	72
Specialties: As Served			
Crispy Chicken Tender Dinner	1410	81	126
Ribs: Half Rack	1320	76	88
Full Rack	2200	124	132
Salads: Entrée Size, w/ Dressing, w/out Breadstick			
Apple Pecan, with Chicken	1060	59	87
Caesar: Without Chicken	670	57	28
With Chicken	880	67	28
Sides: Onion rings	280	17	28
Herb Rice	250	2	51
Sweet And Treats:			
Banana Cream Pie	990	61	107
Triple Choc. Cake, with Ice Cream	1270	65	157

McAlister's Deli® (Feb '14)

Sandwiches: Per Whole Sandwich

	C	F	Cb
Classic: Grilled Chicken	680	37	46
Harvest Chicken Salad	760	53	51
The Italian	760	36	51
Tuna Salad	540	27	45
Veggie Pita	590	40	45
Club: Black Angus	810	40	68
Grilled Chicken	780	34	73
McAlister	770	36	73
Grilled Sandwiches:			
Four Cheese Griller	800	43	64
Smoky Pepper Jack Turkey	800	39	72
Spicy Southwest Chicken	920	52	74
Sweet Chipotle Chicken	640	19	75
Hot Sandwiches:			
California Turkey Reuben	850	50	66
French Dip	540	20	43
Ham Melt	610	25	52
Reuben	780	41	62
Roast Beef Melt	600	24	49
The Big Nasty	770	24	66
The New Yorker	740	30	51
Spuds: *Without Butter or Sour Cream*			
Bacon Angus Roast Beef	920	26	124
Cheese	710	18	118
Grilled Chicken	820	19	120
Max	940	33	120
Soups: *Per Bowl*			
Cheddar Potato	390	26	30
Chicken Noodle	140	2	20
Clam Chowder	400	22	39
Traditional Chili	540	34	25
Drinks:			
Lemonade	190	0	50
Sweet Tea	120	0	30

McDonald's® (Mar '14)

Burgers/Sandwiches:

	C	F	Cb
Big Mac	550	29	46
Cheeseburger	300	12	33
Double Cheeseburger	440	23	34
Hamburger	250	9	31
McDouble	390	19	33
Quarter Pounder: With Cheese	520	26	41
Double with Cheese	750	43	42
Filet-O-Fish	390	19	39
McChicken	360	16	40
McRib	500	26	44
Southern Style Crispy Chicken	420	19	43

McDonald's® cont... (Mar '14)

Premium Chicken Sandwiches:

	C	F	Cb
Classic: Crispy Chicken	510	22	55
Grilled Chicken	350	9	42
Club: Crispy Chicken	670	33	58
Grilled Chicken	510	20	44
Premium McWraps:			
Crispy: Chicken & Bacon	620	31	54
Chicken & Ranch	580	29	55
Chicken Sweet Chili	520	22	57
Grilled: Chicken & Bacon	460	18	40
Chicken & Ranch	420	16	41
Chicken Sweet Chili	360	9	43
Snack Wraps:			
Crispy Chicken: Chipotle BBQ	330	15	34
Honey Mustard	330	15	34
Ranch	350	18	32
Grilled Chicken: Chipotle BBQ	250	8	27
Honey Mustard	250	8	27
Ranch	270	12	25
Chicken:			
Spicy McBites: Snack Size, 3 oz	270	17	18
Shareable, 10 oz	910	55	61
McNuggets:			
6 pieces	280	18	18
10 pieces	470	30	30
Strips, 5 pieces	640	38	36
French Fries:			
Kids, 1.1 oz	100	5	13
Small, 2.5 oz	230	11	29
Medium, 4 oz	380	19	48
Large, 5.5 oz	500	25	63
Poutine, (Canada),	510	29	44
Sauces: Chipotle BBQ, 1 oz	50	0	11
Creamy Ranch, 0.8 oz	110	12	1
Spicy Buffalo, 0.8 oz	35	3	1
Sweet 'N Sour; Tangy BBQ, 1 oz	50	0	12
Snack, Apple Slices	15	0	4
Breakfast:			
Bagel, Classic Steak, Egg & Cheese	680	35	57
Big Breakfast: With Regular Biscuit	740	48	51
With Hotcakes	1090	56	111
Biscuits:			
Bacon Egg & Cheese: Reg. Bisc.	460	26	38
Large Biscuit	520	30	43
Sausage with Egg: Regular Bisc.	510	33	36
With Large Biscuit	570	37	42
Southern Style Chicken:			
Regular Biscuit	410	20	41
Large Biscuit	470	24	46
Steak & Egg:			
Regular Biscuit	540	32	38
McMuffin	420	23	31

Continued Next Page...

McDonald's® cont... (Mar'14)

Breakfast (Cont):

	C	F	Cb
Burrito, Sausage	300	16	26
Cinnamon Melts, 4 oz	460	19	66
Fruit & Maple Oatmeal:			
With Brown Sugar	290	4	58
Without Brown Sugar	260	4	49
Hash Brown, (1), 2 oz	150	9	15
Hotcakes: Plain (3)	350	9	60
W/ Margarine (2 pats),w/o Syrup	430	18	60
W/ Margarine (2 pats), w/ Syrup (1)	610	18	105
McGriddles: Bacon, Egg & Cheese	460	21	48
Sausage	420	22	44
Sausage, Egg & Cheese	550	31	48
McMuffins: Egg	290	12	31
Sausage	360	22	29
Sausage with Egg	440	27	30
Steak & Egg	420	23	31

Happy Meals:

	C	F	Cb
4 Chicken McNuggets:			
+ Fries + Apple Juice	390	17	48
+ Fries + 1% Low Fat Milk	390	20	37
+Apple Slices + Fat-Free Choc Milk	335	12	39
Hamburger:			
+Fries + Apple Juice	450	14	67
+Fries + 1% Low Fat Milk	450	17	56
+ Apple Slices + 1% Low-Fat Milk	365	12	47
Cheeseburger:			
+Fries + Apple Juice	500	17	69
+Fries + 1% Low-Fat Milk	500	20	58
+ Apple Slices + Fat-Free Choc Milk	445	12	60

Mighty Kids Meals:

	C	F	Cb
With 6 Chicken McNuggets:			
+Fries, 1.1 oz + Apple Juice	480	23	54
+ Apple Slices+ Fat-Free Choc Milk	425	18	45
With Double Cheeseburger:			
+Fries, 1.1 oz + Apple Juice	640	28	70
+ Apple Slices + 1% Low-Fat Milk	555	26	50

Premium Salads: Without Dressing

	C	F	Cb
Bacon Ranch: Without Chicken	140	7	10
With Crispy Chicken	390	22	24
With Grilled Chicken	230	9	10
Southwest: With Crispy Chicken	450	21	42
With Grilled Chicken	290	8	28

Salad Dressings: Per Package

	C	F	Cb
Newman's Own: Ranch, 2 fl.oz	170	15	9
Low-Fat: Balsamic Vinaig., 1.5 fl.oz	35	2.5	3
Family Recipe Italian, 1.5 fl.oz	50	2.5	7

McDonald's® cont... (Mar'14)

Desserts & Cookies:

	C	F	Cb
Baked Apple Pie, 2.7 oz	250	13	32
Cookies: Choc. Chip Cookie (1)	160	8	21
Oatmeal Raisin (1), 1 oz	150	6	22
Fruit & Yogurt Parfait	150	2	30
McFlurry: M&M Candies, 12 fl.oz	650	23	96
Oreo Cookies, 12 fl.oz cup	510	17	80
Soft Serve: Kiddie Cone	45	1.5	7
Vanilla Reduced Fat, Cone	170	4.5	27
Sundaes: Hot Caramel, 6.4 oz	340	8	60
Hot Fudge, 6.3 oz	330	9	53
Strawberry, 6.3 oz	280	6	49

McCafe:

	C	F	Cb
Shakes: Chocolate; Strawberry, average:			
12 fl.oz cup	555	16	91
16 fl.oz cup	695	20	114
22 fl.oz cup	850	24	140
Vanilla: 12 fl.oz	530	15	86
16 fl.oz	660	19	109
22 fl.oz	820	23	135
Hot Chocolate:			
Whole Milk:			
Small, 12 fl oz	360	13	50
Medium, 16 fl oz	440	16	61
Large, 20 fl oz	540	20	73
Nonfat Milk:			
Small, 12 fl oz	280	3.5	50
Medium, 16 fl oz	340	3.5	61
Hot Mocha:			
Whole Milk:			
Small, 12 fl oz	340	11	49
Medium, 16 fl oz	410	14	60
Large, 20 fl.oz	500	17	72
Nonfat Milk: Small, 12 fl oz	270	3.5	49
Medium, 16 fl oz	330	3.5	60
Large, 20 fl.oz	390	4	73

Iced Coffee:

	C	F	Cb
Regular:			
Small, 16 fl.oz	140	4.5	23
Large, 22 fl.oz	190	7	31
Mocha:			
Small, 12 fl.oz	290	11	41
Large, 22 fl.oz	480	16	70

Continued Next Page...

McDonald's® cont... (Mar '14)

Milk:	C	F	Cb
1% Low-Fat, 8 fl.oz	100	2.5	12
Fat-Free Chocolate	130	0	23
Juice: Apple Juice, 6.8 fl.oz box	100	0	23
Orange Juice: Small, 12 fl.oz	150	0	34
Medium, 16 fl.oz	190	0	44
Large, 22 fl.oz	280	0	65
Beverages: With Ice, approximately 30%			
Coca-Cola or Sprite:			
Child, 12 fl.oz cup	100	0	29
Small, 16 fl.oz cup	140	0	38
Medium, 21 fl.oz cup	205	0	55
Large, 30 fl.oz cup	280	0	76
Diet Coke	0	0	0
Hi-C Orange Lavaburst:			
Child, 12 fl.oz	110	0	31
Small, 16 fl.oz	160	0	43
Medium, 21 fl.oz	230	0	61
Large, 30 fl.oz	310	0	84
Powerade, Mountain Berry Blast:			
Childs, 12 fl.oz	60	0	15
Small, 16 fl.oz	80	0	21
Medium, 21 fl.oz	150	0	39
Large, 30 fl.oz	220	0	58

For Complete Menu & Data ~ see CalorieKing.com

Mimi's Cafe® (Feb '14)

Breakfast: Without Sides	C	F	Cb
Benedicts: Original	1020	69	55
Croissant Eggs	1020	71	52
Quiche Lorraine	895	60	58
Omelettes: Basquaise	800	53	35
Le California BLT	895	66	34
Le Griddle			
Cinnamon Brioche French Toast	1120	37	179
Mimi's Original Pain Perdu	620	22	96
Lunch & Dinner: Without Sides			
Les Burgers: Le French Quarter	1160	73	76
au Fromage	650	36	54
de Madame	980	63	55
Sandwiches:			
Artisan: Brioche Croque Madame	890	59	44
Turkey Pesto Ciabatta	1040	58	61
Cafe: Chicken Salade Croissant	490	28	45
Tuna Au Gratin	930	52	67
Specialties:			
Coq Au Vin	860	38	65
Grilled Salmon & French Lentils	490	25	24
Pasta Carbonara a la Mimi's	1060	61	87
Poulete a l 'Orange Crepes	680	31	64

Mr. Goodcents® (Feb '14)

Cold Subs:	C	F	Cb
Per 8" Wheat Bread Sub With Standard Toppings			
Centsable	440	17	55
Italian Sub	630	37	52
Mr. Goodcents Original	510	24	54
Oven Roasted Chicken Breast	340	6	52
Penny Club	350	5	53
Pepperoni	685	42	52
Roast Beef	340	6	52
Tuna Salad	475	20	59
Veggie Sub	295	4	57
Toasted Sub: Per 8" Wheat Bread Sub With Standard Toppings			
Chicken Bacon Ranch, w/ Cheddar	665	30	57
Chkn Chipotle Chsesteak, w/ P.Jack	660	29	63
Meatball w/ Mozzarella	760	37	70
Pasta:			
Alfredo Sauce	1235	42	183
Chicken Alfredo	1380	45	187
Chicken Parmesan	1090	12	190
Marinara Sauce, with Meatballs	1205	27	197
Breadstick, 1 piece, 2 oz	170	8	23

Mr. Hero® (Feb '14)

7" Hot Subs & Burgers:	C	F	Cb
Burgers: Cheeseburger	775	55	47
Classic Gourmet HERO burger	990	72	45
Romanburger	860	62	48
Subs:			
Chicken,			
Grilled Chicken Philly	540	22	48
Deli Subs: Per 7" Sub with Menu Board Toppings			
Original Italian	640	39	47
Tuna & Cheese	725	54	44
Turkey	470	20	46
Ultimate Italian	675	40	46
Steak Subs:			
Hot Buttered Cheesesteak	670	42	45
Zesty Bacon & Swiss	615	32	42
Taste Buddies: Per 4 ½" Sandwich with Menu Board Toppings			
Bacon Cheeseburger	430	30	33
Grilled Italiano	440	32	32
Tuna 'n Cheese	485	38	31
Zesty Chicken	495	25	48
Sides:			
Mozzarella Sticks, w/ Marinara Sce	565	43	12
Onion Petals, w/ Tangy Sce, 5.75 oz	595	37	58
Fries: Potato Waffer, w/o Sce, 5.75 oz	430	30	38
With Cheese Sauce, 1.5 oz	485	34	42
Zesty Fries, 4.7 oz	435	34	30
Desserts: Oreo Cookie Cheesecake	260	17	24
Snickers Cheesecake	270	18	23
Strawb. Swirl Cheesecake	280	19	22

Updated Nutrition Data ~ www.CalorieKing.com
Persons with Diabetes ~ See Disclaimer (Page 22)

Mrs Fields Cookies® (Feb '14)

	C	F	Cb
Brownies: *Per 2.15 oz Brownie*			
Butterscotch Blondie	260	10	38
Double Fudge; Pecan Fudge, av.	265	14	33
Special Walnut Fudge & Blondie	260	13	35
Toffee Fudge; Walnut Fudge, av.	265	14	33
Brownie Bites:			
Double Fudge (3)	200	10	27
Toffee Fudge (3)	200	11	26
Coffee Cake,			
Choc. Chip, small, 2.35 oz	240	11	30
Cookies:			
Bite Size Nibblers: Cinn. Sugar (3)	180	8	25
Peanut Butter (3)	170	9	19
Semi-Sweet Chocolate (3)	170	8	23
Triple Chocolate (3)	160	8	22
White Chunk Macadamia (3)	180	9	22
Butter (1)	200	8	29
Cut Out (1)	280	11	44
Debra's Special (1)	200	9	27
Oatmeal, Raisins and Walnuts (1)	200	9	27
Peanut Butter (1)	200	12	24
Semi-Sweet: Chocolate (1)	210	10	29
With Walnuts (1)	220	11	28
Triple Chocolate (1)	210	10	28
White Chunk Macadamia (1)	230	12	28
Muffins: *Per 2 oz*			
Blueberry	190	9	24
Chocolate Chip	200	10	26

For Complete Nutritional Data ~ see CalorieKing.com

My Favorite Muffin® (Feb '14)

	C	F	Cb
Jumbo Muffins: *Per 5¾ oz*			
Regular: Blueberry	505	24	66
Choc. Chip; Cinn Swirl Cheesecake	635	33	81
Deep Dish Apple Pie	530	24	75
Pumpkin Spice	545	24	78
Fat Free: Blueberry	325	0	78
Chocolate Marble	375	0	87
Cinnamon Bun	505	0	126

Nathan's Famous® (Feb '14)

	C	F	Cb
Burgers:			
Bacon Cheeseburger, 5 oz	900	61	43
Double Beefburger, 10 oz	1030	73	41
Hamburger, 5 oz	620	38	41
Super Cheeseburger, 5 oz	960	67	48
Nathan's Famous Hot Dogs: *With Natural Casings*			
Original, 3.5 oz	290	17	24
Cheese Dog, 5.5 oz	390	25	30
Chili Dog, 5.5 oz	420	28	30
Chili Cheese, 6.5 oz	460	31	33
Corn Dog, on a stick, 3.2 oz	380	21	39

Nathan's Famous® cont... (Feb '14)

	C	F	Cb
Chicken:			
Chicken Tenders, Krispy, 3 pcs, 6.3 oz	520	31	32
Grilled: Chicken Sandwich, 8.2 oz	470	21	43
Chicken Caesar Wrap, 9.2 oz	570	22	57
Krispy: Chicken Sandwich, 8.8 oz	620	32	59
Chicken Tenders, 3 piece	520	31	32
Fries:			
French: Regular, 7.5 oz	510	34	42
Large, 11.5 oz	780	52	64
Family, 15.5 oz	1050	70	86
Cheese: Regular, 9 oz	570	38	46
Large, 13.5 oz	860	58	70
Philly Cheesesteak, 14.4 oz	680	33	52

New York Fries® ~ *See CalorieKing.com*

Ninety Nine (Feb '14)

	C	F	Cb
Standout Starters: *As Served*			
Baked Stuffed Shrimp	800	63	21
Boneless Wings & Skins Sampler	1660	110	73
Fried Mozzarella	780	48	57
Outrageous Potato Skins	1130	84	45
Burgers: *Without Sides*			
All Star Steakburger	1300	97	53
Bacon & Cheese Steakburger	1010	68	44
Steakburger: Without Cheese	850	55	42
With Cheese	930	62	44
Sandwiches: *Without Sides*			
Honey BBQ Chicken Wrap	930	40	94
Triple-Decker Turkey Club	940	38	110
Meals: *Served with Menu Set Sides Unless Indicated*			
Chicken Caesar Crowd Pleazer	2700	210	67
Fish & Chips	1840	123	122
Macadamia Crusted Chkn	1130	69	80
New England Shoreline Combo	2190	144	161
NY Stip Sirloin, without sides	680	28	1
Prime Rib: 12 oz, without sides	920	72	2
18 oz, without sides	1370	107	2
Smothered Sirloin Tips, w/o sides	1010	56	12
Salads: *As Served*			
Chicken Caesar	830	54	50
Fire Grilled SW Cobb	890	58	30
Tropical Chicken	740	40	58
Sides:			
Double Bleu Iceberg Wedge	460	42	9
Honey Butter Bisc., w/ Honey Butter	210	8	29
Loaded Baked Potato	580	34	52
Dessert,			
Little Midnight Fudge Hero	490	25	60

219

Noodles & Company® (Feb '14)

Noodles & Pasta: Regular Size	C	F	Cb
BBQ Pork Mac	1270	56	133
Buttered Noodles	930	39	115
Bangkok Curry	510	16	82
Indonesian Peanut Saute	840	19	149
Japanese Pan Noodles	620	15	110
Mushroom Stroganoff	790	32	101
Pad Thai	830	19	151
Pasta Fresca	790	25	115
Penne Rosa	790	35	97
Spaghetti & Meatballs	920	39	102
Steak Stroganoff	1030	46	104
Wisconsin Mac & Cheese	1040	43	124
Sandwiches: BBQ Pork	560	18	70
Mmmeatball	670	33	59
Spicy Chicken Ceasar, without Dressing	330	9	40
The Veggie Med	300	9	45
Salads: Per Regular Size			
Chinese Chicken Chop Salad	480	25	39
Grilled Chicken Caesar	500	34	17
Pork Med Salad	490	22	44
Spinach & Fresh Fruit Salad	650	42	50
Soups: Per Regular Size			
Chicken Noodle	380	13	44
Thai Curry	460	18	69
Tomato Basil Bisque	520	38	43
Extras: Cheesy Garlic Bread (3)	330	18	32
Cucumber Tomato Salad	110	0	24
Lettuce Wraps (3)	260	10	30
Potstickers, regular, w/o sauce	340	10	45

Nothing But Noodles® (Feb '14)

Noodle Bowls:	C	F	Cb
American: Beef Stroganoff	510	31	33
Buttery Noodles	650	44	46
Santa Fe Pasta	705	54	40
Southwest Chipotle	715	58	41
Spicy Cajun Pasta	660	50	44
Asian: Pad Thai Noodles	600	10	118
Sesame Lo Mein	410	11	64
Spicy Japanese Noodles	420	8	74
Thai Peanut	570	20	89
Italian: Basil Pesto	575	42	36
Cappellini Primavera	500	28	56
Fettuccini Alfredo	725	56	36
Margherita Pasta	475	31	36
Marinara Pasta	485	11	77
Three-Cheese Macaroni	445	21	45

For Complete Menu & Data ~ see CalorieKing.com

O'Charley's® (Feb '14)

Appetizers: As Served	C	F	Cb
Chicken Tenders, Chipotle	960	37	99
Over-Loaded Potato Skins	1260	98	44
Spicy Jack Cheese Wedges (7)	860	59	52
Top Shelf Combo Platter	1900	131	106
Chicken & Pasta:			
Bruschetta Chicken	400	15	14
Cajun Chicken Pasta, dinner size	1730	106	131
Chicken Italia	1250	66	94
Chicken Tenders, Buffalo	1060	59	77
Prime Rib Pasta	1470	97	89
Classic Combos: Without Sides			
Panko-Crusted Shrimp & Battered Cod	1240	63	66
Steak & Chicken Tenders	980	55	53
Steak & Grilled Atlantic Salmon	620	33	5
Steak & Panko-Crusted Shrimp	590	23	39
Steak & Shrimp Scampi	520	31	11
Steaks & Ribs:			
O'Charley's:			
Baby Back Ribs, without Sides:			
Full Rack	1480	96	76
Half Rack	740	48	38
Homestyle Pot Roast Dinner	600	26	34
Prime Rib, 10 oz, without Sides:			
W/ Pepper, Sauted Onions, & Bleu Cheese	1270	102	18
W/ Mushrooms & Gravy	1180	95	11
Seafood: Without Sides			
Bayou Tilapia	830	52	40
Grilled Atlantic Salmon, 6 oz	400	26	3
Hand Battered Fish & Chips	1340	77	43
Panko Crusted Shrimp Dinner	570	26	53
Sides: Bacon Smashed Potatoes	400	14	47
Broccoli	145	10	11
French Fries, 1 serve	520	33	53
Premium: Loaded Baked Potato	545	34	52
Sweet Potato Fries	470	31	46
Salads: With Dressing Unless Indiated			
Black & Bleu Caesar	950	71	22
California Chicken, w/out Dressing	570	26	46
Southern-Fried Chicken Salad	1140	63	69
Soup: Per Cup			
Chicken Harvest	160	8	12
Chicken Tortilla	100	4	7
Overloaded Potato	170	10	16
Desserts:			
Double Crust Peach Pie, 1 slice	440	23	54
Ooey Gooey Caramel Pie, 1 slice	440	21	57

For Complete Menu & Data ~ see CalorieKing.com

Olive Garden® (Feb '14)

	C	F	Cb
Appetizers:			
Bruschetta	950	13	173
Calamari	890	54	64
Spicy Shrimp Scampi Fritta	550	34	34
Stuffed Mushrooms	280	19	15
Entrees:			
Lunch:			
Chicken Alfredo	910	52	71
Eggplant Parmigiana	620	26	70
Fettuccine Alfredo	800	48	69
Five Cheese Ziti al Forno	770	32	89
Lasagna Classico	580	32	35
Spaghetti with Meatballs	680	30	63
Spicy Shrimp Vesuvio	490	14	63
Dinner:			
Eggplant Parmig.	850	35	98
Fettucini Alfredo	1220	75	99
Five Cheese Ziti al Forno	1050	48	112
Lasagna Classico	850	47	39
Ravioli di Portobello	670	30	74
Stuffed Chicken Marsala	800	36	40
Tour of Italy	1450	74	97
Desserts: Black Tie Mousse Cake	760	48	73
Tiramisu	510	32	48
Zeppoli	920	35	131

Old Spaghetti Factory® (Feb '14)

	C	F	Cb
Appetizers: As Served			
Shrimp, Spinach & Artichoke Dip	590	40	39
Sicilian Garlic Cheese Bread	1320	77	111
Entrees, Lunch/Dinner:			
Classics:			
Spaghetti: With Clam Sauce, 15 oz	810	31	107
With Marina Sauce, 15 oz	560	5	108
With Meat Sauce, 15 oz	650	11	108
With Sicilian Meatballs, 21 oz	1040	36	115
Factory Favorites:			
Chicken Parmigiana, 18 oz	750	29	70
Spinach & Cheese Ravioli, 11 oz	470	16	63
Spinach Tortellini w/ Alfredo Sce	940	56	86
Managers Favorites:			
Marinara: Clam, 15 oz	690	18	107
Meat, 15 oz	600	8	108
Mushroom, 16.5 oz	610	10	109
Signature Selection:			
Chicken Penne, 18.8 oz	870	38	102
Baked Chicken, 16.55 oz	970	60	61
Crab Ravioli, 11 oz	810	45	73

On the Border® (Feb '14)

	C	F	Cb
Appetizers: As Served			
Border Sampler	2060	142	101
Fajita Quesadillas: Chicken	1180	82	55
Steak	1210	88	54
Burritos: Includes Rice, Without Beans & Sauce			
Classic Chicken	920	36	103
Classic Shredded Beef	1020	41	102
Chimichangas: Includes Rice, Without Beans & Sauce			
Chicken	1300	79	103
Ground Beef	1420	90	105
Dinner: Includes Rice, Without Beans			
Enchiladas: Gr. Pepper Jack Chkn	1050	48	106
Ranchiladas	1260	66	96
Suiza	1000	45	106
Fajitas, Signature: Without Rice, Beans, Tortillas or Condiments			
Monterey Chicken Ranch	650	43	12
The Ultimate	1160	96	26
Fresh Grill: Served As Listed			
Carne Asada	970	38	105
Chicken Salsa Fresca	520	9	60
Queso Chicken	1030	41	110
Tomatillo Chicken	850	24	109
Salads: Without Dressing			
House, side size	200	12	20
Grande Taco Salad: With Chicken	1180	75	79
With Ground Beef	1280	85	80
Sides: Per Serving			
Black Beans	180	3	29
Mexican Rice	280	5	55
Pico de Gallo	10	1	1
Sour Cream	60	5	2
Dressings: Per Serving			
Ranch Dressing	230	24	2
Smoked Jalapeno Vinaigrette	250	24	8

For Complete Nutritional Data ~ see CalorieKing.com

Orange Julius® (Feb '14)

	C	F	Cb
Julius Originals: Per Small Size			
Berry Pomegranate	330	0	83
Mango Pineapple	350	0	87
OrangeBerry	250	0	63
Strawberry Banana	400	6	87
Premium Fruit Smoothies: Per Medium Size			
Berry Pomegranate	380	0	91
Pina Colada	340	0	80
Strawberry	300	0.5	71
Light Smoothies: Per Medium Size			
Orange	170	0	41
Strawberry	200	0	50
Triple Berry	210	0	55
Boost, Banana, Small drink	30	0	7

Outback Steakhouse® (Feb '14)

Aussie-Tizers: Per Whole Dish, With Selected Dressing/Sauce

	C	F	Cb
Alice Springs Chicken Quesadilla:			
Small, serves 2	900	61	47
Regular, serves 4	1505	92	86
Aussie Cheese Fries:			
Small, serves 3	1220	91	70
Regular, serves 6	1915	134	126
Bloomin' Onion, serves 6	1950	160	117
Coconut Shrimp, serves 2	615	35	54
Seared Ahi Tuna, small, serves 2	405	15	21
Spinach Artichoke Dip, serves 4	1000	67	66

Burgers & Sandwiches:

	C	F	Cb
Aged Cheddar Bacon Burger	1005	72	36
With Fries	1385	92	80
Classic Cheeseburger w/ Am. Chse	790	49	39
With Fries	1170	69	84
The Bloomin Burger	1030	70	50
With Fries	1405	90	95
The Outbacker Burger	685	40	39
With Fries	1065	60	83

Steaks: Without Sides

	C	F	Cb
New York Strip, 14 oz	765	49	0
Outback Special: 6 oz Sirloin	255	13	0
9 oz Sirloin	380	19	0
12 oz Sirloin	510	25	0
Porterhouse, 22 oz	1110	78	5
Ribeye, 14 oz	760	49	0
Victoria's Filet: 6 oz	220	9	0
8 oz	300	12	0

Outback Favorites: Without Sides

	C	F	Cb
Alice Springs Chicken	1120	65	57
Baby Back Ribs, full order	1165	77	24
Grilled Chicken on the Barbie	310	4	11
New Zealand Rack of Lamb	600	40	1
No Rules Parmesan Pasta:	880	51	73
With Grilled Chicken	1305	69	77
With Grilled Chicken & Scallops	1315	70	81
With Grilled Chicken & Shrimp	1305	69	80
With Grilled Scallops	1275	70	84
With Grilled Shrimp	1195	70	78
With Grilled Shrimp & Scallops	1270	71	81
Sweet Glazed Pork Tenderloin	305	9	14
Wood-Fired Grilled Pork Chop	385	12	17

Straight From The Sea: Without Sides

	C	F	Cb
Lobster Tails, 4 oz	440	26	2
Royal Port Tilapia	750	49	7

Outback Steakhouse® cont... (Feb '14)

Specialty Cuts & Combos: W/o Sides

	C	F	Cb
Filet & Grilled Shrimp On The Barbie	425	23	6
Filet, 6 oz & Lobster Tail, 4 oz	620	41	3
Sirloin:			
6 oz: With Coconut Shrimp	595	30	36
With Grilled Shrimp	490	28	6
9 oz: With Coconut Shrimp	690	36	27
With Grilled Shrimp	620	35	6

Salads: Without Dressing Unless Indicated

	C	F	Cb
Aussie Chicken Cobb:			
Crispy	790	50	42
Grilled	475	25	15
Chicken Caesar with Dressing	700	15	19
Sesame, with Ahi Tuna	445	25	23
Steakhouse	1025	72	46

Soups: Per Bowl

	C	F	Cb
Clam Chowder	695	45	45
Too Right French Onion	486	31	28

Add Ons:

	C	F	Cb
Blue Cheese Crumb Crust	305	29	6
Grilled Shrimp	235	16	6
Horseradish Crumb Crust	280	26	10
Lobster Tail	315	23	2
Sauteed Mushrooms	145	7	11

Sides:

	C	F	Cb
Aussie Fries	380	20	45
Baked Potato:			
Plain	230	1	49
With Bacon & Sour Cream	280	5	51
With Butter	360	16	49
With Butter, Cheese & Bacon	395	19	49
With Chse, Chives & Sour Cream	290	5	51
Fresh Seasonal Mixed Veggies	95	3	11
Garlic Mashed Potatoes	255	14	27
Sweet Potato: Plain	320	5	63
With Honey Butter	420	16	66

Desserts: Per Single Serving

	C	F	Cb
Carrot Cake, ½ dish	320	15	45
Chocolate Thunder, ¼ of dish	395	27	35
Classic Cheesecake, w/o sce, ½ slice	165	12	11

For Complete Menu & Data ~ see CalorieKing.com

Panda Express® (Mar '14)

Appetizers:

	C	F	Cb
Chicken Egg Roll (1), 3 oz	200	12	16
Chicken Potsticker (3), 3.3 oz	220	11	23
Cream Cheese Rangoon (3), 2.4 oz	190	8	24
Veggie Spring Rolls (2), 3.4 oz	160	7	22

Continued Next Page...

Panda Express® cont... (Mar '14)

Entrees:

	C	F	Cb
Beef: Beijing Beef, 5.6 oz	690	40	57
Broccoli Beef, 5.4 oz	120	4	13
Shanghai Angus Beef, 5.4 oz	220	7	19
Chicken: Kung Pao Chicken, 5.8 oz	240	14	13
Mandarin Chicken, 5.8 oz	310	16	8
Orange Chicken, 5.7 oz	420	21	43
Potato Chicken, 5.2 oz	190	9	19
SweetFire Chicken Breast, 5.8 oz	440	18	53
Shrimp: Crispy Shrimp (6), 3.5 oz	260	13	26
Golden Treasure Shrimp, 5 oz	390	19	39
Honey Walnut Shrimp, 3.7 oz	370	23	27

Rice & Noodles: Per Serving

	C	F	Cb
Chow Mein, 9.4 oz	490	22	65
Fried Rice, 9.3 oz	470	19	64
Steamed White Rice, 8.1 oz	380	0	86

Panera Bread® (Feb '14)

Bagels:

	C	F	Cb
Asiago Cheese	330	6	55
Cinnamon Crunch	420	6	81

Breakfast Sandwiches, Grilled:

	C	F	Cb
Asiago Cheese Bagel, with Bacon	610	28	54
Bacon, Egg & Cheese on Ciabatta	510	25	43
Sausage, Egg & Cheese on Ciabatta	550	29	44

Cafe Sandwiches: Per Full Sandwich

	C	F	Cb
Sierra Turkey, on Asiago Cheese Foccacia	810	37	78
Smoked Turkey Breast on Country	430	3.5	67
Tuna Salad on Honey Wheat	510	16	64

Signature Sandwiches: Per Full Sandwich:

	C	F	Cb
Asiago Steak on Asiago Chse Demi	710	31	58
Bacon Turkey Bravo on Tomato Basil	790	28	84
Napa Almond Chicken Salad, on Sesame Semolina	700	27	89

Hot Paninis: Per Full Panini

	C	F	Cb
Chipotle Chicken on Artisan French	840	38	72
Frontega Chicken on Focaccia	800	32	83
Tomato & Mozzarella on Ciabatta	740	27	95

Salads: Full Size, With Dressing, without Bread

	C	F	Cb
Asian Sesame Chicken	420	22	25
Caesar, with Chicken	440	26	19
Greek	360	32	13
Thai Chicken	490	19	42

Panera Bread® cont... (Feb '14)

Soups: Per 1½ Cups, w/o Bread

	C	F	Cb
All Natural Low Fat Chicken Noodle	130	1.5	23
Baked Potato	350	21	32
Broccoli Cheddar	330	21	23
Cream of Chicken & Wild Rice	310	20	24
Creamy Tomato with Croutons	450	32	33
New England Clam Chowder	720	62	31

Pastries & Sweets:

	C	F	Cb
Bear Claw, 4.5 oz	550	28	68
Cheese Pastry, 3.75 oz	400	22	44
Chocolate Pastry, 3.5 oz	410	23	47
Cobblestone, 7 oz	640	13	122
Oatmeal Raisin Cookie, 3.25 oz	390	14	62
Pecan Roll, 5.5 oz	740	39	89
Muffins: Apple Crunch, 5 oz	450	12	80
Pumpkin, 6 oz	590	22	91
Wild Blueberry, 4.5 oz	440	17	66

Papa Gino's® (Feb '14)

Appetizers: Small, Per 2 Servings

	C	F	Cb
BBQ Chicken Tenders, 8.25 oz	520	18	60
Buffalo Chicken Tenders, 9.65 oz	660	42	38
Cheese Breadsticks, 20 oz	1240	44	158
Chicken Tender, 6.6 oz	420	18	36
Burgers: Cheeseburger, 6.25 oz	520	28	36
Classic Double, 12.85 oz	1040	67	43
Hamburger, 6.25 oz	520	28	36
French Fries, 4 oz	170	7	25

Pastas: Entree Size Without Breadstick

	C	F	Cb
Papa Platter, Penne, 22 oz	1020	34	145
Ravioli, 12.4 oz	560	21	67
Spaghetti & Meatballs, 19.8 oz	780	28	109

Pizzas:

Thin Crust: *Per Slice of Large Pizza*

	C	F	Cb
Boss BBQ Chicken	340	12	41
Cheese	230	7	32
Meat Combo	330	16	32
Paparoni	340	16	32
Pepperoni	280	11	32
Super Veggie	250	8	35
Works	330	14	34

Subs: Per Small Sub

	C	F	Cb
BLT	690	35	67
Italian	590	24	64
Meatball Parmesan	790	38	79
Steak & Cheese	710	33	63
Super Steak	750	33	72
Tuna	730	39	64
Turkey Club	600	22	67

223

Fast - Foods & Restaurants

Papa John's® (Feb '14)

Pizzas:

	C	F	Cb
Original Crust (14"): *Per ⅛ of Large 14" Pizza*			
Double Bacon 6 Cheese	350	14	38
Spicy Italian, 5.25 oz	380	18	38
Spinach Alfredo, 4 oz	280	10	36
The Meats, 3.75 oz	370	17	38
The Works, 5.5 oz	330	14	39
Thin Crust (14"): *Per ⅛ of Large 14" Pizza*			
Double Bacon 6 Cheese	290	16	22
Spicy Italian, 4 oz	320	20	22
Spinach Alfredo, 2.75 oz	220	12	21
The Meats, 3.75 oz	310	19	22
The Works, 4.25 oz	270	15	23
Wings: *Without Sauce*			
BBQ, 2 wings, 2.5 oz	190	12	6
Spicy Buffalo, 2 wings, 2.5 oz	170	13	3
Dipping Sauces: *Per 1 oz Container*			
Barbeque	45	0	11
Blue Cheese	160	16	1
Buffalo	15	0.5	2
Ranch	100	10	1
Sides: *Without Dipping Sauce*			
Breadsticks (2)	290	4.5	54
Cheesesticks (4)	370	16	41
Parmesan Breadsticks (2)	340	10	54

Papa Murphy's® (Feb '14)

Pizzas:

	C	F	Cb
Original Crust: *Per ½ of Family Size Pizza*			
BBQ Chicken	330	12	36
Cheese	270	10	29
Cowboy	335	16	30
Gourmet: Chicken Garlic	320	13	30
Classic Italian	350	18	31
Vegetarian	300	13	31
Hawaiian	295	11	33
Murphy's Combo	350	17	31
Papa's Favorite	350	17	31
Pepperoni	320	15	31
Rancher	325	15	30
Specialty of the House	310	14	30
Vegetarian	280	12	32
Stuffed Pizzas: *Per ¹⁄₁₆ of Family Size Pizza*			
5 Meat	370	16	39
Big Murphy	370	15	40
Chicago Style	370	16	40
Chicken and Bacon	370	15	39

Papa Murphy's® cont... (Feb '14)

Pizzas (Cont):

	C	F	Cb
Thin Crust deLITES: *Per ¹⁄₁₀ of Large Pizza*			
Cheese	145	7	13
Hawaiian	160	7	15
Pepperoni	170	9	13
Salads: *Per Whole Salad, 2 Servings, Without Dressing or Croutons*			
Club, 13 oz	280	16	12
Garden, 14.5 oz	190	11	15
Italian, 13 oz	265	19	13

Pei Wei Asian Diner (Feb '14)

Small Plates: *Per Full Dish, w/out Sauce*	C	F	Cb
Crab Wontons (4)	340	20	26
Crispy Potstickers (4)	300	16	24
Tradt'nl Chicken Lettuce Wraps (2)	670	22	72
Vegetable Spring Rolls (6)	690	30	78
Sauces: Lettuce Wrap	60	4	3
Potsticker	50	3	3
Sweet Chile	130	0	32
Thai Peanut Dipping Sauce	160	10	16
Noodle & Rice Bowls: *Per Full Dish, Original Size*			
Dan Dan Noodle, Chicken, without Rice	780	16	119
Fried Rice: With Chicken	1180	27	178
With Steak	1220	34	183
Lo Mein Noodles: *Without Rice*			
With Chicken	1010	24	150
With Steak	910	24	132
Teriyaki Rice:			
With Chicken	1170	19	206
With Shrimp	1080	13	211
With Steak	1150	19	207
Signature Dishes: *Per Full Dish, Original Size*			
Honey Seared: With Chicken	1580	50	228
With Shrimp	1470	48	222
Pei Wei Spicy: With Chicken	1430	34	222
With Steak	1700	53	260
Sweet & Sour: With Chicken	1470	40	232
With Shrimp	1350	37	226
Soup:			
Hot & Sour, 1 Cup	70	2.5	6
Thai Wanton, 1 Cup	80	2	11
Salads: *Per Full Dish*			
Asian Chopped Chicken	800	46	54
Pei Wei Spicy Chicken	990	44	111

Pepe's Mexican *~ see CalorieKing.com*

224

Perkins® (Feb '14)   C   F   Cb

Breakfast:

Benedicts: *With Muffin, Breakfast Potatoes & Fruit Cup*

	C	F	Cb
Classic	850	49	70
Country Cookin'	1210	84	74

Classics: *With Fruit Cup*

Country Fried Steak & Eggs	1080	59	91
Tremendous Twelve	950	55	75

Griddle Greats:

Belgian Waffles:

With Wh. Butter & Pdr Sugar	470	23	57
With Blueberries, Pwdr. Sugar, and Non Dairy Topping	640	18	112
With Strawberries Pwdr. Sugar, and Non Dairy Topping	580	18	97
Berry Blueberry Pancakes, with Non-Dairy Topping	860	24	145
Brioche French Toast Platter	890	47	74

Omelettes: *With Fruit Cup & White Toast & Butter*

Everything	680	49	24
Farmer's	1050	72	52
Granny's Country	840	53	54

Hearty Extras:

Breakfast Potatoes, 5 oz	250	12	32
English Muffin, w/ butter, 2.7 oz	230	11	28
French Fries, 4 oz	320	20	31
Fruit Cup, 4 oz	50	0	12
Hash Browns, 4 oz	490	13	87
Oatmeal, w/ 2% Milk & Br. Sugar	330	6	60
Sausage Links (4)	460	44	2

Burgers: *With Standard Toppings, Without Fries*

BBQ Bacon Supreme	900	52	56
Hamburger	620	33	44

Melts: *With French Fries*

Chicken Strip	1380	90	87
Reuben Melt, on Rye	1020	62	55

Sandwiches: *With Standard Toppings, w/out Fries*

French Dip, with Au Jus	610	31	46
Kickin' Chicken	990	57	80
Triple Decker Club	880	55	54

Wraps: *With French Fries*

Ham & Turkey BLT	1080	69	89
The Buffalo Wrap	1460	98	104

Perkins® cont... (Feb '14)   C   F   Cb

Dinners:

Fork Worthy Entrees: *With Menu Selected Sides and Bread Roll*

	C	F	Cb
Butterball Turkey & Dressing	1210	52	129
Captain's Catch	2290	134	215
Chicken Strips	1200	70	89
Country Fried Steak	900	53	72
Grilled Pork Chops	880	52	35
Grilled Salmon	870	48	61
Homestyle Pot Roast	630	34	41
Jumbo Shrimp Dinner	880	53	75
Steak Medallions, & Portabella Mushrooms	760	44	32
Tilapia Grille	870	42	70

Sides:

Baked Potato, with Sour Cream, & Whipped Butter, 8.64 oz	390	22	42
French Fries, 7 oz	570	36	56
Macaroni & Five Cheese, 5.2 oz	300	16	26
Side Salad with Croutons, and Ranch Dressing, 6.5 oz	300	25	15

Super Soups: *Per Bowl*

Homestyle Chicken Noodle	150	5	16
Tomato Basil	410	33	26

Salads:

Chef Deluxe	510	30	16
Chicken & Spinach, with Bacon Dressing	790	54	23
Honey Mustard Chicken, with Honey Mustard Dressing	1010	66	65

Dessert: *Per Slice*

Bakery: Apple Granola Muffin	570	22	85
Cherry Cheesecake, with Whipped Cream, 1 slice	600	37	59
Red Velvet Silk Cake, with Whipped Cream, 1 slice	910	60	84
Pies: Caramel Apple, 7.15 oz	500	22	68
Chocolate French Silk, with Whipped Cream, 6 oz	760	54	66
Southern Pecan, 5.5 oz	670	33	86
Wildberry, 7 oz	460	27	50

Beverages:

Cherry Coke, 12.35 oz	160	0	42
Raspberry Iced Tea, 11.64 oz	130	0	34

Peter Piper Pizza® (Feb '14)

	C	F	Cb
Appetizers: *Per Serving*			
Boneless Wings: *Per Regular Size*			
Buffalo	395	19	22
Plain	305	11	19
Garlic Cheese Bread, 3.25 oz	310	14	37
Signature Pizzas: *Per Slice*			
Original Crust: *Per ⅛ of Large 14" Pizza*			
5 Meat Supreme	350	13	38
California Veggie	200	6	23
Chicago Classic	300	10	38
New York 3 Cheese w/ Pepperoni	380	16	38
Pepperoni & Sausage	310	11	37
The Werx	320	11	38
Original Crust: *Per ½ of Extra Large 16" Pizza*			
5 Meat Supreme	320	13	33
California Veggie	240	6	33
Chicago Classic	270	9	33
New York 3 Cheese w/ Pepperoni	340	14	32
The Werx	290	10	33
Hand-Tossed: *Per ⅛ of Large 14" Pizza*			
5 Meat Supreme	350	13	38
California Veggie	270	7	39
Chicago Classic	300	10	39
New York 3 Cheese w/ Pepperoni	380	16	39
Pepperoni & Sausage	310	11	38
The Werx	310	11	39
Hand-Tossed Crust: *Per ½ of Extra Large 16" Pizza*			
5 Meat Supreme	320	13	34
California Veggie	240	6	34
Chicago Classic	270	9	34
New York 3 Cheese w/ Pepperoni	340	14	34
The Werx	280	10	34
Pan Crust: *Per ⅛ of Large 14" Pizza*			
5 Meat Supreme	380	13	46
California Veggie	300	7	47
Chicago Classic	340	10	46
New York 3 Cheese w/ Pepperoni	410	16	46
Pepperoni & Sausage	340	11	45
The Werx	350	11	46
Pan Crust: *Per ½ of Extra Large 16" Pizza*			
5 Meat Supreme	340	13	39
California Veggie	260	6	39
Chicago Classic	290	9	39
New York 3 Cheese w/ Pepperoni	360	15	39
The Werx	310	10	39

Peter Piper® ...cont (Feb '14)

	C	F	Cb
Signature Pizzas (Cont):			
Thin Crust: *Per ⅛ of Large 14" Pizza*			
5 Meat Supreme	180	8	14
California Veggie	130	4.5	15
Chicago Classic	150	6	15
New York 3 Cheese w/ Pepperoni	200	10	14
Pepperoni & Sausage	150	7	14
The Werx	160	7	14
Thin Crust: *Per ¹⁄₁₆ of Extra Large 16" Pizza*			
5 Meat Supreme	190	9	14
California Veggie	130	4	14
Chicago Classic	150	6	14
New York 3 Cheese w/ Pepperoni	200	10	14
The Werx	160	7	14

P.F. Chang's® (Feb '14)

	C	F	Cb
Starters: *Per Whole Dish*			
Crab Wontons (6), without sauce	475	29	40
Spicy Plum Sauce, 2 oz	100	0	26
Crispy Green Beans, without sauce	760	55	63
Crispy Bean Sauce, 2 oz	310	33	3
Egg Rolls (4), without sauce	560	20	75
Lettuce Wraps: Chicken (4)	530	24	47
Vegetarian (4)	610	36	39
Pork Dumplings:			
Pan-Fried, with sauce, (6)	420	16	45
Steamed, with sauce, (6)	370	13	45
Salt & Pepper Calamari	610	37	44
Shrimp Dumplings:			
Pan-Fried, with sauce, (6)	300	7	40
Steamed, with sauce, (6)	270	2.5	43
Spring Rolls, without Sauce, (4)	230	10	25
Main Menu:			
Beef: *Per Whole Meal, Without Rice*			
A La Sichuan	680	32	54
Mongolian	720	39	31
Orange Peel	720	36	55
Chicken: *Per Whole Dish, Without Rice*			
Chang's Spicy	830	35	74
Kung Pao Chicken	1100	66	56
Orange Peel Chicken	860	41	66
Sesame Chicken	790	36	50
Sweet & Sour Chicken	840	44	71

Continued Next Page...

Updated Nutrition Data ~ www.CalorieKing.com
Persons with Diabetes ~ See Disclaimer (Page 22)

P.F. Chang's® cont... (Feb '14)

Main Menu (Cont):

	C	F	Cb
Seafood: *Per Whole Meal, Without Rice*			
Lemongrass Grilled Norw. Salmon	640	37	20
Crispy Honey Shrimp	660	38	53
Kung Peo Shrimp	830	54	46
Sichuan Shrimp	360	16	32
Vegetarian Plates: *Without Rice*			
Coconut Curry Vegetables	1050	75	52
Ma Po Tofu	1030	70	44
Stir-Fried Eggplant	1010	88	50
Noodles Meins & Rice:			
PF Chang's Fried Rice, with Beef	1240	28	203
PF Chang's Lo Mein, with Pork	760	25	100
Singapore Street Noodles	700	17	105
Sides: *Per Small Dish*			
Shanghai Cucumbers	70	3	7
Sichuan-Style Asparagus	110	4	15
Spinach Stir-Fried with Garlic	120	8	8
Soups: Hot & Sour: 1 cup	70	2	9
1 bowl	380	11	48
Egg Drop: 1 cup	60	2.5	4
1 bowl	290	12	39
Desserts: *Per Whole Dish*			
Banana Spring Rolls	950	38	143
New York Style Cheesecake	900	57	83
Tiramisu	180	11	18

Pita Pit® ~ *See CalorieKing.com*

Pizza Hut® (Mar '14)

Hand-Tossed Style: *Per 1/8 of 12" Pizza*

	C	F	Cb
Cheese Only	210	8	26
Chicken Supreme	210	7	26
Meat Lover's	300	16	26
Pepperoni	230	10	25
Pepperoni Lover's	270	13	26
Supreme	260	12	27
Super Supreme	270	13	27
Ultimate Cheese Lover's	230	9	26
Veggie Lover's	200	7	27

Pan: *Per 1/8 of 12" Pizza*

	C	F	Cb
Cheese Only	240	10	26
Chicken Supreme	230	9	27
Meat Lover's	320	18	26
Pepperoni	260	13	26
Pepperoni Lover's	300	16	26
Supreme	280	14	27
Super Supreme	300	15	27
Ultimate Cheese Lover's	260	12	26
Veggie Lover's	220	9	27

Pizza Hut® cont... (Mar '14)

Personal Pan: *Per 6" Pizza*

	C	F	Cb
Chicken Supreme	590	25	68
Meat Lover's	850	48	68
Pepperoni	620	28	68
Pepperoni Lover's	730	37	68
Supreme	730	38	69
Super Supreme	760	40	70
Ultimate Cheese Lover's	630	29	67
Veggie Lover's	540	20	69

Thin 'n Crispy: *Per 1/8 of 12" Pizza*

	C	F	Cb
Cheese Only	190	8	22
Chicken Supreme	190	6	23
Meat Lover's	280	16	22
Pepperoni	210	10	21
Pepperoni Lover's	260	14	22
Supreme	230	12	23
Super Supreme	250	13	23
Ultimate Cheese Lover's	210	10	21
Veggie Lover's	180	6	23

P'Zone: *Per 1/2 P'Zone*

	C	F	Cb
Classic	470	17	61
Meaty	550	24	61
Pepperoni	460	16	60

Stuffed Crust: *Per 1/8 14" Pizza*

	C	F	Cb
Cheese Only	310	13	35
Meat Lover's	440	25	36
Supreme	380	16	35
Ultimate Cheese Lover's	340	15	35
Veggie Lover's	300	11	37

Wings: *Per 2 Pieces, Without Dipping Sauce*

	C	F	Cb
Bone Out: Buffalo, all flav., 2.5 oz	200	9	19
Honey BBQ, 3 oz	230	9	28
Crispy Bone In:			
Buffalo, all flavors, 2.5 oz	240	15	19
Honey BBQ, 3 oz	270	14	28
Traditional: Buffalo, all flav, 2 oz	130	6	8
Garlic Parmesan, 2 oz	200	17	1
Dipping Sauces: Blue Chse, 1.5 oz	230	24	2
Ranch, 1.5 oz	220	23	2

Pastas, Tuscani: *Per 1/2 Pan*

	C	F	Cb
Creamy Chicken Alfredo	520	27	46
Meaty Marinara	450	21	44
Desserts: Cinnamon Sticks, 2 pcs	160	4.5	26
Hershey's: Choc. Dunkers, 2 pcs	190	8	26
Chocolate Sauce, 1.5 oz	120	2	25
White Icing Dipping Cup, 2 oz	170	0	44

Pizza Ranch® (Feb '14)

	C	F	Cb
Original Crust: *Per 1/10 Slice of Medium Pizza*			
Bacon Cheeseburger	240	9	29
BLT	280	14	29
Bronco	250	10	29
Buffalo Chicken	240	9	28
California Chicken	260	11	28
Chicken Bacon Ranch	270	12	28
Chicken Broccoli Alfredo	230	8	28
Garlic Cheese	240	11	27
Italian Sausage	230	8	29
Pepperoni	240	9	29
Prairie (Veggie)	220	7	30
Roundup	240	9	30
Stampede	250	9	30
Sweet Swine	220	6	30
Texan Taco	270	9	37

For Complete Menu & Data ~ see CalorieKing.com

Pollo Tropical® ~ See CalorieKing.com

Popeye's® (Feb '14)

	C	F	Cb
Chicken Pieces: *Mild & Spicy With Skin*			
Breast, average	430	27	14
Leg, average	165	10	5
Thigh, average	270	20	8
Wing	210	14	8
Nuggets: 4 pieces, 1.75 oz	150	9	10
6 Pieces 2.65 oz	230	14	14
Tenders: Mild, 3 pieces, 4.45 oz	340	14	26
Spicy, 3 pieces, 4,45 oz	310	15	16
Sandwiches & Wraps: *Each*			
Blackened BBQ Chicken Po'Boy	340	7	49
Chicken & Sausage Jambalaya	220	11	20
Chicken Po'Boy	660	34	61
Chicken Livers	1190	80	65
Loaded Chicken Wrap	310	13	33
Shrimp Po' Boy	690	42	66
Seafood: Catfish Fillets, 5 oz	460	29	27
Butterfly Shrimp (8)	290	17	21
Popcorn Shrimp, 3 oz	330	9	28

Popeye's® ... cont (Feb '14)

	C	F	Cb
Sides:			
Biscuit, 2 oz	260	15	26
Cajun Fries, regular, 3 oz	260	14	30
Cajun Rice, regular, 4.34 oz	170	5	25
Cole Slaw, regular, 4.87 oz	220	15	19
Corn on the Cob (1), 7.75 oz	190	2	37
Mashed Potatoes, regular, 5 oz	110	4	18
Onion Rings (12)	560	38	50
Red Beans & Rice, regular, 5.15 oz	230	14	23
Breakfast:			
Biscuits: Bacon	400	25	37
Chicken	490	26	47
Egg	510	29	41
Egg & Sausage	690	45	43
Sausage	540	36	41
Sausage & Gravy	510	33	42
Grits	370	5	80
Hashbrowns	360	20	41
Desserts:			
Hot Sweet Potato Pie 3.35 oz	350	19	41
Mardi Gras Cheesecake, 3 oz	310	19	32
Mississippi Mud Pie, 3 oz	280	7	51
Sliced Pecan Pie, 3.35 oz	410	21	52

Port of Subs® (Feb '14)

Figures Based on West Coast Outlets

	C	F	Cb
Cold Submarine S'wiches: Per 5" Sub with Cheese, Lettuce, Tomato Vinegar, Oil, Salt & Oregano			
#1 Ham, Salami, Capicolla & Pepperoni with Provolone	435	18	42
#2 Ham & Turkey, with Provolone	355	9	42
#3 Salami & Turkey, with Provolone	390	13	43
#4 Ham & Salami with Provolone	385	14	42
#5 Smkd Ham & Turkey, with Chedd.	370	10	41
#6 Vegetarian, with 3 Cheeses	450	21	45
#7 Roast Beef, with Provolone	365	10	42
#8 Turkey, with Provolone	360	8	44
#10 Rstd Chicken Brst, w/ Provolone	350	8	44
#11 Ham, with American Cheese	405	14	44
#12 Salami, with Provolone	395	16	42
#13 Peppered Pastrami Turkey Swiss	375	12	43
#15 Salami & Pepperoni, w/ Provolone	405	18	42
#16 BLT Sandwich	470	26	39
#17 Tuna, with Provolone	475	25	43
#18 Rst Beef & Turkey, w/ Provolone	360	9	43

Continued Next Page...

Port of Subs® ... cont (Feb '14)

Figures Based on West Coast Outlets **C** **F** **Cb**

Light Submarine S'wiches: Per 5" Sub,
(318 Calories or less) w/out Cheese, Oil or Mayo

	C	F	Cb
#2 Ham Turkey	305	5	42
#5 Smoked Ham & Turkey	318	6	43
#6 Vegetarian	248	5	42
#7 Roast Beef	314	6	42
#8 Turkey	310	5	44
#9 Peppered Pastrami	267	4	41
#10 Roasted Chicken Breast	300	4	42
#18 Roast Beef & Turkey	312	5	43

Wraps: With 12" Flour Tortilla, Cheese, Lettuce,
Tomato, Onion, Vinegar, Oil, Salt & Oregano

	C	F	Cb
#4 Ham, Salami, with Provolone	600	28	56
#8 Turkey, with Provolone	565	21	59
#11 Ham, with American Cheese	615	27	58

Fresh Salads: With Lettuce, Tomato & Onion, w/o Dressing

	C	F	Cb
Caesar: With Parmesan, 6 oz	35	0	11
Add Grilled Chicken, 10 oz	190	3	10
Chefs, 11 oz	300	18	10
Garden, 10 oz	70	2	11
Grilled Chicken, 10 oz	190	3	10
Tuna, 9 oz	250	18	9

Salad Dressings: Per 1.5 oz package

	C	F	Cb
Blue Cheese	220	23	2
Ranch	260	28	2
Fat Free Ranch	50	0	13

Sides: Per Regular, 8 oz

	C	F	Cb
Caesar Bow Tie Pasta Salad, 8 oz	355	18	37
Potato Salad	325	13	52

Desserts:

	C	F	Cb
Brownie, 4.5 oz	535	12	96
Chocolate Chunk Cookie, 4.5 oz	560	29	72

Pret A Manger® (Feb '14)

Baguettes: Per Pack **C** **F** **Cb**

	C	F	Cb
Albacore Tuna & Cucumber	490	28	35
Brie, Tomato & Basil	540	17	72
Chicken Mozzarella	620	19	73
Ham & Cheese	610	21	69
Roast Beef & Parmesan	550	15	70

Hot Food: Per Pack

Toasties:
	C	F	Cb
Ham & Cheddar	520	24	49
Mozzarella & Pesto	430	16	52

Wraps:
	C	F	Cb
Buffalo Chicken	490	23	46
New York Meatball	540	32	50

Sandwiches: Per Pack
	C	F	Cb
Albacore Tuna Salad	450	28	24
California Club	430	24	30
Chicken & Bacon	340	17	35
Slims: Balsamic Chicken & Avocado	215	12	17
California Club	215	12	15

Pret A Manger® ... cont (Feb '14)

Wraps: Per Pack **C** **F** **Cb**

	C	F	Cb
Avocado Pine Nut	460	29	41
Bang Bang Chicken	510	30	37
Pret's: Crunch Wrap	370	15	49
Greek Falafel	390	6	63
Spicy Shrimp & Cilantro	380	17	32

Soups: Per Regular Size Pack

	C	F	Cb
Broccoli & Cheddar	510	39	23
Chicken Noodle	150	3	15
Chipotle Black Bean	330	4.5	57
Mediterranean Eggplant	135	7	20
New England Lobster Bisque	390	26	27

Salads: Per Pack, Without Dressing

	C	F	Cb
Chicken & Avocado	440	27	34
Chicken Caesar	370	16	23
Market Fresh	250	10	33
Pret's Cobb	430	22	35

Breakfast: Per Pack

Baguettes:
	C	F	Cb
Cream Cheese, Tomato & Basil	330	11	47
Egg & Bacon	440	21	45
Egg & Roasted Tomato	430	20	45

Pots:
	C	F	Cb
Egg & Spinach	170	11	2
Egg & Quinoa	240	14	18
Oatmeal, Steel Cut, regular	210	3.5	39

Bakery: Per Pack
	C	F	Cb
Classic Carrot Cake	370	26	29
Croissants: Plain	300	16	30
Almond	410	23	41
Pain au Chocolat	300	15	34
Muffins: Blueberry	420	20	54
Cranberry Orange	370	12	62

Beverages: Per Pack
	C	F	Cb
Grapefruit Juice, 15 fl.oz	200	0	46
Lemonade, 15 fl.oz	220	0	58

Pretzelmaker® (Feb '14)

Pretzels: Per Serving **C** **F** **Cb**

	C	F	Cb
Bites: Plain, salted, large, 3.5 oz	250	1	52
Cinnamon Sugar, 3.8 oz	330	4	65
Whole: Caramel Crunch, 4.2 oz	300	4	58
Cinnamon Sugar, 3.88 oz	330	4	65
Garlic; Salted, average, 4.2 oz	310	4	60
Iced Cinnamon Swirl, 3.88 oz	330	4	65
Ranch, 4.2 oz	320	4.5	60
Pretzel Dogs: Mini (6)	300	19	23
Jalapeno	410	19	32
Rolls, Pepperoni (1)	560	22	73

Continued Next Page...

Fast - Foods & *Restaurants*

Pretzelmaker® cont... (Feb '14)

	C	F	Cb
Sauces: Per Single Portion			
Caramel	140	0	35
Cheddar Cheese	80	5	4
Cream Cheese	200	20	2
Honey Mustard	80	0	20
Icing	180	0	45
Ketchup	20	0	4
Mustard	10	0	1
Nacho Cheese	80	5	4
Pizza	20	0.5	6

Beverages: Per 20 fl.oz Unless Indicated

Blended Drinks:

	C	F	Cb
Cool Cappuccino	640	21	107
Lemon Twist	540	16	99
Mango Madness	520	16	89
Mocha Mania	620	20	106
Power Pomegranate	490	16	86
Strawberry Bananza	650	20	115
Lemonade, Original, 44 oz	380	0	91

Qdoba® (Feb '14)

	C	F	Cb
Burritos: Each with Flour Tortilla, Cilantro-Lime Rice, Black Beans, Salsa Verde, Sour Cream and Shredded Cheese			
Grilled Chicken	985	32	120
Pulled Pork	955	26	129
Ground Beef	1035	38	121
Signature Flavors: With Flour Tortilla, 3-Cheese Queso, Pinto Beans, Lettuce, Shredded Cheese, Guacamole & Sour Cream			
Grilled Chicken	995	46	90
Grilled Steak	995	45	93
Pulled Pork	965	40	99
Seasoned Ground Beef	1045	52	91
Grilled Quesadillas: With Flour Tortilla, Shredded Cheese and Grilled Vegetables			
Grilled Chicken	1000	56	61
Shredded Beef	1000	53	66
3-Cheese Nachos: Per Serving, with Tortilla Chips, 3-Cheese Queso, Salsa Roja, Guacamole & Sour Cream			
Grilled Chicken	1110	62	96
Pulled Pork	1080	56	105

Qdoba® cont... (Feb '14)

	C	F	Cb
Tacos: Each, With Lettuce, Cheese, Guacamole, Pico de Gallo & Sour Cream			
Crispy Shell: Grilled Chicken	250	16	11
Pulled Pork	235	14	14
Seasoned Ground Beef	265	19	14
Shredded Beef	245	16	13
Taco Salads: With Crunchy Flour Tortilla Bowl, Lettuce, Black Bean & Corn Salsa, Shredded Cheese, Sour Cream, Guacamole, Fat Free Picante Ranch Dressing			
Grilled Chicken	985	54	68
Seasoned Ground Beef	1035	60	69
Chips & Dip: Includes Tortilla Chips			
3- Cheese Queso	740	40	82
3-Cheese Queso, Guac. & Salsa Roja	945	54	99
Breakfast Burritos: With Flour Tortilla			
Chorizo, Egg & Potato:			
With 3-Cheese Queso Sauce	845	39	76
With Shred. Cheese & Salsa Roja	995	50	78

Quiznos Subs® (Mar '14)

	C	F	Cb
Subs: Per Regular, with Standard Menu Toppings on White Italian Roll			
All Natural Chicken:			
Baja Chicken	860	38	74
Chicken Carbonara	950	48	71
Honey Bourbon Chicken	610	11	84
Mesquite Chicken	910	43	72
Steak:			
Black Angus Steak	860	32	83
Double Swiss Prime Rib	830	38	78
French Dip	910	48	80
Peppercorn Prime Rib	880	48	75
Deli Classics:			
Classic Italian	870	47	74
Honey Bacon Club	860	39	85
Italian Meatball	1110	59	86
Spicy Monterey Turkey	630	20	78
The Traditional	760	37	73
Tuna	790	37	74
Veggie Guacamole	760	43	71
Grilled Flatbreads: Per Small			
Basil Pesto Chicken	370	15	36
Chicken Bacon Ranch	480	24	36
Greek Chicken	420	19	37
Honey Bourbon Chicken	290	5	43
Sonoma Turkey	440	25	35

Continued Next Page...

Updated Nutrition Data ~ www.CalorieKing.com
Persons with Diabetes ~ See Disclaimer (Page 22)

Quiznos Subs® cont... (Mar '14)

	C	F	Cb
Wraps: Includes Dressing			
Cobb Chicken	820	48	64
Honey Mustard Chicken	840	45	73
Salads: Per Large, with Dressing			
Honey Mustard Chicken	800	62	29
Peppercorn Caesar Chicken	820	17	15
Savory Soups: Per Regular Bowl, with 2 Crackers			
Broccoli Cheese	180	9	17
Chicken Noodle	140	4.5	19
Desserts: Choc. Chunk Cookie	390	19	54
Chocolate Brownie	310	16	40
Cinnamon Sugar Cookie	400	17	58
Oatmeal Raisin Cookie	360	12	58

Rally's/Checkers® (Feb '14)

	C	F	Cb
Burgers/Sandwiches:			
Bacon Double Cheeseburger	650	42	32
Big Buford	570	36	31
Cheese Double Cheese	510	31	31
Chili Cheeseburger	320	15	30
Rallyburger	390	22	32
Classic Wings: Extra Hot, 5 pieces	355	21	2
Honey BBQ, 5 pieces	390	17	18
Parmesan Garlic, 5 pieces	480	35	1
Fries:			
Chili Cheese, 7.75 oz	550	34	48
French: Medium, 4.25 oz	420	27	40
Large, 6 oz	590	38	57

Ranch 1® (Feb '14)

	C	F	Cb
Sandwiches:			
Chicken & Cheese	390	12	40
Chicken Philly, 9.25 oz	410	13	40
Original: Crispy Chicken, 11.5 oz	640	31	60
Grilled Spicy Chicken, 10.25 oz	360	7	46
Other Favorites:			
Chicken Fajita, 5.5 oz	540	24	53
Chicken Platter, with Rice, 11.85 oz	270	6	28
Popcorn Chicken: Small, 5.5 oz	310	10	30
Large, 7.5 oz	420	14	40
Kids, 2 oz	120	4	11
Salads: Completed			
Grilled Chicken Caesar, 13.25 oz	430	30	14
Southwest Chicken, 17.5 oz	680	43	44
Fries: Medium, 5.75 oz	380	19	43
Large, 8 oz	530	27	58
Kids, 4.25 oz	280	14	31
Cheese: Medium, 7.3 oz	490	27	44
Large, 11 oz	760	44	66

Red Hot & Blue® (Feb '14)

	C	F	Cb
Entrees: Per Serving			
Delta Double: With Memphis Chkn	900	54	12
With Pulled Pork	795	60	9
Five Meat Treat	935	63	15
Ribs, Half Slab: Dry	935	72	14
Sweet	950	71	22
Sandwiches: Regular, Without Sides			
Beef Brisket	390	15	37
Carolina Chopped Pork	360	14	34
Pulled Pork	370	15	37
Salads: Without Dressing			
Grilled Chicken Caesar Salad	770	46	47
Pulled Chicken Salad	295	8	14
Smokehouse Salad	670	36	36
Southern Fried Chicken Salad	710	31	60
Soup, Memphis Corn Chowder,			
1 bowl	270	12	23
Sides: BBQ Beans	255	2	48
Mashed Potatoes with Gravy	310	14	44
Memphis Fries, 6 oz	345	19	38
Potato Salad	405	28	33

Red Lobster® (Feb '14)

Lunch Menu: Without Condiments, Dipping Sauces or Optional Side Dishes.

	C	F	Cb
Seaside Starters:			
Chilled Jumbo Shrimp Cocktail	120	0.5	9
Crispy Calamari & Vegetables	1390	88	110
Lobster Pizza	680	31	66
Shrimp Nachos	1290	78	98
Classics:			
Cajun Chicken Linguini Alfredo,			
lunch serve	720	34	55
Crab Linguine, lunch serve	810	46	64
Crunchy Popcorn Shrimp	380	18	38
Garlic Shrimp Scampi	130	8	0
Sailor's Platter	290	9	5
Walleye: Beer-Battered	350	21	12
Blackened	150	3.5	5
Fried	290	15	6
Lighthouse/Fresh Fish Menu: Includes Broccoli			
Rainbow Trout, half portion	220	10	6
Salmon, half portion	270	9	6
Tilapia, half portion	210	3	9

Continued Next Page...

Red Lobster® cont... (Feb '14)

Dinner Menu: Without Condiments, Dipping Sauces Or Optional Side Dishes Unless Indicated

Seaside Starters:	C	F	Cb
Battered Crawfish	1280	81	99
Lobster, Artich. & Seafood Dip	1050	61	96
Lobster, Crab & Seafood, Stuffed Mushrooms	320	18	20
Mozzarella Cheesesticks	710	42	50
Sweet Chili Shrimp	1140	80	78

Soup: *Per Cup*			
Lobster Bisque	210	14	12
Manhattan Clam Chowder	80	1	12
Seafood Gumbo	230	8	25

Lobster & Crab Entrees:			
Crab Linguine Alfredo, full serve	1580	89	127
Live Main Lobster, steamed, with Corn & Potatoes, 20 oz	520	12	45
Rock Lobster Tail	170	1	1
Snow Crab Legs, with Corn & Potatoes, 16 oz	470	13	45

Shrimp Entrees:			
Chesapeake Shrimp	660	35	54
Parrot Isle Jumbo C'nut Shrimp	880	60	56
Shrimp Linguini Alfredo, full sve	1130	49	108
Walt's Favorite Shrimp	550	30	39

Side Dishes:			
Baked Potato: Plain	200	0.5	43
With Butter	290	11	44
With Sour Cream	230	3	44
Coleslaw	200	15	13
Creamy Lobster Mashed Potatoes	370	22	30
Fresh Broccoli	40	0	5
French Fries	330	17	40
Mashed Potatoes	210	10	27
Wild Rice Pilaf	160	3.5	30

Salads: *Includes Dressing*			
Caesar Salad: With Chicken	660	52	15
With Shrimp	630	53	16

Sauces:			
Cocktail Sauce	40	0	9
Honey Mustard Dipping Sauce	280	26	12
Tartar Sauce	190	19	6
100% Pure Melted Butter	350	38	2

Desserts:			
Carrot Cake	600	36	63
Chocolate Wave	1490	81	172
Key Lime Pie	580	22	88
New York-Style Cheesecake with Strawberries	590	41	48
Warm Apple Crostada	670	32	85
Warm Chocolate Chip Lava Cookie	1070	51	142

For Complete Nutritional Data ~ see CalorieKing.com

Red Robin® (Feb '14)

Nutritional Information varies between restaurants. Please refer to Red Robin's website for further information

Appetizers:	C	F	Cb
Chili Con Queso	730	37	61
Creamy Artichoke & Spinach Dip	770	44	63
Guacamole, Salsa & Chips	840	35	98

Jump Starters:			
Jalepeno Coins, fried, w/out Dress.	490	31	17
Swt Potato Fries, w/out Dressing	285	15	35
Zucchini, Breaded & Fried, without Dressing	215	15	17
Towering Onion Rings, w/ Ranch Dressing & Mayo	2530	149	265
Warm Pretzel Bites, w/ Beer Chse	635	19	96
Yukon Chips & French Onion Dip	810	62	46

Entrees: *With Standard Menu Components*			
Arctic Cod Fish & Chips	1175	69	98
Clucks & Fries: Regular Style	905	59	45
Buffalo Style	1190	94	45
Clucks & Shrimp Combo	905	54	62
Ensenada Chicken Platter, 1 piece	265	9	13
Prime Rib	700	27	67
Red's Nantucket Seafood Scatter	1210	73	91

Gourmet Burgers:			
A.1. Peppercorn	1395	87	96
All American Patty Melt	1150	80	63
Bleu Ribbon	1380	85	100
Burnin' Love	895	52	61
Fiery Ghost Style Big Tavern	805	44	63
Guacamole Bacon	1010	65	54
Prime Chophouse	1395	81	114
Royal Red Robin	1230	87	51
Sauteed Mushroom	855	49	56
Whiskey River BBQ	1410	89	98

Sandwiches & Wraps:			
Baja Turkey Club Sandwich	880	49	48
BLTA Croissant	795	52	45
Chicken Caesar Sandwich	765	42	54
Whiskey River BBQ Chicken Wrap	820	39	69

Continued Next Page... . . .

Red Robin® cont... (Feb '14)

Soups: **C F Cb**

Chicken Tortilla: *Includes Tortilla Strips*

	C	F	Cb
1 Cup	205	11	17
1 Bowl	400	19	35

Clam Chowder: *Includes Garlic Bread*

1 Cup	325	19	23
1 Bowl	605	39	37

French Onion: *Includes Garlic Bread*

1 Cup	245	14	20
1 Bowl	340	19	28

Salads: Without Side Bread or Dressing

Avo Cobb-O	455	25	16
Crispy Chicken Tender	820	47	45
Simply Grilled Chicken	465	15	40
Southwest Grilled Chicken	670	36	40
Whiskey River BBQ Chicken	780	38	64

Desserts:

Gooey Chocolate Brownie Cake	795	28	132
Mountain High Mudd Pie	1370	58	193

Milkshakes:

Classic: Banana

Classic: Banana	505	20	75
Chocolate	715	20	126

Smoothie, Hawaiian Heart Throb | 375 | 2 | 91

Roly Poly® (Feb '14)

Wraps: **C F Cb**

Per 6" White Tortilla Unless Indicated

Ham & Smoked Pork:

	C	F	Cb
Italian Classic	335	12	32
Key West Cuban Mix	330	9	44
Peachtree Melt	310	11	27
Pork Melt	310	11	26
Porky's Nightmare	320	12	28
Chicken: Basil Cashew Chicken	300	10	30
Catalina Chicken	315	11	28
Chicken Caesar	310	11	30
Chicken Fajita	315	9	28
Cobb Salad	255	12	27
Oriental Chicken	270	4	29
Santa Fe Chicken	305	11	28
Tuna: Classic Tuna Melt	340	17	26
Popeyes Tuna on Wheat	305	11	31
Texas Tuna Melt	310	12	30
Thai Hot Tuna	340	11	30
Turkey: California	330	12	30
Tuscan	220	2	31

Round Table Pizza® (Feb '14)

Appetizers: **C F Cb**

	C	F	Cb
Buffalo Wings, 6 pieces	420	30	6
Buffalo Wings, 6 pieces	480	27	12
Garlic Bread: 6 pieces	360	18	36
With Cheese, 6 pieces	540	36	72
Garlic Parmesan Twists, 1 twist	170	5	24
Honey BBQ Wings, 6 pieces	420	30	6

Pizzas: Per ½ of Large 14" Pizza

Original Crust: Cheese

Original Crust: Cheese	220	9	24
Chicken & Garlic Gourmet	250	11	24
Gourmet Veggie	230	10	26
Guinevere's Garden Delight	210	9	25
Hawaiian	220	8	26
Italian Garlic Supreme	270	14	24
King Arthur Supreme	270	13	25
Maui Zaui, with Polynesian Sce	260	10	29
Montague's All Meat Marvel	290	15	24
Smokehouse Combo, Chicken	290	14	26
Triple Pepperoni	250	12	24
Pan Crust: Cheese	300	11	36
Chicken & Garlic Gourmet	330	13	37
Gourmet Veggie	320	12	39
Guinevere's Garden Delight	290	10	38
Hawaiian	300	10	38
Italian Garlic Supreme	350	16	37
King Arthur Supreme	330	14	37
Maui Zaui w/ Polynesian Sauce	340	12	41
Montague's All Meat Marvel	350	15	37
Smokehouse Combo, Chicken	350	14	38
Triple Pepperoni	330	14	36
Skinny Crust: Cheese	190	9	17
Chicken & Garlic Gourmet	210	11	18
Gourmet Veggie	200	10	19
Guinevere's Garden Delight	180	8	19
Hawaiian	190	8	20
Italian Garlic Supreme	240	14	17
King Arthur Supreme	230	13	18
Maui Zaui w/ Polynesian Sauce	220	10	21
Montague's All Meat Marvel	260	15	17
Smokehouse Combo, Chicken	240	12	19
Triple Pepperoni	220	12	17

Sandwiches:

Chicken Club	800	43	59
Ham Club	740	40	60
RT Veggie	630	32	65
Turkey Club	720	38	59
Turkey Sante-Fe	730	40	57

For Complete Nutritional Data ~ see CalorieKing.com

Rubio's Mexican Grill® (Feb '14)

	C	F	Cb
Burritos: Each, with Corn Tortilla, without Chips			
Baja: Grilled Chicken	630	28	55
Steak	650	32	55
Bean & Cheese	760	37	78
Beer-Battered Fish	830	49	70
Grilled: Mahi Mahi	730	32	79
Shrimp	720	34	74
Veggie	770	35	83
Burrito Especial: Chicken	820	31	102
Steak	850	35	102
Health Mex, Chicken	500	10	74
Nachos: Regular	1270	78	112
With Chicken	1340	78	114
Quesadillas: Three Cheese	1120	70	87
Three Cheese Chicken	1200	70	89
Tacos: Each, with Corn Tortilla			
Grilled Gourmet: Chicken	320	17	24
Steak	330	19	24
Seafood:			
Blackened: Atlantic Salmon	250	10	26
Pacific Mahi Mahi	250	9	26
Grilled: Gourmet with Shrimp	340	19	23
Grilled Tilapia	220	8	22
Mango Habanero Mahi Mahi	250	8	29
Salsa Verde Shrimp	240	12	22
Add Ons:			
Black Beans & Chips, 6 oz	360	14	50
Black Beans & Rice, 7 oz	240	3	44
Pinto Beans & Chips, 6 oz	370	15	55
Pinto Beans & Rice, 7 oz	250	4	49
Pinto & Black Beans, 8.2 oz	210	2	39
Rice & Chips, 4.8 oz	400	15	60
Salad & Bowls: Entree Size, Includes Dressing			
Chipotle Ranch with Chicken	450	31	22
Chopped Chicken	460	24	36
Grilled Grande Bowl: With Chicken	640	28	62
With Shrimp	630	31	61
Salsas: Per 1 oz			
Picante	20	1	2
Other Varieties	5	0	1

Ruby Tuesday® (Feb '14)

	C	F	Cb
Shareables: Per Serve, w/out Sauce			
Asian Dumplings	65	2	8
Fried Mozzarella	135	8	11
Southwestern Spring Rolls	160	8	18
Spinach Artichoke Dip	310	19	27
Burgers: With Fries			
Avocado Turkey	1390	71	137
Buffalo Chicken	1240	57	149
Chicken BLT	1250	55	149
Ruby's Classic	1310	70	130
Smokehouse	1610	86	155
Turkey	1220	59	136
Triple Prime: Original	1365	74	135
Bacon Cheddar	1585	91	135
Cheddar	1525	86	135
Fit & Trim Choices: Includes Menu Set Sides			
Chicken Bella	460	23	15
Grilled Salmon	425	23	9
Hickory Bourbon Chicken	485	23	25
Top Sirloin	445	27	15
Fork-Tender Ribs: Without Sides			
Classic BBQ, Half	470	24	21
Memphis Dry Rub, Half-Rack	410	24	6
Premium Seafood: Without Sides			
Crab Cake Dinner	270	17	14
French Quarter Gumbo	800	45	49
Herb-Crusted Tilapia	400	24	11
Jumbo Skewered Shrimp	275	15	0
Louisiana Fried Shrimp	560	29	47
New Orleans Seafood	365	19	2
Smart Eating,			
Grilled Chicken Wrap, w/o sides	495	17	47
Steakhouse Steaks: Without Sides			
Black Fire New York Strip	505	28	6
Rib Eye	935	74	7
Top Sirloin	350	22	6

Continued Next Page...

Updated Nutrition Data ~ www.CalorieKing.com
Persons with Diabetes ~ See Disclaimer (Page 22)

Ruby Tuesday® cont... (Feb '14)

	C	F	Cb
Pasta Classics: Without Sides			
Cajan Jambalaya	990	48	84
Chicken & Broccoli	1500	95	93
Chicken & Mushroom Alfredo	1220	66	87
Parmesan Chicken	1345	74	110
Spaghetti Squash Marinara	260	11	32
Dressing: Per 1 oz			
Balsamic Vinaigrette	40	2	5
Blue Cheese	180	19	1
Honey Mustard	90	8	5
Italian	130	14	1
Ranch	90	9	1
Signature Parmesan	150	16	1
Thousand Island	80	7	5
Fresh Sides:			
Baked Potato: Plain	260	2	52
Loaded Baked Potato	570	29	54
French Fries	480	18	78
Garlic Cheese Biscuit	110	5	12
Mashed Potatoes	290	17	29
Onion Rings	340	19	37
Rice Pilaf	160	3	30
Roasted Spaghetti Squash	55	3	6
Mashed Potatoes	290	17	29
Kid's Menu: Includes Set Menu Sides			
Chicken Breast	350	12	39
Chicken Tenders	585	21	48
Grilled Cheese	660	26	92
Desserts:			
Blondie for One	540	23	77
Cake, Double Chocolate	795	31	119
Cookies: Chocolate Chip	180	9	24
White Choc. Macadamia Nut	200	12	23
Cupcakes: Carrot Cake (1)	325	16	45
Red Velvet (1)	285	11	45
New York Cheesecake	740	60	76
Tiramisu	535	30	69

For Complete Menu ~ see CalorieKing.com

Runza® (Feb '14)

	C	F	Cb
Burgers:			
¼ lb BBQ Bacon & Swiss	530	32	26
¼ lb Bacon Cheeseburger	510	31	26
Deluxe	540	34	26
¼ lb French Onion	490	29	26
¼ lb Jalapeno	530	35	25
¼ lb Legend Supreme	520	32	26
¼ lb Spicy Jack Hamburger	570	38	23
¼ lb Swiss Mushroom	480	29	24
Runza Way: ¼ lb Cheeseburger	420	22	28
¼ lb Hamburger	370	18	26
½ lb Double Cheeseburger	670	39	30
½ lb Double Hamburger	570	31	26
Sandwiches:			
Grilled: BBQ Chicken	400	11	40
Buffalo Chicken	360	11	37
Deluxe Chicken	360	10	37
Sides:			
Onion Rings: Medium	320	19	35
Large	550	31	58
French Onion Dip	110	7	5
Salads:			
Asian Grilled Chicken w/ dressing	410	7	59
Southwest Chicken Salad w/ Salsa	320	15	31
Sweet Berry Chicken w/o dressing	370	19	21
Dressings: Honey Mustard	290	27	13
Ranch	270	27	4
Soups: Per Bowl			
Broccoli Cheese	250	18	13
Chicken Tortilla	145	7	13
Homemade Chili	320	15	23
New England Clam Chowder	290	16	34
Wisconsin Cheese	280	18	18
Kids:			
Junior: Cheeseburger, plain	250	13	18
Hamburger, plain	200	9	16
Swiss Cheese Mushroom Burger	300	17	17
Runza Way: Cheeseburger	270	13	22
Hamburger	220	9	20
Desserts:			
Ice Cream Cones, all flavors	260	7	40
Ice Cream Dish, all flavors	230	7	34
Sundaes: Caramel; Chocolate	300	7	51
Turtle	360	13	53
Shakes: Per Regular, 16 oz			
Cappucino	490	12	82
Chocolate	480	12	81
Vanilla	430	12	66

Ryan's Grill Buffet & Bakery® (Feb '14)

Entrees: Without Sides

	C	F	Cb
Beef: BBQ'd, 4 oz	140	5	16
Country Fried Steak, w/ gravy, 2.6 oz	220	13	16
Meatloaf, 3 oz	180	11	7
Perfect Pot Roast, 5 oz	160	7	9
Salisbury Steak, 3.5 oz	150	9	8
Chicken:			
Breasts: Country BBQ, 5.8 oz	310	16	6
Rotisserie, 5.3 oz	310	17	1
Traditional, Baked, 5.3 oz	310	17	0.5
Chicken & Dumplings, 5 oz	160	5	17
New Orleans Bourbon Street, 3 oz	180	8	9
Orange Chicken, 3 oz	340	22	26
Fish/Seafood: Baked Fish, 2 oz	90	4.5	0
Butter Crumb Alaskan Pollock, 1.75 oz	110	5	2
Butterfly Shrimp (6), 2.3 oz	210	9	24
Carved Salmon Filet, 3 oz	190	11	0
Clam Strips, 3 oz	320	20	28
Fried: Fish, 3 pieces, 3 oz	240	12	27
Shrimp (22), 3 oz	240	12	24
Wood Seared Salmon, 1 pce, 3 oz	220	16	0
Pasta/Spaghetti: *Per 5 oz Serving*			
Country Pasta Gratine	160	4	24
Creamy Penne Carbonara	260	17	17
Fire Grilled Chicken Alfredo	220	14	14
Grilled Italian Sausage Penne	180	11	14
Pork:			
Carved: Grilled Loin, 3 oz	140	10	0
Ham, 3 oz	100	5	0
Honey Glazed Baked, 1 sl, 3 oz	120	5	1
Ribs, BBQ/County-Style (3), 3.5 oz	420	27	15
Steak: Grilled, 2 oz	140	9	0
BBQ, grilled, 2 oz	150	9	3
Salads: *Without Dressing*			
Asian Chopped, 3.55 oz	90	4	13
Caesar, 1 cup, 2.5 oz	70	5	4
Greek, 2.65 oz	120	8	10
Seafood, 4.15 oz	310	26	15
Sides:			
Baked Potato, plain, 4.25 oz	150	0	36
BBQ Baked Beans, 3 oz	130	3	26
Cauliflower Au Gratin, 3 oz	50	2	8
French Fries, 2 oz	170	9	23
Fried Okra, 3 oz	220	12	28
Mashed Potatoes, 4 oz	70	0.5	13
Desserts: Cheesecake, plain, 1 sl.	230	12	28
Key Lime Pie, scratch, 1 sl., 2.5 oz	220	9	31
Lemon Meringue Pie, 2.25 oz	130	4.5	23

7-Eleven® (Feb '14)

7-Select Burritos:

	C	F	Cb
Bean and Cheese, 5 oz	320	10	47
Beef & Bean, 5 oz	360	16	44
Beef, Bean & Green Chile, 5 oz	360	15	44
Red Hot Beef, 5 oz	340	15	41
Bites: *Without Bun or Toppings*			
Big Bite Hot Dog, 2 oz	180	17	1
Breakfast Bite Sausage, 3 oz	250	21	2
Cheeseburger Bite Link, 4.2 oz	440	38	2
Qtr Pound Big Bite Hot Dog, 4 oz	360	34	2
Breakfast Sandwiches:			
Biscuits: Egg, Cheese & Ssg, 5.45 oz	460	32	31
Sausage, 3.3 oz	330	22	28
Croissant, Egg, Cheese & Ssg, 4.75 oz	410	30	20
Eng. Muffin, Egg, Chse & Ssg, 5 oz	390	25	24
Fresh:			
Cilantro Lime Chicken Flatbread	570	25	51
Turkey Sandwich	560	28	48
Very Berry Salad	210	15	12
Yoplait yogurt Parfait	230	2.5	47
Other Selections:			
Chicken Tenders (1), 3.3 oz	160	5	11
Maple Pancake Sausage (1), 2.6 oz	270	19	19
Pepperoni Pizza, 1 slice, 3.9 oz	300	14	30
Rollers: Buffalo Chicken (1), 3 oz	190	7	16
Corn Dog (1), 3.4 oz	320	21	23
Taquitos: *Per 1.3 oz Taquito*			
Bacon, Egg, Cheese & Potato	190	8	23
Jalapeno Cream Cheese	240	13	27
Monterey Jack & Chicken	280	14	30
Steak & Cheese	210	11	22
Wings, Bone In, Spicy Wing Zings,			
1 wing	80	4.5	3
Sides: Hash Browns (1), 2 oz	100	5	12
Potato Wedges (6), 0.65 oz	240	4.5	27
Slurpees: average all flavors:			
12 oz cup	95	0	26
22 oz cup	175	0	44
28 oz cup	220	0	56
Sugar Free, 12 oz cup	30	0	9

Saladworks® (Feb '14)

Salads: Without Dressing

	C	F	Cb
Autumn Harvest	300	12	40
Bently	245	10	11
Buffalo Bleu	250	7.5	24
Chicken Caesar	285	4	19
Cobb	270	16	13
Fire Roasted Cabo Jack	390	19	31
Greek	185	10	18
Nuevo Nicoise	230	4	31
Sophie's Salad	310	14	35
Tivoli	430	19	31

Focaccia Fusion: Without Spread

	C	F	Cb
BLT	345	13	32
Chicken Monterey	385	12	35
Fajitalicious	380	12	33
Turkey Ranch	365	10	33

Dressings: Per 1 oz Ladle

	C	F	Cb
Balsamic: Regular	170	18	4
Fat Free	20	0	5
Classic French	130	12	6
Green Goddess	150	15	3
Oriental Sesame	90	4.5	12
Parmesan Caesar	150	17	1
Rustic Thousand Island	140	13	5

Extra Menu Items ~ See CalorieKing.com

Sandella's® (Feb '14)

	C	F	Cb
Grilled Flatbread: With Standard Toppings			
Brazilian Bacon	560	17	79
Brazilian Chicken	510	10	73
Pesto Chicken	610	28	56
Spinach & Bacon	660	39	52
Paninis: With Standard Toppings			
Philly Cheese	590	25	55
Spinach, Ham & Swiss	550	20	61
Tuscan Chicken	540	21	55
Quesadillas: With Standard Toppings			
California	500	23	53
Mediterranean	400	16	53
Salads: Includes ½ Flatbread & Dressing			
Fiesta	360	8	54
Greek	310	15	37
Rice Bowls: Includes Flatbread & Standard Toppings			
Black Bean & Rice	840	20	130
Chicken Fajita	750	20	104
Wraps: With Standard Toppings			
California Turkey	410	10	55
Chicken Fajita	520	20	53
Pesto Turkey	460	15	54
Sweet & Spicy Chicken	400	7	64

Sarku Japan® (Feb '14)

D'Lite Meals:

	C	F	Cb
Rice & Chicken Tempua, 15 oz	970	58	81
Rice & Shrimp Tempura, 11 oz	540	21	70
Vegetarian, 14 oz	360	0.5	79
Vegetarian Soba Noodle, 14 oz	710	24	106

Combos:

	C	F	Cb
Tempura: Chicken, 23 oz	1270	78	102
Chicken & Shrimp, 20 oz	980	53	95
Teriyaki: Beef, 19 oz	690	26	81
Beef & Shrimp, 21 oz	630	11	85
Chicken, 22 oz	640	13	90
Chicken & Shrimp, 24 oz	700	14	90
Shrimp, 19 oz	500	2.5	83
Sauce, Teriyaki, 1.5 oz	45	0	9
Sides: Maki Roll, 2 oz	140	11	9
Rice: Steamed, 9 oz	290	0	64
Fried, 9 oz	330	4.5	62
Tempura Chicken, 1 piece, 2 oz	230	19	8
Tempura Shrimp, 1 piece, 0.8 oz	90	7	4

Schlotzsky's® (Feb '14)

Oven-Toasted Sandwiches: Per Medium Size

	C	F	Cb
Angus: Beef & Provolone	760	28	82
Corned Beef	500	7	69
Corned Beef Reuben	870	37	78
Pastrami Reuben	870	36	78
Pastrami & Swiss	800	29	77
BLT	540	17	74
Chicken & Pesto	560	11	79
Chicken Breast	490	3	82
Chipotle Chicken	530	9	78
Homestyle Tuna	580	16	75
Santa Fe Chicken	660	19	78
Smoked Turkey Breast	500	6	80
Smoked Turkey Reuben	850	35	78
Turkey & Guacamole	520	11	78
Turkey Bacon Club	770	29	81
Original Style: The Original	780	33	79
Deluxe	980	46	81
Ham & Cheese	730	25	81
Turkey	820	33	82

Wraps: Per Medium Size

	C	F	Cb
Chicken & Pesto	510	18	54
Homestyle Tuna	540	22	55
Santa Fe Chicken	590	24	55

Continued Next Page...

Fast - Foods & Restaurants

Schlotzsky's® cont... (Feb '14)

8" Pizzas: Per Pizza

	C	F	Cb
BBQ Chicken & Jalapeno	660	15	100
Combination Special	660	27	79
Double Cheese	600	21	76
Fresh Veggie	610	21	79
Grilled Chicken & Pesto	670	21	78
Pepperoni & Double Cheese	740	33	77
Smoked Turkey & Jalapeno	650	20	81

Salads: Without Dressing or Breadsticks

Cranberry, Apple, Pecan & Chicken	640	26	68
Hearts of Romaine, Chicken Caesar	400	16	29
Garden	40	2	9
Potato	240	13	29
Turkey Avocado Cobb	610	33	42
Turkey Chef	415	25	17
Garlic Breadsticks, entree portion (2)	60	2	10

Dressings: Per 3 oz

Butttermilk Ranch	320	33	4
Chunky Blue Cheese	455	49	3
Red Wine Vinaigrette	425	43	9
Robusto Italian	285	28	3
Tuscan Caesar	425	45	2

Soup: Per Bowl

Broccoli Cheese	170	10	17
Chicken & Wild Rice	270	15	20
Creamy Chicken Tortilla	300	15	22
Potato, with Bacon	340	27	34
Timberline Chili	450	22	33
Tomato Basil	310	24	24

Chips:

Baked: Regular; BBQ, average	130	3	26
Other varieties, average	230	14	24

Kid's Meals: Without Cookie or Drink

Cheese Pizza	540	16	78
Cheese Sandwich	390	14	49
Ham & Cheese Sandwich	420	15	50
Pepperoni Pizza	590	21	78
Turkey Sandwich	290	3	50

Desserts:

Brownie (1)	370	19	49
Carrot Cake, 1 slice	715	42	80
Creamy Cheesecake, 1 slice	540	33	50
Cookies: Per Cookie			
Chocolate/Fudge Choc. Chip, av.	160	7	23
Oatmeal Raisin; Sugar, average	150	6	24
Macadamia Nut	170	9	22

Second Cup® ~ see CalorieKing.com

Shakey's® (Feb '14)

Pizzas: Per Slice, ⅛ Large Pizza

	C	F	Cb
Cheese: Pan Crust	185	6	26
Thin Crust	150	5.5	18
Firehouse: Pan Crust	255	12	27
Thin Crust	220	12	19
Garden Veggie: Pan Crust	185	5.5	27
Thin Crust	150	5	19
Margherita: Pan Crust	175	5	26
Thin Crust	135	4.5	18
Rustic Garlic Chicken: Pan Crust	190	5.5	26
Thin Crust	155	5.5	18
Shakey's Special: Pan Crust	210	6.5	31
Thin Crust	195	10	18
Texas BBQ Chicken: Pan Crust	205	5	29
Thin Crust	170	5	21
Ultimate Meat: Pan Crust	280	14	26
Thin Crust	245	13	18
Additional Toppings: Beef	35	3	0
Cheese	15	1	0.5
Chicken	15	0.5	0
Pepperoni	25	2.5	0
Sausage	45	4	0.5

Shareables: Per Serving, Unless Indicated

Chicken Strips (5)	620	31	48
Mojo Potatoes (5)	215	11	25
Mojo Supreme, serves 4-6	1950	120	160
Shakey's Spicy Wings (6)	495	29	27

Shakey's Famous Chicken: Per Piece

Fried Chicken: Breast	475	26	16
Leg	170	19	6
Thigh	350	24	10
Wing	130	9	3.5

Shari's® (Feb '14)

Breakfast:

	C	F	Cb
Favorites:			
Farmhouse Biscuit Breakfast	1170	73	94
The Breakfast Sampler, with Butter Syrup	1460	84	133
Traditional Eggs Benedict, with Hashbrowns	810	46	61
Fruit Crepes: Apples; Strawb., av.	685	36	79
Burst O Berry	630	36	67
Omelettes: BMP	930	77	8
Denver; Spring Spinach, average	655	52	11
Fajita Chicken	700	52	13
Sauteed Shrimp & Cheese	550	38	8
Pancakes: B'milk, w/ Butter & Syrup, entree size	770	15	151
Shari's Potato Pancakes	570	17	96

Continued Next Page...

Shari's® cont... (Feb '14)

Breakfast (Cont):

	C	F	Cb
Specialties:			
Breakfast Panini			
Classic Quiche: BMP	610	29	63
Lorraine	610	30	61
Meat Lover's Skillet,			
w/o side choices	1140	91	34

Lunch:

	C	F	Cb
Flame-Grilled Burgers: *Without Sides*			
Brioche Garlic-Mshrm Swiss	1070	74	55
Old-Fash. Classic Hamburger	600	29	46
With Bleu Cheese	650	33	46
With Cheddar Cheese	680	35	46
With Pepperjack Cheese	700	38	46
With Swiss Cheese	670	34	46
The: Bavarian	1030	47	59
Caprese	860	49	51
Flatbread Paninis: *Without Sides*			
All American	740	34	61
Classic Reuben	860	37	67
Salads: *Entrée Size*			
American Chopped, w/o Dress.	620	29	44
Classic Grilled Chicken Caesar,			
with dressing	700	45	41
Sandwiches: *Per Whole Sandwich, w/o Side Choices*			
Applewood Smoked BLT	420	22	40
Handcrafted:			
Baja Chipotle Chicken	840	48	59
Cuban, on Ciabatta	620	30	45
Prime Rib Dip	820	51	47

Dinner:

	C	F	Cb
Down-Home BBQ Favorite,			
Baby Back Ribs, as served	1470	63	123
Flame Grilled Favorites: *With Garlic Herb Bread & Onion Rings*			
Center Cut NY Strip Steak	970	64	39
Surf & Turf Grilled Steak:			
With Shrimp	1070	50	95
With Shrimp Scampi	960	62	42
With Shrimp Skewers	790	43	41
T-Bone Steak, 16 oz	1130	67	41
Top Sirloin Steak	600	32	40
Homestyle Classic,			
Pot Roast & Veggies, as served	1440	79	82

Shari's® cont... (Feb '14)

Dinner (Cont):

	C	F	Cb
Seafood Favorites: *As Served*			
Alask. Cod & Shrimp Combo Platter	1280	79	119
Hand Cut Alaskan Cod & Chips	1220	77	111
Desserts:			
Classic Pies: *Per Slice, as Served*			
Banana Cream Dream	600	36	56
Chocolate Cream Supreme	590	33	67
Gourmet Pies: *Per Slice, As Served*			
Creamy Caramel Pecan Crunch	710	45	71
Peanut Butter Chocolate Silk	660	45	60
S'mores Galore	570	31	68
Velvet Chocolate Silk	640	46	55

Sheetz® (Oct '13)

Breakfast:

Plain Bagel, Without Add Ons Or Dressing

	C	F	Cb
Shmagelz: Bacon & Egg	530	27	53
Egg & American Cheese	440	19	50
Egg, Ham & Provolone	525	21	55
Shmscuitz: Bacon & Egg	540	35	39
Egg & American Cheese	450	27	36
Egg, Ham & Swiss Cheese	550	30	41
Egg, Sausage & Amer. Cheese	625	44	36
Shmuffins: Bacon & Egg	410	25	29
Egg & American Cheese	320	17	26
Egg & Ham	310	11	30
Egg, Sausage & Cheddar Cheese	495	34	26
Egg & Steak	395	16	27

Cold Subz: *Per 6" White Sub, w/o Add Ons or Dressing*

	C	F	Cb
American Cheese	350	11	45
BLT	445	19	48
Chicken Salad	490	23	54
Roast Beef	280	4	46
Turkey	295	4	47

Hot Subz: *Per 6" White Sub, w/out Add Ons or Dressing*

	C	F	Cb
Chicken	360	6	45
Meatball	370	13	48
Pepperoni	440	20	45
Hot Dogz, with Chili & Onions	310	19	27
Nachoz, Bueno/Grande,			
with Nacho Cheese	515	23	65

Saladz: *Without Dressing*

	C	F	Cb
Chef, with Shredded Cheese	250	12	13
Crispy Chicken, w/ Shredded Chse	370	16	31
Garden, with Shredded Cheese	130	8	8
Steak	210	8	8
Taco, with Shredded Cheese	355	18	39

Continued Next Page...

Fast - Foods & Restaurants

Sheetz® cont... (Oct '13)

	C	F	Cb
Add Ons:			
Bacon	150	12	2
Black Olives	15	1	0.5
Cheeses: American; Cheddar; Swiss	110	9	0
Hot Pepper Provolone	100	8	1
Parmesan	5	0.5	0.5
Green/Jalapeno Peppers	5	0	0.5
Shredded Lettuce; Diced Onions, av.	5	0	1
Tomatoes, sliced	5	0.5	1
Dressings/Sauces:			
Honey Mustard	10	0	4
Italian Romano	60	6	2
Marinara	10	0.5	1
Mayo; Ranch, average	145	16	1
Sidez:			
Chili, Mac & Cheese, 6.7 oz	130	6	14
Cole Slaw, 5 oz	200	9	28
Fryz: Bag, 3.2 oz	160	6	23
Cup, 5 oz	260	10	36
Cheese, 14.4 oz	670	32	81
Smokehouse, 15.38 oz	985	53	103
Beverage, Hot Chocolate, medium	290	1	56

Sizzler® (Feb '14)

	C	F	Cb
Burgers/Sandwiches: With Standard Toppings			
Burgers: Mega Bacon Cheeseburger	1040	63	48
Sizzler Burger: ⅓ lb	620	30	48
½ lb	760	39	48
Sandwiches: Grilled Chicken Club	640	29	48
Malibu Chicken	980	67	59
Hot Entrees: Includes Sauces & Toppings, Without Vegetable Side Dishes			
Chicken: Grilled Fettuccini Alfredo	1035	61	64
Hibachi Chicken, Single	165	3.5	10
Lemon-Herb Chicken, Single	175	8	2
Malibu Chicken, Single	640	55	12
Pork Chop, Single	570	37	24
Spareribs: Includes Cole Slaw			
St Louis: Half Rack	920	54	72
Full Rack	1540	99	87
Seafood:			
Grilled Salmon, 8 oz, without Rice	405	25	0.5
Grilled Shrimp: Fettuccine Alfredo	1130	51	82
Skewers (2)	340	23	4.5
Steaks: Bacon Wrapped Sirloin Filet	540	32	5
Big Appetite Trio	1130	51	82
Burgundy Beef Tip Skewers	595	27	40
Classic Trio	1120	75	42
Trip Tip: 8 oz	390	22	0.5
10 oz	490	27	1
12 oz	590	32	1

Sizzler® cont... (Feb '14)

	C	F	Cb
Prepared Salads: Per 1 Serving Spoon, W/out Dressing			
Seafood	90	6	6
Sicilian Pasta	70	4	6
Three Bean	50	1	9
Tuna Pasta	135	10	6.5
Waldorf	65	4	6.5
Salad Dressings:			
Blue Cheese	320	30	10
Honey Mustard	220	16	18
Italian	265	28	2
Ranch	275	29	1.5
Thousand Island	275	28	6
Sides:			
Baked Potato, plain	265	4	51
Broccoli	50	0.5	7.5
French Fries	285	13	42
Rice Pilaf	180	3.5	32

For Complete Menu & Data ~ see CalorieKing.com

Skyline Chili® (Feb '14)

	C	F	Cb
Burritos:			
Chili Burrito Deluxe	640	33	44
Vegetarian Black Bean Deluxe	700	32	73
Ways: Per Regular Serving			
Chili & Cheddar Cheese Spaghetti:			
3 Way	780	41	52
4 Way Onion	800	41	58
4 Way Bean	850	42	65
5 Way	870	42	70
Bowls: Coney	780	61	8
Loaded Chili	510	31	23
Vegetarian Black Beans & Rice	370	14	47
Chili Spaghetti, regular	440	13	51
Potatoes: 3-Way Potato	600	25	63
Cheddar Potato	700	42	61
Sour Cream Potato	520	28	61
Salads: Without Dressing Unless Indicated			
Buffalo Chicken	190	8	10
Garden, with Croutons	140	8	13
Greek, regular size, with dressing	380	37	7
Wraps:			
Buffalo Chicken, w/ Ranch Dress.	680	39	56
Classic Chkn w/ Chili Ranch Dress.	650	36	56
Greek Chicken, w/ Greek Dressing	670	38	58
Sides: Chicken, 2.5 oz	70	1	1
Crackers, 1 bowl	60	1.5	11
Fries: Chili Cheese	750	40	66
French	390	13	63

Smoothie King® (Feb '14)

Fruit Smoothies: Per 20 fl.oz Cup

Figures Include Turbinado. Without Turbinado, deduct 100 calories and 23 carbs.

	C	**F**	**Cb**
Local Selection: Acai Adventure	435	5	92
Cherry Picker	275	1	66
Pina Colada Island	600	10	110
Nutritional Smoothie Meals:			
Banana Boat	475	4	101
High Protein: Almond Mocha	365	9	42
Banana	320	9	32
Chocolate	365	9	42
Lean 1: Chocolate	295	10	28
Strawberry	275	6	35
Vanilla	270	9	26
Slim-N-Trim: Chocolate	295	2	57
Orange Vanilla	210	1	46
Strawberry	375	1	84
The Hulk: Chocolate	800	31	108
Strawberry	965	32	145
Vanilla	800	32	105
The Shredder: Chocolate	310	3	36
Strawberry	355	1	56
Vanilla	285	2	30
Refreshing Fruit:			
Angel Food	355	0	84
Banana Berry Treat	365	0	86
Fruit Fusion	355	1	76
Strawberry X-Treme	320	0	82

32 fl.oz Cup: Multiply 20 oz figures by 1.5
40 fl.oz Cup: Multiply 20 oz figures by 2

Kids Kup Smoothies: Per 12 fl.oz Cup

Berry Interesting	260	0	65
Choc-A-Laka	210	4	32
CW Jr.	255	0	64
Lil' Angel	210	0	52

Snappy Tomato (Feb '14)

Pizza: Per Slice, 1/8 of Large Pizza

	C	**F**	**Cb**
Buffalo Grilled Chicken	250	5	32
Cheese	220	7	30
Hawaiian	370	18	33
Meat Topper	430	23	31
Pepperoni	340	17	31
Ranch	370	21	31
Snapperoni	390	22	31
Snappy Ultimate	460	26	33
Supreme	340	17	32
Veggie	240	8	33
Snappetizers, Snappy Wings (3), Plain, without sauce, 2.6 oz	160	11	0

Sonic Drive-In® (Feb '14)

Burgers: With Standard Toppings

	C	**F**	**Cb**
Cheeseburger, with Mustard	710	43	42
Green Chile Cheeseburger	710	43	43
Jr.	330	17	30
Jr. Deluxe	360	20	32
Sonic: W/ Mayonnaise	690	42	43
With Mustard	640	37	42
Bacon Cheeseburger, w/ Mayo	820	54	43
Super Sonic:			
Bacon Dble Cheeseburger, w/ Mayo	1240	87	44
Dble Cheeseburger, w/ Mayo	1160	81	44
Coneys:			
Chili Cheese	420	26	30
Footlong, 1/4 pound	830	55	54
Toaster Sandwiches: Chicken Club	740	39	61
Bacon Cheeseburger	850	50	59
Wraps: Crispy Chicken	510	22	57
Grilled Chicken	430	14	42
Chicken:			
Super Crunch Chicken Strips (5)	550	26	42
Jumbo Popcorn Chicken:			
Small, without Sauce, 4 oz	380	22	27
Large, without Sauce, 6 oz	650	37	47
Sides: Per Medium Serving			
French Fries: Plain, 4 oz	360	17	49
With Cheese, 5.5 oz	490	26	53
With Chili & Cheese, 7.25 oz	560	31	57
Mozzarella Sticks, w/o sauce, 5 oz	440	22	40
Onion Rings, 5.5 oz	440	21	55
Tater Tots: Plain, 5 oz	360	19	43
With Cheese, medium, 6 oz	450	28	43
With Chili & Cheese, med., 8.2 oz	540	34	48
Breakfast:			
Burritos: Bacon	480	26	39
Sausage	500	29	39
Steak & Egg	600	33	44
SuperSonic	580	32	49
Ultimate Meat & Cheese	800	56	46
French Toast Sticks: With Syrup (4)	590	31	71
Without Syrup (4)	500	31	49
Sandwiches:			
Breakfast Bagel: With Bacon	600	24	68
With Sausage	680	32	68
CroisSonic, Sausage	650	49	28

Continued Next Page...

Sonic Drive-In® cont... (Feb '14)

Desserts:	C	F	Cb
Banana Split	490	18	76
Single Topping Sundaes:			
Chocolate	500	22	69
Hot Fudge	520	26	64
Pineapple	440	22	55
Sonic Blasts: M&M's, small size	900	48	106
Oreo small size	900	47	106
Beverages: Per Small Size			
Floats/Blended:			
Coca-Cola; Dr Pepper, average	330	14	49
Fanta	340	14	51
Malts: Chocolate	630	31	80
Strawberry	580	31	69
Vanilla	550	31	61
Shakes: Banana	620	31	80
Chocolate	670	31	89
Pineapple; Strawberry, average	575	31	67

For Complete Nutritional Data ~ see CalorieKing.com

Souplantation® (Feb '14)

Soups: Per Cup	C	F	Cb
Chesapeake Corn Chowder	290	17	30
Classical Minestrone	120	2	20
Cream of Mushroom	280	22	15
New Orleans Jambalaya	210	11	18
Vegetarian Harvest	200	10	23
Pasta: Per 1 Cup			
Arizona Marinara	360	11	47
Carbonara Pasta with Bacon	290	10	43
Creamy Bruschetta	360	16	43
Chicken Tetrazzini	480	23	47
Creamy Cilantro Lime Pesto	360	20	37
Fettuccine Alfredo	390	18	41
Fire-Roasted Tomato Basil Alfredo	370	14	44
Garden Vegetable with Meatballs	310	10	44
Vegetarian Marinara with Basil	260	4	44
Prepared Salads: Per ½ Cup			
BBQ Potato	170	9	21
Carrot Raisin	90	3	17
Dijon Potato with Garlic Dill Vinegar	150	12	9
Greek Couscous w/ Feta & Pinenuts	210	10	25
Thai Noodle w/ Chkn & Peanut Sce	190	10	19

Souplantation® cont... (Feb '14)

Bakery:	C	F	Cb
Muffins: Chocolate Brownie	180	8	26
Chocolate Chip	170	8	22
French Quarter Praline	250	10	35
Fruit Medley Bran	130	0.5	29
Breads: Per Piece			
Buttermilk Cornbread	190	7	28
Garlic Asiago Focaccia	70	2	11
Sourdough	150	0.5	27
Desserts: Per ½ Cup			
Apple Medley	70	0	18
Banana Royale	80	0	20
Caramel Apple Cobbler	390	12	68
Rice Pudding	110	2	20

For Complete Nutritional Data ~ see CalorieKing.com

Southern Tsunami® (Feb '14)

Rolls:	C	F	Cb
Hybrid: *With White Rice*			
Berry, 6 oz	230	5	44
Blueberry: Salmon, 8 oz	350	15	45
Shrimp, 8 oz	330	12	45
Done Deal, 7 oz	370	17	39
Happy Mango, 8 oz	440	21	53
Jalapeno, 8 oz	310	7	48
Mango Shrimp, 6 oz	370	19	41
Red Rock Fujisan, 7 oz	400	15	42
Spicy Mango Roll, 8 oz	400	17	46
Ultimate Chili Combo, 6 oz	290	9	41
Hybrid Rolls: *With Brown Rice*			
Berry, 6 oz	200	6	33
Blueberry: Salmon, 8 oz	320	15	34
Steelhead, 8 oz	310	14	34
Crunchy: Dragon, Hot, 6 oz	270	10	30
Tempura, 6 oz	260	7	37
Jalapeno, 8 oz	270	7	35
Mango Shrimp, 6 oz	350	19	33
Red Rock Fujisan, 7 oz	370	16	31
Ultimate Chili Combo, 6 oz	250	1	30
Chef Samplers: A, 9.5 oz	410	2	65
B, 7.5 oz	360	6	57

Continued Next Page... . . .

Southern Tsunami® cont... (Feb '14)
Rolls (Cont):

	C	F	Cb
Plus Rolls: *Per Two 3 oz Servings*			
California	230	4	44
Cream Cheese Plus: Salmon	290	11	39
Shrimp	260	8	39
Tuna	280	8	39
Eel	300	9	46
Seaside Plus: Eel	380	15	47
Salmon	290	7	45
Shrimp	230	1	45
Steelhead	270	7	39
Tuna	280	1	45
Spicy Plus: Salmon	280	9	39
Shrimp	240	5	39
Steelhead	270	7	39
Tuna	270	5	39
Vegetable	230	4	46
Wraps: *Avocado Salad Roll, 4.6 oz*	130	5	21
Berry, 4.6 oz	180	8	25
California, 6.6 oz	270	17	28
Smoked Salmon Salad, 4.6 oz	210	10	21
Salads: *Without Dressing*			
Edamame, 4 oz	120	7	9
Seared Tuna, 9 oz	210	8	18
Dressings/Sauces: *Eel Sauce, 1 T.*	40	0	8
Ginger Dressing, 2 Tbsp	50	2	8
Peanut Sauce, 2 Tbsp	30	1	6
Sweet Chili, 3 fl.oz	300	0	72
Wasabe Dressing, 2 Tbsp	30	2	2

Starbucks® (Mar '14)
Brewed Coffee: Figures based on 16 fl.oz Grande without Whipped Cream

	C	F	Cb
Caffe Misto (Au Lait): W/ Whole Milk	130	7	10
With Nonfat Milk	70	0	10
With Soy Milk	100	3	13
Hot Espresso Beverages:			
Caffe Latte: With Whole Milk	220	11	18
With Nonfat Milk	130	0	19
With Soy Milk	170	4.5	23
Cappuccino: With Whole Milk	140	7	12
With Nonfat Milk	80	0	12
With Soy Milk	120	3.5	16
Caramel Macchiato: W/ Whole Milk	270	11	34
With Nonfat Milk	190	1	35
Cinn. Dolce Latte: With Whole Milk	300	10	40
With Nonfat Milk	210	0	40
Espresso: 1 Doppio, 2 fl.oz	10	0	2
1 Solo, 1 fl.oz	5	0	1
Espresso Con Panna, 1 Solo, 1 fl.oz	30	2.5	2

Starbucks® cont... (Mar '14)
Chocolate:
Per Grande, 16 fl.oz Without Whipped Cream

	C	F	Cb
Hot Chocolate:			
With Whole Milk	330	13	47
With 2% Milk	290	9	47
With Soy	290	7	51
White Hot Chocolate:			
With Whole Milk	450	17	61
With 2% Milk	410	12	61
With Soy Milk	410	11	65
Iced Espresso: *Per 16 fl.oz Grande without Whipped Cream*			
Caffe Latte:			
With Whole Milk	150	7	13
With Nonfat Milk	90	0	13
With Soy Milk	130	3.5	17
Vanilla Latte:			
With Whole Milk	210	6	30
With Nonfat Milk	160	0	31
With 2% Milk	190	4	30
Frappuccino: *Cold, Per 16 fl.oz Grande With Whole Milk, With Whipped Cream*			
Caffe Vanilla	430	14	72
Caramel	410	15	66
Cinnamon Dolce	380	14	60
Hazelnut	390	14	62
Java Chip	460	18	72
Mocha	400	15	64
White Chocolate Mocha	440	16	69
Frappuccino Creme: *Cold, Per 16 fl.oz Grande with Whole Milk and Whipped Cream*			
Cinnamon Dolce Creme	350	16	49
Tazo Chai	360	15	52
Vanilla Bean Creme	400	16	59
White Chocolate Creme	420	18	59
Smoothies: *Per16 fl.oz Grande with 2% Milk, without Whipped Cream*			
Orange Mango	270	1.5	53
Strawberry	300	2	60
Teas: *Per 16 fl.oz Grande with Whole Milk*			
Hot Tea Latte: Awake	210	7	31
Chai	270	7	45
Earl Grey	200	7	39
Green Tea	390	13	57
Iced Tea Latte: Awake	120	2	24
Chai	260	7	44
Green Tea	320	9	51
Kid's Drinks & Others:			
Apple Juice, Cold, 12 fl.oz	190	0	49
Apple Juice, Steamed, 8 fl.oz	120	0	30

Continued Next Page... ...

Fast - Foods & *Restaurants*

Starbucks® cont... (\Mar'14)

	C	F	Cb
Drink Extras:			
Caramel Drizzle, 1 teaspoon	15	0.5	2
Flavored Syrup: 1 Pump	20	0	5
Sugar-Free, 1 Pump	0	0	0
Mocha Syrup, 1 Pump	25	0.5	6
Sweetened Whipped Cream:			
Grande/Venti, cold drinks, average	115	11	3
Grande/Venti, hot drinks	70	7	2
Breakfast:			
Bacon, Gouda & Parmesan Frittata, on Artisan Roll	350	18	30
Egg White, Spinach, Feta Wrap	290	10	33
Oatmeal, w/o sugar			
1.4 oz	150	2.5	27
Reduced-Fat Turkey Bacon S'wich	230	6	28
Bistro Boxes:			
Cheese & Fruit, 5.3 oz	480	28	39
Chicken & Hummus, 6.3 oz	270	7	29
Protein, 6.8 oz	380	19	37
Sandwiches & Paninis:			
Ham & Swiss Panini	340	10	42
Rstd Tomato & Mozzarella Panini	390	18	44
Roasted Vegetable Panini	350	12	48
Turkey & Havarti	450	33	31
Turkey Rustico Panini	480	18	53
8-Grain Roll, with Raisins	380	7	67
Bagels:			
Everything with Cheese	270	2	54
Multigrain	290	3	58
Plain	270	1	57
Bars & Brownies:			
Double Chocolate Brownie	410	24	46
Marshmallow Dream Bar	240	5	45
Cakes: Per Slice			
Banana Walnut Bread, 4.25 oz	490	19	75
Pound: Iced Lemon, 4.5 oz	500	23	67
Marble, 3.75 oz	350	13	54
Starbuck's Classic Coffee, 4 oz	440	19	63
Reduced Fat Cakes:			
Banana Chocolate Chip Coffee	400	8	80
Cinnamon Swirl Coffee	340	9	62
Very Berry Coffee	350	10	59
Cookies: Chocolate Chunk	370	19	50
Outrageous Oatmeal	360	15	52
Croissants: Butter	310	18	32
Chocolate	300	17	34
Doughnuts, Old-Fashioned Glazed	480	27	56

Starbucks® cont... (Mar'14)

	C	F	Cb
Muffins:			
Bountiful Blueberry	350	12	55
Chocolate Caramel	410	20	56
Sweet Rolls & Danish:			
Apple Fritter	420	20	59
Cheese Danish	420	25	39
Morning Bun, small	350	16	45
Yogurt Parfaits:			
Greek Yogurt with Berries	220	3	36
Greek Yogurt with Honey	260	4.5	41

Ice Cream ~ See Page 107

Bottled Drinks ~ See Page 37

Coffee Mix (VIA) ~ See Page 35

Steak Escape® (Feb '14)

Sandwiches: With Menu Board Toppings

	C	F	Cb
Regular: Cajun Chicken	660	23	68
Grand: Chicken	620	19	68
Escape	660	19	68
Gobbler	530	13	68
Turkey Club	550	14	65
Vegetarian	550	20	71
Wild West BBQ	700	20	75
Wraps: With Menu Board Toppings			
Cajun Chicken	470	17	50
Grand: Chicken	490	18	51
Escape	520	18	50
Gobbler	440	14	51
Turkey Club	440	15	49
Vegetarian	430	17	52
Wild West BBQ	550	19	56
Salads:			
Grilled: Chicken	410	25	14
Ham	360	22	17
Steak	440	24	15
Turkey	360	21	15
Without Meat	280	20	13
Loaded Potatoes: Bacon & Ranch	670	46	51
Cheddar & Bacon	430	17	56

For Complete Nutritional Data ~ see CalorieKing.com

Fast - Foods & Restaurants

Steak 'n Shake® (Feb '14)

The Original Steakburgers:

	C	F	Cb
Single, without Cheese	280	11	30
Double: With Cheese	440	25	31
Bacon 'n Cheese	480	28	31
Cheesy Cheddar	480	27	32
Guacamole	700	48	47
Wisconsin Buttery	710	49	45
Triple, without cheese	510	30	30
Chili: 3-Way (1)	830	36	94
5-Way (1)	1170	63	99
Deluxe, bowl	1220	74	81

Sandwiches:

Guacamole Grilled Chicken	580	31	59
Jalapeno Crunch Chicken	560	24	66
Spicy Chicken	490	21	51

Signature Steak Franks: Regular 380 27 22

Cheesy Cheddar	490	36	24
Chicago Style	420	27	30
Chili Cheese	620	44	31

Salads: Without Dressing

Apple Pecan Grilled Chicken	330	8	39
Fried Chicken	470	26	34
Southwest Grilled Chicken	490	26	46

Fries: French, regular 440 21 60

Large	640	30	87
Cheese: Regular	610	34	67
Large	810	43	94

Breakfast:

Bagels Sandwich: With Bacon	450	16	51
With Sausage	570	29	50
Biscuits: Bacon, Egg & Cheese	520	35	32
Egg & Cheese	450	30	31
Sausage & Egg	600	44	31
Sausage, Egg & Cheese	650	48	31
With Sausage Gravy: Half order	540	37	43
Full Order	1070	74	86
Hash Browns: Shredded	290	23	19
Side order, 5 pieces	260	17	23
Perfect Start Oatmeal	340	11	57
Skillets: Country	1230	93	63
Portobello & Swiss	1040	87	27

Hand Dipped Milk Shakes: Per Regular

Banana; Mocha	610	20	100
Butterfinger	830	29	135
Chocolate; Vanilla, average	620	20	101
Cookies 'n Cream	760	25	124

Subway® (Mar '14)

6" Sandwich: 6g Fat Or Less

Figures Based on 9 grain wheat bread, lettuce, tomatoes, onions, green peppers and cucumbers. Oil or mayo not included.

	C	F	Cb
Black Forest Ham	290	4.5	46
Oven Roasted Chicken	320	5	47
Roast Beef	320	5	45
Subway Club	310	4.5	46
Sweet Onion Chicken Teriyaki	370	4.5	57
Turkey Breast	280	3.5	46
Turkey Breast & Black Forest Ham	280	4	46
Veggie Delite	230	2.5	44

6" Sandwiches: Figures based on 9-grain wheat bread, lettuce, tomatoes, onion, green peppers, cucumbers. Oil or mayo not included.

Big Philly Cheesesteak	500	17	51
BLT	320	9	43
Chkn & Bacon Ranch Melt w/ Chse	570	28	47
Cold Cut Combo	360	12	46
Italian B.M.T.	410	16	46
Meatball Marinara	480	18	59
Spicy Italian	480	24	46
Steak & Cheese	380	10	48
Subway Melt, with Cheese	370	11	47
Tuna	480	25	44

Kids Meal Sandwiches: Figures based on 9-grain wheat bread, lettuce, tomatoes, onions, green peppers and cucumbers. Oil or mayo not included.

Black Forest Ham	180	2.5	30
Roast Beef	200	3	30
Turkey Breast	180	2	30
Veggie Delite	150	1.5	29

Condiments & Sauces: For 6" Sandwiches

Chipotle Southwest, 0.75 oz	100	10	1
Honey Mustard, Fat-Free, 0.75 oz	30	0	7
Mayonnaise: 1 Tbsp, 0.5 oz	110	12	0
Light, 1 Tbsp, 0.5 oz	50	5	1
Mustard, Yellow or Deli Brown. 2 tsp	5	0	0.5
Olive Oil Blend, 1 tsp	45	5	0
Ranch Dressing	110	11	1
Sweet Onion, Fat-Free, 0.75 oz	40	0	9

Extras: For 6" Sandwiches

Bacon Strips (2)	45	3.5	0
Cheese: American, 2 triangles, 0.25 oz	40	3.5	1
Cheddar, 2 triangles, 0.25 oz	60	5	0
Swiss, 2 triangles, 0.25 oz	50	4.5	0

Continued Next Page....

Subway® cont... (Mar '14)

Breakfast:

6" Egg White Omelet Sandwiches: *Figures based on 9-grain*

	C	F	Cb
Bacon, Egg White & Cheese	370	11	45
Egg White & Cheese	320	8	44
Egg White & Cheese with Ham	350	9	45
Steak, Egg White & Cheese	390	10	47
Sunrise Melt, with Egg White	430	13	48

6" Omelet Sandwiches: *Figures based on 9-grain bread, cheese & regular egg*

	C	F	Cb
Bacon, Egg & Cheese	410	16	45
Egg & Cheese	360	12	44
Egg & Cheese with Ham	390	13	45
Steak, Egg & Cheese	430	15	47
Sunrise Melt	470	17	48

Egg White on 3" Flatbread: *Figures based on flatbread, cheese and egg whites.*

	C	F	Cb
Bacon, Egg White & Cheese	190	7	21
Egg White & Cheese	170	5	21
Egg White & Cheese with Ham	180	5	22
Steak, Egg White & Cheese	190	6	22
Sunrise Melt, with Egg White	220	8	23

Regular Egg On 3" Flatbreads: *Figures based on flatbread, cheese and regular egg.*

	C	F	Cb
Bacon, Egg & Cheese	210	9	21
Breakfast B.M.T. Melt	250	12	22
Egg & Cheese	190	7	21
Steak, Egg & Cheese	210	8	22
Sunrise Melt	240	10	23

Sides, Hash Browns, 4 pieces — 210 | 10 | 28

Salads (6g Fat or Less): *Figures based on lettuce, tomatoes, onions, green peppers, olives & cucumbers. Dressing or croutons not included.*

	C	F	Cb
Black Forest Ham	110	3	12
Oven Roasted Chicken Breast	130	2.5	10
Roast Beef; Subway Club, av.	140	3.5	11
Sweet Onion Chicken Teriyaki, with Sweet Onion dressing	240	3	34
Turkey Breast & Ham	110	2.5	12
Veggie Delite	50	1	9

Salad Dressings:

	C	F	Cb
Italian, fat free, 2 oz	35	0	7
Ranch, 2 oz	320	35	3

Subway® cont... (Mar '14)

Soups: Per 8 oz Bowl

	C	F	Cb
Beef Chili	350	24	17
Chicken Noodle	100	1	12
Clam Chowder	200	11	20
Loaded Baked Potato	220	11	23
Minestrone	90	1	17
Poblano Corn Chowder	150	7	18
Vegetable Beef	90	2	15

Cookies & Desserts:

	C	F	Cb
Apple Pie	250	10	37
Apple Slices, 1 package, 2.5 oz	35	0	9
Chocolate Chip Cookie, 1.5 oz	220	10	30
Oatmeal Raisin Cookie, 1.5 oz	200	8	30
Raspberry Cheesecake, 1.6 oz	200	9	29

Sweet Tomatoes®

Same Menu & Data as Souplantation ~ See Page 242

Swiss Chalet® (Feb '14)

Starters:

	C	F	Cb
Caesar Salad without Dressing	90	3	13
Chalet Chicken Wings (8), with sauce	550	34	23
Cheese Perogies (7)	420	10	69
Garlic Loaf, without Cheese, 8.5 oz	700	40	73

From The Grill: Without Sides

	C	F	Cb
Burgers: Classic Hamburger	710	39	43
Classic Bacon & Cheese	890	54	46
Veggie	470	13	57
BBQ Ribs: Half Rack	650	42	17
Full Rack	1300	85	34

Rotisserie Chicken: Meat Only

	C	F	Cb
Double Leg, with Skin	490	31	0
Half Chicken, with Skin	530	27	0
Quarter Chicken:			
Dark meat, without Skin	160	8	0
Dark meat, with Skin	240	16	0
White meat, without Skin	220	6	0
White meat, with Skin	290	11	0
Chicken Pot Pie, 1 pie	560	32	39

Sandwiches: Without Sides

	C	F	Cb
Classic Hot Chicken, white meat	520	11	51
Flatbread: Hickory Chicken	700	32	70
Southwest Chicken	710	37	64

Continued Next Page...

Updated Nutrition Data ~ www.CalorieKing.com
Persons with Diabetes ~ See Disclaimer (Page 22)

Swiss Chalet® cont...(Feb '14)

Wrap,

	C	F	Cb
Rotisserie Chicken Club	710	32	57

Entree Salads: Without Dressing

Spinach Chicken Salad	410	25	28
Sweet Heat Salad with Chicken	340	9	30
West Coast Salad with Chicken	460	21	21

Dressings/Sauces:

Caesar Dressing, 1 oz	180	18	2
Chalet Dressing, 1 Tbsp, 1 oz	160	14	6
Chalet Dipping Sauce, 3.5 oz	25	0.5	5

Sides:

Gravy, 4 oz	45	1.5	7
Mashed Potatoes, 5 oz	150	4	27
Sauteed Mushrooms, 6 oz	140	1	30
Seasoned Rice, 6 oz	240	3.5	48

Desserts/Pies:

Apple Pie	440	19	65
Coconut Cream Pie	540	33	57
Lemon Meringue Pie	400	11	73
Old Fashioned Carrot Cake	260	16	24
Pecan Pie	590	29	79

Taco Bell® (Mar '14)

Burritos:

	C	F	Cb
½ lb Cheesy Potato	510	24	56
½ lb Combo	450	18	51
7-Layer	430	17	57
Beefy 5-Layer	510	20	64
Cantina, Chicken	730	26	92
Chicken	410	18	46
Chili Cheese	370	16	39
Supreme: Beef	410	16	51
Chicken; Steak, average	395	13	49

XXL Grilled Stuft:

Beef	870	41	91
Chicken; Steak, av.	830	35	88

Cantina Bell:

Bowl: Chicken, 14.6 oz	530	21	59
Steak, 14.6 oz	550	23	59
Veggie, 13.9 oz	510	20	69
Burrito: Chicken	730	26	92
Steak	750	28	92
Veggie	720	25	104

Chalupas:

Supreme: Beef	370	22	31
Chicken	340	18	30
Steak	350	19	30

Fresco:

Crunchy Taco	150	8	13
Soft Tacos: Original	160	7	17
Chicken; Grilled Steak, av.	145	4	17
Supreme, Chicken; Steak, av.	340	9	48

Taco Bell® cont... (Mar '14)

Gorditas:

	C	F	Cb
Cheesy Crunch	490	28	40
Supreme: Beef	290	13	31
Chicken	270	9	30
Steak	280	10	30

Nachos:

Regular	310	17	34
BellGrande	760	39	85
Cheesy	280	15	32

Specialities:

Cantina Bowl, Chicken	530	21	59
Cheese Roll-Up	180	9	15
Chilli Cheese Burrito	370	16	39
Crunchwrap Supreme	540	21	71
MexiMelt	250	14	19
Mexican Pizza, 7.5 oz	550	31	48

Quesadillas:

Cheese	460	26	37
Steak	520	28	38
Tostada	270	11	31

Tacos:

Crunchy: Regular	170	10	12
Supreme	200	12	15
Double Decker: Regular	320	14	36
Supreme	350	16	38
Soft: Beef	190	9	17
Beef Supreme	220	11	20
Chicken	160	5	16
Crispy Potato	250	12	28
Fresco Chicken	140	3.5	16
Grilled Steak	200	10	16

Taco Salads:

Express with Chips	580	29	57
Fiesta: Beef	780	42	74
Chicken	730	35	71
Steak	750	37	71

Sides:

Cheesy Fiesta Potato	270	15	31
Cinnamon Twist, 1.25 oz	170	7	26
Latin Rice	100	2.5	18
Pintos 'n Cheese	190	7	21

Condiments & Sauces:

Avocado Ranch Dressing, 0.5 oz	80	8	1
Creamy Jalapeno Sauce, 0.5 oz	70	7	1
Green Tomatillo Sauce, 1 oz	10	0	2
Guacamole, 0.75 oz	35	3	2
Pepper Jack Sauce, 0.5 oz	70	7	1
Sour Cream, Reduced Fat, 0.75 oz	30	2	2

Continued Next Page...

247

Fast - Foods & *Restaurants*

Taco Bell® cont... (Mar '14)

Breakfast:	C	F	Cb
AM Crunchwrap: Bacon	660	41	51
Sausage	710	46	51
AM Grilled Taco: Bacon	230	14	15
Sausage	220	14	15
Burritos: Bacon	490	28	36
Sausage	470	28	36
Cinnabon Delights, 2 pack	160	9	17
Hash Brown, 1.9 oz	160	11	14

Note: Nutritional data in New York outlets may vary slightly. Please check Taco Bell website

Taco Cabana® (Feb '14)

Cabana Burritos:	C	F	Cb
Includes Flour Burrito & Menu Set Toppings			
Beef	980	47	97
Chicken	900	37	98
Steak Fajita	910	39	96
Quesadillas: *Personal, with Guacamole & Sour Cream*			
Cheese	710	39	61
Chicken Breast Fajita; Steak, av.	765	41	62
Shrimp Tampico	820	45	63

Sizzling Skillets: *Includes Flour Tortilla, Grilled Onion, Bell Pepper, Rice, Shredded Cheese, Sour Cream, Guacamole, Lettuce & Pico de Gallo*

½ lb, 1 serving: Brisket	960	46	95
Chicken Fajita	775	26	95
Mixed Fajita Steak & Chicken	785	28	95
Shrimp Tampico; Steak Fajita, av.	795	30	97

Tacos:			
Crispy: Ground Beef	200	12	12
Stewed Chicken	160	7	12
Soft: Beef, ground	240	12	22
Black Bean	190	4	34
Carne Guisada	190	6	20
Chicken, stewed	200	7	22

Sides & Add-Ons: *Per Serving*			
Black Beans, 4 oz	80	1	15
Borracho Beans, 4 oz	140	3	20
Guacamole, 3 oz	110	9	7
Queso, 3 oz	110	8	5
Refried Beans	260	14	25
Rice	120	0.5	25
Salsa: Fuego; Roja, 1 oz	5	0	1
Verde, 1 oz	10	0	1
Sour Cream, 3 oz	160	15	3

Taco Del Mar® (Feb '14)

Baja Bowls: *Per 14.3 oz Bowl with Standard Menu Toppings, without Guacamole, Sour Cream, Jalapenos or Sauce*

	C	F	Cb
Mondo: Carne Asada Steak	490	15	62
Chicken; Shredded Beef	520	17	62
Fish, 14.85 oz	570	34	46
Ground Beef	570	23	62
Pork	500	15	61

Burritos: *Per Standard Menu Toppings, without Guacamole, sour Cream, Jalapenos or Sauce*

Mondito: *Per 9.6 oz Unless Indicated*			
Carne Asada Steak	440	13	65
Chicken; Shredded Beef	460	14	65
Fish, 10.7 oz	520	23	61
Ground Beef	480	17	65
Pork	450	13	65

Mondo: *Per 18.45 oz Unless Indicated*			
Carne Asada Steak	820	23	118
Chicken; Shredded Beef	860	25	118
Fish, 19 oz	900	42	102
Ground Beef	900	32	118
Pork	840	24	117

Platters: *Per 2 Corn Tortillas and Standard Menu Toppings, without Jalapenos or Sauce*

Enchilada: Carne Asada Steak	780	28	104
Cheese	870	38	104
Chicken; Shredded Beef, average	820	30	104
Ground Beef	860	36	105
Pork	800	28	103

Enchilada/Taco: *Per 1 Enchilada & 1 Taco, Includes Standard Menu Toppings, without Jalapenos or Sauce*

Carne Asada Steak	820	30	109
Chicken; Shredded Beef	850	32	108
Ground Beef	900	38	109
Pork	830	30	108

Quesadillas: *Includes Standard Menu Toppings, without Jalapenos and Sauce*

Carne Asada Steak	1170	49	135
Chicken; Shredded Beef	1200	51	135
Ground Beef	1250	57	136
Pork	1180	50	134

Nachos: *Includes Standard Menu Toppings, without Jalapenos and Sauce*

6 Layer Cheese	1050	62	96
Super: Carne Asada Steak	1140	65	98
Chicken; Shredded Beef, av.	1170	67	97
Ground Beef	1220	74	98
Pork	1150	66	97

continued next page...

Updated Nutrition Data ~ www.CalorieKing.com
Persons with Diabetes ~ See Disclaimer (Page 22)

Taco Del Mar® cont... (Feb '14)

Salads: Includes Standard Menu Toppings & Dressing, without Jalapenos

	C	F	Cb
Cabo: Chicken; Shredded Beef	420	19	36
Fish	450	22	47
Taco: Carne Asada Steak	610	29	59
Ground Beef	690	37	60

Note: Nutritional Information varies from state to state. Please refer to Taco Del Mar Website

Taco John's® (Feb '14)

Burritos:

	C	F	Cb
Bean Burrito	370	11	53
Beef Grilled Burrito	590	32	53
Beefy Burrito	440	21	42
Chicken & Potato Burrito	480	21	56
Chicken Grilled Burrito	590	30	50
Combination Burrito	410	16	47
Crunchy Chicken & Potato Burrito	580	27	67
Meat & Potato Burrito	520	25	57
Super Burrito	450	20	50

Tacos:

Soft Shell, Chicken	190	6	21
Taco Bravo	330	13	38

Specialties:

Taco Salad w/o dressing	540	33	40
Chicken Taco Salad w/o dressing	500	27	39
Crunchy Chicken Taco Salad w/o dress.	630	36	53
Super Nachos: Small	420	25	37
Regular	790	47	72
Super Potato Oles: Small	650	40	59
Regular	1090	67	98
Quesadilla Melt: Cheesy	450	24	40
Fajita Beef	550	29	46
Fajita Chicken	520	25	43
Crunchy Chicken without sauce	370	18	29

Snacks: Chips & Queso — 430 / 25 / 43
Cini-Sopapilla Bites — 200 / 8 / 34

Sides: Potato Oles: Small — 480 / 27 / 52
Medium — 670 / 38 / 73
Large — 860 / 49 / 94
Refried Beans: With Cheese — 320 / 7 / 46
Without Cheese — 260 / 2.5 / 45
Mexican Rice — 250 / 6 / 45

Condiments:

Bacon Ranch, 1.5 oz	120	9	10
House Dressing, 1.5 oz	70	7	2
Nacho Cheese, 3 oz	110	9	5
Salsa, 2 oz	10	0	2
Sour Cream, 2 oz	120	10	3

Desserts:

Apple Grande	260	11	39
Choco Taco	390	21	48
Churro	200	9	29

Taco Mayo® (Feb '14)

Burritos:

	C	F	Cb
Bean	495	16	71
Beef	490	23	41
Super: Beef	540	23	57
Chicken	405	16	39

Melts: Tamale — 615 / 34 / 50
Tostada — 525 / 32 / 35

Quesadillas: Chicken — 675 / 37 / 46
Fajita Chicken — 700 / 39 / 47
Fajita Steak — 725 / 40 / 47

Tacos: Crispy Taco, Beef — 160 / 9 / 10
Soft Taco: Beef — 230 / 11 / 17
Chicken — 185 / 6 / 16

Salads: As Per Menu Description
Acapulco: Chicken — 680 / 50 / 35
Steak — 705 / 51 / 35
SalsaLita Steak — 305 / 8 / 33
Taco Steak — 445 / 25 / 30

Sides: Mexicali Rice — 160 / 1 / 36
Refried Beans — 295 / 9 / 43
Potato Locos, Small — 380 / 24 / 36

Taco Time® (Feb '14)

Burritos:

	C	F	Cb
Beef, Bean & Cheese	490	17	55
Chicken B.L.T.	690	39	43
Big Juan: Chicken	580	16	70
Ground Beef	630	23	73
Casita: Chicken	490	17	42
Ground Beef	540	24	46
Crisp Burrito: Chicken	380	17	33
Ground Beef	430	21	36
Pinto Bean	360	14	47
Soft Burrito: Ground Beef	430	16	43
Pinto Bean	370	10	54
Veggie	520	17	73

Tacos:
Soft Tacos: *Per 7 oz*
Chicken — 360 / 9 / 40
Ground Beef — 420 / 16 / 43

Other Favorites: Cheddar Melt — 250 / 12 / 25
Nachos Grande — 930 / 43 / 96
Tostada: Bean — 230 / 13 / 21
Chicken — 320 / 13 / 22
Ground Beef — 380 / 20 / 25

Breakfast:
Burritos: Egg & Bacon, 7.5 oz — 510 / 24 / 49
Egg & Cheese, 5.75 oz — 370 / 16 / 40
Ultimate, 11 oz — 860 / 58 / 52
Omelets: Cheese, 8 oz — 490 / 36 / 6
Country, 13.25 oz — 720 / 54 / 20
Nacho, 15.5 oz — 740 / 48 / 26

continued next page...

249

Fast - Foods & *Restaurants*

Taco Time® cont... (Feb '14)

Sides:	C	F	Cb
Chips, Taco, oz	150	3.5	27
Fries: Cheddar, medium, 7 oz	500	35	39
Mexi, medium, 6 oz	390	26	38
Stuffed, medium, 7 oz	460	28	42
Mexi-Rice, 3.5 oz	80	0.5	17
Refritos, with Chips, 6 oz	230	7	29
Salads:			
Regular: Chicken Taco, 9.5 oz	310	13	22
Ground Beef Taco, 9 oz	370	20	24
Tostada Delight: Chicken, 9 oz	450	19	35
Ground Beef, 9 oz	490	26	36
Desserts: Crustos	290	6	58
Churro: Plain	210	16	17
With Cinnamon & Sugar	250	16	27

Target Food Court® (Oct '13)

Entrees: Per Order	C	F	Cb
Beef Hot Dog	370	24	27
Chicken Tenders	270	10	18
Kids: Chicken Nuggets	180	7	12
Grilled Cheese	300	17	27
Personal Pan Pizza: Per Order			
Cheese	590	24	69
Italian Sausage	750	39	69
Pepperoni	610	26	67
Sandwiches: Ham & Swiss, 6.1 oz	370	10	40
Turkey & Havarti	720	40	47
Turkey & Provolone	330	12	36
Toasted Flatbreads:			
Chicken Marinara	180	8	15
Chicken Spinach Artichoke	160	7	17
Salads: California Chicken	680	40	39
Chicken Caesar, 13 oz	560	38	20
Harvest Chicken	620	37	38
Soups: Chicken Noodle	120	4	16
Tomato Basil	300	27	13
Snacks: French Fries	230	9	33
Popcorn	300	16	33
Yogurt Parfait	320	5	59
Treats: Chocolate Chip Cookies	510	26	68
Churro	180	5	32
Pretzels: Bavarian, with Butter	490	6	93
And Cinnamon Sugar	520	6	102
Sugar Cookie	500	23	69
Smoothies: Mango; Strawb., av.	230	0	57
Strawberry	240	0	60
ICEE's: Coca Cola, 20 oz	180	0	45
Dr Pepper, 20 oz	330	0	75
Pepsi, 32 oz	240	0	61

TCBY® (Feb '14)

Soft Serve Froz. Yogurt: Per 4 fl.oz	C	F	Cb
Cheesecake	110	2	23
Golden Vanilla	120	2	23
Peanut Butter	130	2	26
No Sugar Added, Fat Free,			
average all flavors	80	0	22
Sorbet,			
average all flavors, 4 fl.oz	100	0	25
Hand-Scooped Frozen Yogurt:			
Butter Pecan: Kid's, 4 fl.oz	150	7	17
Small, 6.4 fl.oz	240	11	27
Regular, 12.8 fl.oz	480	22	54
Choc. Chunk Cookie Dough:			
Kid's, 4 fl.oz	150	6	23
Small, 6.4 fl.oz	240	10	37
Regular, 12.8 fl.oz	480	19	74
Peaches & Cream:			
Kid's, 4 fl.oz	110	2.5	18
Small, 6.4 fl.oz	175	4	29
Regular, 12.8 fl.oz	350	8	58
Peanut Butter Delight: Kid's, 4 fl.oz	170	8	21
Small, 6.4 fl.oz	270	13	34
Regular, 12.8 fl.oz	540	26	68
Vanilla Bean: Kid's, 4 fl.oz	110	3	18
Small, 6.4 fl.oz	175	5	29
Regular, 12.8 fl.oz	350	10	58
Cakes: Per 1/10 Cake			
Choc. & Van. Yogurt Dble	350	18	43
White Choc. Mousse Yog. w/ choc.	310	14	42
Pies: Per 1/10 Pie			
Chocolate Decadence	330	13	49
Cookies & Creme	320	15	42

TGI Friday's® (Feb '14)

Appetiers: As Served	C	F	Cb
Individual: Crispy Green Bean Fries	900	65	69
Fried Mozzarella	770	46	54
Pan Seared Potstickers	770	42	77
Sesame Jack Chicken Strips	1090	35	159
Taste & Share:			
Ahi Tuna Crisps	280	14	25
Bacon Mac & Cheese Bites	600	40	41
Corned Beef & Swiss Sliders	480	23	46
Garlic & Basil Bruschetta	360	22	34
Hibachi Skewers: Beef	510	20	63
Chicken	480	14	63
Parmesan Meatballs	790	61	39
Thai Pork Tacos	280	14	25

Continued Next Page...

Updated Nutrition Data ~ www.CalorieKing.com
Persons with Diabetes ~ See Disclaimer (Page 22)

TGI Friday's® cont... (Feb '14)

Hand-Crafted Burgers: As Served	C	F	Cb
Cheeseburger	1240	76	105
Jack Daniel's Burger	1490	86	132
NY Cheddar & Bacon Burger	1540	100	104
Sedona Black Bean Burger	1240	76	105
Turkey Burger	930	50	77
Sandwiches: Without Sides			
California Club	750	46	40
Jack Daniel's Chicken	1220	62	108
Triple Stack Reuben	960	53	75
Black Angus Steaks: Without Sides			
Flat Iron	380	27	2
Sirloin: 6 oz	370	24	3
With Half Rack Ribs	850	44	40
Sirloin: 10 oz	600	45	2
With Grilled Shrimp Scampi	900	71	7
Chicken & Pasta: As Served			
Crispy Chicken Fingers	1020	54	89
Dragonfire Chicken	660	15	95
Pasta: Bruschetta Chicken	920	42	90
Cajun Shrimp & Chicken	1110	58	87
Chicken Florentine Piccata	1020	54	89
Jack Daniels Grill: Without Sides			
Chicken	620	8	79
Chicken & Shrimp	570	11	77
Flat Iron Steak	590	16	80
Ribs & Shrimp	1730	74	181
Sirloin & Shrimp	1010	41	102
Salads: Includes Dressing			
Balsamic-Glazed Chicken Caesar	490	26	25
Chipotle Yucatan Chicken	850	59	46
Pecan-Crusted Chicken	1080	71	76
Dressing: Balsamic Vinaigrette	300	31	7
Bleu Cheese	320	34	2
Honey Mustard	310	29	12
Ranch	210	22	2
Sides: Ginger-Lime Slaw	80	4.5	9
Mashed Potatoes	210	10	21
Parmesan Steak Fries	660	49	47
Seasoned Fries	290	22	21

TGI Friday's® cont... (Feb '14)

Soups: Per 10 oz Bowl	C	F	Cb
Broccoli Cheese	300	25	11
French Onion	290	18	20
Soup Of The Day: Chicken Noodle	250	7	33
New England Clam Chowder	500	30	45
Tomato Basil	300	24	20
Tortilla	250	13	23
Desserts:			
Brownie Obsession, ½ serve	620	30	80
Oreo Madness, 1 serving	490	13	92
Vanilla Bean Cheesecake, 1 serving	970	61	91
Signature Slushes: Per 22 oz Tumbler			
Blue Rasperry	310	0	75
Mango Peach Lemonade	150	0	41
Red Bull Passion	220	0	54
Red Bull Ruby	200	0	51

Thundercloud Subs® (Feb '14)

Subs: Small, w/ Standard Toppings	C	F	Cb
Classic: BLT	405	17	40
Smoked Chicken	295	4	40
Turkey	280	4	41
Hot Subs: Meatball	650	32	56
Hot Pastrami	430	13	41
Signature Subs: Club	480	19	43
California Club	510	23	45
NY Italian	570	30	42
Office Favorite	850	40	81
Texas Tuna	700	45	44
Veggie Delite, with Hummus	360	10	53

Tim Hortons® (Feb '14)

Breakfast:	C	F	Cb
Bagel BELT, with Cheese	460	16	59
Biscuit: Bacon, Egg & Cheese	440	25	35
Egg & Cheese	390	21	35
Sausage, Egg & Cheese	560	37	36
English Muffins: Bacon, Egg & Chse	320	16	28
Sausage, Egg & Cheese	440	28	28
Wraps: Bacon, Egg & Cheese	270	16	18
Egg & Cheese	220	12	17
Sausage, Egg & Cheese	390	28	18
Hash Brown, (1), 1.75 oz	100	5	12

Continued Next Page...

Tim Hortons® cont... (Feb '14)

Paninis & Sandwiches: With Menu Board Toppings

	C	**F**	**Cb**
Paninis: Chipotle Turkey	350	17	32
Pesto Chicken	460	23	29
Smoked Ham & Cheese	340	15	29
Sandwiches: BLT	410	18	45
Chicken Salad	340	9	46
Ham & Swiss	390	12	46
Turkey Bacon Club	370	7	53
Wrap Snackers: *Per 3.5 oz Wrap*			
BBQ Chicken; Chicken Ranch, av.	185	7	18
Chicken Caesar	210	7	29
Cookies: Chocolate Chunk	230	9	35
Oatmeal Raisin Spice	220	8	35
Peanut Butter	280	16	27
Triple Chocolate	250	13	31
Donuts:			
Cake: Chocolate, glazed	260	10	39
Old Fashioned Plain	260	19	20
Sour Cream Glazed	340	17	46
Filled: Boston Cream	250	9	37
Canadian Maple	260	9	41
Strawberry	230	8	36
Honey Cruller	320	19	37
Yeast: Apple Fritter	300	11	49
Blueberry Fritter	330	10	55
Chocolate/Maple Dip	210	8	30
Vanilla Dip with sprinkles	290	10	46
Timbits:			
Cake: Chocolate, glazed	70	2.5	10
Sour Cream, glazed	90	4.5	12
Old Fashion, plain	70	5	5
Filled, all varieties	60	2	10
Yeast, Apple Fritter; Honey Dip, av.	55	2	9
Low Fat Yogurt: Creamy Vanilla	160	2.5	33
Strawberry	150	2.5	30
Beverages:			
Cafe Mocha, 10 fl.oz	170	6	27
Coffee, 1 cream, 1 sugar, 10 fl.oz	70	3.5	9
Hot Chocolate, 10 fl.oz	240	6	45
Iced Cappuccinos: *Per Small, 12 fl.oz*			
Original: With milk	180	1.5	39
With cream	310	16	40

T.J. Cinnamons® (Feb '14)

Bakery:

	C	**F**	**Cb**
Cinnamon Roll, Original, 5.25 oz	505	10	73
Cinnamon Twist (1), 2.5 oz	260	14	33
Sticky Bun Smear w/ Pecans, 1.25 oz	180	12	18
T.J. Cream Cheese Icing, 1 oz	115	5	18
Beverages: *Per 12 fl.oz Serving*			
Mocha Chill, w/o Whipped Cream	265	4	46

Togo's Eatery® (Feb '14)

Sandwiches:

	C	**F**	**Cb**
Cold: *Per Regular White Bread With Standard Toppings, Without Dressing*			
Albacore Tuna	550	17	73
Roast Beef & Avocado	570	13	69
The Italian	780	34	71
Turkey & Avocado	530	15	74
Turkey, Bacon Club	530	16	67
Turkey, Ham & Cheese	540	13	67
Vegetarian: Avocado & Cucumber	450	11	75
Egg Salad & Cheese	640	28	70
Hummus	650	27	85
Hot: BBQ Beef	670	19	85
Chicken	480	4	71
French Dip	690	17	66
Pastrami	770	37	66
Roast Beef	580	9	66
Toasted Sandwiches: *Per Regular With Menu Board Featured Bread*			
Clubhouse	660	23	80
Pepper Jack Pastrami	980	57	68
Uncle Toby's Italian	880	47	73
Salad Wraps: *Includes Whole Wheat Wrap, Standard Toppings & Dressings*			
Asian Chicken with Asian Dressing	670	32	74
BBQ Chicken Ranch w/ Buttmlk Ranch	640	30	72
Chicken Caesar w/ Caesar Dress.	550	20	67
Santa Fe Chicken with Spicy Pepitas	800	44	75
Salads: *Per Full Salad, Without Dressing*			
BBQ Chicken Ranch	390	20	32
Chicken Caesar	210	6	17
Farmer's Market	160	6	20
Santa Fe Chicken	370	16	33

Updated Nutrition Data ~ www.CalorieKing.com
Persons with Diabetes ~ See Disclaimer (Page 22)

Tropical Smoothie Cafe® (Feb '14)

Breakfast:

	C	F	Cb
Wraps: Early Bird, regular size	850	51	54
All American, regular size	620	26	53

Toasted Sandwiches: Without Chips or Fruit

Cranb. Walnut Ckn Salad, on Wheat	635	36	59
Turkey Bacon, w/ Ranch, on Ciabatta	520	15	52
Turkey Guacamole, on Wheat	500	10	66
Ultimate Club, w/ Chipotle Mayo on Ciabata	605	25	52

Toasted Wraps: On Garlic Herb Tortilla, Without Chips Or Fruit

Hummus Veggie	615	25	78
King Caesar, with Caesar Dressing	625	29	56
Thai Chicken	605	17	81
Totally Turkey, w/ Ranch Dressing	575	20	56

Fresh Salads: Includes Standard Dressing

Chicken Caesar	325	21	10
Southwest Chicken, w/ SW Ranch	540	29	44
Thai Chicken	375	11	43

Simply Indulgent Smoothies: 24 oz with Turbinado

Beach Bum	510	5	123
Chocolate Chiller	530	7	118
Peanut Butter Cup	655	21	117
Tropi-Colada	460	1	129

Low Fat Smoothies: Per 24 oz with Turbinado

Blimey Limey	475	0.5	124
Blue Lagoon	305	1	79
Hawaiian Breeze	370	0.5	93
Rockin Raspberry	380	0.5	99
Strawberry Beach	440	0.5	113
Sunrise Sunset	425	0.5	109

Supercharged: Per 24 oz with Turbinado

Health Nut	490	5.5	97
Lean Machine	425	0.5	111
Muscle Blaster	430	3	89
Peanut Paradise	650	19	99

With Splenda, deduct 200 calories & 50g carbs

Tubby's® (Feb '14)

Subs: Per Regular, w/o Condiments

	C	F	Cb
Deli-Subs: Classic Italian	610	14	75
Ham & Cheese	500	10	76
Turkey Breast & Cheese	530	12	76
Grilled Burger Subs: Big Tub	630	25	75
Burger Special	760	33	78
Cheeseburger Italiano	740	33	76
Pizza Burger	630	25	75

Tubby's® Cont... (Feb '14)

Subs (Cont): Per Regular Size

	C	F	Cb
Grilled Chicken Subs:			
Chicken	440	4.5	73
Chicken & Broccoli	520	10	75
Chicken & Cheddar	510	10	73
Chicken Fajita	520	10	75
Grilled Steak Subs:			
Portobella Mushroom Steak	600	17	80
Pepper Steak & Cheese	570	15	76
Steak & Cheese	560	15	74
Steak Special	590	16	76
Specialty Items: BLT	580	23	73
Cold Veggie	470	9	79
Italian Sausage	630	26	77
Tuna	530	9	74
Veggie Stir Fry, hot	470	9	79

Uno Chicago Grill® (Feb '14)

	C	F	Cb
Appetizers: Per Whole Dish			
Mozzarella Sticks, 11.4 oz	850	47	80
Pizza Skins, 25 .4 oz	2070	140	147
Shrimp & Crab Fondue, 16.4 oz	1120	81	64
Burgers: Without Sides			
BBQ, with Bacon & Cheddar	1100	60	33
Buffalo Cheddar	970	51	29
Uno	860	42	28

Entrees:

Chicken: Per Whole Dish, Without Sides Or Breadstick

Baked Stuffed Spinoccoli, 11.8 oz	360	14	10
Chicken Milanese, 22.5 oz	850	56	46
Chicken Thumb Platter, 10.5 oz	480	17	34

Steak & Seafood: Per Whole Dish w/o Sides Or Breadstick

Baked Haddock, 11.85 oz	580	35	12
Brewmasters Grill NY Sirloin	510	14	21
Grilled Shrimp & Sirloin, 17 oz	820	53	8
Lemon Basil Salmon, 8.65 oz	490	34	0

Thin Crust Pizza: Per Whole Pizza

Traditional Crust: Mediterranean	920	46	99
Pepperoni, Flatbread	990	46	96
Roasted Eggplant, Spinach & Feta	880	32	113
Sides: French Fries, 5.53 oz	350	27	25
Red Bliss Mashed Potatoes	270	14	34
Roasted Seasonal Veggies, 7.2 oz	80	4.5	10
Farro Salad, 7.5 oz	180	7	31

Villa Fresh Italian® (Feb '14)

Pizzas: Per Slice

	C	F	Cb
Neapolitan: Cheese, ⅙ pizza	405	13	49
Bacon & Tomato, ⅙ pizza	500	20	50
Deluxe, ⅙ pizza	505	21	52
Stuffed: Baked Ziti, ⅛ pizza	815	28	100
Meat, ⅛ pizza	840	41	74
Spinach and Mshrm, ⅛ pizza	730	33	77

Pasta & Italian Specialties:

Baked Spaghetti Bolognese, 15.8 oz	590	22	69
Baked Ziti, 15 oz	595	25	66
Chicken Alfredo, 16 oz	580	11	80
Meat Lasagna, 13.5 oz	695	21	94
Pasta Primavera, 23.5 oz	715	25	86
Spinach Lasagna, 19 oz	995	45	106
Spaghetti, 12 oz	755	34	94

Vegetables,

Sauteed, Fresh, 5.45 oz	215	20	7.5

Vocelli Pizza® (Feb '14)

Pizzas:

Artisan: Per ⅛ of Medium Pizza

	C	F	Cb
Basil Pesto Primavera	240	10	28
Buffalo Chicken	224	9	26
Chicken Carbonara	250	10	27
Chicken Spinaci	220	8	27
Deluxe	260	10	29
Hawaiian	280	11	30
Meat Magnifoco	280	12	26
Mexican	300	15	28
Philly Steak	270	13	25
Quattro Cheese	270	11	28
Spring Veggie	210	7	28
Pasta: Chicken Alfredo, 18 oz	1080	55	100
Chicken Parmesan, 20 oz	1030	35	132
Chicken Pesto, 18 oz	1110	59	99
House Baked Subs: *On Ciabatta*			
Chicken Alfredo, 18 oz	1080	55	100
Chicken Parmesan, 20 oz	1030	35	132
Meatball Marinara, 18.6 oz	950	34	121
Salads: *Per Regular Size, Without Dressing*			
Antipasta, 16 oz	270	16	17
Caesar, 8 oz	130	3	5
Mediterranean, 16 oz	270	18	17
Tuscan Grilled Chicken, 14 oz	290	13	12
Wings:			
BBQ, 9 oz	760	53	14
Buffalo, 9 oz	720	54	2
Garlic Romano, 9 oz	970	80	3
Hot Versuvius, 9 oz	720	54	2

Wahoo's Fish Taco® (Feb '14)

Bowls: With White Rice & Black Beans

	C	F	Cb
#7 Blackened/Charbroiled Chkn, av.	860	15	127
# 8 Charbroiled/Teriyaki Fish, av.	930	22	126
#9 Veggie	760	11	141
#10 Carnitas/Kahlua Pig, average	1025	25	131

Burritos: With Brown Rice & White Beans

Banzai:

Blackened or Charbroiled:			
Chicken	575	16	77
Fish, average	620	21	34
Mushroom	490	14	81
Carne Asada	565	17	34
Carnitas	685	23	79
Shrimp	475	14	77
Vegetarian	485	14	82
Side Kicks: Brown Rice	350	7	64
White Beans	285	3	54
Salads: *Chips Not Included*			
Blackened Chicken	415	22	14
Charbroiled Chicken	415	21	14
Charbroiled Fish	485	29	14
Sandwiches: *Blackened or Charbroiled*			
Chicken	510	18	51
Fish, average	555	22	51
Carne Asada	500	19	52

For Complete Nutritional Data ~ see CalorieKing.com

WAWA® (Mar '14)

Breakfast:

	C	F	Cb
Bagels: Plain	290	1	60
Plain, with Butter	490	23	60
Cinnamon Raisin	290	1	63
Cinnamon Raisin w/ Crm Cheese	410	13	65
Everything	310	6	56
Bowls: *Without Syrup*			
Creamed Chipped Beef On White	230	6	36
French Toasts: Plain	340	13	54
With Bacon	420	19	55
With Sausage Crumble	540	32	55
With Turkey Sausage	430	20	55
Scrambled Egg: With Bacon	470	34	10
With Sausage Crumble	590	47	10
Burritos: *Without Extra Toppings*			
Bacon & Cheddar Cheese	480	28	36
Beef Steak & Cheddar Cheese	450	23	37
Chicken Steak with Cheddar Chse	450	22	37
Sizzlis: *Per Sizzli*			
Bagels: Bacon, Egg & Cheese	410	18	43
Pork Roll, Egg & Cheese	420	19	42

Continued Next Page...

Continued Next Page...

WAWA® cont... (Mar '14)

Breaded Chicken Strips:	C	F	Cb
3 piece	240	13	16
5 piece	400	22	27

Cold Hoagies: *On Shorti Roll without Toppings*

	C	F	Cb
Egg Salad	650	37	61
Tuna Salad	690	39	63
Turkey	370	5	59

Hot Dogs: *Without Toppings, Mustard or Sauce*

	C	F	Cb
¼ Pound	420	28	21
Big Bacon Cheese Dog	810	47	57

Hot Hoagies: *On Shorti Roll without Toppings*

	C	F	Cb
Beef Steak & Cheddar Cheese	550	19	59
Chicken Steak & Cheddar Cheese	550	17	59
Meatballs & Cheddar Cheese	730	34	75

Soups: *Per Medium Serving*

	C	F	Cb
Baked Potato w/ Cheddar & Bacon	450	32	28
Chicken Noodles	150	3	23
Lobster Bisque	470	38	20
Italian Wedding	210	7	21
New England Clam Chowder	330	21	24

Quesadillas: *Without Toppings*

	C	F	Cb
Beef & Cheddar Cheese	450	22	36
Cheddar Cheese	390	20	39
Chicken & Cheddar Cheese	450	20	36

Sides: *Per Medium Serving*

	C	F	Cb
Chili	350	11	43
Macaroni & Beef	350	11	43
Macaroni & Cheese	500	25	49
Mashed Potatoes	470	28	50
Meatballs in a Cup	320	21	17

Bakery:

	C	F	Cb
Croissant, Plain	280	14	35
Muffins: Banana Walnut	670	34	83
Blueberry	610	30	78
Chocolate Chip	680	34	86
Corn	640	29	87

Hot Beverages: *Per 16 oz, without Extras*

	C	F	Cb
Hot Cappuccino, with 2% milk	130	5	13
Mocha Latte, with 2% milk	330	7	59

Smoothie, Strawberry Banana,

	C	F	Cb
without whipped cream, 24 oz	690	0	180

Wendy's® (Mar '14)

Old Fashioned Hamburgers: *With Standard Toppings*

	C	F	Cb
Dave's ¼ lb Single, w/ Cheese	580	31	42
Dave's ½ lb Double w/ Cheese	820	47	42
Dave's ¾ lb Triple w/ Cheese	1090	66	43
Baconator	940	56	41
Son of Baconator	670	37	41
Double Stack	420	21	26
Jr. Bacon Cheeseburger	390	22	26
Jr. Cheeseburger	290	13	26
Jr. Cheeseburger Deluxe	350	19	27

Sandwiches: *With Standard Toppings*

	C	F	Cb
Asiago Ranch Club, with Homestyle or Spicy Chicken	670	32	57
Crispy Chicken	350	19	34
Homestyle Chicken	510	20	54
Spicy Chicken	510	20	55
Ultimate Chicken Grill	370	7	43

Go Wraps: Grilled Chicken

	C	F	Cb
Grilled Chicken	260	10	25
Spicy Chicken	330	16	30

Chicken Nuggets, Regular:

	C	F	Cb
6 pieces	270	18	14
10 pieces	450	30	24

Sauces:

	C	F	Cb
Barbecue Nugget	45	0	11
Honey Mustard Nugget	80	6	7

Garden Sensations Salads: *Full, without Toppings or Dressing*

	C	F	Cb
Apple Pecan Chicken	350	11	27
BBQ Ranch Chicken	390	15	28
Spicy Chicken Caesar	480	27	24

Dressings: *Half Salad Size*

	C	F	Cb
Classic Ranch, 1 pkt	100	10	2
Italian Vinaigrette, 1 pkt	70	6	4
Thousand Island, 1 pkt	160	15	5

Sides:

	C	F	Cb
Baked Potatoes: Plain	270	0	61
Sour Cream & Chives	320	3.5	62
Chili Cheese Fries, 10 oz	530	28	55
Natural Cut Fries: Value	220	11	28
Small, 4 oz	310	15	40
Medium, 5 oz	410	20	52
Large, 6.5 oz	500	24	65
Rich Meaty Chili, small, 8 oz	180	5	20
Frosty, Chocolate/Vanilla, small	285	7	47

Frosty Shakes: *Per Large, With Whipped Cream*

	C	F	Cb
Caramel, 18.1 oz	990	18	195
Chocolate, 17.5 oz	810	16	153
Strawberry, 17.3 oz	750	15	139

For Complete Nutritional Data ~ see CalorieKing.com

Fast - Foods & *Restaurants*

Whataburger® (Feb '14)

	C	F	Cb
Burgers:			
A.1. Thick & Hearty Burger	1050	64	65
BBQ Cheddar Burger	1060	63	67
Chop House Cheddar Burger	1160	75	59
Green Chili Double	1010	62	68
Honey BBQ Chicken Strip S'wich	1070	56	96
Justaburger	310	16	29
Whataburger: Original	640	32	61
Bacon & Cheese	800	44	61
Double Meat	880	51	61
Patty Melt	1100	75	54
Triple Meat	1130	70	61
Jr.	330	16	32
Jalapeno & Cheese	730	39	61
Chicken:			
Whatachick'n: Burger	570	27	64
Bites: 6 pieces, without sauce	390	19	31
9 pieces, without sauce	540	27	42
Strips, 3 pieces, without sauce	610	34	42
French Fries: Small, 3 oz	260	13	31
Medium, 4.5 oz	390	20	47
Large, 6 oz	520	27	63
Onion Rings: Medium, 4.25 oz	400	25	37
Large, 6½ oz	590	38	56
Salad, Garden, without dressing	180	9	15
Breakfast:			
Cinnamon Roll	400	9	71
Biscuits: Plain	300	17	32
With Bacon	350	20	32
With Gravy	510	30	48
With Jelly	340	16	41
With Sausage	490	33	32
Honey Butter Chicken	590	36	50
Biscuit Sandwiches:			
With Bacon	490	31	34
With Sausage	640	44	34

Whataburger® cont... (Feb '14)

	C	F	Cb
Breakfast (Cont):			
On A Bun: With Bacon	370	21	30
With Sausage	510	34	30
Platters: With Bacon	640	41	34
With Sausage	780	54	34
Taquitos: With Bacon	370	20	27
With Bacon, Egg & Cheese	420	24	28
With Cheese	370	20	28
Desserts:			
Chocolate Chunk Cookie	230	11	31
Hot Apple Pie, 3 oz	270	14	34
Beverages:			
Malts: Chocolate, 20 oz	670	16	123
Vanilla, 20 oz	590	17	99
Shake, Chocolate, 20 oz	630	16	111

White Castle® (Feb '14)

	C	F	Cb
Sliders:			
Original	140	6	13
Double	240	12	21
Chicken Breast with Cheese	390	28	20
Fish, with Cheese	340	24	18
Surf & Turf with Cheese, 6 oz	540	38	27
Sides:			
Chicken Rings: 6 rings, 5 oz	530	47	12
9 rings, 7.5 oz	790	71	18
Clam Strips, small, 4.5 oz	210	17	5
Fish Nibblers, small, 5 oz	320	16	28
French Fries, small, 5.6 oz	350	21	34
Mozzarella Cheese Sticks, 3 sticks	440	33	22
Onion Chips, small, 4.4 oz	480	36	33
Onion Rings, Homestyle, med., 5 oz	480	33	40
Sauces & Condiments: Per Packet			
Ketchup	10	0	2
Mayonnaise	60	7	0
Sauces: BBQ	10	0	3
Tartar Sauce	25	1.5	1
Desserts: On A Stick			
Fudge Dipped Brownie	250	12	33
Fudge Dipped Cheesecake	180	10	21

Wienerschnitzel® (Feb '14)

Hot Dogs:	C	F	Cb
Original: *On Standard Bun*			
Chili	270	12	31
Chili Cheese	320	16	31
Deluxe	250	11	30
Kraut	240	11	28
Plain	240	11	27
Pastrami	350	19	29
Original: *On Pretzel Bun*			
Chili	400	14	57
Kraut; Mustard; Plain	370	13	54
Stadium	380	13	56
Angus All Beef: *On Pretzel Bun*			
Chicago	570	26	67
Chili Cheese	600	32	57
Bacon Wrapped: On Standard Bun			
Original	340	21	27
Street Style	370	24	29
Corn Dogs:			
Regular	250	17	15
Mini (6 pack)	320	22	22
Junkyard Dog, on Seeded Bun	460	24	45
Sides: Chili Cheese Fries	540	38	39
Fries: Regular	300	22	25
Large	430	31	35
Jalapeno Poppers (3)	210	11	21
Breakfast:			
Biscuits: Egg, Bacon, Cheese	440	25	36
Egg, Sausage, Cheese	540	34	40
Burritos: Egg, Bacon, Cheese	490	25	39
Egg, Sausage, Cheese	590	34	43
French Toast Sticks	490	29	49
Syrup, 1 oz	120	0	31
Desserts:			
Cones, Regular: 5 oz	250	9	41
Chocolate Dipped, 5 oz.	450	27	50
Freezees: Butterfinger	620	24	100
Oreo; M&M	630	25	99
Reese's Peanut Butter Cup	630	26	97
Sundaes: Caramel; Hot Fudge, av.	400	15	64
Chocolate	390	14	64
Pineapple; Strawberry	370	14	59
Shakes, average all flavors	650	23	110
Drinks: 16 fl.oz, without ice			
Lipton Raspberry Iced Tea	180	0	45
Mountain Dew	230	0	61
Mug Root Beer	210	0	57

Winchell's® (Feb '14)

Donuts: Per Donut	C	F	Cb
Buttermilk Bars, Choc Iced; Glazed	420	19	61
Jelly Filled:			
Apple with Cinnamon Crumb	370	15	53
Raspberry with Glaze	390	13	61
Strawberry with Sugar	380	13	60
Old Fashioned, Glazed; Maple Iced	410	17	60
Raised Ring: Choc. Iced	270	10	41
Sugared	230	9	34

WingStreet (Feb '14)

Chicken:	C	F	Cb
Crispy Bone In Wings: *Per 2 Pieces*			
Buffalo, Mild/Med./Hot, 2.75 oz	240	15	19
Garlic Parmesan, 2.5 oz	310	25	12
Honey BBQ, 3 oz	270	14	28
Naked	200	14	11
Bone Out Wings: *Per 2 Pieces*			
Buffalo, Mild/Medium, 2.5 oz	200	9	19
Garlic Parmesan, 2.5 oz	270	20	12
Honey BBQ, 3 oz	230	9	28
Lemon Pepper	250	14	21
Traditional Wings: *Per 2 Pieces*			
Buffalo, Medium/Hot, 2 oz	130	6	8
Garlic Parmesan, 2 oz	200	17	1
Spicy Asian, 2.3 oz	150	6	13
Spicy BBQ	140	6	11

Woody's Bar-B-Q® (Feb '14)

Starters:	C	F	Cb
Breaded Wings (10)	700	47	13
Beef Chili Cheese Fries	805	38	63
Dinner Entrees: Without Sides			
½ Chicken	840	56	0
Baby Back Ribs, ½ Rack	260	20	1
Beef Prime Rib	760	62	1
Sandwiches: Per Regular, Without Sides			
Beef	390	14	28
Pork	490	26	29
Wraps: Without Sides			
Beef BBQ	380	13	31
Pork	440	21	31
Extras: BBQ Beans	170	8	20
Cobettes	80	1	18
French Fries	185	7	28
Garlic Toast	120	6	14
Green Beans	50	2.5	6
Okra	95	1	21
Squash	140	1	28

For Complete Nutritional Data ~ see CalorieKing.com

257

Yoshinoya® (Feb '14)

Appetizers: As Served

	C	F	Cb
Sesame Wings: 4 pieces	280	18	1
6 pieces	420	27	2

Entrees: As Served

	C	F	Cb
Bento: Beef	880	25	131
Teriyaki Chicken	1010	29	137
Beef Bowl: *With Sauce*			
Regular	730	27	91
Large	1040	38	131
With Vegetables: Regular	650	20	95
Large	960	29	141
Beef & Teriyaki Chicken Combo:			
Large, with skin	1190	36	151
Large, without skin	1150	33	151
Teriyaki Chicken Bowl:			
Regular, with skin	790	18	190
Large, with skin	1140	25	165
Grilled Fish:			
With Rice, Slaw & Ponzu Sauce	530	14	78
With Rice, Veggies & Ponzu Sce	460	6	75
With Rice, Slaw & Teriyaki Sauce	550	14	83
With Rice, Veggies & Teriyaki Sce	470	7	79
Yaki Udon: With Beef & Noodles	740	22	106
With Beef & Rice	810	21	126
With Chicken & Noodles	750	18	103
With Chicken & Rice	820	17	123
Desserts: Cheese Cake, 3.5 oz	330	19	35
Chocolate Cheesecake, 3.5 oz	370	22	37

Please note: Relates only to Northern California Menu

Z Pizza® (Feb '14)

Pizzas: Small, Per Slice

	C	F	Cb
Creations: Berkeley Vegan	150	5	21
California	140	4.5	18
Casablanca	180	8	18
Greek	140	5	17
Italian; Mexican, average	165	7	17
Provence; Santa Fe	150	6	17
Thai; ZBQ, average	165	5	19
Rusticas: *Per Slice*			
Chicken Sausage	100	3.5	12
Curry Chicken & Yam	130	3.5	16
Mediterranean; Moroccan, av.	140	8	13
Pear & Gorgonzola	130	6	14
Calzones: Meat Calzone	790	36	82
Veggie Calzone	630	22	86
Salads: *Small*			
Arugula, with Balsamic Vinaigrette	450	37	23
Caesar Side, with Caesar Dressing	200	16	8
California, with Chipotle Ranch	180	13	16

Zaxby's® (Feb '14)

Zappetizers: With Sauce

	C	F	Cb
Fried White Cheddar Bites w/ sce	820	51	62
Onion Rings, 5 oz	780	58	59
Spicy Fried Mushroom, 5.7 oz	620	46	43
Tater Chips, 5.2 oz	940	69	72
Meal Dealz: *With Sauce, without Drink*			
Big Zax Snak	950	53	82
Buffalo Wings, without sauce	900	57	51
Chicken Finger Nibbler	1330	72	137
Most Popular: *As Served*			
Chicken Finger Plate: Regular	1260	72	99
Large	1775	105	129
Wings & Things, regular	1490	94	85
Sandwich Baskets: *Includes Fries*			
Cajun Club	1070	51	90
Club	1250	74	99
Wings & Fingerz: *With Sauce*			
Buffalo Fingerz:			
5 pieces	630	43	15
10 pieces	1270	87	30
Buffalo Wings:			
5 pieces	540	41	3
10 pieces	880	61	4
Chicken Fingerz:			
5 pieces	610	39	19
10 pieces	1230	79	36
Zax Kidz: *Without Drink*			
Kiddie Cheese	800	51	69
Kiddie Finger	570	36	40
Kiddie Nibbler	550	29	59
Zalads: *With Texas Toast, Without Dressing*			
Blue, with Blackened Chicken	630	29	35
Caesar Zalad:			
With Fried Chicken	730	39	39
With Grilled Chicken	590	27	29
House Zalad: With Fried Chicken	760	42	44
With Grilled Chicken	620	30	34
Salad Dressings:			
Blue Cheese, 1 packet, 1.25 oz	180	19	2
Honey French, 1.25 oz	150	12	9
Honey Mustard, 1.25 oz	150	13	6
Lite Ranch, 1.25 oz	90	8	3
Mediterranean, 1.25 oz	140	14	4
Ranch, 1.25 oz	160	16	2
Thousand Island	230	24	3
Sides: Celery Basket,			
with 2 cups Ranch Sauce	420	42	10
Cole Slaw, 2.2 oz	140	11	12
Crinkle Fries, regular, 5 oz	360	16	48
Texas Toast, basket, 3 wedges, 4.3 oz	440	20	60

Zero Sub's® ~ *see CalorieKing.com*

Updated Nutrition Data ~ www.CalorieKing.com
Persons with Diabetes ~ See Disclaimer (Page 22)

Notes on Cholesterol

- **Cholesterol** is a white waxy substance produced mainly by our liver. It is also found in animal food products. Plant foods have no cholesterol.

- **Cholesterol is essential to life.** It is a structural part of every body cell wall and is the building block for vitamin D, sex hormones, and bile acids which help in the digestion of dietary fats.

- **The body makes sufficient cholesterol** for its needs and does not rely on cholesterol in the diet. Dietary fats have a major influence on blood cholesterol levels - more so than dietary cholesterol.

- **A high blood cholesterol level increases** the risk of atherosclerosis - the thickening of arteries that can reduce or block blood flow to the heart, brain, eyes, kidneys, sex organs and other body parts.

  This in turn increases the risk of heart attack, stroke, blindness, kidney failure, impotence and other blood circulatory problems.

  Other risk factors which increase the risk of atherosclerosis include high blood pressure, smoking, obesity and uncontrolled diabetes.

BLOOD CHOLESTEROL

CHECK YOUR RISK!

Total Cholesterol Level (mg/dl)		Risk of Heart Attack
▼		▼
240 and above	~	High Risk
200 - 239	~	Borderline/High
Below 200	~	Desirable

♥ **Know your cholesterol level, particularly if there is a family history of heart disease or stroke. If level is high, see your doctor.**

♥ **All adults should have their cholesterol, HDL and triglycerides tested at least every 5 years.**

HEART ATTACK WARNING SIGNALS

Many victims die before reaching the hospital by ignoring warning signals and delaying medical help.

Symptoms vary and commonly include:

- **Chest pain,** vice-like squeezing or burning sensation in center of the chest or between the shoulder blades, or in the mid-back. Pain may even feel like severe indigestion.

- **Pain** may be felt in the arms, shoulders, neck or jaw.

- **Shortness of breath** often occurs with or before chest discomfort.

- **Other signs,** with or without pain, include a cold sweat, nausea or light-headedness.

If you experience any of the above symptoms call IMMEDIATELY for medical help. Every minute counts.

Call 9-1-1 *or your emergency number*

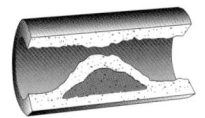

▲ Atherosclerosis can clog arteries and impede blood flow to the heart or other body organs.

▼ A thrombus (blood clot) can form on unstable, festering athero-sclerotic plaque and rapidly block blood flow. A heart attack or stroke can result.

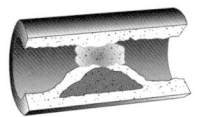

Fats & Cholesterol Guide

The amount and type of dietary fat has the greatest influence on blood cholesterol levels.

Fats in food are a mixture of 3 basic types: saturated, monounsaturated, and polyunsaturated. Animal fats are mainly saturated while plant oils and fish oils are mainly mono- and polyunsaturated.

Saturated fats have subgroups known as long-chain, medium-chain, and short-chain fats. Most of the long chain fats raise blood cholesterol, and increase the risk of blood clots and thrombosis leading to artery blockage.

Long-chain saturated fats are found mainly in full-cream milk, cheese, butter, cream, fatty meats and sausages, and processed foods.

Monounsaturated fats tend to more selectively lower 'bad' LDL cholesterol and maintain the protective 'good' HDL cholesterol in the bloodstream – but only if they replace saturated fats in the diet.

Foods rich in monounsaturates include canola and olive oils, canola margarine, peanuts, and avocados.

Polyunsaturated fats consist of two main classes. **Omega-6** polyunsaturates tend to lower blood cholesterol. Rich sources include safflower, sunflower and corn oils.

Omega-3 polyunsaturated fats can lower blood cholesterol; significantly lower blood triglycerides; and reduce the rise of thrombosis, heart arrythmmia, and artery spasm.

Best practical omega-3 sources include canola oil and margarine, soybean oil and fish.

A balanced intake of the two omega classes is important for optimal health. For most Americans, slightly increasing omega-3 intake would help attain a more ideal balance.

Trans fats from hydrogenated vegetable oils and shortenings should also be avoided. They are common in commercial baked and fried food products such as cakes, muffins, pastries, doughnuts, fried snacks and french fries.

Note: All fats are high in calories and need to be limited for weight control.

DIETARY FATS COMPARISON

■ Saturated Fat ■ Monounsaturated Fat
Polyunsaturated Fats:
□ Linoleic (Omega-6) ■ Alpha-Linolenic (Omega-3)

OILS — PERCENTAGE CONTENT

OILS	Saturated	Monounsaturated	Linoleic (Omega-6)	Alpha-Linolenic (Omega-3)
CANOLA OIL	7	63	20	10
LINSEED/FLAX OIL	9	19	17	55
SAFFLOWER OIL	9	14	77	
GRAPESEED OIL	10	22	68	
SUNFLOWER OIL	11	23	66	
CORN OIL	14	32	52	2
OLIVE OIL	14	76	10	
SOYBEAN OIL	15	23	54	8
PEANUT OIL	19	45	34	2
COTTONSEED OIL	26	16	58	
PALM OIL	51	39	10	

SPREADS & FATS

Saturated Fat includes 'Trans Fats'   □ WATER CONTENT

SPREADS & FATS	Saturated	Monounsaturated	Linoleic (Omega-6)	Alpha-Linolenic (Omega-3)	Water Content
LIGHT MARGARINE	14	14	21		51
CANOLA MARGARINE	18	45	12	6	19
POLYUNSATURATED MARG	24	20	36		20
BUTTER	57	18	2		24
LARD	41	47			12
BEEF FAT	44	37	4		15

GOOD SOURCES OF OMEGA-3 FATS

Plant Sources	Omega-3 Fats (Grams)
Canola Oil, 1 Tbsp, ½ fl.oz	1.5g
Flaxseed Oil, 1 Tbsp	8g
Soybean Oil, 1 Tbsp	1.2g
Canola Margarine, 1 Tbsp, ½ oz	1g
Soybeans, cooked, ½ cup, 4 oz	0.5g
Walnuts, ½ oz	0.5g

FISH - *Per 4 oz Serving*

High Content: Salmon (Chinook), Tuna, Trout (Lake), Sardines, Herring, Mackerel — 3g / 3g

Medium Content:
Salmon, (Pink/Red/Coho), 4 oz — 2g

Fair Content: *Per 4 oz Serving*
Bass, Catfish, Cod, Grouper, Hake, Halibut, Kingfish, Perch, Pollock, Shark, Trout (Rainbow), Tuna, Crab, Oysters, Blue Mussels, Shrimp, Squid — 0.5-1g

How Much Is Needed?

As little as 1-2 grams daily of omega-3 fats may benefit general health. High doses of fish-oil supplements should only be taken as directed by your doctor.

Dietary Cholesterol

Cholesterol in food varies in its effect on blood cholesterol level (BCL) from person to person. Much depends on the amount and type of fat and fiber eaten at the same meal.

Any elevating effect of dietary cholesterol on BCL is more likely to occur when the diet is high in saturated fat. Little elevation, if any, generally occurs when dietary fats are balanced in favor of monounsaturated and polyunsaturated fats (including omega-3 fats).

For example, while fish does contain cholesterol, the omega-3 fats can prevent any increase in BCL. Conversely, a meal containing no cholesterol but rich in saturated fat may result in a significant increase in BCL.

Consequently, the need to be overly concerned about dietary cholesterol is being de-emphasized in favor of the approach of limiting total fat, saturated fat, and trans fat in particular – and substituting unsaturated fats.

The liver usually cuts back its own cholesterol production in response to cholesterol in the diet. Many people can consume normal amounts of high-cholesterol foods without concern.

However, it is difficult to identify just who is at risk - the so-called 'hyper-responders'. Because over 50% of Americans have a BCL above ideal levels, the **American Heart Association** advises all Americans to be prudent and limit their cholesterol intake to less than 300mg daily, as well as to adopt a heart-healthy diet.

This limitation still allows the inclusion of most foods that are regularly eaten – even the overly maligned egg.

Eggs contain a modest 5 grams of fat per large egg. Barely 2 grams is saturated, the rest being monounsaturated or polyunsaturated.

By comparison, a cup of whole milk has 8g fat of which almost 5g is saturated.

CHOLESTEROL COUNTER

Cholesterol is found only in foods of animal origin. Plant foods contain no cholesterol.

	Cholesterol mg
Meat - Average all types:	
Lean Meat, cooked, 120g	100
Fatty Meat, cooked, 120g	100
Fat, thick strip, 60g	40

Note: While lean meat and fat have similar amounts of cholesterol, choose lean meat to limit fat intake.

Chicken/Turkey, average, 120g	100
Organ Meats: Liver, fried, 4 oz	500
Brains, beef, pan fried, 3 oz	1700
Sausages: Frankfurter, 40g	25
Salami, 2 slices, 55g	40
Bacon: 3 slices, cooked, 30g	20
Fish: Fish fillets, average, ckd, 120g	70
Tuna/Salmon, canned, 100g	50
Scallops, 9 medium, 3 oz	30
Prawns, raw, 100g	110
Oysters, raw, 6 medium, 85g	45
Crayfish, Crab, cooked, 100g	70
Eggs (Chicken), 1 large	210
1 medium	180
Egg White, *Scramblers*	0
Milk/Yoghurt: Whole, 1 cup, 250ml	30
Light/low-fat Milk (1%), 1 cup	10
Skim/Non-fat, 1 cup	10
Soy Milk, Tofu, Tempeh	0
Cheese: Natural/Hard/Cream, 30g	30
Cottage, low-fat, 2 Tbsp, 40g	5
Cream Cheese, 30g	25
Fats: Butter, 1 Tbsp, 20g	45
Margarine, Oils (vegetable)	0
Mayonnaise, 1 Tbsp	0
Cream: Heavy, whipping, 2 Tbsp, 40g	40
Light/Sour, 2 Tbsp	10
Ice Cream: Full-fat (10-11%), 100ml/50g	20
Low-fat (less than 4%), 50g	5
Fruit, Vegetables, Avocados	0
Nuts, Seeds, Grains	0
Coffee, Tea, Beer, Wine	0

For Comprehensive Food Listings ~ see CalorieKing.com

Blood Cholesterol ~ Diet Hints

DIETARY HINTS TO LOWER BLOOD CHOLESTEROL

1. **Maintain a healthy weight.**
   If overweight, lose weight with a sensible, low-fat meal plan and daily exercise.

2. **Reduce saturated fat intake by:**
   (a) eating less dairy fat. Choose low-fat or fat-reduced varieties of milk, yogurt, soy drinks, cheese, and ice cream.

   (b) replacing saturated fats with fats and oils rich in monounsaturated and polyunsaturated fats. Choose vegetable oils such as canola, olive, sunflower and soybean. Avoid solid frying fats.

   Note: *Promise Active* and *Benecol* spreads contain plant stanol esters which can lower total and LDL cholesterol.

   (c) eating less fat from meat and poultry. Choose lean cuts of meat and skinless chicken. Go easy on lunch meats, salami and fatty sausages. Enjoy fish.

   (d) eating less saturated and trans fats from baked and fried fast-foods. Avoid deep-fried foods. Avoid donuts, cakes, pastries and cookies unless made with healthier fats and oils.

3. **Increase your soluble fiber intake.**
   Foods rich in soluble fiber include beans, lentils, chick peas, hummus, nuts, seeds, psyllium-seed husks and psyllium-fiber supplements. Oat bran, rice bran and barley are also good sources, as are fruit, vegetables and avocados.
   (*See Fiber Guide - Page 264-269*).

4. **Eat more soy bean products** such as: soy drinks, tofu, tempeh (cultured soy beans), soy flour, soy vegetarian foods and edamame (fresh green soybeans).

   Soy protein in place of animal protein can significantly decrease high blood cholesterol levels as well as 'bad' LDL cholesterol and blood triglycerides while 'good' HDL cholesterol is maintained. For best results, eat at least 25g of soy protein per day (from 3-4 servings).

5. **Eat more fruit, vegetables, and whole grains** in place of high-fat foods. Aim for 2 fruits and 5 servings of vegetables per day. They also contain valuable antioxidants. The fat of avocados (and most nuts) is mainly unsaturated and can lower blood cholesterol levels.

6. **Limit cholesterol to 300mg per day.**
   (Extra Notes ~ See Previous Page)

7. **Avoid brewed unfiltered coffee** (espresso; plunger-style). Several cups per day may raise blood cholesterol. Filtered coffee is fine.

8. **Spread your food intake over the day.**
   Have 5-6 small meals per day rather than just 2-3 large meals. Nibbling, versus gorging, favors lower blood cholesterol.

ALCOHOL – WINE

Alcohol is a mixed bag. Moderate amounts of 1-2 drinks daily appear to reduce the risk of heart attack and ischemic stroke in older persons.

However, larger amounts increase the risk of high blood pressure, obesity, heart failure and hemorrhagic stroke, and can aggravate hypertriglyceridemia: as well as many other health hazards. (*See Alcohol Guide – Page 23*)

The speculative benefits of moderate alcohol intake have been overstated in the media. The overriding harmful effects of excess alcohol do not allow its recommendation for any aspects of health promotion.

Fruit, Vegetables & Tea Also Protect:
Red wine and red grapes (more so than white) contain antioxidants which may help protect cholesterol in the blood from becoming oxidized.

Many fruits, vegetables, grains, nuts and tea also contain protective antioxidants.

How Fats Affect Blood Flow

Fats in the diet affect more than blood cholesterol levels. They can also strongly influence blood clot formation and thrombosis, as well as blood flow and ultimate oxygen delivery to body parts and organs.

While advanced atherosclerosis can impede blood flow to the heart and other organs, it is thrombosis (complete blockage by blood clots) or arterial spasm which commonly results in a heart attack or stroke.

Plant and fish oils rich in omega-3 fats lessen the risk of blood clots, thrombus formation, and artery spasm by reducing platelet stickiness and adhesion to artery walls. This reduces the risk of atherosclerotic plaque becoming unstable and reactive.

Omega-3 fats also improve blood flow by reducing blood viscosity and increasing the flexibility of red blood cells (RBC) that need to flex and twist on themselves in order to squeeze through tiny narrow capillaries often half their diameter.

A diet high in saturated fats has the opposite effect by stiffening RBC membranes and increasing blood viscosity, thereby hindering blood flow. The stiffening of the RBC membrane also reduces its ability to release vital oxygen to body cells and take up carbon dioxide.

Stiff red blood cells may also form aggregates that resemble coin stacks. In narrow blood vessels, this further impedes blood flow and impairs oxygen release through the much-lessened surface area of red blood cell membranes exposed to blood. (Smoking, lack of exercise, and stress can have similar adverse effects on thrombosis, red blood cell flexibility, and blood flow.).

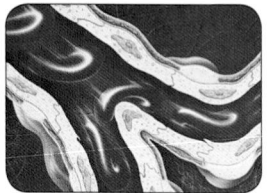

▲ Picture of Healthy Blood Flow

Flexible red blood cells twist and slide through tiny capillaries - often half the diameter of red blood cells.

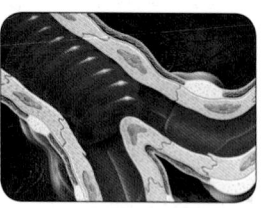

▲ A Not-So-Healthy Picture!

Red blood cells have lost their flexibility and ability to twist and slip through capillaries. They are stacked up, thereby impeding blood flow.

A diet high in saturated fats can contribute to this picture - as can smoking, lack of exercise, and stress.

Fiber Guide

Introduction

`Fiber`

Fiber is the general term for those parts of plant food that we cannot digest (although bacteria in the large bowel partly digests fiber through fermentation). It is not found in foods of animal origin (meats, dairy products).

Fiber promotes intestinal health, bowel regularity, can benefit diabetes and blood cholesterol levels, and may help prevent colon cancer. High-fiber foods also assist weight control.

Most Americans don't eat enough fiber – less than 20 grams/day - instead of a healthier 25 to 35 grams/day.

Types of Fiber

Plant foods contain a mixture of different fibers in varying proportions. Insoluble and soluble fiber categories are based on their solubility in water. All types of fiber are beneficial to the body.

◆ Insoluble fibers (cellulose, hemi-celluloses, lignin) make up the structural parts of plant cell walls.

Best food sources are wheat bran, corn bran, rice bran, wholegrain cereals and breads, beans and peas, nuts, seeds, and the skins of fruits and vegetables.

These fibers absorb many times their own weight in water. They create a soft bulk and hasten the passage of waste products through the intestines.

They promote bowel regularity, and aid in the prevention and treatment of uncomplicated forms of constipation, diverticulosis and hemorrhoids.

The risk of colon cancer may also be reduced by fiber's diluting effect on potentially harmful substances.

◆ Soluble fibers (pectin, gums, mucilages) are found mainly within plant cells, soy milk (whole bean) and products.

Fiber promotes good health, and better control of diabetes and cholesterol.

'*An apple a day keeps the doctor away.*' ... it just might!

Types of Fiber (Cont)

Best Sources of Soluble Fiber: Fruits and vegetables, oat bran, barley, beans and peas, prunes, psyllium and flax seed.

These fibers form a gel which slows both stomach emptying and the absorption of sugars from the intestines. **This helps to control blood sugar levels.**

Weight control is also aided by the slower emptying of the stomach and the feeling of **fullness provided by soluble fiber.**

Some soluble fibers can lower **blood cholesterol** by binding bile acids and excreting them. More body cholesterol must then be broken down to supply bile acids for emulsification of dietary fats. **Rice bran, while not high in soluble fiber, can also lower blood cholesterol.**

◆ **Resistant starch** is that part of starchy foods (approx. 10%) which is tightly bound by fiber and resists normal digestion. Friendly bacteria in the large bowel ferment and change the resistant starch into short-chain fatty acids, which are important to bowel health and may protect against colon cancer.

Starchy foods include bread, cereals, rice, pasta, potatoes and legumes.

Fiber & Weight Control

Fiber can assist weight control in several ways. Fiber-rich foods such as fresh fruit and vegetables, potatoes and wholegrain bread contain few calories for their large volume (due to their low-fat, high-water content).

Their bulk fills the stomach and satisfies the appetite much sooner than fiber-depleted foods. The extra chewing time also contributes to satiety, and gives the stomach time to register a feeling of fullness. Excessive calories are less likely to be consumed.

Fiber-depleted foods and drinks are more concentrated in calories; e.g. fats, sugar, candy, soft drinks, fruit juices, alcohol. They require little or no chewing. Large amounts with excessive calories can be consumed before the appetite is satisfied.

Example: Whereas one fresh apple might satisfy the appetite, an apple juice drink with the equivalent sugars and calories of 2-3 apples only minimally satisfies the appetite. (See illustration below.)

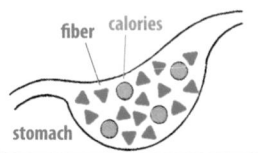

High-fiber foods fill the stomach. Fewer calories are consumed.

Low-fiber foods are more concentrated in calories. More food must be eaten to fill the stomach.

EFFECTS OF REMOVING FIBER FROM FOOD

2-3 pieces of fresh fruit produces 1 glass of fruit juice. The removal of fiber concentrates the sugar and calories.

FIBER REMOVED

Fresh Fruit	Fruit Juice
High Fiber	Negligible Fiber
Low Calorie Density	High Calorie Density
Long Eating Time	No Eating Time (Drink)
Satisfies Hunger	Does Not Satisfy Hunger
Sugar Slowly Absorbed	Sugar More Quickly Absorbed
Less Insulin Required	More Insulin Required

Fiber Guide ~ Constipation

Constipation

Constipation can reasonably be defined as a failure to have a bowel movement at least every second day – and just as importantly, without straining or pain.

Typically, constipated stools are too hard, too narrow and too small.

The **main cause** is simply a lack of dietary fiber. Other contributing factors include insufficient fluids, too little exercise, emotional stress, gastrointestinal disease, lack of proper dentition to chew high-fiber foods, and some medications (e.g. some antacids, antidepressants, pain medications).

Note: Check with your doctor to rule out any underlying medical problem – especially if you have a change in bowel habits in middle-age or later years.

HINTS TO INCREASE FIBER AND AVOID CONSTIPATION

❶ **Breakfast is an important** contributor to daily fiber intake. Eat high-fiber breakfast cereals (bran-based cereals, oatmeal etc.). Add 1-2 tablespoons of unprocessed bran.

Dried fruits, chopped nuts, soy grits, and seeds are also excellent additions to cereals.

Note: A gradual increase in fiber will prevent bloating, gas or pain. People intolerant to bran may benefit from psyllium-based fiber supplements and cereals.

❷ **Drink adequate water daily.** Fiber works by absorbing many times its own weight in water.

❸ **Eat wholegrain breads,** or fiber-enriched breads. They have over double the fiber of regular white bread.

❹ **Enjoy fruit as fresh fruit** with skin rather than as fruit juice. Enjoy wholegrain pasta, barley, brown rice, nuts and seeds.

❺ **Eat more vegetables,** salads and legumes – especially cooked beans, lentils, potatoes with skins, avocado, broccoli, brussels sprouts, cabbage, carrots, celery, and peas.

❻ **Add bran** (barley/rice/wheat) or soy grits to soups, casseroles, yogurt, desserts, cookies, cakes. Also use whole-meal flour or soy flour in place of white flour. Use nuts, seeds, and ground linseed.

❼ **Snack** on fresh or dried fruits, carrot or celery sticks, popcorn, nuts or seeds, wholegrain crackers, high-fiber bars (low-fat). Limit amounts if overweight.

❽ **Exercise regularly** to strengthen abdominal muscles and stimulate the gut. Keep up water intake, especially in warm weather.

❾ **Avoid** indiscriminate and regular use of harsh laxatives. They can overstimulate the intestinal muscles and may make normal bowel activity impossible. It may take several weeks to restore normal bowel function.

FOODS WITH ZERO FIBER

- **Dairy Products (Milk, Cheese, etc)**
- **Meats, Poultry, Fish, Eggs**
- **Fats/Oils, Sugar/Syrups**

(Only foods of plant origin contain fiber.)

Fiber ~ Fiber (grams)

Breakfast Cereals

	Fiber
General Mills:	
Basic 4, 1 cup, 2 oz	3
Cheerios (Honey Nut; Multigrain), 1 c., 1 oz	2
Fiber One, ½ cup, 1.1 oz	14
Multi-Bran Chex, 1 cup, 2 oz	7
Oatmeal Crisp Almond, 1 cup, 2 oz	4
Raisin Nut Bran, 1¼ cup, 2 oz	6
Total, average all types, ¾ cup, 1 oz	3
Wheat Chex, 1 cup, 2 oz	6
Wheaties ¾ cup, 1 oz	3
Health Valley:	
Amaranth Flakes, ¾ cup, 1 oz	3
Crunches & Flakes, ¾ cup, 1.9 oz	4
Fiber 7 Flakes, ¾ cup, 1 oz	7
Golden Flax, ¾ cup, 1.9 oz	6
Granola (Low-Fat), ⅔ cup, 2 oz	6
Healthy Fiber Flakes, ¾ cup, 1.1 oz	4
Oat Bran Flakes, all types, ¾ cup, 1 oz	2
Oat Bran O's, ¾ cup, 1 oz	3
Real Oat Bran, ½ cup, 1.7 oz	5
Kellogg's:	
All-Bran, ½ cup, 1.1 oz	10
All-Bran w. Extra Fiber, ½ cup, 1 oz	13
All-Bran Bran Buds, ⅓ cup, 1.1 oz	13
Corn Flakes, Fruit Loops, Smacks 1 cup, 1 oz	1
Cocoa/Rice Krispies Treats, 1¼ cup, 1 oz	0
Complete: Wheat Flakes, ¾ c., 1 oz	5
Oat Bran Flakes, ¾ cup, 1.1 oz	4
Corn Pops, 1 cup, 1.1 oz	0
Cracklin' Oat Bran, ¾ cup, 1.7oz	6
FiberPlus Antioxidants:	
Berry Yogurt Crunch, 1 c., 1.9 oz	10
Cinnamon Oat Crunch ¾ c., 1.1 oz	9
Frosted Mini Wheats, 24 bisc., 2 oz	5
Granola w. Raisins, ⅔ cup, 2.1 oz	3
Raisin Bran, 1 cup, 2.1 oz	7
Smart Start, Strong Heart, Cinnamon Raisin, 1 cup, 1.8 oz	4
Special K, 1 cup, 1.1 oz	0.5

Breakfast Cereals (Cont)

	Fiber
Kashi:	
GoLEAN Cereal, 1 cup, 1.8 oz	10
GoLEAN Crunch!, 1 cup, 1.9 oz	8
GoLEAN Bars, avg. (1)	6
Good Friends: Original, 1 cup, 1.9 oz	12
Cinna-Raisin Crunch, 1 cup, 1.8 oz	8
Heart to Heart, ¾ cup, 1.2 oz	5
7 Whole Grain Pilaf, ½ cup, cooked, 5 oz	7
7 Whole Grain Puffs, 1 cup, 0.7 oz	1
Quaker:	
Cap'n Crunch, ¾ cup, 1 oz	1
100% Natural Granola, avg., ½ cup, 1.8 oz	3
Crunchy Corn Bran, 1 cup, 1 oz	5
Life Cereal, ¾ cup, 1.1 oz	2
Oat Bran, ½ cup, 1.4 oz	6
Oatmeal, average, 1 packet	3
Post:	
100% Bran, ⅓ cup, 1 oz	9
Alpha Bits, 1 cup, 1 oz	2
Blueberry Morning, 1 cup, 1.9 oz	5
Cranberry Almond Crunch, 1 cup, 1.8 oz	3
Fruit & Bran, 1 cup, 1.9 oz	6
Grape-Nuts, ½ cup, 2 oz	7
Great Grains, ⅔ cup, 1.9 oz	5
Honey Bunches of Oats, ¾ cup, 1.1 oz	2
Shredded Wheat & Bran, ½ cup, 2 oz	8

Brans & Supplements, Metamucil

	Fiber
Oat Bran: 1 Tbsp (level)	1
⅓ cup, (5⅓ Tbsp), 1 oz	5
Rice Bran, raw. ¼ cup, 1 oz	6
Wheat Bran, Unprocessed:	
Raw, 1 Tbsp	1.5
2 Tbsp (level), ¼ oz	3
¼ cup, (4 Tbsp), ½ oz	6
Wheat Germ, Raw, ¼ cup, 1 oz	4
Psyllium Seed Husks, 2 Tbsp	8
Fibersure, 1 heaping tsp	5
Metamucil: Orange, 1 rnd Tbsp, 11g	3
Fiber Wafers (2)	6

Hot Cereals, Oatmeal

	Fiber
Bulgur (cracked Wheat), ckd, 1 cup	8
Corn/Hominy Grits, dry, 3 Tbsp, 1 oz	0.5
Cream of Wheat, cooked, ¾ cup	1
Oatmeal (uncooked ⅓ cup), ckd, ⅔ cup	3

Fiber Counter

Breads & Crackers

	Fiber
Bread: White, 1 slice, 1 oz	0.6
Whole-wheat, 1 slice, 1 oz	1.5
Wholegrain, 1 slice, 1 oz	2
Rye, Pumpernickel, 1 oz	1.5
Bagel/Roll/Bun, 1 medium, 2 oz	1.5
Pita, whole wheat, 6½" pocket	4.5
Crackers: Graham, average, 2	0.4
Saltine, 4 crackers	0.4
Crispbreads, average, 2	4
Matzo, 1 board, 1 oz	1
Rice Cakes, average, 1 cake	0.3
Tortilla: Regular, 6"	0.5
Whole-wheat, 6"	1.3

Barley, Pasta, Rice & Flours

	Fiber
Barley, pearled, raw, ¼ cup, 1.7 oz	8
Rice:	
White, cooked, 1 cup	0.6
Brown, cooked, 1 cup	3.5
Rice-A-Roni, average, 1 cup, prepared	1.5
Spaghetti/Noodles: Cooked, 1 cup	2
Whole-Wheat, cooked, 1 cup	4
Flour: Wheat, All-purpose, 1 cup, 4½ oz	3.5
Whole-wheat, 1 cup, 4½ oz	15
Cornmeal, stone ground, 1 cup, 4½ oz	13
Carob Flour, 1 cup, 4½ oz	41
Rye Flour, 1 cup, 3½ oz	15
Soy Flour: Defatted, 1 cup, 3½ oz	17
Full-fat, raw, 1 cup, 3 oz	8
Soy Meal, defatted, 1 cup, 4½ oz	14

Frozen Entrees & Dinners

Average All Brands: Per Serving

	Fiber
Beans/Chili base, average	6-10
Potato/Pasta base, average	4-6
Vegetable base, average	3
Meat/Chicken base, average	2-3
Pizzas, ¼ large, average	3
Vegetarian Soy Burgers, 1 pattie	4

Soups

	Fiber
Chicken Noodle, 1 cup	0.5
Tomato Soup, average, 1 cup	0.5
Vegetable Soup, average, 1 cup	3
Health Valley: *Per 1 Cup*	
Black Bean; Minestrone	8
Tomato	
5 Bean Vegetable; Lentil & Carrots	10
Mushroom Barley; Vegetable	4
Split Pea	
Progresso, High Fiber, all flavors, 1 cup	7

Fast Foods & Restaurants

	Fiber
Hamburgers: Small, average	1.5
Large/Whopper, average	2.5
Hot Dog, Regular	1.5
French Fries: Small serving, 2½ oz	2.5
Regular/Medium, 3½ oz	3.5
Chicken Nuggets, 6 pack	0.5
Chicken Sandwich, average	2
Taco, average	4
Sundaes, Shakes, Soft Drinks	0
Arby's, Classic Roast Beef Sandwich	1
Denny's: Grilled Chicken Salad, no bread	4
Classic Burger, no fries	4
Club Sandwich, no fries	2
Grilled Chicken Sandwich, no fries	4
Domino's: 12", Classic/Thin, 1 slice	1
Deep Dish, 1 slice	3
Feast Pizza, Classic/Thin, 1 slice	3
McDonald's: Big Mac	3
Hamburger; Quarter Pounder	3
Egg McMuffin	2
Grilled Chicken Caesar Salad	4
Pizza Hut: *Per 1 Slice, Medium*	
Pan Pizza: Cheese, Pepperoni	1
Supreme	2
Thin 'n Crispy, Supreme	2
Hand-Tossed, average all varieties	2
Subway: Sandwich, white roll, av.	4
With Honey Wheat Roll, average	3
Salads, average	4

Cakes, Cookies, Snack Bars

	Fiber
Apple/Fruit Pie, 1 serving, 4 oz	2
Cake: With plain flour, 1 serving, 3.4 oz	1.5
With whole-wheat flour, 1 serving	3
Carrot Cake, 4 oz	4
Cookies, oatmeal, (3 small/1 large)	1
Donuts, medium, 1.7 oz	0.7
Fruit Cake, 1 serving, 1½ oz	2
Fig Bars, 1 cookie, ½ oz	0.7
Muffins, Oat Bran (2 small, 1 large), 4 oz	5
Granola Bars, average, 1 bar	2
Atkins Advantage Bars, average	7
Clif Bars, 2.5 oz	5
Curves, Chocolate Peanut Bar, 25g	5
Fi-Bar Chewy & Nuttly, 1 bar	1
Fiber One (Gen. Mills), 1.4 oz bar	9
FiberPlus, all bars, 1.2 oz	9
Health Valley: Fruit/Granola Bars	3
Cereal Bars	1
Luna Bars, avg., 1.7 oz	3
Special K, Protein Meal Bar, 1.6 oz	5

Chocolate, Chips, Popcorn

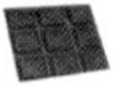

	Fiber
Cheese Balls/Curls/Twists	1
Chocolate, Hard Candy, 1 oz	0
Chocolate with nuts/fruit, 2 oz bar	1.5
Mars Bar, 1.8 oz	1
Potato Chips; corn chips, 1 oz	1
Popcorn, 3 cups	3
Pretzels, Twists (6)	1

Nuts, Seeds

Almonds: Natural, 25 nuts, 1 oz	3.5
Blanched (skins removed), 1 oz	3
Cashews, Filberts, Pecans, 1 oz	1.7
Peanuts, Mixed Nuts, Coconut, 1 oz	2.5
Peanut Butter, 2 Tbsp, 1 oz	2
Pistachio Nuts, dried, shelled, 1 oz	3
Walnuts, Black/English, dried, 1 oz	2
Seeds: Amaranth, 2½ Tbsp, 1 oz	3.5
Flax Seeds, 3 Tbsp, 1 oz	7
Psyllium Seed Husks, 5 Tbsp, 1 oz	20
Quinoa Seeds, 3 Tbsp, 1 oz	1.7
Sesame Seeds, whole, 1 oz	3.4
Sesame Butter/Tahini, 2 Tbsp, 1.1 oz	1.4
Sunflower kernels, ¼ cup, 1 oz	3.8
Teff Seeds, 1 oz	3.8

Fruit – Fresh

Apples: 1 medium, 5½ oz (whole)	
with skin + core	3.7
with skin, no core	3.2
without skin, no core	1.7
Apricots, 2 medium, 4 oz	1.5
Avocado, average, ½ medium	6
Banana, 1 medium, 6 oz (w. skin)	3
Blueberries, raw, ½ cup, 2½ oz	1.7
Cherries, sweet, raw, 8 fruits, 1.6 oz	1
Grapefruit, average, ½ fruit, 10 oz	1.4
Grapes, 1 medium bunch, seedless, 7 oz	2
Kiwifruit, 1 medium, 2.7 oz	2.3
Mango, 1 medium, 11 oz (whole)	1.6
Melons, Cantaloupe, 4 oz (edible)	1
Nectarine, 1 medium, 4 oz	1.9
Olives, average all types, 7 jumbo, 2 oz	1.5
Oranges, 1 medium (7-8 oz w. skin)	
5½ oz (peeled)	3.8
Passionfruit, 2 medium, 2½ oz	2
Peaches, 1 large, 6 oz	2
Pears, raw, 1 medium, 6 oz	4.5
Pineapple, 1 slice, 3 oz	1.2
Plums, 2 medium, 6 oz	1.8
Strawberries, 6 medium/3 large, 2 oz	1
Watermelon, 4 oz (edible)	0.5

Fruit – Dried, Juice

	Fiber
Dried Fruit: Apricots, 8 halves, 1 oz	2.2
Dates (3 med); Raisins (2 Tbsp), 1 oz	1.5
Figs, 3 medium, 1½ oz	5
Prunes, 4 medium, 1 oz	2
Fruit Juice: Orange/Apple etc, 1 glass	<0.5
Prune Juice, 5 oz	1.4
Carrot Juice, 8 oz	1.8

Vegetables

Asparagus, 4 medium spears	1.3
Bean Sprouts, ½ cup, 2 oz	1
Beans: Snap/Green, ½ cup, 2 oz	2
Baked Beans in Tom Sce, ½ c, 4½ oz	5
Dried Beans, ckd, average, ½ cup	7
Beets, ckd, slices, ½ cup, 3 oz	1.7
Broccoli, cooked, ½ cup, 3 oz	2.4
Brussels Sprouts, ckd, ½ cup, 3 oz	3.5
Cabbage: White, ckd, ½ cup, 2.5 oz	1
Red, ckd, ½ cup, 2.5 oz	2
Carrots, 1 medium (7½"), ½ cup, 3 oz	2.5
Cauliflower, cooked, 3 flowerets, 2 oz	1.5
Celery, raw, diced, 1 cup, 3½ oz	1.6
Chickpeas (Garbanzos), ckd, ½ c., 3 oz	6.5
Corn: Kernels, cooked, ½ cup, 2½ oz	2
Corn on the Cob, 1 ear, 5 oz	4
Cucumber/Lettuce/Mushrooms, 2 oz	0.5
Eggplant, raw, sliced, ½ cup, 1½ oz	1
Lentils, cooked, ½ cup, 3.5 oz	8
Mixed Vegetables, frozen, cooked, ½ cup	3
Onions: Raw, 1 medium, 4 oz	1.5
Spring Onions, chop., ¼ cup, 1 oz	0.7
Peas: Green, raw, ½ cup, 2.5 oz	3.7
Cowpeas (Black-eyed), ckd, ½ cup	10
Split Peas, cooked, ½ cup, 3.5 oz	8
Peppers, sweet, raw, 1 large, 6 oz	3
Potatoes: 1 medium, with skin, 5 oz	4
1 medium, without skin	2.5
½ cup mashed, 3.5 oz	1.5
French Fries, small, 2.6 oz	3
Spinach, cooked, ½ cup, 3 oz	2.2
Squash: Summer, cooked, ½ cup, 3 oz	1.5
Winter, cooked, ½ cup, 3.5 oz	2.4
Tomatoes: 1 medium, 4.5 oz	1.5
Tomato Sauce, 1 cup	0.3
Soybean Products: Miso, ½ c., 5 oz	7.4
Tempeh, cooked, 1 piece, 3 oz	2
Tofu, ½ cup, 4.4 oz	0.4

Salads:

Side Salad, average	1
Bean Salad, ½ cup	5
Coleslaw, ½ cup	1
Potato Salad, ½ cup	2

Protein Guide

General Notes

- **Protein has many important body functions.** It builds and repairs muscle, and is the basis of our body's organs, hormones, enzymes, and antibodies to fight infection.

- **Protein is also an emergency fuel** in the absence of sufficient carbohydrate and fats. For this reason, weight loss should be gradual so as to preserve protein levels in muscle, the heart and other body organs.

- **It is easy to obtain sufficient protein,** even if vegetarian. **Plant proteins are not inferior to animal proteins.** In fact, eating more soy and other plant proteins, and less animal protein, may help to build stronger bones and prevent osteoporosis, and may help to control blood cholesterol levels.

- **When changing to a vegetarian diet,** include soybeans, and other beans, soy milk drinks (calcium-enriched), lentils, tofu, tempeh, nuts and wholegrain breads and cereals. Milk, yogurt, cheese and eggs can enhance nutrient intake.

Elderly people (and dieters) must eat sufficient food to ensure adequate protein intake.

Inadequate protein leads to a drop in immune response with greater susceptibility to illness and infections. Muscle strength and muscle mass also drop.

Protein needs are easily met with sensible eating. Athletes who eat enough food for their energy needs can obtain sufficient protein.

Protein & Muscle

- Although muscles are built of protein, protein is not a special fuel for working muscle cells – carbohydrates and fats are.

- In fact, a diet high in protein (and fat) and low in carbohydrate can significantly reduce the performance of endurance sports athletes. **Carbohydrates** are the best fuel for muscles exercised for long periods.

- Any **extra protein** required by athletes and body-builders can easily be obtained from the extra food eaten to satisfy hunger and energy needs.

- Remember, **excessive protein** intake will not build bigger muscles. Any excess is converted and stored as fat. Excess protein can also strain the kidneys, which excrete the waste products of protein metabolism.

RECOMMENDED DAILY PROTEIN INTAKE
~ HEALTHY RANGE ~
(Lower figure is RDA)

		PROTEIN
Children:	1-3 yrs	13g-26g
	4-8 yrs	19g-38g
	9-13 yrs	34g-64g
Males:	14-18 yrs	52g-120g
	19+	56g-120g
Females:	14+	46g-110g
Pregnancy:		71g-120g
Breastfeeding:		71g-120g

Note: On lower-calorie diets, aim for higher amounts of protein within the Healthy Range.

Pro ~ Protein (grams)

Meat

	Pro
Steak: Average all cuts, lean (no fat)	
Small (4 oz raw/3 oz cooked)	23
Medium (6 oz raw/4¼ oz cooked)	34
Large (10 oz raw/7¼ oz cooked)	57
Roast Beef, lean, 2 slices, 3 oz	24
Ground Beef patty, lean, cooked, 3 oz	21
Lamb chop, broiled, 3 oz	22
Liver, cooked, 3 oz	23
Veal cutlet, 1 medium	23
Pork, cooked, lean, 3 oz	24
Bacon, 3 medium slices	6
Ham, roasted, 2 pieces, 3 oz	18
Ham, luncheon, 2 slices, 1½ oz	7
Pastrami, 3 sl., 1¾ oz	10
Sausages: Bologna, 2 sl., 2 oz	7
Braunschweiger, 2 sl., 2 oz	8
Pork link, thick, 2 oz	6
Frankfurter, 1⅓ oz	5
Salami, hard, 3 slices, 1 oz	7
Vegetarian, 1 pattie	13
Chicken/Turkey: *Without Skin*	
Chicken, cooked: Breast, Roasted, 4 oz	36
Leg/Thigh,Roasted, 2 oz	14
½ Whole Chicken	60
Drumstick, Rstd, 1 med., 3 oz	13
Turkey: Light meat, cooked, 3 oz	28
Dark meat, lean, 3 oz	24

Fish

Fresh Fish: *Per 4 oz, cooked*	
Cod, Flounder/Sole, Pollock	28
Catfish, Haddock, Halibut, M/Mahi	28
Ocean Perch, Swordf., Orange Roughy	28
Canned Fish: Tuna, Light, 3 oz	25
White, 3 oz	23
Salmon, pink, 3 oz	17
Salmon, red, 3 oz	17
Sardines, 3 whole (3"), 1¼ oz	9
Anchovies, 1 can, 1½ oz	13
Shellfish: Crabmeat, 3 oz	17.5
Clams, raw, 4 large/9 sml, 3 oz	11
Crayfish, cooked, 3 oz	20
Lobster, cooked, 3 oz	17
Oysters, raw, 6 medium, 3 oz	7
Scallops, 2 lge/5 small, 1 oz	5
Shrimp, raw, 6 large, 1½ oz	8.5
Fish Products: Fish Sticks, 4 sticks	10
Fish Portions, in batter, 4 oz	13
Gefilte Fish, 1 medium ball, 2 oz	8

Eggs

	Pro
1 Large Egg, whole	6
Egg Yolk	3
Egg White	3
Omelet: Plain, 2 eggs	13
Ham & cheese	17
Egg Substitutes, (liquid):	
Egg Beaters, ¼ cup, 2 oz	4.5
Better 'n Eggs/Scramblers, ¼ cup, 2 oz	6

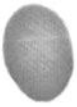

Milk, Yogurt, Ice Cream

Milk: Whole: 2%, 1 cup	8
Low-Fat (1%), Fat-Free, 1 cup	8.5
Chocolate Milk, 1 cup	8
Thick Shake: Chocolate, 10 oz	9
Vanilla, 10 oz	11
Soymilk, (fortified), average, 1 cup	7
Soy Dream, Enriched, shelf-stable, 1 cup	7
Yogurt, average all brands:	
Plain, 6 oz	8
Fruit flavors, 6 oz	7
Chobani, Greek, Plain, 6 oz	14
Soy, fruit flavors, 6 oz	7
Ice Cream: Rich, ½ cup	2
Regular, Vanilla, ½ cup	2.5
Sherbet, ½ cup	1
Custard, baked, ½ cup	7

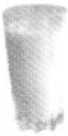

Cheese

Hard Cheeses, average, 1 oz	7
Cottage Cheese, ½ cup	13
Cream Cheese, avg., 1 oz	2
Ricotta, part skim, ½ cup	14

Bread, Bagels, Biscuits

Bread: *With enriched flour*	
1 slice, 1 oz	2
4 thin slices, 4 oz	8
4 thick slices, 6 oz	1.2
Bagel, plain 2 oz	6
Biscuits, 1 oz	2
Pita Bread, 1 pita, 1½ oz	4
Pumpernickel, 1 slice, 1 oz	3

Infant/Baby Foods

	Pro
Infant Formula Milk:	
Enfamil/Gerber/Similac,	
Regular/Low Iron , 5 fl.oz	2.2
Isomil/Nursoy/ProSobee,	3
Baby Cereals: *Average all brands*	
Dry, 4 Tbsp, ½ oz	1
Jars, with fruit, 4½ oz	1

Protein Counter

Breakfast Cereals

	Pro
Hot Cereals ~ *Cooked:*	
Bulgur, cooked, 1 cup, 5 oz	9
Oatmeal: Reg., non-fortified, 1 cup	6
Instant, fortified, avg., 1 pkt	4
Quaker, all flavors, ½ cup	5
Corn/Hominy Grits: 1 cup	3
Quaker: Reg., 3 Tbsp, 1 oz	2
Instant White, 1 packet	2
Cream of Wheat, 1 cup	4
Brands ~ *Ready-To-Eat*	
General Mills:	
Cheerios, Original, 1 cup, 1 oz	3
Kix, Original, 1¼ cups, 1 oz	2
Multi-Bran Chex, ¾ cup, 1.65 oz	4
Lucky Charms, Original, ¾ cup, 1 oz	2
Total Raisin Bran, 1 cup, 1.8 oz	3
Wheaties ¾ cup, 1 oz	2
Health Valley:	
Oat Bran Flakes, 1 cup, 1.75 oz	5
Amaranth Flakes, 1¼ cups, 2 oz	6
Bran Flakes, with Raisins, 1 cup, 1.8 oz	5
Corn Crunch-Ems, 1 cup, 1 oz	2
Rice Crunch-Ems, 1¼ cups, 1 oz	2
Kashi:	
Good Friends, 1 cup, 1.9 oz	5
GoLean Crunch!, 1 cup, 1.9 oz	9
7 Whole Grain Flakes, 1 c., 1.75 oz	6
Kellogg's:	
All-Bran, ½ cup, 1 oz	4
Apple Jacks, 1 cup, 1 oz	1
Corn Flakes, 1 cup, 1 oz	2
Low-fat Granola	
with Raisins ⅔ cup, 2.1 oz	5
Product 19, 1 cup, 1 oz	2
Raisin Bran, Original, 1 cup, 2 oz	5
Rice Krispies, 1¼ cup, 1.2 oz	2
Smart-Start Strong Heart, 1 c., 1.75 oz	4
Special K: Regular, 1 c., 1.1 oz	6
Protein, ¾ cup, 1.1 oz	10
Post:	
Raisin Bran, 1 cup, 2 oz	5
Grape Nuts, Original, ½ cup, 2 oz	8
Quaker:	
Corn Bran Crunch, ¾ cup, 1 oz	2
Honey Graham Oh's, ¾ cup, 1 oz	1
Life, ¾ cup, 1.1 oz	3
Natural Granola, ½ cup, 1.7 oz	5

Brans & Wheatgerm

	Pro
Oat Bran, raw, 1 Tbsp	2
Rice Bran, raw, 2 Tbsp	1
Wheat Bran, unprocessed, 2 T.	1
Wheat Germ, 2 Tbsp, ½ oz	4

Grains & Flours, Yeast

Amaranth, ½ cup, 3.4 oz	14
Barley, ½ cup, 3.2 oz	12
Buckwheat Flour, Whole-groat, 1 cup	15
Carob Flour, 1 cup, 3.6 oz	5
Corn Flour, 1 cup, 4 oz	11
Corn Meal, 1 cup, 4½ oz	8
Flour: White, 1 cup, 5.6 oz	9
Wholegrain, 1 cup, 4¼ oz	16
Millet, wholegrain, 1 cup, 3½ oz	12
Rye Flour: Dark, 1 cup, 4½ oz	18
Light, 1 cup, 3½ oz	9
Soy Flour, full fat, 1 cup, 3 oz	29
Yeast: Brewers, 2 Tbsp, ½ oz	8
Nutritional Yeast Flakes *(Red Star)*,	
1 heaping Tbsp, ½ oz	8

Rice, Spaghetti, Macaroni

Rice: Brown/White, average	
1 cup cooked, 6½ oz	5
Spaghetti/Macaroni/Noodles (enriched):	
Cooked, 1 cup, 4½ oz	7
Canned: in Tomato Sce, ½ cup	2
with Meatballs, 1 cup, 8 oz	10
Macaroni & Cheese, 1 cup, 9 oz	8

Soups

With Noodles/Vegetables, 1 cup	3
With Meat/Beans/Peas, 1 cup	8

Fruit

Fresh/Canned:	
Average, all types,	
1 medium/2 small fruit	1
Avocado, ½ medium	2
Dried Fruit: Apricots, 8 halves, 1 oz	1
Dates, 6 dates, 2 oz	1.5
Figs, 4 medium figs, 2 oz	2
Prunes, 5 medium, 1½ oz	1
Raisins, 1 oz	1
Fruit Juice: Average, 1 cup	0.5
Prune Juice, 6 fl.oz	1
Tomato Juice, 1 cup, 8 fl.oz	1.5

Protein Counter

Vegetables | Pro

Beans: Snap/green, ½ cup, 2 oz — 1
Dried: Average all types, cooked, ½ cup — 7
Baked Beans, ½ cup 4½ oz — 5
Bean Sprouts, mung, 1 c., 4 oz — 3
Broccoli, 3raw, ½ cup, 1½ oz — 1.5
Cabbage; Cauliflower, raw, 1 c. 3 oz — 1.5
Corn: Raw, ½ cup kernels, 3 oz — 2.5
1 ear trimmed to 3½" — 2
Lentils, cooked, ½ cup, 3½ oz — 9
Mushrooms, raw, ½ c., sliced — 1
Peas: Green, raw, ½ c., 2½ oz — 4
Split Peas, cooked, 1 cup, 7 oz — 16
Potatoes: Cooked:
1 medium, with skin, 5 oz — 3.3
without skin, 4 oz — 2.3
French Fries, small, 2.6 oz — 2
Potato Salad, ½ cup, 4 oz — 3.5
Pumpkin, ½ cup mashed, 4.3 oz — 1
Seaweed, kelp, 1 oz — <1
Spinach, cooked, ½ cup, 3 oz — 2.7
Squash, ckd, all types, ½ cup — 1
Tomatoes, 1 medium, 4½ oz — 1
Vegetables, mixed, ckd, 1 cup — 2.5
Soybeans, cooked, ½ cup, 3 oz — 14

Tofu, Tempeh, Miso

Tofu, raw, firm, ½ cup, 4½ oz — 10
Tempeh, ½ cup, 3 oz — 16
Miso, ½ cup, 5 oz — 16
Miso Soup, 1 cup — 3
Soybean Protein (TVP), 1 oz — 18

Cakes, Pastries, Pies

(Made with enriched flour)
Carrot w. cream cheese frosting, 4 oz — 4
Cheesecake, 1 piece, 4 oz — 6
Chocolate, 1 piece, 2 oz — 2
Fruitcake, 1 piece, 3 oz — 4
Plain, 1 piece, 3 oz — 4
Croissant, plain, 2 oz — 5
Danish Pastry, 1 pastry, 2¼ oz — 4
Donuts, average, 2 oz — 4
Muffins, average, 1 med., 1½ oz — 3
Pancakes, 4" diam., two, 2 oz — 4
Pies: Fruit, 1 piece, 5½ oz — 4
Pecan, 1 piece, 5 oz — 7
Puddings, average, ½ cup, 4½ oz — 4
Waffles, 1 large, 2½ oz — 7

Peanut Butter | Pro

Regular: 2 Tbsp, 1.1 oz — 8
Peter Pan Plus, 2 Tbsp, 1.1 oz — 8

Sugar, Honey, Jam

Sugar: White — 0
Brown, 1 Tbsp — 0
Molasses: Light/Med., 1 Tbsp — 0
Blackstrap, 1 Tbsp, ¾ oz — 0
Corn Syrup, 1 Tbsp, ¾ oz — 0
Honey, Jams, Jelly — 0

Candy, Chocolate, Carob

Candy, sugar-based — 0
Chocolate: Plain, 2 oz bar — 4
with nuts, 2 oz bar — 6
Carob, plain, 2 oz — 6

Cookies, Crackers, Chips

Cookies, average, 4 cookies — 2
Crackers, Graham, 2½" sq., (2) — 1
Rice Cakes, average, one — 1
Corn/Potato Chips, 1 oz — 2

Nuts:

Almonds, shelled, 20-25 nuts — 6
Brazil Nuts, 7-8 medium nuts, 1 oz — 4
Cashews, 12-16 nuts, 1 oz — 5
Macadamias, 1 oz — 2
Peanuts, dry rsted, 40 nuts, 1 oz — 6
Pecans, 24 halves, 1 oz — 2
Walnuts, 15 halves, 1 oz — 4

Seeds:

Sesame Seeds, dry, 1 Tbsp — 2
Pumpkin Kernels, dry, hulled, 1 oz — 7
Sunflower Seeds, dried, hulled, 1 oz — 6
Tahini, 1 Tbsp, ½ oz — 2.5

Granola & Food/Protein Bars

Granola Bars, avg., 1 bar, 2 oz — 2
Anytime Health,
Meal Repl. Bars, 80g — 20
Snack Bars, 50g — 12
Balance Bars, Orig. 1.76 oz — 14
Bariatrix, Proti-Bars (1), 1.4 oz — 15
Dr Soy, Protein Bars, 1.76 oz — 11
GeniSoy, Protein Bars, 1.6 oz — 15
Jenny Craig, Bars, 1.8 oz — 4
Met-Rx, "Big 100", 3.5 oz — 27
Myoplex, Carb Sense Bar, 2.5 oz — 26
Optifast, Peanut Butter, 1.59 oz — 8
PowerBar: Harvest/Performance — 10
Slim-Fast, High Protein Meal, 1.7 oz — 15
Optima Meal, 2 oz bar — 8
Special K: Protein Meal, 1.6 oz — 10
Protein Snack, 0.9 oz — 4

Protein Counter

High Protein Drinks   **Pro**

Anytime, Health,
  Whey Prot. Isolate, all flav., 1 oz   25
Atkins, Shakes, 11 fl.oz can   18
Boost, High Protein, 8 fl.oz bottle   15
Carnation, B'fast Essentials, 11 fl.oz   14
Curves, Protein Drink, 2 scoops, dry   15
dotFIT, First String,
  Choc., 2 scps, 2.65 oz   21
Whey Smooth, Van., 2 scps, 2.2 oz   40
Ensure, Plus, 8 fl.oz bottle   13
Gatorade: Nutrition Shake, 11 oz   20
  Protein Recovery Shake, 11 oz   20
GeniSoy, Shake, 1 scoop, 1.2 oz   14
Met-Rx, Meal Replacement, RTD   40
Myoplex, Original Nutrition Shake, 1 pkt   42
Optifast 800, made up, 8 fl oz   14
Resource (Novartis), Standard, 8 fl.oz   15
Slim-Fast Shakes: Meal, 11 oz can   10
  High Protein, 10 fl.oz bottle   20
Special K₂O, Protein Water, 16 fl.oz   5
Weider, Mass 1000, 4 scoops, 7 oz   34

Coffee, Tea, Soda

Coffee, Coffee Substitutes, 1 cup, 8 fl.oz   0
Coffee, with 2 oz milk, 1 cup, 8 fl.oz   2
Caffe latte, large, 16 fl.oz   12
Cappuccino, large, 16 fl.oz   8
Frappuccino, average, 16 fl.oz   6
Hot Chocolate, with milk, 1 cup, 8 fl.oz   8
Soft Drinks/Soda   0
Tea, all types   0

Beer, Wine, Spirits

Beer, 12 fl.oz   1
Wines, red/white, 1 glass   0
Spirits/Liquor   0

Fast-Foods/Burgers

Pancakes, Average all outlets, 3   8
Shakes, Chocolate, 16 fl.oz   12
Sundaes, Average all outlets   7
Arby's:
  Chopped Farmhouse Salad, Crispy Chicken   30
  Roast Beef Sandwich: Classic   23
  Max   21
Burger King: Whopper Sandwich   25
  Double Bacon Cheeseburger   26
  Prem. Alaskan Fish Sandwich   18

Fast Foods/Burgers (Cont)   **Pro**

Carl's Jr:
  Famous Star Hamburger with Cheese   28
  Charbroiled Chicken Club Sandwich   36
  Super Star Hamburger with Cheese   48
Domino's Pizza: Hand Tossed (12")
  Feast, Ultimate Pepperoni, 1 slice   11
  Legend: Buffalo Chicken, 1 slice   13
  Honolulu Hawaiian, 1 slice   9
KFC: Original, Breast   36
  Extra Crispy Tenders, 3 strips   33
  Filet, Original   23
McDonald's: Big Mac   25
  Cheeseburger   15
  Chicken McNuggets (6)   13
  Crispy Chicken Classic Sandwich   24
  Filet-O-Fish   15
  Hamburger   12
  Quarter Pounder with Cheese   30
  French Fries: Small, 2.5 oz   3
    Large, 5.4 oz   6
  Salad, with Chicken, average   26
  Shake, McCafe, average, 12 fl.oz   12
  Breakfast: Egg McMuffin   18
    Bacon, Egg & Cheese McGriddles   19
    Sausage Burrito   12
    Sausage McMuffin with Egg   21
Pizza Hut: Per Medium, 1 slice, ⅛ Pizza
  Thin 'n Crispy, Supreme   10
  Pan Pizzas, average   11
  Hand Tossed: Pepperoni Lover's   12
    Ultimate Cheese Lover's   10
Subway: 6" Subs with standard toppings, no oil
  Applewood Pulled Pork   25
  Meatball Marinara   21
  Spicy Italian   20
  Subway Melt   23
  Turkey Jalapeno Melt   21
Taco Bell: Bean Burrito   15
  Cheesy Gordita Crunch   20
  Chicken Quesadilla   27
  Chicken/Steak Chalupas   16
  Steak Burrito Supreme   20
  Taco Supreme   9
Wendy's:
  Asiago Ranch Chicken Club   38
  Dave's ¼ lb Single Burger   30
  Jr Hamburger   14

High Blood Pressure

Many American adults have hypertension (high blood pressure), and are unaware of it. It is generally symptomless, so **have your blood pressure checked annually** – particularly if it runs in the family.

Untreated hypertension overworks the heart, damages arteries and promotes atherosclerosis. This in turn greatly increases the risk of heart disease, stroke, blindness, kidney disease and impotence. The earlier hypertension is detected, the sooner it can be brought under control.

BLOOD PRESSURE CLASSIFICATION

For Adults Age 18 & Older ~ Not Acutely ill or on Medication (American Heart Association)

	DIASTOLIC		SYSTOLIC
Normal ➤	Below 80	and	Below 120
Prehypertension ➤	80-89	or	120-139
Hypertension:			
Stage 1 ➤	90-99	or	140-159
Stage 2 ➤	100 or more	or	160 or more

Treating Hypertension

Prehypertension (in the chart above) means you don't have high blood pressure now but are likely to develop it in the future.

You can take steps to lessen the risk by adopting healthy lifestyle habits such as:
- reducing sodium intake
- eating adequate fruit and vegetables
- losing weight if overweight
- limiting alcohol to 2 drinks or less daily
- quitting smoking
- exercising regularly, managing stress.

Stage 1 hypertension can often be treated with the above lifestyle changes.

Stage 2 hypertension usually requires drug therapy. However, salt restriction, abstaining from alcohol, and the above lifestyle changes will improve the success of drug therapy, and enable smaller drug doses to be prescribed.

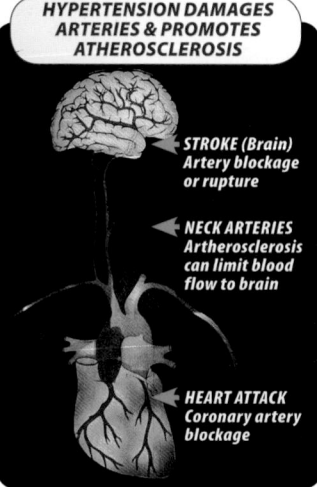

HYPERTENSION DAMAGES ARTERIES & PROMOTES ATHEROSCLEROSIS

STROKE (Brain) Artery blockage or rupture

NECK ARTERIES Artherosclerosis can limit blood flow to brain

HEART ATTACK Coronary artery blockage

STROKE KNOW THE WARNING SIGNS

Stroke is a medical emergency! If you notice one or more of these signs, call 9-1-1 or your doctor immediately.

These signs may be signalling a possible stroke or transient ischemic attack:

- **Sudden weakness** or numbness in your face, arm, or leg on one side of your body.
- **Sudden confusion,** trouble speaking or understanding. Slurred speech.
- **Sudden trouble seeing,** in one or both eyes
- **Sudden trouble walking,** dizziness, loss of balance or coordination.
- **Sudden severe headache** - 'a bolt out of the blue' – with no apparent cause.

Extra Info: www.stroke.org

Salt & Sodium Guide

Salt & Sodium

- **Sodium is a mineral element** most commonly found in salt (sodium chloride). It also occurs naturally in much smaller amounts in animal and plant foods, and water – normally sufficient for our needs without having to add salt to our diet.

- **Sodium is required** for nerve and muscle function, as well as to balance the amount of fluid in our tissues and blood. Sodium acts like a sponge to attract and hold fluids in body tissues.

- **Excess sodium** can cause water retention, and increase the risk of developing hyper-tension. Very high salt intake may also increase the risk of stomach cancer.

- **Too little sodium** may cause low blood pressure (hypotension), and decrease blood flow to the heart, brain and kidneys – especially during exercise. (A certain blood volume is required to sustain the blood pressure needed for adequate blood flow in the capillaries).

Salt-Sensitive Persons

- Normally, our kidneys excrete excess dietary sodium. The thirst we feel after a salty meal is the body calling for water to dilute the sodium, and enable the kidneys to flush out excess sodium.

- However, 'salt - sensitive' persons (up to 70% of adults) tend to retain excess sodium (above approximately 3000mg daily) instead of excreting it. Such persons are more likely to develop hypertension and would benefit most from sodium restriction. Assume you are susceptible if there is a family history of hypertension.

- Although not everyone will benefit, **all Americans are being asked to moderate their salt and sodium intake** as a public health measure – particularly because so many do not know whether or not they have hypertension, and also because we do not know just who is salt-sensitive.

The American Heart Association recommends a **maximum sodium intake of 1500mg per day** for adults with normal blood pressure.

Persons with hypertension and kidney ailments are usually restricted to as little as **1000mg sodium per day**. Your doctor will discuss the correct sodium level for you.

On average, **less than one third of our sodium intake comes from the salt shaker.**

The rest is hidden in processed foods that have salt added during manufacture.

Sodium compounds added to food or medicinals can also contribute significant sodium.

Sodium bicarbonate in particular is widely used in antacid tablets (such as *Alka Seltzer*) and powders. Sodium bicarbonate contains 27% sodium by weight. Each gram contributes 270mg sodium. Large amounts of sodium can be unwittingly consumed – up to 600mg per tablet. (See Antacids ~ Page 280)

Example: 2 *Alka-Seltzer* Tablets = 1000mg sodium

Other sodium compounds include monosodium glutamate (MSG), sodium ascorbate, sodium nitrite, and sodium citrate.

POTASSIUM BALANCES SODIUM

Potassium helps to balance sodium by helping the kidneys to excrete excess sodium.

Fruit and vegetables are rich sources of potassium – another reason to ensure you have your 5-7 servings every day.

Nuts also provide potassium as well as magnesium and other heart-healthy nutrients and anti-oxidants. Eat them unsalted.

Note: This info is only for people with normal kidney function. Also not for persons on potassium-sparing diuretics.

ALCOHOL DANGER

Excessive alcohol intake contributes to hypertension. Susceptible persons should limit alcohol intake to 1-2 drinks per day.

Salt Sodium Guide

Sodium accounts for only 40% of the weight of salt (sodium chloride). Examples:
1 gram (1000mg) Salt has 400mg Sodium
1 teaspoon (5g) Salt has 2000mg Sodium

HINTS TO REDUCE SODIUM

- **Cut down use of the salt shaker.** Start with an easy 50% cut in sodium by using Lite Salt (*Morton*) or *Cardia* Salt. Then gradually cut back until you can leave the salt shaker off the table. Sea salt is still high in sodium.

- **Use fresh herbs,** and salt-free seasonings to add flavor to food.

- **Choose low-sodium,** sodium-free, and reduced-sodium products in place of regular, salted products.

- **Check food labels for sodium levels.** FDA Guidelines for sodium descriptors are:
  - **Reduced Sodium:** At least 25% less sodium than the original product
  - **Low Sodium:** 140 mg or less/serving
  - **Very Low Sodium:** 35mg or less/serving
  - **Sodium Free:** Less than 5mg/serving
  - **No Salt Added:** Made without the salt normally added, but still contains the sodium that is a natural part of the food

- **Use reduced-sodium breads,** butter and margarine. Regular varieties are considered high in sodium in view of their significant contribution to our diet.

- **Go easy on salty condiments and sauces** such as ketchup, mustard, soy sauce, spaghetti sauces, and salad dressings. Use low-sodium varieties.

- **Limit pizzas and salty fast-foods.** Check the *CalorieKing.com* food database.

- **Avoid salty snack foods** such as potato chips, corn chips, salted nuts, pretzels and cheesy-flavored snacks. **Choose unsalted** popcorn, nuts or seeds. Eat more fruit.

- **Don't salt children's food** to your taste.

- **Avoid antacids with** sodium bicarbonate (such as *Alka-Seltzer*). They are high in sodium. Look for low-sodium alternatives.

- Cheese, Butter, Margarine
- Pickles, Sauerkraut, Olives
- Condiments, Sauces
- Salad Dressings
- Canned vegetables/salads/beans
- Deli Salads (with dressing)
- Frozen/Packaged Meals/Entrees
- Soups: Canned/dry; bouillon cubes
- Meats: Ham, bacon, sausage, luncheon meats, smoked meats
- Canned Fish (in brine/salt)
- Sea Salt, Garlic/Celery Salt
- Snack Foods (potato chips, pretzels)
- Tomato Juice (Canned), V8 Vegetable Juice
- Fast Foods: Pizza, Burgers, Chicken
- *Alka-Seltzer* Antacid
- Bread (regular)

MODERATE SODIUM

- Meat, Fish, Poultry - Unprocessed
- Milk, Yogurt, Soy Drinks, Eggs
- Peanut Butter
- Breakfast Cereals (less than 200mg/serving)
- Chocolate Candy, Fruit/Nut Bars
- *Reduced Sodium & Low Sodium* Products

FOODS LOW IN SODIUM

- Products labelled *Very Low Sodium*, or *Sodium Free*
- Bread (No Salt Added)
- Fresh fruits and vegetables
- Canned and Dried Fruits
- Potatoes, Rice, Pasta
- Dried Beans & Lentils, Tofu
- Nuts & Seeds (unsalted)
- Corn & Popcorn (unsalted)
- Pepper, Spices, Herbs
- Jam, Honey, Syrup
- Candy, Gum
- Hard & Jelly Candy
- Coffee, Tea, Alcohol
- Fresh Fruit Juices, Water

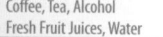

Sodium Counter

The American Heart Association recommends a sodium intake of less than 1500mg/day

Milk & Dairy Products

	Sodium
Milk: Whole/lowfat/skim, average	
1 glass, 8 fl.oz	120
Whole, low sodium, 1 cup	5
Choc Milk, 1 cup	130
Soy Milk, 8 fl.oz	30
Buttermilk, cultured, 8 fl.oz	250
Dry/Powder, skim, ¼ cup, 1 oz	110
Yogurt, with fruit average, 8 oz	130
Cheese: Bleu, 1 oz	330
Cottage Cheese, Creamed, ½ cup, 4 oz	450
Kraft: Cheddar Singles, 2% milk, 0.7 oz	290
Philadelphia Cream Cheese Brick, Orig.,1 oz	105
Parmesan, 1 oz	450
Process Cheese., average,1 oz	430
Ricotta Cheese, ½ cup, 4 oz	150
Swiss, Deli Style, 1 oz	60

Ice Cream, Frozen Yogurt

Icecream, average, ½ cup	50
Frozen Yogurt, ½ cup	50

Fats/Oils

Butter/Margarine:	
Regular, 2 Tbsp, 1 oz	230
Unsalted, reg., 2 Tbsp, 1 oz	5
Mayonnaise, avg., 2 Tbsp, 1 oz	160
Oils/Lard/Drippings	0
Cream, average, 1 Tbsp	5
Coffee-Mate: Powdered, 1 tsp	2
Liquid, 1 Tbsp	5

Eggs

Whole, 1 large	70
Omelet: 2 egg, plain	220
with cheese	400
Egg Beaters: Original, ¼ cup	115
Flavors, average, ¼ cup	230

Meats

Meat, average all types, cooked	
Beef/Lamb/Veal/Pork, 4 oz	80
Corned Beef, cooked, 3 oz	800
Bacon, cooked, 2 sl., ½ oz	270
Ham, 3 oz	1100

Chicken & Turkey

Chicken/Turkey, cooked, unsalted, 4 oz	80
Stuffing Mixes, average., ½ cup	500

Sodium ~ Sodium (mg)

Sausages & Meats

	Sodium
Bologna, 1 oz	280
Frankfurter, 2 oz	640
Ham, chopped, ¾ oz slice	290
Liverwurst (Braunschweiger), 1 oz	320
Pepperoni, 5 slices, 1 oz	570
Salami: Cooked, 1 oz	350
dry/hard, 1 oz	600
Sausage, 1 oz link	220
Pork, 2 oz patty	260
Spam: Classic, 2 oz	790
25% Less Sodium, 2 oz	580
Turkey Roll, 1 oz	160

Fish:

Fresh Fish: average, plain	
Cooked, 4 oz, without bone	60
Broiled w. butter, 4 oz	150
Breaded & fried, 4 oz	320
Fish fillets, batter-dipped 3 oz	350
Fish sticks, 1 oz stick	160
Gefilte Fish, with broth, 1 pce, 1½ oz	220
Herring, pickled, 2 pces, 1 oz	260
Lobster, meat only, 4 oz	180
Oysters, fresh, 6 med., 3 oz	95
Salmon: Canned, 3 oz	460
No Salt Added, 3 oz	65
Smoked fish, average, 3 oz	650
Tuna: Canned, drained, 3 oz	160
Light, drained, 3 oz	200
No Added Salt, 3 oz	40
Spicy Flavored, 5 oz can	260

Entrees & Meals

Frozen Meals, average	600-900
Lean Cuisine, average	700
Stouffer's, average	900-1200
Dinners, average	900-1200
Side Dishes, average	400-600
Pizza, frozen, ¼ large, 6 oz	800-1200
Microwave, Cup Meals	900-1200
Cup O'Noodles, average	1500

More Sodium Counts:
www.CalorieKing.com

Soups

	Sodium
Condensed: Average, 1 cup, 8 oz	800–1000
Low Sodium, average	70
Chicken Noodle, average, 1 cup	900
Bouillon Cube, average	950
Ramen Noodle Soup, av., 3 oz pkg	1500
Soup Cups, average	850
Soup Mixes, average, 1 cup	900

Condiments, Sauces, Dressings

	Sodium
A-1 Sauce, 1 Tbsp	280
Barbecue Sauce, 1 Tbsp	130
Bragg's Liquid Aminos, 1 tsp	220
Chili Sauce, 1 Tbsp	230
Ketchup: Tomato, 1 Tbsp	180
Low Sodium, 1 Tbsp	20
Mayonnaise, 1 Tbsp	80
Mustard, 1 tsp	70
Pizza Sauce, ½ cup	700
Salad Dressings, 2 Tbsp, 1 oz	160–400
Spaghetti Sauce, ½ cup	500
Soy Sauce: 1 Tbsp	900
Lite, 1 Tbsp	600
Sweet & Sour, ½ cup	250
Tabasco, 1 tsp	25
Vinegar, Lemon Juice	0
Worcestershire, 1 Tbsp	65
Tomato: Sauce, 1 cup	1200
Paste/Puree (salted), ½ cup	1000
No Salt Added, ½ cup	75

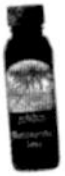

Salt & Salt Substitutes

	Sodium
Table Salt: 1 teaspoon, 6g	2400
Single Serve package, 1 g	400
Cardia Salt, 1 teaspoon	1080
Lite Salt, 1 teaspoon, 6g	1200
Morton, No Salt Substitute, 1 tsp	5
Garlic/Onion/Seasoned Salt, 1 tsp, 4g	1350
Garlic/Seasoned Salt, 1 teaspoon, 4g	1300
Sea Salt, 1 teaspoon, 5g	2250

Seasonings, Herbs & Spices

	Sodium
Baking Powder, 1 tsp, 3g	340
Baking Soda (Sodium bicarb), 1 tsp, 3g	810
Accent, Flavor Enhancer, 1 tsp	600
Chili Powder, 1 tsp, 3g	25
Curry Powder	0
Lemon Pepper 1 tsp	340
Meat Tenderizer, 1 tsp, 5g	1750
MSG (Monosodium Glutamate), 5g	500
Mrs Dash, Blends/Marinades	0
Old Bay, Seasoning (Less Sodium), 1 teaspoon, 2.4g	380
Pepper, Mustard (dry), 1 tsp	1
Yeast, Nutritional, 1 Tbsp	10

Breakfast Cereals

	Sodium
Kellogg's:	
All-Bran, Original, ½ cup, 1 oz	80
Special K, Original, 1 cup, 1.1 oz	220
Corn Flakes, 1 cup, 1 oz	200
Frosted Mini Wheats, Blueb./Strawb., (25)	0
Raisin Bran, 1 cup	210
Quaker:	
Corn Bran Crunch, ¾ cup, 1 oz	210
Natural Granola, average, ½ cup, 1 oz	30
Oh's, ¾ cup, 1 oz	170
Puffed Rice/Wheat, 2 cups, 1 oz	1
General Mills, Total, ¾ cup, 1 oz	140
Oatmeal: Regular, ¾ cup	1
Quaker, Instant, ⅔ cup (1 pkt)	260

Breads, Bagels, Crackers

	Sodium
Bread: Thin Slice, average 1 oz	140
Thick Slice, 1½ oz	210
Low Sodium, 1 oz	10
Bagels: Plain, medium, 2 oz	200
Large, take-out, average, 4 oz	550
Panera Bread, 3.75 oz	460
Biscuits, average, 1 oz	180
Bun/Roll: 1 medium, 1½ oz	200
Large, 4 oz	560
Crackers: Saltine, 2 crackers	70
Low Salt, 2	25
Graham, 2 regular	25
Croissant, Plain, average, 2 oz	280
Rice Cakes, average	25
Ritz Crackers, Low-Sodium, 1 oz	60
Ry-Krisp, Crispbread, Sesame, 2	90

Cookies, Cakes, Desserts

	Sodium
Cookies: Average, 2-3 cookies, 1 oz	100
Average, 1 cookie, 2½ oz	180
Baked Custard, ½ cup	100
Brownie, 1½ oz	130
Carrot Cake, 8 oz	650
Cheesecake, 7 oz	350
Cinnamon Sweet Roll, 2 oz	250
Danish, Apple/Fruit	250
Donut, average	150
Muffins: 1 medium, 2 oz	150
1 extra large, 4 oz	300
Pancakes, (4"), x 3	360
Fruit Pies, average, 7 oz	600
Pudding: Average, ½ cup	160
Jell-O (Mix), Instant, 0.9 oz	350
Waffles: Home-made, 7", 2½ oz	350
Frozen: Average, 1¼ oz	260
Aunt Jemima, av., 2.45 oz	336

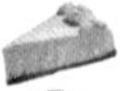

Sodium Counter

Fruit & Juices | Sodium
Fresh Fruit, average all types, 1 serving	1
Dried/Canned Fruit, ½ cup	1
Fruit Juice: Fresh, sqz'd, 6 fl.oz	1
Commercial, aver., 6 fl.oz	20
Tomato Juice *(Campbell's),* 6 fl.oz	570
Low Sodium (No Salt Added)	20
V8 Vegetable *(Campbell's):* 5.5 fl.oz can	290
12 fl.oz bottle	630
Low Sodium, 5.5 fl.oz can	95

Vegetables
Fresh/Frozen (No Salt Added): Per ½ Cup
Asparagus, Bean Sprouts, Corn	3
Beets, Carrots, Celery, ½ cup	40
Broccoli, Cabbage, Cauliflower	10
Cucumber, Green Beans, Mushroom, Okra	3
Onions, Peas, Potato, Pumpkin, Squash	3
Peppers, Hot Chili, raw, each	3
Spinach, Turnips, ½ cup, ckd	40
Tomato, 1 medium, 5 oz	10
Canned: Asparagus, 4 spears	300
Beans, baked in tomato sauce	450
Beets, ½ cup, 3 oz	240
Corn Kernels, ½ cup, 3 oz	190
Creamed, ½ cup, 4½ oz	330
Mushrooms w. butter sce, 2oz	550
Peas, ½ cup, 3 oz	250
Sauerkraut, ½ cup, 4 oz	750

Pickles, Olives
Olives: pickled: Green, 1 large	90
Ripe/black, 1 large	40
Pickles: Bread & Butter, 4 sl., 1 oz	200
Dill, 1 pickle, 2½ oz	900
Sweet, 1 gherkin, ½ oz	130

Soybean Products
Miso (Soy Paste), ¼ c., 2½ oz	2500
Soybean Protein Isolate, 1 oz	280
Tempeh, Natural, ½ cup, 3 oz	5
Tofu, average, ½ cup, 4 oz	5

Jam, Honey, Syrups
Jam/Jelly, 1 Tbsp	2
Honey/Maple Syrup, 1 Tbsp	1
Log Cabin, Syrup, 1 fl.oz	35
Lite, 1 fl.oz	90

Peanut Butter
Peanut Butter: Regular, 2 Tbsp, ½ oz	190
Jif, Low Sodium, 2 Tbsp	65
Trader Joe's, Unsalted, 2 Tbsp	5

Snacks, Nuts | Sodium
Cheese Balls/Curls, 1 oz	280
Cheetos, 1 oz	290
Corn/Tortilla Chips: average, 1 oz	220
Fritos, Lightly Salted, 1 oz	80
Granola bars, average, 1 bar	80
Nuts: Plain, unsalted, 1 oz	1
Lightly salted, 1 oz	80
Salted or Honey Roasted, 1 oz	160
Popcorn: Plain (unsalted), 1 cup	1
Flavored, average, 1 cup	60
Salt added, 1 cup	180
Potato Chips: Plain, 1 oz	160
Lay's, Lightly Salted, 1 oz	90
Flavored, average, 1 oz	250
Pretzels: Regular, 3, 1 oz	450
Soft, salted, large	1000

Candy, Chocolate
Chocolate, milk, 1 oz	30
Fudge, chocolate, 1 oz	55
Candy Bars, average, 1½ oz	60
Hard Candy, 1 oz	10
Licorice, 1 oz	30

Beverages, Alcohol
Coffee or Tea, 1 cup	1
Cocoa: Dry, plain, 1 Tbsp	0
Mix, average, 1 envelope	120
Quik, 2 tsp	35
Soft Drinks, average, 8 fl.oz	25
Mineral Water: Perrier, 8 fl.oz	5
Gatorade, Thirst Quencher, 8 fl.oz	110
Red Bull, 8½ fl.oz can	200
Water, Average, 1 cup, 8 fl.oz	5
Alcohol: Beer, average, 12 fl.oz	15
Wines, average, 4 fl.oz	10
Spirits (distilled), 1½ fl.oz	1

Antacids ~ Alka-Seltzer | Sodium
Alka-Seltzer: *Per Tablet*	
Original; Heartburn	570
Extra Strength	590
Lemon Lime	500
Gold	310
Alka-Mints, chewable	0
Bromo Seltzer, ¾ capful	760
Picot, 1 packet, 5g	670
Rolaids, All types	0
Tums, Regular/Extra Strength	0

Cold & Flu ~ Alka-Seltzer Plus
Effervescents, average, 1 tablet	480
Fast Crystal Packs; Liquid Gels	0

Sodium Counter

Fast-Foods & Restaurants	Sodium
Burger King:	
Burgers: Cheeseburger	690
Double Bacon Cheeseburger	940
Hamburger	460
Whoppers: Original	980
With Cheese	1380
Whopper Jr. with Cheese	730
Chicken Sandwich, Original	1390
Sides: French Fries, medium, salted	570
Onion Rings, medium	1080
Breakfast: Ham, Egg & Cheese Croissan'wich	1030
Denny's:	
Burgers: Bacon Avocado Cheeseburger	1830
Macho Nacho Burger	1980
Sandwiches: Club	1850
Prime Rib Philly Melt	2000
Dinner: Brooklyn Spaghetti & Meatballs	2460
Sirloin Steak with bread	1590
Sides: Broccoli	20
French Fries, salted, 6 oz	110
Red-Skinned Potatoes	627
Soup: Chicken Noodle, 12 oz bowl	1130
Clam Chowder, 12 oz bowl	1870
Breakfast: Buttermilk Pancakes (2)	1170
Moons Over My Hammy Omelette, w/ Hash	2530
Hearty Breakfast Skillet	2130
Sides: Hash Browns, 1 serving	650
Hearty Breakfast Sausage	830
Desserts: Apple Pie, 7 oz	580
Hot Fudge Brownie al la Mode, 9 oz	520
Jack In The Box:	
Burgers: Bacon Untimate Cheeseburger	2190
Hamburger	680
Jumbo Jack with Cheese	1310
Sandwiches: Homestyle Ranch Chicken Club	2010
Sourdough Grilled Chiken Club	1490
KFC:	
Chicken Breast: Original	1130
Extra Crispy	1140
Grilled	730
Popcorn Chicken,	
Value Box	2160
Sandwich, Crispy Twister	1260
Strips, Extra Crispy Tenders, 3 pieces	940
Sides: Macaroni & Cheese	830
Mashed Potatoes with Gravy	530
Potato Wedges	810
Wings, HBBQ Hot (1)	160

Fast-Foods & Restaurants	Sodium
McDonalds:	
Burgers: Big Mac	970
Cheeseburger	680
Double	1050
Hamburger	480
Quarter Pounder with Cheese	1100
Chicken McNuggets: 6 pieces	540
Chipotle BBQ Sauce, 1 package, 1 oz	140
Sandwich, Prem. Grilled Chicken Ranch BLT	1210
French Fries: Small, 2.5 oz	160
Medium, 4.1 oz	270
Large, 5.4 oz	350
Ketchup, 1 package, 10g	100
Breakfast: Egg McMuffin	780
Big Breakfast, reg. size Biscuit	1560
Hash Browns, 2 oz	310
Hotcakes, with Syrup & Whipped Margarine	665
Sausage Burrito	790
Southern Style Chicken Biscuit, regular bisc.	1180
Desserts/Shakes: Hot Fudge Sundae	170
Strawberry McCafe Shake, 12 fl.oz	240
Pizza Hut:	
Pan Pizza: *12", Per ½ Pizza, 4 Slices*	
Meat Lovers	3280
Cheese; Chicken Supreme; average	2110
Pepperoni; Supreme, average	2560
Pepperoni Lover's: Super Supreme, av.	3120
Subway:	
6" Lowfat Sandwich: *W/ Set Menu Board Toppings, no oil*	
Chicken, oven roasted	610
Roast Beef	660
Subway Club	850
Sweet Onion Chicken Teriyaki	840
6" Sandwiches: *With Set Menu Board Toppings, no Oil*	
BLT; Tuna, average	625
Meatball Marinara	920
Spicy Italian	1490
12" Footlong ~ Double above figures	
Taco Bell:	
Burritos: Combo, 8.2 oz	1380
Supreme; Chicken; Steak, average	1065
Chapulas, Chicken; Steak, average	515
Gorditas, Cheesy Crunch	830
Nachos: Regular	420
BellGrande	1270
Specialties, Cheese Quesadillas	990
Tacos: Chicken, Soft	480
Crunchy Supreme	340

Index A - C

A-1 Steak Sauce 144
A&W Cream Soda 51
Agave Nectar 157
Ahi Tuna 95
Albertson's Sodas 51
Alcoholic Drinks 24
Alcohol Guide 23
Al-Bran Bkfast Cereal 60
Alligator 168
Almond Breeze 49
Almond Butter 131
Almond Dream 49
Almond Joy 68
Almond Paste 30
Almonds 130
Aloe Vera Juice 156
Alouette Cheese 60
Alpina: Oat Smoothies 49
  Greek ogurt 162
Alta Dena Yogurt 162
Amaranth Flour 98
Amazake 49
AMP Energy Drink 38
Anchovies 95
Ant Eggs/Larvae 174
Antacids 156
Apple Danish 62
  Dunkin Donuts 197
Apple Fritter,
  Dunkin Donuts 197
Apple Pie 134
Apple Sauce 80, 102
Applebee's 176
Apples 99
Apricots 99
Arbor Mist Blenders 26
Arbor Mist Wine 26
Arby's 177
Arizona Teas 53
Arroz Con Pollo 174
Asian Foods 168
  Panda Express 222-223
  Pei Wei 224
Asparagus 158
Atkins Bars 31
Au Bon Pain 178-179
Aunt Jemima:
  Pancakes 132
  Waffles 132
Austin S'wich Crackers 151
Avocado 99

Baba Ghannouj 172
Baba Ghanoush 79
Baby Ruth 68
Babybel 76
Bacardi & Coke 28
Bacardi Silver 27
Bacon 126
Bacon Bits 126
Bagels:
  Chips 56
  Dogs 128
  S'wiches:
    Dunkin Donuts 198
  Spreads 56
Big Apple Bagels 182
Bruegger's Bagels 185
Manhattan Bagel 215
Baileys Irish Cream 29
Baking Ingredients 30
Baking Mix 30
Baking Powder 30
Baklava 62

Balance Bars 31
Ball Park Franks 127
Balsamic Vinaigrette 142
Banana 99
Banana Chips 102
Banana Flakes 102
Banquet Meals 111
Barbecue Sauce 80
Bariatrix: Shakes 38
  Proti-Bar 38
Barley 98
Bars: Granola 31-34
  Meal/Nutrition 31-34
  Sports & Diet 31-34
Bartles & Jaymes 27
Baskin-Robbins 181
Beans 158
Bear Claw 62
Beaver Tails 169
Bee Maggots 174

Beef 124
  Beef Ribs 124
  Franks 127
  Ground Beef 124
  Jerky 124
  Roast Beef 124
  Tallow 94
Beer: Alcoholic 24-25
  Non-Alcoholic 95
Beerwurst 128
Beiglach 171
Ben & Jerry's:
  Ice Cream 104
  Ice Cream Bars 108
Benecol Spread 93
Bernstein's Dressings 142
Best Foods Dressings 142
Betty Crocker::
  Cake Mixes 65
  Muffin Mixes 67
Biggest Loser:
  Entrees 112
  Shakes 38
Big Mac 216
Birds Eye Frozen Veg. 160

**FAST-FOODS INDEX
~ PAGE 175 ~**

Biscotti 81
Biscuits Packaged 55
  Burger King 186
  Hardee's 204
  Jack in the Box 207
  McDonald's 216
Bison Steak 124
Blintzes 171
Bloody Mary 29
Bloomin' Onion 222
BLT Sandwich 165
Blue Bunny: Novelties 108
  Ice Cream 104
Blue Cheese Dressing 142
Blue Sky Sodas 51
Bob Evans 183
Boca Burgers 112
Bok Choy 158
Bologna 128
Bolthouse Juice 41
Boost Drinks 38

Borscht Soup 152
Boston Market 184
Boston's Pizza 184-185
Brach's Candy 68
Brain 126
Bran 57
Brandy 27-29
Bratwurst 128
Braunschweiger 128
Brazil Nuts 130
Bread 55
Bread Crumbs 55
Bread: Buns/Rolls 55
  Breadsticks 55
Breakfast Cereals 57-61
Breakfast Meals,
  Denny's 194
Breakfast Sausages 127
Brewer's Yeast 156
Breyers: Ice Cream 104
  Ice Cream Bars 108
Brioche Cake 168
Broccoli 158
Brownies 62-65
Brownie Mixes 65
Bruegger's 185
Bruschetta 170
Brussels Sprouts 158
Bubble Tea 160
Bubble Yum 75
Buckwheat: 98
  Groats 57
Budweiser Beer 24
Buffalo Wings,
  Domino's 196
Buitoni Pasta 133
Bulgur: Grain 57, 98
  Salad 141
Bumble Bee Tuna 95
Burger King 186
Burritos: Qdoba 230
  Taco Bell 247
  Taco John's 249
  Taco Mayo 249
  Taco Time 249
Butter & Margarine 93
Butter Balls, deep fried 166

Butter Substitutes: 93
  Butter Buds 93
  Molly McButter 93
Butterfinger 69
Buttermilk 47
Butterscotch 69
Butter Tart 169
Cabbage 158
  Cabbage Rolls 171
Cactus Fruit 99
Cactus Leaf 158
Caesar Dressing 142
Cadbury Candy 69
Cafeteria Foods 165
Cajun Foods 168
Cake Frosting/Mixes 65
Cakes 62
Calamari: Fried 95, 169
  Macaroni Grill 214
Calcium Chews 156
California Pizza Kitchen 196
Calorie Countdown 47
Camembert 76
Canada Dry Sodas 51
Canadian Bacon 126
Canadian Foods 168
Candied Apple 167
Candied Fruit 102
Candy 68-74
Cannelloni 170
Cannoli 62
Cantaloupe 99
Cappuccino 36
Capri Sun 42
Caramello 69
Caramels 69
Carb Smart: Ice Cream 104
  Ice Cream Bars 108
Cardini's Dressings 142
Caribou 126
Carob 75
Carrots 158
Cashews 130
Caterpillars 174
Catfish 95
Caviar 95
Cereal Drinks 49
Challah Bread 54
Chalupas, Taco Bell 247
Champagne 26
Chapati 54
Cheerios Cereal 59
Cheese 76-79
Cheese:
  Balls 76, 150
  Cheese Whiz 76

Cheese Fries,		Chili's	189	Coffee:	35-37	Cranberries: Dried	102	Dolmades	169

Cheese Fries,
  Nathan's Famous 219
Cheese Puffs 150
Cheeseburgers::
  Burger King 186
  Hardee's 204
  Jack in the Box 207
  McDonald's 216
Cheesecake 62
Cheesecake Factory 150
Cheetos 150
Cheez-It Crackers 150
Chef Boyardee 113
Chef's Salad 141
Cherries 99
Chestnuts 130
Chex Breakfast Cereal 59
Chex Mix 150
Chia Seeds 131
Chi Chi's 29
Chick Peas 150
Chicken Alfredo 170
Chicken 189
  Chik-fil-A 210
  Church's Chicken 190
  KFC 210
  S'wich, McDonald's 216
Chicken Buffalo Wings:,
  KFC 210
Chicken Helper 112
Chicken Katsu 169
Chicken Korma 170
Chicken Kung Pao:
  P.F. Chang's 226
  Panda Express 223
Chicken McNuggets 216
Chicken of the Sea 97
Chicken Strips:
  KFC 210
  McDonald's 216
Chili Sauce 113
Chili: Con Carne 113
  Gold Star Chili 202
  Stagg Meals 150
  Trader Joe's Meals 121

Chili's 189
Chimichangas 172
Chinese Food 168
  P.F. Chang's 226
Chipotle 190
Chips Ahoy! 85
  Snacks 150
Chocolate Candy 68-74
Chocolate Baking Chips 30
Chocolate Chip Cookies 81
Chocolate Milk 48
Chocolate Cake 62
Chocolate Éclair 62
Cholent 171
Chopped Liver 171
Chorizo 127
Churros 62
Ciabatta 54
Cider, Alcoholic 26
Cinnabon 67
Cinnamon Rolls 62
  T.J.Cinnamons 252
Claim Jumper 191
Clam Chowder 152
  Long John Silver's 213
Clamato Juice 42
Clams 95
Clif Bars 31
Coca-Cola 51
Coca-Cola Zero 51
Cocktail Mixers 27
Cocktails 28
  Premixed 27
Cocoa 35
Cocoa Powder 30
Coconut: Desiccated 130
  Fresh 99, 130
Coconut: Cream 89
  Drink 50
  Milk 89
  Water 89
  Zico 40

Coffee: 35-37
  Biggby Coffee 182
  Caribou Coffee 187
  Creamers 89
  Espresso 36
  Flavored Mixes 35
  Instant 35
  Iced 35,
  McCafe 217
  Ready To Drink, Cold 37
  Starbucks 37, 243
Coffee-Mate 89
Cola Drinks 51-52
Coldstone Creamery 191
Coleslaw Dressing 142
Combos 150
Concha 62
Condensed Milk 47
Condiments/Sauces 80
Cookie Dough,
  Toll House 82
Cookies 81-88
Cooking Sprays Pam 94
Cool Whip 89
Coors Beer 24
Coq au Vin 168
Corn 158
Corn Chips 149
Corn Dog 128
Corn Flakes 58
Corn Grits 98
Corned Beef 128
Cornmeal 98
Cornstarch 98
Cosmopolitan 28
Cottage Cheese 76
Cough/Cold Syrups 156
Cough Drops 75
Country Choice Cookies 82
Cous Cous 98, 172
Crab 95
Crab Cakes 95
Cracker Jack 148
Crackers 81-88

Cranberries: Dried 102
  Fresh 99
Cranberry Sauce 80-102
Crawfish 168
Cream 89
Cream Cheese 79, 84
Cream of Wheat 57
Creamers, Bailey's 89
Creamsicle 108
Creole Foods 168
Crepe Suzette 169
Crispbreads 88
Croissant-Donuts 66
Croissants: Plain 134
  Sandwiches 165
  Dunkin Donuts 198
  Sweet 134
Cronuts 66
Croutons 55
Crunch 'N Munch 148
Crystal Light 52
Cup-a-Soup 154
Cupcakes 62
Curves, Protein Drinks 38
Custard, Frozen 103
Custard 90
D'Angelo's 192
Daiquiri 28
Dairy Ease 47
Dairy Queen 193
Danish Pastry 62
Dates 99
Deer 126
Del Taco 194
Deli Meats 128
Denny's 194-195
Desserts/Puddings 90
Dibs 110
Diet Drinks/Shakes 38
Diet Sodas 51-52
DiGiorno Pizzas 136
Dill Pickle 82
Dippin' Dots 105, 195
Dips/Spreads 79

Dolmades 169
Domino's Pizza 196
Donnairs 168
Donuts 66
  Tim Horton's 252
  Winchell's 257
dot.FIT:
  Bars 31
  FirstString 274
Dove: Candy 69
  Ice Cream 105
  Ice Cream Bars 108
Dr Pepper Sodas 51
Dried Fruit 102
Dried (Powdered) Milk 47
Drippings 94
Duck 139
Dumplings 168
  P.F. Chang's 226
Duncan Hines,
  Cake Mixes 65
Dunkin' Donuts 197
Ears, Pork 126
EAS Bars 31
Edamame 158, 171
Eel 95
Eggplant 159
Egg Roll Wrappers 133
Egg Rolls 92
Eggs: Egg Whites 91
  Better'n Eggs 91
  Egg Beaters 91
  Egg Nog 91
  Eggs Benedict 91
Eggo: French Toast 132
  Pancakes 132
Empanadas 173
Enchilada 172
Endive 159
Energy Drinks 38-40

e-BOOK EDITIONS

NOW AVAILABLE FOR
KINDLE • 0 iPAD • iPHONE
Fully Searchable & Enhanced

English Muffins	56
Ensure Drinks	38
Entenmann's: Cakes	63
Cinnamon Bun	67
Equal	157
Espresso Coffee	36
Starbucks	243
Evaporated Milk	47
Extra Gum	75
Fair/Carnival	**166-167**
Fajitas	172
Chili's	189
Falafel	166
Famous Amos	82
Fanta	51
Feet, Pork	126
Feta Cheese	77
Fettuccine Alfredo	170
Fiber One: Bars	31
Cereal	59
Muffin Mix	67
Fibersure	156
Fiddle Faddle	148
5th Avenue	70
Fig Bars	62
Figs	100
Filet Mignon Steak	123
Fish	95
Fish & Chips	95
Fish Oil	94
Capsules	156
Flame Broiler	201
Flaxseeds	131
Fleischmann's Spread	93
Flours	98
Fortune Cookie	168
Franks	127
Frappuccino,	
Starbucks	243
French Foods	168-169
French Fries:	166
Burger King	186
McDonald's	216
Fr./Italian Dressing	142
French Stick	54
French's Fried Onions	114
Fresca	51
Freschetta Pizzas	136
Freshens	201
Fried Dough	167
Fried Oreos	167

Fried Rice,	
Panda Express	223
Fried Twinkie	167
Frissants	66
Fruit Snacks	151
Fruit Spreads	157
Frog Legs	168
Froot Loops	60
Frosting, cake	65
Frozen Custard	103
Frozen Vegetables:	
Birds Eye	160
Green Giant	161
Ore-Ida	161
Frozen Yogurt	103
FrozFruit	108
FRS Energy Drink	38
Fruit Juices	41-46
Fruit Leather	102
Fruit Pies	134
Fruit Sauces	102
Fruit Smoothies	48
Orange Julius	221
Fruit Snack Cups	102
Fruit: Fresh	99-101
Candied	102
Canned/Bottled	102
Dried	102
Fruit Leather	101
Sauces	102
FryBread	167
Fudge	70
Fudgesicle	109
Full Throttle Energy	38
Funnel Cake	167
Fuze: Energy Drinks	38
Iced Teas	53
GardenBurger	**114**
Garlic	159
Garlic Bread	54
Gazpacho Soup	172
Gatorade	38
Gefilte Fish Balls	171
Gelati-da	105
Gelatin: Parfait	90
Snacks	90
Gelato	103
GeniSoy	32
Genisoy Powder Shakes	38
German Foods	169
Ghee	93

Ghirardelli	70
Gin	27
Ginger	159
Glaceau Drinks	38
Glowelle	156
Gluhwein	26
GNC: Bar	32
Protein Drinks	32
Gnu Foods	32
Goat Meat	126
Goat's Milk	47
Goat's Milk Cheese	77
Godiva Candy	70
Goldfish	150
Goober P'nut Butter	131
Good Humor	109
Goose	139
Gorditas, Taco Bell	247
Graham Crackers	81
Grains	98
Grandma's Cookies	82
Granola	58
Granola Bars	31-34
Grapefruit	100
Grapes	100
Gravy	144
Great Value: Bars	32
Meals	114
Greek Foods,	
Daphne's Café	193
Ground Pork	126
Guacamole	172
Guava	100
Gum	75
Gum Drops	70
Gummi Bears	70
Gyros	169
Haagen-Dazs:	
Ice Cream	105, 204
Ice Cream Bars	109
Haggis	174
Half & Half	89
Halls Drops	75
Ham:Roasted/ Sliced	128
Ham Steak	126
Lunch/Deli	128

Hamburger:	
Carnival/Fair	166
Jack in the Box	207
McDonald's	216
Hamburger Helper	112
Hansen's:	
Energy Drinks	39
Iced Teas	53
Juices	42
Sodas	51
Hardee's	204
Hash Browns:	92
Burger King	186
McDonald's	217
Hawaiian Foods	169
Healthy Choice: Meals	114
Heart	126
Hebrew National Links	127
Heineken Beer	24
Herring	96
Hershey's: Candy/Choc.	70
Chocolate Mix	35
Hidden Valley Dressings	142
Hissho Sushi	205
Hoagies, Davanni's	193
Honey	157
Honeycomb	71
Honeydew	100
Horchata	172
Horseradish	80
Hostess: Cup Cakes	63
Ding Dongs	63
Donettes, Mini	66
Fruit Pies	134
Twinkies	63
Hot & Sour Soup	155
Hot Chocolate	35
Hot Dogs/Franks:	
Carnival	166
WAWA	255
Wienerschnitzel	257

Hot Dog On A Stick	205
Hot Dog Toppings	128
Hot Pockets	115
Hummus	79, 172
Hunt's Snack Pack	90
Hushpuppy,	
Long John Silver	214
Ice Cream	**103-107**
Ice Cream Novelties	108-110
Butterfinger	108
Drumstick	109
Klondike	109
Oreo	109
Slim-a-Bear	109
Ice Cream: Carvel	188
Dippin' Dots	195
Starbucks	107
Ice Cream Toppings	157
Iced Tea	53
Mixes	53
Icee Drinks	51
IHOP	206
Indian Foods	170
Italian Dressing	142
Italian Foods:	170
Fazoli's	200
Macaroni Grill	214
Italian Sausage	128
Jack In The Box	**207**
Jam	157
Jamba Juice	208
Jambalaya	168
Japanese Foods:	171
Edo Japan	199
Yoshinoya	258
Java Monster Energy	39
Jellies	71
Jell-O: Gel Snacks	90
Gelatin Mixes	90
No Bake Cheesecake	65
Puddings	90
Jelly Beans	71
Jif Peanut Butter	131
Jolly Rancher	71
Junior Mints	71

FAST-FOODS INDEX
~ PAGE 175 ~

Kahlua 29
Kahlua Mudslide 28
Kaiser Roll 55
Kalua Chicken 169
Kashi: Bars 32
  Cereal 59
  Cookies/Crackers 83
Keebler: Cookies 83
  Crackers 83
Kefir Milk 47
Kellogg's:
  Bars 32
  Breakfast Cereals 59
  To Go B'Fast Shakes 39
KFC 210
Kid Cuisine 115
Kidneys 126
Kielbasa 121, 128
Kimchee 172
Kind Bars 32
Kisses 71
Kit Kat 71
Kiwifruit 100
Knish 171
Kombucha Drink 39
Kool-Aid 53
Korean Foods 172
Kosher Deli Foods 171
Kozy Shack 90
Kraft: Cheese 76-78
  Dressings 143
  Mayonnaise 94
  Meals 116
Krispy Kreme Donuts 66
Kudos Bars 32

Lactaid 100 47
Lactose-Free Drinks 47
Lamb 125
Lamb Pilaf 170
Land O'Lakes Spread 93
Lard 94
Lasagna: Villa Pizza 254
  Chicken, Fazoli's 200
Latkes, Potato Patty 171
Lau Lau 169
Lean Cuisine: 116-117
  Deep Dish Pizza 136
Lean Pockets 117
Lebanese Foods 172
Lecithin Granules 57
Lemons 100
Lemon Cake 62
Lemon Crème 134
Lettuce 159

Lettuce Wraps:
  P.F.Chang's 226
  Pei Wei 224
Licorice 71
Life Breakfast Cereal 61
Lifesavers 71
Lighter Bake 30
Limes 100
Lindora Bars 32
Lindt 72
Linguine 133
Lipton: Brisk 53
  Green/Iced Tea 53
Liqueur, Coffee 29
Liqueurs 29
Liquor 27
Little Caesar 213
Little Debbie: Cakes 63
  Cookies 84
  Donut Stick 66
  Honey Buns 67

Liver: 126
  Liver Pate 128
  Liver, Chopped 128
Liverwurst 128
Lobster 96
Lochshen 171
Locusts 174
Lollipops 72
Lox 96
Luna Bar 32
Lunchables 117
Lunchmakers 117

M & M's 72
Macadamia Nuts 130
Macaroni & Cheese 133
Macaroni Salad 141
Mamey Apple 100
Manapua 169
Mandarin 100
Mandelbrot 171
Mango 100
Manhattan Clam Chowder,
  Campbell's 153
Manischewitz 84
Marathon Bars 32
Marble Cake 62
Margarita 27

Marie Callender's,
  Dinners 117
Marie's Dressings 143
Marsala 26
Marshmallows 72
Maruchan Noodles 117
Masa 172
Matzos: 88
  Balls 171
  Ball Soup 152
Mayonnaise 94
Mazola Spray 94
McDonald's: McCafe 217
  McMuffin 217
Meals:
  Amy's 111
  Betty Crocker 112
  Gorton's 114
  Hungry Man 115
  Thai Kitchen Meals 121
  Trader Joe's 121
  Worthington 122

FAST-FOODS INDEX
~ PAGE 175 ~

Meat Snacks 128
Meat Spreads 129
Meats 123-126
Melons 100-101
Mentos 72
Meringues 90
Met-Rx: Bars 33
  Energy Drinks/Shakes 39
Metamucil 156
Mexican:
  Carnival 166
  Cheese 76
Mexican Foods 172
Michelob Beer 25
Middle Eastern Foods 172
Mike's Hard Lemonade 27
Milk: Canned 47
  Dried 47
  Flavored 48
  Plain 47
Milky Way 72
Miller Beer 25
Millet 98
Minestrone Soup 152
Mint Julep 28
Mints 72

Minute Maid: Juices 43
  Lemonade; Punch 43
Minute Rice 118
Miracle Whip 94
Miso Soup 171
Mojo Bar, Clif 31
Molasses 157
Morningstar Farms 118
Mounds 72
Mountain Dew 52
Moussaka 169
Mozzarella Cheese 77
Mr Goodbar 72
MRM Protein Drinks 39
Mrs Dash Seasonings 146
Mrs Fields Cookies 219
Mud Cake 62
Muffin Mixes 67
Muffins 67
  Dunkin Donuts 197
Mulled Wine 26

Munchies 150
Muscle Milk: Powders 39
  Ready To Drink 48
Mushrooms 159
Mussels 96

Naan Bread 170
Nachos: 166, 172
  Chili's 189
  Qdoba 230
  Taco Bell 247
Naked Juice 43
Nanaimo Bar 169
Nathan's Famous 219
Nature's Path Bars 33
Nayonaise 94
Nectarines 100
Nesquik 35, 48
Nestea, Iced Tea 53
Nestle Crunch: Bar 72
  Ice Creams Bars 110
New England,
  Clam Chowder,Blimpie 182
Newman's Own:
  Cookies 86
  Dressings 143

Juice 44
Newtons Cookies 85
Nissin Noodles 118
No Fear Energy 39
Noni Juice 39
Noodles 133
  Pei Wei 224
Noodles & Company 220
Nopal Cactus Salad 172
Nopales 159
NOS Energy 39
Nothing But Noodles 220
Nut Spreads 131
Nutella 131
Nutri-Grain Bars 33
Nutrilite: Bars 33
  Protein Drinks 39
NutriSystem: Bars 33
  Breakfast Cereals 61
Nuts 130

Oat Bran 57
Oatmeal 57
Oatmeal Raisin Cookies 81
Oats 98
Ocean Spray, Juice 44
Odwalla Bars 33
Oils: Fish 94
  Vegetable 94
Okra 159
Old El Paso:
  Dinner Kits 118
  Dip 79
  Refried Beans 118
  Salsa 79
Olive Garden 221
Olive Loaf 128
Olives 100
Omelets: 91
  Ham & Cheese 92
  Western 92
  Bob Evans 183
Onion Flower 166
Onions 159
Onion Rings::
  Burger King 186
  Dairy Queen 193
  Jack in the Box 207
  Zaxby's 258
Optifast: Bars 33
  Shakes 40
Orange Juice 41
Orange Julius 221
Oranges 100

Orangina 44
Oreo: Cakesters 64
    Cookies 85
    Snacks 150
Ostrich 126
Outback Steakhouse 222
Ovaltine 35
Oyster & Soup Crackers 81
Oysters 96
Pad Thai 174
Paella 174
Palmier Cookie 62
Pancakes 132
    IHOP 206
Pancreas 126
Panda Express 223
Panera Bread 223
Paninis:
    Hot Pockets 115
    Lean Cuisine 116
Papaya 100
Pappadum 170
Parfait 90
Parkay Spread 93
Parmesan Cheese 78
Parsnip 159
Passionfruit 100
Pasta: Fresh 133
    Macaroni Grill 214
    Pizza Hut 227
Pasta Roni 118
Pasta Sauces 144-147
Pastrami 129
Pastries 62-64
Pastry Crust 134
Pate 128
PayDay Bar 72
Peach Melba 62
Peaches 100
Peanut Butter Cookie 81
Peanut Butter Cups:
    Newman's Own 72
    Reese's 73
Peanut Butter 131
    & Jelly S'wich 131
Peanuts 130
Pears 100
Peas 159
Pecan Pie 134
Pecans 130
Pepperidge Farm: Cakes 64
    Cookies 86
Peppermints 73
Peppers 159
Pepsi 52
Persimmons 100

Pez 73
Philadelphia Cheese 78
Pickles & Relish 80
Pie Crust 134
Pie Fillings 30, 134
Pies 134
Pilaf 140
Piloncillo Sugar Cone 157
Pina Colada 28
Pine Nuts 130
Pineapple 101
Pinkberry 106
Pirate's Booty 150
Pistachios 130
Pizza Hut 227
Pizzas: Frozen 136, 137
    Ready-To-Eat 135
Planters, Peanuts 130
Plums 101
Poi 169
Poke Salad 173
Polenta 98
Polish Foods 173
Pom Wonderful: Juices 44
    Pomegranate Teas 53
Pomegranate 101
Popcorn: Plain 148
    Caramel 148
    Orv. Redenbacher's 148
Popcorners 148
Popchips 149
Pop Tarts, Kellogg's 64
Pops, Ice Cream 108-110
Pork: Meat
    Cracklings 173
    Rinds/Skins 150
    Sausages 127
    Spareribs 125
Port Wine 26
Porterhouse Steak 123
Post Cereals 61
Potato Salad 141
Potatoes: 159
    Carnival 166
    French Fries 166
Poutine, Canadian 168
PowerAde ION4 40
PowerBar: Bars 33
    Shakes 40
Pretzelmaker 229
Pretzels: Flipz 149
    Rold Gold 149
Prickly Pear 101
Probiotics 164

Progresso Soup 154
Promise Spread 93
Proscuitto 129
Protein Drinks/Shakes 38
Prunes 101
Psyllium Husks 57, 98
Puddings 90
Pumpkin Pie 134
Pumpkin Seeds 131
Pumpkin 160
Qdoba 230
Quail 139
Quaker: Bars 34
    Breakfast Cereals 57, 61
Quakes Rice Snacks 151
Quarter Pounder 216
Quesadilla 166, 172
    Qdoba 230
Quiche 91
Quinoa 98
Rabbit 126
Radish 160
Raisin Bran 58
Raisin Bread 54
Raisinets 73
Raisins 101
Rambutan 101
Ranch Dressing 142
Raspberries 101
Ravioli 112-119
    Fazoli's 200
Red Bull & Vodka 28
Red Bull Energy 40
Reddi-Wip 89
Red Mango,
    Frozen Yogurt 106
Reese's 73
Refried Beans 112, 118-120
Relishes 80
Reuben Sandwich 165
Revival Soy Shakes 140
Rice:
    Bran 57, 98
    Cakes 56
    Crackers 81
    Drinks 49
    Snacks 151
Rice Dream 49
Rice Krispies 73
Rice Noodles 133
Rice, Sticky Thai 174
Rice-A-Roni 119
Ricola 101
Ricotta Cheese 78

Ritz Crackers 86
Rockstar Energy 40
Rogan Josh 170
Rolo 73
Root Beer 51
Rugulah 62
Rum 27-28
Russell Stover Candy 73
Rye Bread 54
Rye Flour 98
Sabritones Snacks 151
Sake 26
Salad Dressings 142
Salad Toppings: 141
    Bacon Bits 141
Salads: Deli 141
    Packaged 141
Salami 129
Salmon 96
Salsa 79, 80
Saltines 81
Sandwiches: Cosi 191
    D'Angelo's 192
    Denny's 194
    Einstein Bros 199
    Mr. Hero 218
    Schlotzsky's 237
    Subway 245
Sara Lee: Bagels 56
    Croissants 134
    Frozen Cakes 64
    Pies 134
Sardines 97
Sashimi 171
Sausages 127
Sauces: 144
    Prego Pasta Sauces 146
    Ragu 147
    Worcestershire 145
Sarku Japan 237
Scallops 96
Scone, Fruit 62
Scotch 27
Screwdriver 28
Seagram's Coolers 27
Seaweed 156
See's Candies 73
Seeds 131
Semolina 98
Sesame Butter 131
Sesame Seeds 131
7-Eleven 236
7-UP Soda 52
    Shakes 48
Shasta Sodas 52

Shaved Ice 103
Shellfish 95-97
Shawourma 172
Sherry 26
Shooters 28
Shish Taouk 168
Shrimp 97
Silk: Creamer 89
    Soy Drinks 49
Simply Asia Meals 119
Sirloin Steak 123
Sizzler 240
Skippy Peanut Butter 131
Skittles 73
Skyline Chili 240
Slim-Fast: Bars 34
    Shakes 40
Slurpees, 7-Eleven 236
Smart Balance Spread 93
Smarties 73
Smirnoff Ice 27
Smoked Sausage 127
Smoothies: 41
    Freshens 201
    Jamba Juice 208
    Smoothie King 241
    Tropical Smoothie 253
Smucker's Goober 131
    Snacks 148-151
Snow Cone 167
Snackwell's Cookies 85
Snails 169
Snake 174
Snapple 45, 53
Snickers 74
So Delicious: Yogurt 106
    Coconut Milk 50
SoBe: Energy Drinks 40
    Green Tea 53
Soft Drink Mixes 50
Soft Drinks/Soda 51-52
Sonic Drive-In 240-241
Sopapillas Pastry Puffs 173
Soul Foods 173
Soup: 152-155
    Campbell's 152-153
    Progresso 154
Sour Cream 89
Sourdough Bread 54

Southern Comfort 27
Souvlaki 169
Soy Dream: Drinks 50
  Ice Cream 107
Soy Flour 98
Soy Milk/Drinks 49
Soy Nuts 130, 151
Soy Powder Mix 50
Soybeans 160
Spaghetti:
  & Meat Sauce 117-119
  & Meatballs 111, 113
  Cooked 133
  Dry/Fresh 133
  Old Spagh. Factory 221
Spam: Canned 129
  Musubi 169
Spanish Foods 174
Spareribs 125
  P.F. Chang's 226
Sparks 27
Special K: Bars 34
  Cereals 60
Spreads 79
Spices & Herbs 147
Spinach 160
Spirulina 156
Splenda 157
Spring Roll: Chinese
  Panda Express 222
  Pei Wei Asian Diner 224
Sprite 52
Squash 160
Squaw Bread 54
Squid 97
Stadium Foods 167
Stagg Chili Meals 120
Starbucks: Coffee 243
  Bottled Coffee 37
  Cakes/ Bakery 244
  VIA Mix 35
Starburst 74
Starkist 97
Steak Subs Mr. Hero 218
Steaks 123
  Chili's 189
  Lone Star 213
  Outback Steakhouse 222
  Ruby Tuesday 234
Steaz: Energy Drink 40
  Green Teas 53
Stella D'Oro Cookies 157
Stevia 157
Stouffer's 120

Strawberries 101
String Cheese 77
Stromboli:
  Stouffers 120
  Villa Fresh Italian 254
Stonyfield Farm Yogurt 163
Strudel 62
Stuffing Mix 55
Subway 245-246
Succotash 160
Sugar 157
Sugar Substitutes 157
Sukiyaki 171
Sundaes 103
  McCafe 217
Sunflower Seeds 131
Sunkist, Sodas 52
SunnyD 45
Sunsweet: Lighter Bake 93
  Prune Juice 41
Supplements 156
Surimi 97
Sushi 97
Southern Tsunami 242
Swanson Pot Pies 120
Sweet 'N Low 157
Sweet Buns/Rolls 67
Sweetbreads 126
Sweet Potatoes 160
Swiss Miss: Drinks 35
  Pudding Snacks 90
Swordfish 97
Syrups 157

TAB Soda 52
Tabouli 141
Tacos 172
  Qdoba 230
  Taco Bell 247
Taco Salad Qdoba 230
Taco Shell 56, 172
Tahini 131
Tahini Sauce 172
Take 5 74
Tamales 172
Tamarillo 101
Tamarind 101
Tandoori Chicken 170
Tang 52

Tangelo 101
Tangerine 101
Tapioca 90
Taramasalata 169
Tartar Sauce 80
Tassot, Beef/Goat 168
Tasti D-Lite 107
TCBY 250
Tea 53
Tempura 171
Teppan Yaki 171
Tequila 27
Tequila Sunrise 28
Teriyaki: Beef 171
  Chicken 171
  Salmon 171
TGI FRiday 250-251
  Frozen Meals 120
Thai Foods 174
Thai Kitchen Meals 121
Thousand Is. Dressing 142
3 Musketeers 68
Tia Maria 29
Tilt Energy 40
Tim Hortons 251-252
Tiramisu 62
Toblerone 74
Tofu Fresh/Packaged 156
Tofurky Meals 121
Tofutti 107
Tofutti Cheese 78
Tomatillos 101, 160
Tomato: Fresh 101
  Ketchup 144
  Paste/Puree/Sauce 144
  Sundried 144
Toaster Streudel 64
Tombstone Pizzas 137
Tongue 126
Tony's Pizzas 137
Torte 169
Tortellini 133
Tortillas: Chips 149
  Dorritos 149, 151
  ...Shells 56
Tostada 172
Tostitos 149, 151

Tostitos Dip 79
Toutiere 168
Trader Joe's: Bars 34
  Breakfast Cereals 61
  Cakes 64
  Cookies 87
  Juices 45
  Meals 121
  Yogurt 163-164
Trail Mix 130, 151
Tripe 126
Tuna 97
Turkey 139
  Breast, Deli 129
  Loaf; Pastrami 129
Turnip 160
Turnovers, Fruit 62
Twinkies 63
Twix 74
Twizzlers 74

Udon Noodles 121
Uncle Ben's Meals 121

V8 Juice 46
Veal 125
Veal Parmigiana 170
Vegetable Juices 41-46
Vegetable Oils 94
Vegetable Shortening 94
Vegetables 158-160
  Frozen 160-161
  Canned/Bottled 161
Vending Machine Snacks 151
Vermouth 26
Via® Iced Coffee 35
Vienna Sausage 173
Vietnamese Foods 174
Vinegar 30, 80
Vitamins 156
VitaMuffins 67
Vodka 27

Waffles 132
Walgreens Sodas 52
Walnuts 130
Wasabi Peas 151
Water Crackers 81
Water Chestnuts 160
Watermelon 101
  Seeds 101
WAWA 254-255
Weetabix 61

Weight Watchers:
  Candy 74
  Pizzas 137
  Smart Ones::
    Cakes 64
    Meals 119
Weiners 127
Wendy's 255
Werther's 75
WestSoy: Rice Drinks 49
  Soy Milk 50
Wheat Germ 57, 98
Wheat Thins 85
Whipped Toppings 89
Whipping Cream 89
Whiskey 27
Whitman's Chocolates 75
Wienerschnitzel 257
Wine 26
Wishbone Dressings 143
Wonton Wrappers 133
Wonder Bread 55
Wonka 75
Worthington 122
Wraps, Sandella's 236
Wrigley's 75
Wyder's Cider 26

Yams: 160
Yakult 164
Yeast 30
Yogurt 162-164
Yogurt Drinks 164
Yogurt Raisins 151
Yonique Yogurt 164
Yoo-Hoo 48
York Peppermint Pattie 75
Yorkshire Pudding 124
Yucca Root 160
Yves Veggie Cuisine 122

Zatarain's 122
Ziti, Fazoli's 200
Zola Acai Drink 46
Zone Perfect Bars 34
Yoplait 164
Zucchini 160

**FAST-FOODS INDEX
~ PAGE 175 ~**